THE AMERICAN CONSTITUTIONAL SYSTEM

BY

JOHN MABRY MATHEWS, Ph. D.

Professor of Political Science,
University of Illinois

FIRST EDITION

McGRAW-HILL BOOK COMPANY, Inc.

NEW YORK AND LONDON

1932

THE MAPLE PRESS COMPANY, YORK, PA.

To
JAMES WILFORD GARNER
With True Regard

PREFACE

This treatise on "The American Constitutional System" is the result of the author's experience of many years in teaching a course on the subject for upperclassmen at the University of Illinois. He undertook the writing of this text because of his failure to find a book which seemed to him altogether suitable for a college text for a semester's course. Existing texts were found to be, on the one hand, either too full or too meager, or, on the other, either too elementary or too advanced or technical. In the present volume, the endeavor has been made to strike a mean between these extremes.

This book is not intended to be exhaustive, but an effort has been made to include a consideration of all the more important topics in constitutional law with which college students of the subject should be familiar. With respect to the topics taken up, consideration has been given to the principles involved therein, as far as they have been formulated in decisions of the Supreme Court of the United States rendered up to January, 1932. It is thought that all important cases have been adequately explained, but since, in a number of respects, the Constitution has not been authoritatively interpreted by the courts, the discussion in the text has been supplemented by considerations of reason and usage.

In general the purpose of the book is to furnish both the general reader and especially the undergraduate student in American colleges and universities with a thorough, comprehensive text on the constitutional system of the United States in all its important phases, giving adequate attention to both the legal and the governmental sides of the subject, avoiding technicalities wherever possible, and laying the emphasis on those main features and general principles which should be understood by all intelligent citizens and by all careful students of American public affairs.

Without attempting to shift responsibility for the shortcomings of the work, I wish to acknowledge my indebtedness for helpful suggestions and criticisms which I have received from Professors C. G. Haines, of the University of California at Los Angeles, R. E. Cushman, of Cornell University, F. W. Coker, of Yale University, O. P. Field, of the University of Minnesota, J. Hart, of the Johns Hopkins University, and from my colleagues, Professors J. W. Garner, C. A. Berdahl, C. M. Kneier, and C. S. Hyneman, of the University of Illinois. Finally, my thanks are due to my former teacher, Professor W. W. Willoughby, of the Johns Hopkins University, who originally inspired in me an interest in the subject, for permission to use as the title of this volume one borne by a noteworthy product of his pen which appeared nearly three decades ago.

UNIVERSITY OF ILLINOIS,
May, 1932.

J. M. M.

CONTENTS

PART II

THE NATIONAL GOVERNMENT: ORGANIZATION AND POWERS

CHAPTER VII

CHAPTER VIII

CHAPTER XIII

CHAPTER XIV

PART III

GOVERNMENT AND THE INDIVIDUAL

CHAPTER XXI

CHAPTER XXII

CHAPTER XXIII

CHAPTER XXIV

PART I
PRINCIPLES OF THE FEDERAL SYSTEM

CHAPTER I

INTRODUCTION

The Approach to the Constitution.—The Constitution of the United States is the oldest existing written constitution of a sovereign state, having been in operation without fundamental change for almost a century and a half. Its roots go far into the past: we can trace some of its provisions to Magna Carta, to the Bill of Rights, and to the writings of such famous men as John Locke, Coke, Hobbes, and Blackstone. It is an instrument, however, which has most vital significance not only for the past but also for the present and for the future. It is worthy of the closest study and attention by the lawyer and by the careful observer of American public affairs. Moreover, every intelligent citizen should be acquainted with its main features. Nicholas Murray Butler has declared that "the highest public duty of an American citizen is silently to take for himself the oath which the Constitution prescribes to be taken by the President before entering upon his office: *viz.*, to the best of his ability to preserve, protect, and defend the Constitution of the United States." Although such an oath might be of some value even if taken by a person who is ignorant of the contents of the Constitution, it would be of greater value if the citizen who takes it has an intelligent conception of the instrument which he is swearing to defend.

At various times the Constitution has been both highly praised and also severely condemned. The celebrated English statesman Gladstone is reported to have described it as "the most wonderful work ever struck off at a given time by the brain and purpose of man." This statement is frequently quoted by writers on the Constitution as a sort of straw man to be set up and immediately knocked down. The statement is true merely to the extent that the language of the original Constitution was drafted by a group of able men during the summer of 1787. The statement fails to notice two important factors in the greatness of the Constitution: first, that it was the product of the long experience and wisdom of the past and, second, that it is a dynamic document which has been molded and developed until today it is something very different from what it was in 1787. The Constitution as a written document has not been greatly changed, but the law of the Constitution has enormously expanded, mainly through judicial interpretation.

Some of the highest praise accorded to the Constitution has come from a recent President of the United States who says that.

3

The Constitution of the United States is the final refuge of every right that is enjoyed by any American citizen. So long as it is observed, those rights will be secure. Whenever it falls into disrepect or disrepute, the end of orderly organized government, as we have known it for more than one hundred and twenty-five years, will be at hand. The Constitution represents a government of law. There is only one other form of authority, and that is a government of force. Americans must make their choice between these two. One signifies justice and liberty; the other tyranny and oppression. To live under the American Constitution is the greatest political privilege that was ever accorded to the human race.[1]

These expressions are in striking contrast with the characterization of the Constitution by the leader of the abolitionists before the Civil War as "a covenant with death and an agreement with hell." Since the adoption of the Eighteenth Amendment, some arch anti-prohibitionists have denounced the Constitution in almost equally extreme terms. It would seem that one's attitude toward the Constitution depends to a considerable extent upon whether he thinks it protects his interests or stands in the way of the accomplishment of his purposes. It should be noted, however, that the quarrel of the critics is not so much with the Constitution as originally drawn up or even as amended, but rather with the interpretations which have been placed upon it.

The careful student of the Constitution will indulge in neither blind worship nor intemperate criticism. It should be his purpose to understand it and to have an intelligent knowledge of its provisions. He will find that, like all human works, the Constitution is not perfect. It is not the Ark of the Covenant: we shall not fall dead if we touch it. It is not inspired in the sense in which many Christians believe the Bible to be. Nevertheless, it is generally wise and a noble heritage which the American citizen should cherish. He should also be willing to admit that it has defects, which, when demonstrated, should be remedied as soon as possible by regular methods of constitutional change. Only in this way can it be kept abreast of modern conditions.

The Study of Law.—The subject of constitutional law opens up to many students their first direct acquaintance with the field of law. It is therefore desirable at the outset to have some knowledge of law in general. Law may be defined as consisting of those rules of conduct which the government compels the people to follow. If law is to be regarded as more than mere moral precept, it should have some definite sanction or means of enforcement. In the last analysis, municipal law or law within the state consists of those rules of conduct which the courts will enforce. Even though rules are embodied in constitutions or statutes, if the courts will not enforce them, they are dead letters.

---

[1] COOLIDGE, CALVIN, Foreword to James M. Beck, *The Constitution of the United States* (New York, 1924).

Although the content of law may be based to a large extent upon men's ideas of morality prevalent at the time the law is made, a distinction should be drawn between law and morality. The law does not prohibit a state of mind, but only outward acts. By the Tenth Commandment a man is prohibited from coveting his neighbor's property. This is a moral precept, violation of which may be a sin but is not a crime. It is not against the law to covet. But if a man's covetousness should be translated into the act of taking what does not belong to him, the law steps in to prohibit and to punish.

Law may be classified in several ways. One classification is into written and unwritten law. Written law consists of those rules of law which have been formally enacted by a law-making body and the exact language of which has been reduced to writing. Examples are constitutions and statutes. Unwritten law consists of those rules of law which are binding but which have not been embodied in a definite set of words. An example is the common law as embodied in the decisions of the courts. The rule in this case may have to be derived from a series of decisions by a process of induction. Custom, if recognized by the courts as binding, may also be a form of unwritten law.

The classification of law into written and unwritten suggests also a classification of the sources of law. Formally adopted enactments consisting of those written forms of law—constitutions and statutes—are important sources of law in modern times. Unwritten rules embodied mainly in court decisions and to some extent in customs are also still an even more important source of law but were relatively more important in former times than at present. An example of a mere custom which in time became a law is the rule of the road that vehicles should pass to the right. The custom existed as such before the law recognized it as binding. The law finally adopted it as a convenient and generally recognized rule.

When law is created through the adoption of a previously well-established custom, it is naturally more easily enforced than when it attempts to introduce an innovation not already embodied in custom. The ease or difficulty with which a law is enforced depends to a considerable extent upon whether it is generally supported by public opinion. American constitutions and laws in their basic principles are for the most part designed to operate upon the people of a fairly homogeneous democracy, in which approximately the same ideals of liberty and law are generally held throughout the community. Unfortunately, the population, especially in cities with their various racial elements, does not measure up to this standard. Moreover, the problem of law enforcement in the United States becomes continually more acute and pressing on account of the constantly increasing number of laws to be enforced. The growth of civilization and the increasing complexities of modern conditions invite the constant growth of statute law enacted to regulate such conditions.

Another classification of law is into public and private. All rules of law are made, either formally and expressly or tacitly and impliedly, by public authority, *i.e.*, by the state. In public law, however, the state or the government is a party to the relations thereby set up. Among the branches of public law are international law, constitutional law, and administrative law.

International law is the body of rules and regulations which has grown up through the centuries and governs the conduct of nations in their relations with one another. It is partly unwritten, resting upon usage and custom. In part it has been reduced to writing in the form of general international treaties. International law is supposed to regulate the conduct of nations not only in time of peace but also in time of war. Under the latter condition, however, violations of international law are likely to be more serious and frequent. International law still depends largely upon the public opinion of the civilized nations for its enforcement. Gradually, however, more definite machinery for this purpose is being developed. In case of conflict between international law and formally enacted internal or municipal law, the courts as a rule follow the latter.

Administrative law consists of the body of rules which provide for the detailed organization of the executive and administrative authorities and determine the scope and limits of their powers, duties, and functions. Administrative law and constitutional law may overlap or supplement each other to some extent, for the latter is peculiarly concerned with the structure or organization of governmental departments and authorities. Criminal law may also be considered as a branch of public law, because every crime is an offense not only against the particular individual injured but also against the state. It is for this reason that the state sets up an officer with authority to prosecute the offender and does not leave this matter to be attended to solely by the injured person.

Private law consists of those legal rules which regulate the relations between private individuals and/or private corporations. Examples are contracts, torts, and property. These are the branches of law with which the practicing lawyer is mainly concerned, but they need to be only incidentally considered by the student of constitutional law.

The development of the law in all its branches has been one of the most important influences in the establishment and maintenance of justice between man and man. Law proceeds by general rules which embody the consensus of opinion as to what is fair, just, and right and does not depend upon the mere whim or caprice of any particular individual, however highly placed he may be. This, at any rate, is the ideal of the law, although, like all human institutions, it does not fully reach this ideal. It was doubtless with this ideal in mind that the Massachusetts bill of rights of 1780 declares that "this government shall be a government of laws and not of men."[1] This principle was familiar to the men who framed the Federal Constitution. In reality, however, we cannot have a government without both laws and men—laws to govern conduct and men to interpret and administer the laws. Whether a government is to be considered as one of laws or one of men is a relative matter or a question of where the emphasis is placed.

What Is Constitutional Law?—The branch of public law with which we are particularly concerned in this volume is constitutional law. This may be defined as the fundamental body of laws which determine the general organization of the government in its various organs and departments and define the extent of their powers. Although this definition is probably as satisfactory as any, it is somewhat lacking in precision because there may well be a difference of opinion as to what laws are fundamental. It will be noticed from this definition that the functions of a constitution are (1) to determine the structure of the government and (2) to indicate what limits, if any, rest upon the exercise of its powers. Most modern constitutions place limits upon the power of the government. Even if this power were unlimited, however, the state would still have a constitution, although, under these circumstances, there would be little practical utility in formally embodying the constitution in a written document. An absolutism might in time be transformed into a democracy without the adoption of a written constitution, but a democracy formed without such antecedents must almost necessarily be equipped with a written constitution.

In every state there is a constitution of some sort, although it may sometimes be very rudimentary. Furthermore, it need not be put in writing but may consist of unwritten customs, usages, and understandings. To put a constitution in writing makes it more definite and certain, and the tendency in most countries nowadays is to reduce to writing a large part of the constitution. Even in the United States, however, which was the pioneer in adopting written constitutions, they remain partly unwritten. The written document, ordinarily spoken of as the Constitution, is really only the core of the constitution. In order to get a view of the constitution in the broad sense, we must consider not only the written document but also custom and usages which modify it, statutes which elaborate the structure of the government, and decisions of the courts which interpret and apply provisions of the written constitution.

The term constitution may be used in the formal sense or in the material sense. These concepts overlap to some extent but not altogether. Whatever is found in the written document known as the Constitution is

---

[1] On the distinction between a government of laws and one of men, see Aristotle, *Politics*, Bk. III, Chap. XVI.

constitutional in the formal sense, regardless of the essential nature of the provision.   Thus, the provision in the Constitution of the United States that a census of the population shall be taken every ten years is constitutional in the formal sense but not in the material sense.   On the other hand, provisions of law relating to the organization of the lower Federal courts, although embodied merely in acts of Congress, are nevertheless a part of the constitution in the material sense.   The divergence between the meaning of the term constitution in these two senses is not so great in the case of the Federal Constitution as it is in the case of most of the state constitutions.   The former is confined for the most part to the statement of fundamental principles.   The latter in many instances, however, are veritable codes of law, largely statutory in essential nature and therefore not constitutional in the material sense.

The function of the constitution in defining the powers of the government may be exercised either by making a positive grant of power, with the implied limitation that the power shall extend no further than the grant, or by placing an express prohibition upon the exercise by the government of certain powers.   One of the principal purposes usually involved in the adoption of written constitutions is the protection of individual rights against invasion by the arbitrary or tyrannical action of the government.   For this reason, constitutions usually contain bills of rights, for the protection of fundamental civil rights and of persons accused of crime.   Political rights, such as the right to vote, are also frequently provided for in constitutions. It should be remembered, however, that individual rights cannot be protected from the state or, more accurately, that there are no legal rights capable of being enforced as against the state, which stands above the constitution and can amend it in any way or to any extent.   As far as the government is concerned, however, the constitution is both fundamental and paramount law.   Since the constitution determines the powers of the government, including usually its law-making power, the latter power cannot as a rule be exercised in violation of the constitution. Therefore, a statute or act of the ordinary legislature is usually to be considered as a grade of law subordinate to the constitution.   This is especially true in a country, such as the United States, where the courts assume to exercise the power of refusing to give effect to statutes which they deem to be in conflict with the constitution.   It should be noted, however, that the courts do not do this in England, which is without a written constitution and in which a statute is legally superior, or at least equal, to the constitution.   Nor do the courts do so in most countries of Continental Europe, in which, although the constitution is written, the courts do not uphold it as against allegedly conflicting statutes.

As indicated above, an important function of the constitution is to indicate the scope and limits of the powers not only of the government as a whole but also of its component parts or departments, legislative, executive, and judicial. These limits are drawn not only in the relations of the respective departments to private individuals or corporations but also in their relations to one another. In the case of the Constitution of the United States, another important function, which is performed only by constitutions establishing federal forms of government, is that of distributing governmental powers between the National Government and the states and of drawing a line of demarcation between them. To perform this function satisfactorily is a difficult undertaking. Moreover, even though it were possible to draw a dividing line at any given time which would be perfectly adapted to the existing economic, social, and political conditions in the country, it would probably not long remain suited to such conditions, since they are constantly changing. For this reason, it is desirable that the Constitution should contain adequate means of amendment, either formally or by judicial interpretation, or both, in order to keep it abreast of such changing conditions. It is not sufficient that unchanging provisions should be adapted to changing conditions: the provisions themselves must change. As to where the line of division between the American National Government and the states is actually drawn at any given time, the Supreme Court of the United States is the final arbiter, except under such unusual conditions as those which produced the Civil War. In a federal form of government the power of the courts to declare laws unconstitutional is especially necessary in order to keep the central and local governments within their respective spheres. Although, in exercising this power, the courts follow a legalized form of procedure, they may really be marking out the boundaries of government.

From what has been said above, it will be perceived that the contents of most constitutions may, as a rule, be classified as follows: (1) the bill of rights, (2) the main body of the constitution dealing with the structure of the government, (3) administrative provisions, and (4) provisions relating to amendment and revision of the constitution. In addition to the above, there is also usually found a preamble and a schedule. The preamble is of legal significance in so far as it embodies an enacting clause, but it usually contains other provisions. The latter are sometimes a mere preliminary euphemistic flourish and add little to the body of the constitution, except that they throw light upon the general intentions of the framers. The schedule consists of merely temporary provisions designed to bridge over the transition from the old constitution to the new.

Classification of Constitutions.—Theoretically, constitutions may be classified into written and unwritten, although in practice, as noted above, any particular constitution is likely to partake partly of both kinds, and this classification, therefore, is not very satisfactory. In the course of time a written constitution naturally becomes overgrown with political customs, which may even go so far as practically to nullify certain provisions of the written document. Constitutions may also be classified in accordance with the character of the government set up by them, as, for example, into democratic, oligarchical, and autocratic. From the standpoint of the relations set up between the central and the local governments within the state, they may be classified into federal and unitary. A federal constitution is almost necessarily written.

Still another classification sometimes made is into rigid and flexible, which has reference to the process of amendment. In a rigid constitution, in order to emphasize its greater dignity and importance, the process of amending it is different from, as well as more difficult than, the process of passing an ordinary statute by the legislature. In this sense the Constitution of the United States and practically all of the American state constitutions are rigid, while in some other countries, notably England, there is no difference in the methods of changing the constitution and of enacting statutes, and the constitution is therefore said to be flexible. This distinction, however, is rather legalistic than pragmatic, because, as a matter of fact, American constitutions have been more frequently amended than the English. Since customs change slowly, any constitution having a high customary content naturally changes slowly, regardless of the legal procedure of amendment.

In this book we shall be concerned primarily with the Constitution of the United States rather than with those of the states of the American Union. Incidentally, however, we shall also be concerned with the latter, since the Constitution of the United States is a part of the constitution of all the states in the Union in so far as it applies to them.

Sources of Constitutional Law.—A thorough knowledge of the constitutional law of the United States cannot be obtained from the most thorough study of the mere language of the Constitution, although the language itself is the starting point on the road to such knowledge. Further information must be sought because it is not always clear or obvious how the language of the Constitution is to be applied to cases and situations that are constantly arising. The sources of this further information may be classified into official and unofficial.

Official sources of information with reference to the meaning of the Constitution of the United States consist of interpretative acts performed by the various departments of the government, or by members thereof, in the course of their official duties. Some questions regarding the interpretation of the Constitution cannot be easily raised in the courts or, at least, may not have been so raised. For light on such questions we may rely to some extent upon interpretative acts performed by the legislative and executive departments. An example of this was the so-called "legislative decision of 1789" regarding the removal power of the President.[1]

[1] See below, Chap. XII.

By far the most important official source of information regarding the meaning and interpretation of the Constitution, however, is the opinions and decisions of the courts, especially those of the Supreme Court of the United States, which has final authority to interpret its provisions. Although there are numerous decisions of the Supreme Court which do not relate to the interpretation of the Constitution, many of them do. The latter, taken as a body, constitute the most valuable and authoritative source of information in existence upon the meaning and application of the fundamental law of the United States. The judiciary is *par excellence* that department of government whose business it is to interpret the laws, including the Constitution. The courts, however, do not regard this as their primary concern. On the contrary, their primary concern is to determine the legal rights of the particular parties to the cases or controversies before them for decision. In reaching such decisions, however, it is necessary for them incidentally to find the law applicable to the case and, in applying such laws, they necessarily construe and interpret them.

The cases decided by the Supreme Court of the United States are printed in a long series of volumes. The student of the Constitution will derive much benefit by looking up the more important cases construing that instrument as published in the official reports. For most cases, however, it will be sufficient to consult the report as presented in condensed form in any one of the useful and handy collections of cases on constitutional law which have been edited by private individuals. In either event, he will find that the report of a case may usually be classified into three parts: (1) the facts, (2) the opinion, and (3) the decision. The facts are those pertinent events or circumstances which gave rise to the case or controversy which is presented to the Court for its decision. The decision is the order which the Court issues affecting the rights of the parties to the case. The opinion is the chain of legal reasoning which impels the Court to reach that decision. The opinion contains the doctrine of the case, which is a general proposition of law from which the decision, in view of the facts, logically follows. In the course of its opinion, however, a court may make various incidental remarks not involved in the chain of legal reasoning and not essential to the decision. These are known as *obiter dicta*.

In order to reach a decision, a majority of the judges of the Court must agree, but the opinion is usually written by a particular judge and is likely to reflect his particular point of view in approaching the case. John Marshall, the greatest jurist whom the United States has produced, was chief justice of the Supreme Court during a third of a century of its formative period and himself wrote the opinions of the Court in many important constitutional cases. His usual method was to arrive at his conclusion by a process of deduction from the fundamental principles which he conceived the Constitution to embody. His method was due in part to the fact that he was breaking new ground. Other judges, however, have been inclined to rely more largely upon the inductive method and have made copious citations of judicial decisions in previous cases in arriving at their conclusion.

As a general rule, with but few exceptions, courts follow the principle of *stare decisis, i.e.*, they decide the case before them in accordance with the previous most authoritative decision or series of decisions involving substantially similar circumstances, unless later overruled by a higher court or modified by statute or constitutional amendment. This practice is desirable in that it makes for certainty and prevents unsettlement in the law bearing on the subject. On the other hand, it does not sufficiently allow for flexibility and the adaptability of the law to changing conditions. In case the courts find that justice will be better subserved by not following the principle of *stare decisis*, they sometimes reverse themselves, but, more usually, they prefer to whittle down or differentiate previous cases. As a rule, a reversal is more likely to be made by the Supreme Court than by a lower court.

Unofficial sources of information regarding the meaning of the Constitution consist principally of formal textbooks or treatises, briefs filed by able lawyers in important constitutional cases, and the speeches and letters of leading students of the fundamental law. These sources may be used by the courts in reaching decisions on constitutional questions, but they have merely persuasive and not binding authority. The weight to be accorded them by the student will naturally depend upon the ability and thoroughness with which they present the principles of constitutional law.

CHAPTER II

THE FORMATION AND ADOPTION OF THE FEDERAL CONSTITUTION

The Constitution of the United States did not spring full-grown from the mind of man. It was the product of experience and had its roots deep in the past. In order to understand its formation, therefore, it is necessary to consider some of the events which preceded it. Such an inquiry might logically lead us back into early English constitutional history, but for practical purposes it will be sufficient to start at a much later date.

The Continental Congresses.—The first general meeting of the American colonies, which was called on their own initiative, was the Stamp Act Congress, composed of representatives from nine colonies, which met in New York City in 1765. It had no legal authority but adopted resolutions protesting against the Stamp Act of the British Parliament, which was deemed to be obnoxious as embodying "taxation without representation." This congress was only a temporary affair, but the incident formed a precedent for united action of the colonies against objectionable practices of the mother country and paved the way for later efforts in this direction.

The grievances against the British policies toward the colonies, especially in matters of taxation, continued to accumulate. The colonies were thrown more closely together by their common interests in the impending struggle against the mother country. In 1774, upon call of Virginia and Massachusetts, the First Continental Congress, composed of delegates from eleven colonies, met at Philadelphia. Since that date there has always been some form of central government in the United States. This Congress also had no legal authority to act, but its strength rested rather upon the common consent of the people. It recommended a boycott on British goods, issued a call for another congress to meet the following year, and then adjourned.

The Second Continental Congress, composed of delegates from all the colonies, met in 1775 in pursuance of the call issued by the First Congress. It was as clearly a revolutionary body as the First Congress had been illegal. Before it met, actual fighting had broken out between the colonists and British troops. This Congress was chiefly occupied in carrying on the Revolutionary War. It also recommended that the various states adopt constitutions fitted to their new condition. This was done by all of them except Connecticut and Rhode Island, which continued

13

for some years to live under their old colonial charters, with only slight changes.

The Declaration of Independence.—Another important act of the Second Continental Congress was the issuance, in 1776, of the immortal Declaration of Independence. This document, written by Thomas Jefferson, is a landmark in the history of democracy. It stated eloquently the grievances of the colonies against Great Britain and laid down certain fundamental political principles. The most important of these principles were couched in the following memorable words:

We hold these truths to be self-evident—That all men are created equal; that they are endowed by their Creator with certain inalienable rights; that among these are life, liberty, and the pursuit of happiness. That, to secure these rights, governments are instituted among men, deriving their just powers from the consent of the governed.

These principles are not literally a part of the Constitution or the laws of the United States; nevertheless they have exerted a powerful influence upon the political history of this country and, indeed, of the world.

The Articles of Confederation.—The Continental Congresses exercised authority by virtue of the common consent of the people during a war emergency, but the extent and nature of their authority was not regulated by any constitution or fundamental law. Even while the Revolutionary War was still raging, it was felt that this situation should be remedied through the adoption of a body of fundamental law. Consequently, in 1776, the Second Continental Congress appointed a committee to draw up the Articles of Confederation. Two years later this document, having meanwhile been accepted by the Congress, was submitted to the various state legislatures for adoption. It was not to go into effect until ratified by every one of the thirteen states. Nearly all of the states ratified within about a year, but Maryland held back on account of her desire to have the question settled as to the conflicting claims of several of the states to Western lands. When this question appeared to be in process of settlement through cession of the disputed land to the United States, Maryland finally ratified the Articles, and they went into effect in March, 1781, almost at the end of the Revolutionary War.

Government under the Articles.—The form of government provided under the Articles, although a decided advance over that which existed under the Continental Congresses, was still rather rudimentary. It was a somewhat loosely constructed league or confederation, and not a national government. Each state was declared to remain sovereign and independent and to retain all powers not expressly delegated to the Confederate Government. Although the Confederation was expressly declared to be perpetual, there seems to be little doubt that each state retained the right to withdraw therefrom if it so desired.

The Confederate Government was not divided into legislative, executive, and judicial departments, but such governmental powers as were granted to the Confederate Government were concentrated in the hands of its one organ, the unicameral Congress. This body was a sort of congress of ambassadors from sovereign states, each of which paid its own delegates, who were annually appointed in such manner as the state legislature might direct and might be recalled by their respective states at any time. Regardless of the number of its delegates, and regardless of its size or population, each state had only one vote in Congress.

Certain important powers, such as those to declare war, make treaties, and to coin, borrow, and appropriate money, were vested in Congress, although it could not exercise them except by a vote of nine states. On the other hand, the states were prohibited, without the consent of Congress, from declaring war, maintaining warships, and from making treaties or sending ambassadors to foreign countries. The Congress was authorized to obtain revenue by making requisitions upon the states in proportion to the value of improved land. It might also make requisitions upon the states for troops in proportion to the white population. There was no system of Confederate courts, but disputes between states might be decided by special tribunals set up under the supervision of Congress. There was no effective way, however, of enforcing the decisions of such tribunals. Congress was also authorized to establish prize courts and courts for the trial of piracies and felonies committed on the high seas. Since there was no executive, Congress was authorized to appoint a committee composed of one delegate from each state to assume direction of affairs during the recess of Congress. In reality, Congress was more of an executive than a legislative body, but it had no effective means of enforcing its authority.

Certain provisions were included in the Articles which were intended to bind the states more closely together. Thus, the inhabitants of each state were declared to be entitled to the privileges and immunities of free citizens in the several states. Moreover, the people of each state were accorded free movement to and from any other state. This, however, did not, in general, apply to goods. Interstate extradition of criminals was provided for, and, finally, each state was enjoined to give full faith and credit to the records, acts, and judicial proceedings of every other state. Although these provisions had a nationalizing tendency, they were quite insufficient to counteract the widespread tendencies of a centrifugal character which manifested themselves under the Articles.

Defects of the Articles.—The language of the Articles exhibits a painstaking care on the part of its framers to avoid offending the susceptibilities of those whose first allegiance was to their respective states and who believed strongly in state sovereignty. The states, which were declared to be sovereign and independent, retained so much power that the central government was rendered weak and ineffective. Although Congress was vested with the power to make treaties, and although the Articles declared that no state should lay any imposts or duties which might interfere with the stipulations of treaties, there was no means of enforcing this limitation upon the states.

The central government was not well organized. There were no separate organs to exercise executive and judicial powers. The scope of the grant of such powers to the central government was, in fact, hardly large enough to justify the creation of separate organs. The requirement of the assent of nine states to the passage of important measures often operated to impede action simply because the representatives of as many as nine states were not present. The lack of interest in the proceedings of Congress was so great that the representatives of the smaller and more distant states were frequently absent.

An important defect of the Articles was that the Confederate Congress acted on states and not directly on individuals. There were citizens of the states, but under the Articles there were no citizens of the United States. Congress had no power of levying taxes directly on individuals. For the raising of revenue it was dependent upon grants made by the states at the request of Congress. The same procedure must also be followed in the raising of troops. Frequently, such requests were not granted, and a state might always refuse for any reason that seemed to it sufficient.

A final defect of the Articles was that the Confederate Congress had no power to regulate commerce among the states. Nor could it regulate commerce with foreign nations except through the making of treaties which, as we have seen, might be disregarded by the states. Each state could levy its own tariff on goods imported from abroad and from other states.

Experience under the Confederate Government amply demonstrated the inconveniences resulting from the defects mentioned above, and attempts were made from time to time to remedy them through amending the Articles. Provision was made in the Articles for their amendment, but the provision proved to be unworkable because of the strict requirement of unanimous consent of the states. To whatever amendment might be proposed, there was always at least one state that objected.

The Movement for the Constitution.—The fundamental defects of the Articles listed above showed that they did not provide a form of government adequate to the needs of the country. The defect which brought to a head the movement for revision of the Articles was the lack of power of Congress to regulate commerce. There were as many different sets of commercial regulations as there were states. The lack of unity and harmony in commercial regulations was a great burden to the business interests of the country. Since they were so adversely affected by existing conditions, it was natural that they should have taken a leading part in the movement for a change. Moreover, many of the leading statesmen of the country felt, regardless of business interests, that the future welfare of the nation depended upon the establishment of some stronger form of government.

The first link in the chain of events which led to the constitutional convention of 1787 was the holding of a conference at Mt. Vernon in 1785 between commissioners of Virginia and Maryland in order to reach an agreement regarding the navigation of the Potomac River. Encouraged by the success of this conference, the legislature of Virginia issued in the following year a call for a convention of delegates of all the states to meet at Annapolis to consider the general need of a uniform system of commercial regulations. When the convention assembled in September, 1786, however, it was found that only five states were represented. This was deemed to be too small a representation to accomplish the purpose for which the convention was called, but, before adjourning, a proposal was adopted that a convention of representatives of all the states should meet in Philadelphia in May, 1787,

. . . to take into consideration the situation of the United States; to devise such further provisions as shall appear necessary to render the constitution of the federal government adequate to the exigencies of the Union, and to report such an act for that purpose to the United States in Congress assembled, as, when agreed to by them and afterwards confirmed by the legislatures of every state, will effectually provide for the same.

This proposal on its face evidently contemplated a mere revision of the Articles in order to render them "adequate to the exigencies of the Union," although its author, Hamilton, doubtless hoped to bring about a more fundamental change than was implied in such a revision. The proposal having been transmitted to the Confederate Congress, that body issued a call for the holding of the proposed convention

. . . for the sole and express purpose of revising the Articles of Confederation, and reporting to Congress and the several legislatures such alterations and provisions therein as shall, when agreed to in Congress and confirmed by the states, render the federal Constitution adequate to the exigencies of government and the preservation of the Union.

All of the states except Rhode Island responded to this call and sent delegates to the convention. In no case were these delegates chosen directly by the people; they were either elected by the state legislature or appointed by the governor. The instructions given to the delegates either expressly or by implication limited their power to a revision of the Articles of Confederation.

The Constitutional Convention.—Pursuant to call, the convention assembled at Philadelphia in May, 1787. The leading men in the political life of the country, such as Washington, Franklin, Madison, and Hamilton, were sent as delegates by their respective states. Most of them had had practical experience and contact with governmental affairs through membership in the Continental or Confederate Congresses or in their state legislatures. Some of them had been signers of the Declaration of Independence.

In the convention the delegates voted by states, each state having one vote. The convention decided to hold its sessions behind closed doors, and this move was probably a wise one, since it enabled the delegates to reach compromises on controversial matters which otherwise would have been impossible. In spite of the secrecy of the proceedings, we now know the main trend of the discussions in the convention through the publication of Madison's notes.

The two principal plans looking toward a change in the central government which were presented to the convention were known as the New Jersey and the Virginia plans. The New Jersey plan was in the main a mere revision of the Articles of Confederation. Although it provided to some extent for separate executive and judicial departments, it retained the salient feature of the Articles in that it preserved the equality of the states. The central legislature was still to consist of a single house, in which each state was to have one vote. This arrangement naturally appealed to the small states.

The Virginia plan, on the other hand, proposed a much more radical reconstruction of the central government. It was not a mere revision of the Articles. It not only provided for separate executive and judicial departments but also divided the national legislature into two branches. The lower branch was to be elected by direct popular vote, and in both houses the states were to have not equal, but proportional, representation. This arrangement naturally commended itself to the large states, because it gave them greater weight in national legislation. While the New Jersey plan was based on the federal principle, the Virginia plan was based to a greater extent on the national principle.

In the conflict which ensued between the large and small states, it soon appeared that the only solution was some sort of compromise. In the main the large states prevailed, but some concessions were made to the small states. A national government was provided for, although state's rights were to a considerable extent preserved. The attempt was made to effect a compromise whereby the government would be strong enough to be stable and effective, while at the same time it would not be so strong as to endanger the principle of local or state autonomy.

A most important compromise from the standpoint of reconciling the interests of the large and small states was the so-termed Connecticut compromise, which provided that the states should have equal representation in the upper house and representation according to population in the lower house. When this had been agreed to, the question then arose as to how the negro slaves should be counted in determining the population of the various states as a basis of representation in the lower house. This difficulty was settled by a compromise whereby, somewhat arbitrarily, three-fifths of the slaves were to be counted for purposes of representation. This fraction of the slaves was also adopted in determining the population of the states for purposes of apportioning direct taxes among them.

Another important compromise of the convention was that relating to commerce. Inasmuch as the unsatisfactory condition of commerce was, as we have seen, one of the principal causes leading to the calling of the convention, it was natural that special attention should have been given to this matter. Congress was given the power to regulate commerce, both with foreign nations and among the states. On the other hand, Congress was prohibited from levying taxes on goods exported from the country and, until the year 1808, the importation of slaves into the United States was not to be forbidden.

In spite of the concessions made to the small states it was evident that the proposed new government was constructed on a radically different plan from that provided under the Articles. Inasmuch as the delegates had been instructed merely to propose a revision of the Articles, some of the more timid delegates argued that the convention ought either to keep within its powers or ask for new instructions. As opposed to this view, however, it was pointed out that the delegates had been sent to the convention to frame a proposed government which would be adequate to meet the needs of the country and to preserve the Union and that a mere revision of the Articles would not be sufficient to accomplish this purpose. When the very safety of the country was at stake, no mere scruple as to the extent of power should be allowed to prevent the delegates from doing their full duty in proposing such form of government as they thought necessary for national salvation. Moreover, as Madison pointed out, the action of the convention was merely advisory and recommendatory and the proposed new government could not be put into operation unless the constitution framed by the convention was ratified.

These arguments prevailed and a majority of the delegates—thirty-nine altogether, including at least two from every state except Rhode Island—indicated their approval by signing the proposed new constitution. Some of those who signed were not enthusiastic about it but accepted it as the best instrument of government obtainable under the circumstances.

The Ratification of the Constitution.—After the proposed new Constitution had been finally agreed upon by the convention, it was transmitted to the Confederate Congress with the request that it be submitted to the several states for ratification. Although the convention was not a mere committee of Congress (as had been the body which drafted the

Articles of Confederation), it nevertheless did not assume to exercise the power of transmitting the proposed constitution directly to the states for ratification. As to methods of procedure, the convention made two important recommendations. The first was that the Constitution be referred for action to conventions in each state specially elected by the people for this purpose rather than to the regular legislatures. This plan was designed to give the new Constitution a more popular basis than could be claimed for the Articles of Confederation or, indeed, for most of the state constitutions.

The second important recommendation made by the convention was that, as soon as nine of the thirteen states should have ratified, steps should be taken to put the new constitution into effect as between the states so ratifying. Such a provision was, in fact, embodied in the instrument itself. This provision was intended to facilitate the process of putting the government under the new Constitution into operation and to avoid the delay which had been experienced in putting the Articles of Confederation into effect, due to the requirement of unanimous consent. The departure from the requirement of unanimity was also to some extent a recognition that the new Constitution provided for a national government rather than for a mere confederation of sovereign states. Nevertheless, this provision, if carried out, would constitute a sort of legal or bloodless revolution, because it would produce a lack of legal continuity between the Confederation and the government under the new Constitution. The Articles of Confederation, it will be remembered, required the unanimous consent of all the states merely to amend them. The new Constitution was, of course, not a mere amendment of the Articles and putting it into effect was a much greater exercise of power than the adoption of an amendment to the Articles would have been. Yet it was proposed that this greater power should be exercised not by all of the states but merely by nine of them.

Nevertheless, both of the recommendations made by the convention were accepted by the Confederate Congress. That body promptly transmitted the proposed new Constitution to the several states to be ratified in specially elected conventions. Although some of the states, principally small ones, ratified with little delay, in several of the state conventions debate on ratification was long and heated. There was also considerable excitement over the matter throughout the country. Upon the question of ratification the members of the state conventions and the people generally were divided into three classes. The first class consisted of those who favored ratification and were known as Federalists. The second class opposed ratification and came to be known as Anti-Federalists. The third class consisted of those persons who had not made up their minds on the question but reserved their judgment until convinced by one side or the other. Many arguments on both sides were made, the most celebrated and convincing being a series of newspaper articles written by Hamilton, Madison, and Jay, arguing with great cogency in favor of ratification. These essays were collected and published in book form under the title of *The Federalist*. It is valuable not only as containing arguments in favor of ratification but also as giving a contemporaneous exposition as to the meaning of the new Constitution by a group of men who had taken part in drafting it and were among the ablest students of government of their time.

The arguments of the Federalists were successful, and state after state ratified in rapid succession until the necessary number of nine had acted favorably. Among those that still held off, however, were Virginia and New York. Without these important and pivotal states, union under the new Constitution could hardly have been a practical success. In the conventions of those states, as well as in others, one of the principal arguments against the new Constitution was that, unlike most of the existing state constitutions, it did not contain an enumeration or bill of rights for the protection of individual liberty. To this argument the Federalists answered that a bill of rights was unnecessary because the new government was to have no powers except those conferred upon it. The Anti-Federalists, however, did not deem this to be a sufficient answer, especially in view of the rather indefinite extent of the powers conferred upon Congress by the "necessary and proper" clause of the Constitution. Some of them were willing to vote for ratification on condition that a bill of rights should be inserted. Such a conditional ratification, however, would have complicated the situation and was finally avoided. The friends of the new Constitution succeeded in winning over the conventions by promising to use their best efforts to secure the subsequent insertion of a bill of rights through the regular process of amendment.

Virginia and New York thus fell into line, bringing the number of ratifying states up to eleven. Steps were taken toward putting the new government into operation through the election of senators, representatives, and presidential electors. Meanwhile, the old congress of the Confederation, already moribund, quietly expired through lack of a quorum and the new government went into effect on March 4, 1789. Within a year thereafter, the two remaining states, North Carolina and Rhode Island, finally ratified the Constitution and came under the "Federal roof."

CHAPTER III

GOVERNMENT UNDER THE CONSTITUTION

The Nation and the States.—The Constitution of the United States provides for a federal form of government as distinguished from unitary or centralized government on the one hand and, on the other, from such a loose confederation as existed before its adoption. That instrument assumes the existence of the states and marks out a sphere of operation for them wherein they are not subject to control or interference by the National Government. The powers of the latter are also delimited by the Constitution, and, in its own sphere, it is not subject to control by the states. The National Government has those powers that are granted to it by the Constitution, while the states have reserved powers, *i.e.*, all powers not granted exclusively to the National Government and not prohibited to the states.[1] There are some powers which cannot be exercised by any government in the United States, because they have been prohibited to the states and have not been granted to the National Government. Such powers are said to remain in the people, the original source of all governmental power.

The distribution of power between the National Government and the states may be indicated by the following classification:

1. Powers granted exclusively to the National Government. These are powers which from their nature require unity or uniformity in their exercise. Examples are making treaties, declaring war, and coining money.

2. Powers reserved exclusively to the state governments. These are the powers which by the Constitution have not been prohibited to the states and have not been granted to the National Government. Examples are the maintenance of a public-school system and the regulation of marriage and divorce.

3. Concurrent powers, *i.e.*, those which may be exercised by both nation and states, such for example as the levying of taxes. It should be noted that, as a general rule, if Congress and the states have power to regulate the same matter by law, and such laws conflict with each other, the laws of Congress override those of the state.

4. Powers prohibited to the National Government. Since the National Government could exercise no powers except those granted to it either expressly or impliedly, it may seem strange that it should have

[1] Constitution, Amendment X.

22

been thought necessary to insert in the Constitution any express prohibitions on that Government. Nevertheless, either out of superabundant caution or because it was felt that some of the more indefinite grants of power to the National Government might be abused or unduly extended unless limitations were placed upon them, some prohibitions on that Government were placed in the original Constitution, such as those relating to the suspension of the writ of habeas corpus and the levying of a direct tax. The prohibitions upon the National Government were considerably extended by the first eight amendments to the Constitution.

5. Powers prohibited to the state governments. These may be either expressly prohibited or impliedly through exclusive grant to the National Government. The powers expressly prohibited to the states are forbidden either absolutely or in the absence of the consent of Congress. Thus, the states are absolutely forbidden to enter into treaties, alliances, or confederations, but, unless Congress refuses its consent, they are not forbidden to make agreements or compacts with one another or with a foreign power.

6. Powers prohibited to both the nation and the states. These are the powers which still remain in the people, the original source of all power. Examples are passing bills of attainder and *ex post facto* laws, and granting titles of nobility.

One difficulty which arises in operating the federal form of government is that there may be conflicts between the laws passed by the National Government and those passed by the states. This possibility was foreseen and provided for by the Constitution in the following words: "This Constitution and the laws of the United States which shall be made in pursuance thereof . . . shall be the supreme law of the land."[1] The laws of the National Government operate not on the states, as under the Articles of Confederation, but directly on individuals. They are enforced, for the most part, not by state but by national officers. In case of doubt or controversy, the supremacy of national law in its own sphere is enforced by the courts. If the state courts or lower Federal courts should fail to do so, appeals may be taken to the Supreme Court of the United States, which is the final arbiter of the controversy. That tribunal, which is an organ of the central government, stands over both state and national governments as a sort of sentinel or umpire for the purpose of keeping each strictly to the sphere which has been marked out for it.

The drawing of a line of demarcation between the powers of the National Government and those of the states is by no means an easy matter. An attempt was made in the original Constitution to draw such a line and changes in the location of the line have since been made from time to time. In spite, however, of elaborate precautions designed to avoid them, conflicts sometimes take place between the central and state

[1] Art. VI.

governments. Moreover, even though it were possible to draw a dividing line at any given time which would be perfectly adapted to the existing economic, social, and political conditions in the country, it would not remain long suited to such conditions, since they are constantly changing. Amendment of the Constitution so as to provide a new and more suitable distribution of powers is a difficult undertaking. From one point of view, the Civil War may be considered as a struggle to determine whether slavery was under the control of the states or of the nation. The regular legal means of settlement having failed, the issue was submitted to the "arbitrament of the sword."

In ordinary times, however, by constitutional amendment, by Congressional legislation, and by judicial interpretation, the distribution of powers is being gradually changed to suit new conditions. Happily, with a national Supreme Court as the arbiter of disputes between the central and state governments, the danger of conflict is greatly minimized. By this means the balance between the Union and the states is harmoniously preserved. In cases of doubt, however, the Supreme Court, as an organ of the National Government, would naturally be inclined, either consciously or unconsciously, to favor the extension of national power at the expense of the states. Many exceptions to this general rule, however, may be found in the decisions of the Court. During the time that Marshall was chief justice of the Supreme Court, the decisions of that tribunal undoubtedly favored the extension of national power, but, after he was succeeded by Taney, an at least temporary reaction towards the preservation of state power set in. This was brought about by giving a more liberal interpretation of state powers and a more strict interpretation of national powers than Marshall had done. Even Taney, however, did not deny the supremacy of national law in its sphere and some of his judicial utterances have a strongly nationalistic trend. Thus, in a case decided in 1859 he held that the state court of Wisconsin had no right by writ of habeas corpus to interfere with a person held in the custody of a Federal officer under the authority of the fugitive slave law passed by Congress in 1850.[1]

Although [he declared] the state of Wisconsin is sovereign within its territorial limits to a certain extent, yet that sovereignty is limited and restricted by the Constitution of the United States . . . The Constitution was not formed merely to guard the states against danger from foreign nations, but mainly to secure union and harmony at home . . . and to accomplish this purpose, it was felt by the statesmen who framed the Constitution and by the people who adopted it, that it was necessary that many of the rights of sovereignty which the states then possessed should be ceded to the general government; and that, in the sphere of action assigned to it, it should be supreme and strong enough to execute its

[1] Ableman v. Booth, 21 How. 506 (1859).

own laws by its own tribunals, without interruption from a state or from state authorities.[1]

The Separation of Powers.—It is the primary function of a constitution to set up the main organs of the government, to indicate the relations between its different departments, and to delimit the sphere of their powers. At the time of the adoption of the Constitution of the United States, the principle of separation of powers was regarded by the leading political thinkers as fundamental and essential to a constitutional government. If this principle were disregarded, the result would be autocratic and tyrannical government. As Madison expressed it in *The Federalist:* "The accumulation of all powers, legislative, executive, and judiciary, in the same hands, whether of one, a few, or many, and whether hereditary, self-appointed, or elective, may justly be pronounced the very definition of tyranny."[2]

Under the Constitution, the powers of the National Government are distributed among three departments—legislative, executive, and judicial. There is no general distributive clause, as in many of the state constitutions, but separate clauses confer legislative powers upon Congress, executive powers upon the President, and judicial powers upon the Supreme Court and such lower courts as Congress may establish. The doctrine of the separation of powers was thus accepted by the framers of the Constitution not only as a fundamental political maxim of government but also as a rule of American public law. This rule will, in proper cases, be enforced by the courts, except in so far as express exceptions to it may be made in the Constitution itself. In order to insure the independence of departments, various provisions are inserted in that instrument, such as those making each house of Congress the judge of the elections and qualifications of its own members and prohibiting Congress from diminishing the salaries of judges during their continuance in office.

On the other hand, in order still further to place limits on the separate departments, the Constitution also provides for a system of "checks and balances," whereby each department is checked by one or both of the others. For example, Congress is checked by the power of the President to veto acts of Congress, while, on the other hand, the President is checked through the possibility of his impeachment and removal from office by Congress.

It will be noticed that the operation of such interdepartmental checks involves an intermingling of the spheres of power and, to that extent, constitutes exceptions to the principle of separation of powers. Thus, through his veto power, the President participates in the work of legislation. In granting pardons to persons convicted by the courts of criminal

[1] *Ibid.*
[2] *The Federalist*, No. 47.

offenses, he exercises a quasi-judicial power. In impeachment cases, Congress, or at least the Senate, exercises a power of a similar nature. Finally, the power of the courts to set aside acts of Congress as being in excess of its constitutional powers is substantially the exercise of a legislative power.

The authors of *The Federalist* realized that a mere paper demarcation of the proper spheres of the several departments of government by constitutional provision would not necessarily keep them from exceeding these limitations. They held that there was a need for some practical security against encroachment by one department upon the sphere of another. They deemed that it was not practicable constantly to recur to the people to correct such breaches of the Constitution. Although they probably did not foresee the extent to which the courts would come to exercise the power of declaring legislative acts unconstitutional, they presented a very cogent argument in favor of the need for the exercise of this power in a limited government.[1]

Compact versus National Theories.—Since a state must exist before a constitution can be adopted, the question arises as to the nature of the American state which was in existence at the time of the adoption of the Constitution of the United States. In spite of the fact that some authorities have denied that the original thirteen states ever were sovereign, there seems to be little doubt that they were sovereign during the period of the Confederation. They were declared to be sovereign and independent states both by the treaty of peace of 1783 with Great Britain and also by the Articles of Confederation themselves. Such paper declarations, while not conclusive in themselves, are confirmed and supported by the overwhelming evidence of the practical conditions existing under the Confederation.

Admitting, then, that the thirteen states were sovereign prior to the adoption of the Constitution of 1787, the question may be raised as to whether the establishment of the Constitution was the result of a compact between the thirteen sovereign states or was the result of the consent of the people acting through the ratifying conventions. The compact theory as to the origin and nature of the Union was the one most widely held at the time of the adoption of the Constitution. Moreover, it was the prevalent view of the current political philosophy that organized society itself rests upon the basis of contract. This view was reflected in the statement of the Declaration of Independence that government rests upon "the consent of the governed." Some indication that the Constitution was considered to be a compact between the states was found in the language of that instrument itself in the provision that "the ratification of the conventions of nine states shall be sufficient for the establishment of this Constitution *between the states so ratifying the same.*"[2]

[1] *The Federalist*, No. 78.
[2] Art. VII. (Italics are mine.)

On the other hand, the Constitution also declares in the preamble that "We, the people of the United States . . . do ordain and establish this Constitution." This seems to indicate that the act of establishing the Constitution was a national act resting on the popular will rather than a compact between states. It is not clear, however, whether the "people" referred to in the preamble were the people of the whole country considered *en masse* or the people of the several states considered separately. In *The Federalist*, however, Madison declared that "this assent and ratification is to be given by the people not as individuals composing one entire nation, but as composing the distinct and independent states to which they respectively belong."[1] He added that "the act establishing the Constitution will not be a national but a federal act."[2]

The evidence of contemporaneous understanding as to the nature of the act establishing the Constitution, considered as a whole, is ambiguous and even contradictory. If, as Madison stated, the act was not national but federal in character—that, in other words, the Constitution was based on a compact between sovereign states—then it follows that any state that had ratified the Constitution might subsequently secede from the Union if it saw fit. The Constitution itself is discreetly silent upon the question of the right of the states to secede. In the state conventions called to ratify the Constitution, the general feeling seemed to be that the act of a state in ratifying would not be subject to recall. No claim was put forth in those conventions that a state would have the right to secede. On the contrary, in the Virginia convention, George Mason declared without contradiction that the Constitution "will be paramount to everything. After having once consented to it, we cannot recede from it." This statement implied not only that the states had no right to secede but that national law would be supreme over state law in case of conflict. The statement was, in fact, put forth as an argument against ratification.

Again, when New York proposed to ratify on condition that a bill of rights be added to the Constitution and that, if this were not done within a stipulated time, the state would be at liberty to withdraw from the Union, Madison declared that such a conditional ratification would not effect the entrance of New York into the Union. He maintained that "any condition whatever must vitiate the ratification" and added that "the Constitution requires an adoption in toto and forever."

In spite of these authoritative statements as to the irrevocable character of the act of ratification and in spite of the fact that a "more perfect Union" was formed based on ratifications by conventions specially chosen by the people of each state instead of by state legislatures (as in the case of the Articles of Confederation), it was nevertheless believed that

[1] *The Federalist*, No. 39.
[2] *Ibid.*

the Constitution was the result of a compact between sovereign states. The reason for this apparent contradiction was that the people of that time saw no difficulty in holding that sovereignty was divided between the states and the nation. They would have perceived no dilemma if asked whether the states or the nation were sovereign and would have answered that both were sovereign. They had, they thought, succeeded in creating a new national sovereign state while at the same time not sacrificing the sovereignty of the thirteen component states. The impossibility of such a situation was not perceived by them. What they probably meant by sovereignty was the exercise of governmental power, which was, of course, divided between the states and the nation. Ultimate sovereignty they would have held to rest in the people, but it was not clear whether this meant the people of the nation as a whole or the people of the separate states. It was not until the time of Calhoun that the view came to be widely held that sovereignty is indivisible and must rest either in the states or in the nation, but not in both. Whether it rested in one or the other was not determined by the language of the Constitution, which, as we have seen, is ambiguous on this point, but was a fact to be determined by future developments in the interpretation and application of the Constitution.

The Development of Nationality.—Although the states were admittedly sovereign during the period of the Confederation, the failure of the movement for secession at the time of the Civil War demonstrated that they were no longer such, but that sovereignty had meanwhile shifted to the nation. This shift was not brought about immediately by the adoption of the Constitution, although such action was an important step in this direction. While the Constitution was ambiguous on the question of the location of sovereignty, it did not, like the Articles of Confederation, contain any express statement that the states were sovereign. It placed no insuperable obstacles in the way of the development of national sovereignty but, on the other hand, contained provisions which might be interpreted as tending in that direction.

An incident which clearly showed the greater vigor of the new National Government under the Constitution was the decisive manner in which it put down the Whiskey Rebellion in 1794 in western Pennsylvania. In view of the fact that the collection of the whiskey tax levied by the National Government upon individuals was resisted in that region, President Washington called out the militia of several states and ordered them to the scene of trouble. Upon their appearance, the rebellion collapsed and national authority was vindicated.

During the first few decades after the adoption of the Constitution, one of the most important centralizing and nationalizing influences was the attitude of the Supreme Court, presided over by Chief Justice Marshall, as exemplified in its leading decisions. For example, in 1796

was decided the case of Chisholm v. Georgia,[1] in which the Court
jurisdiction of a case in which one of the states was defendant
rendered judgment against the state. This was considered by the
as striking a blow at state sovereignty and an amendment to the Con
tion was adopted designed to prevent the Federal courts from
jurisdiction in future cases of like character. The fact that a co
tional amendment was deemed necessary in order to prevent this me
being done was an admission of the increased power and strength of the
National Government.

In spite of the Eleventh Amendment, the Supreme Court continued
to act as the final arbiter in cases of conflict between state and national
power and usually decided such cases in favor of the extension of national
power. By the Constitution the judicial power of the United States
was extended to all cases, in law and equity, arising under the Constitution, laws, and treaties of the United States,[2] which were declared to be
the supreme law of the land, regardless of conflicting provisions in state
constitutions or laws.[3] Through the operation of these provisions and
through the establishment of the doctrine of implied power, the Federal
courts built up a strongly nationalistic basis for the constitutional law of
the United States. Thus, to mention only one case, in Marbury v.
Madison[4] it was shown that questions as to the extent of the power of
Congress under the Constitution are to be finally determined not by
Congress, much less by the states, but by the Supreme Court of the
United States.

The decision in Marbury v. Madison, rendered in 1803, may be considered as in a way an answer to the doctrine put forth in 1799 in the
Virginia and Kentucky resolutions. Written by Madison and Jefferson,
and occasioned by the alien and sedition laws passed by Congress, they
clearly stated that the Constitution is a compact to which the states are
parties and that "each party has an equal right to judge for itself as well
of infractions as of the mode and measure of redress." In a second
series of Kentucky resolutions, it was declared that "nullification . . .
of all unauthorized acts . . . is the rightful remedy." Nevertheless,
the alien and sedition laws were enforced in Virginia and most of the
other states failed to join with Kentucky and Virginia in support of
these doctrines.

After the passage of the tariff of abominations in 1828, however, a
convention held in South Carolina passed an ordinance of nullification
which declared the tariff act as passed by Congress null and void and
without force in that state and prohibited the payment of the duties

[1] 2 Dall. 419.
[2] Art. III, sect. II.
[3] Art. VI, sect. II.
[4] 1 Cranch 137 (1803).

specified in the act.   The ordinance further threatened secession if the
National Government attempted to enforce the act in that state.   Congress made some concessions in the duties, but the determined stand of
President Jackson, who threatened to use any amount of force that might
be necessary to carry out the laws of the Union in South Carolina, caused
the nullificationists to recede from their extreme position.

Nullification was not secession, but for a state to nullify the laws of the
Union while continuing to remain therein was an illogical and impracticable position.   Nullification, if not put down, leads almost inevitably to
secession.   The action of South Carolina, therefore, while not successful
at that time, may be considered as the forerunner of the secession movement of 1861.   By that date, however, the course of events had established
the sovereign character of the Union.   The failure of every previous
movement based on the theory of state sovereignty foreshadowed the
failure of secession.   Sovereignty is a matter of fact rather than of law.
By 1861 the fact was that the nation had become sovereign.   If that
premise were correct, it followed that the states had no legal right to
secede.   The result of the Civil War demonstrated that the premise
was correct.   And the Supreme Court, summing the matter up after
that war, declared that the Constitution "looks to an indestructible
Union, composed of indestructible states."[1]

[1] Texas v. White, 7 Wall. 724 (1869).

CHAPTER IV

THE DEVELOPMENT OF THE CONSTITUTION

Constitutional Changes.—The transition from the Articles of Confederation to the Constitution was, as we have seen, revolutionary although bloodless. The Articles had required a unanimous vote of the states even for their amendment, whereas a new constitution was put into effect by the vote of a fewer number of states. Although our Constitution is thus revolutionary in origin, that fact does not affect its validity. The defect of its origin, if such it may be called, was completely cured by the general acquiescence of the people in the new *regime*. The government set up by the Confederate states during the Civil War was extralegal in origin. In this case, however, the Northern states did not acquiesce. Had the rebellion of the Southern states been successful, it would have been a revolution.

As a fundamental extralegal fact, the people always retain the right of revolution. Only extraordinary circumstances, however, give moral justification for the exercise of this right. As a rule, it is better that the orderly processes of constitutional amendment should be resorted to whenever such change seems desirable. For this reason constitutions should contain provisions for their own amendment that are not too difficult to operate.

Some of the early state constitutions in this country contained no provision for their own amendment. This was probably due to two reasons or influences. The first was the idea which was held in France shortly after the revolution of 1789 that it was possible to draw up a constitution which would be so perfect that it would never need amendment. More important, however, was the idea that, since the people, who are the ultimate source of all political authority, must be assumed to have the right to change their instruments of government, it was unnecessary expressly to provide for this right in the constitution. The framers of later state constitutions, however, have adopted the view that it is desirable to insert in the constitution an express provision for its amendment. This may be made an expressly exclusive method, in which case no other method may be followed. If, however, it is not expressly exclusive, it seems that a convention elected by the people may be held for the purpose of submitting proposed amendments for popular ratification.

A constitution should be adapted to the political, economic, and social conditions of the country. Since these conditions are constantly

31

changing, it is clear that adequate means should be available for amending the constitution so that it will not be too ill-adapted to such changing conditions.

The Constitutional Provision for Amendment.—The framers of the Constitution of 1787 did not make the mistake of some of their French contemporaries of believing it possible to construct a perfect constitution. They realized that, even were such a thing possible, the instrument would not remain perfect for any great length of time and that, as conditions changed, the need for constitutional revision would arise. At the same time, they felt that the Constitution, as the fundamental law, should not be needlessly tinkered with and should not be subject to easy change in order to conform to some passing whim of popular fancy. It is to be remembered that they performed their labors in the eighteenth century and that the idea which became prevalent in the nineteenth that the people should be directly consulted about constitutional changes had not yet become established. In order to carry out their ideas as to methods of constitutional change, it was necessary for them to insert in the instrument itself a provision for its amendment, and this was accordingly done.

If Article V of the Constitution, which contains the provision for amendment, is analyzed, it will be found to stipulate alternative methods of both proposing and ratifying amendments. The two methods of proposing amendments are, first, by a two-thirds vote of Congress and, second, two-thirds of the state legislatures may apply to Congress which is then required to call a national constitutional convention for the purpose of proposing amendments.

Likewise, two methods of ratifying amendments are provided. These are, first, by the action of three-fourths of the state legislatures and, second, by the action of specially called state conventions in three-fourths of the states. Congress is empowered to determine which of the two methods of ratification shall be followed.[1] The selection of the three-fourths vote of the states for ratification was the result of a compromise in the convention between those who favored an easier process and those who advocated the more difficult requirement of unanimous consent. This latter requirement, it will be remembered, was that found in the Articles of Confederation, which proved to be practically prohibitive, and the framers of the Constitution fortunately avoided the mistake of following that precedent.

It will thus be seen that the process of amendment, while giving great weight to the states, is based on a compromise between the federal and national principles. The failure to give the people any direct share in the process is a departure from the national principle. The requirement of a stipulated percentage of the states for ratification, rather than a

[1] United States v. Sprague, 282 U. S. 716 (1931).

unanimous vote, is a departure from the federal principle. A group of states fewer in number than one-fourth of the whole, no matter how much they might be opposed to an amendment ratified by the other states, would be powerless to prevent it from going into effect and would be as much bound by it as if they had voted in favor of its ratification. The participation of the lower house of Congress, whose membership is based upon population, in the process of proposing amendments is to that extent a departure from the federal principle; but, on the whole, the federal principle seems to be given greater weight in the process than the national.

Since Congress is a body of delegated rather than of general residuary powers, it cannot propose amendments in any other way than that expressly provided in the Constitution. It probably could not call a national constitutional convention except upon the application of the legislatures of two-thirds of the states. On the other hand, if two-thirds of the state legislatures should apply to Congress for a convention, there seems to be no legal means whereby Congress could be compelled to call one, notwithstanding the fact that the language of the Constitution is mandatory and that the act is a ministerial one. In fact, taking our history as a whole, more than two-thirds of the state legislatures have at one time or another applied to Congress for a convention. Congress has thus far ignored such applications and apparently with good reason because they were spread over a long period of time and were made for no concerted purpose or particular constitutional change.[1]

The Constitution makes no provision regarding the organization and procedure of a national convention, in case one should be called, nor as to the number of delegates of which it should be composed nor as to the manner of choosing them. It would seem, however, that Congress in calling the convention should appropriate for its expenses and would have the implied power to specify the number of delegates and to determine whether they should be elected by popular vote or otherwise. It would also seem desirable that Congress should designate some person to act as *ex officio* presiding officer of the convention temporarily until permanent organization could be effected. Thereafter, the convention, as an independent deliberative body, should be deemed to be completely in control of its own proceedings to the extent that might be necessary to perform its function of proposing amendments. It hardly seems that either Congress or the state legislatures would have the right to dictate to the convention as to what amendments it should or should not propose.

In actual practice only one method of amending the Constitution has yet been followed, *viz.*, proposal by two-thirds of Congress and ratification by the legislatures of three-fourths of the states. In selecting this method,

---

[1] Some of the proposed changes have already been adopted.

Congress has followed the conservative policy of pursuing the line of least resistance and of utilizing the existing machinery rather than stipulating the creation of the additional machinery of state conventions.

The Proposal of Amendments.—Several questions have arisen in connection with the process actually followed in proposing amendments. One question was as to whether the requirement of a two-thirds vote in Congress means that fraction of the total membership or merely of a quorum of the two houses. The validity of the Eighteenth Amendment was attacked on the ground that the resolution proposing it had not received a two-thirds vote of the total membership of the House of Representatives. It was contended that if less than two-thirds of the total membership were sufficient, the Constitution would have so indicated by the use of appropriate words to that effect, as in the case of the number of senators necessary to approve a treaty. On the other hand, it was maintained that, since a legislative body ordinarily acts by vote of a quorum, the constitutional provision should be interpreted as meaning two-thirds of a quorum unless language is expressly inserted so as to avoid such a conclusion. In the national prohibition cases the Supreme Court adopted the latter view, holding that

. . . the two-thirds vote in each house which is required in proposing an amendment, is a vote of two-thirds of the members present—assuming the presence of a quorum—and not a vote of two-thirds of the entire membership, present and absent.[1]

It would seem to be sufficiently obvious that, if Congress passes by the required vote a resolution proposing an amendment to the Constitution, the members so voting deem such an amendment to be necessary and that an express declaration by them to that effect is not essential. The Supreme Court so held in the national prohibition cases, cited above.

Another question which has arisen is as to the part, if any, that the President plays in the process of proposing amendments. The Constitution provides that "every order, resolution, or vote to which the concurrence of the Senate and House of Representatives may be necessary (except on a question of adjournment) shall be presented to the President."[2] This language would seem to be broad enough to include resolutions passed by Congress for proposing amendments. Nevertheless, this seems to be an instance in which the letter of the Constitution has

[1] National prohibition cases, 253 U. S. 350 (1920). This decision was based in part upon a previous holding of the court that the provision in almost identical language regarding the vote necessary to pass a bill over the President's veto means two-thirds of a quorum. Missouri Pacific Ry. Co. v. Kansas, 248 U. S. 276 (1919). Although a two-thirds vote is required on final passage of the amendment, an amendment to the proposed amendment may be adopted by a mere majority vote.

[2] Art. I, sect. 7.

been modified by the practice under it. It has not been the practice for resolutions proposing amendments to be submitted to the President. In 1865, the proposed Thirteenth Amendment was inadvertently submitted to President Lincoln for his approval. The Senate thereupon adopted the following resolution:

Resolved, that the article of amendment proposed by Congress to be added to the Constitution of the United States respecting the extinction of slavery therein having been inadvertently presented to the President for his approval, it is hereby declared that such approval was unnecessary to give effect to the action of Congress in proposing said amendment, inconsistent with former practice in reference to all amendments to the Constitution heretofore adopted, and being inadvertently done, should not constitute a precedent for the future.[1]

Two reasons for the practice have been put forth. One is that, since the vote of Congress required to propose an amendment in the first place is the same as that by which a presidential veto may be overridden, there is no need of submitting the proposal to the President, for his veto would be without its usual effect in this case.[2] This argument, however, overlooks the fact that the reasons assigned by the President for vetoing a proposed amendment may be sufficiently cogent to win over to his side some members of Congress who voted for the proposal on its first passage and whose votes are necessary to make the required two-thirds. Indeed, regardless of the President's reasons, the mere fact that it is known that he has publicly and officially taken a stand against the proposed amendment may be sufficient to have the same effect.

A better reason for the practice is that the action of Congress in proposing an amendment is not an expression of ordinary legislative power. This view is supported by an early decision of the Supreme Court, in which the validity of the Eleventh Amendment was upheld notwithstanding the fact that it had not been submitted to the President. In the course of the argument in that case, Justice Chase declared that "the negative of the President applies only to the ordinary cases of legislation: he has nothing to do with the proposition or adoption of amendments to the Constitution."[3]

When Congress has once submitted to the states a proposed amendment, the function of that body is complete. Congress cannot reconsider

---

[1] Quoted by W. W. Willoughby, *Constitutional Law of the United States*, 2d. ed., vol. I, p. 593.

[2] BURDICK, C. K., *The Law of the American Constitution*, p. 38.

[3] Hollingsworth v. Virginia, 3 Dall. 378 (1798). It should be noted that the apparent conflict between the letter of the Constitution and the practice under it may be avoided by construing the provision "Every order, resolution, or vote to which the concurrence of the Senate and House of Representatives may be necessary" to mean "necessary to give such order, resolution, or vote the force of law." Since resolutions proposing amendments to the Constitution do not have the force of law, the provision does not apply.

its action nor effect the recall of the proposal. The fate of the amendment is no longer within its control but has been transferred to the control of the states.

The Ratification of Amendments.—As noted above, the only method of ratification heretofore adopted in practice is that by the legislatures of three-fourths of the states. It seems clear that this means three-fourths of the number of states in existence, not at the time the amendment is proposed, but at the time it is ratified. In the case of the amendments adopted shortly after the Civil War, the question arose as to whether the states which had attempted to secede and which had not yet been readmitted to the full enjoyment of the privileges of states of the Union should be counted among the whole number of states of which three-fourths were needed for ratification. With respect to the Thirteenth Amendment, the unreconstructed states were so counted and some of them were also counted among those ratifying the amendment. The unreconstructed states were required to ratify the Fourteenth and Fifteenth Amendments as a condition precedent to their readmission to the full enjoyment of the privileges of states of the Union. As has been pointed out, the imposition of this requirement by Congress was one which "it is difficult constitutionally to justify."[1] But the courts would not interfere to prevent such an imposition, deeming themselves to be precluded from doing so by the action of the political department of the government.[2]

Official notification of the action of state legislatures in ratifying an amendment is transmitted to the secretary of state at Washington. By an act of 1818 Congress has placed upon the secretary the duty to proclaim an amendment adopted when he has received official notices from the required number of states. The validity of the Nineteenth Amendment to the Constitution was attacked in the Supreme Court on the ground that the ratifying resolutions of Tennessee and West Virginia were adopted in violation of the rules of legislative procedure obtaining in those states. It was held, however, that official notice from the states to the secretary of state that they had ratified is "conclusive upon him, and, being certified by his proclamation, is conclusive upon the courts."[3] This doctrine, however, should not be pushed to the point where the amendment of the Constitution would substantially depend upon the approval of the secretary of state. Moreover, it has been held that the duty of the secretary of state to proclaim the adoption of an amendment involves no discretion and is purely ministerial and that an amendment is brought into effect not by his proclamation but by the

---

[1] WILLOUGHBY, W. W., *Constitutional Law of the United States*, 2d. ed., vol. I, p. 594.

[2] White v. Hart, 13 Wall. 646 (1872).

[3] Leser v. Garnett, 258 U. S. 130 (1922), citing Field v. Clark, 143 U. S. 649 (1890).

ratifying action of the required number of states.[1] Unless otherwise specified in the amendment itself, it goes into effect not on the date of the secretary's proclamation but on the date of the consummation of its ratification.[2]

The Eighteenth Amendment is peculiar in that it contains a provision that the amendment should not take effect until one year after its ratification. It has not been directly decided that Congress could by mere legislation place such a limitation upon the force of the states' ratification, but the Court has declared that "as a rule the Constitution speaks in general terms, leaving Congress to deal with subsidiary matters of detail as the public interests and changing conditions may require; and Article V is no exception to the rule."[3] There would certainly be no objection to such a provision contained in the amendment itself, for it then rests not merely upon the authority of Congress but also upon the consent of the state legislatures. It was, in fact, in the case of the Eighteenth Amendment, acted upon without question.

Another unusual feature of the Eighteenth Amendment is that declaring it to be inoperative unless ratified by three-fourths of the state legislatures within seven years from the date of submission. This provision was an attempt on the part of Congress to limit to a reasonable length of time the period during which an amendment might be ratified after it had been submitted. Here again, although it has not been directly decided that Congress could make such a restriction by mere legislation, there is certainly no constitutional objection to placing such a provision in the amendment itself. Indeed, there might be some advantage in having such a provision in the amending clause of the Constitution and applying to future amendments generally.

There are several amendments which have been proposed by Congress, some of them more than a century ago, but have never been ratified by the requisite number of states. It would be absurd to suppose that, after such a great lapse of time, such amendments are to be considered as still pending and still capable of becoming part of the Constitution through additional ratifications. The Constitution itself sets no express limit upon the time within which amendments may be ratified, but it must be supposed that a reasonable limit is necessarily implied. The reasons for this view are: first, that proposal and ratification should be considered as two related and almost contemporaneous steps in a single process; second, that it is only when Congress deems a necessity to exist that amendments are to be submitted to the states for ratification and it could not be supposed that the Congressional estimate of necessity should continue to exist for longer than a reasonable time; and, third,

[1] United States v. Colby, 265 Fed. 998 (1920).
[2] Dillon v. Gloss, 256 U. S. 368 (1921).
[3] *Ibid.*

that it is fairly implied that the acts of ratification by the states, in order to represent an effective expression of popular approval, should take place within the same general period of time. This view has in fact been upheld by the Supreme Court.[1] The term "reasonable limit," however, is of course somewhat vague and it seems desirable that a more definite limit, such as that of the Eighteenth Amendment, should be set. In the case just cited the Supreme Court declared that:

Of the power of Congress, keeping within reasonable limits, to fix a definite period for the ratification we entertain no doubt . . . Whether a definite period for ratification shall be fixed, so that all may know what it is and speculation on what is a reasonable time may be avoided, is, in our opinion, a matter of detail which Congress may determine as an incident of its power to designate the mode of ratification. It is not questioned that seven years, the period fixed in this instance, was reasonable, if power existed to fix a definite time; nor could it well be questioned considering the periods within which prior amendments were ratified.[2]

The Court here speaks as if it were under the impression that the seven-year limit was contained in a mere act or joint resolution of Congress rather than in the amendment itself, whereas the latter was the case. If the Court intended to hold, as seems to be the case, that Congress could on its sole authority enforce such a time limit, then its statement was *obiter*, for this question was not directly before it. As pointed out above, however, there is no doubt of the constitutionality of placing such a time limit in the amendment itself.[3]

A question of practical importance which has arisen in connection with ratification is whether a state which has once ratified an amendment may later rescind or withdraw its ratification. Obviously, this could not be done after the amendment has received the requisite number of ratifications and gone into effect. The question relates rather to the case where a state attempts to withdraw its ratification before the amendment has been proclaimed. The courts have not directly passed upon this question, but practice indicates that a state cannot withdraw its ratification. Ohio and New Jersey attempted to withdraw their ratifications of the Fourteenth Amendment. The secretary of state issued his proclamation in hypothetical form, declaring the amendment to be in effect if the ratifications of those states were to be counted, notwithstanding their subsequent attempt to withdraw ratification. Later, however, he issued another proclamation declaring positively that the amendment was in force, and Congress passed a concurrent resolution to the same effect. This decision seems wise in view of the

---

[1] Dillon v. Gloss, 256 U. S. 368 (1921).

[2] *Ibid.*

[3] The proposed Twentieth Amendment, submitted by Congress to the states in 1932, also contains the seven-year limit. See below, Appendix.

fact that to allow states to withdraw their ratifications at will would be likely to produce confusion in determining whether or not an amendment has been adopted.

On the other hand, there is nothing to prevent a state which has rejected an amendment from later ratifying it, and such ratification, if made within a reasonable time, may be counted among the necessary number. This, in fact, has been done. Thus, North Carolina and South Carolina, having rejected the Fourteenth Amendment, later ratified it and were counted among the necessary three-fourths to secure its adoption. The rejection of an amendment signifies mere failure to ratify for the time being. In legal effect, there is no difference between rejection and failure to act at all.

Lack of Direct Popular Participation.—As already noted, the framers of the amending clause of the Constitution, in accordance with eighteenth century ideas, made no provision for direct popular participation in the amending process. There has been a widespread feeling that the process should be democratized and in some quarters it had been supposed until recently that this object might be accomplished to some extent through the power of the states to regulate the manner of ratification. Many states have introduced the popular referendum on state-wide legislation, and it was thought that this right of the people might be invoked with respect to the action of the legislature in ratifying an amendment to the Federal Constitution. Ohio even went so far in 1918 as to embody in her constitution a provision expressly authorizing the invocation of the referendum upon proposed Federal amendments. Moreover, the state supreme courts of Ohio and Washington held the referendum to be applicable to the Federal amending process. The Ohio case involved the right of the opponents of prohibition to invoke the referendum upon the action of the legislature in ratifying the Eighteenth Amendment. This right having been upheld by the state court, the case was appealed to the Supreme Court of the United States, which reversed the decision of the state court.[1]

The decision of the Supreme Court in this case turned upon the proper interpretation of the word "legislatures" as used in the amending clause. By those who favored the use of the referendum it was argued that the word meant the legislative power of the state, one means of exercising which was through the referendum. The Court pointed out, however, that, at the time the Constitution was drawn up, the word "legislature" meant not the electorate but "the representative body which made the laws of the people" and held that it still bore the same meaning. If it were objected to this conclusion that it might take away altogether the power of passing on Federal amendments in the case of a state which, having abolished its legislature, depended upon the popular

[1] Hawke v. Smith, 126 N. E. 400 (1919); 253 U. S. 221 (1920).

initiative as the sole means of legislation, the answer obviously would be that a state could not do so without violating the constitutional guarantee of a republican form of government.   One of the essential reasons behind the decision of the Court in this case was expressed in the following passage from the opinion:

The argument to support the power of the state to require the approval by the people of the state of the ratification of amendments to the Federal Constitution through the medium of a referendum rests upon the proposition that the Federal Constitution requires ratification by the legislative action of the states through the medium provided at the time of the proposed approval of an amendment.   This argument is fallacious in this—ratification by the state of a constitutional amendment is not an act of legislation within the proper sense of the word.   It is but the expression of the assent of the state to the proposed amendment.[1]

The Court added that

. . . the power to ratify a proposed amendment to the Federal Constitution has its source in the Federal Constitution.   The act of ratification by the state derives its authority from the Federal Constitution to which the state and its people have alike assented . . . Any other view might lead to endless confusion in the manner of ratification of Federal amendments.   The choice of means of ratification was wisely withheld from conflicting action.[1]

The principle laid down in Hawke v. Smith is of importance as applied not only to the situation in Ohio but also to the situation which later arose in Tennessee in connection with the ratification by that state of the Nineteenth Amendment.   The Constitution of Tennessee provides that:

No convention or General Assembly of this state shall act upon any amendment of the Constitution of the United States, proposed by Congress to the several states, unless such convention or General Assembly shall have been elected after such amendment is submitted.[2]

This provision was evidently intended to secure a popular expression upon the proposed amendment indirectly through the election of representatives who are either favorable or opposed to it.   If the legislature chosen before the amendment is submitted acts upon it, the people would obviously have no opportunity of passing upon it even in this indirect manner.   Nevertheless, the legislature of Tennessee elected before the Nineteenth Amendment was submitted proceeded to ratify it in disregard of the above-quoted provision of the constitution of that state.   When, on that account, the validity of the Nineteenth Amend-

[1] *Ibid.*
[2] Art. II, sect. 32.

ment was attacked in the Supreme Court, that tribunal denied the contention, holding on the strength of Hawke v. Smith, that the state legislature, in ratifying a proposed amendment to the Federal Constitution, is acting as a Federal agency and its act is a Federal function derived from the Federal Constitution and transcends any limits sought to be imposed by the people of a state through the state constitution.[1]

If the people of a state through their state constitution cannot require their state legislature to wait until after a legislative election before ratifying an amendment to the Federal Constitution, neither can Congress make such a requirement. Although the legislature is acting as an agent or organ of the Federal Government and not of the state government, it is still a state legislature which is acting and Congress could not regulate the procedure in the legislature in ratifying an amendment.

A final question which has arisen with reference to ratification by state legislatures is as to whether the governor of the state has any right to veto the legislature's action in this respect. The President, as we have seen, has no similar power and the governor is clearly in the same situation. Since the legislature in ratifying is not performing an ordinary act of legislation and is not acting under the state constitution, the veto of the governor does not apply. In a few cases the resolution of the legislature ratifying a Federal amendment has been sent to the governor and vetoed by him, but his right to do so has not been upheld by the state courts and has been ignored by the secretary of state at Washington in issuing his proclamation declaring the amendment adopted.

There is nothing, however, to prevent a governor from sending a message to the legislature recommending the rejection ef an amendment, as Governor Hughes of New York did in the case of the Sixteenth Amendment. When the legislature has ratified, the governor may transmit to the secretary of state at Washington the certification of the state's ratification, but this is a mere ministerial act.

Express Limits on the Subject Matter of Amendments.—The amending clause contains two express limits upon the amending power. The first prohibited any change prior to the year 1808 in the case of two specified provisions of the Constitution dealing with direct taxes and with the importation of slaves. This limit was only temporary and is now of merely historical significance. The second limit, which is still in force, was inserted as a concession to the small states and prohibits a state from being deprived, without its consent, of its equal representation in the Senate. It has been suggested that "this limitation may be evaded by adopting a constitutional amendment eliminating this limitation upon the amending power, and thus opening the way to subsequent amendments providing for unequal representation of the states in the

[1] Leser v. Garnett, 258 U. S. 130 (1922).

Senate."[1] This, however, would be an attempt to nullify a provision of the Constitution by two steps instead of one and would manifestly violate the spirit, if not the letter, of that instrument. States have occasionally been without equal representation in the Senate, owing to their failure to elect or to the refusal by the Senate to seat the person elected on the ground of lack of qualifications, but this deprivation has been, technically at least, with the consent of the state concerned and therefore not a violation of the constitutional limitation. The better view would seem to be that the provision establishing the right of the states to equal representation in the Senate is one which can be changed only by a process different from that which applies to the amendment of other provisions of the Constitution, unless the state which it is proposed to deprive of equal representation is numbered among the three-fourths ratifying the amendment. Since, however, a state would not be likely to consent to its own deprivation of this right, the constitutional limitation is practically unamendable by ordinary methods. Assuming, however, that ultimate authority rests in the people of the United States who are outside the governmental machinery set up by the Constitution, it would seem to follow that, by revolution if necessary, any change desired by the people in the fundamental law may be made. In other words, while, from the standpoint of constitutional law, the amending power is not competent to deprive a state of its equal representation in the Senate without its consent; from the standpoint of political theory, no one generation can so firmly fix the fundamental law of the land as absolutely to bind all future generations.

Are There Implied Limits upon the Amending Power?—This question seems scarcely to have been raised until after the adoption of the Eighteenth Amendment prohibiting the manufacture, sale, or transportation of intoxicating liquors. The validity of that amendment was attacked in the Supreme Court on the ground that it violates certain implied limits upon the amending power which were alleged to exist. Among these allegations was, first, that the amendment was not, properly speaking, an amendment but rather an addition of new matter which was beyond the amending power to introduce. There is nothing, however, in the proceedings of the Constitutional Convention of 1787 to indicate that the framers intended any such narrow construction of the scope of the amending power. On the contrary, it seemed to be understood by the members of that convention that any changes might be made except those expressly prohibited.

In the second place, it was alleged that the amendment contains matter which is essentially statutory legislation in character, in that it lays down a self-executing rule governing the personal conduct of indi-

---

[1] WILLOUGHBY, W. W., *Constitutional Law of the United States*, 2d ed., vol. I, p. 598, citing Von Holst, *Constitutional Law*, p. 31, note.

viduals, and therefore has no proper place in a constitution. This argument would not be conclusive even though no similar provision had previously been incorporated in the Constitution, but it may be pointed out that the Thirteenth Amendment prohibiting slavery also embodied a self-executing rule governing the personal conduct of individuals and affecting the ownership of private property. The validity of both amendments is equally beyond successful attack on this ground.

The third ground of attack upon the Eighteenth Amendment was of a more fundamental character. It was alleged that the Ninth and Tenth Amendments must be construed as limitations upon the amending power so as to prevent any change which would deprive the states of such an essential ingredient of the police power as the regulation of the liquor traffic. If this fundamental governmental power of the states could be encroached upon, other essential powers of the states might be taken away to such an extent as virtually to destroy the states as members of the Union, which would be in violation of the spirit of the Constitution. An argument of the same general character was made against the validity of the Nineteenth Amendment, it being alleged that the determination as to which of its citizens shall be allowed to vote is an essential governmental power of the state which cannot be taken away by the amending power. The addition of such a large number of persons to the electorate of a state without its consent, it was argued, destroys its autonomy as a political body. In answer to this argument, however, the Supreme Court pointed out that the Nineteenth Amendment was couched in language quite similar to that of the Fifteenth, whose validity it was now too late to question.[1] Moreover, in the case involving the validity of the Eighteenth Amendment, all of these arguments were summarily brushed aside by the Supreme Court which simply upheld the validity of that amendment in a series of conclusions without a reasoned opinion.[2]

It would have been easy, however, for the Court to find reasons for upholding the validity of the Eighteenth Amendment in spite of the arguments made against it. Among such reasons the following may be mentioned. In the first place, if, as the courts frequently affirm, the benefit of doubt should be resolved in favor of the validity of legislative acts, it would certainly seem that the same rule should apply with all the more force to a constitutional amendment. When two-thirds of Congress and three-fourths of the states have in due form adopted an amendment, which violates no express prohibition of the Constitution, it would certainly be a great stretch of power for the Court to set it aside and thus defeat the will of the amending power on the ground of a violation of some implied limitation upon that power which is alleged to exist. This would constitute an assumption of political power by

[1] Leser v. Garnett, 258 U. S. 130 (1922).
[2] National prohibition cases, 253 U. S. 350 (1920).

the judiciary which it would be difficult to justify.   It would mean, in effect, that actual power over the subject matter of amendments would be transferred to the judiciary with scarcely any possibility of reversal short of revolution.   The courts would then be in a position to decide, regardless of the wishes of the amending authority, what proposed changes should or should not be inserted in the Constitution, without any legal rule to guide them but merely according to their own notions of expediency or propriety.   It would be manifestly unwise for the courts to take such a position.

In the second place, some of the arguments against the validity of the Eighteenth and Nineteenth Amendments were based upon the outworn theory that the Constitution is a compact between the states or between the states and the central government.   Although this doctrine does not seem to have been specifically stated in the arguments against those amendments, such arguments are logically based on this theory.   Were this the correct theory, it might with force be maintained that a state's electorate could not be enlarged nor its police powers taken away without its consent.   As we have seen, however, the compact theory has long since been discarded in favor of the national theory, under which there would be no logical objection to any changes in the character or position of the states that the amending power might in its discretion wish to make except only those expressly prohibited.

Another attack upon the validity of the Eighteenth Amendment was the holding of a Federal district judge in New Jersey that a distinction should be made in the method of ratification according to the subject matter of the amendment.   Amendments changing constitutional provisions respecting governmental machinery may be submitted to state legislatures.   But amendments that affect so fundamentally the sphere of individual liberty as does the Eighteenth Amendment could not, he held, be properly ratified except by state conventions. Consequently, he held that this amendment had not been validly ratified.   Upon appeal to the Supreme Court, however, the lower court was reversed, and the amendment was upheld as having been validly adopted.[1] Admittedly, there is good ground for the argument that, as matter of policy, the convention method of ratification should have been selected. But, as a matter of law, by the plain language of the amending article, the choice of the mode of ratification lies in the sole discretion of Congress, regardless of the nature of the subject matter of the amendment.

Our conclusion is that there is no judicial sanction for the proposition that there are any implied limitations upon the subject matter of constitutional amendments.   If the amending authority so desires, there would seem to be nothing to prevent the transformation of the government from a federal to either a unitary or a confederate government.

[1] United States v. Sprague, 282 U. S. 716 (1931).

The Exercise of the Amending Power.—Of the formal amendments which have thus far been adopted, the first ten were ratified so soon after the original Constitution went into effect as to be practically contemporaneous with it. The first eight amendments embodied the bill of rights, the lack of which in the original Constitution, as we have seen, caused opposition in the state conventions to ratification, which was only overcome by a promise that such amendments would be proposed by Congress. One argument that had been made against the insertion of a bill of rights in the Constitution was that to do so was not only unnecessary (since the new government was one of delegated powers) but also dangerous, because it was almost impossible to enumerate all private rights in the Constitution and from the failure to enumerate certain rights the inference might be drawn that such rights were not protected as against the action of the central government. The Ninth Amendment was adopted to overcome this objection and the Tenth embodies the general principle which controls the distribution of power between the central government and the states.

The Eleventh was the first of the series of amendments adopted which were not contemporaneous with the original Constitution. It resulted from a decision of the Supreme Court holding that a state is subject to suit by a citizen of another state.[1] This doctrine was so objectionable to believers in states' rights that they secured the adoption of an amendment so as to prevent such a construction from being placed upon the power of the courts.

The Twelfth Amendment, ratified in 1804, was adopted for the purpose of remedying a defect in the system of electing the President which had been disclosed by the presidential election of 1800.

More than sixty years elapsed between the dates of adoption of the Twelfth and the Thirteenth Amendments. Then, beginning in 1865, three amendments, known as the war amendments, were adopted in rapid succession. The Thirteenth abolished slavery, while the Fourteenth and Fifteenth were intended to protect the newly acquired rights of the freedmen. One incidental effect of the adoption of the Thirteenth Amendment was to render obsolete the three-fifths compromise of the Constitutional Convention of 1787 whereby that fraction of the slaves were counted as the basis of representation in the lower house of Congress and as the basis for levying direct taxes. The result was to increase the representation in Congress of the Southern states in which lived the bulk of the former slaves. In order to overcome this unintended result of the Thirteenth Amendment, the second section of the Fourteenth Amendment was adopted, whereby Congress was empowered to reduce the representation of those states unless they allowed the former slaves to vote. When this threat of loss of representation did not have the

[1] Chisholm v. Georgia, 2 Dall. 419 (1793).

intended effect, the Fifteenth Amendment was adopted which prohibited discrimination in the matter of voting on account of race, color, or previous condition of servitude.

From the time of the adoption of the last of the war amendments until the Sixteenth was placed in the Constitution, forty-three years elapsed. After this long period of inactivity, four amendments dealing with unrelated matters were adopted. These matters were the income tax, the election of senators, prohibition, and woman suffrage. They were embodied in the Sixteenth, Seventeenth, Eighteenth, and Nineteenth Amendments adopted between 1913 and 1920.

Criticism of the Amending Process.—The first twelve amendments were adopted to cure defects early discovered in the original Constitution. During the century following the adoption of the Twelfth Amendment, thousands of proposed amendments were introduced in Congress which failed to pass that body and only three amendments—the Thirteenth, Fourteenth, and Fifteenth—were placed in the Constitution. The latter were war amendments, adopted in order to bring the fundamental law of the land into conformity with the new conditions resulting from the Civil War. When, at the end of the century, none except the war amendments had been adopted during that time, the feeling became widespread that the Constitution is substantially unamendable except during a period of great national emergency and public excitement. As a result, however, of the adoption of four amendments in rapid succession between 1913 and 1920, this feeling has been largely dissipated and the impression has been created in the minds of many people that the Constitution is capable of fairly easy amendment.

This impression, however, seems hardly justified when we remember that a long and hard struggle preceded the adoption of each of these four amendments. The movement for the income tax amendment of 1913 had begun nearly two decades before when the income tax law of 1894 was invalidated by the Supreme Court. The movement for the popular election of senators had been of even longer duration and was not successful until after a widespread popular demand for it had made itself felt for some time. The movements for prohibition and woman suffrage had been equally long and probably would not have succeeded as soon as they did had it not been for the unsettling of conditions resulting from the World War.

The fact that thousands of proposed amendments have been introduced in Congress but thus far only twenty-five have received the necessary two-thirds vote in that body, while nineteen of these twenty-five have been adopted shows that the principal difficulty is in securing the consent of Congress to submit proposals rather than in obtaining the ratification of the states.

It does not follow that, because it is difficult to amend the Constitution, the process should be made more easy. We have become accustomed in this country to the fundamental difference between a constitution and a statute, and it would hardly be wise to minimize this difference by making it as easy to change the Constitution as to pass a statute. Moreover, the Federal Constitution fortunately confines itself mainly to matters of fundamental importance, such as the outline of the organization of the National Government and the distribution of power between that government and the states. It does not go very much into detail but wisely leaves minor matters for legislative determination. Such a Constitution should be fairly permanent and it is not essential that it should be easily amendable.

It must be admitted, however, that if there is need of change in the amending process, it is rather in the direction of greater ease than otherwise. This is shown by the fact that there are a number of provisions of comparatively minor importance in the Constitution, about which there is little difference of opinion as to the need for change but no change is made because of the difficulty of amendment. It is difficult to arouse widespread popular excitement over such minor matters, and so we put up with relatively unimportant inconveniences rather than attempt to invoke the cumbrous machinery of constitutional amendment. It would probably facilitate the process of adopting needed changes without making change too easy, if Congress were allowed to submit proposed amendments by a mere majority vote of all members elected to both branches.

The amending process has also been criticized on the ground that it is too undemocratic. It was, as we have seen, with the purpose of remedying to some extent this defect that constitutional provisions were adopted in Ohio and Tennessee relating to the Federal amending process, but these provisions were held to be invalid by the Supreme Court. At the present time, therefore, the people, in accordance with the provisions of our eighteenth century Constitution, have no direct participation in the amending process and their indirect influence is limited to acting through their representatives in the legislatures who may not be, and usually have not been, elected with special reference to their attitude upon prospective Federal amendments.

Various proposals have been made from time to time in order to give the people a larger share in the amending process. Thus the LaFollette proposal, made in 1912, would have directed that a Federal amendment be proposed by Congress on application of ten states either by legislative resolution or by majority vote of the people. It would have allowed ratification by a majority of the electors voting in the majority of the states, provided this constituted a majority of the total vote cast on the proposal in the whole country. On the other hand, the Wadsworth-

Garrett proposal of 1923, while making no change in the method of proposing amendments, provided that ratification might be effected by popular vote in three-fourths of the states after affirmative or negative action by the respective legislatures.[1] It has also been suggested that the Federal Constitution should be so amended as to embody the changes sought to be accomplished by the Ohio constitutional provision permitting the referendum on Federal amendments and also by the Tennessee constitutional provision mentioned above, at least to the extent of requiring that the members of at least one house in each of the ratifying legislatures should have been elected after the amendment should have been proposed.

None of the above suggestions has been adopted nor does it seem that they are likely to be placed in the Constitution, because they are more or less abstract propositions about which it is difficult to get the people of the country sufficiently aroused to set in motion the amending process. Nor does it seem necessary to amend the Federal amending clause in order to democratize it, in view of the fact that greater popular control might be introduced under the clause as it stands. This could be accomplished by resorting to the alternative method of ratification by specially chosen state conventions. Although popular control would still be indirect, it would be distinctly greater under the convention method than under the present practice. In fact, under this method of ratification, any state could introduce what would virtually be a popular referendum on the amendment by providing for voting by general ticket on two slates of candidates for delegates to the state convention, one pledged to ratify, and the other pledged to reject, the proposed amendment.

Development of the Broad Constitution.—As pointed out in a preceding chapter, the Constitution may be considered from two points of view. In the first place, it is the written document drawn up in 1787 together with the nineteen formal amendments adopted thereto. In the broad sense, the Constitution includes not only this core but also statutory amplification, judicial decisions interpreting the written Constitution, and customs, usages, and unwritten rules which have come to have the force of law.

Although the formal written Constitution is more or less rigid, in the broad sense it is much more flexible and has been more extensively changed. The framers of the Constitution confined themselves in the main to fundamentals and included few details in the written instrument. They did not even provide fully for the framework of govern-

---

[1] The texts of the LaFollette and Wadsworth-Garrett proposals are reprinted in Mathews and Berdahl's *Documents and Readings in American Government*, pp. 54–55. The Wadsworth-Garrett proposal was intended to make the process of amendment more difficult.

ment. Although indicating that there should be executive departments and inferior courts, these were not definitely created in the Constitution but were left to be established by act of Congress. Upon the latter body also devolves the function of providing for succession to the Presidency after the Vice President. In these and various other ways, Congress fills in the gaps in the Constitution, so that, in the material as contrasted with the formal sense, that instrument is frequently being developed by statutory elaboration.

Much of constitutional law is found not in the written Constitution but in the opinions of the courts interpreting and applying its provisions to concrete cases brought before them. Through the exercise of this function, the courts actually do make constitutional law. They may broaden or narrow the meaning of constitutional provisions so as to include or exclude various matters to which they might possibly apply. Thus, the Supreme Court has interpreted the term commerce, used in the Constitution, as broad enough to include not only traffic but also intercourse,[1] while, on the other hand, it has held that the insurance business is not included in the term.[2] Through hundreds of decisions defining and applying its provisions, the Constitution is thus being constantly developed by judicial interpretation.

Finally, the Constitution in the broad sense is being developed by usages, customs, and conventions. These go to make up what may be called the unwritten constitution, which is superadded to, and to some extent inconsistent with, the written constitution. In developing the unwritten constitution, the operations of political parties are especially important. Through their agency, the actual method of electing the President has been made quite different from that intended by the theory of the Constitution. Through the holding of caucuses outside the regular meetings of Congress, political parties may exercise a controlling influence upon its deliberations. The powerful committee system in Congress and the third-term tradition also rest upon usage and compose parts of the unwritten constitution. Customs and usages change from time to time, although not so quickly or readily as do other methods of constitutional development.

The development of the Constitution in the broad sense is a continuous process. Further illustrations of this process will be found throughout this volume.

[1] Gibbons v. Ogden, 9 Wheat. 1 (1824).
[2] Paul v. Virginia, 8 Wall. 168 (1868).

CHAPTER V

NATIONAL AND STATE RELATIONS

A considerable part of the whole body of constitutional law is concerned with the relations between the National Government and the states. Such relations crop up in connection with many important topics, such as the amendment of the Constitution, presidential elections, taxation, and the regulation of commerce, and will be considered incidentally in the chapters dealing with those topics. Other phases of the relations between the National Government and the states are considered in the present chapter. A consideration of these matters shows that neither the state government nor the National Government is a complete government in all respects, but each is dependent to a certain extent upon the other for the performance of several essential functions.

The Admission of New States.—The states already existed prior to the adoption of the Constitution. These were the thirteen original states which came into the Union through their respective acts in ratifying that instrument. The claims of certain of the original states to Western territory had been ceded to the general government, prior to establishment of the government under the Articles of Confederation in 1781, with the understanding that Congress would eventually organize that territory into states and admit them into the Union. By the Northwest Ordinance, passed by the Confederate Congress in 1787, it was provided that the Northwest Territory should be divided into not less than three or more than five states and that "whenever any of the said states shall have sixty thousand free inhabitants therein, such state shall be admitted, by its delegates, into the Congress of the United States, on an equal footing with the original states, in all respects whatever."

In view of the foregoing matters, it was natural that the Constitution should have contained a provision for the admission of new states into the Union in addition to the original thirteen. This provision declares that "new states may be admitted by the Congress into this Union."[1] In order to safeguard the territory of existing states against the exercise of this power, it is further provided by way of limitation thereupon that (1) "no new state shall be formed or erected within the jurisdiction of any other state" and (2) that no state shall "be formed by the junction of two or more states or parts of states, without the consent of the legislatures of the states concerned as well as of the Congress."[2]

[1] Art. IV, sect. III.
[2] *Ibid.*

Construed in the light of the practice under this group of provisions, the two limitations quoted may be reduced to one, *viz.*, that Congress cannot take away from any state, without the consent of its legislature, a part of its territory and admit the latter into the Union as a new state. In addition to the express limitations quoted, there are also the implied limitations that Congress cannot admit new states except on an equal footing with the states already in the Union and that Congress cannot admit a new state into the Union whose government is not republican in form.

Practice in Admission.—Altogether, thirty-five states have been admitted into the Union by act of Congress. Of these, five—Vermont, Kentucky, Tennessee, Maine, and West Virginia—have been carved out of the territory of older states. In these five instances the consent of the legislature of the older state was obtained, except in the case of West Virginia in 1862. The consent of the legislature of Virginia, which was then in military opposition to the Union, was not obtained, but the consent of a newly formed legislature in the western portion of the state, claiming to be the legal legislature, was deemed by Congress to be sufficient.[1] The question as to what procedure should be followed in case the older state had no legislature that could even claim to be legal has not arisen.

On account of unsatisfactory conditions existing in some cities as the result of their treatment by the respective states in which they are situated, some agitation has arisen at times in certain cities, notably New York and Chicago, in favor of the admission of those cities as states. The dissatisfaction of Chicago has been due principally to the failure of the legislature to reapportion the state into legislative districts since 1901 in disregard of a constitutional provision that this shall be done after each decennial census. It has even been contended in some quarters that this disregard of the state constitution leaves Illinois without a legally established legislature. Even if this were true, the existing legislature is the *de facto* legislative body, and its consent as well as that of Congress would doubtless have to be secured before Chicago could be admitted into the Union as a state.

Two states have been admitted into the Union without having had previously an organized territorial government. These were Texas and California. The former had been an independent state before its annexation and admission in 1845. By the joint Congressional resolution of admission, it was provided that Texas might subsequently be divided

---

[1] RANDALL, J. G., *Constitutional Problems under Lincoln*, p. 452. The attorney-general rendered an opinion that the legislature which, meeting at Wheeling on May 13, 1862, gave its consent to the dismemberment of Virginia was not a legislature competent to give consent, on behalf of Virginia, to the formation of West Virginia. 10 Op. U. S. Atty.-Gen. 426.

into not more than five states, but the state has apparently never desired to carry out this plan in spite of the increased representation in the Senate which it would afford.

The remaining twenty-eight states have been formed out of preexisting organized territory under the jurisdiction of the National Government. The Constitution makes no provision as to the procedure to be followed by a territory desiring to become a state. The movement for admission has usually started in the territory itself, which sends a petition to Congress asking that that body take the necessary steps for the admission of the territory as a state. If this petition is accorded a favorable reception, Congress passes an "enabling act" authorizing the territorial government to provide for holding a popularly elected convention to draw up a proposed state constitution. If this instrument is ratified by the voters of the territory, it is then submitted to Congress for its approval. In case the proposed constitution is acceptable to Congress, that body passes the statehood bill or resolution which has the effect of transforming the territory into a state. As in the case of other bills, the statehood bill must be submitted to the President for his approval, and he may veto the bill if the proposed state constitution is not satisfactory to him. If that happens, the territory cannot come into the Union under that constitution unless Congress repasses the statehood bill over the President's veto. As the final stage in the procedure, the President, in accordance with the direction of Congress, sometimes issues a proclamation declaring the admission of the new state.

In some instances, territories have not waited for the passage by Congress of an enabling act but have on their own initiative framed proposed state constitutions for submission to Congress. On rare occasions they have even established governments under such constitutions before admission by Congress as states. Although this procedure is irregular, it is validated if Congress subsequently passes the statehood bill.

It is doubtful whether Congress could compel a territory to become a state of the Union against its will. This is not a question that has actually arisen, however, because territories have usually been only too glad to become states. On the other hand, there is no doubt that a territory has no means of compelling Congress to admit it as a state. The power, position in the Union, and prestige of a state, as compared with a territory, are of course much greater and more important. On the other hand, the power of Congress over a state is correspondingly less than over a territory. In view of this situation, it is remarkable that Congress has admitted new states so readily and in some cases, indeed, when there was little doubt that they were not yet fitted for statehood. This readiness on the part of Congress may be explained, in part, by the exigencies of practical politics. Thus, before the Civil War, states were admitted in rapid succession in order to maintain approximate equality in the numbers of slave and free states. During that war, Nevada, although very thinly populated, was admitted in order to secure the vote of the necessary number of states for the ratification of the thirteenth or antislavery amendment to the Constitution of the United States.[1] Even allowing for the exigencies of practical politics, however, the policy of Congress in admitting new states seems generous to a fault. With the possible exception of Alaska, however, there seems to be no prospect of the admission of any more states.

Ordinarily, Congress has the power to repeal any act or joint resolution which it has the power to pass. A statehood act, however, is irrepealable, or, in other words, any attempt at repeal would be without legal effect. If the contrary were true, Congress would have the power of expelling a state from the Union or, at least, of demoting it from the status of a state to that of a territory, but no such power has been granted to it. Since, therefore, the step taken by Congress in admitting a new state is irrevocable, it should be taken only after careful consideration.

Conditions on Admission.—Numerous illustrations might be cited of requirements which Congress has imposed upon territories as a condition of admission to statehood. Thus, Nevada was admitted in 1864 on condition that she should not deny any persons the right to vote on account of their color. A similar requirement was imposed upon Nebraska in 1867 and also upon the Southern states which had attempted secession as the condition of their readmission to full privileges in the Union. Utah was admitted in 1894 on condition that she make "by ordinance irrevocable without the consent of the United States" provision for religious toleration and for the abolition of polygamy in perpetuity.

The proposed state constitution, as framed by a territory, has sometimes been unsatisfactory in certain respects to Congress or to the President, and the territory has been required to amend the instrument so as to meet these objections. Thus, the first draft of the constitution of Arizona provided for the recall of elected officials, including judges. President Taft vetoed the resolution providing for the admission of the state with this constitutional provision, and she was required to amend her constitution by excepting judges from the operation of the recall before she was finally admitted in 1912. Very shortly after her admission, however, she again amended her constitution and reinserted the provision for the recall of judges.

With respect to the validity of conditions placed by Congress on the admission of new states, it is necessary to make a distinction between conditions precedent to admission and those intended to be operative subsequent to admission. Since Congress may refuse or delay indefinitely

[1] See MATHEWS and BERDAHL, *Documents and Readings in American Government*, pp. 147–149.

the admission of a state, it follows that it may impose such conditions precedent as it sees fit.   There is no constitutional limitation upon Congress as to the number of states which it may admit nor as to the population which such states shall have attained at the time of admission.   A state cannot secure admission until it complies with the conditions laid down by Congress, no matter how arbitrary they may be.   Of course, Congress would have no right to impose conditions which violate those fundamental limitations of the Constitution that are binding on Congress even when dealing with the territories.

With regard, however, to conditions intended to be operative after the admission of the territory as a state, the situation is different.   Upon admission into the Union, a state becomes a member of a society of equals. Most of the Congressional acts looking to the admission of new states contain the provision that the state in question shall be admitted "on an equal footing with the original states in all respects whatever."[1] Such a provision, however, is surplusage, because Congress could not admit a state on anything but an equal footing.[2]   With reference to alleged limitations found in the Northwest Ordinance of 1787 upon the power of the state of Illinois to make police regulations affecting the navigation of the Chicago River, the Supreme Court of the United States declared that:

Whatever the limitation upon her powers as a government while in the territorial condition, whether from the Ordinance of 1787 or the legislation of Congress, it ceased to have any operative force, except as voluntarily adopted by her after she became a state of the Union.   On her admission, she at once became entitled to, and possessed of, all the rights of dominion and sovereignty which belonged to the original states.   She was admitted and could be admitted only on an equal footing with them.[3]

Since there is nothing in the Constitution of the United States which prohibits any state from providing for the recall of judges by popular vote, it follows that Arizona, in providing, after becoming a state, for the popular recall of judges in spite of the restriction placed upon her admission, was acting within her constitutional rights.   If, in spite of the limitation placed upon her at the time of admission, Utah should desire to permit polygamy within her boundaries, she would doubtless have the legal power to do so, since the regulation of marriage and divorce is among the reserved powers of the states.   This situation is further illustrated by the case of Oklahoma, which was admitted in 1907 upon

[1] See, for example, the act of 1818 for the admission of Illinois.   3 Stat. at L. 536.

[2] DUNNING, W. A., "Are the States Equal under the Constitution?" Polit. Sci. Quart., vol. 3, pp. 425–453 (1888).

[3] Escanaba and Lake Michigan Transportation Co. v. City of Chicago, 107 U. S. 678 (1883).

condition that the state capital should be located at Guthrie and should not be changed for a period of years. Prior to the expiration of this period, the capital was removed by act of the state legislature to Oklahoma City. The validity of this act was upheld by the Supreme Court of the United States in a case wherein the Court remarked that "the constitutional equality of the states is essential to the harmonious operation of the scheme upon which the Republic was organized."[1] As far as the exercise of political rights is concerned, therefore, the states are equal. Furthermore, this proposition seems logically to follow from the Tenth Amendment to the Constitution of the United States, which reserves "to the states" powers not delegated to the United States or prohibited to the states.

A condition placed by Congress upon a new state which is impliedly imposed upon all the states by the Federal Constitution does not affect the power of the state after admission but merely changes an implied limitation into an express one. For example, Missouri was admitted in 1821 on condition that she should never exclude citizens of other states from the enjoyment of privileges and immunities derived from the Constitution of the United States. This would have been impossible anyway. Again, the enabling act of 1857 authorizing the people of Minnesota to form a constitution contained a proviso that the constitutional convention should provide "by a clause in said constitution or by an ordinance irrevocable without the consent of the United States" that "no tax shall be imposed on lands belonging to the United States, and that in no case shall nonresident proprietors be taxed higher than residents." Such a clause was inserted in the Minnesota Constitution of 1857.[2] However, the conditions were largely superfluous because, in general, no state can tax land belonging to the United States,[3] while to tax land belonging to residents of other states at a higher rate would violate the interstate citizenship clause of the Constitution.

Congress, however, has sometimes gone further, as in the case of Ohio in 1802, and admitted a state on condition that for a period of years she should not levy taxes on land owned by private individuals which they had purchased from the United States Government. In the absence of such a condition, taxes levied by the state on such land would be valid, provided they were not discriminatory and did not single out such lands especially for taxation on account of the fact that they had previously been owned by the United States Government. Such taxes, however, could not be levied, during the period specified, by a state upon which Congress had imposed such a condition. The acceptance of the condition by the state at the time of its admission creates a valid compact

---

[1] Coyle v. Smith, Secretary of State of Oklahoma, 221 U. S. 559 (1911).
[2] Art. II, sect. 3.
[3] Van Brocklin v. Tennessee, 117 U. S. 151 (1886).

between the United States and the state. As the Supreme Court of the United States has declared:

There may be agreements or compacts attempted to be entered into between two states, or between a state and the nation, in reference to political rights and obligations, and there may be those solely in reference to property belonging to one or the other. That different considerations may underlie the question as to the validity of these two kinds of compacts or agreements is obvious. It has often been said that a state admitted into the Union enters therein in full equality with all the others, and such equality may forbid any agreement or compact limiting or qualifying political rights and obligations; whereas, on the other hand, a mere agreement in reference to property involves no question of equality of status, but only of the power of a state to deal with the nation or with any other state in reference to such property. The case before us is one involving simply an agreement as to property between a state and the nation.[1]

Guarantee of a Republican Form of Government.—As already pointed out, Congress, in admitting a new state into the Union, does so subject to the implied limitation that no state can be admitted unless it has a republican form of government. This implication arises from that provision of the Constitution which declares that "the United States shall guarantee to every state in this Union a republican form of government."[2] Although couched in the form of a right accorded to the states, this provision also operates as a continuing limitation upon a state after admission so as to prevent it from changing its form of government into one not republican. It is thus not only a right accorded to the states but necessarily implies a duty imposed upon them. Since it is the only limitation in the Federal Constitution upon the internal governmental organization of a state, it indicates the full extent of national control over a state's internal affairs and, provided it be republican in form, a state may construct its government according to any plan it desires. Its government may be autocratic in spirit and essence, provided only it is republican in form. Nevertheless, this provision implies that the people of the United States, as represented in the general government, may control the people of a particular state so as to prevent them, even against their will, from establishing or maintaining a government which does not comply with this requirement.

The provision, while distinguishing between a state or political community and its government, does not undertake to define what is meant by a republican form of government. A general rule of construction of the Constitution, however, is that terms used in that document which are not defined are to be understood in the sense generally accepted at the time the Constitution was adopted. It can be safely assumed that the governments of the original states existing at the time of the establish-

[1] Stearns v. Minnesota, 179 U. S. 223, at p. 244 (1900).
[2] Art. IV, sect. 4.

ment of the new National Government under the Constitution were considered to be republican in form. By implication the governments of the states subsequently admitted to the Union must also have been so considered. Although these state governments were clearly republican in form, it does not follow that there are no other forms of government which might properly be classed as republican. In fact, Madison declared in *The Federalist* that "whenever the states may choose to substitute other republican forms, they have the right to do so and to claim the federal guaranty for the latter."[1] In general, however, it appears from contemporaneous writings that the constitutional guaranty was intended to insure a representative form of government in the states, as distinguished from a monarchy or oligarchy on the one hand and from a pure or direct democracy on the other.[2] It has recently been defined as "one in which the will of the people is the highest source of authority and looks for its interpretation and execution to responsible agents acting under the forms of law."[3]

It is not to be supposed, however, that any departure from the representative principle or any admixture in the government of a state of institutions based on the principle of direct democracy will necessarily cause such government to lose its republican character.[4] This question has come up in connection with the adoption in several states of the popular initiative and referendum in matters of ordinary legislation, while continuing the representative legislature as an alternative agency for enacting laws. Under such a plan of direct legislation in Oregon, a law was enacted in 1906 imposing certain taxes on corporations, the payment of which was resisted on the ground that the incorporation of the popular initiative and referendum into the constitution of the state deprived its government of the republican form in violation of the guaranty in the Federal Constitution. The Supreme Court of the United States, however, refused on this ground to restrain the enforcement of the tax.[5] The Court held that the determination in any given case whether a state has a republican form of government is a political question which is to be settled not by the courts but by the action of the political departments of the National Government. In this case, Congress, by admitting senators and representatives from Oregon to membership in that body had determined that that state had a republican form of government.

During the reconstruction period after the Civil War, the question was raised as to whether a state in which women were not allowed to vote had a republican form of government. In the light of the fact

[1] *The Federalist*, No. 43.
[2] MADISON in *The Federalist*, Nos. 10, 14, 39.
[3] HOLCOMBE, A. N., *State Government in the United States*, 2d ed., p. 41.
[4] See, however, *per contra*, a Delaware case, Rice v. Foster, 4 Harr. 479.
[5] Pacific States Telephone and Telegraph Co. v. Oregon, 223 U. S. 118 (1912).

that only one of the original thirteen states (New Jersey) allowed women to vote, the Court held that the grant of this privilege is not an essential ingredient of the republican form of government.[1]

The power of Congress to refuse to admit senators and representatives from a state which, it deems, does not have a republican form of government enables that body to exercise a sort of censorship over a state and to put pressure upon it so as to bring about certain governmental changes. Thus, during the reconstruction period after the Civil War, Congress assumed to exercise the power of imposing new governments upon the former Confederate states against the will of the great majority of their citizens. Furthermore, Congress refused to readmit the representatives of those states to their seats in Congress until they had amended their constitutions so as not to discriminate against persons in the matter of voting on the ground of race and color and had ratified the Fourteenth and Fifteenth Amendments to the Constitution of the United States. This action deprived those states for the time being of their constitutional right to equality with the other states in the Union and extended the power of Congress under the guaranty provision far beyond the intention of the framers of the Constitution.[2]

The constitutional provision under consideration declares that the "United States shall guarantee," etc., without specifying in which department of the government of the United States the power is vested or the duty is imposed. It would seem that all three departments should cooperate in enforcing the provision in connection with the exercise of their appropriate functions. Since, however, as pointed out above, the determination as to whether or not a particular state government is republican in form is a political question, both the power and the duty reside primarily in the political departments of the National Government, i.e., in Congress and the President, and especially in Congress because the power is in the main one appropriately to be exercised by a legislative body.

The power of Congress under this provision of the Constitution is not confined to a mere passive refusal to receive senators and representatives from a state whose government it deems not to be republican in form, but it may go further and take positive action, or confer upon the President power to take positive action, to enforce the guarantee. This might become necessary particularly in the closely allied situation where there exist in a state two rival governments, each claiming to be the legally established government. In such circumstances, Congress would have to decide which is the established government before determining whether it is republican in form. If the rival governments are in armed conflict with each other, it may be necessary for the political depart-

---

[1] Minor v. Happersett, 21 Wall. 162 (1874).

[2] Cf. WILLOUGHBY, W. W., The American Constitutional System, pp. 120–121.

ments of the National Government forcibly to intervene both to put down the disturbance or insurrection and also to enforce the constitutional guaranty of a republican form of government.

Dorr's Rebellion.—The situation thus outlined in general terms was illustrated in a concrete way by Dorr's rebellion in Rhode Island in 1841–1842. Up to that time, that state had continued to operate under its old colonial charter as a constitution, with only slight changes. Under that document, the suffrage was on a very narrow basis, its exercise depending on the ownership or possession of property. Only a minority of the adult male citizens were qualified to vote, and the constitution contained no provision for its amendment. The disfranchised citizens, under the leadership of Thomas W. Dorr, rose in rebellion. They held a convention, adopted a new and more liberal constitution, and attempted to put into operation the government provided for under that instrument. The old charter government, however, refused to recognize the validity of these proceedings. It resorted to force by calling out the militia, but, fearful that this force would not be sufficient, it appealed through its governor to the President of the United States to furnish military aid to put down the insurrection.

The National Government might have intervened in the Rhode Island situation on its own initiative but did not do so until appealed to by the governor of the old charter government. Thereupon, the President recognized that government as the legally established government of the state and took measures to call out the militia to support its authority. In doing so, he acted in accordance with the provisions of an act of Congress of 1795 which purported to make it lawful for the President, upon application by the proper authority of any state against whose government an insurrection had broken out, to use the militia for its suppression. No actual armed conflict between the insurrectionary forces and those under command of the President took place, however, because, when the position taken by the President became known, the Dorr rebellion collapsed. Subsequently, the controversy as to which of the rival governments was the legitimate one having been carried to the Supreme Court of the United States, that tribunal refused to decide this question on the strength of its own independent examination but merely followed the determination of the President.[1]

Since, in this case, no senators or representatives in Congress were elected by the insurrectionary government, Congress was not called upon to decide which of the rival governments was the legitimate one, and this decision consequently devolved upon the President. New governments have sometimes been established in the states by methods not in accordance with the provisions of the existing state constitutions and the new government, although thus irregular in origin, has been

[1] Luther v. Borden, 7 How. 1 (1848).

recognized as legitimate by the political departments of the National Government. But in those cases the new government was generally acquiesced in and its validity was not contested by the old government. In this respect the Rhode Island case was different. In that case both of the contending governments were republican in form. If we disregard its origin, the new government, being based on a broader suffrage, would seem to have been even more republican in form than the old. But its origin could not be disregarded, and, since it did not come into existence by regular legal means whose validity the old government recognized, the National Government properly intervened for the support of the latter.

If the legally established government of a state is in danger of overthrow, not through an internal insurrection but through invasion by some foreign power, it becomes all the more the duty of the National Government to intervene for the protection of the established government of the state.

If there should happen to be in a state not two rival governments but two organs of the government, such as two governors or two legislatures, each claiming to be the legitimate one, such a contest would normally be left to be settled by the state itself without the intervention of the National Government. Indirectly, however, it might become necessary for some department of the National Government to decide, in the regular discharge of its duties, which of the rival state organs is deemed to be the legitimate one. Thus, the Supreme Court of the United States, in a suit brought by a state through its attorney-general, may be called upon to decide whether such officer is an agent of the legally established government of the state. Again, when there are in a state two persons, each claiming to be the legally elected governor of the state, and one of them calls upon the President of the United States for assistance in putting down domestic violence, it becomes necessary for the President, in the first place, to determine which of the two claimants to the governorship is the constitutionally established one.[1]

Protecting the States against Invasion and Domestic Violence.— The two sources from which disturbance of peaceful conditions in a state may come are invasion from outside and violence or insurrection arising from within. The territory of a state might be invaded by hostile forces coming either from another state or states of the Union or from some foreign country. A state has the right to have its territorial integrity respected and, as we have seen, it cannot be divided without the consent of its legislature. In case its safety or territorial integrity should be threatened by invasion of hostile forces from outside, it would have the right to use such force as it might have at its disposal in order to repel the invasion. Since, however, by the Constitution, a

[1] *Cf.* 14 Op. U. S. Atty.-Gen. 394 (1874).

state is prohibited, without the consent of Congress, from keeping troops or ships of war in time of peace, it would probably not have at its disposal sufficient force for this purpose. Consequently, it would be under the necessity of calling upon the Government of the United States for aid in warding off the invasion, unless the latter Government came to its assistance without being requested to do so. Since the invasion of any state would at the same time be an invasion of the United States, it would be the imperative duty of the United States Government to furnish protection to the state against such invasion, without waiting for any request for aid or for any independent effort on the part of the state to repel the invasion. When the United States is a neutral, the President may take steps to seize and intern the troops of a belligerent power found violating the territory of the United States.[1]

The other source from which disturbance of peaceful conditions in a state may come is, as noted above, domestic violence. The state is ordinarily expected to deal with such a situation by the use of its own law-enforcing officers and by calling out the state militia if necessary. There are two sorts of cases, however, in which the National Government may intervene in a state in order to put down domestic violence or insurrection. The first is that in which the state government claims to be unable to put down the disturbance and applies, through its legislature or through its governor when the legislature cannot be convened, to the national authorities for assistance. In 1795, Congress passed an act which purported to make it lawful for the President, upon receipt of such an application, to furnish sufficient military force to suppress the insurrection. In the absence of such an application, the President will not act to put down a mere local disturbance. On the other hand, the President, even when applied to by the proper state authority, is not required to act and if, in his judgment, the need is not clear or the claim of the state that it is unable to cope with the disorder is not well founded, he may decline to send assistance, provided that the disorder does not interfere with the enforcement of national law. Thus, in 1921, President Harding declined at first to accede to the request of West Virginia for assistance.

The second sort of case in which the National Government may intervene in a state in order to put down domestic violence is where such violence endangers national property or interferes with the enforcement of national laws. More specifically, if domestic violence in a state, although confined to a local area, interferes with the movement of the United States mails, with the processes of the Federal courts, or with the free flow of goods and passengers through the channels of interstate commerce, it becomes not only the right but also the duty of the President to intervene and to send such forces, including the entire standing army

[1] *Ex parte* Toscano, 208 Fed. 938.

of the United States if necessary, as may be sufficient to put down the disturbance. In this case, the President not only need not wait for a request for aid from the state authorities but may proceed to send Federal forces into the state even over the protest of the state authorities. The most striking illustration of this situation was the action of President Cleveland in sending Federal forces into Illinois in order to put down the disturbances incident to the Chicago railroad strike of 1893–1894. He did so over the protest of Governor Altgeld of that state, but his position was subsequently sustained by the Supreme Court of the United States in a unanimous decision.[1] In its opinion in this case the Court declared that:

The entire strength of the Nation may be used to enforce in any part of the land the full and free exercise of all national powers and the security of all rights entrusted by the Constitution to its care. The strong arm of the National Government may be put forth to brush away all obstructions to the freedom of interstate commerce or the transportation of the mails. If the emergency arises, the army of the Nation and all its militia are at the service of the Nation to compel obedience to its laws.

Secession.—Not only is there no power in Congress to expel a state, but a state, after admission to the Union, cannot withdraw. The Constitution, as we have seen, is silent upon the question as to the right of secession. That the states have no such right was apparently decided for all time by the result of the Civil War. After that conflict the Supreme Court of the United States declared that the "Constitution, in all its provisions, looks to an indestructible Union, composed of indestructible states."[2] The Court then further held that:

When, therefore, Texas became one of the United States, she entered into an indissoluble relation. All the obligations of perpetual union, and all the guaranties of republican government in the Union, attached at once to the state. The act which consummated her admission into the Union was something more than a compact; it was the incorporation of a new member into the political body. The union between Texas and the other states was as complete, as perpetual, and as indissoluble as the union between the original states. There was no place for reconsideration or revocation except through revolution, or through the consent of the states.

The Court then went on to hold that the ordinance of secession adopted by Texas was null and void and that, notwithstanding it, Texas continued to be a state of the Union. It would seem, however, that, as a practical fact, a state could withdraw from the Union if neither the National Government nor the other states raised any objection; but this would be a revolutionary act.

[1] *In re* Debs, 158 U. S. 564 (1895). See also Grover Cleveland, *Presidential Problems*, Chap. II (New York, 1904).

[2] Texas v. White, 7 Wall. 700 (1868).

National Grants in Aid.—A form of the extension of national control over the states which has within recent years grown to be of considerable importance is that through conditional grants of money by the National Government to be spent in the states for such purposes as the promotion of education, good roads, national defense, and public health. To some extent these purposes are purely non-Federal. In his budget message to Congress of December, 1925, President Coolidge called attention to this development and deprecated its further extension, both because of its drain upon the National Treasury and also because it interfered with the performance by the states of properly state functions. Nevertheless, the tendency continues apace. The money is appropriated by Congress to be spent in the states for these purposes on condition that the states shall appropriate an equal amount and that activities for the accomplishment of these ends shall be carried on in accordance with specifications and standards laid down by the National Government. In this way that Government is extending its practical control over matters which, constitutionally, are within the sphere of state action.

In order to combat through judicial action the tendency outlined above, an original proceeding was brought in the Supreme Court of the United States by the State of Massachusetts to test the constitutionality of the Sheppard-Towner Act,[1] passed by Congress in 1921, which was entitled an act "for the promotion of the welfare and hygiene of maternity and infancy." The question as to the constitutionality of this particular act was probably raised because the subject matter of the act was clearly not within the scope of direct action by Congress but was just as clearly within the reserved powers of the states. The plaintiff state sought an injunction from the Court to forbid the secretary of the treasury from carrying out the act, claiming a right to relief both on its own behalf and also on behalf of its citizens who were taxpayers. The Court, however, unanimously denied the state's application for an injunction and dismissed the suit on the ground that it did not present a justiciable controversy. The Court did not directly pass upon the constitutional questions involved but, in *obiter dicta*, outlined its attitude toward the subsidy system as follows:

It is alleged that the statute constitutes an attempt to legislate outside the powers granted to Congress by the Constitution and within the field of local powers exclusively reserved to the states. Nothing is added to the force or effect of this assertion by the further incidental allegations that the ulterior purpose of Congress thereby was to induce the states to yield a portion of their sovereign rights; that the burden of the appropriations falls unequally upon the several states; and that there is imposed upon the states an illegal and unconstitutional option either to yield to the Federal Government a part of their reserved

---

[1] See text of this act reprinted in Mathews and Berdahl, *Documents and Readings in American Government*, pp. 528–531.

rights, or lose their share of the moneys appropriated. But what burden is imposed upon the several states, unequally or otherwise? Certainly there is none, unless it be the burden of taxation, and that falls upon their inhabitants, who are within the taxing power of Congress as well as that of the states where they reside. Nor does the statute require the states to do or to yield anything. If Congress enacted it with the ulterior purpose of tempting them to yield, that purpose may be effectively frustrated by the simple expedient of not yielding.[1]

---

[1] Massachusetts v. Mellon, 262 U. S. 447 (1923). An attempt made at the same time by an individual taxpayer to secure relief also failed, the Court holding that no judicial remedy was available. Frothingham v. Mellon, *ibid*. See also E. S. Corwin, "The Spending Power of Congress—Apropos the Maternity Act," *Harvard Law Rev.*, vol. 36, pp. 548–582.

CHAPTER VI

INTERSTATE RELATIONS AND OBLIGATIONS

The general principle governing the relations between the states is that they are foreign to each other except in so far as this condition is modified by provisions of the Federal Constitution. Among such provisions are those relating to interstate privileges and immunities, full faith and credit, the rendition of fugitives from justice, and compacts between states.

Interstate Privileges and Immunities.—One of the few provisions of the Articles of Confederation which were inserted in the Federal Constitution is that known as the interstate citizenship clause. It declares that "the citizens of each state shall be entitled to all privileges and immunities of citizens in the several states."[1] Anyone who is a citizen of the United States and has acquired a legal residence in a particular state is a citizen of that state. The interstate citizenship clause tends toward cementing together the various states of the Union. It prevents undue or special discrimination being practiced by any state against citizens of other states in the exercise of ordinary civil rights or privileges. Supplementing the commerce and postal powers of Congress, it tends to break down the boundary lines between states by conferring on the citizens of each state the privilege of freely moving into and out of other states.

The object of the interstate citizenship clause, as explained by the Supreme Court, was

. . . to place the citizens of each state upon the same footing with citizens of other states, so far as the advantages resulting from citizenship in those states are concerned. It relieves them from the disabilities of alienage in other states; it inhibits discriminating legislation against them by other states; it gives them the right of free ingress into other states, and egress from them; it insures to them in other states the same freedom possessed by the citizens of those states in the acquisition and enjoyment of property and in the pursuit of happiness; and it secures to them in other states the equal protection of their laws. It has been justly said that no provision of the Constitution has tended so strongly to constitute the citizens of the United States one people as this.[2]

A citizen or resident of one state may change his residence by settling in another state. But if a resident of Ohio owns property in Illinois, the interstate citizenship clause prevents Illinois from levying upon such

[1] Art. IV, sect. 2.
[2] Paul v. Virginia, 8 Wall. 168, 180 (1869).

65

property taxes at a higher rate than it levies upon property in the same class owned by residents of Illinois.   It also prevents Illinois from levying higher taxes on residents of Ohio engaged in selling goods in Illinois than it levies on its own residents similarly engaged.   It does not prevent Illinois, however, from requiring citizens of Ohio who bring suit in Illinois courts to post a bond to guarantee payment of court costs, although not requiring such a bond of its own citizens.

Persons changing their residence from one state to another do not carry with them the rights and privileges which they enjoyed in the state of their former residence, but, in the state of their newly acquired residence, they are entitled to the same privileges and immunities as are enjoyed generally by the citizens of the latter state.   In general, each state must accord both to citizens of other states and to its newly acquired citizens who have migrated from other states the same ordinary private rights, such as access to its courts and the ownership and disposition of property, and on the same terms as it accords them to all its other citizens. The discrimination which the interstate citizenship clause prohibits a state from making includes not only that between its own citizens and citizens of other states but also that between citizens of different other states.

To the operation of the interstate citizenship clause, however, certain exceptions or qualifications should be noted.   In the first place, the clause protects private rights but does not protect public or political rights. Thus, a person who is legally qualified to vote or hold office in Ohio does not become qualified to exercise those rights in Illinois immediately upon his arrival in the latter state but must first undergo the period of residence required by Illinois.   Again, a person who is entitled to engage in certain professions, such as the practice of law or medicine, in a given state, is not entitled, under the interstate citizenship clause, to engage in such professions in another state.   This exception to the general rule does not apply to any ordinary occupation, such as that of a barber, but only to those professions wherein the practitioner comes into such close relations with clients or patients that the state, in the interests of the public welfare, is deemed to have the right, as well as the duty, to subject him to special conditions before admission to the practice of such profession.

As expressed by the Supreme Court in the case already quoted:

The privileges and immunities secured to citizens of each state in the several states, by the provision in question, are those privileges and immunities which are common to the citizens in the latter states under their constitution and laws by virtue of their being citizens.   Special privileges enjoyed by citizens in their own states are not secured in other states by this provision.   It was not intended by the provision to give to the laws of one state any operation in other states. They can have no such operation, except by the permission, express or implied, of those states.   The special privileges which they confer must, therefore, be enjoyed at home, unless the assent of other states to their enjoyment therein be given.[1]

Another exception to the general rule is found in the fact that the exercise of rights which may deplete the natural resources of a state, such as fish and game, may be restricted to the citizens of such state. Thus, a statute of New Jersey, which forbade nonresidents, under certain circumstances, from gathering oysters within the state, was upheld.[2] By parity of reasoning, a state may restrict to its own citizens the use and enjoyment of public property, such as state parks and state charitable and educational institutions. This does not include state courts or other public offices, access to which is necessary incidentally to the maintenance of private rights. It follows that, if the state may exclude nonresidents entirely from the use of such public property, it may admit them on conditions in excess of those required of its own citizens. Thus, a state may allow nonresidents to hunt or fish in its public parks, but subject to the payment of higher fees than are charged its own citizens. Similarly, a state may admit nonresidents as students in its state university or other state educational institutions, subject to the payment of higher tuition fees than are exacted from resident students.

Foreign Corporations.—The right to be a corporation and the right to do business in the corporate form are special privileges granted by a state. The enjoyment of these privileges is not secured in other states by the interstate citizenship clause. It is true that within the meaning of the diverse citizenship clause of the Federal Constitution regulating the jurisdiction of the Federal courts, corporations are considered for practical purposes to be citizens of the state in which incorporated; but, within the meaning of the interstate citizenship clause, they are not citizens and cannot, therefore, invoke this clause in order to secure free entry into another state for the purpose of doing business there. It follows, therefore, that a state may refuse to allow outside corporations to enter its borders for this or other purposes. To this statement, however, an exception must be made in the case of corporations engaged in interstate commerce. Another exception is that of a corporation chartered by the United States Government to construct railroads or public buildings or otherwise to aid in the discharge of governmental functions. Subject to these exceptions, a state may exclude foreign corporations altogether.

If foreign corporations, with the exception of the two classes mentioned, may be excluded altogether, it follows that, in general, they may be admitted on such conditions as the state may see fit to impose. Thus, they may be required to obtain a license from the secretary of state as a prerequisite to doing business, to pay the fees required by law, and to

[1] Paul v. Virginia, 8 Wall. 168 (1869).
[2] Corfield v. Coryell, Fed. Cas. No. 3230 (1825).

designate an agent or attorney in fact within the state upon whom process may be served in all suits brought against the corporation. A foreign insurance company, which the courts have held not to be engaged in interstate commerce, may be taxed by a state at a higher rate than that levied upon such corporations of domestic creation.

If a foreign corporation is not seeking admission but is already doing business in a state, it may be treated differently from domestic corporations if there is a reasonable basis for the distinction. The right of a foreign corporation to continue to do business in a state may be withdrawn through the expiration of the period of time for which its license was granted. As far as securing a renewal of its right to do business therein is concerned, a corporation under such circumstances is in the same position as an outside corporation seeking admission. After having been admitted, however, a foreign corporation is held to be a person within the jurisdiction and, under the equal-protection clause of the Fourteenth Amendment, cannot be subjected to arbitrary discrimination in such a matter as that of taxation, especially where it has invested within the state a substantial amount of property of a fixed and permanent character. Both the equal-protection clause and the constitutional right of citizens of one state to resort to Federal courts in another prevent a state from forbidding a foreign corporation within its jurisdiction to remove cases from state to Federal courts or from revoking its license for doing so.[1]

Full Faith and Credit.—In the absence of treaty stipulation, there is no legal requirement that the state or Federal courts of the United States shall give full faith and credit to the judgments of courts of foreign countries, although this may be done as a matter of international comity. The states, however, are required by the Constitution to give full faith and credit to the public acts, records, and judicial proceedings of every other state.[2] Congress is authorized by general laws to prescribe the manner in which such acts, records, and proceedings shall be proved, and the effect thereof, and this it has done. The words "acts, records, and judicial proceedings," as here used, refer to legislative acts, statutes, ordinances, records of deeds, wills, births, marriages, contracts, and the decisions, judgments, and decrees rendered by courts of a state

---

[1] Terral v. Burke Construction Co., 257 U. S. 529 (1921). It was held, however, in Railway Express Agency v. Virginia, 282 U. S. 440 (1931), that a company incorporated in Delaware to do both an interstate and an intrastate business could be prohibited from doing an intrastate business in Virginia unless it becomes incorporated in the latter state, in spite of the fact that the effect of such local incorporation would be to deprive the corporation of the right to sue in the Federal courts and to remove suits to them on the ground of diversity of citizenship. "If the corporation," said the Court, "sees fit to acquire a new personality under the laws of Virginia, it cannot complain that the new person has not the same rights as itself."

[2] Art. IV, sect. 1.

in civil cases. The clause does not require a state to assist in enforcing the criminal laws of another state.[1]

The full-faith-and-credit clause does not mean that acts, records, and judicial decisions of one state shall, of their own force, have extraterritorial effect or operation in another state, but rather that they shall be recognized as conclusive evidence of the facts of the case, without the necessity for a retrial of the case upon its merits. Thus, if A residing in Illinois buys on credit a radio set worth $500 from a dealer in his home town and later, upon his refusal to pay, the dealer sues him in the Illinois court and gets judgment, but, before the judgment can be executed, A has moved to Pennsylvania taking the radio set with him, the dealer may then apply to the Pennsylvania court to compel payment of the judgment, presenting with his application a duly certified or authenticated copy of the judgment. A may claim that the Illinois court did not have jurisdiction of the case, or that he was not properly served with notice of the suit against him; but if these claims are overruled, the full-faith-and-credit clause requires that the Pennsylvania court shall give effect to the judgment of the Illinois court, without reexamining the case on its merits.

The fact that the law of Pennsylvania may be different from that of Illinois with reference to the collection of such claims would not relieve the Pennsylvania court from the necessity of sustaining the judgment of the Illinois court. A will with two witnesses, if made according to the law of the state in which it was drawn up, will be given effect by the courts of another state even though the law of the latter state requires three witnesses to wills. Likewise a gambling contract, if made in a state where such contracts are legal, will be enforced by the courts of another state, even though by the law of the latter state such contracts are illegal.

With reference to some matters uniform laws have by agreement been adopted in the various states. With reference to other matters, however, diverse laws exist. One of the subjects on which the greatest diversity is found is that of marriage and divorce. The full-faith-and-credit clause requires each state to recognize divorces granted in other states, even though the law of the respective states in reference to such matters may be different, provided the court granting the divorce had jurisdiction and the defendant in the case was properly notified. Difficulties have been caused by differences between states in regard to such matters as methods of determining the jurisdiction of the court granting the decree of divorce, the domicile of the parties, and methods of serving notice upon the defendant. A decree of divorce granted by a court of a state where the court did not have jurisdiction, or the parties were not domiciled in that state, or the defendant was not properly notified, need

[1] Wisconsin v. Pelican Insurance Co., 127 U. S. 265 (1888).

not be recognized by the courts of another state. If, on the other hand, the parties are both residents of the state in which the divorce is granted, or the defendant alone is not a resident of that state but nevertheless is actually notified, such a decree of divorce must be recognized by other states. Furthermore, such a decree will be valid in other states even though the defendant residing in another state was not actually notified, provided the state in which the decree was granted was the "last matrimonial domicile" of the parties and the defendant was constructively notified, *i.e.*, by mail or publication, as required by law.

Thus, in the case of Atherton v. Atherton,[1] the last matrimonial domicile of the parties was in Kentucky. A wife can change her domicile from that of her husband only in case of misconduct on his part. In this case, the wife left her husband in Kentucky and went to New York where she obtained a decree of divorce from him on the ground of cruel and abusive treatment. Meanwhile, however, the husband had obtained in Kentucky a decree of divorce from her upon constructive notice. This decree he set up in the New York court as a defense against her suit for divorce, but the New York court refused to give it effect. Upon appeal, the Supreme Court of the United States held that the New York court erred in that the full-faith-and-credit clause required it to give effect to the divorce decree in Kentucky, since the latter state was the last matrimonial domicile of the parties.

Although, as pointed out above, there are cases of divorces granted in one state which the full-faith-and-credit clause does not require other states to recognize, nevertheless they are recognized by many other states as a matter of interstate comity.[2]

Interstate Rendition of Fugitives.—The laws of one state have no operation in another state. This is especially true of criminal laws. Nor do the courts of one state have any legal right to punish crimes committed in another state. As between foreign governments, the international extradition of criminals is a matter which is regulated by treaty. Since, however, the states of the American Union are prohibited from making treaties with each other, it is proper that this matter should be regulated by the Constitution. International extradition, however, differs from interstate rendition in several respects. As a rule, a criminal will not be extradited from one nation to another unless an extradition treaty subsisting between them specifically covers the crime with which he is charged. Offenses of a political character are regularly excluded. As a usual rule, a nation will decline to extradite its own citizens or subjects. Furthermore, when a criminal has been extradited from one

---

[1] 181 U. S. 155 (1901).

[2] Full faith and credit are not required to be given to a judgment of a Federal court in one state by a Federal court in another state. Baldwin v. Iowa State Traveling Men's Assoc., 283 U. S. 522 (1931).

nation to another, he cannot be tried for any offense other than the one for which he was extradited.

The constitutional provision relating to interstate rendition declares that "a person charged in any state with treason, felony, or other crime, who shall flee from justice and be found in another state, shall, on demand of the executive authority of the state from which he fled, be delivered up, to be removed to the state having jurisdiction of the crime."[1] No specific authority is granted to Congress to enforce this provision, but, since it is not self-executing, Congress in 1793 passed legislation for its enforcement. State laws may also be passed in aid of, or supplementary to, the constitutional provision and the act of Congress. Although territories are not mentioned in the constitutional provision, the act of Congress extends to the governors of territories, whether incorporated or unincorporated, the power to make requisitions and to grant extradition. Indian reservations, however, are not included.

As sometimes used in the Constitution, the word crime refers only to serious offenses. In the interstate rendition clause, however, it apparently includes minor offenses and misdemeanors. It also applies to persons who break parole and flee to another state, but they must be demanded on the ground of the former crime. It need hardly be said that the words "treason, felony, or other crime" as used in the interstate rendition clause refer to offenses against a state and not to those against the United States. By including treason against a state, which is a political offense, the clause departs from the usage in international extradition.

The Constitution fails to indicate upon what officer of the state the demand for the criminal shall be made, and thus no obligation is specifically placed by the Constitution upon any particular state officer to comply with the demand. Congress, however, has undertaken to supply this omission in the Constitution by providing that it shall be the duty of the executive authority of the state to comply with the demand by causing the arrest of the fugitive and his delivery to the agent of the demanding state. Until the arrest takes place, it is not usually known to what state a person charged with crime has fled. Consequently, the arrest ordinarily takes place before formal extradition papers are issued containing a demand for the criminal's return. From considerations of reciprocity, police officers in cities of different states frequently make arrests or hold suspected persons upon telegraphic or wireless information that they are wanted for certain crimes by police officers in other states. In practice, when the arrest has been made, the governor of the demanding state, upon the request of local police officers, sends to the governor of the state in which the prisoner is being held a requisition for his return, together with a certified copy of the indictment or affidavit

[1] Art. IV, sect. 2, cl. 2.

against him, in order that he may be placed on trial in a court of the demanding state.

Upon receipt of the requisition by the governor of the state in which the prisoner is being held, the question arises as to the nature of the duty resting upon him. Can the governor refuse to comply with the demand? Or, if he appears inclined to do so, can he be compelled by writ of mandamus to deliver the prisoner to agents of the demanding state? These questions arose and were settled in 1860 in the case of Kentucky v. Dennison.[1] In that case, Dennison, the governor of Ohio, had refused to comply with the request of the governor of Kentucky to surrender a fugitive from the latter state. Application was thereupon made to the Federal court for a writ of mandamus to compel compliance with the request, but the court refused to issue it. Chief Justice Taney, in rendering the opinion of the court, said:

The words "it shall be the duty" were not used as mandatory and compulsory, but as declaratory of the moral duty which this command created, when Congress had provided the mode of carrying it into execution. The act does not provide any means to compel the execution of this duty, nor inflict any punishment for neglect or refusal on the part of the executive of the state; nor is there any clause or provision in the Constitution which arms the government of the United States with this power.

It follows from this decision that the word "shall" as used in the interstate rendition clause of the Constitution and also in the act of Congress for its enforcement is to be construed as if it were "may." Whether the governor will give up the prisoner on demand is therefore one to be decided by him in his discretion, and numerous instances have occurred in which a governor has declined to issue a warrant for the arrest of a fugitive or an order for his surrender to the agent of the demanding state. For example, the governor of Indiana on one occasion declined to deliver up to the authorities of Kentucky former Governor Taylor of the latter state, who was alleged to have been implicated in the murder of Governor Goebel of Kentucky. The reasons for which a governor may refuse to permit extradition may be any that seem to him good and sufficient. Among such reasons are that the alleged offense is not a crime in the state to which the fugitive has escaped or that the fugitive would probably not receive a fair trial in the demanding state or, perhaps, mere personal hostility between governors.

In the great majority of cases, however, governors comply with demands for extradition, if properly made. It is nevertheless the duty of the governor upon whom the demand is made to determine, in the first instance, whether the demand is in accordance with the law and whether the person whose return is sought is actually a fugitive from jus-

[1] 24 How. 66.

tice. If he satisfies himself that these questions should be answered in the negative, it is his duty to refuse to grant extradition. If, on the other hand, he permits the warrant of arrest or the order of extradition to issue, the legality of his action is subject to revision in habeas corpus proceedings in either a state or a Federal court. The right of the prisoner to secure release through such proceedings is substantially the same as if he had been arrested in the state in which the crime is alleged to have been committed.

In order to be a fugitive from justice within the meaning of the interstate rendition clause, it is necessary that the accused person should have been actually, and not merely constructively, present in the state at the time the crime was committed and that he should subsequently be found in another state. The fact that he did not know that his act constituted a crime in the demanding state or that he had no intention of fleeing from that state does not free him from liability. As illustrating the necessity of actual presence may be mentioned the controversy which occurred in 1925 between Illinois and Wisconsin in the Sovetsky case. Sovetsky was arrested in Chicago upon the request of the governor of Wisconsin and charged with being the directing head of a gang of burglars whom he sent into Wisconsin to steal merchandise for him, which he sold in Illinois. He might have been tried in Illinois for receiving and selling stolen goods, but, since he had not himself gone into Wisconsin to commit the burglaries, the governor of Illinois properly refused to deliver him up to the Wisconsin authorities.

If, while a governor is considering a request for extradition or after he has refused to grant such a request, the fugitive is kidnapped and illegally brought back into the demanding state by force or a ruse, he is then within the jurisdiction of the demanding state and may be placed on trial, convicted, and punished just as if he had been regularly extradited. It does not seem to matter whether the kidnappers were private individuals acting on their own initiative or officers of the demanding state acting under its direction. By way of illustration may be mentioned the case of Mahon v. Justice[1] which arose in 1888. Mahon, accused of murder in Kentucky, fled into West Virginia. The governor of Kentucky requested the governor of West Virginia to bring about the arrest and delivery of Mahon, but before this was done a group of persons from Kentucky went into West Virginia, kidnapped Mahon, and brought him back into Kentucky where he was put in jail. He petitioned the Federal court for a writ of habeas corpus in order to secure his return to West Virginia. The court, however, declined to free him from the custody of the Kentucky authorities merely because he had been illegally kidnapped in West Virginia. The kidnappers, however, had committed a crime in West Virginia whose governor might make a demand upon the

[1] 127 U. S. 700.

governor of Kentucky for their extradition to stand trial for this crime in West Virginia. When kidnapping follows refusal of the governor of the refuge state to grant extradition, however, it is not likely that the governor of the demanding state will agree to the extradition of the kidnappers, especially when, as sometimes happens, the kidnappers are agents of the demanding state acting under the direction or connivance of its law-enforcing authorities. Under these circumstances the kidnapped prisoner finds himself practically in the anomalous situation of being wronged but without having a remedy. Congress might possibly supply a remedy in such a case but has not yet done so.

In a case of international extradition, the rules of international law, unless modified by treaty, require that the fugitive shall be tried only for the crime for which he was extradited and, after discharging his liability for this offense, if not a capital one, must be allowed a reasonable time to depart from the country before being arrested and tried for another offense. In a case of interstate rendition, however, no such rule prevails. Whether regularly extradited or not, when once brought within the jurisdiction of the demanding state, the fugitive may be there tried for offenses other than that for which his extradition was demanded.

Inasmuch as the control over foreign intercourse is in the hands of the National Government, the governor of a state from which a fugitive from justice has fled to a foreign country must, as a rule, act through the secretary of state at Washington in securing from the foreign government the return of the fugitive in accordance with extradition treaties between the two countries. By treaty or act of Congress, however, state governors may be authorized to conduct extradition proceedings directly with the authorities of a foreign government. Thus, the United States has entered into treaties or conventions with Mexico, Denmark, and the Netherlands authorizing the governors of our border states and insular possessions to make requisitions and to grant extradition in certain cases. In such cases, the state or territorial governor is acting primarily as the agent of the United States Government.[1]

Compacts between States.—Sovereign nations may regulate their relations with each other in the form of treaties, and an elaborate network of such formal agreements exists between the members of the family of nations. The Constitution of the United States, however, provides that "no state shall enter into any treaty, alliance, or confederation."[2] This is an absolute prohibition resting upon the states of the American Union and prevents them from entering into arrangements or combinations of a distinctly political nature, either with one another or with foreign nations. The confederation of the Southern states at the time of the Civil War was the sort of combination which is prohibited

[1] MATHEWS, J. M., *American Foreign Relations*, pp. 253–254.
[2] Art. I, sect. 10.

by this clause of the Constitution. Of course, those states maintained that, having seceded from the Union, they were no longer bound by the Constitution of the United States. The result of the war, however, was to render this position untenable.

Although the states are absolutely prohibited from entering into any treaty, alliance, or confederation, they are allowed, with the consent of Congress, to enter into agreements or compacts with one another or with foreign powers.[1] A distinction is thus drawn in the Constitution between treaties and alliances on the one hand and agreements and compacts on the other, although the exact location of the line of division between them is not always clear. It is obvious that the states may enter into agreements or compacts provided, first, that they do not amount to treaties or alliances and, second, that the consent of Congress be given. Since the states of the Union, unlike foreign nations, cannot settle their controversies by war or diplomacy, it is proper that they should be given the opportunity to do so by agreement. It has been held that the compacts and agreements which may be made only with the consent of Congress are those "tending to the increase of political power in the states."[2] Thus, an agreement between two states whereby one ceded to the other a considerable portion of its territory would require the consent of Congress. Such increase of the territory of one state might increase its political power including a possible increase of its representation in Congress.

When the consent of Congress is given to a compact or agreement between states, there is no stipulated form in which it shall be given, but it may be and has been given in various ways. It may be given either expressly, impliedly, or tacitly, and it may be given either before or after the agreement has been entered into. Furthermore, such consent need not be given specifically in each particular agreement but general consent may be given by Congress in advance to interstate agreements made in regard to a given subject, such as those designed to conserve water supplies and forests.

By way of illustration, it may be mentioned that the admission by Congress of Kentucky as a state constituted an implied consent to the agreement between Virginia and Kentucky for the separation of the latter from the former, while the admission of West Virginia into the Union constituted similar consent of Congress to the arrangement between her and Virginia regarding the apportionment of their joint debt. While neither Kentucky nor West Virginia was a state at the time the agreements were first entered into, such agreements were of continuing validity after their admission as states and embodied legal, and not merely moral, obligations upon the respective parties.[3] The compact

---

[1] Art. I, sect. 10.

[2] Virginia v. Tennessee, 148 U. S. 503 (1893).

[3] Virginia v. West Virginia, 246 U. S. 565 (1918).

between Oregon and Washington regarding the limitation of the right of the respective states to issue licenses to fish in the Columbia River was ratified in 1918 by act of Congress.

The constitutional prohibition against states' entering into agreements or compacts except with the consent of Congress does not apply to those of a nonpolitical or merely business character. Thus, a *bona fide* agreement between two states for the mere settlement of a boundary line could be made without the consent of Congress, because it merely serves to define what existed before but was in doubt and does not affect the political influence of either state. Again, such consent would not be required for a state to buy land within its boundaries which happened to be owned by another state. This situation is well brought out in the following extract from the opinion of the Court in the case cited above:

There are many matters upon which different states may agree that can in no respect concern the United States. If, for instance, Virginia should come into possession and ownership of a small parcel of land in New York which the latter state might desire to acquire as a site for a public building, it would hardly be deemed essential for the latter state to obtain the consent of Congress before it could make a valid agreement with Virginia for the purchase of the land. If Massachusetts, in forwarding its exhibits to the World's Fair at Chicago, should desire to transport them a part of the distance over the Erie Canal, it would hardly be deemed essential for that state to obtain the consent of Congress before it could contract with New York for the transportation of the exhibits through the state in that way. If the bordering line of two states should cross some malarious and disease-producing district, there could be no possible reason, on any conceivable public grounds, to obtain the consent of Congress for the bordering states to agree to unite in removing the cause of disease. So, in the case of threatened invasion of cholera, plague or other causes of sickness and death, it would be the height of absurdity to hold that the threatened states could not unite in providing means to prevent and repel the invasion of the pestilence without obtaining the consent of Congress, which might not be at the time in session.[1]

The power of the states to enter into agreements and compacts with one another has been not infrequently exercised. Thus, in 1921, by agreement between New York and New Jersey, the "Port of New York Authority" was established for the comprehensive development of the port. Several interstate agreements have been made regarding the use of the waters of rivers flowing through or among several states, such as the tristate agreement of 1925 in reference to the Delaware River and the four-state agreement of the same year regarding the Columbia River. One of the best-known agreements of this sort is that negotiated in 1922 by the seven states having water rights in the Colorado River, which undertook to allocate such rights. This agreement was supervised and approved by Secretary of Commerce Hoover,

[1] Virginia v. Tennessee, 148 U. S. 503 (1893).

representing the Government at Washington. The refusal of one of the seven states, however, to ratify the agreement illustrates some of the difficulties of state cooperation in accomplishing common purposes.[1]

Controversies between States.—As pointed out above, the states cannot settle controversies between themselves by war or diplomacy and they are sometimes unable to do so by agreement. Hence, some means of settling such difficulties must be provided by judicial settlement. This means is found in the jurisdiction granted to the Supreme Court of the United States over controversies between states. A number of such suits have been brought regarding boundary disputes, rights in public waters, and other matters. In hearing and determining such cases, the function of the Court has some similarity to that of an international tribunal, but the analogy is not perfect, since a state of the Union cannot refuse to recognize the jurisdiction of the Court.[2]

[1] See the Boulder Dam case, Arizona v. California, 283 U. S. 423 (1931).
[2] For further discussion of this topic, see Chap. XIV.

PART II

THE NATIONAL GOVERNMENT: ORGANIZATION AND POWERS

CHAPTER VII

THE ORGANIZATION OF CONGRESS

The Bicameral System.—For thirteen years preceding the adoption of the Constitution, a central representative body had existed, which exercised governmental powers of various kinds. In response to the needs of the situation, the framers of the Constitution decided to create a more elaborate and more highly developed governmental structure. It was natural that they should have made the representative body the central organ in the new national government. The New Jersey plan as brought forward in the Convention of 1787 proposed the continuation of a congress consisting of but one house. This plan, however, was rejected. The most conspicuous feature of the organization of Congress as actually adopted is that it is composed of two branches. These are known as the Senate and the House of Representatives.

What were the reasons for the adoption of the bicameral system in the organization of Congress? There were three main reasons. In the first place, there was the historical precedent for this plan. It is true that the Continental and Confederate Congresses had been composed of only one house, but, in this respect, they were exceptional. In the colonies the legislature had consisted of two branches, the lower of which was the popular assembly while the small governor's council constituted the upper. This body was in turn modeled upon the English Parliament, composed of the House of Commons and the House of Lords. Moreover, with three exceptions, the thirteen states of the Union had, at the time of the adoption of the Constitution, two-branch legislatures, and these three states subsequently fell into line.

In the second place, the bicameral system carried out the principle of checks and balances which the framers of the Constitution thought it desirable to embody in the organization of the new national government, not only as between separate departments but, in this case, within the same department. They feared that a one-branch legislature, especially if elected by direct popular vote, might become too powerful. It might also pass legislation without sufficient consideration. It was thought that in the bicameral system each branch would act as a check upon the other in preventing the enactment of hasty and ill-considered legislation. With two branches, a broader basis of representation could be secured and some dissimilarity in the composition and terms of office of the two bodies might be brought about. Thus, in *The Federalist,*

81

attention is called to the need of "dissimilarity in the genius of the two bodies" and to the desirability of distinguishing "them from each other by every circumstance which will consist with a due harmony in all proper measures, and with the genuine principles of republican government."[1]

In the third place, a very practical reason presented itself to the members of the convention for the adoption of the bicameral system. This was the need of effecting a compromise between the contentions and conflicting desires and interests of the large and small states. As we have seen above, the large states wanted representation in Congress to be based on population, while the small states demanded equal representation. This difficulty, which at one time seemed likely to wreck the convention, was finally solved by the adoption of the Connecticut compromise, whereby each state was to have equal representation in the Senate, while representation in the House of Representatives was to be based on population. Thus, in the Senate, representation was based on the federal principle, which places the emphasis on the member governments of which the Union is composed. In the House of Representatives, on the other hand, representation is based on the national principle, which emphasizes the immediate relation of the people of the whole country to the National Government. It should be noted, however, that senators do not vote as a unit but separately, as each one chooses, and that each state has at least one representative in the lower house, no matter how small its population may be.

The Apportionment of Representatives.—The representation of each state in the Senate is definitely fixed. Since there seems little likelihood of any increase in the number of states in the near future, the total number of members of the Senate is also fixed with a fair degree of definiteness.

This, however, is not true in the case of the House of Representatives. Since the number of representatives from each state in that House is based on its population, the total number of members in the House, as well as the number from each state, is likely to vary from time to time. The Constitution provided originally that there should be sixty-five members in the lower house, divided among the states according to a rough estimate of their respective population. It was required that a census of population should be taken every ten years, and the representation of each state in the lower house was to be based on its total population except that only three-fifths of the slaves were to be counted and that Indians not taxed were excluded.

This three-fifths rule for counting the slaves was, of course, abrogated by the adoption of the Thirteenth Amendment freeing the slaves. Thereafter the former slaves were counted in full and, since most of

[1] *The Federalist*, No. 62.

them continued to live in the Southern states, the adoption of this Amendment had the incidental result of increasing the representation of those states in the lower house of Congress. Since this result was not deemed to be desirable by those who were then in political control of the National Government, provision was made in the second section of the Fourteenth Amendment for the reduction of the representation of any state which denied to any of its adult male citizens the right to vote, except for participation in rebellion or other crime. This provision was aimed at the Southern states, where the former slaves were not generally allowed to vote, but it has proved to be impracticable and has never been put into operation. This seems to be partly due to the fact that any plan of reduction of representation would probably also affect some Northern states which have established educational and other qualifications for voting. In spite of the adoption of the Fifteenth Amendment, any state which disfranchises any of its adult male citizens is probably still liable to have the penalty of reduction of representation imposed upon it.

There has recently been some discussion of the question of excluding aliens from the basis of representation. In almost every state they are excluded from voting and it might be desirable also to exclude them from being counted in determining the representation of the respective states. Such a plan, however, could probably not be carried out without an amendment to the Constitution.

Although the Constitution requires that membership in the House of Representatives shall be apportioned among the several states in accordance with their respective populations, and that the latter is to be determined by a census to be taken every ten years, it does not require that there shall be a reapportionment every ten years unless there has been a relative change in the respective state populations. In practice, however, every decennial census reveals such a change and therefore a reapportionment is required if the constitutional provision for representation on the basis of population is to be carried out. The Constitution does not expressly indicate what organ of the government shall have the power, or the duty, to make the reapportionment, but, since Congress is authorized to provide for the taking of the decennial census, it is apparently implied that this power or duty rests in Congress. At any rate, practice has established such an implication. However, during the decade between the censuses of 1920 and 1930 Congress failed to make a new apportionment based on the census of 1920. It was suggested that this failure might invalidate the presidential election of 1928, if it were close, because of the fact that the number of presidential electors to which a given state is entitled is based in part upon the number of representatives accorded it in the lower house of Congress. Fortunately, no such question actually arose.

Another question raised by the failure of Congress to make a reapportionment after the census of 1920 was as to whether there is any means of compelling that body to perform its constitutional duty in this respect. It seems clear that there is no judicial process by which Congress can be compelled to act. The only remedy is the political responsibility of Congress to the people. Finally, as the result largely of such political pressure, Congress passed in 1929 an act providing for the taking of a census in the spring of 1930 and further providing that the election of a new Congress in November, 1930, should be based upon a reapportionment to be made under the 1930 census.

The Constitution provided originally that the number of representatives should not exceed one for every 30,000 inhabitants, but in fact the number is much less than that, since such a ratio would make the House much too large. In practice, Congress first decides what shall be the total membership of the House. This number is divided into the total population of the country. The result is the ratio of representation, and this ratio, when divided into the population of each state, gives, at least roughly, the number of representatives to which it is entitled. With the growth of population, the total number of members of the House has steadily increased until, under the reapportionment made by Congress after the census of 1910, it was 435.

Terms of Senators and Representatives.—The term of representatives is two years, which seemed fairly long to the framers of the Constitution but now seems too short. On the other hand, the term of senators was fixed at six years. This gives the Senate greater continuity of personnel. The shorter terms of members of the lower house indicate that that body is more likely to be influenced by the changing currents of public opinion, whereas the Senate is likely to be more stable and conservative. The shortness of the term in the lower house gives new members of that body little opportunity to learn the methods of procedure before they find it necessary to start their campaigns for reelection. In practice, members of both houses are frequently reelected, but there are also numerous instances in which members serve for but one or two terms.

Qualifications of Senators and Representatives.—Legal qualifications for senators and representatives in the lower house are laid down in the Constitution. These relate to age, citizenship, and residence. The requirements as to age and length of citizenship differ somewhat; senators must be thirty years of age and have been for nine years a citizen of the United States, while representatives need be only twenty-five years old and have been for only seven years a citizen of the United States. In other respects, the qualifications for senators and representatives are the same. Both are required to be inhabitants of the state for or in which they are chosen. This condition of being an inhabitant must exist at the time of election and has been interpreted as meaning not merely habitancy but also legal residence.

It is clear that a state cannot, by constitutional or statutory provision, add other qualifications to those mentioned in the Constitution of the United States. Nevertheless, by custom and usage an important additional qualification for representatives in the lower house has been established. This is that they must be residents not only of the state but also of the district in which they are elected. This custom runs counter to the apparent intent of the Constitution, but it is almost as firmly established as if required by law. The reason for this requirement is that a representative is regarded by his constituents as an agent in Congress to look out for the interests of his local district, and it is supposed that he can do so better if he is a resident of it. In this respect the American plan is in striking contrast with that in England where it frequently happens that a member of Parliament is elected from a district other than that of which he is a resident. Among the disadvantages of the American practice is that the best available man in the district has no chance of election if he happens to belong to the political party which is in a hopeless minority in that district. Moreover, if among the residents of a particular district there are several good men belonging to the same party, it is impossible for the people of the state to avail themselves of the services in Congress of more than one of them at the same time.[1]

Disqualification to Hold Federal Office.—In addition to the qualifications above mentioned, the Constitution also provides that

. . . no senator or representative shall, during the time for which he was elected, be appointed to any civil office under the authority of the United States, which shall have been created, or the emoluments whereof shall have been increased during such time; and no person holding any office under the United States shall be a member of either house during his continuance in office.[2]

This provision was inserted for the purpose of establishing as a rule of the fundamental law the principle of separation of powers in respect to the membership in the legislative and executive departments of the government. It requires the maintenance of the presidential form of government as distinguished from the parliamentary form. Historically, it may be traced back to an act of Parliament of 1701, which undertook to prohibit "placemen," *i.e.*, royal appointees, from holding seats in the House of Commons. This law was subsequently modified so as to permit the development of the British cabinet system, wherein leading members of the controlling party in the House of Commons are placed at the head of the important executive departments. In the United States Government, there is also a cabinet but it differs from the British

[1] HORWILL, H. W., *The Usages of the American Constitution*, Chap. IX.
[2] Art. I, sect. 6, cl. 2.

cabinet in that its members are not at the same time members of Congress. There is nothing in the Constitution to prevent Congress from according to the heads of executive departments seats in that body without the right to vote, but this has not been done. On the other hand, there is nothing to prevent the President from constituting the chairmen of important Congressional committees as a group of confidential advisers to be known as his cabinet, but this would differ from the existing cabinet in that its members could not be placed in charge of the executive business of the government.

The disqualification under discussion prevents members of Congress from holding not only cabinet positions but also any other civil office under the Federal Government, as well, of course, as military or naval offices. A member of Congress, however, if appointed to any such office, could accept it and enter upon the discharge of its duties after resigning his seat in Congress, provided the office was not one which had been created, or its emoluments increased, during the term for which such appointee had been elected to Congress. In the latter case, he would have to wait until the expiration of such term before entering upon the office. If a Federal officer is elected to a seat in Congress and chooses to accept such election, he must resign his Federal office, but the necessity for such resignation does not arise at the time of his election but only when he is sworn in and takes his seat. Until he takes his seat, he is not a member of Congress.[1]

The Constitution is not clear as to whether a member of Congress may accept a Federal office the emoluments of which have been increased during his term, provided the entire increase has been subsequently wiped out by law. Such a case arose during President Taft's administration when he appointed Senator P. C. Knox as his secretary of state, a position the salary of which had been increased during Mr. Knox's term in the Senate. Although the proceeding was of doubtful constitutionality, Mr. Knox was allowed to enter upon the office after Congress had reduced the salary of the position to the former figure.

What Is a Federal Office?—Although it is well established that members of Congress cannot hold Federal office, it is not always clear as to whether a given position under the Federal Government is or is not an office within the meaning of this disqualifying provision. One phase of this question has arisen in connection with the appointment of members of Congress to special or temporary diplomatic positions. For example, on the commission to negotiate the Treaty of Ghent in 1814, President Madison appointed, with the advice and consent of the Senate, James A. Bayard, a member of the Senate, and Henry Clay, at that time speaker of the House. Both men, however, apparently considered their new

[1] 14 Op. U. S Atty.-Gen. 408 (1874).

duties incompatible with membership in Congress, because they resigned from that body. On the commission to negotiate the treaty of peace with Spain in 1898, President McKinley appointed three members of the Senate, one being president *pro tempore* of that body and another being chairman of the committee on foreign relations. Their names were not submitted to the Senate for confirmation, nor did they resign from that body. The President appointed them, however, during a recess of the Senate, and the negotiations were practically completed during this interim.[1]

In 1898, the Senate declined to confirm the appointment of three of its members as members of the commission to propose legislation for the government of the Hawaiian Islands. Nevertheless the three served on the commission as mere presidential appointees, with no compensation beyond their salaries as senators.[2]

The question again arose in 1903 upon a proposed amendment to the Sundry Civil Appropriation Bill providing that senators and representatives should be ineligible for service on foreign missions. The amendment failed to pass, but the debate upon it in the Senate indicated that the opinion of that body was strongly opposed to the service of senators on such missions, especially when they were appointed to negotiate treaties which must later come before the Senate for action, since it might give the President an undue influence over the Senate.

In this debate the argument of unconstitutionality was also brought forward against the practice in question. Senator Bacon of Georgia declared that it was "distinctly in opposition to the express policy, if not the express command, of the Constitution." At the same time, however, he indicated the basis upon which the practice may be defended against this charge: "The only possible escape from the [constitutional] prohibition is to say that a position on one of these commissions is not an office."[3]

It appears, therefore, that persons designated by the President to serve on special missions to negotiate treaties need not be considered officers of the United States. The power of the President to appoint commissioners to negotiate treaties rests not upon his power to appoint officers but upon his power to negotiate treaties. The President merely employs agents to perform certain specific duties under his direction. Their compensation for these special services is not definitely fixed by law. Although the President may voluntarily send their nominations to the Senate, this is not done as a rule, and the constitutional requirement as to the confirmation by the Senate of presidential appointments is not applicable.[4]

[1] MATHEWS, J. M., *American Foreign Relations: Conduct and Policies*, pp. 327–328.
[2] *Cong. Rec.*, vol. 36, p. 2695 (Feb. 26, 1903).
[3] *Cong. Rec.*, *loc. cit.* p. 2696.
[4] MATHEWS, J. M., *op. cit.*, pp. 328–329.

The point here under discussion was elucidated in a House report as follows:

It is not contended that every position held by a member of Congress is an office within the meaning of the Constitution, even though the term office may usually be applied to many of these positions . . . In United States v. Hartwell (6 Wall. 385), it is laid down that "an office is a public station or employment conferred by the appointment of government. The term embraces the ideas of tenure, duration, emolument, and duties." Elsewhere it is held that an office is "an employment on behalf of the government, in any station of public trust, not merely transient, occasional, or incidental."[1]

As thus stated, the distinction seems in general to be fairly clear, but in its application to concrete cases it is found that some of them fall on the border line. Such a case was that of the World War Foreign Debt Commission, which had been created by Congress to fund the war debts and to membership on which President Harding in 1922 appointed Senator Smoot and Representative Burton. The attorney-general gave an opinion upholding the legality of these appointments, and the Senate finally confirmed them, but the Senate Judiciary Committee filed a report holding that positions on the commission were offices within the meaning of the Constitution and that Senator Smoot and Representative Burton were therefore ineligible thereto.[2] The committee based its opinion mainly on the fact that the commission had been created by act of Congress, a circumstance not found in those cases where members of Congress had been appointed as commissioners to negotiate treaties.

There is no constitutional limitation which debars a member of Congress from holding a state office. A proposal to include such a limitation in the Constitution was rejected by the Convention of 1787. In practice, however, it rarely occurs that any member of Congress holds a state office.

Can Further Qualifications Be Required?—The question as to whether any qualifications for members of Congress in addition to those expressly mentioned in the Constitution can be required may be considered under two heads. First, can a state require additional qualifications and, second, can Congress, or either branch thereof, do so?

In accordance with the general rules of legal construction, the laying down of certain express qualifications carries with it the implication that no others can be required, for the constitutional provision shows an intention on the part of the framers that all persons having the expressed qualifications should be eligible. Consequently any law of a state requiring qualifications in addition to those mentioned in the Constitu-

---

[1] *House Rep.* 2205, 55th Cong., 3d Sess., quoted by W. W. Willoughby, *Constitutional Law*, vol. I, p. 605.

[2] For texts of the attorney-general's opinion and of the committee's report, see Mathews and Berdahl, *Documents and Readings in American Government*, pp. 303–311.

tion is doubtless invalid. To obtain a court decision holding it invalid, however, may not always be easy. As pointed out above, custom has established an additional qualification for representatives in Congress: that they must reside in the districts from which they are elected. A few states have embodied this customary rule in a formal statute. When, as in this case, the statute is merely declaratory of existing custom which is so strong as to have virtually the force of law, there is ordinarily no legal or judicial process whereby such statute, in spite of its probable unconstitutionality, may be so declared.

As to the power of Congress to require additional qualifications, the situation is somewhat different. On general principles it would seem that neither Congress nor either branch thereof has legally any such power. The fact remains, however, that such a power has been exercised on several occasions. Contrary to the English practice, the Constitution confers upon each house of Congress the essentially judicial power of judging as to the elections, returns, and qualifications of its own members.[1]

As far as qualifications are concerned, this provision was probably intended to enable each house to determine whether or not any person claiming to be elected to that body possessed those stipulated in the Constitution. As interpreted in practice, however, it enables each house to require qualifications other than those which the Constitution specifies.

The following examples of the exercise of this power may be cited. In 1862, Congress passed the Test Oath Act which required every member of that body, as well as every Federal officer, to take an oath that he had not participated in rebellion against the United States, thus imposing a qualification not mentioned in the Constitution. In 1900, the House refused to seat Brigham H. Roberts of Utah on the ground that he was a polygamist, thus in effect setting up as an additional qualification that a member must be a monogamist. In 1919, Victor L. Berger of Wisconsin was refused a seat by the House because of the fact that he was at that time under conviction for opposing the war and violating the Espionage Act. Having been reelected, he was again in the following year denied a seat. Subsequently, however, having been elected for a third time and his conviction having meanwhile been reversed by the Supreme Court, he was allowed to take his seat.

Frank L. Smith of Illinois was elected to the Senate in 1926, but it appeared that large sums of money had been contributed to his campaign fund by public utility corporations which came under the jurisdiction of the Illinois Commerce Commission of which Smith was, at the time, chairman. Early in 1928, therefore, the Senate formally and finally refused to seat him on the ground that the acceptance and expenditure of these sums of money on behalf of his candidacy "is contrary to sound

[1] Art. I, sect. 5, cl. 1.

public policy, harmful to the dignity and honor of the Senate, dangerous to the perpetuity of free government, and taints with fraud and corruption the credentials for a seat in the Senate."

From the cases above cited, it appears that both the House and the Senate have on occasion refused to seat persons who had all the qualifications laid down in the Constitution and who, on the face of the returns, had been elected by a clear majority of the votes. There was no tribunal to which the person thus excluded could appeal except to that of public opinion and his constituents. On broad grounds of public policy the action of the House and Senate in most, if not all, of these cases may have been justifiable, but, from the standpoint of strict constitutionality, it would seem that the better course would have been to seat the member-elect and later to expel him. The latter action, however, would require a two-thirds vote, while refusal to seat requires merely a majority vote.

The power of either the House or the Senate to add qualifications not mentioned in the Constitution and its power to waive any or all of the qualifications stipulated therein rest upon virtually the same footing. The latter power has occasionally been exercised, as at the time of the admission of Texas into the Union. Neither power is clearly valid constitutionally, but precedents establish the existence of both of them.

The Election of Representatives.—It was the intention of the framers of the Constitution that the lower house of Congress should, in contrast with the Senate, have a broadly popular base. They therefore provided that the members of the House should be elected "by the people of the several states."

It was not deemed advisable to prescribe in the Constitution definite qualifications for those who are privileged to vote for representatives in the lower house. Such a prescription would almost necessarily have involved uniformity in qualifications throughout the country and the creation of a national electorate distinct from that of the state. The composition of the state electorates varied considerably from state to state on account of the varying qualifications for voting found in the different states. In order to conform in each state to the voting requirements laid down by that state, the Constitution merely provides that the voters or "electors" in each state for members of the lower house "shall have the qualifications requisite for electors of the most numerous branch of the state legislature."

For practical purposes it is accurate to say that the state, when determining the right of its residents to vote for members of the lower house of its legislature, thereby incidentally or indirectly determines also who has the right to vote for members of the lower house of Congress. The voter, as determined by state law, becomes *ipso facto* a voter in Congressional elections. The right, however, to vote for a member of Congress is derived not merely from the state but from the Federal Constitution.[1] This distinction has been stated by the Supreme Court as follows:

It is not correct to say that the right to vote for a member of Congress does not depend upon the Constitution of the United States. The office, if it be properly called an office, is created by that Constitution and by that alone. . . . The states, in prescribing the qualifications of voters for the most numerous branch of their own legislatures, do not do this with reference to the election for members of Congress. Nor can they prescribe the qualifications for voters for those *eo nomine*. They define who are to vote for the popular branch of their own legislature, and the Constitution of the United States says the same persons shall vote for members of Congress in that state. It adopts the qualification thus furnished as the qualification of its own electors for members of Congress. It is not true, therefore, that electors for members of Congress owe their right to vote to the state law in any sense which makes the exercise of the right to depend exclusively on the law of the state.[2]

Since the right to vote for a member of Congress is a Federal right, Congress has the power to enact appropriate legislation for the protection of its enjoyment and has in fact done so.[3]

The Regulation of Elections.—The times, places, and manner of holding elections for senators and representatives are prescribed in the first instance by the several state legislatures, but Congress is authorized by the Constitution to make or alter such regulations at any time. Unless and until Congress interferes, this matter is subject wholly to state regulation. If and when Congress interferes, it may supersede the state regulations either wholly or in part. It was not until 1842 that Congress exercised this power. To some extent state regulations on this subject have now been superseded by those of Congress. The latter require that representatives in the lower house shall be elected on a uniform date throughout the country, *viz.*, on Tuesday next after the first Monday in November of the even-numbered years. It is also required that the votes shall be cast by written or printed ballots or by voting machines. Congress could probably not assume full control over all elections where candidates for Congressional positions are chosen in conjunction with those for state and local offices. On the other hand, Congress has been held to have the power to control state election officials in the execution of state laws relating to the holding of Congressional elections.[4]

Congressional Districts.—Prior to 1842 some states elected representatives in the lower house on a general ticket. Under this plan the minority

[1] Wiley v. Sinkler, 179 U. S. 62 (1900).
[2] *Ex parte* Yarborough, 110 U. S. 651, 663 (1884).
   Cf. Wiley v. Sinkler, 179 U. S. 58, 62 (1900).
[3] United States v. Mosley, 238 U. S. 383 (1915).
[4] *Ex parte* Siebold, 100 U. S. 371 (1880).

party in a given state was not likely to secure any representation whatever. Consequently, in the reapportionment act of 1842, Congress provided that, in all states entitled to more than one representative, members of the lower house should be elected by districts rather than from the state at large. If, after a reapportionment, a state becomes entitled to additional representatives, the latter may be elected at large, but, in general, the district plan is followed, one representative being elected from each district.

The work of dividing the state into districts is assigned to the state legislature, but it does not have a completely free hand in this matter. The act of Congress requires that the districts into which a state is divided shall be composed of compact and contiguous territory and shall contain, as nearly as practicable, an equal number of inhabitants. These limitations, however, are so flexible that they do not prevent the legislature from dividing the state into districts in such a way as to favor the party in power. For this purpose, the state may be divided into districts in such a way that the opposition party will have a large majority in a few districts, while the party in power will have a small majority in a large number of districts. This is known as "gerrymandering." Under this plan some districts may exhibit very queer shapes, and in practice the districts are sometimes very unequal in population.

The Election of Senators.—The original Constitution provided that the senate "shall be composed of two senators from each state, chosen by the legislature thereof, for six years; and each senator shall have one vote."[1] This provision, as we have seen, was the result of one of the compromises of the Constitutional Convention whereby, as a concession to the small states, equal representation of the states was accorded in the upper house as an offset to the plan of representation in proportion to population in the lower. It was also thought that sufficient concession to the democratic principle had been made by providing for popular election of representatives in the lower house. Consequently, it was provided that senators should be chosen by the state legislatures. This was in accordance with the idea that the Senate should represent the state governments, rather than the people of the states. On the other hand, the states do not vote as units in the Senate, but each senator is privileged to vote independently.

At first the state legislatures were left to their own devices regarding the procedure to be followed in choosing senators. In 1866, however, Congress, under its constitutional power to make or alter regulations regarding the times, places, and manner of holding Congressional elections, passed an act providing, among other things, that if the two houses of the state legislature voting separately were unable to elect a senator, they should meet in joint session and choose a senator by majority vote.

[1] Art. I, sect. 3, cl. 1.

In spite of the improvement resulting from this act, the method of electing senators by state legislatures became continually more unsatisfactory. For one thing, it distracted the legislature from its main work of legislation. Sometimes deadlocks and long-drawn-out contests occurred in the legislature. Moreover, it was alleged that senatorial elections in the legislatures were sometimes controlled by powerful special interests through bribery and other illegitimate means. A movement was therefore set on foot to change the method of choosing senators to that of popular election. As early as 1893, a resolution proposing an amendment to the Constitution designed to bring about this change was passed in the House of Representatives by the necessary two-thirds vote but failed in the Senate. In some states, however, a form of senatorial primary was introduced by state law which, to all intents and purposes, had the effect of bringing about popular election of senators. Finally, in 1913, the Seventeenth Amendment was adopted, which provides that senators shall be elected by direct popular vote. The amendment also provides that, as in the case of the House of Representatives, those who are privileged to vote for senators are all persons qualified to vote for members of the "most numerous branch of the state legislature."

Although all members of the lower house are chosen every two years, only about one-third of the senators are chosen every two years by the voters. The ninety-six senators are divided into three classes of about thirty-two each, and the terms of one class, containing about one-third of the whole body, come to an end every two years. The result is, therefore, that the membership of the Senate is gradually renewed, and the Senate is a more stable and continuous body than the lower house.

The Filling of Vacancies.—Vacancies in either branch of Congress may occur through death, resignation, expulsion, or the acceptance of a disqualifying office. When such a vacancy occurs in the lower house, the governor of the state wherein the vacancy is to be filled is authorized and required to issue a writ for an election to fill such vacancy. By the Seventeenth Amendment, the same method is also provided for filling a vacancy in the Senate. In this case, however, the state legislature may authorize the governor to make temporary appointment pending the holding of an election. Just how long such a "temporary" appointment may last is not settled but in practice has sometimes been for a longer period than a reasonable interpretation of the word would seem to imply.

May Congress Control the Nomination Process?—In a series of acts Congress has undertaken to provide for the punishment of corrupt practices at Congressional elections. For example, by an act of 1910, as amended the following year, Congress imposed stringent restrictions upon the amounts of money that might be expended in campaigns for nomination and election to the offices of senator or representative in Congress. The question as to the constitutionality of this provision, in so far as it applied to the process of nomination through party primaries or conventions, came before the Supreme Court in the Newberry case.[1] Five of the justices, or a bare majority, held that the power granted to Congress in the Constitution to regulate the manner of holding elections did not extend to the process of nomination. "If," said Justice McReynolds speaking for these five justices, "it be practically true that, under present conditions, a designated party candidate is necessary for an election—a preliminary thereto—nevertheless his selection is in no real sense part of the manner of holding the election." The word "election" as used in the Constitution, he held to mean merely "the final choice of an officer by the duly qualified electors."

Although this is called the opinion of the Court, nevertheless its force is weakened by the fact that one of the five justices expressly reserved his opinion as to whether the act in question would have been constitutional if enacted subsequent to the adoption of the Seventeenth Amendment. It is further weakened by the cogent reasoning of the minority, who hold that an election is a complex process including the entire mode of procedure by which the popular choice is arrived at. They declare that "the relation of the primary to the election is so intimate that the influence of the former is largely determinative of the latter," and therefore Congress, under the "necessary-and-proper" clause, should be held to have the power to regulate the primary. Moreover, they point out that the power of the states to regulate the manner of holding elections for senators and representatives is a delegated and not a reserved power, is coextensive with that of Congress, and consequently, if Congress does not have the power to regulate the nomination procedure, neither do the states.

A somewhat stronger argument of the minority, however, is that in which they challenge the position of the majority that the only power which Congress has over this subject is that which it derives from the express grant in Article I, section 4, of the Constitution. The minority hold that, entirely aside from this grant, Congress has the inherent power, necessary for its self-preservation, to take appropriate measures for safeguarding the purity of the whole process whereby its own members are selected.

Nevertheless, the opinion of the majority was that, as the Constitution stood in 1910, Congress did not have control over any of the preliminaries leading up to the final election. It may be of some significance that, in passing a new corrupt practices act in 1925, Congress provided expressly that it should not be applicable to primary elections or party nominating conventions.[2] Nevertheless, when a member of Congress

---

[1] Newberry v. United States, 256 U. S. 232 (1921).

[2] As noted above, one of the majority justices in the Newberry case expressly reserved his opinion as to the effect of the Seventeenth Amendment. This raises the

was indicted for having received funds from officers and employees of the United States for use in his primary campaign for renomination to the House of Representatives, and the Federal district court quashed the indictment under the doctrine of the Newberry decision, the Supreme Court reversed the lower court. The basis of the higher court's holding, however, was not that Congress can regulate corrupt practices in primary elections but that it may protect officers and employees of the government from being subjected to pressure for money for political purposes.[1]

A case which apparently further weakens the authority of the Newberry case is the Texas White Primary case, decided in 1927.[2] A law of that state excluding negroes from participation in the primary elections of a political party was held to be unconstitutional as violative of the equal-protection-of-the-laws clause of the Fourteenth Amendment. The opinion in this case, however, was prepared by Justice Holmes, who had been one of the majority justices in the Newberry case.

Determination of Elections and Returns of Members.—The Constitution makes each house of Congress the judge as to the elections and returns of its members.[3] This would appear on its face to be an essentially judicial function. In fact, in England and in some of the British dominions, it is assigned to the courts. This was not the case, however, at the time of the adoption of our Constitution and we followed the plan then existing in that country whereby the House of Commons passed on election contests. In certain respects this plan is probably less desirable than the other. The conclusions reached by the committees on privileges and elections appointed by each house to pass on election contests are doubtless more likely to be influenced by considerations of party advantage. On the other hand, it to this extent avoids the possibility of getting the courts mixed up in politics. This power enables each house to go behind the formal certificates of election presented by would-be members to determine whether irregularities have taken place which vitiate the result. The returns from state authorities are merely *prima facie* evidence of an election and not binding upon the House. It is not necessary that there should be a contestant, but each house may on its own initiative institute an investigation into the right of would-be members to seats.

---

question as to whether an act, unconstitutional at the time of its enactment, might not be rendered constitutional and effective without reenactment by a subsequent change of the Constitution. In order to reach this conclusion, it must be assumed that the act was not utterly void but was in a state of suspended animation during the period prior to the amendment of the Constitution. Some courts have taken this view but the contrary view seems to be more generally held. *Cf.* People v. Roberts, 148 N. Y. 360 (1896).

[1] United States v. Wurzback, 280 U. S. 396 (1930).
[2] Nixon v. Herndon, 273 U. S. 536 (1927).
[3] Art. I, sect. 5, cl. 1.

The Expulsion of Members.—A power distinct from that of refusing to seat would-be members is that of expelling members after they have been seated. In the case of expulsion, however, the Constitution requires a two-thirds vote.[1] The Constitution does not specify the particular reasons for which a member may be expelled and each house is apparently the conclusive judge as to whether the reasons are sufficient. A member may be expelled for treason, high crimes, or misdemeanors, or for irregularities in connection with his election. The offense need not be an indictable one but anything which in the judgment of the house renders him unfit to continue as a member. The requirement of a two-thirds vote is a safeguard against the abuse of this power for mere partisan purposes. The precedents would seem to indicate a feeling on the part of Congress that a member should be subject to expulsion only for acts committed subsequent to his election and not for those committed before that event, but the language of the Constitution draws no such distinction. It should be noted that members of Congress, not being civil officers of the United States, are not subject to impeachment.

Sessions of Congress.—Under the original Constitution, unless Congress provides for meeting at some other time, the regular sessions of Congress begin on the first Monday in December every year. The result is that a new Congress, elected in November, and with terms beginning on the fourth of March following, would not convene in regular session until about thirteen months later. During the two-year period covered by a Congress, there are two regular sessions. Of these the first is known as the long session, because it may extend over almost an entire year if Congress so desires; the second is the short session which must end by constitutional limitation not later than the fourth of March, thus covering only about three months. In addition to regular sessions the President may also, in his discretion, call extra or special sessions of Congress, or of either branch thereof, and in practice he frequently exercises this power. There is no provision in the Federal Constitution, such as is found in many state constitutions, enabling the chief executive to limit the matters acted upon in the special session.

The short regular session of Congress is also sometimes called the "lame-duck" session, because it usually contains a number of members who have failed of reelection at the preceding November election and have thus been repudiated by the voters of their districts. They nevertheless continue to sit in Congress and to participate in the work of legislation during the short session. Some of them may have the opportunity arbitrarily to prevent the passage of laws simply by consuming time. An even more serious objection to this arrangement is the possibility that a House of Representatives, which has been thus discredited at the polls, might have the opportunity to elect a President through the

[1] Art. I, sect. 5, cl. 2.

failure of any candidate for that office to receive a majority of the electoral votes.

Although Congress can by law change the date for the beginning of regular sessions, it cannot change the date of the beginning of the terms of senators and representatives, since this would affect the length of their terms as fixed by the Constitution. Hence a constitutional amendment is necessary to effect this change. A proposed constitutional amendment, known as the Norris amendment, intended to overcome the disadvantages of the existing arrangement was passed by Congress in 1932. This amendment, if adopted, would do away with the short, or lame-duck, session. It provides that the first session of the new Congress shall begin in January following the Congressional election in November and that the terms of the senators and representatives chosen at that election shall begin at the same time. It thus shortens from thirteen months to two months the length of time intervening between the election of members and the taking of their seats in regular session. Incidentally, it also changes the date of the inauguration of the President and Vice President from March to January.[1]

The proposed Norris amendment would thus prevent representatives who have been repudiated by their constituents from passing on important measures and would thus increase the efficiency of popular control. Since, under this plan, there would be no definite limitation laid upon the length of sessions, the danger of holding up important legislation through filibusters, i.e., by talking a bill to death during the closing hours or days of a session which must expire on a given date by constitutional limitation, would be greatly decreased.

Compensation of Members.—Unlike the system of compensation which prevailed under the Articles of Confederation, members of Congress are not paid by their respective states but are paid a compensation for their services out of the treasury of the United States. This emphasizes the fact that members owe allegiance to the nation and are not mere state agents. Inasmuch as the proper amount of compensation is liable to change rather frequently from various causes, it was not deemed practicable to fix the amount in the Constitution itself. The framers of that instrument, therefore, left it to Congress to determine the amount from time to time, and in doing so Congress is subject to no constitutional restrictions, such as apply in the case of the salaries of the President and of Federal judges. There is no constitutional requirement that the members of the two houses shall be paid at the same rate, but in practice this is always done. In practice, however, the presiding officers of the two houses receive somewhat larger salaries than ordinary members. This would naturally be expected, especially in the case of the presiding officer of the Senate, since he is also Vice President.

[1] For text of the proposed Norris amendment see below, Appendix.

Privileges and Immunities of Members.—The Constitution provides that senators and representatives

. . . shall in all cases, except treason, felony, and breach of the peace, be privileged from arrest during their attendance at the session of their respective houses, and in going to and returning from the same; and for any speech or debate in either house, they shall not be questioned in any other place.[1]

This provision may be traced back to the struggle between the Crown and Parliament in England. It was embodied in the English Bill of Rights, from which it was substantially copied into the Articles of Confederation. As found in the Articles and in our Constitution, however, it is aimed not so much at the executive as at interference with the legislative duties of members of Congress through trumped-up charges or private suits. It is a special privilege which ordinary private citizens do not enjoy, and it is intended to inure not to the private benefit of members of Congress but to promote the public welfare through enabling them to perform their public duties free from the restraint which a lack of such privilege would entail. The extent of the privilege is to be determined in the light of this fundamental purpose for which it exists.

It is to be noted that the privilege of freedom from arrest exists not only while a member is attending a session of Congress but also while going to and returning from the same. The period of exemption before and after a session hardly extends for forty days, as Blackstone averred in the case of members of Parliament, but only for a reasonable time. The privilege of exemption from arrest probably applies to a newly elected member on his way to the capital before he has been seated. The value of the privilege thus granted is not as great as it may seem because the constitutional provision contains a joker in the form of the weasel words "except treason, felony, and breach of the peace." These words have been construed to include all indictable offenses.[2] Consequently the exemption from arrest does not apply to the processes of the criminal law but only in civil actions. Occasions for making arrests in civil actions, however, seldom arise. During sessions of Congress, members could not be compelled to serve on juries. Although they might be served with summonses to appear in court to testify as witnesses, they could not with propriety be arrested for failure to appear.

Of more importance is the privilege extended to members of Congress that "for any speech or debate in either house, they shall not be questioned in any other place." If the proceedings of Congress were secret, there would not be so much need of this provision, but in view of the publicity of the proceedings the privilege granted in this provision seems obviously desirable in order to enable members to express themselves freely upon all questions relating to the public business. The "other

---

[1] Art. I, sect. 6, cl. 1.

[2] Williamson v. United States, 207 U. S. 425 (1907).

place" mentioned in this provision is primarily a court in which a member might be sued for libel or slander, and the provision thus prevents such a proceeding being brought against him. It has been held that the constitutional provision is to be liberally construed. Consequently, it is not limited to words spoken in debate. It also covers reports, resolutions, and votes, whether in the House proper or in the course of committee proceedings, and, in general, everything done in a session of the House by one of its members in relation to the business before it.[1] The constitutional provision, however, does not protect from suit for damages a member who goes out of his way to make unnecessary and malicious attacks upon the reputation of others, when such attacks do not relate to the business before the House. Furthermore, the provision does not protect a member from responsibility for unwarranted personalities contained in outside publications.

Adjournment.—The Constitution prohibits either house to adjourn, without the consent of the other, for more than three days. Although the President may call a special session of either or both houses, he has no power of dissolving Congress. In case, however, the two houses should disagree as to the time of adjournment, whether in a regular or in a special session, the President is authorized to adjourn them to such time as he sees fit. This is a power, however, which he has not found occasion to exercise.

[1] Kilbourn v. Thompson, 103 U. S. 168, 204 (1880).

CHAPTER VIII

CONGRESSIONAL PROCEDURE

Organization for Work.—The lower house differs from the Senate in that it has to reorganize itself at the beginning of each new Congress. The Constitution provides that the House of Representatives "shall choose their speaker and other officers."[1] The usual practice is for the clerk of the preceding House to preside until the speaker, or permanent presiding officer, has been chosen. Before the House meets, the members of each political party represented in the House usually hold a caucus at which they select their respective candidates for the speakership. When the House meets in its first session, the candidate of the political party having a majority of the members is elected speaker. In reality, since this candidate may be the choice of only a bare majority of the caucus held by the party having possibly only a bare majority of the total membership, the speaker actually chosen may be favored by only a minority of the House. There are no constitutional qualifications laid down for this important office. The speaker need not even be a member of the House, but in practice he always is.

The powers and duties of the speaker are determined not by the Constitution but by the rules of the House. Unlike the speaker of the English House of Commons, the speaker of the House of Representatives is a party man and may sometimes exercise his powers in such a way as to favor the interests of his own party.

In addition to the speaker, the House also chooses its other officers, including the clerk, sergeant at arms, doorkeepers, etc. Their selection is controlled by the majority party, but they are never chosen from among the members of the House.

Unlike the lower house, the Senate is a permanent and continuously organized body. Although at the beginning of a new Congress all of the members of the House might conceivably be new members, there are always at least two-thirds of the senators who have served in one or more previous Congresses. Moreover, unlike the House, the Senate does not have to engage in a contest at the beginning of each new Congress for the selection of its presiding officer. This is because the Constitution provides that the Vice President of the United States shall be president of the Senate. The Senate, however, is authorized by the Constitution to choose its other officers, including a president *pro tempore* who

---

[1] Art. I, sect. 2, cl. 5.

presides in case of the absence of the Vice President or in case of his succession to the presidency.

Although the president *pro tempore* of the Senate is always a member of that body, the Vice President never is. The latter officer, unlike the speaker of the House, merely presides and does not participate in the general work of legislation. He does not enter into debate and has ordinarily no vote on measures before the Senate. This prevents the state from which he comes from having three votes in comparison with only two from the other states. The Constitution provides, however, that in case the Senate should be equally divided, the Vice President may vote in order to break the tie. This power has been rather frequently exercised, and occasionally with reference to important measures, the fate of which was determined by the Vice President's casting vote.

The Rules of Procedure.—Since the houses of Congress are set up as legislative and deliberative bodies, it is to be presumed that, even in the absence of any specific constitutional provision, they would have impliedly the right to adopt rules of procedure within the limits of the Constitution, but, in order to remove any possible doubt of this, that instrument so provides.[1] It has been held that the only limitations upon this power of either house is that "it may not by its rules ignore constitutional restraints or violate fundamental rights, and there should be a reasonable relation between the mode or method of proceeding established by the rule and the result which is sought to be attained."[2] Subject to these restrictions, each house may make or change its rules at pleasure.

Quorum.—Among the constitutional rules which restrict the freedom of each house in determining its rules of procedure is that which stipulates that "a majority of each shall constitute a quorum to do business." This contrasts with the rule of the English House of Commons where forty members constitute a quorum. The Constitution does not indicate how the presence of a quorum is to be determined, and consequently it is left to each house to provide by rule any method of determination reasonably certain to ascertain the fact. On this basis, a rule of the House of Representatives which provided for counting members actually present but not voting in making up a quorum was upheld.[3] Even in the absence of a quorum, those present may proceed with some kinds of business unless or until some member makes objection or suggests the lack of a quorum. It was not felt proper by the framers of the Constitution that members should be allowed to break up the proceedings by merely failing to attend. Consequently, they provided that a smaller number than a quorum might adjourn from day to day and might "be authorized to compel the attendance of absent members, in such manner

---

[1] Art. I, sect. 5, cl. 2.
[2] United States v. Ballin, 144 U. S. 1 (1892).
[3] *Ibid.*

and under such penalties as each house" might provide.[1] The penalty for failure of absent members to attend may be imprisonment.[2] The constitutional requirement as to the presence of a quorum may be practically evaded by the House of Representatives through the device of resolving itself into the Committee of the Whole, in which one hundred members, or much fewer than a majority, constitute a quorum.

The Journals.—The Constitution provides that "each house shall keep a journal of its proceedings, and from time to time publish the same, excepting such parts as may in their judgment require secrecy."[3] This provision was obviously intended to secure publicity to a reasonable extent in Congressional proceedings. The lower house may hold secret sessions but has not done so since 1811. The Senate, however, frequently goes into executive session, which is supposed to be secret. Subsequently, by order of the Senate, the injunction of secrecy as to such sessions may be removed, whereupon the journal of proceedings in executive session is published. The Constitution does not indicate how full a journal shall be kept nor what particular items of business it shall contain. These are matters which are left to the discretion of the respective houses.[4]

The question has been raised as to how far the records of Congressional proceedings as shown in the journals are conclusive and binding upon the courts in considering the question as to whether a law has been legally enacted. They have been inclined to hold that where the passage of a bill has been duly attested by the presiding officers of the two houses, has been approved by the President of the United States, and deposited as a law in the public archives, the courts must accept it as authentic in spite of any contrary evidence adduced from the journals.[5] It would seem, however, that this position should be subject to some modification. If, for example, a given law is a revenue measure, which under the Constitution must originate in the lower house, and its validity is impeached on the ground that it originated in the Senate, it would seem that the Court should be able to have the journals of the two houses admitted as evidence upon this point and decide in accordance with such evidence even though the decision may be that the law is null and void in spite of the signatures of the presiding officers. As was pointed out by a Federal district court,

When the Congress, through its proper officials, certifies that it has gone through the forms of law making in violation of an express constitutional mandate, is the result a law at all? Of course it is not; the question answers itself, unless there be some different treatment due to an act created in a fundamentally illegal manner and that accorded to one created for an unconstitutional purpose.

[1] Art. I, sect. 5, cl. 1.

[2] Kilbourn v. Thompson, 103 U. S. 190 (1880).

[3] Art. I, sect. 5, cl. 3.

[4] Field v. Clark, 143 U. S. 649 (1892).

[5] Field v. Clark, 143 U. S. 649 (1892); Flint v. Stone Tracy Co., 220 U. S. 107 (1911); United States v. Ballin, 144 U. S. 1 (1892).

There can be no such difference logically. Any and all violations of constitutional requirements vitiate a statute.[1]

The Court then held invalid the Cotton Futures Act of 1914 on the ground that although a revenue measure, it had not originated in the lower house.

The Yeas and Nays.—A final restriction upon the two houses of Congress in freely determining their own rules is the provision of the Constitution that "the yeas and nays of the members of either house on any question shall, at the desire of one-fifth of those present, be entered on the journal."[2] This method of voting is also required on the question of passing a bill over the presidential veto.[3] The obvious purpose of the requirement in both cases is to put the members on record and to enable the people to know how their representatives vote. On account of the length of time consumed in taking a roll call, however, this method of voting is frequently used for mere purposes of delay and obstruction. In this connection, it should be noted that this method of voting is not used in Committee of the Whole, so that by the device of going into such committee, members may avoid being put on record.

[1] Hubbard v. Lowe, 226 Fed. 135, quoted by W. W. Willoughby, *Constitutional Law of the United States*, 2d ed., vol. II, p. 655.

[2] Art. I, sect. 5, cl. 3.

[3] Art. I, sect. 7, cl. 2.

CHAPTER IX

THE POWERS OF CONGRESS: GENERAL VIEW

If we analyze the constitutional functions of Congress, we find that it is by no means a body created for the purpose merely of enacting laws. That is one of its most important but not its sole function. This and other powers granted to it by the Constitution, either expressly or impliedly, may be classified as follows: (1) constituent, (2) electoral, (3) executive, (4) administrative, (5) legislative, (6) inquisitorial and investigative, and (7) judicial.[1]

Some of these functions are dealt with in other connections and need only be mentioned at this point. Thus, in considering the method of formally amending the Constitution, we have seen that the action of Congress is indispensable and may be exercised in various ways. Congress may take the initiative in proposing the amendment and may also determine whether it shall be ratified by conventions or by legislatures in the states. Congress is also authorized to call a national constitutional convention upon the request of two-thirds of the state legislatures.

The opportunity for the exercise by Congress of its electoral function arises when no candidate for President has a majority of the electoral vote, in which case the House of Representatives chooses the President from the three candidates having the highest number of votes. Furthermore, in case of a similar contingency with reference to the Vice President, the Senate chooses the latter officer from the two highest candidates. This situation does not often happen, but in every presidential election Congress acts as a board to canvass the vote cast in the electoral college and declare the results. Usually this function involves mere clerical work but may occasionally assume great importance, as in the case of the Hayes-Tilden contest of 1876.

It was apparently the expectation of the framers of the Constitution that the Senate would act as a general executive council to advise and consult with the President on important matters. In actual practice, however, this expectation has not been fully realized. Mainly because of the fact that the President does not choose the members of the Senate, among whom may be many persons belonging to the opposite political party, the President is more inclined to turn to his cabinet for advice rather than to the Senate. Nevertheless, it is constitutionally necessary for him to obtain the approval of the Senate to treaties and to important

[1] Cf. WILLOUGHBY, W. F., *The Government of Modern States*, pp. 291ff.

appointments. In practice, moreover, the President sometimes consults in person with the Senate Committee on Foreign Relations.

The administrative function of Congress is apt to be confused with its legislative function because both functions are exercised in the same form, *i.e.*, through the enactment of laws. Many enactments having the form of laws, however, are not laws in the sense of embodying general and relatively permanent rules for governing the conduct of individuals in their relations with each other and with the government. Rather, they are directions to administrative officials to carry on certain activities or authorizations permitting them to do so. Much of the work of any legislative body consists in creating new organs, offices, and functions in the executive department, or rearranging those already in existence, and giving detailed directions as to the exercise of their powers and duties by the designated organs.[1]

Of great importance in this connection is the legislative control of the public purse. New organs cannot be created, nor new functions undertaken, nor can the old ones be maintained without provision being made by the legislature for the necessary financial support. By means of detailed appropriations, the legislature is able to exert an influence which permeates every branch of the administrative system. This power of the legislature is not properly legislative, but administrative. The legislature enters so intimately into the business of regulating the administration that it has been aptly called the "board of directors of the public corporation."[2]

The Inquisitorial Powers of Congress.—In order intelligently to exercise its power of directing the administration, as well as many of its other powers, Congress, or either branch thereof, may find it desirable to secure information by conducting investigations. Congress does not have a general power of making inquiry into any or all of the private affairs of the citizens.[3] On the other hand, it may make investigations in order to elicit information which is reasonably conducive to the effective exercise of its constitutional powers. As stated by the Supreme Court in a recent case:

The power of inquiry—with process to enforce it—is an essential and appropriate auxiliary to the legislative function . . . A legislative body can not legislate wisely or effectively in the absence of information respecting the conditions which the legislation is intended to affect or change; and where the legislative body does not itself possess the requisite information—which not infrequently is true—recourse must be had to others who do possess it.[4]

[1] MATHEWS, J. M., *Principles of American State Administration*, pp. 10–12 (New York, 1917).

[2] WILLOUGHBY, W. F., *op. cit.*, p. 302.

[3] Kilbourn v. Thompson, 103 U. S. 190 (1880).

[4] McGrain v. Daugherty, 273 U. S. 135 (1927).

Among the powers of Congress, or either branch thereof, to which the power of investigation may be auxiliary are those of legislation, impeachment, passing upon contested elections of members, the admission or expulsion of members, the approval of treaties, and the confirmation of appointments.

There are two kinds of constitutional limitations upon the power of Congress to conduct investigations. The first kind arises from the fact that the information to be elicited from certain investigations is not auxiliary to the exercise of any power constitutionally granted to Congress. The second kind of constitutional limitation is that, in conducting such investigation, Congress must not violate those provisions designed to protect the individual against the arbitrary power of the government, such as the prohibitions against self-incrimination and against unreasonable searches and seizures.

Investigations are not usually conducted by Congress, or by either branch thereof, as a whole, but rather by standing or special committees of either house to which the function has been entrusted. Except in connection with the presentation of articles of impeachment, investigations are more usually conducted by committees of the Senate than by those of the lower house, on account of the more strict party control in the latter body.[1] The extent of the constitutional power of a Congressional committee to make investigations may be equal to that of either house of Congress itself. This power may be used incidentally to hold executive officers to accountability for their acts or failure to act. Such an exercise of power is judicial rather than legislative in character and, in deference to the principle of separation of powers, would not be sustained unless it is clearly implied in some power expressly granted to Congress. Although the courts would probably not uphold an inquiry conducted solely for the purpose of holding an executive officer to accountability for his acts or failures to act, the existence of such a purpose will not invalidate an investigation capable of being sustained on other grounds. This was shown in the Daugherty case, decided in 1927,[2] which involved an attempt on the part of the Senate to hold the attorney-general to accountability for his failure to enforce the laws of Congress. The investigation was sustained by the Supreme Court on the ground that it was capable of facilitating future legislation.[3] The Court declared that "the power of inquiry with process to enforce it is an essential and appropriate auxiliary to the legislative function." In this case the point was raised that the Congress which had ordered the investigation had

[1] ROGERS, L., *The American Senate*, Chap. VI.

[2] McGrain v. Daughterty, 273 U. S. 135 (1927).

[3] DIMOCK, M. E., "Congressional Investigating Committees," *Johns Hopkins Univ. Stud. in Hist. and Polit. Sci.*, Ser. XLVII, No. 1, p. 145. It should be noted that since the inquiry could be sustained only on the ground that it was an aid to legislation, the witness might refuse to answer any questions not conducive to this end.

expired, but the Court held that this fact did not invalidate the investigation because the Senate has a continuous organization and authority.

The business of government is becoming so complicated that Congress is compelled to delegate many important regulatory functions to permanent administrative commissions. To such bodies it may also delegate the power to make investigations in order to promote the effective performance of their regulatory functions. In such case, the work of fact finding is auxiliary to the work of regulation. Some of these bodies, such as the United States Tariff Commission, are mere fact-finding agencies, without power of regulation. The Supreme Court has held, as a matter of statutory construction, that such a regulatory body as the Interstate Commerce Commission does not have power to make fact-finding investigations as such, except with regard to matters tending to interfere with the enforcement of the acts of Congress regulating interstate commerce.[1]

It should be noted that, although the power of Congress to make investigations is not general but limited, the contrary is true of the state legislatures, because they are bodies not of delegated but of general residuary powers.

Power to Punish for Contempt.—If Congress in making investigations were dependent upon the voluntary attendance and testimony of witnesses, its power in this respect would probably be of comparatively little importance. As the Court declared in the Daugherty Case, "Experience has taught that mere requests for such information often are unavailing, and also that information which is volunteered is not always accurate or complete; so some means of compulsion are essential to obtain what is needed." In order that such investigations may be successful in bringing to light the desired information, it may be necessary for Congress to summon witnesses and to require the production of books and papers. But if witnesses refuse to appear when summoned or refuse to testify about matters into which Congress has jurisdiction to inquire, it may then become necessary for Congress to exercise its power to punish for contempt—a power derived by implication from its power to make the investigation. This power of punishment exists not primarily for the purpose of punishment, but rather for the purpose of self-preservation or of preventing or overcoming obstruction to the performance by Congress, or either branch thereof, of its official duties.[2] Such punishment for contempt may be meted out directly by either house without criminal prosecution. In addition, Congress may, and in fact has, passed an act making it a misdemeanor for witnesses to refuse to testify about matters into which Congress has jurisdiction to inquire.[3] The

[1] Harriman v. Interstate Commerce Commission, 211 U. S. 407 (1908); and *cf.* Brimson v. Interstate Commerce Commission, 154 U. S. 447 (1894).

[2] Marshall v. Gordon, 243 U. S. 521 (1917).

[3] *In re* Chapman, 166 U. S. 661 (1897).

courts may, of course, be appealed to in cases of dispute as to the extent of the jurisdiction of Congress, and, under the statute just mentioned, a contumacious witness may be indicted, tried, and punished in the courts.

The power of Congress to punish for contempt is broader than its power to make investigations. It may apply, for example, to one who creates a disturbance in the House or Senate chamber intended to interfere with the orderly procedure of those bodies, or possibly to one who makes slanderous and defamatory charges impugning the motives of Congress or of a committee of either branch thereof. The Supreme Court has approved of punishment by the houses of Congress for contempt in the following instances:

Either physical obstruction of the legislative body in the discharge of its duties, or physical assault upon its members for action taken or words spoken in the body, or obstruction of its officers in the performance of their official duties, or the prevention of members from attending so that their duties might be performed, or finally with contumacy in refusing to obey orders to produce documents or give testimony which there was a right to compel.[1]

In the case just cited, however, the Court declared that "the power, even when applied to subjects that justified its exercise, is limited to imprisonment and such imprisonment may not be extended beyond the session of the body in which the contempt occurred."

What has been said above applies primarily to the jurisdiction of Congress over outsiders or nonmembers who may become recalcitrant witnesses or disturbers of proceedings. Congress, or rather each house thereof, also has disciplinary power over its own members. The Constitution provides that "each house may punish its members for disorderly behavior, and, with the concurrence of two-thirds, expel a member."[2] Disorderly behavior of members might be declared to constitute contempt of the house and, if persisted in, might furnish ground for punishment by imprisonment. In the Chapman case, the Supreme Court upheld the right of the Senate to conduct an investigation and to punish a contumacious witness for contempt under its power to expel its members for misconduct.[3]

In a recent case involving a contest over the seating of one Vare as senator from Pennsylvania, the Supreme Court held that the Senate has the right to compel a witness to appear and give evidence in aid of its judicial function of passing upon the elections, returns, and qualifications of its own members.[4]

[1] Marshall v. Gordon, 243 U. S. 521, 542 (1917).
[2] Art. I, sect. 5, cl. 2.
[3] *In re* Chapman, 166 U. S. 661 (1897).
[4] Barry v. United States *ex rel.* Cunningham, 279 U. S. 620 (1929).   *Cf.* the case of Sinclair v. United States, 279 U. S. 263 (1929).

In punishing either members or nonmembers for contempt, Congress is limited by the fundamental provisions of the Constitution for the protection of individual liberties, such as that of the Fifth Amendment requiring due process of law.

Impeachment.—Public officers whose records are unsatisfactory may be retired to private life at the end of their terms through failure to be reelected. This method of retirement, however, can not be applied to Federal judges, whose tenure is during good behavior. Moreover, even in the case of officers elected for a term of years, occasional instances of gross misconduct may occur which render it inadvisable that the officer should be allowed to serve out his term. The Constitution makes no express provision for administrative removal from office. It is true that it has nevertheless been established that the President has the power of administrative removal. This power, however, does not apply to Federal judges nor, of course, to the President himself. Moreover, there might be cases of officers who are guilty of misconduct, whom the President could remove but fails to do so. These considerations point to the need for some other method of removal, and this is found in the provision of the Constitution for impeachment. This is a judicial power exercised by the legislative department, or the upper branch thereof, and was well established in English constitutional practice at the time of the adoption of the Constitution.

In considering the process of impeachment, a distinction must be made between the act of accusation, or impeachment proper, and trial and conviction on impeachment. The act of accusation, technically known as impeachment, is entrusted to the House of Representatives. When charges are made against an officer, that body may in its discretion pass, by majority vote, so-called "articles of impeachment" which are then sent to the Senate. It would seem that the Senate has no right to refuse to hear the case, although, if it should refuse to do so, there would probably be no legal means of compelling it to do so. Such a situation has not actually arisen. In practice, the Senate, upon receipt of the articles of impeachment from the House, notifies the accused officer of the charges against him and designates the time for the trial to begin. At such trial the House acts as official prosecutor, through a committee of managers appointed by it, while the Senate sits as a court with its regular presiding officer in the chair, unless the President of the United States is on trial. In the latter case the Constitution requires that the chief justice of the Supreme Court shall preside. The reason for this provision is obviously that the Vice President, who would ordinarily preside, should not be allowed to do so in a trial the result of which would greatly affect his personal interests. Curiously enough, in the only case in which a President has been on trial—that of President Johnson—there was no Vice President at the time and the officer who, under the law as it then stood, would have succeeded to the presidency in case of the conviction of Johnson, *viz.*, the president *pro tempore* of the Senate, quite unembarrassed by his personal interest in the result, cast his vote for conviction. It would seem that the chief justice should preside when the Vice President is under impeachment, as in the case of the President, but the Constitution contains no express provision for this situation.

It would seem that, when the chief justice presides, he has such privileges in the matters of voting and ruling on questions of law and procedure as the Vice President would have in other cases. It would also seem that, on questions preliminary to the final vote of guilty or not guilty, such as the admission of evidence, the Senate may proceed by mere majority vote. Although the Senate sits as a court, it is not compelled to follow all the technical rules of judicial procedure, such as those, for example, relating to the admissibility of evidence. In practice, however, the Senate ordinarily accords to the accused various rights which he would have if on trial in an ordinary court, such as the benefit of counsel and compulsory process for obtaining witnesses on his behalf. In order to secure conviction, the Constitution requires a two-thirds vote of the senators present, without regard to who may be on trial. If only one less than the requisite two-thirds vote "guilty"—as happened in President Johnson's case—the result is acquittal. The decision of the Senate is final and not subject to appeal. Moreover, the President's power of granting pardons for offenses against the United States does not apply to cases of impeachment.

The penalty, in case of conviction on impeachment, is removal from office. The imposition of this penalty is required by the Constitution and, it would seem, is automatic. Nevertheless in practice the Senate, after voting to convict, takes another vote to remove from office. If the latter vote should fail to be adopted, however, the result would probably be the same as if it had carried. The Constitution also specifies another penalty which is not required but may or may not be imposed within the discretion of the Senate. This is "disqualification to hold and enjoy any office of honor, trust or profit under the United States."[1] Aside from these two, no further penalties can be imposed as the result merely of conviction on impeachment, but the convicted person, after removal from office, is nevertheless "liable and subject to indictment, trial, judgment, and punishment, according to law."[2] In other words, the officer who has been convicted on impeachment, after retirement to private life, may be prosecuted and punished in a court of law just like any private person if the offense of which he was accused is criminal or indictable. Upon conviction in the court of law, however, he may be pardoned by the President.

[1] Art. I, sect. 3, cl. 7.
[2] *Ibid.* This does not constitute double jeopardy.

Who May Be Impeached?—Under the English law of impeachment as it stood at the time of the adoption of our Constitution, "all the King's subjects were liable to impeachment, whether officials or not, and for any offense."[1] In the United States, however, impeachment has been construed to apply only to officials. Curiously enough, the Constitution does not delimit expressly the class or group of persons who may be impeached. It does declare, however, that "the President, Vice President, and all civil officers of the United States shall be removed from office on impeachment for, and conviction of, treason, bribery, or other high crimes and misdemeanors."[2] Without definitely saying so, this provision seems clearly to imply that no other persons except those mentioned are subject to impeachment. It follows, therefore, that officers of the army and navy, not being civil officers, are not subject to impeachment.

For the purpose of impeachment at least, members of Congress are held not to be civil officers of the United States. This is implied in that provision of the Constitution which declares that "no senator or representative shall, during the time for which he was elected, be appointed to any civil office under the authority of the United States," etc.[3] Moreover, as we have seen, any member of either house may be removed from his position by a two-thirds vote cast for his expulsion. The only case of an attempt to impeach a member of Congress was that of Senator Blount in 1797. Prior to his impeachment he had been expelled by the Senate. When his trial came on, he claimed that the Senate had no jurisdiction because a senator is not a civil officer of the United States, within the meaning of the constitutional provision. This plea to the jurisdiction was upheld by the Senate.

The further question arises as to when civil officers may be impeached. It was formerly held by some, including Judge Story, that, since the Constitution requires removal from office as the result of conviction on impeachment, no one can be impeached unless he was in office at the time of conviction on impeachment or at least at the time of impeachment. This reasoning, however, is not conclusive. In the Blount case the plea was made that, since he had been expelled from the Senate, he was not impeachable, although it was intimated by counsel that if he had resigned instead of being expelled, this plea would not have been good. As it turned out, it was unnecessary for the Senate to pass on this plea. In 1912, Judge Archbald of the Commerce Court, although convicted on impeachment, was acquitted on certain charges of misconduct alleged to have been committed by him while holding a previous judicial office.

---

[1] THOMAS, D. Y., "The Law of Impeachment in the United States," *Amer. Polit. Sci. Rev.*, vol. 2, p. 378 (May, 1908).

[2] Art. II, sect. 4.

[3] Art. I, sect. 6, cl. 2.

In 1876, Secretary of War Belknap resigned and his resignation was immediately accepted by President Grant. The House of Representatives shortly thereafter impeached him and the Senate proceeded with the trial. He pleaded to the jurisdiction of the Senate on the ground that he was no longer a civil officer of the United States and had not been at the time of his impeachment. The Senate nevertheless voted (but by less than two-thirds) that it had jurisdiction and later voted that, in order to decide the matter of jurisdiction, a two-thirds vote was not necessary. In the end, however, Belknap was acquitted. In several cases where judges of the lower Federal courts have been impeached by the House of Representatives or where the House committee recommended impeachment, proceedings have been dropped upon notice of the resignation of the judges accused.

It will be observed that the above precedents are not conclusive upon the question as to whether or not an officer is still subject to impeachment after his separation from the office. It is submitted, however, that upon reason he should be considered as still subject to impeachment. The principal reason for this view is that the Constitution specifies as a possible penalty for conviction on impeachment not only removal from office but also disqualification to hold office in the future. If this view were not correct, it would be a simple matter for any officer about to be impeached to avoid this disqualification by the mere device of resigning.[1] It may be desirable to impose this disqualification not merely for purposes of punishment but also for the sake of public security. It may be argued that after resignation he would still be subject to be prosecuted in a court of law. But to this argument two answers may be made. First, even if prosecuted and convicted in a court of law, he might be granted a pardon by the President, which could not be done in case of conviction on impeachment. In the second place, as shown below, impeachment might apply to misconduct which is not indictable and therefore not punishable by a court of law.

What Are Impeachable Offenses?—Under the English law and practice, as pointed out above, impeachment might be had for any offense. The framers of our Constitution did not see fit to follow this precedent but deemed it wise to specify the offenses on which impeachment charges might be based. This they did in the words "treason, bribery, or other high crimes and misdemeanors." Treason is defined in the Constitution and bribery is sufficiently definite. The phrase "high crimes and misdemeanors," however, is rather flexible and indefinite.

It has been supposed in some quarters that this phrase refers to indictable offenses only or those made penal by Federal statute, but it seems clear that this is a mistaken view. A consideration of the charges actually brought in impeachment trials shows that many of them did

---

[1] Provided, at least, that his resignation were accepted.

not specify indictable offenses. Thus, President Johnson was accused, among other things, of making public speeches denunciatory of Congress, while District Judge English, impeached in 1926, was accused of showing partiality and favoritism. Although, in most of these cases, the accused official was not convicted, his acquittal was not based on the ground that the charges did not specify indictable offenses. It would seem, therefore, that any misconduct which affects the public welfare or indicates the unfitness of the official renders him subject to impeachment. This misconduct, moreover, need not be committed while in the discharge of official duties. In convicting Judge Archbald of the Commerce Court in 1912, the Senate acted on charges involving acts which were not indictable and were not committed in the exercise of judicial power. The Senate is the final judge as to whether the alleged misconduct indicates the officer's unfitness, and from its decision there is no appeal.

This does not mean that the power of impeachment is absolutely unlimited or that it may be exercised, for example, on entirely baseless charges or merely because a judge has rendered a mistaken decision. Even in this case, however, it is difficult to perceive what redress an official would have if the Senate proceeded on this ground to convict him. But assuming that the Senate rests under a sense of political responsibility, such action on its part, although theoretically possible, is extremely improbable. So little has the power of impeachment been used and so cumbrous is it in operation that we may almost agree with Jefferson's characterization of it that it "is not even a scare-crow."

The Separation of Powers.—Although Congress, as we have seen, has various kinds of power, such as judicial or administrative, its principal power is that of law making. The Constitution declares that "all legislative powers herein granted shall be vested" in Congress. It results that Congress is the great policy-determining organ of the government. It cannot exercise powers that are not legislative in character unless they are delegated to it by the Constitution or are properly incidental to the exercise of its legislative functions. Legislative, executive, and judicial functions are sometimes thought of as if they occupied separate and distinct spheres. It would be more accurate, however, to consider them as occupying overlapping spheres. To the extent that they overlap, a function is legislative, executive, or judicial according to the way it is exercised rather than according to its essential nature, which is not always susceptible of exact determination.

The significance of the principle of the separation of powers in American public law has been discussed above.[1] As was there pointed out, the Constitution does not merely create separate departments and allots to them their appropriate powers, with certain exceptions for the sake of checks and balances, but also undertakes to secure the inde-

[1] Chap. III.

pendence of departments. Thus, the independence of the legislative department is secured by such provisions as those making it the sole judge of the qualifications of its members and exempting its members from arrest, except on certain grounds, and from suits for libel or slander for statements made in Congressional speeches.

It should be noted that the principle of separation of powers as found in the Federal Constitution does not prevent a state from providing in its constitution for the merging of departments. The principle is considered much less applicable in local government than in either national or state government.

The Delegation of Legislative Power.—In view of the constitutional provision that "all legislative powers herein granted shall be vested in Congress," it follows that, as a general principle, Congress cannot delegate its legislative power to any other body or agency. It has been declared by an eminent authority that

. . . the power to whose judgment, wisdom, and patriotism this high prerogative has been entrusted cannot relieve itself of the responsibility by choosing other agencies upon which the power shall be devolved, nor can it substitute the judgment, wisdom, and patriotism of any other body for those to which alone the people have seen fit to confide this sovereign trust.[1]

It does not follow, however, that Congress cannot delegate to another agency any power which it might have exercised itself. The prohibition against delegation applies only to the essential legislative power of Congress. The same principle also prohibits the delegation of legislative power by the state legislatures. In both cases, however, there is one exception to the principle which has been established by custom and usage. This is that legislative power may be delegated to local governing bodies in order to comply with the long-established rule of local self-government. Thus, the state legislatures may grant to municipal councils the power of enacting local ordinances, while Congress may delegate similar powers to territorial legislative bodies.

The question as to whether or not a given law unconstitutionally delegates legislative power to executive and administrative authorities has given rise to a number of adjudications. This question may arise in two aspects: first, when the law as passed by Congress provides that its operation may be suspended upon the occurrence of a certain fact or situation to be ascertained by an executive or administrative officer and, second, when the law stipulates that its provisions shall become effective only when a certain fact or situation is found by such officer to exist. An illustration of the first aspect was the act passed by Congress in 1809 prohibiting importation of goods from certain foreign countries but permitting such prohibition to lapse in case the President ascertained and

---

[1] Cooley, *Constitutional Limitations*, 7th ed., p. 163.

proclaimed that those countries were no longer preying on the sea-borne commerce of the United States. The constitutionality of this law was affirmed by the Supreme Court.[1]

The leading case, however, on this subject was one which dealt with the second aspect mentioned above. By the tariff act of 1890, it was provided that, with a view to securing reciprocal trade, the free importation of certain .articles into the United States should be suspended whenever the President proclaimed such suspension as a result of his ascertainment that the exporting countries were imposing reciprocally unequal and unreasonable duties upon American products. It was provided by the act that, upon the issuance of his proclamation to this effect, certain specified rates of duty were to be imposed upon the importation of these articles. The act was attacked in the Supreme Court as a delegation of legislative power, but the Court denied the contention, saying:

Legislative power was exercised when Congress declared that the suspension should take effect upon a named contingency. What the President was required to do was simply in execution of the act of Congress. It was not the making of law. He was the mere agent of the law-making department to ascertain and declare the event upon which its expressed will was to take effect . . .

The true distinction . . . is between the delegation of power to make the law, which necessarily involves a discretion as to what it shall be, and conferring authority or discretion as to its execution, to be exercised under and in pursuance of the law. The first cannot be done; to the latter no valid objection can be made.[2]

The doctrine thus stated is a salutary one in view of the complexity of modern governmental conditions, and the impossibility for the legislature in enacting laws to foresee future events which may make changes in their operation desirable. As has been said, to deny the power of the legislature to make a law to delegate a power to determine some fact or state of things upon which the law makes its own operation depend would almost "stop the wheels of government."[3] It should be added, however, that the facts on which the executive action depends should be clearly described in the law and should be capable of definite ascertainment by the executive without the exercise of independent judgment or discretion on his part. If such independent discretion is involved, it is difficult to distinguish the situation from a delegation of legislative power. The courts, however, for the sake of policy, endeavor to make such a distinction.

Numerous illustrations might be given of ways in which the operation of laws is dependent upon the ascertainment of facts by executive or administrative officers. Thus, Congress has by law prohibited the

[1] The Brig Aurora, 7 Cranch 383 (1813).
[2] Field v. Clark, 143 U. S. 649 (1892).
[3] *Ibid.*

construction of bridges over the navigable waters of the United States in such a way as to constitute an unreasonable obstruction of navigation and delegated to the secretary of war the power to determine in each case whether such unreasonable obstruction is involved.[1] By the flexible provision of the tariff act of 1922, the President was authorized, whenever satisfied that the rates of duty specified in the act did not equalize the differences in the cost of production in the United States and in the principal competing country, to proclaim changes in the rates, either upward or downward to the extent of 50 per cent of the amounts imposed by the law, in order to equalize such differences.[2] Congress has passed acts appropriating large sums of money for good roads in the states, but the expenditure in any given state is contingent upon the appropriation by that state of an equal sum for this purpose. Again, Congress might provide that the color of postage stamps should be determined in accordance with the color specified by the International Postal Union for stamps of like denominations.

The work of fixing rates for carrying passengers and freight in interstate commerce is an intricate business which Congress realizes that it is not a suitable body to perform, since it requires expert knowledge and careful investigation. Consequently, by an act of 1906, it prohibited interstate carriers from charging unreasonable rates but delegated to the Interstate Commerce Commission the function of determining what rates should be considered reasonable. Congress thus contents itself with setting up the general standard that rates shall be just and reasonable, leaving to the Commission the detailed work of fixing rates in conformity with this standard. This delegation of authority has been sustained by the courts.[3]

Administrative Ordinances.—The President and other officers of the executive department may exercise what amounts to a subsidiary legislative power through the issuance of rules, regulations, and ordinances. In the case of the President, this power is sometimes derived by implication directly from the Constitution. Thus, the President, by virtue of his constitutional position as commander-in-chief, issues regulations for the government of the army and navy. On the other hand, the President's power in this respect is sometimes derived from acts of Congress, either expressly or by implication, and this is generally true in the case of other executive officers. Thus, the heads of Federal executive departments are authorized by act of Congress to prescribe regulations, not inconsistent with law, for the government of their respective departments,

---

[1] Held constitutional in Union Bridge Co. v. United States, 204 U. S. 364 (1907).

[2] Held constitutional in Hampton v. United States, 276 U. S. 394 (1927), upon the authority of Field v. Clark, cited above.

[3] Interstate Commerce Commission v. Illinois Central R. R. Co., 215 U. S. 542 (1910).

and other more specific ordinance powers are frequently conferred upon them, either expressly or as implied in the general grant of authority contained in the law. No such ordinance or regulation is valid, of course, if in conflict with any act of Congress, but the exercise of this power is necessary in many instances in order to supplement acts of Congress, to carry them into execution, and to fill in the details of administrative organization and procedure. Such regulations can be changed by executive order at any time, which makes them much more flexible than they would be if embodied in the act as passed by Congress.

Under modern conditions, the frequent exercise by the executive authorities of the ordinance-making power is necessary in order to deal adequately with the complicated work of government. At first sight, this practice might seem to violate the rule against the delegation of legislative power. It may be sustained, however, on the ground that it does not constitute a delegation of essential legislative power but is rather the means which the executive authorities are under the necessity of adopting in order efficiently to execute the law.[1]

The Referendum as a Delegation of Legislative Power.—Except in the case of local option laws, or unless expressly authorized to do so by the state constitution, a state legislature cannot submit to the voters the question as to whether or not a proposed measure shall become a law. A number of state constitutions have, however, provided for the introduction of the popular referendum on legislative acts. As pointed out in another connection, when the popular initiative and referendum were attacked on the ground that they violated the requirement of the Federal Constitution that each state should have a republican form of government, the Supreme Court declined to interfere, holding that this was a political question.[2]

Although there has been no attempt to introduce the national referendum as applied to acts of Congress, there is little question that this would involve an unconstitutional delegation of legislative power if the action of the voters were to be the determining factor in creating the law. There would seem, however, to be no constitutional objection to a national referendum of a purely advisory character, which would leave Congress free to legislate as it chooses regardless of the result of the referendum.

Special Powers of Each House.—Although the powers of the two houses are for the most part the same, to some extent they are different. Thus, while the House of Representatives has the power to choose its own presiding officer, the Vice President, who is not chosen by the Senate, ordinarily presides over the latter body. As already pointed out, in impeachment proceedings, the House accuses while the Senate judges. As indicated elsewhere, the House and the Senate have special functions

[1] For further discussion of this topic, see below, Chap. XII.
[2] Pacific States Telephone and Telegraph Co. v. Oregon, 223 U. S. 118 (1912).

in connection with the election of the President and the Vice President when no candidate for those offices has a majority of the electoral votes. The Senate has two important powers in which the House does not participate, *viz.*, the approval of treaties and the confirmation of presidential appointments.

Revenue Bills.—In matters of ordinary legislation, the two houses have equal power except that the Constitution requires that "all bills for raising revenue shall originate in the House of Representatives; but the Senate may propose or concur with amendments as on other bills."[1] This provision conformed to the well-established rule in England under which the House of Commons controlled the national purse. Inasmuch as the general burden of taxes is borne by the mass of the people and since, under the original Constitution, the House of Representatives is the only body in the National Government elected directly by the people, the framers of that instrument deemed it appropriate that the House should have the exclusive power to originate revenue bills. They were also impelled to this decision by the consideration that thereby they would be giving a compensatory advantage to the larger states which would help to offset the great advantage which the small states derived from their equal representation in the Senate.

This constitutional provision, however, has not worked out in practice as the framers intended. They apparently did not foresee the extent to which the Senate would utilize to its advantage the permission granted it to propose amendments to revenue bills. The mere technical requirement that the bill must originate in the House is of little importance if the Senate can amend it at will, especially in view of the broad construction given by the Senate to the term "amendment." In practice the Senate usually amends revenue bills quite freely, even having gone to the extent of striking out the whole of the House bill after the enacting clause and substituting therefor its own bill on the subject. This was done in 1883 and the bill as thus amended was accepted by the House. Other instances have occurred, notably in 1872 and 1894, when the Senate amended revenue bills out of all semblance to their original form. The House has usually acquiesced in the Senate amendments with little or no alteration. This attitude of the House appears to be due to its greater tractability, owing to the stricter party discipline over its members and to the more rigorous limitation of debate in that body than in the Senate. It would certainly seem that amendment by complete substitution is hardly in accordance with the spirit of the constitutional provision. Nevertheless the power of the Senate in this respect seems well established as a part of the unwritten constitution.[2]

---

[1] Art. I, sect. 7, cl. 1.
[2] HORWILL, H. W., *The Usages of the American Constitution*, pp. 152–154.

The meaning of the phrase "revenue bill" as used in the Constitution is not always perfectly clear. For example, the question may be raised as to whether a bill to repeal a law imposing taxes is a revenue bill in such sense that it must originate in the House. On this question the House and Senate have taken contrary positions. A few cases have arisen in the courts in which acts of Congress have been attacked as being invalid because, in spite of the alleged fact that they were revenue measures, they originated in the Senate. It has been held that a bill which incidentally raises revenue but which is intended primarily for other purposes is not a bill which, under the Constitution, must originate in the House.[1] Other bills held not to be bills to raise revenue within the meaning of the constitutional provision are bills to increase the rates of postage and bills to levy taxes in the District of Columbia.[2]

As far as the language of the Constitution is concerned, the prohibition against the origination of bills in the Senate applies only to revenue bills. There is no express limitation upon its power to originate appropriation bills, and it exercises this power in the case of bills carrying appropriations for a single object. In practice, however, the great annual appropriation bills are now uniformly first introduced in the House. This limitation on the power of the Senate may also be regarded as a part of the unwritten constitution.[3]

Implied Powers of Congress.—One of the important functions of the Federal Constitution is to draw a general line of division between the powers of the National Government and those of the states. That instrument does not contain a list of the powers of the states but enumerates the powers of the National Government and places certain limitations upon the states as well as upon the National Government. These provisions might have indicated sufficiently the distribution of power between the nation and the states, but, in order to make the situation clear by a general statement of principle, the Tenth Amendment was added. The Articles of Confederation had provided that "each state retains its sovereignty, freedom and independence, and every power, jurisdiction and right which is not by this confederation *expressly* delegated to the United States in Congress assembled."[4] The Tenth Amendment to the Federal Constitution, however, significantly omits the word "expressly" and provides that "the powers not delegated to the United States by the Constitution, nor prohibited by it to the states, are reserved to the states respectively or to the people."

This omission of the word "expressly" from the Tenth Amendment would in itself have been sufficient to indicate that the National Govern-

[1] United States v. Norton, 91 U. S. 569 (1875); Twin City Bank v. Nebeker, 167 U. S. 196 (1897).

[2] Millard v. Roberts, 202 U. S. 429 (1906).

[3] HORWILL, H. W., *op. cit.*, p. 155.

[4] Art. II.

ment might exercise incidental powers in addition to those expressly granted.   In order, however, to make this clear as far as the powers of Congress were concerned, the Constitution, after enumerating a list of expressly granted powers of that body, goes on to provide that it shall have power "to make all laws which shall be necessary and proper for carrying into execution the foregoing powers, and all other powers vested by this Constitution in the Government of the United States, or in any department or officer thereof."[1]   This is known as the elastic or "necessary-and-proper" clause of the Constitution.   This general grant of implied power was inserted by the framers of the Constitution because they did not think it was feasible to enumerate all the powers that it might be appropriate for Congress to exercise as incidental to the execution of its expressly granted powers.   To have prohibited the exercise of any such incidental or implied powers would, in their view, have reduced the National Government to hopeless impotence.[2]

After the adoption of the Constitution, the strict constructionists were inclined, in theory at least, to limit the application of the elastic clause to the exercise of such powers as were absolutely necessary for carrying out the express powers.   To take a single step beyond this limit was, in Jefferson's view, "to take possession of a boundless field of power, no longer susceptible of any definition."   Subsequent events have shown that there was a good deal of truth in Jefferson's view, but, on the other hand, the practical need that the National Government should be deemed to have larger powers than those absolutely necessary for the execution of its express powers was demonstrated by the course of Jefferson himself when, as President, he brought about the acquisition of the Louisiana Territory.

Those who favored a broad, or liberal, construction of the Constitution held that Congress might exercise any power that would be useful or appropriate for carrying out the express powers.   Had the Constitution established a compact between states, the view of the strict constructionists would have been logical.   Assuming, however, that the Constitution established a real national government which was something more and stronger than a mere interstate compact, we are forced to the conclusion that the broad constructionists had the better of the argument. Their view, moreover, has prevailed, since it was adopted by the Supreme Court under the leadership of Chief Justice Marshall, who held that this interpretation of the Constitution was the correct one in the light of the purpose for which it was adopted: *viz.*, to establish a national government which should be adequate for the needs of the country.

As early as 1804 Marshall declared that

. . . it would be incorrect and would produce endless difficulties if the opinion should be maintained that no law was authorized which was not indispensably

[1] Art. I, sect. 8, last paragraph.
[2] *Cf.* Hamilton in *The Federalist*, No. 33.

necessary to give effect to a specified power. Where various systems might be adopted for that purpose, it might be said with respect to each that it was not necessary because the end might be obtained by other means. Congress must possess the choice of means which are in fact conducive to the exercise of a power granted by the Constitution.[1]

The leading case, however, in which Marshall upheld the doctrine of implied powers is that of McCulloch v. Maryland,[2] decided in 1819. This is one of the most celebrated cases ever decided by the Supreme Court. It involved the constitutionality of the act passed by Congress in 1816 incorporating the Bank of the United States, under which a branch had been established at Baltimore. There was admittedly no express grant to Congress of the power to establish a bank nor to create a corporation. But Congress was expressly granted the powers to collect taxes and to borrow money. Marshall, in the opinion of the Court, argued that

. . . it must have been the intention of those who gave these powers to insure, as far as human prudence could insure, their beneficial execution. This could not be done by confining the choice of means to such narrow limits as not to leave it in the power of Congress to adopt any which might be appropriate and which were conducive to the end . . . Let the end be legitimate [he declared] let it be within the scope of the Constitution, and all means which are appropriate, which are plainly adapted to that end, which are not prohibited, but consist with the letter and spirit of the Constitution, are constitutional.

As the result of this line of reasoning, the Court held that Congress had the power to establish the bank.

The implied powers of Congress are more numerous and extensive than its express powers. Thus, Congress can provide for the punishment not only of the four crimes expressly mentioned in the Constitution but also of all violations of the laws of the United States. Under the express power "to establish post offices and post roads," Congress has the implied power to provide for carrying the mail along the post road from one post office to another. Moreover, from this implied power, Congress has the further implied powers of punishing theft of the mails and the use of the mails for fraudulent purposes. Another illustration of implied power is found in the national police power, exercised by Congress for the protection of the public safety, morals, and health. For example, Congress has passed a pure food and drugs act as implied in its express power to regulate interstate commerce. This act prohibits the sending in interstate commerce of articles which are not properly labeled or which are detrimental to health.

Congress may exercise some powers by virtue of double implication, *i.e.*, a power may be implied from a power which is itself implied from an

[1] United States v. Fisher, 2 Cranch 358 (1804).
[2] 4 Wheat. 316.

express power. Again, a power may be implied not from any one specific power but from a group of powers or from the aggregate of powers granted to Congress. These are sometimes called resulting powers. An example is the building of a capitol.

As is more fully pointed out in another connection, in its international relations the National Government is fully sovereign except in so far as it is limited by the Constitution. Congress may sometimes pass laws for the enforcement of treaties which it would have no power to enact in the absence of such treaties.[1] It must not be supposed, however, that the National Government is endowed with inherent sovereign powers, *i.e.*, powers neither expressly nor impliedly granted but arising merely from the sovereignty of the nation. It is true that in the legal tender cases[2] the Court came dangerously near to enunciating such a doctrine, but its statements in that respect were *obiter* and such a doctrine has usually been repudiated.

Another doctrine as to the extent of the power of the National Government which the Court has repudiated is that known as the Wilson-Roosevelt doctrine. It was put forward by James Wilson of Pennsylvania even before the adoption of the Constitution and subsequently espoused by President Roosevelt. This doctrine, as stated by Wilson was that "whenever an object occurs, to the direction of which no particular state is competent, the management of it must, of necessity, belong to the United States in Congress assembled." This doctrine is quite different from that of implied powers and was rejected by the Supreme Court as in violation of the Tenth Amendment and of the doctrine that the National Government is one of enumerated powers.[3]

[1] Missouri v. Holland, 252 U. S. 416 (1920).
[2] 12 Wall. 457. (1870).
[3] Kansas v. Colorado, 206 U. S. 46 (1907).

CHAPTER X

THE PRESIDENT: ELECTION AND GENERAL POSITION

One of the conspicuous defects of the government under the Articles of Confederation was that it had no distinct executive head, and the exercise of executive functions by Congress or its committees proved unsatisfactory. The framers of the Constitution undertook to remedy this defect by erecting the executive into a separate and coordinate department of the government and giving it a distinct head. Whether this head should be single or multiple was a question which gave rise to some difference of opinion. A single executive was thought by some to resemble a monarchy too closely and to embody dangers of executive tyranny. Fortunately, however, the contrary view prevailed that a single executive was more satisfactory and should be established because it embodied greater unity, energy, and more definite responsibility. It also followed the analogy of the state executives or governors. Constitutional safeguards, such as length of term, were adopted so as to prevent the President from assuming the position of a monarch.

The President's Term.—Although Hamilton was willing to accord the President life tenure, the members of the Constitutional Convention were generally agreed that he should have a term of years, but there was difference of opinion as to whether he should have a fairly long term, such as seven years, and be made ineligible to succeed himself, or whether he should be given a shorter term, such as four years, with no restriction upon reeligibility. Eventually, the latter plan was adopted.

Although no legal restriction upon reeligibility was placed in the Constitution, there has grown up a usage known as the third-term tradition which has apparently become so well-established as to be a rule of the unwritten constitution. President Washington declined a third term, not, however, on grounds of principle but for personal reasons. Jefferson could probably have been elected for a third term but declined the honor upon the ground of principle, and thereafter the rule came to be generally considered a sound one. As was illustrated by the case of President Roosevelt, however, the rule is not considered so strong when one of the terms is not an elective term and especially when the third term is not consecutive. In the latter case, the aspirant for a third term is not, of course, in a position to use the great prestige of the office in securing his renomination and reelection. It has been suggested that the strength of the rule against a third term is due mainly to the unwilling-

123

ness of the American people to accord to any man a greater honor than President Washington received.[1]

Qualifications of the President.—The most important of the legal qualifications for the President laid down in the Constitution is that he must be a natural-born citizen of the United States.   This was obviously intended to prevent possible foreign influence on our government through the election of a man of alien nativity.   Exception, however, was made in the case of persons who were naturalized citizens at the time of the adoption of the Constitution, some of whom—for example, Hamilton— were members of the Convention.   This exception was, of course, of only temporary significance.

Other legal qualifications laid down in the Constitution are that the President must be at least thirty-five years of age and must have been for fourteen years a resident of the United States.[2]   This does not mean that he must have been physically present in the United States for fourteen years, but merely that he has retained a legal residence therein for that length of time.   The fourteen years, moreover, need not be consecutive nor need they immediately precede his election to the presidency. Legally, there are no disqualifications on account of race, creed, or sex.

The Vice President.—The only office in the executive department, besides that of the President, directly created by the Constitution is that of the Vice President.[3]   He is elected at the same time and in the same manner as the President is, and for the same term, and must have the same legal qualifications.   Although nominally classified as an executive officer, the Vice President has no executive functions, except when he succeeds to the presidency, but, when this event occurs, he ceases to be Vice President.   In reality, therefore, the normal function of the Vice President is merely that of presiding over the Senate, but he is not a member of that body and has no right to vote, except in the case of a tie. It is true that, in some instances, he has attended meetings of the President's cabinet and even presided over that body in the absence of the President, but this arrangement has not become established as a usage of the Constitution.

The cabinet, in fact, is unknown to the Constitution.   It is established by the President and, technically at least, could be abolished by him. The Constitution, however, does make incidental mention of heads of executive departments,[4] from whom the President may require information in writing regarding the discharge of their duties.   The framers of the Constitution, however, seem in the main to have supposed that the

[1] HORWILL, H. W., *The Usages of the American Constitution*, p. 98.

[2] Art. II, sect. 1, cl. 5.

[3] For a general account of the office of vice president, see an article by O. P. Field in *Amer. Law Rev.*, vol. 56, p. 365 (1922).

[4] Art. II, sect. 2, cls. 1 and 2.

Senate would act as an advisory council for the President, but, in this respect, the expectation of the framers has not been fully realized in practice.

Election of the President.—The question of the most desirable method of choosing the President and Vice President was one which gave considerable difficulty to the framers of the Constitution. The two most obvious methods—election by the people and election by Congress—were both unsatisfactory. Most of the members of the Convention of 1787 had no great confidence in the political capacity of the people to make intelligently such a momentous choice as that of the chief magistrate of the country. Moreover, the lack of means of creating an informed public opinion upon such a question made this method seem to them hardly feasible. The delegates from the small states feared that this method of election would give the balance of power to the larger and more populous states. On the other hand, the method of election by Congress was deemed unsatisfactory because it violated the principle of separation of powers and might upset the balance and coordination which it was thought should exist between the executive and legislative departments.

The framers of the Constitution finally hit upon a method of choosing the President which they thought avoided the disadvantages of both of those previously mentioned. This was the creation of a special agency, known as the electoral college, whose members, known as presidential electors, choose the President. The number of electors to which each state is entitled is equal to the number of senators and representatives which that state has in Congress. Each state is authorized to "appoint, in such manner as the legislature thereof may direct," its quota of electors.[1] Senators and representatives and officers of the United States are declared ineligible to be electors.[2]

The word "appoint" as used in this passage of the Constitution has been broadly construed to include almost any method of choice. Legally, it is entirely within the discretion of each state legislature to decide what method of choice shall be followed in that state. Consequently, there is no requirement of uniformity of method throughout the country. Congress, however, may designate and has designated a uniform time throughout the country for choosing the electors and also a uniform date on which the electors are to cast their ballots for President and Vice President. Although performing a federal function, the electors are regarded, strictly speaking, as state officers.[3]

---

[1] Art. II, sect. 1, cl. 2.

[2] If a presidential elector should be chosen who is constitutionally ineligible, it is not settled whether the state would lose its vote or whether the elector with the next highest popular vote could take his place. State law may provide for this contingency.

[3] *In re* Green, 134 U. S. 377 (1890).

At first the legislature itself in most states chose the electors. Gradually, however, this method was displaced by that of popular election, which has everywhere prevailed for more than half a century. The method of popular election is probably not in accordance with the intention of the framers, but it has now become so well established that it may be regarded as required by the usage or unwritten rule of the Constitution. Formerly, it was not infrequently the custom to choose the electors under the district system, and this was done in Michigan as late as 1892.[1] This plan, however, has everywhere given way to the general ticket system, under which the political party that has a plurality of the popular vote usually controls the entire electoral vote of the state.

The Electoral Process.—Under the original Constitution, the presidential electors were required to meet in their respective states and vote by ballot for two persons, of whom one at least should not be an inhabitant of the same state with themselves, but they were not required to indicate which of the two was their choice for President and which for Vice President. The person who received the highest number of votes as well as a majority of them was to be President and the person having the next largest number of votes was to be Vice President. In case two persons had a majority of the votes and were tied for the highest number, the House of Representatives should choose one of them for President. In case no one had a majority of the votes, the House should choose the President from the five highest on the list. After the President was chosen, the person having the next largest number of votes should be the Vice President.

The plan thus provided by the original Constitution contained certain defects which were quickly brought to light. Thus, it was possible under this plan for a Vice President to be chosen who did not have a majority of the electoral votes. Again, it was possible for the President and Vice President chosen under this plan to be of opposite political parties, as happened when Adams and Jefferson were paired in 1796. The most serious defect, however, was brought to light by the election of 1800. In that election Jefferson and Burr each received a majority of the electoral votes and were also tied for the highest number. The election of the President therefore devolved upon the House of Representatives. Probably without exception, the electors voting for Jefferson and Burr had intended that Jefferson should be President. There was nothing, however, to prevent the House from choosing Burr for President and, in fact, the danger of its doing so was only narrowly averted.

The Twelfth Amendment.—In order to prevent this danger from again arising, the Twelfth Amendment was adopted in 1804. The principal change which it makes in the original Constitution is the requirement that the electors shall cast separate ballots for President and for

[1] The Michigan law was upheld in McPherson v. Blacker, 146 U. S. 1 (1892).

Vice President and keep the votes cast for each officer in distinct lists. Another change is the provision that, in case no candidate for President has a majority and the election devolves upon the House of Representatives, that body shall choose the President from among the three (instead of the five) highest on the list. Finally, it is provided that the candidate for Vice President who has the highest number of votes, provided it is a majority, shall be deemed elected, but that, if no one has a majority, the Senate shall choose the Vice President from the two highest on the list.[1]

Working of the Electoral Process.—The provision for the election of the President has worked out less in accordance with the intention and expectation of the framers than almost any other provision of the Constitution. This has been due largely to the fact that they did not understand the function of political parties in a modern democratic government. They regarded them as factions and dangerous excrescences upon the body politic. Consequently, they did not foresee the necessary rôle which they would play in operating the machinery for the election of the President. The expectation of the framers was that the presidential electors would exercise full discretion in casting their ballots for the person who, in their opinion, would most satisfactorily fill the office. This expectation was fulfilled at first, but beginning with the election of 1800 the influence of the parties becomes noticeable. The party organizations recognized that, if the whole strength of the party was to be exerted to control the presidency, they must unite upon a definite candidate for whom the presidential electors affiliated with them would be expected to vote. Consequently, methods of nominating party candidates arose—at first the Congressional caucus and later the national nominating convention.

The presidential electors are not usually formally pledged to vote for the nominees of their party, but this has become the usage or unwritten rule, almost as strongly established as if it were required by the written Constitution. The presidential electors are mere dummies or "animated rubber stamps." As soon as the popular vote is cast and counted in November of the presidential year, it is known that the nominee of that party which has chosen the majority of the presidential electors will become the next President. Probably the only situation in which the electors of the successful party would not cast their ballots for the party's nominee would be when the latter should die so shortly before the time for the casting of the electoral votes that there would be afforded to the national committee or party leaders no opportunity to select another nominee.

[1] The proposed twentieth amendment would authorize Congress to provide for the case of the death of any of the persons from whom the House may choose a President or of those from among whom the Senate may choose a Vice President. See below, Appendix.

Although the presidential electors are mere automata with no discretion whatever, the existence of the electoral college still has some effect upon the method of choosing the President. He is not chosen by the direct vote of the people of the country as a whole but by a majority of the electors voting by states, so that it is possible for a President to be chosen in spite of the fact that the electors who voted for him received only a minority of the popular votes or even a smaller number than were cast for the electors of another party. Nevertheless, in spite of the theory of the Constitution, the President is virtually chosen by popular vote and this adds greatly to his prestige and influence.

There is still another way in which the operations of political parties have caused the presidential electoral machinery to work out in a different way from that expected by the framers. The latter supposed that the election of President would frequently devolve upon the House of Representatives. In fact, however, that body has had the opportunity of choosing the President only twice, in 1801 and in 1825. The existence of a strong third party would have caused this situation to arise more frequently. In the main, however, the two-party system has prevailed, with the result that the presidential election has seldom been thrown into the House.

As noted above, the number of presidential electors to which each state is entitled is equal to the number of senators and representatives which that state has in Congress. While the number of senators is fixed, the number of representatives varies from time to time as new decennial apportionment acts are passed by Congress. After the census of 1920, however, Congress failed to pass a new apportionment act, with the result that some states had more, and others had fewer, representatives in Congress than they would have been entitled to if such an act had been passed. Consequently, in the presidential election of 1928, some states had more, and others had fewer, electoral votes than they would have been entitled to if an apportionment act had been passed based on population as determined by the census of 1920. Indirectly, therefore, the failure of Congress to pass a reapportionment act might conceivably have changed the result of the presidential election of 1928 and, if so, would, in the opinion of some observers, have rendered it invalid. Fortunately, however, the election was not close enough to make this factor one of any consequence.

Counting the Electoral Vote.—The Twelfth Amendment, following in this respect the original Constitution, provides that the lists of electoral votes cast in the several states shall be transmitted sealed to the seat of government of the United States, directed to the president of the Senate, who, in the presence of the two houses of Congress, shall open all the certificates and "the votes shall then be counted." The framers apparently supposed that the counting of the votes would be a mere clerical function and consequently that it was not necessary particularly to specify who should do the counting. This omission in the fundamental law occasioned little difficulty until the presidential election of 1876, in which there were two sets of disputed electoral ballots sent up from several of the states. The election was so close that, if any one of the disputed votes should be counted for Tilden, he would have been elected; while if all of them should be counted for Hayes, he would have been elected by a margin of one vote. Whoever had the right to count the ballots also had the power to decide which ballots should be counted and this power, under the circumstances, would enable whoever exercised it to determine the result of the election. The situation was still further complicated by the fact that each of the two houses of Congress was controlled by a different political party, so that the houses were unable to agree as to which set of votes should be counted. The controversy was finally settled through the creation of a special commission of fifteen persons, drawn equally from the Senate, the House of Representatives, and the Federal judiciary.

This special electoral commission was entirely extraconstitutional and Congress probably exceeded its authority in creating it. This technical lack of authority, however, may be overlooked in view of the serious emergency with which the country was confronted and the apparent absence of any other available method of meeting the difficulty. In order to provide for such a situation if it should again arise, Congress in 1887 passed the Disputed Presidential Elections Act, the detailed provisions of which need not be mentioned here.[1] Suffice it to say that it places upon the states the responsibility of settling their own disputes and that, if they fail to do so, the two houses of Congress shall by concurrent action decide which set of votes shall be counted. If the two houses are unable to agree, the vote of the state is presumably lost. The constitutionality of this act has been questioned on the ground that Congress has no constitutional power over the electoral system. It also has practical defects, but no occasion has yet arisen for its actual application.

Succession to the Presidency.—The Constitution might have required that, upon the occurrence of a vacancy in the office of President, a special election should be held for the purpose of filling it, but this plan was not adopted. The principal reason for creating the office of Vice President was not to supply a presiding officer for the senate but rather to supply a successor to the President whenever he should be unable to serve out his term, either through death, resignation, removal, or inability to discharge the powers and duties of the office.

The question has been raised as to whether, when the Vice President succeeds to the presidency, he becomes President or merely acting

[1] For further information, see J. H. Daugherty, *The Electoral System of the United States*, Chap. IX.

President. The language of the Constitution seems to indicate that it was the intention of its framers that he should become merely acting President.[1] In this respect, however, usage has stepped in to change the letter of the Constitution. Beginning with the case of Tyler who succeeded upon the death of Harrison in 1841 (the first instance of the sort), a Vice President succeeding to the presidency has been generally regarded as having become the President and not merely acting President. Thus far, however, no Vice President has succeeded except upon the death of the President. The same procedure would probably be followed in the case of the President's resignation or removal on impeachment, but no instance of vacancy by these methods has occurred.[2] If, however, the President should become unable to discharge his powers and duties and the Vice President should thereupon assume to exercise the duties of the office, it would seem that he would become not President but merely acting President. Otherwise, we would have two presidents at the same time. The President's inability might be removed, whereupon the Vice President presumably would cease to act as President, while he who had all along been President would resume the discharge of his powers and duties. Therefore, in answering the question as to whether the Vice President becomes President or merely acting President, it seems reasonable to make a distinction based on the reasons causing the vacancy in the presidency, although no such distinction is found in the language of the Constitution.[3]

No Vice President has as yet attempted to take over the powers of the President upon the latter's inability, although cases of such inability have occurred. There was no doubt in fact that Presidents Garfield and McKinley were disabled during the period after they were shot by assassins. There was some doubt as to whether President Wilson was completely disabled during his illness. The failure of the Vice President to take over the office in these instances was probably due, in part at least, to the lack of any definite provision for a legal method of establishing the President's inability. In case, however, a Vice President should, under these circumstances, assume to discharge the duties of the presi-

---

[1] *Cf.* the language of the Twelfth Amendment providing that, upon the failure of the House to choose a president, "then the vice president shall act as president, as in the case of the death or other constitutional disability of the president."

[2] While no President has resigned, Vice President John C. Calhoun resigned in 1832 in order to enter the Senate and transmitted his resignation to the secretary of state in accordance with an Act of Congress of Mar. 1, 1792 (R. S., sect. 151).

[3] The proposed twentieth amendment, however, makes such a distinction, providing that the Vice President-elect shall become President in case of the death of the President-elect before the beginning of the latter's term. If, however, no President has been chosen or the person chosen has failed to qualify before the beginning of his term, the Vice President-elect shall merely act as President until a President shall have qualified. See below, Appendix.

dential office and any question were raised as to the legality of his acts, the courts would probably be able, in a proper proceeding, to decide whether or not he was within his constitutional rights. Congress might by concurrent resolution declare when a disability exists or might even direct the attorney-general to bring an action in mandamus against the Vice President to compel him to take over the powers and duties of the office. For all practical purposes, however, the provision of the Constitution authorizing the Vice President to exercise the office in case of the president's inability may be regarded as a dead letter.[1]

If, upon the death of the President, the Vice President becomes President, he ceases to be Vice President and the latter office becomes vacant. This conclusion is necessary in order to avoid the supposition that one man could simultaneously hold both offices. Upon succeeding to the presidency, the Vice President does not serve for a full term but merely for the unexpired portion of his predecessor's term.

The Succession Act of 1792.—In addition to the succession of the Vice President to the presidency, the Constitution also contemplates the situation where a vacancy occurs in the offices of both President and Vice President. It does not, however, undertake to designate the officer who shall succeed upon such a contingency but empowers Congress to do so. In the exercise of this power, Congress passed an act in 1792 providing that, upon the contingency mentioned, the president *pro tempore* of the Senate or, in case there should be no president of the Senate, the speaker of the House of Representatives should "act as President of the United States until the disability be removed or a President shall be elected." The act further provided that a special election of President and Vice President should be held, prior to the expiration of the term of the previous incumbents, and that the persons chosen at such election should serve for the full term of four years. Such an intermediate election, while not clearly authorized by the Constitution, is apparently permitted by that instrument. But the holding of such an election would be objectionable inasmuch as it might cause the presidential election to fall at a different time from that of senators and representatives.

The act of 1792 was also objectionable in several other respects. One objection was based on the doubt as to whether members of Congress are properly to be regarded as officers of the United States. If they cannot be so regarded, Congress exceeded its powers in designating them to succeed. A more important objection, however, was that there was no assurance that the president *pro tempore* of the Senate or the speaker of the House would, at the time when the vacancy occurred, be affiliated with the same political party as that of the President, with the result that such a vacancy would bring about an accidental change in party control over the government. Another important objection was that,

[1] *Cf.* HORWILL, *op. cit.*, pp. 80 *ff.*

if the vacancy occurred while Congress was not in session, there would be nobody holding the position of speaker of the House and the position of president *pro tempore* of the Senate might also be vacant. Neither of these positions was filled, for example, at the time when Vice President Arthur succeeded to President Garfield in 1881, so that, if President Arthur had died before the convening of Congress, there would have been no one designated by law to take his place.

The Succession Act of 1886.—These objections to the act of 1792 finally caused Congress, in 1886, to pass a new presidential succession act, repealing the previous act and providing that in case of vacancy in the offices of both President and Vice President, the secretary of state should succeed and, after him, other heads of executive departments in a designated order. It is necessary, however, that each such executive officer, in order to be eligible to succeed, shall have been appointed by the advice and consent of the Senate and shall have the qualifications for President laid down in the Constitution. The act provides that the person thus succeeding "shall act as President until the disability of the President or Vice President is removed or a President shall be elected." No specific provision is made in the act for an intermediate election. In case Congress is not in session, however, or about to convene at the time the acting President assumes the duties of the office, he is directed to call an extraordinary session of that body which may, upon convening, pass an act providing that such an intermediate election should be held. This act would, of course, be subject to the veto power of the acting President and there would, moreover, be no method immediately available of compelling him to call the extraordinary session.

The only situations in which the Constitution expressly authorizes Congress to provide for the succession after both the President and Vice President are the cases of the death, removal, resignation, or inability of both these officers. There is still another cause, however, which may bring about a vacancy in both these offices. This is through the failure of the electoral process to select successors to fill these offices before the expiration of the terms of the incumbents. If none of the candidates for President and Vice President has a majority of the electoral votes and the election is thrown into the House and Senate respectively, it is possible that a deadlock might ensue in the House which would not be broken prior to the expiration of the term of the incumbent on March 4. A deadlock in the Senate over the election of the Vice President is less likely, since that body chooses from only two candidates, but it is conceivable that it might happen when the Senate is equally divided and there is no Vice President to break the tie. The existing statutes of Congress do not cover this situation and a technical question might be raised as to whether it has the constitutional power to cover it. If the probable failure of the electoral process to function were realized before the fourth of March, this technical difficulty could be overcome through the resignation of the President and Vice President before that date, whereupon the secretary of state would without doubt become acting President in accordance with the succession act of 1886. Moreover, since he serves for no definite term, he would hold over into the next quadrennial period. Probably he would also succeed on March 4 in case of the failure of the electoral process to function, even though the incumbents neglected to resign before that date. His succession would also seem to be the most likely solution of the difficulty which would be presented by the death or incapacity of both the President-elect and the Vice President-elect after the electoral colleges have adjourned and before the fourth of March. Technically, however, there has been no provision of law regarding the succession under these circumstances. The proposed twentieth amendment, however, undertakes to cover this situation by providing that,

. . . Congress may by law provide for the case wherein neither a President-elect nor a Vice President-elect shall have qualified, declaring who shall then act as President, or the manner in which one who is to act shall be selected, and such person shall act accordingly until a President or Vice President shall have qualified.[1]

The President's Compensation.—The Constitution does not undertake to fix the amount of the President's compensation but leaves this to the determination of Congress, subject to the limitation that it "shall neither be increased nor diminished during the period for which he shall have been elected."[2] He is prohibited from receiving any other emolument from the United States or from any state. The latter prohibition, however, is not construed to prevent Congress from making special allowances for travel and other incidental expenses.

It has been held that the constitutional prohibition against the diminution of the compensation of Federal judges during their continuance in office prevents the application to them of a Federal income tax upon their official salaries.[3] The question as to whether the President is subject to an income tax on his salary has not been raised in the courts, but, by analogy, it would seem that he is entitled to the same exemption that Federal judges enjoy.

The President's Immunities.—As the chief magistrate of the nation and head of one of the three coordinate departments of the Government, the President is not amenable to compulsory judicial process and cannot be controlled by the courts in the exercise of his powers, whether discretionary or ministerial. His person is inviolable, so that he is not sub-

[1] For full text of the proposed twentieth amendment, see below, Appendix.
[2] Art. II, sect. 1, cl. 7.
[3] Evans v. Gore, 253 U. S. 245 (1920).

ject to arrest, no matter what offense he may commit. He cannot be removed from office except by impeachment. After removal in that manner, however, or after the expiration of his term of office, it would seem that he might be prosecuted like a private individual for any violation of the ordinary criminal law which he is alleged to have committed while in office, but not in connection with his official duties. Fortunately, no case of this sort has actually arisen.

CHAPTER XI

THE PRESIDENT AND LAW MAKING

The President is not only the chief executive but, as noted above, is an important factor in the determination of policies. It is a mistake to think of the President as separate and distinct from the legislative department. The framers of the Constitution did not adhere rigidly to the principle of separation of powers. They recognized that the President's experience in the enforcement of law would give weight to his opinion as to what the law should be. His function in connection with the determination of legislation attracts more public attention than does the work of administration and enforcement. On account of the lack of leadership in Congress in matters of legislation, the people look to the President to supply it. The success of his administration of public affairs depends largely upon the ability and clear-sightedness with which he rises to meet this popular demand. The political leadership of the President varies with circumstances, with the personalities of the particular incumbents of the office, and with their theories as to the proper scope of their functions. To a considerable extent it is dependent upon extra-constitutional methods. To some extent, however, the Constitution expressly grants power to the President in matters of legislation, and these powers have tended to increase through usage.

The Sessions of Congress.—The time for the meeting of the regular annual session of Congress is stipulated in the Constitution subject to change by Congress, and the President, therefore, has no control over it. Moreover, the President has no power to dissolve Congress, and in this respect his power differs from that of the chief executive in several European countries. Nor can he adjourn Congress unless there should be disagreement between the two houses as to the time of adjournment. Incidentally, he may exert some influence over the length of the long session by urging the consideration of certain important measures therein and by threatening to call a special session unless they are considered.

The President has never exercised his power of adjourning the two houses of Congress. On the other hand, he has frequently exercised his power of calling special sessions of Congress. The Constitution authorizes him to do this on extraordinary occasions, and the power extends to calling into special session either house separately.[1] In recent years

[1] Art. II, sect. 3. The Senate is sometimes called separately in order to deal with executive business, *i.e.*, the approval of treaties and/or the confirmation of appointments.

the regular sessions have apparently not been sufficient to enable Congress to complete its legislative work, and Presidents have called special sessions so frequently that Congress has been in almost continuous session. It is especially likely to happen that the President will call a special session at the beginning of his administration in order to get his legislative program started without delay. As to whether the occasion is an extraordinary one justifying the calling of a special session is a matter for the President to decide entirely within his own discretion.

In some of the states of the Union, the governor, at the time of calling a special session of the legislature, can limit the matters to be acted upon by it at such session. This enables him to concentrate the attention both of the legislature and of the people upon the few important items of his legislative program. The President of the United States, however, has no such power, so that Congress, in a special session, may consider and act upon as wide a range of matters as it can in regular session.

Presidential Messages.—The Constitution provides that the President "shall from time to time give to Congress information of the state of the Union, and recommend to their consideration such measures as he shall judge necessary and expedient."[1] This is both a power and a duty. It is a function which logically belongs to the President because his position as head of the national administration puts him in possession of information derived from many sources which it is necessary for Congress to secure in order to exercise intelligently its law-making function. The Constitution does not say when nor how often nor in what manner the President shall communicate with Congress but leaves these matters to his discretion. In practice, it has been customary for Presidents to make a general or comprehensive communication at the opening of Congressional sessions and then to send in special messages relating to particular matters as occasion may require during the session.

Presidents Washington and John Adams communicated their general messages orally before a joint session of Congress. Jefferson, however, began the practice of sending written messages to Congress which were read by the clerks and this practice continued until the time of Wilson. At the beginning of his first administration, President Wilson reverted to the earlier practice initiated by Washington and explained his reason for doing so by saying that "the President of the United States is a person, not a mere department of the government hailing Congress from some isolated island of jealous power, sending messages, not speaking naturally and with his own voice; he is a human being trying to cooperate with other human beings in a common service."

The oral message has the advantage of emphasizing the close relation between the two departments of government. It also draws the attention both of Congress and of the country more definitely to the President's

[1] Art. II, sect. 3.

recommendations.   If, through the publicity attaching to the President's message, public opinion is mobilized to support his recommendations, they will naturally have more weight with Congress.   The President may also indirectly enhance the strength of his recommendations through the exercise, or potential exercise, of his power of patronage.   Legally, however, such recommendations are in the nature of advice, which Congress is under no compulsion to follow.

Submission of Bills.—The constitutional provision authorizing the President to "recommend measures" to the consideration of Congress has not usually been construed in practice as authorizing him to send to Congress completely drafted bills designed to carry out his recommendations.   Occasional instances of this, however, have occurred during time of war when the usual formalities are more likely to be dispensed with. Ordinarily the President merely recommends the general subjects of legislation and leaves to Congress the function of selecting the detailed means embodied in a bill for carrying the recommendations into effect. It should be noted as an exception, however, that the President sends to Congress a fully detailed budget, which is prepared by the director of the budget subject to the President's approval.

If the President should adopt the practice of sending to Congress completely drafted bills, he would naturally be accused by Congress of usurping the proper function of the legislative body.   In order to avoid such an accusation, the President may prepare a bill himself, or have one of his principal administrative officers do so, and then secure its introduction by one of his supporters in Congress.   This is frequently done in the case of bills relating to the work of the administrative departments.   Such bills are known as administration measures and will usually be accorded priority of consideration.   Sometimes the formality of securing introduction by a member of Congress is dispensed with and the head of one of the executive departments may send a communication to the presiding officer of one or both branches of Congress containing a draft of a proposed bill, who may then refer it to a committee, which may in turn report it back in the shape of an original bill.   Such communications may be considered technically as merely in the nature of information for the use of Congress but have nevertheless given rise to criticism by members of that body.[1]

Congressional Requests for Information.—Although, as already noted, the power of the President to give Congress information of the state of the Union is also a duty, nevertheless it is one the performance of which there is no direct means of enforcing.   In practice, therefore, it may amount to a power to withhold information.   The President is in control of many sources of information which are not available to Congress, but

[1] For an example of such criticism, see Mathews and Berdahl, *Documents and Readings in American Government*, pp. 183–187.

which may be essential in order that it may exercise intelligently its function of legislation. If the President withholds such information, Congress may have to act in partial darkness. Under such circumstances the Constitution does not confer upon Congress the right to demand information, but it may nevertheless request it and this is frequently done. Such requests may be addressed either to the President or to the head of an executive department. The request is usually made with the proviso "if not incompatible with the public interests." Any information transmitted to Congress, however, is likely to become public and, especially in connection with the conduct of foreign relations, the President may deem secrecy desirable.

Except when the Congressional request is based upon contemplated action relating specifically to the conduct of the executive, the President has full discretion to withhold the information requested, if he so desires, even though it relates to a matter regarding which the Constitution authorizes Congress to legislate. If the Congressional request is addressed to a head of an executive department, the President may direct him not to furnish it, regardless as to whether or not the request is conditioned upon the proviso stated. With the President's permission, express or tacit, heads of departments may appear before Congressional committees and give information regarding matters falling within the scope of their respective departments, and this is often done. The President himself does not appear before committees. In 1919, however, President Wilson summoned the Senate Foreign Relations Committee to the White House to discuss a treaty upon which he desired to secure the Senate's advice and consent.[1]

Approval and Veto.—The President is associated with Congress not only through the suggestion of measures for legislative consideration but also in the actual process of legislation. All bills after having been passed by the two houses in identical form are signed by the presiding officers of the respective houses and then go to the President for his approval or disapproval. The rule on this point cannot be better stated than in the language of the Constitution itself, which declares that:

Every bill which shall have passed the House of Representatives and the Senate shall, before it becomes a law, be presented to the President of the United States; if he approves he shall sign it, but if not he shall return it, with his objections, to that house in which it shall have originated, who shall enter the objections at large on their journal and proceed to reconsider it. If after such reconsideration two thirds of that house shall agree to pass the bill, it shall be sent, together with the objections, to the other house, by which it shall likewise be reconsidered, and if approved by two thirds of that house it shall become a law. But in all such cases the votes of both houses shall be determined by yeas and

[1] For further discussion of Congressional requests for information, see J. M. Mathews, *American Foreign Relations: Conduct and Policies*, pp. 231–235.

nays, and the names of the persons voting for and against the bill shall be entered on the journal of each house respectively. If any bill shall not be returned by the President within ten days (Sundays excepted) after it shall have been presented to him, the same shall be a law, in like manner as if he had signed it, unless the Congress by their adjournment prevent its return, in which case it shall not be a law.[1]

The framers of the Constitution deemed it desirable to give the President some check over legislation, but they were not willing to go so far as to give him an absolute veto, such as had been possessed by the colonial governors and the King of England. Consequently, they effected a compromise between an absolute veto and no veto at all by giving the President what is known as a qualified veto.

A careful reading of the constitutional provision quoted above will disclose that, when a bill which has passed the two houses is sent to the President, any one of four things may happen. In the first place, he may indicate his approval by signing it. This is the usual course in the case of the large majority of bills.

In the second place, the President may disapprove the bill and indicate his disapproval by returning it within ten days to that house in which it originated. In this case he does not sign the bill but accompanies it with a statement of his objections. The bill is then said to be vetoed, but the veto power is qualified by the possibility that Congress may override the veto. This it does by repassing it in both houses by a vote of at least two-thirds, which has been construed to mean not two-thirds of the entire membership but merely two-thirds of a quorum.[2] Each house is required to enter the President's objections at large upon its journal, and the vote on repassage of the bill is taken by "yeas and nays"; *i.e.*, the roll is called and the way each member votes is recorded in the journal for the purpose of putting him under a greater sense of responsibility in taking this important action. When the veto has been overridden in accordance with these formalities, the bill becomes a law in spite of the President's objections.

In the third place, the President may do nothing with a bill; *i.e.*, he may take no action on it indicating either approval or disapproval but merely hold it. When he has thus held it for ten days it becomes a law without his signature, provided Congress is still in session. This procedure may be taken by the President when he has not made up his mind as to the merits of a measure or prefers, for political reasons, not to take any definite stand upon it.

The Pocket Veto.—The fourth possibility is like the third as far as the President's course is concerned. In both cases he does nothing with

[1] Art. I, sect. 7, cl. 2. It will be noticed that this provision is found in the article of the Constitution dealing with the legislative department.
[2] Missouri Pacific Ry. Co. v. Kansas, 248 U. S. 276 (1919).

the bill. But if Congress adjourns within the ten-day period which the President is given for the consideration of bills, it fails to become a law. The President's inaction in this case results in what is known as his "pocket veto." This form of veto differs from that described above in two important respects. In the first place, the President does not have to make any formal statement of his objections to the bill. In the second place, the pocket veto is an absolute veto because Congress, by adjourning, has precluded the possibility of repassing it over his veto. Many bills are pocket-vetoed because of the practice of Congress in passing them during the last few days of a session.

It should be noted that the ten-day period which the President is given for the consideration of bills does not include Sundays and does not begin to run until the bill has been presented to the President. Therefore any delay involved in presenting a bill to him after it has passed the two houses does not have the effect of shortening his time for consideration. This was illustrated by the situation during Wilson's administration when the President was abroad while Congress was in session.

Moreover, Congress cannot, by adjourning, shorten the ten-day period which the President has for the consideration of bills. This was held by the Supreme Court in 1929 in what is known as the pocket veto case.[1] This case involved the question as to whether a bill authorizing certain Indian tribes to sue in the Court of Claims had been enacted into law in spite of the fact that it had been presented to the President within ten days of the adjournment of the session and no action had been taken by him upon it. This was not the final adjournment of the Congress but merely the adjournment of the first session of the Sixty-ninth Congress. The Court held that the bill had been pocket-vetoed. The reasons for this decision were that the word "adjournment" as used in the constitutional provision allowing the pocket veto means not only the final adjournment of a Congress but any temporary adjournment which prevents the President from returning the bill to the house in which it originated; that a bill cannot be returned to a house unless it is in session; and that the ten days allowed the President for consideration of bills refers to calendar days and not legislative days.

May the President Sign after Adjournment?—As noted above, Congress passes many bills during the closing days and even during the closing hours of a session. Such bills the President may pocket-veto. But suppose he wants to have such a bill become a law. On account of the mass of legislation dumped on his desk during the end-of-the-session rush, he may not have adequate opportunity to separate the wheat from the chaff and decide what bills he wants to approve before Congress adjourns. May he nevertheless sign a bill and thus enact it into law after Congress has adjourned?

[1] 279 U. S. 655 (1929).

Until the administration of President Wilson, the practice indicated the general belief that the President could not secure the enactment of a bill into law by signing it after Congress had adjourned. It had been held by the Court of Claims in 1894[1] and by the Supreme Court in 1899[2] that the President might sign bills during the recess of Congress, such as that which it takes over the Christmas holidays. This did not clear up the question as to whether the President could sign after the adjournment of Congress. In June, 1920, President Wilson, acting in accordance with an opinion of the attorney-general upholding his right to do so,[3] signed several bills after the adjournment of Congress. The validity of this practice seems now to be generally acquiesced in and is in accordance with the analogous practice in most of the states, which usually allow the governor a certain length of time after the legislature has adjourned for the signature of bills. It seems desirable that this rule should be established in the Federal Government, since it gives the President more time for careful consideration of the mass of legislation dumped upon his desk at the close of a Congressional session. It should be noted, however, that the adjournment of Congress after which President Wilson signed bills in 1920 was not a final adjournment marking the formal termination of a definite Congress but merely an interruption of legislative activity between two sessions of the same Congress.

What Measures Go to the President?—The question may be raised as to whether all measures of whatever character passed by Congress or either branch thereof should be sent to the President for his approval or disapproval. The Constitution expressly excepts from this requirement resolutions relating to adjournment, but it is not clear from the language of the Constitution what other, if any, acts of Congress are also excepted. In terms, the Constitution requires that:

Every order, resolution, or vote to which the concurrence of the Senate and House of Representatives may be necessary (except on a question of adjournment) shall be presented to the President of the United States; and before the same shall take effect shall be approved by him, or being disapproved by him, shall be repassed by two thirds of the Senate and the House of Representatives according to the rules and limitations prescribed in the case of a bill.[4]

In spite of this apparently very inclusive language, it has become established in practice that certain kinds of measures (besides those relating to adjournment) do not go to the President. As pointed out in an earlier chapter, resolutions of Congress proposing amendments to the Constitution are not sent to the President.[5] The provision of the Constitu-

---

[1] United States v. Alice Weil, 29 Ct. Cl. 526 (1894).
[2] La Abra Silver Mining Co. v. United States, 175 U. S. 423 (1899).
[3] 32 Op. Atty.-Gen. 225 (1920).
[4] Art. I, sect. 7, cl. 3.
[5] See above, pp. 34–35.

tion regarding "Every order, resolution, or vote to which the concurrence of the Senate and House of Representatives may be necessary" has been construed to mean "necessary to give such order, resolution, or vote the force of law." Resolutions passed by Congress proposing amendments to the Constitution do not have the force of law and therefore do not come within the scope of the requirement for submission to the President.[1]

Joint resolutions of Congress ordinarily go to the President, but concurrent resolutions and simple resolutions do not. In 1897, the Judiciary Committee of the Senate made an elaborate report in which it declared that the settled practice of Congress for a century had been not to present concurrent resolutions to the President. In this report, the committee goes on to say that such resolutions

. . . have uniformly been regarded by all the departments of the Government as matters peculiarly within the province of Congress alone. They have never embraced legislative provisions proper, and hence have never been deemed to require Executive approval . . . Whether concurrent resolutions are required to be submitted to the President must depend not upon their mere form but upon the fact whether they contain matter which is properly to be regarded as legislative in its character and effect . . . The clause of the Constitution which declares that every order, resolution, or vote must be presented to the President to which the concurrence of the two Houses may be necessary, refers to the necessity occasioned by the requirements of the other provisions of the Constitution, whereby every exercise of legislative power involves the concurrence of the two Houses; and every resolution not involving the exercise of legislative power need not be presented to the President.[2]

Reasons for Exercising the Veto.—In formally vetoing a bill, the President is required by the Constitution to state his objections. There is no indication in the Constitution, however, as to what the nature of his objections may be and this is a matter which is apparently left entirely within the President's discretion. In discussing the veto power, Hamilton expressed the opinion that its use would primarily be for the purpose of self-defense by the executive against the encroachments of Congress. He further declared that it would "furnish an additional security against the enaction of improper laws."[3]

Both of the reasons stated by Hamilton have been used by Presidents as the bases of the exercise of the veto. President Johnson especially used the power in order to defend his office against what he deemed to be the encroachments of Congress. Most of the Presidents, beginning with Jackson, have vetoed bills because they deemed them to be unwise, inexpedient, or not expressive of the will of the American people. The

[1] *Cf.* Hollingsworth v. Virginia, 3 Dall. 378 (1798).
[2] *Senate Rep.* 1335, 54th Cong., 2d. Sess.
[3] *The Federalist*, No. 73.

Presidents prior to Jackson seem to have exercised the power only for the purpose of preventing the enactment of measures which they deemed to be unconstitutional, or inherently defective, but this reason is also frequently found as the basis of vetoes by subsequent Presidents. They have not hesitated to veto measures on this ground in spite of the argument sometimes put forth that the question of constitutionality should be left to the courts. President Taft averred that since he was required to take an oath to support the Constitution, it was his duty to veto measures of doubtful constitutionality.[1]

Presidents Jackson and Cleveland were noted for the frequency with which they exercised the veto power, especially on the ground of inexpediency. On the whole, however, the power has not been frequently exercised. It is, of course, true that the efficacy of the veto power is not to be measured solely by the frequency of its exercise. President Johnson exercised the power frequently, but his vetoes were regularly overridden by Congress. Moreover, it should be noted that the threat of a veto may sometimes be as effective as its actual exercise. If the President, either publicly or privately, lets it be known that he is opposed to a bill in the form in which it is being considered by Congress, it either may never be passed or may be amended so as to conform with the President's views.

No Item Veto.—The veto power, as granted to the President in the Constitution, does not extend to him the power of vetoing parts of bills. In this respect the power of the President is inferior to that of the governors of the large majority of the states, upon whom the power has been conferred of vetoing items in appropriation bills. In some of these states the governor is allowed to disapprove sections in any bill. In a few states the governor has exercised the power not only of vetoing whole items but also of reducing items in appropriation bills. The framers of the Constitution of the Confederate states, adopted in 1861, were familiar with the working of the Federal Constitution and, in the light of their experience, conferred upon the President of the Southern Confederacy the power to veto items.

It results from the inability of the President of the United States to veto items that many wasteful and unnecessary items of expenditure are slipped into appropriation bills, which the President, however vigilant and conscientious in the performance of his duties, cannot eliminate without vetoing the whole bill and thus possibly stopping the wheels of governmental machinery, which of course he is loath to do. Moreover, since the President is under the necessity of either approving or dis-

[1] In his message to Congress of Feb. 28, 1913, vetoing the Webb-Kenyon bill. For the texts of two veto messages of President Wilson, one based on the ground of unconstitutionality and the other on that of inexpediency, see Mathews and Berdahl, *Documents and Readings in American Government*, pp. 180–183.

approving a bill as a whole, Congress has adopted the practice of inserting extraneous matter or "riders" in bills embodying in the main necessary legislation, such as appropriations. For example, in an appropriation bill, passed in 1913, Congress inserted as a rider a provision prohibiting the President, without specific authority of law, from calling, or accepting an invitation to, an international conference.[1] The President was practically forced to sign the bill regardless of his opinion as to the wisdom of this particular provision.

In order to remedy this situation, there has been agitation, from time to time, in favor of amending the Constitution, so as to confer the item veto on the President. Whether this is advisable, however, is doubtful. It would form a powerful club which the President might wield over members of Congress who are opposed to him politically. They are mainly interested in securing appropriations for their districts, upon which their political fortunes frequently depend. The President might abuse his power by eliminating items of appropriation for districts of members who oppose him, while approving those desired by members belonging to his own party.

Since the adoption of the executive budget system in 1921, the question of the executive veto of items in appropriation bills is not so acute as it formerly was. Inasmuch as the President controls the drawing up of the annual budget of appropriations, he is under no legal compulsion to insert in the budget any item of which he disapproves. Of course, Congress still retains the legal power of inserting such items later, but in time the tradition or practice may become established whereby Congress feels practically bound to make little or no increase in the President's budget.

Executive Seats in Congress.—The President and the heads of executive departments are, as we have seen, barred by the Constitution from being members of Congress. This would have been, in the opinion of the framers of that instrument, too great a departure from the principle of separation of powers. There is nothing in the Constitution, however, which prevents the President or heads of departments from appearing on the floor of Congress for the purpose of imparting information, answering questions, and participating in debate. This, however, cannot be done without the consent of Congress and it has not become established as a practice. Cabinet officers, it is true, frequently appear before committees of Congress in order to give information and answer questions, but this is a more roundabout, cumbrous, and ineffective method than would be that of giving such officers seats in Congress. From the failure to accord them such seats it results, as former President Taft points out, that:

[1] 37 U. S. Stat. at L. 913.

There has been much lost motion in the machinery, due to lack of cooperation and interchange of views face to face between the representatives of the Executive and the members of the two legislative branches of the Government . . . Time and time again debates have arisen in each house upon issues which the information of a particular department head would have enabled him, if present, to end at once by a simple explanation . . . The presence of the members of the Cabinet on the floor of each House would greatly contribute to the enactment of beneficial legislation.[1]

As President Taft further points out in the message quoted, this reform was urged in 1864 by a select committee of the House of Representatives and again in 1881 by a select committee of the Senate. It was also embodied in the Constitution of the Southern Confederacy, although never put into actual practice. The reform, however, has not been adopted by Congress. In securing information about the working of the executive departments, that body, instead of directing questions to cabinet officers on the floor, frequently resorts to the practice of appointing Congressional committees of investigation. The ostensible reason why Congress does not adopt this reform is that it would violate the spirit of the principle of separation of powers. The real reason, however, would seem to be the fear of Congress that it might enhance the power and influence of the executive at the expense of Congress.

[1] Message to Congress, Dec. 12, 1912, *Cong. Rec.*, vol. 49, Pt. 1, pp. 895–896, reprinted in Mathews and Berdahl, *Documents and Readings in American Government*, pp. 237–239.

CHAPTER XII

THE PRESIDENT AS CHIEF EXECUTIVE[1]

Under the Articles of Confederation, there was no distinct executive authority, and such executive powers as the Confederate Government could exercise were vested in the Congress, or in its committees or appointees. This plan did not work satisfactorily. The framers of the Constitution, profiting by this experience and mindful of the principle of the separation of powers, established the President as head of the executive department, more or less independent of control by Congress. Believing also in the principle of checks and balances, they also conferred upon him certain powers connected with national legislation. The President thus occupies a twofold position. His powers may be broadly classified into executive and political. His position as a political leader has become, in popular estimation at least, even more important than that as chief executive, but the powers involved in the latter position are considerable.

The powers and duties of the President are derived in part from the Constitution but also in part from acts of Congress and from treaties. Considered as a whole, the powers which the President is able to exercise render him one of the most powerful officials on earth. The actual extent of his powers, however, varies from time to time, depending in part upon the personality of the President himself and in part upon whether or not the nation is at war. During the administration of a President with an aggressive personality, such as Roosevelt, his power tends to increase considerably as compared with that of a President who, like Taft, prefers to keep within the strict letter of the Constitution and laws. The difference here, however, is more a matter of political influence than of strict legal power.

The Enforcement of Law.—Certain general grants of presidential power are specifically made in the Constitution. In addition to declaring that the executive power shall be vested in a President, it provides that he "shall take care that the laws be faithfully executed."[2] In this connection should also be noted the oath or affirmation which he is required to take to faithfully execute the office of President and "to the best of my ability preserve, protect, and defend the Constitution of the United States."[3] It will also be remembered that the President is made "com-

[1] The diplomatic, war, and treaty powers of the President are considered in Chaps. XVIII and XIX.
[2] Art. II, sect. 3.
[3] Art. II, sect. 1, cl. 8.

mander-in-chief of the army and navy of the United States, and of the militia of the several states when called into the actual service of the United States."[1]

By virtue of the above provisions, responsibility for the enforcement of the laws of the United States is concentrated in the President. This is a duty as well as a power. In carrying it out, the President may utilize other specific grants of power conferred upon him by the Constitution. It is impossible, of course, for the President personally to see to the enforcement of all laws, and therefore he must have agents subject to his control through appointment and removal, upon whom he can depend for the faithful execution of the laws. The Federal courts also cooperate with the executive department by protecting Federal officers in the performance of their official duties and by punishing those who interfere with them.[2] Whenever resistance to the enforcement of the laws is encountered with which the ordinary civil officers provided for the purpose are unable to cope, the President may resort to the exercise of such military force as may be necessary to overcome this resistance and to enforce the laws of the United States upon every foot of our territory.

The laws which the President is required to see faithfully executed are Federal, rather than state, laws. In cases of doubt as to what the law is or how it is to be interpreted, the President has no authority to set himself up as the final judge. It is rather the function of the courts to decide such matters. The President has no right to refuse to see that a law is executed merely because he thinks it is unconstitutional, especially after it has been upheld as constitutional by the courts. Furthermore, the President would be exceeding his authority if he directed his cabinet officers or heads of departments to do or not to do something forbidden to, or required of, them by valid acts of Congress.

The Neagle Case.—The question may be raised as to whether the President has any inherent executive power. As a general rule, he has only such powers as are either expressly granted in the Constitution, laws, or treaties or may be fairly implied from their provisions. Occasionally, however, the Supreme Court has held that the President may exercise a power without any specific authorization in the Constitution or statutes.

A case of this sort was that of *In re* Neagle.[3] In this case it appeared that Justice Field of the United States Supreme Court had been threatened with violence while traveling on circuit in California by one Terry, who was disgruntled by a decision which Justice Field had rendered. Under these circumstances the President, acting through his attorney-

---

[1] Art. II, sect. 2, cl. 1.
[2] *Cf. In re* Debs, 158 U. S. 564 (1895).
[3] 135 U. S. 1 (1890).

general, ordered Neagle, a United States deputy marshal, to accompany Justice Field and protect him from violence.   While traveling on circuit duty, Justice Field encountered Terry in a railroad restaurant and the latter attempted to make a murderous attack upon the judge, whereupon Neagle shot and killed Terry.   Neagle was thereupon indicted for murder in the California state courts.   He set up the order of the President as his authority for what he had done, however, and secured his release from the state authorities upon a writ of habeas corpus issued by the Federal circuit court, and the judgment of the circuit court was affirmed by the Supreme Court of the United States.

In upholding the right of the President to take the action which he did in the Neagle case, the Supreme Court admitted that there was no special act of Congress which, in express terms, authorized the President to order a deputy marshal or other officer of the United States to accompany the judges of the Supreme Court through their circuits and act as a bodyguard to them.   Nevertheless, the Court held that an assault upon a Federal judge while in the discharge of his official duties was a breach of the peace of the United States, as distinguished from the peace of the state in which the assault took place; and that it was within the power and duty of the President to take measures for the protection of a Federal judge whenever there was just reason to believe that he would be in personal danger while executing the duties of his office.

The President and His Cabinet.—In the Neagle case, cited above, the Supreme Court, after referring to the responsibility of the President to enforce the laws, went on to say that the duty

. . . thus imposed upon him he is further enabled to perform by the recognition in the Constitution, and the creation by acts of Congress, of executive departments, . . . the heads of which are familiarly called cabinet ministers. These aid him in the performance of the great duties of his office, and represent him in a thousand acts to which it can hardly be supposed his personal attention is called, and thus he is enabled to fulfil the duty of his great department, expressed in the phrase that "he shall take care that the laws be faithfully executed."

The cabinet as such, however, is not recognized in the Constitution. But the framers of that instrument evidently intended that Congress should create executive departments.   The heads of such departments are twice mentioned in the Constitution: first, that the President "may require the opinion, in writing, of the principal officer in each of the executive departments upon any subject relating to the duties of their respective offices,"[1] and, second, that Congress may by law vest the appointment of inferior officers in the heads of departments.[2]

[1] Art. II, sect. 2, cl. 1.
[2] Art. II, sect. 2, cl. 2.

As far as the language of the Constitution goes and as far as the intentions of the framers are discoverable, it would appear that the Senate was expected to act as the President's advisory council. This seems also to have been President Washington's understanding, and he appeared personally in the Senate on one or two occasions to seek their advice. His experience in these instances, however, was not satisfactory and the practice was quickly abandoned by him and has not been revived by later Presidents. For advice and counsel, therefore, the Presidents have fallen back upon those heads of executive departments who, by custom and usage, have come to be known as the President's cabinet. The Vice President has occasionally attended cabinet meetings, but his membership in that body has not become established as an unwritten rule.

The provision of the Constitution quoted above seems to indicate that the framers of that instrument expected that the medium of communication between the President and the heads of executive departments would be mainly written reports. The stipulation of written opinions was probably intended to insure greater trustworthiness of the opinions and to put the departmental head under a greater sense of responsibility in giving them. Presidents do sometimes ask for opinions in writing, and some of those submitted to President Washington by leading members of his cabinet—Hamilton and Jefferson—have come to be regarded as important state papers. This method of communication between the President and heads of departments, however, is exceptional. For the most part, communication between them is carried on through personal consultation, especially in cabinet meetings. The President, however, is not bound by any advice given him by members of his cabinet, either singly or collectively. Upon him alone rests the responsibility for the policies of his administration. In exercising their functions, the heads of executive departments act as agents of the President. In legal contemplation, their acts are his acts, except those involving the exercise of his personal judgment.

In creating the various executive departments, Congress has sometimes shown an intention of placing them under its own direction. It is true that, in creating the state and war departments, Congress, in deference to the constitutional powers of the President over war and foreign relations, placed those departments under his direction. The heads of those departments were required to "perform and execute such duties as shall from time to time be enjoined on, or entrusted to them, by the President of the United States." By virtue of his constitutional duty to see that the laws are faithfully executed, the President was also deemed properly to have general direction of the department of justice, under the attorney-general. It was recognized that he might direct that officer to institute prosecutions for violation of Federal law or even, under certain circumstances, to discontinue suits.

On the other hand, the Constitution vests in Congress authority to "establish post offices and post roads" and also provides that "no money shall be drawn from the treasury, but in consequence of appropriations made by law."[1]   Hence, in creating the treasury and post office departments, Congress made their heads subject to its own direction and control. No authority was conferred by Congress upon the President to direct or to assign duties to the heads of those departments.   Moreover, that Congress may assign duties to executive officers was affirmed by the Supreme Court.[2]   In spite, however, of the attempt of Congress to keep these departments under its control, their actual position has been rather under the direction of the President.   This has been brought about in part through practical necessity and in part through the existence and exercise by the President of his powers of appointment and removal. The control by the President over the treasury department was shown by the episode of the withdrawal of funds from the Bank of the United States during Jackson's administration.

Appointment of Officers.—Largely because of the difficulty of amending the Federal Constitution, the democratic wave which swept over the states during the first part of the nineteenth century and brought about the widespread popular choice of state officers did not affect the National Government.   A subsequent reaction led to a movement for a shorter ballot in the states, but, in the case of the National Government, we have had a short ballot continuously from the beginning.[3]   The President and Vice President are the only executive officers of the National Government elected even indirectly by popular vote.   All others are appointed.

Most appointments are vested either directly or indirectly in the President, and this places upon him a great burden and responsibility. Congress has no power of appointment, but each house of Congress may choose its own officers and employees, except in the case of the Vice President as presiding officer of the Senate.   With reference to the method of appointment, officers of the United States are divided by the Constitution into two classes: superior and inferior.   The former class include "ambassadors, other public ministers and consuls, judges

[1] Art. I, sect. 8, cl. 7; Art. I, sect. 9, cl. 7.

[2] Kendall v. United States, 12 Pet. 524 (1838).

[3] Even the practice of voting for the entire list of presidential electors to which a state is entitled has been done away with in some states, e.g., Iowa, Nebraska, and Illinois, through the elimination of their names from the ballot, leaving merely the names of the candidates nominated by each party for the offices of President and Vice President.

of the Supreme Court, and all other officers of the United States, whose appointments are not herein otherwise provided for, and which shall be established by law."[1] This class of officers the President nominates and, by and with the advice and consent of the Senate, appoints. The latter class, or inferior officers, are not defined by the Constitution but may be described as those whose appointment Congress may by law, as it thinks proper, vest in the President alone, in the courts of law, or in the heads of departments.

The phrase "ambassadors, other public ministers and consuls" refers to envoys of various grades sent to represent the United States in foreign countries. Consequently, the only appointive officers with domestic functions which are specifically placed by the Constitution in the category of superior officers are judges of the Supreme Court. Judges of the regular Federal courts below the Supreme Court and even heads of executive departments might, on this ground, be regarded as falling in the class of inferior officers. If so at all, however, they are only potentially, and not actually, inferior officers, because Congress has never attempted to provide that they should be appointed otherwise than by the President with the concurrence of the Senate. There are undoubtedly many thousands of officers, now appointed by the President and Senate, who might be transferred to the class of inferior officers and whose appointment Congress might vest in the President alone, the courts of law, or the heads of departments.

Qualifications of Appointees.—Although officers of the United States are appointed in the manner mentioned above, the discretion of the appointing authority in choosing whom it pleases may be limited by the action of Congress in prescribing qualifications for those who are to fill the offices. Such prescription of qualifications is frequently made by Congress at the time of creating the office. The power of Congress to create offices may be construed as implying the right of prescribing qualifications for them, but this right "is limited by the necessity of leaving scope for the judgment and will of the person or body in whom the Constitution vests the power of appointment."[2] Although there is no adjudication of the Supreme Court in reference to the validity of the exercise of this power by Congress and it might seem, strictly speaking, to be in conflict with the unequivocal grant of the appointing power in the Constitution, it has nevertheless become established in practice and may be regarded as valid, provided it does not go so far as to deprive the appointing authority of its discretion to an undue or unreasonable extent. It would be unreasonable if the qualifications laid down by

---

[1] Art. II, sect. 2, cl. 2. Curiously enough, the convention's committee on style, usually so adept in phraseology, made a slip in this provision. The language implies that "officers," rather than "offices," are established by law.

[2] 13 Op. Atty.-Gen. 520.

Congress so limit selection and so trench upon the choice of the appointing authority as to be in effect Congressional designation.

It is true that, with reference to an act of Congress passed in 1855 providing that the President should appoint no other than citizens of the United States as diplomatic envoys or consuls, the attorney-general held that such an attempted limitation by Congress upon the discretion of the President and Senate in the exercise of the appointing power must be regarded as recommendatory only and not mandatory. "The limit of the range of selection," he said, "for the appointment of constitutional officers depends on the Constitution . . . The President has absolute right to select for appointment."[1] A later incumbent of the office of attorney-general, however, gave a more liberal construction of the power of Congress in prescribing qualifications for office. He held that Congress could require that officers shall be of American citizenship or of a certain age, that judges shall be of the legal profession and of a certain standing in the profession, and still leave a reasonable scope for the exercise by the appointing power of its own judgment and will.[2]

In this connection it should be noted that the power of the President and Senate to appoint whom they please to office is limited to some extent by the provision of the Constitution which prohibits a member of either house of Congress from holding any office under the United States or from being appointed, during the time for which he was elected, to any civil office under the authority of the United States which has been created or the emoluments thereof increased during such time.[3] This limitation, however, applies to the appointment of members of Congress to regular or, comparatively speaking, permanent positions under the Government and does not prevent the President from appointing members of Congress on special or temporary missions to accomplish particular objects, such as the negotiation of a treaty of peace.

Civil Service Appointments.—In the exercise of its power of laying down qualifications for appointment to office, Congress may require that certain classes of inferior officers or employees of the Government shall be appointed only from a list of those who have passed with the highest grades examinations set by a civil service commission appointed by the President and Senate.

To require that the selection shall be made from persons found by an examining board to be qualified in such particulars as diligence, scholarship, integrity, good manners, and attachment to the government, would not impose an unconstitutional limitation on the appointing power. That power would still have a reasonable scope for its own judgment and will.[4]

[1] 7 Op. Atty.-Gen. 215, 267.
[2] 13 Op. Atty.-Gen. 525 (1871).
[3] Art. I, sect. 6, cl. 2.
[4] 13 Op. Atty.-Gen. 524 (1871).

It would probably be unconstitutional, however, for Congress to require that such persons only as receive the highest grade in a competitive examination and are so certified by the commission should be appointed, for this would leave the appointing authority no choice and would virtually transfer the power of appointment to the commission. Moreover, Congress would probably be exceeding its power if it provided for the application of civil service regulations to the appointment of other than inferior officers and employees. The President may, however, by executive order or regulation, voluntarily limit his nominations to such persons as may have attained the highest grades on the examination set by the civil service commission. It has also been held that the President may, under authority derived from Congress, issue such regulations even with reference to positions in the civil service which by law are to be filled by appointees of a head of an executive department.[1]

The Process of Appointment.—In his opinion in Marbury v. Madison,[2] Chief Justice Marshall spoke of the process of appointment as involving

. . . three distinct operations: 1st. The nomination. This is the sole act of the President and is completely voluntary. 2d. The appointment. This is also the act of the President, and is also a voluntary act, though it can only be performed by and with the advice and consent of the Senate. 3d. The commission. To grant a commission to a person appointed might, perhaps, be deemed a duty enjoined by the Constitution. "He shall," says that instrument, "commission all the officers of the United States."

The chief justice declared further that the appointment is complete when the commission is signed and that the delivery of the commission can, in proper cases, be compelled by the issuance of a writ of mandamus by a court having jurisdiction to do so. In spite of the statement of the Chief Justice, however, the President cannot be legally compelled to sign a commission, even though the Senate has given its advice and consent to the appointment.

In giving its advice and consent to an appointment, the Senate acts by a mere majority of a quorum, and not by a two-thirds vote, as in the case of the approval of treaties. The association of the Senate with the President in the process of appointment doubtless operates in many cases to divide the responsibility between them. According to Hamilton, however, the purpose of associating the Senate in the process was not to relieve the President of responsibility for appointments but rather to "check a spirit of favoritism in the President" and "to prevent the appointment of unfit characters from state prejudice, from family connection, from personal attachment or from a view to popularity."[3] It

[1] 13 Op. Atty.-Gen. 524.
[2] 1 Cranch 137 (1803).
[3] *The Federalist*, No. 76.

was suggested by the Supreme Court in the Myers case[1] that the purpose of the consitutional provision associating the Senate with the President in the power of appointment was in order to allay the fears of the small states that the President might make an undue number of appointments from the large states if he were not checked by a body in which the small states had equal representation.

The constitutional provision as to appointments is somewhat ambiguous in regard to the respective functions of the President and the Senate in the process. It apparently gives to the President the sole power of nominating persons for appointment but in the next breath declares that the appointment can be made only with the advice and consent of the Senate. The action of the Senate in giving its consent cannot be performed until it receives a nomination from the President, but it is difficult to see how the Senate can exercise its power of giving advice except by suggesting the names of candidates to the President and thus virtually participate with him in the exercise of the power of nomination. In practice the President does not consult with the Senate as a body in arriving at a decision upon nominations. He may, however, and does consult with individual senators. The requirement of senatorial confirmation in order to validate an appointment may exert an indirect or retroactive influence over the President's action.

Although the Senate has the legal power to reject any and all nominations submitted by the President, there are in practice certain classes of nominations which it almost invariably confirms. The Senate does not often reject the President's nominations to positions in the diplomatic service and on the Supreme Court bench. Recently, however, the Senate rejected President Hoover's nomination to the Supreme Court bench of Judge Parker of North Carolina, largely because of certain decisions which the latter had rendered, which made him unpopular with certain groups. Through its power of confirmation, the Senate thus sometimes attempts to exercise a censorship over the views of those who are to hold important judicial and other office. As a rule the Senate confirms without question the President's nominations to cabinet positions. To this rule there have been only about half a dozen exceptions. One of the latest of these occurred in 1925 when the Senate rejected President Coolidge's nomination of Charles B. Warren to be attorney-general.[2] Although exceptional instances of this sort may be justified, the rule whereby the Senate confirms nominations to cabinet positions as a matter of course is a proper one. Since the cabinet officers are the President's confidential advisers and he is responsible for their acts, he should have a free hand in selecting them. The Warren incident shows

---

[1] Myers v. United States, 272 U. S. 52 (1926).

[2] For an account of the Warren case, see Mathews and Berdahl, *Documents and Readings in American Government*, pp. 196–212.

that the President should exercise circumspection in not sending in nominations to which valid objection may be made, but his right as a general rule to control cabinet appointments is still recognized as well established.

Renomination.—In the Warren case mentioned above, after the first rejection President Coolidge again nominated Mr. Warren for the same position and the Senate again rejected him. The question may be raised as to whether the action of the Senate in rejecting a nomination made by the President is to be regarded as a final and conclusive determination of the matter. There is nothing to prevent the President from renominating the same person for the same place. On the other hand, the Senate is free to reject a renomination as often as it pleases. It might fail to act upon it at all, which would have the same result.

Reconsideration of Confirmation.—A constitutional question for which there was apparently no precedent was raised in 1931 when the Senate attempted to oust George Otis Smith from the chairmanship of the Federal Power Commission. He was nominated to this position by President Hoover and, late in 1930, was confirmed by the Senate and sworn into office. Thereafter the Senate, displeased with the policy of the commission regarding the dismissal of certain of its employees, and acting within its own rules, reconsidered the confirmation of Smith's nomination and requested the President to return to the Senate notification of Smith's confirmation. This the President declined to do, but nevertheless the Senate, upon reconsideration of Smith's nomination, rejected him and adopted a resolution to bring a judicial determination of Smith's right to office. The question thus presented was finally submitted to the Supreme Court which in 1932 handed down a decision upholding the correctness of the President's position that, when the Senate has once confirmed a nomination and officially notified the President to that effect, its action is final and reconsideration cannot bring about ouster of the appointee.

Senatorial Courtesy.—As pointed out above, although the President does not consult the Senate as a body regarding nominations, he does consult with individual senators regarding certain nominations. Profiting by his unfortunate experience in attempting to consult with the Senate as a body in regard to treaties, President Washington made no attempt to consult with them regarding nominations. At the very beginning of his first administration, the Senate, without assigning any reason, refused to confirm a nomination which he had made to the position of naval officer at Savannah, Georgia. The real reason was that the senators from that state were opposed to the nomination, and Washington had to send in another name. This seems to have been the first instance of the operation of a log-rolling device among senators which has been dignified with the appellation "senatorial courtesy."[1]

[1] Horwill, H. W., *The Usages of the American Constitution*, p. 128.

If there is any courtesy involved in this device, it is not the courtesy of the Senate to the President, but the courtesy of the Senate to the senators from the state in which an appointment is to be made. It thus applies, as a rule, only to appointments to positions the duties of which are localized within some particular state, such as collectors of customs, district attorneys, and internal revenue collectors.[1] The constitutional usage involved in senatorial courtesy is not definitely fixed and settled, but, as a rule, it requires the President to consult with the senator or senators from the state in which such appointments are located. If he fails to conform to their wishes in making nominations, the Senate is very likely to refuse to confirm. This is done as a matter of course and without consideration of the qualifications of the President's nominees.[2] If there is no senator belonging to the President's party from the state in which the appointment is located, the President may consult the party leader from that state. In the case of minor offices, he may consult the representative in the lower house of Congress from the district in which the position is located.

Recess Appointments.—If, through the operation of the rule of senatorial courtesy or otherwise, an appointment remains unconfirmed or a position remains vacant, the President has at his disposal a constitutional resource in that provision which empowers him to "fill up all vacancies that may happen during the recess of the Senate, by granting commissions which shall expire at the end of their next session."[3] Inasmuch as neither Congress nor the Senate is continuously in session, this grant of power seems desirable in order to avoid as far as possible interruption in the public service through accidental or unforeseen changes in the personnel of the administration. It enables the President, however, to overcome the opposition of the Senate to an appointment which he desires to make. In the case of Charles B. Warren, whom President Coolidge desired in 1925 to appoint to the position of attorney-general and whose nomination the Senate twice rejected, the President announced his intention of granting him a recess appointment. This announcement was followed by speeches in the Senate declaring the President's course violative of the spirit of the Constitution.[4] The

---

[1] Occasionally, however, nominations to positions of an extralocal character, such as interstate commerce commissioner, have been opposed under the guise of senatorial courtesy by the senator of the state from which the nominee hails.

[2] In connection, however, with appointments to certain Federal offices in New York, President Garfield in 1881 failed to conform to the wishes of Senators Platt and Conkling from that state, whereupon the latter resigned and sought vindication of their course through reelection, but the legislature of New York failed to reelect them.

[3] Art. II, sect. 2, cl. 3.

[4] See extracts from *Congressional Record* reprinted in Mathews and Berdahl, *Documents and Readings in American Government*, pp. 159–162.

President, however, was only deterred from granting Mr. Warren such an appointment by his declination to accept it.

It seems clear that the President might, while keeping within his strict legal powers, exercise the power of making recess appointments to such an extent as to violate the spirit of the provision giving the Senate the power of advising and consenting to appointments. There is nothing legally to prevent the President from keeping in office indefinitely a nominee whom the Senate refuses to confirm by renewing his commission at the expiration of each session of Congress. Whether any President has actually abused his power in this respect is another question, but it is one which has been exercised from the early days of the Republic. Thus President Jefferson kept Robert Smith as his secretary of the navy for four years without senatorial confirmation.

Even where the unconfirmed nominee is not kept in office for so long a period, he may have finished the work for which he was appointed. Thus, President Jackson nominated Roger B. Taney to be secretary of the treasury and, although his appointment was not confirmed by the Senate, he stayed in the office long enough to carry out the financial policy of the administration.[1]

Another noteworthy case of a recess appointment was that of W. D. Crum to be collector of customs at Charleston, South Carolina, made by President Roosevelt in 1902. Senator Tillman of that state objected to the nomination and succeeded in preventing confirmation. President Roosevelt nevertheless continued to send in the nomination at the beginning of each session, Crum meanwhile holding the office but without compensation. One peculiarity of this case was that President Roosevelt reappointed Crum at precisely twelve o'clock noon of the first Monday in December, 1903, when a special session of the Senate ended and the regular session of Congress began. There was no actual interval of time between these sessions but merely a constructive recess.[2]

Presidential Appointment without Senatorial Confirmation.—There are three situations in which the President may make appointments without senatorial confirmation. Two of these have already been discussed, *viz.*, recess appointments and the appointment of inferior officers vested by law in the President alone. The third method of exercising this power is that which the President has developed of appointing special agents without sending their names to the Senate for confirmation. This practice has developed especially in connection with the negotiation of treaties and other matters connected with the conduct of foreign relations.

[1] FORD, H. J., *The Rise and Growth of American Politics*, p. 290.

[2] For the facts of this case, see the letter of Secretary of the Treasury Leslie M. Shaw, reprinted in Mathews and Berdahl, *op. cit.*, pp. 158–159. For further discussion of recess appointments, see J. M. Mathews, *American Foreign Relations: Conduct and Policies*, pp. 339–341

It sometimes happens, in the case of important or delicate negotiations, that the President prefers to entrust them to specially selected agents rather than to the regular diplomatic representatives.

The practice of the President in this respect has been upheld on the grounds of precedent and necessity. The argument from necessity is especially potent where the President deems secrecy in negotiations indispensable to success. The practice has also been upheld on the ground that it is implied in the President's initiative in foreign affairs and also in Congressional appropriation acts, providing special compensation for such presidential agents. The practice, however, has not escaped occasional opposition in Congress and in the Senate. The question may be raised as to whether Congress could curb the practice of the President in appointing special diplomatic agents by passing an act requiring that such agents or delegates should be appointed by and with the advice and consent of the Senate. In general, it may be said that such an act would be entitled to respect but would not necessarily be binding upon the President, unless Congress should make such a position a regular office and should provide that no compensation could be paid out of public funds to the holder of such office unless the Senate has confirmed his appointment.[1]

The Power of Removal.—Curiously enough, the Constitution makes no express provision for the removal of officers except through the process of impeachment. This is the only method whereby Federal judges, who serve during good behavior, can be removed. In creating offices, Congress may specify the length of term of the incumbent, at the expiration of which he automatically goes out of office unless reappointed. Strictly speaking, however, this is not removal, which denotes ousting from office prior to the expiration of the term. It has been held that when Congress by law vests the appointment of inferior officers in the heads of executive departments, it may limit and restrict the exercise by such heads of the power of removal.[2] This proposition was approved in the Myers case decided in 1926, but under the latter case it would seem that Congress probably cannot withdraw officers from the President's power of removal by designating them as inferior and vesting their appointment in the heads of departments. This point, however, is not definitely settled.

The principal question regarding the removal of officers, however, has come up in connection with the removal of those appointed by the President by and with the advice and consent of the Senate. Is the power of removing such officers implied in the power to appoint them? If so, can they be removed by the President only with the consent of the Senate? Or may it be inferred that the President alone has this power

[1] For further discussion of this point, see J. M. Mathews, op . cit., pp. 336–339.
[2] United States v. Perkins, 116 U. S. 484 (1886).

by implication from his general executive power and from his constitutional duty to see that the laws are faithfully executed?

The Decision of 1789.—Although the Constitution is silent upon the question as to the location of the power of removal, light upon this question may be drawn from contemporary sources. Hamilton, a member of the Constitutional Convention, in a paper published in 1788, expressed the opinion that the Senate was associated with the President in the exercise of the power of removal. "The consent of that body," he declared, "would be necessary to displace as well as to appoint."[1] This, however, was of course merely his personal opinion.

A more important contemporary source of information regarding the location of this power is found in the debate on this question which arose in the First Congress in 1789 and in the action taken by that Congress with reference to the matter. This debate was on a bill to establish the department of foreign affairs, which provided that the head of the department should be appointed by the President by and with the advice and consent of the Senate and should "be removable by the President." With reference to this proposal, there were at least three distinct shades of opinion voiced in Congress by (1) those who thought that the Constitution conferred upon the President alone the power of removal, which could not be restricted by Congress; (2) those who thought that the Constitution vested the power of removal in the President and the Senate jointly; and (3) those who thought that the Constitution had left it to Congress under its "necessary and proper" power to provide as it saw fit for removals. Madison was the leader of the first group and argued very forcibly against the view that the Senate should be associated with the President in exercising the power of removal. He based his argument not only on constitutional but also on practical grounds. The plan to associate the Senate with the President, he declared, might have the effect of making an administrative officer who was supposed to be subordinate to the President in reality independent of him. Since the President must bear the responsibility for the general conduct of the office, he should have power of removing the head of the department without interference from the Senate.

Madison's view finally prevailed, although the provision declaring the secretary of foreign affairs removable by the President was stricken out, because it might be construed as an undertaking on the part of Congress to confer on him a power which otherwise he would not have. As finally passed, the act contained a provision that the chief clerk of the department should act in place of the secretary whenever the latter should "be removed from office by the President of the United States." Consequently, as thus finally passed, the act merely implied the existence of the power of removal in the President without attempting expressly

[1] *The Federalist,* No. 77.

to confer it.   If the President did not derive the power from the act of Congress, then he must derive it directly from the Constitution, and, upon this hypothesis, it would seem to follow that Congress could not take away or restrict his exercise of the power.[1]

Development of the Removal Power.—The Congressional decision of 1789 regarding the location of the power of removal may have been influenced in part by the exalted character of the man then occupying the presidential office.   At any rate, it has, with few exceptions, been generally acquiesced in since that date.   It is true that Chief Justice Marshall, in the case of Marbury v. Madison,[2] expressed the opinion that, as the law creating the office of justice of the peace in the District of Columbia "gave the officer the right to hold for five years, independent of the executive, the appointment was not revocable."   This, however, seems to have been an *obiter dictum*, and moreover, the statement would not necessarily apply to an office outside of the District.[3]

In 1820, Congress passed an act providing that district attorneys and other officers should be appointed for four-year terms and in other acts has also stipulated the length of official terms.   Such acts, however, have not been construed as limiting the President's power of removal before the expiration of the term.[4]   Otherwise, the only remedy for dereliction in office would be impeachment.

In actual practice, the President exercised the power of removal without interference from the adoption of the Constitution until the time of the Civil War.   Through the exercise of this power, he developed a powerful means of direction over the principal officers of the administration.   Through control over their tenure of office, he was able to control the policies pursued by them.   This situation was strikingly illustrated by the incident of President Jackson's demand, in 1833, that the secretary

[1] The account of the "decision of 1789" here given is based on that given by the Supreme Court in Parsons v. United States, 167 U. S. 324 (1897), and in Myers v. United States, 272 U. S. 52 (1926).   It should be noticed, however, that the Senate was equally divided upon the bill and it was passed only through the favorable casting vote of Vice President Adams.   Moreover, it has been declared that, as a historical fact, "less than a third of the membership of the House was at any time of the opinion that the Constitution vested the President alone with the power of removal; while even this fraction were by no means in agreement as to the constitutional basis of the power of removal."   Corwin, E. S., *The President's Removal Power under the Constitution*, p. 13 (1927).   It should be noted, furthermore, that the legislative decision of 1789, strictly speaking, did not logically establish the doctrine that the President's power of removal is unlimited or subject to no control by Congress.   Moreover, that decision had reference to a cabinet officer and might have been different as applied to an inferior officer.   These arguments against the controlling force of the legislative decision of 1789 were strongly urged by the dissenting judges in the Myers case.

[2] 1 Cranch 137 (1803).

[3] In the Myers case, Chief Justice Taft maintains that Marshall's statement was *obiter*, but in a dissenting opinion this contention is denied.

[4] *Cf.* Parsons v. United States, 167 U. S. 324 (1897).

of the treasury should remove the Government funds from the National Bank. Duane, at that time occupying the office of secretary, declined to comply with the President's demand, on the ground that he must consult Congress before acting. Jackson thereupon removed Duane from office and subsequently appointed another secretary who carried out his instructions in regard to the removal of the funds.

With the possible exception of an act passed in 1863 regarding the tenure of the comptroller of the currency, no attempt was made by Congress to interfere with the President's removal power until the administration of President Johnson. In 1867, Congress passed the tenure of office act which forbade the removal by the President of the heads of executive departments without the advice and consent of the Senate. The passage of this act was due to the bitter struggle and political animosity between Congress and President Johnson, and one of the principal charges against the President at his impeachment trial was that he had attempted to remove from office Secretary of War Stanton in disregard of the provisions of the tenure of office act. This act was modified in 1869 at the beginning of President Grant's administration and finally in 1887 was repealed altogether. Congress thereby reverted to the earlier construction of 1789 regarding the President's power of removal.

In 1920, Congress passed a budget and accounting bill, which provided, among other things, that the comptroller-general "may be removed at any time by concurrent resolution of Congress . . . and in no other manner, except by impeachment." Since concurrent resolutions are not sent to the President, this provision would have prevented him from even participating in the act of removal. The reason for this provision was the desire to create an office whose incumbent would act as the agent of Congress and would be absolutely independent of the executive in examining the expenditures of the executive officers and departments. President Wilson, however, vetoed the bill on the ground that it unconstitutionally infringed upon the President's power, derived from the Constitution, to remove officers of the United States. Shortly after the beginning of President Harding's administration in 1921, the bill was reenacted, but the section regarding the comptroller-general was changed so as to provide that he should be appointed by the President, with the consent of the Senate, for a term of fifteen years and should be removable only by impeachment or by joint resolution of Congress. In this form it was approved.[1]

On account of the scandal connected with the naval oil leases, the Senate in 1924 passed a resolution declaring it to be the sense of that body that the President should immediately request the resignation of Secretary of the Navy Denby. This resolution raised the question as to the right of the Senate thus to attempt to influence the President with respect

[1] 42 U. S. Stat. at L. 23, 24.

to the removal of a member of his cabinet. The President immediately replied that no official recognition could be given to this resolution and further declared that "the dismissal of an officer of the Government, such as is involved in this case, other than by impeachment, is exclusively an executive function."[1] This incident indicates that the Senate cannot coerce the President into exercising his power of removing members of his cabinet.

The Myers Case.—The constitutional question involved in the tenure of office act passed by Congress during President Johnson's administration did not reach the Supreme Court for final adjudication. It was the opinion of most authorities on the Constitution, however, that the act was invalid. Curiously enough, it was not until 1926 that the Supreme Court finally and clearly passed upon the question of the President's power of removal. This was probably due in part to the fact that the President did not usually remove an officer without at the same time nominating his successor, and the confirmation of this nomination by the Senate implied its consent to the removal.[2] This was not true, however, in the Myers case,[3] so that the Senate did not even impliedly consent to Myers' removal.

This case involved the constitutionality of an act of Congress passed in 1876 which provided that "postmasters of the first, second, and third classes shall be appointed and may be removed by the President by and with the advice and consent of the Senate and shall hold their offices for four years unless sooner removed or suspended according to law." Myers had been appointed to a first-class postmastership in Portland, Oregon, by President Wilson in 1917 for a term of four years. In 1920, the President removed him from office without securing the consent of the Senate to the removal as required by the act of 1876. Myers protested against his removal and, upon the expiration of the four-year period for which he originally had been appointed, brought suit in the Court of Claims for that portion of his salary which he would have received if he had been allowed to serve out his term. His contention was that his removal was in violation of the act of 1876. On the mere ground of undue delay in bringing the suit, the Court of Claims decided against him and, upon appeal to the Supreme Court, the latter tribunal, in a six-to-three decision, affirmed the judgment of the lower court on the ground that "the provision of the law of 1876, by which the unrestricted power of removal of first-class postmasters is denied to the President, is in violation of the Constitution, and invalid." In this case,

[1] Although not requested to do so by the President, Secretary Denby shortly afterward resigned. For the documents in the case, see Mathews and Berdahl, *Documents and Readings in American Government*, pp. 212–224.

[2] So held by the Supreme Court in Wallace v. United States, 257 U. S. 541 (1922).

[3] Myers v. United States, 272 U. S. 52 (1926).

the Government adopted the very unusual procedure of appearing, through its department of justice, for the purpose of contesting the constitutionality of a Congressional act.

The majority opinion was delivered by Chief Justice Taft. The reasons assigned for the decision of the Court fall into two main parts. The first part is based on the legislative decision of 1789 which, the learned chief justice maintains, supports the view that the President has an untrammeled power of removing executive officers appointed by him, even though the consent of the Senate was necessary to make the appointment. This view is further supported by the unbroken practice of all departments of the Government for three-quarters of a century. He attaches no weight to the change in view on the part of Congress as embodied in the tenure of office act of 1867, on account of the heated partisan controversy involved, and points out that this change was not acquiesced in by either the executive or judicial departments.

The second part of the Court's opinion in this case is of more importance. It bases the President's unrestricted power of removing executive officers upon implication from certain provisions of the Constitution. The two most important of these provisions are those which declare that "the executive power shall be vested in a President" and that "he shall take care that the laws be faithfully executed."[1] The reasoning of the Court from these provisions is as follows:

The President alone and unaided could not execute the laws. He must execute them by the assistance of subordinates . . . As he is charged specifically to take care that they be faithfully executed, the reasonable implication, even in the absence of express words, was that as part of his executive power he should select those who were to act for him under his direction in the execution of the laws. The further implication must be, in the absence of any express limitation respecting removals, that as his selection of administrative officers is essential to the execution of the laws by him, so must be his power of removing those for whom he cannot continue to be responsible.

The implied grant of the removal power to the President found in the provisions cited from Article II of the Constitution is further supported by the argument that the removal power is to be inferred from his power of appointment. Even where the Senate's consent to the appointment is necessary, the President alone appoints. Therefore, the implied power of removal rests in the President alone. "A veto by the Senate . . . upon removals," declared the Court, "is a much greater limitation upon the executive branch and a much more serious blending of the legislative with the executive than a rejection of a proposed appointment. It is not to be implied."

[1] Art. II, sects. 1 and 3.

The Court then proceeds to draw a sharp distinction between the powers of appointment and removal and to show as follows the practical objections to associating the Senate with the President in removals:

The power to prevent the removal of an officer who has served under the President is different from the authority to consent to or reject his appointment. When a nomination is made, it may be presumed that the Senate is, or may become, as well advised as to the fitness of the nominee as the President, but in the nature of things the defects in ability or intelligence or loyalty in the administration of the laws of one who has served as an officer under the President, are facts as to which the President, or his trusted subordinates, must be better informed than the Senate, and the power to remove him may, therefore, be regarded as confined, for very sound and practical reasons, to the governmental authority which has administrative control. The power of removal is incident to the power of appointment, not to the power of advising and consenting to appointment, and when the grant of the executive power is enforced by the express mandate to take care that the laws be faithfully executed, it emphasizes the necessity for including within the executive power as conferred the exclusive power of removal.

Evaluation of the Myers Decision.—The arguments presented by the Court in this case to support its decision, in so far as they are based on history and on logical inferences from the language of the Constitution, are not altogether convincing. The weaknesses of these arguments are amply shown in the opinions of the dissenting justices. Nevertheless, from the standpoints of practical expediency and of sound principles of administration, the decision may be approved as wise and far-sighted. It recognizes that the power of the President is equal to his responsibilities as head of the national administration and thus confirms a situation which practical needs had already established in practice. The opinion of the majority of the Court was doubtless influenced by the fact that the chief justice, who wrote it, alone among all those who have occupied that office, had also filled the presidential chair and knew, from practical acquaintance with the problems of the presidential office, the impediments to efficient administration which a different decision would have entailed.

The objection may be raised, however, that the large power of control over the administration which the President is thus recognized as having may be subject to abuse and may give full sway to the spoils system. This objection, however, does not seem serious because civil service regulations embodying the merit system have never been applied to the higher officers in the service but only to the filling of inferior positions. Congress may by law provide that the latter positions shall be filled through appointment by the heads of departments or the courts of law, and the majority opinion in the Myers case expressly recognizes that, when the power of appointment is vested in such agencies, Congress may regulate the exercise by them of the power of removal. It is true that the case does not definitely settle the point as to whether Congress can withdraw officers from the President's power of removal by designating them as inferior and vesting their appointment in the heads of departments. It is true also that the President might control the exercise by heads of departments of their power of removal through his power to remove such heads. Furthermore, the Myers decision also leaves unsettled the question as to whether Congress can restrict the power of the President to remove officers appointed by him alone. Even supposing that these unsettled questions are finally decided in favor of unlimited Presidential power, it should be remembered that powers that are legally unlimited may be practically limited so that they cannot be exercised according to the President's mere whim or caprice. He is still limited by the check of public opinion and by the practical need of working as harmoniously as possible with the leaders in Congress and especially in the Senate.

Another question which the Myers decision leaves unsettled is as to the status, with reference to the President's power of removal, of the independent officers, and members of boards and commissions not placed in any of the executive departments presided over by cabinet officers. The opinion of the Court in the Myers case is addressed specifically to the question of the President's power of removing executive officers. The question may be raised as to whether there are not other officers, not strictly executive in character, to whom the decision in the Myers case does not apply and over whom, therefore, the President does not have an unlimited power of removal. One such officer is the comptroller-general, who, by the Budget and Accounting Act of 1921 cannot be removed except by impeachment or by joint resolution of Congress. He was intended to be the agent of Congress in seeing that the money appropriated is spent in accordance with the will of that body and, consequently, should be removable by Congress rather than by the President. Members of certain independent fact-finding commissions, such as the Interstate Commerce Commission and the Federal Trade Commission, exercise quasi-judicial and quasi-legislative power. Whether the President has power of removing them from office which Congress cannot restrict, the Myers case does not decide, because the question was not before the Court. It would seem, however, that the President should not be regarded as having the same unrestricted power of removing them which he exercises over purely executive officers. The same reasoning applies also to statutory judges as distinguished from those of the regular Federal courts. It would seem that, in the case of all officers exercising judicial powers or discretionary powers of a quasi-judicial or quasi-legislative nature, the President should not be deemed to have unrestricted power of removal. On the other hand, in such cases Congress should be deemed to have power to place limitations on the removal power and to regulate the tenure of office.[1]

Administrative Ordinances and Regulations.—On account of the complexity of modern conditions, it is impossible for Congress to foresee and provide for all conditions and situations that may arise in connection with the operation of laws. In many instances, therefore, Congress must perforce content itself with laying down the general principles in the law and leaving to some administrative officer or commission the power and duty of filling in the details. Such officer may be the President or the head of one of the executive departments. The power of the President to issue orders and regulations is derived in part from acts of Congress and in part by implication from express powers conferred upon him by the Constitution. It is, of course, his constitutional duty to see that acts of Congress are faithfully executed and, in doing so, he may exercise what is virtually a subsidiary or subordinate legislative power.

As commander-in-chief of the army and navy, the President issues regulations for the government of the armed forces of the United States. By virtue of the Civil Service Act passed by Congress in 1883, the President has issued executive orders providing for the merit system of appointment in the classified service. By virtue of his position as the responsible officer in charge of our foreign relations, the President has prescribed and the state department has issued a body of rules and regulations governing the duties of American consuls. Other examples of presidential ordinances are President Lincoln's emancipation proclamation and President Taft's proclamation prescribing the rates of toll to be paid by vessels using the Panama Canal.[2]

An ordinance is really an act of legislation but is issued by some other authority than the regular legislative body. Those issued by the President are usually in the form of proclamations or executive orders.[3] By proclamation the President may also indicate his finding of a fact upon which a law operates. By the tariff act passed by Congress in 1890 the President was authorized by proclamation to suspend the importation of certain articles into the country free of duty whenever he ascertained as a fact that the countries from which such articles were exported were imposing reciprocally unequal and unreasonable duties upon American products. Upon the issuance of his proclamation, certain rates of duty

[1] On this whole question, see J. Hart, *Tenure of Office under the Constitution: a Study in Law and Public Policy* (1930).

[2] The text of this proclamation is reprinted in J. Hart, *The Ordinance Making Powers of the President*, Johns Hopkins University Studies in Historical and Political Science, XLIII, 3, p. 66 (1925). For text of other Presidential orders, see Mathews and Berdahl, *Documents and Readings in American Government*, pp. 173–176.

[3] Some proclamations, however, such as a Thanksgiving proclamation are hortatory and not legislative and therefore are not ordinances.

were to be imposed upon the importation of such articles. The Supreme Court upheld the law as not involving an unconstitutional delegation of legislative power to the President.[1]

As indicated above, the orders and regulations issued by the President may be classified according as the authority to issue them is derived from the Constitution or from Congressional delegation.[2] Again, they may be classified according as they are intended to be binding solely on subordinate administrative officials or as they are primarily binding on, or affect the interests of, private individuals. In the case of the latter class of ordinances, the question may be raised as to whether a penalty may be attached to their violation. The courts are loath to admit the existence of a criminal liability unless clearly provided by law. An executive officer cannot, on his own authority and initiative, attach a criminal liability to the violation of the regulations which he issues, but Congress may, in the law authorizing the issue of regulations, provide specifically that their violation shall be a penal offense. Thus, Congress passed various acts for the management of forest reservations upon the public lands and authorized the secretary of agriculture to make regulations regarding the use of such land by private individuals, the violation of which was to be punishable as a crime. Certain persons were indicted for grazing their sheep on this land in violation of the regulations of the secretary and the imposition of the penalty upon them as specified in the law was upheld by the Supreme Court.[3]

The Pardoning Power.—Just as the President may veto acts of Congress, so he may virtually veto or amend the decisions of the Federal courts in criminal cases through the exercise of his power of granting pardons. There is, however, this difference, that Congress may repass an act over the President's veto by an extraordinary majority, whereas the courts cannot revise the action of the President in granting a pardon. In fact, it would seem that when the President has granted an unconditional pardon and it has been accepted, such action is final and the pardon cannot be modified or rescinded, even by the President. Granting a pardon is the exercise of a quasi-judicial power and, therefore, when exercised by the President, is not in accordance with the principle of separation of powers. Nevertheless, it is evidently needful that the power of pardoning should exist in some department of the government, if for no other reason than that, in every system of the administration

[1] Field v. Clark, 143 U. S. 649 (1892). For further discussion of this case, see p. 115.

[2] In some cases, however, the President may exercise the power of making rules and regulations without any clear or specific constitutional or statutory authority, being nevertheless upheld as necessary for the proper conduct of the administration with which the President is entrusted.

[3] United States v. Grimaud, 220 U. S. 506 (1910).

of justice, unavoidable errors and miscarriages of justice may occasionally occur, as, for example, evidence discovered subsequent to a trial may establish the innocence of a convicted man.

Although the President's pardoning power is not exclusive, nevertheless it is evidently the intention of the Constitution that this power should rest mainly and primarily in him.   This idea was doubtless an outgrowth of the fact that in England the pardoning power was a part of the royal prerogative, being derived from the venerable principle that the King was the fountain of justice.   In order, however, that the President may exercise this power, it is necessary that it should be expressly conferred upon him.   Consequently, we find that the Constitution provides that the President "shall have the power to grant reprieves and pardons for offenses against the United States, except in cases of impeachment."[1]

It will be noticed that the Constitution places two limitations upon the President's pardoning power: first, it does not extend to cases of impeachment, so that he could not, through granting a pardon, automatically restore to office a person who had been removed therefrom as a result of impeachment.   As a further result of his conviction on impeachment, such a person might also be disqualified from being reappointed to office by the President.   In the second place, the President can grant pardons only for offenses against the United States and not for offenses against one of the states of the Union.   Aside from these exceptions, the President can grant pardons at any time after the offense has been committed, whether before or after trial or conviction.   The effect of a pardon is to obliterate the offense and, in general, to make the grantee as innocent as if he had never committed it.[2]

In addition to full pardon, the President may also grant pardons subject to any conditions he may see fit to lay down.   He may also exercise other acts of clemency, such as granting a reprieve in capital cases, which operates to postpone the execution of the sentence, and a commutation, which reduces the length or severity of the penalty.   The President may also issue proclamations of amnesty, as was done by Presidents Lincoln and Johnson.

Amnesty differs from pardon in that it applies to whole classes of persons or communities rather than to individuals.   It also differs from pardon in that it is granted regardless of proof of the fact of guilt and relieves the grantees from prosecution for engaging in disturbances or other political offenses which threaten the government.   Congress may also exercise, prior to conviction, the power of passing acts of general

---

[1] Art. II, sect. 2, cl. 1.

[2] Pardon, however, does not restore property or office that may have been forfeited as the result of conviction.   Willoughby on the Constitution, vol. III, p. 1491.

amnesty.[1] Congress cannot limit the exercise by the President of his pardoning power, but it may authorize some officer other than the President, such as the secretary of the treasury, to remit fines, forfeitures, and penalties.[2] Under some circumstances, the courts may order new trials and have also at times exercised the power of suspending sentences.[3]

Acceptance of Pardon.—The question may be raised as to whether a pardon, in order to be valid, must be accepted by the grantee. In an early case, Chief Justice Marshall declared that "a pardon is a deed, to the validity of which delivery is essential, and delivery is not complete without acceptance. It may be rejected by the person to whom it is tendered, and if it be rejected, we have discovered no power in a court to force it on him."[4] This doctrine was reiterated by the Supreme Court as late as 1915, in a case in which a person to whom the pardon was tendered refused to accept it on the ground that to do so would destroy his immunity from self-incrimination. The Court upheld his right to refuse the pardon.[5]

With reference to this matter, however, it would seem that a distinction must be made between pardon and commutation of sentence. A case illustrating this point arose in 1925. The President issued an order unconditionally commuting the sentence of one Gerald Chapman, then serving a term in Federal prison, to the term already served. The purpose of the order was to permit a sentence of death imposed upon Chapman by a state court to be carried out. On behalf of Chapman, it was argued that the President's order constituted a pardon and that the prisoner had a right to refuse to accept it. The lower Federal court admitted that a pardon involves a grant and cannot be imposed against the grantee's will. It held, however, that the President's order was a commutation, which is merely "a cessation of the exercise of sovereign authority and does not obliterate guilt nor restore civil rights, and need not be accepted by the convict to be operative." It further held that such commutation did not deprive the prisoner of any constitutional right, since the right to imprisonment is not protected by the Constitution.[6]

The doctrine of the case just cited has been affirmed by the Supreme Court in a case in which the President, without the consent of the accused person, commuted his sentence from death to life imprisonment. The

---

[1] Such an act, in the form of a grant of immunity from prosecution to witnesses, on account of evidence given by them, has been upheld as constitutional. Brown v. Walker, 161 U. S. 591 (1896).

[2] The Steamboat Laura, 114 U. S. 411 (1884).

[3] It has been held by the Supreme Court, however, that the Federal courts have no inherent power to suspend sentences, but such a power may be conferred upon them by Congress. *Ex parte* United States, 242 U. S. 27 (1916).

[4] United States v. Wilson, 7 Pet. 150 (1833).

[5] Burdick v. United States, 236 U. S. 79 (1915).

[6] Chapman v. Scott, 10 Fed. (2d) 156 (1925).

Court upheld the President's action as a legitimate exercise of his constitutional power on the ground that "by common understanding, imprisonment for life is a less penalty than death." It points out that, supposing the accused "did not accept the change, he could not have got himself hanged against the Executive order." While not overruling Burdick v. United States, the Court limits the doctrine of that case by declaring that

> . . . a pardon in our days is not a private act of grace from an individual happening to possess power. It is a part of the constitutional scheme. When granted, it is the determination of the ultimate authority that the public welfare will be better served by inflicting less than the judgment fixed . . . Just as the original punishment would be imposed without regard to the prisoner's consent and in the teeth of his will, whether he liked it or not, the public welfare, not his consent, determines what shall be done.[1]

Pardon for Contempt.—It was formerly supposed in some quarters that the President could not grant pardons for contempt of court. The reasons for this position were twofold: first, that the exercise of such a power would constitute an executive interference with judicial proceedings and would thus violate the principle of separation of powers. The second reason was that the President's pardoning power extends only to "offenses against the United States" and that this phrase includes only those created by legislative act and triable by jury.

In the Grossman case, however, the Supreme Court in 1925 denied these contentions and upheld the power of the President to grant pardons in cases of criminal contempt.[2] In violation of an injunction issued by the Federal district court under the provisions of the Volstead Act, Grossman had sold liquor on his premises. As a result of this violation, he was found guilty of contempt of court. He was sentenced to pay a fine and to serve a year in prison. The President granted him a pardon which commuted his sentence to the payment of the fine. Upon the refusal of the prison authorities to release him, the case was brought to the Supreme Court on application for a writ of habeas corpus.

In its opinion in the Grossman case, the Supreme Court held that the principle of separation of powers is not an absolute one, numerous exceptions to it being recognized in the Constitution. To grant pardons in cases of fully completed criminal contempt is no more serious an interference with the independence of the courts than to grant pardons for other offenses. In fact, the Court suggested, "may it not be fairly said that, in order to avoid possible mistake, undue prejudice or needless severity, the chance of pardon should exist at least as much in favor of a person convicted by a judge without a jury as in favor of one convicted

---

[1] Biddle v. Perovich, 274 U. S. 480 (1927).
[2] *Ex parte* Grossman, 267 U. S. 87 (1925).

in a jury trial?" Abuses through excessive use of the pardoning power might arise in either case, but the remedy for such abuse would be impeachment.

The Court further held that the phrase "offenses against the United States" in the Constitution was not intended to limit the pardoning power to statutory crimes but merely to distinguish between offenses against the Federal Government and those against the states. Under the common law the King of England could pardon for criminal contempt, and the framers of our Constitution used the term pardon in the common-law sense. The Court, however, drew a sharp distinction between criminal and civil contempt. Such a distinction was recognized at common law and also clearly appears in the United States. The difference between the two kinds of contempt is not the fact of punishment but rather its character and purpose. "For civil contempts, the punishment is remedial and for the benefit of the complainant, and a pardon cannot stop it. For criminal contempts, the sentence is punitive in the public interest to vindicate the authority of the court and to deter other like derelictions." The Court therefore held that the pardoning power of the President, just as in the case of that of the King, does not extend to civil contempt. That it extends to criminal contempt, however, had been recognized in practice for eighty-five years. This power of the President, moreover, extends to all cases of criminal contempt, whether direct or indirect, *i.e.*, whether committed in the presence of the court, and thus interfering with orderly judicial proceedings, or committed outside the court through violation of its order.

The Grossman case did not directly involve the question as to whether the President can pardon for contempt of a legislative body. By analogy, however, it would seem that the President should be held to have the power to pardon for such a contempt. Pardon for legislative contempt is no more a violation of the principle of separation of powers than is pardon for contempt of court.

CHAPTER XIII

ORGANIZATION OF THE FEDERAL JUDICIARY

The settlement of controversies between individuals and the punishment of crimes are among the most important functions of the modern state. For performing these functions, modern states have established specialized agencies known as courts. Courts may be defined as tribunals established by the state for the administration of justice according to law. Although power of a judicial, or at least of a quasi-judicial, nature may be exercised to some extent by the legislative, executive, or administrative organs of the government, judicial powers, properly speaking, are mainly vested in such judicial tribunals or courts as are provided for by the Constitution or statutes. With the growth of population, the increasing complexity of social and economic conditions and the multiplication of laws, the functions of the courts have gained in importance. Although the legislature determines, within certain limits, what the law shall be, the courts decide what it was at the time when the facts of the case or controversy occurred. On account of the imperfection of human language and of the impossibility of foreseeing all future developments, the legislature can rarely draw up a law in such form that its interpretation and application to specific facts and concrete cases give rise to no controversy. The settlement of such questions of interpretation and application is one of the essential functions of the courts.

Judicial Power under the Confederation.—The lack of a separate judicial department was, as we have seen, one of the defects of the government under the Articles of Confederation. Since the Confederate Government acted chiefly upon states rather than upon individuals, it was not deemed necessary to create a system of courts corresponding to that of the states. There were some matters of a judicial character, however, coming within the province of the central Confederate Government which could not suitably be disposed of by the state courts. These were disputes arising between states and cases arising on the high seas. Consequently, the Articles provided that the Confederate Congress should be the last resort on appeal in all disputes and differences arising between two or more states concerning boundary or other matters and that the Congress should have power to establish prize courts and courts for the trial of piracies and felonies committed on the high seas.[1]

---

[1] Art. IX.

Even in connection with this meager extent of judicial power, however, no provision was made for enforcing the decisions of the Confederate courts. Moreover, the lack of any further extent of judicial power on the part of the Confederate Government led to much embarrassment. That Government was dependent upon the state courts to enforce the provisions of treaties entered into by it, but these courts were under no legal obligation to do so and had little desire to do so, especially in cases involving conflicts between treaties and state laws.

The Federal Convention and the National Judiciary.—The lack of a system of central courts, with the embarrassments and inconveniences flowing therefrom, was one of the defects of the Confederation which the Constitutional Convention of 1787 determined to remedy. All of the proposed plans of government submitted to that body provided for a separate system of national courts. Since a separate legislative department was created with power to enact laws applying directly to individuals, it became necessary to establish a national judiciary with power to interpret those laws and to apply them in cases brought by individual litigants.

The new Constitution was to be the supreme law of the land, and the establishment of a system of national courts was necessary in order to bring about uniformity in the interpretation of this law. The lack of national courts would not only produce diversity in interpretation of the Constitution, laws of Congress, and treaties but would endanger and in all probability undermine their supremacy, for their vindication in cases involving conflicts with state law would have to depend on the state courts. National courts were needed both to enforce the constitutional limitations against the states and also to uphold the authority delegated by the Constitution to the new National Government. Moreover, state courts would not be suitable tribunals for deciding cases arising outside the jurisdiction of any state, such as those arising in American vessels on the high seas, nor in cases involving foreign ambassadors, ministers, or consuls sojourning in this country. Finally, state courts might not be impartial tribunals in cases where the parties are citizens of different states, or a state and a citizen of another state, or two states, or the Federal Government and a state or one of its citizens.

Thus, both from the standpoint of maintaining the supremacy of national law and also from that of furnishing impartial tribunals in certain classes of cases, it was deemed necessary to establish a system of national courts. The Convention of 1787, however, was wise enough to provide for this system in general language and not to attempt to crystallize the details of the judicial organization in the Constitution.

Organization of the Federal Courts.—On the important question of the organization of the Federal courts, the Constitution provides quite simply that "the judicial power of the United States shall be vested in

one Supreme Court and in such inferior courts as the Congress may
from time to time ordain and establish."[1]   It is thus within the discretion
of Congress to determine what Federal courts inferior to the Supreme
Court shall be established, and, although the establishment of the
Supreme Court is mandatory, the determination of the number of
judges on that court and the amount of their compensation are matters
which are left to the discretion of Congress.   In the impeachment clause,
however, the Constitution implies that there shall be a chief justice of
the Supreme Court.[2]

Although the Constitution requires the establishment of one supreme
court, this provision is not automatic.   Its operation is dependent not
only upon the action of Congress in stipulating the number and compensation of the judges but also upon the action of the President in nominating,
and that of the Senate in confirming the appointment of, the judges.

By the judiciary act of 1789, Congress provided that the Supreme
Court should be constituted with a bench of a chief justice and five
associate justices.   By various acts passed by Congress since that time,
the number of associate justices has varied from four to nine, while the
present number is eight.   In 1866, during President Johnson's administration, Congress passed an act prohibiting the filling of vacancies
among the associate justices until the number should be reduced to six.
This was evidently intended to curtail the power of the President over
the personnel of the Court.

If Congress should fail to make any provision whatever for the Court,
its nonaction would violate the spirit of the Constitution, but there
would be no legal or judicial means of compelling it to take action.   The
only remedy would be a political one.   The question might be raised as
to whether, in the absence of any act of Congress creating Supreme
Court judgeships, the President could make appointment to fill such
position.   This question has never been raised in a practical form, but
the analogous situation may be noted in which President Washington
nominated and commissioned several consuls prior to any act of Congress
creating the position of consul.

By the judiciary act of 1789, Congress also adopted the suggestion
contained in the Constitution that a system of inferior Federal courts be
created.   This has been called the most noteworthy feature of that act,[3]
because it might have been quite possible to stop with the creation of the
Supreme Court as the only Federal court and to utilize the state courts as
inferior courts with appeals to the Supreme Court in cases involving
Federal questions.   Congress, however, created two sets of inferior
Federal courts—the district courts at the bottom of the Federal judicial

---

[1] Art. III, sect. 1.
[2] Art. I, sect. III, cl. 6.
[3] FRANKFURTER and LANDIS, *The Business of the Supreme Court*, pp. 4–11.

system and the circuit courts occupying a position between the district courts and the Supreme Court. Except for changes in the number of districts and in the number of circuits which were made by Congress from time to time, the system of inferior Federal courts as provided for in 1789 remained unchanged until 1891 when Congress, in order to relieve the Supreme Court of some of the work that was piling up on it, created a system of circuit courts of appeal, one of which was to be established in each of the circuits into which the country was divided. In 1911, the act of Congress providing for the abolition of the circuit courts went into effect, so that at the present time the system of regular Federal courts consists, from top to bottom, of the Supreme Court, the circuit courts of appeals, and the district courts.

Special Federal Courts.—In addition to the regular Federal courts, there have been established from time to time tribunals of specialized jurisdiction. Among these are the court of claims, the courts of customs and of customs appeals, the courts of the District of Columbia, territorial courts, and consular courts.

The courts of the District of Columbia and of the territories are not inferior Federal courts in the strict meaning of the term. They are created by act of Congress, not under its power to establish inferior Federal courts but under its grant of exclusive authority over the District of Columbia and under its power to make all needful rules and regulations for the government of the territories.[1] In this connection should also be mentioned consular courts exercising extraterritorial jurisdiction in certain foreign countries and the United States Court for China, created by act of 1906. These courts have been established by Congress under its power to enact legislation for the enforcement of treaties.

The Court of Claims.—The Government of the United States cannot be sued by an individual without its consent. Persons having claims against the Government may be able to induce Congress to make appropriation to pay for them. This, however, involves the exercise of political influence which may not always be a fair test of the validity of the claim. In 1855, Congress, exercising a power implied from its power to appropriate money to pay claims against the United States, provided for the establishment of the Court of Claims. This tribunal sits at Washington and is composed of a chief justice and four associate justices.

At first this so-called "court" was not really a judicial body but rather a group of commissioners to whom was delegated the function of investigating claims against the Government arising under the Constitution or laws of the United States (except for pensions) or under executive regulations or contracts, and, if the court found the claim to be valid, it was directed to prepare a bill to pay the claim and to submit it for the consideration of Congress. By later legislation, however, the court has been

---

[1] Constitution, Art. I, sect. 8, cl. 17; Art. IV, sect. 3, cl. 2.

given the power to render final judgment, subject to an appeal to the Supreme Court of the United States.   In view, however, of the provision of the Constitution that no money shall be drawn from the treasury of the United States except in consequence of appropriations made by law,[1] the action of Congress is still necessary in order to make available the money required to pay the claim.   In practice, the judgments of the court are usually paid out of a lump-sum appropriation made by Congress and estimated to be sufficient to satisfy all judgments handed down by the court during a given fiscal period.

In this connection it should be noted that the district courts also have jurisdiction over certain claims against the United States.

Other Special Courts.—As implied in its power to regulate commerce, Congress has created a body known at first as the Board of General Appraisers but whose name was changed in 1926 to the United States Customs Court.   By this change of name Congress seems to have indicated its belief that this body is to be regarded as a part of the Federal judicial system.   It consists of a chief justice and eight associate judges. It hears cases arising out of protests by importers against the classification and valuation of merchandise made by customs collectors at ports of entry.   From its decisions appeals may be taken to the Court of Customs Appeals, created by Congress in 1909 and consisting of a presiding judge and four associate judges.   The jurisdiction of the latter court has now been extended to include appeals from the patent office in patent and trade-mark cases and the name of the court has been changed to the United States Court of Customs and Patent Appeals.   Appellate jurisdiction over the decisions of the patent office has been held to be non-judicial in character,[2] but it is not unconstitutional to confer such jurisdiction upon the Court of Customs and Patent Appeals because it is a legislative, and not a constitutional, court.[3]

Powers of a quasi-judicial nature may be exercised by other bodies, such as the United States Board of Tax Appeals, but these are not properly regarded as parts of the Federal judicial system.

The Selection of Judges.—The office of judge of the Supreme Court is created by the Constitution, which provides that such judges shall be appointed by the President, by and with the advice and consent of the Senate.   The judges of the lower Federal courts are also appointed in the same way, although this is not required by the Constitution.   Congress might designate the latter as inferior officers and provide that their appointments might be made by the President alone or by the Supreme Court but has not done so.   No legal qualifications of Federal judges are laid down by the Constitution so that, except for the necessity of

[1] Art. I, sect. 9, cl. 7.
[2] Postum Cereal Co. v. California Fig Nut Co., 272 U. S. 693 (1927).
[3] *Ex parte* Bakelite Corporation, 49 Sup. Ct. 411 (1929).

securing senatorial confirmation of his nominees, the President is untrammeled in his choice. Several Presidents—Washington, Jackson, Lincoln, and Taft—have appointed a controlling number of the judges of the Supreme Court.

Although the Senate usually confirms the President's nomination to positions on the Supreme Court, it nevertheless, as a rule, scrutinizes carefully the personal, legal, and political qualifications of the nominee and sometimes rejects him. A recent instance of this was the rejection of President Hoover's nomination of Judge Parker of North Carolina in 1930, partly because his lower court decisions had rendered him unacceptable to organized labor. The Senate's rejection in this case may have been partly due to its unusual procedure of considering the nomination in open session.

It will be seen that, while the members of Congress are elected directly by the people and the President is virtually chosen in the same manner so that neither the legislative nor executive department is dependent upon the other in the method of its selection, the Federal judiciary is dependent for its selection upon the joint action of the President and the upper branch of Congress. Logically it might seem that, in order to secure independence from the political departments, the judges ought to be elected by the people—a plan which is followed in most of the states. This plan, however, would have seemed much too radical to the framers of the Constitution and was not seriously considered by them.

On the whole, the method of selection provided in the Constitution has worked satisfactorily. As a rule, the justices of the Supreme Court have been men of high character, legal learning, and judicial experience. It must be admitted, however, that other considerations than these have often been taken into account by Presidents and the Senate in making appointments. In general, a fair distribution of appointees among the different sections of the country is attempted but not strictly adhered to. A more important consideration is the political affiliations and the social and governmental views of the appointees. Only rarely does the President appoint to the Supreme Court a man of the opposite political party. Seward declared that the opinions and bias of each of the justices were carefully considered by the President and Senate at the time of appointment. In a letter to Senator H. C. Lodge in 1902 President Roosevelt said: "I should hold myself as guilty of an irreparable wrong to the nation if I should put (on the Supreme Court) any man who was not absolutely sane and sound on the great national policies for which we stand in public life."[1]

The Tenure of Judges.—The desired independence of the Federal judiciary was attempted to be secured by the framers, not through the

---

[1] *Cf.* Mathews and Berdahl, *Documents and Readings in American Government*, pp. 372–374.

method of selection but through security of tenure and compensation. It was provided that "the judges, both of the Supreme and inferior courts, shall hold their offices during good behavior."[1]   No specific provision was made, however, as to the method to be pursued in determining when a judge is guilty of misbehavior nor as to what should be considered as constituting misbehavior.   Since, however, judges are civil officers, they can undoubtedly be removed through the process of impeachment. It is true that the grounds of impeachment, as stated in the Constitution are "treason, bribery, or other high crimes and misdemeanors."   But, as we have seen, this language has been broadly construed, so that it may include "misbehavior."   Several judges of the lower Federal courts have been removed as the result of impeachment, and in 1804 an attempt was made to impeach Justice Chase of the Supreme Court, but the attempt failed.   District Judge Pickering was removed by impeachment in 1803 on the ground of insanity and Judge Archbald of the Commerce Court was impeached in 1913 on grounds of misbehavior not involving indictable offenses.

It has frequently been assumed that the only way of removing Federal judges is by impeachment.   But there is no express provision to this effect in the Constitution.   The question may be raised as to whether Congress might not by law define "good behavior" and provide that a Federal judge may be removable for cause, by the President on the joint address of Congress, after notice and hearing.   Such a provision, which Congress has never attempted to make, would probably not be in accordance with the intentions of the framers of the Constitution.[2]   Several of the early state constitutions provided that judges may be removed upon joint address of the two houses of the legislature, a method copied from England.   Such a plan of removal, however, when proposed in the Federal Convention, was rejected on the ground that it might interfere with the desired independence of the judiciary.   Shortly after the failure of the impeachment proceedings against Justice Chase, John Randolph moved in the House of Representatives that the Constitution be amended so as to make Federal judges removable by the President on the joint address of Congress.   The fact that this proposal was in the form of a constitutional amendment indicated his belief that this could not be provided for by a mere act of Congress.

The Judiciary Act of 1802.—When the Jeffersonian party came into power in 1801, it controlled the executive and legislative branches of the Federal Government but found that the Federalist party was intrenched

---

[1] Art. III, sect. 1, cl. 1.

[2] It is true that by act of Congress it is provided that the judges of the United States Customs Court may be removed by the President for neglect of duty, inefficiency, or malfeasance in office, but this court is created under the power of Congress not to create inferior Federal courts but to regulate commerce.

in the judiciary behind the security of tenure granted by the Constitution to Federal judges. Shortly before the loss of their power over the political departments, the Federalists had secured the passage of an act creating a number of new Federal judgeships which they filled with partisan appointees. In 1802, the Jeffersonians proceeded to repeal this act and not only to abolish the additional Federal judgeships which had just been created but also to legislate out of office the Federalists who had been appointed to fill them. There was no allegation that these judges were guilty of misbehavior. The theory on which this method of removing judges was attempted to be sustained was that there can be no such thing as an officer without an office and that when Congress abolished the judgeship the judge also ceased to exist.

Support for this position was also found in the language of the Constitution with reference to the salaries of judges, which prohibits the diminution thereof "during their continuance in office."[1] This, it was alleged,

> . . . literally excludes the idea of paying a salary when the officer is not in office; and it is undeniably certain that he cannot be in office when there is no office. There must have been some other mode by which the officer should cease to be in office than that of bad behavior, because, if this had not been the case, the Constitution would have directed that the judges should hold their offices *and salaries* during their good behavior, instead of directing that they should hold their salaries during their continuance in office.[2]

In spite of this reasoning most authorities on the Constitution are of the opinion that Congress exceeded its powers in legislating these judges out of office. There was no judicial determination to this effect, because the act was so drawn that the courts had no opportunity of declaring it unconstitutional. At all events, there has been no other instance of an attempt by Congress to exercise this questionable power. On other occasions, as in 1801, 1911, and 1913 certain lower Federal courts have been abolished, but in these cases Congress has provided for the transfer of the judges to other courts. The better view would seem to be that the Constitutional provision that judges shall hold office during good behavior forbids Congress, through the device of abolishing their offices, from removing them from all judicial office in the absence of misbehavior. This limitation does not prevent Congress from making changes in the organization of the lower Federal courts.

Although Congress probably has no valid power to remove from office judges who are guilty of no misbehavior, it may pass laws intended to induce judges to resign when they have reached an age at which they may be assumed to be no longer as efficient as they were when younger.

[1] Art. III, sect. 1.
[2] Quoted by W. S. Carpenter, *Judicial Tenure in the United States*, p. 64.

In the exercise of this power, Congress enacted in 1869 that when judges of the United States courts reach the age of seventy years, after at least ten years of service, they may retire on full pay. In many cases, however, the prospect of retirement on full pay does not seem to have been sufficiently attractive to induce judges who have reached that age to resign.

Compensation of Judges.—The desire of the framers of the Constitution to secure independence of the judiciary extended not only to the matter of tenure of office but also to that of compensation. They consequently provided that the "judges, both of the supreme and inferior courts . . . shall, at stated times receive for their services a compensation, which shall not be diminished during their continuance in office."[1] Congress is thus restrained from attempting to punish or intimidate the judges by reducing, or threatening to reduce, their salaries. In the Convention, Madison expressed the view that, in order still further to insure the independence of the judiciary, Congress should not be allowed to increase their salaries during their terms of office, but this provision, while adopted in the case of the President, was not applied to the judges. This decision seems wise because judges ordinarily serve for much longer periods than the President does, and consequently greater need for increasing their salaries may arise. In practice, the existence of the power in Congress to increase judicial salaries has not led to any loss of judicial independence.

In 1920, the question came before the Supreme Court as to whether the salaries of Federal judges were subject to taxation under the general Federal income tax law, and it was held that they were not so subject, because protected by the constitutional provision against diminution of salaries during continuance in office.[2] Although based to some extent upon precedent, this decision seems to be erroneous. An income tax law which laid a special or discriminatory tax upon the salaries of Federal judges would undoubtedly be unconstitutional, but to say that the Constitution prevents Congress from requiring Federal judges to bear their share of the general burden of income taxation seems to be a very strained construction. As Justice Holmes pointed out in his dissenting opinion, there is no sound reason why a Federal judge should be exempted "from the ordinary duties of a citizen, which he shares with all others."

A few years later, the Court went further and held that the exemption from Federal income taxation extends to the salaries even of those Federal judges who assumed office after the enactment of the tax law.[3] This decision has at least the advantage of putting all the Federal judges upon a parity in the matter.

[1] Art. III, sect. 1.
[2] Evans v. Gore, 253 U. S. 245 (1920).
[3] Miles v. Graham, 268 U. S. 501 (1924).

Tenure and Compensation of Special Court Judges.—There are certain courts which, although created by act of Congress, are not Federal courts in the strict sense of the word. Therefore, the Constitutional provisions regarding tenure of office and diminution of compensation of Federal judges do not apply to the judges of such courts. This distinction was brought out by Chief Justice Marshall in an early case in which he said:

The jurisdiction with which they [the territorial courts] are invested, is not a part of that judicial power which is defined in the third Article of the Constitution, but is conferred by Congress in the exercise of those general powers which that body possesses over the territories of the United States.

The judges of the territorial courts do not, as a rule, hold office during good behavior but may be appointed for a short term of years. In certain cases the act of Congress establishing certain territorial courts, such as the supreme courts of Porto Rico and of the Philippines, confers upon the judges tenure during good behavior, but this is not required by the Constitution.

Procedure in the Supreme Court.—Each member of the Supreme Court is assigned to one (or more) of the judicial circuits into which the country is divided and formerly he "rode the circuit" and helped the circuit court judges to hear cases. This was objectionable, however, both because of the burden of traveling it placed upon the Supreme Court judges and also because a case heard by them in the circuit court might subsequently come before them in the Supreme Court. For a long time the work of the latter tribunal has been so heavy that its judges no longer travel on circuit but give their whole time to hearing and deciding cases brought before the Supreme Court. The sessions of this Court are held annually, beginning in October and lasting until about the first of June.

By Congressional act of 1922, the chief justice of the Supreme Court was made presiding officer over the Federal judicial council, composed of senior circuit judges, and this position makes him, in a sense, the directing head of the Federal judicial system. He also, of course, presides at sessions of the Supreme Court, but he has only one vote in that body and legally no more control over its decisions than any one of the associate justices. Some chief justices, however, notably John Marshall, have dominated the Court through the strength of their personality and ability. Six of the nine justices constitute a quorum for the hearing of arguments in a case, and five, or a bare majority, must concur in order that the Court shall reach a decision. The chief justice usually either prepares the opinion of the Court himself or directs one of the associate justices to do so. If a majority of the justices are unable to agree upon a decision after the first hearing of the case, a rehearing may be ordered.

The decisions of the Court are collected and regularly published in a series of volumes. They form the most authoritative source of the constitutional law of the United States. The report of any particular case usually consists of three parts: the facts, the opinion, and the decision. The decision is the judgment or order of the Court touching the parties to the particular case. The opinion consists of the line of legal reasoning whereby the Court reaches the decision.[1] Although it is necessary that a majority of the members should concur in order to reach a decision, it is not absolutely necessary that a majority should concur in the opinion. Justices who dissent from both the decision and the opinion, as well as those who dissent merely from the opinion, may file their dissenting or "concurring" opinions, as the case may be, and these are published in the official reports along with the opinion of the Court.[2] In some relatively unimportant cases, the decision of the Court is not accompanied by an opinion.

In accordance with the principle of *stare decisis*, the Court usually follows its previous decisions in later cases involving substantially similar circumstances. This principle, however, is not inexorable, and there are a number of Supreme Court decisions by which earlier decisions are overruled.[3] There are a still larger number of cases in which the Supreme Court has modified, evaded, or whittled down the doctrine of earlier cases without ostensibly overruling them. The reason for the principle of *stare decisis* is that the law should be as far as possible certain and stable, and it should therefore be followed in most cases. Departures from it tend to unsettle the law, and this is considered by the courts especially undesirable in cases affecting property rights. In other cases, however, it may be clear that greater harm would result from standing by a previous decision than from overruling it. Departures from the principle of *stare decisis* are more justifiable in the case of a high court passing on constitutional questions than they would be in the case of a lower court passing on questions of private law. In the latter case, mistakes may be corrected either by the higher court or by legislation, while in the former there is no method of correction available except through the overruling of mistaken decisions.[4]

[1] Sometimes the opinion also contains incidental remarks not an essential part of the line of legal reasoning. These remarks are called *obiter dicta*.

[2] Justice Holmes is noted for the number and ability of his dissenting opinions. In some instances they have foreshadowed positions later taken by the Court.

[3] Among these are Legal Tender cases, 12 Wall. 457, overruling Hepburn v. Griswold, 8 Wall. 603; Leisy v. Hardin, 135 U. S. 100, overruling Pierce v. New Hampshire, 5 How. 504; and Pollock v. Farmers' Loan and Trust Co., 158 U. S. 601, overruling Hylton v. United States, 3 Dall. 171.

[4] Except, of course, further, that decisions may be overruled by amending the Constitution. Thus, the case of Pollock v. Farmers' Loan and Trust Co., which overruled an earlier case, was itself overruled by the Sixteenth Amendment.

CHAPTER XIV

JURISDICTION OF THE FEDERAL COURTS

Jurisdiction in General.—The powers of courts in general may be classified into jurisdictional and inherent. The former is the power to hear and decide particular kinds of cases. Inherent powers, such as the power to punish for contempt, may be exercised without being expressly granted. Courts cannot exercise jurisdiction, however, unless it is specifically conferred upon them by constitution or statute.[1] Jurisdiction may be of various kinds, such as original, appellate, final, concurrent, and exclusive—terms which are largely self-explanatory.

The jurisdiction of the Federal courts in general or, in other words, the extent of the judicial power of the United States is sketched in main outline in Art. III, sect. 2 of the Constitution. The cases coming before the Federal courts may be classified according to (1) the subject matter, without regard to the parties, and (2) the parties, without regard to the subject matter. The first class includes all cases in law and equity arising under the Constitution, laws, and treaties of the United States. It also includes cases of admiralty and maritime jurisdiction, *i.e.*, cases arising on the high seas and on the navigable waters of the United States.

The second class of cases coming before the Federal courts includes (*a*) those affecting ambassadors, other public ministers, and consuls; (*b*) those to which the United States is a party; (*c*) those between two or more states; (*d*) those between citizens of different states; and (*e*) those between a state and citizens of another state or of a foreign country, except that, under the Eleventh Amendment, an alien or a citizen of one of the states of the Union cannot bring suit against another state. Another kind of case coming before the Federal courts which falls under both of the above classes is that between citizens of the same state claiming lands under grants from different states, but this kind of case is now of little importance.

The above-mentioned are the only classes of cases that may be brought in the Federal courts. All other kinds of cases are tried in the state courts. The Federal courts do not necessarily have exclusive jurisdiction of the kinds of cases mentioned above. Some such cases of lesser importance may be tried in the state courts. Thus, by act of Congress it is provided that suits between citizens of different states may be brought

---

[1] Except that a court has jurisdiction over any case to the extent necessary to determine whether or not it has jurisdiction.

in the Federal Courts only when the sum of $3,000 or more is involved. If less than this amount is involved, such suits are heard in the state courts. In some sorts of cases, however, such as prize cases, bankruptcy cases, and suits against ambassadors or consuls,[1] the Federal courts have exclusive jurisdiction.

Jurisdiction of the Supreme Court.—The Supreme Court, as the name implies, is the court of final resort in all cases over which it has jurisdiction. In other words, under the Constitution, cases cannot be appealed from the Supreme Court to any higher tribunal. If, therefore, a case once decided in the Supreme Court should subsequently be brought before the Permanent Court of International Justice or an international prize court (if one should be established), it would have to be considered not by way of appeal from the United States Supreme Court but as a case *de novo*.

For practical purposes, the jurisdiction of the Supreme Court may be classified into original and appellate. Its original jurisdiction is defined in the Constitution as extending to "all cases affecting ambassadors, other public ministers and consuls, and those in which a state shall be a party."[2] By the judiciary act of 1789 Congress attempted to give the Supreme Court original jurisdiction also in mandamus cases, but the Court held this provision unconstitutional, declaring that Congress could not extend its original jurisdiction beyond those cases expressly mentioned in the Constitution.[3]

Appellate Jurisdiction of the Supreme Court.—In all other cases to which the Federal judicial power extends, the Supreme Court "shall have appellate jurisdiction, both as to law and fact, with such exceptions and under such regulations as the Congress shall make."[4] The operation of this provision is limited by the Seventh Amendment which provides that "no fact tried by a jury shall be otherwise reexamined in any court of the United States, than according to the rules of the common law." On this account, jury cases in the Supreme Court are rare. That Court may reverse the decision of a lower court for legal error and remand the case for a new trial but cannot review findings of fact by a jury in the lower court.[5] Although Congress can neither restrict nor enlarge the original jurisdiction of the Supreme Court, it has power, subject to the above limitations, to regulate its appellate jurisdiction. It may

---

[1] Except in divorce actions.   Ohio *ex rel.* Popovici v. Agler, 280 U. S. 379 (1930).

[2] Art. III, sect. 2.   The original jurisdiction of the Supreme Court is not necessarily exclusive, for Congress may authorize lower Federal courts also to take jurisdiction of cases to which a state is a party.   United States v. Louisiana, 123 U. S. 32 (1887).

[3] Marbury v. Madison, 1 Cranch 137 (1803).

[4] Art. III, sect. 2.

[5] Capital Traction Co. v. Hof, 174 U. S. 1 (1899).

even do so in such a way as to deprive it of jurisdiction over a case already pending before it.[1]

The appellate jurisdiction of the Supreme Court is of two kinds: first, cases appealed from the lower Federal courts and, second, cases appealed from the state courts. Congress has enacted a judicial code regulating specifically the kinds of cases that may be appealed from the various lower Federal courts. Its provisions are of interest to the practicing lawyer but need not be described in detail here. In general, it may be said that the Federal district court is the court of general original jurisdiction in both civil and criminal cases and in both law and equity.[2] Some cases decided in the district courts may be carried directly to the Supreme Court for final decision. Other cases go to the Circuit Court of Appeals, where they are either decided finally or may be carried further to the Supreme Court. The Circuit Court of Appeals is given some final jurisdiction in order to relieve the Supreme Court of the burden of deciding cases of lesser importance. But more important cases, especially those involving constitutional questions, may be carried up to the Supreme Court for final determination. The Circuit Court of Appeals has no original jurisdiction.

It thus appears that the Supreme Court may entertain appeals in certain cases from the district courts and from the Circuit Courts of Appeals. Other courts from which cases may be appealed to the Supreme Court are the Court of Claims, the Court of Customs and Patent Appeals, the Court of Appeals of the District of Columbia, and the Supreme Court of the Philippine Islands. Cases decided in the supreme courts of other territories and dependencies may be carried to some designated Circuit Court of Appeals.

Methods of Taking Appeals.—When a case, after being decided in a lower court, is taken to a higher court for further consideration and determination, the process is ordinarily spoken of as an appeal. The word "appeal" may thus be used as a general term covering all methods of taking cases from lower to higher courts, but it may also be used in a more specialized and technical sense as applying to only one of these methods, *viz.*, where the case is an equity or an admiralty suit, and the party losing the suit in the lower court endeavors to have the judgment or decree reversed or modified by the higher court. In a law case, on the other hand, the usual method of securing a ruling by the higher court upon an alleged mistaken decision of a lower court is through a writ of error directed by the higher court to the lower.

---

[1] *Ex parte* McCardle, 7 Wall. 506 (1868), a case involving a reconstruction act passed by Congress shortly after the Civil War.

[2] The district courts have a limited appellate jurisdiction from the orders and judgments of United States Commissioners in cases involving the Chinese Exclusion laws.

The above methods of taking cases up for review—by appeal or writ of error—are within the control of litigants.   The exercise of this control by litigants may unduly clog the dockets of higher courts with cases of no great public importance.   Consequently, there has been a tendency recently for Congress to provide for the taking of cases to the Supreme Court for review by other methods, *viz.*, by certificate and by writ of *certiorari*, which leave the process under the control of the court rather than under that of the litigant.   Thus, by act of 1925, Congress provided that, in taking cases from the Circuit Court of Appeals to the Supreme Court, the process, for the most part, should be by certificate or by writ of *certiorari* rather than by appeal or writ of error.[1]   The Circuit Court of Appeals may by certificate request the opinion of the Supreme Court on some point or points of law involved in a case before the lower court, while by writ of *certiorari* the Supreme Court may, in its discretion, bring before it for review decisions of the lower court.

The *right* of a litigant to carry his case to the Supreme Court by appeal or writ of error has been so limited by successive enactments that today at least one-half of the cases which are argued before the Supreme Court reach that court only because it has in its discretion granted a petition for *certiorari* filed by the aggrieved party in the court below.[2]

Appellate Jurisdiction over State Courts.—Cases may be carried to the Supreme Court of the United States not only from the lower Federal courts but also, under certain circumstances, from the state courts.   This is true when there is a "Federal question" involved, *i.e.*, a question the decision of which depends on the interpretation of the Constitution, laws, or treaties of the United States.   In view of the fact that the Constitution, laws, and treaties of the United States are declared by the Constitution to be the "supreme law of the land," it was not deemed feasible to allow the state courts final jurisdiction in cases involving their interpretation.   Hence, in the Judiciary Act of 1789, Congress provided that

. . . a final judgment or decree in any suit, in the highest court of law or equity of a state in which a decision of the suit could be had, where is drawn in question the validity of a treaty or statute of, or an authority exercised under the United States, and the decision is against their validity, or where is drawn in question the validity of a statute of, or an authority exercised under any state, on the ground of their being repugnant to the Constitution, treaties or laws of the United States, and the decision is in favor of their validity . . . may

---

[1] 43 Stat. at L. 936.   An act of 1928 abolishes writs of error and provides that all relief formerly obtainable by writs of error may now be obtained by appeal.

[2] PEACOCK, J. C., "Purpose of Certiorari in Supreme Court Practice," *Amer. Bar Assoc. Jour.*, vol. 15, p. 681 (November, 1929).

be reexamined and reversed or affirmed in the Supreme Court of the United States.[1]

The significance of this provision as a means of upholding national supremacy was quickly perceived by the advocates of states' rights, who attacked both its constitutionality and its expediency. In several important cases, however, its constitutionality was upheld by the Supreme Court of the United States.[2] That tribunal, through the jurisdiction conferred upon it by the section of the Judiciary Act just quoted, is able to assume the rôle of final arbiter of questions as to the boundary between Federal and state power.

The judges of the state courts are bound by the provisions of the Federal Constitution, as well as of Federal laws and treaties in conformity therewith. Formerly, if a state supreme court decided in favor of the validity of a statute or treaty of the United States or against the validity of a state statute on account of its repugnancy to the Constitution, laws, or treaties of the United States, its decision was final. In other words, when the Federal right set up was not denied by the state court, there was deemed to be no need for an appeal to the Federal Supreme Court. It was found, however, that some of the more reactionary state courts were prone to hold progressive state laws invalid because of conflict with Federal limitations, which they construed more strictly than did the Federal Supreme Court. A need was felt for extending the protecting arm of the latter Court to rescue such laws from the effect of the unduly strict attitude of the state courts. Consequently, by amendments to the Federal judicial code, adopted in 1914 and 1916, Congress provided that, even when the decision of the state court does not deny the Federal right set up, the determination of the state court may be reviewed by the Federal Supreme Court.[3] Such review by the Federal Supreme Court, however, may be had only by certificate or by writ of *certiorari* and is thus not within the control of the aggrieved litigant but within the discretion of the higher court. Through these amendments to the Federal judicial code, greater uniformity can be secured in the interpretation of Federal constitutional limitations.

Removal of Cases from State Courts.—In certain classes of cases the Federal and state courts have concurrent jurisdiction; *i.e.*, the case may be brought in the first instance in either a state or a Federal court at the

---

[1] Sect. 25. Although Congress could probably provide for the taking of cases under these circumstances from the state court to a lower Federal court, it has not done so, doubtless out of deference to the sensibilities of the advocates of states' rights. It will be noticed that cases where a Federal question is involved may be carried to the Federal Supreme Court not only from the state supreme court but from any state court that is the highest state court having jurisdiction of the case.

[2] Martin v. Hunter's Lessee, 1 Wheat. 304 (1816); Cohens v. Virginia, 6 Wheat. 264 (1821).

[3] 38 Stat. at L. 790; 39 Stat. at L. 726.

option of the plaintiff.   These are cases in law or equity arising under the Constitution, laws, or treaties of the United States and cases of diverse citizenship, *i.e.*, cases where the parties are domiciled in different states.   When the plaintiff has a choice of courts, he usually brings the case in the court in which he thinks he has the better chance of securing a favorable decision.   If, however, in either of the two classes of cases mentioned above, over which both state courts and Federal district courts have jurisdiction, a litigant should bring his case in the state court, it may subsequently be removed into the Federal district court.   The removal would have to take place prior to final judgment by the state court.   The removal would usually, but not invariably, be made at the request of the party made defendant in the state court.   Removal is a kind of jurisdiction sometimes considered as appellate,[1] and sometimes as an indirect method of exercising original jurisdiction.[2]

The right of removal from state to Federal courts is exercisable only in accordance with the provisions of the Federal judicial code.   It may be exercised not only in civil suits but also in criminal prosecutions.   As a rule, the purpose of allowing removal in civil suits is to assure to the defendant a tribunal which is likely to be more impartial than the state court.   In criminal prosecutions, the purpose of allowing removal may be to maintain the supremacy of Federal law.   This would be true where a person prosecuted in the state courts for violation of state law claimed that his act was justified by Federal law or by authority granted to him by some Federal department or officer.   In the case of a Federal revenue or prohibition officer, the Federal judicial code provides that upon arrest and even before indictment for an act in violation of state law which he claims to have committed in pursuance of Federal authority, the case may be removed to the Federal court.   For example, one Davis, a Federal revenue officer was arrested in Tennessee by state officers on the charge of killing a man.   When brought to trial, his defense was that the killing occurred in pursuance of his duties as a collector of Federal revenue, and he petitioned to have the case removed from the state court to the Federal court.[3]

The question at issue in the Davis case was finally passed upon by the Supreme Court of the United States, which admitted that the act of which Davis was accused was a crime against state and not Federal law but nevertheless upheld the right of removal to the Federal court.   Its reasoning was that the General Government

. . . can only act through its officers and agents, and they must act within the states.   If, when thus acting and within the scope of their authority, those officers can be arrested and brought to trial in a state court for an alleged offense

---

[1] Martin v. Hunter's Lessee, 1 Wheat. 304 (1816).
[2] Railway Co. v. Whitton, 13 Wall. 270 (1871).
[3] Tennessee v. Davis, 100 U. S. 257 (1880).

against the law of the state, yet warranted by the Federal authority they possess, and if the General Government is powerless to interfere at once for their protection—if their protection must be left to the action of the state courts—the operations of the General Government may at any time be arrested at the will of one of its members . . . And even if, after trial and final judgment in the state court, the case can be brought into the United States court for review, the officer is withdrawn from the discharge of his duty during the pendency of the prosecution, and the exercise of acknowledged Federal authority arrested . . . The constitutional right of Congress to authorize the removal before trial of civil cases has long since passed beyond doubt . . . The same power may order the removal of a criminal prosecution . . . Such a jurisdiction is necessary for the preservation of the acknowledged powers of the government. It is essential also to a uniform and consistent administration of national laws.[1]

It will thus be perceived that the rather technical right of removal of cases from state to Federal courts, although sometimes granted in order to provide an impartial tribunal for the hearing of suits, especially between citizens of different states, is in other instances closely bound up with the important matter of the maintenance of the supremacy of Federal authority within its sphere. Some states have attempted to place restrictions upon the right of foreign corporations to remove cases from state to Federal courts. In most instances such attempts have been held invalid. Thus, the Federal Supreme Court held unconstitutional a state law which provided that when a foreign corporation should remove a suit into the Federal court, its license to do business within the state should be revoked.[2] In its opinion, the Court said:

A state may not, in imposing conditions upon the privilege of a foreign corporation's doing business in the state, exact from it a waiver of the exercise of its constitutional right to resort to the Federal courts, or thereafter withdraw the privilege of doing business because of its exercise of such right, whether waived in advance or not. The principle does not depend upon the character of the business the corporation does, whether state or interstate . . . It rests on the ground that the Federal Constitution confers upon citizens of one state the right to resort to Federal courts in another, that state action, whether legislative or executive, necessarily calculated to curtail the free exercise of the right thus secured is void because the sovereign power of a state in excluding foreign corporations, as in the exercise of all others of its sovereign powers, is subject to the limitations of the supreme fundamental law.[3]

Federal Jurisdiction by Habeas Corpus.—In cases of special urgency a prisoner held in the custody of state authorities for an act committed in the course of duties vested in him by Federal authority may be released through the issuance of the writ of habeas corpus by the Federal courts.

---

[1] *Ibid.*
[2] Terral v. Burke Construction Co., 257 U. S. 529 (1921). This case overruled two earlier cases in which the majority of the court took a different view.
[3] *Ibid.*

Authority to issue the writ under such circumstances was granted by act of Congress passed in 1833 and growing out of the nullification laws passed in South Carolina and the interference in that state with Federal revenue officers.

In 1842, the power of Federal judges to issue the writ to release prisoners in state custody was extended as the result of a celebrated case, in which one McLeod, held by the New York state authorities on the charge of murder, claimed that he was a British subject and that the act for which they had arrested him was committed under the authority of his government, that it was a matter for adjustment by international negotiation, and that the New York state court had no right to try him. McLeod was one of a force of British soldiers who, during the Canadian rebellion of 1837, made an attack upon the *Caroline,* a vessel in New York waters. The British Government communicated with the Federal Government at Washington, assuming responsibility for McLeod's act and demanding his release. The Federal executive authorities attempted to secure his release from the New York authorities but failed. The Federal courts found themselves unable to intervene on his behalf on account of lack of jurisdiction to issue the writ of habeas corpus in such cases. Fortunately, McLeod was acquitted in the New York court, and threatened international complications were thus avoided. Nevertheless, in order to meet a similar situation in the future, Congress in 1842 extended the power of Federal judges to issue the writ to cases where the prisoner claims that the act for which the state authorities are holding him in custody was done under the sanction of some foreign government and where the validity and effect of his plea depend upon international law.

In the Neagle case occurred a rather extreme example of the exercise by Federal courts of the power of issuing writs of habeas corpus to release prisoners from state custody. Neagle, a United States deputy marshal, was charged with murder but claimed justification on the ground that he was acting under the orders of the President in protecting the life of a Federal judge. The President was admittedly acting here not under any Federal statute but merely under his general constitutional power of seeing that the laws of the Union are faithfully executed. Nevertheless Neagle was released from state custody by writ of habeas corpus issued by the Federal court.[1]

A broad ground provided by statute for issuance of the writ is when the prisoner is in custody in violation of the Constitution or of a law or treaty of the United States.[2] Although the Federal courts have the

---

[1] *In re* Neagle, 135 U. S. 1 (1890).

[2] In this connection, it should be noted that the converse of the proposition here stated is not true, that is to say, state courts do not have the power, by issuing a writ of habeas corpus, to release a prisoner who is in the custody of Federal authorities.

power to issue the writ under the various circumstances mentioned, the question as to whether, in a given case, they will do so is a matter to be decided within their discretion. As a rule they will not do so except in cases of special urgency. If the writ is not issued, the person in the custody of state authorities still has his remedy of appealing the case from decision of the highest state court to the Supreme Court of the United States.

Cases in Law and Equity.—As pointed out above, the Federal judicial power is declared by the Constitution to extend to "all cases in law and equity" arising under the Constitution, laws, and treaties of the United States.[1] It thus appears that the Federal courts are to be considered as equity courts as well as law courts. The distinction between law and equity is one which arose historically through the development in England of a separate system of courts and of jurisprudence established for the purpose of dispensing justice to litigants who were unable to secure it in the common-law courts, which were bound by precedents and rigid rules. Equity undertakes not only to provide more adequate remedies in certain cases than can be secured under the common law but also to enforce new rights not protected by the common law. Thus, for injuries to person or property, the only remedy at common law is a suit for damages. In cases, however, where the injury is likely to be irreparable and, consequently, the recovery of damages is not an adequate remedy, an equity court may issue a writ of injunction forbidding the commission of the injury by any person threatening to do so.

The rules of equity jurisprudence have now become almost as rigid as those of the common law. Formerly, in England and in some of the states of the American Union, separate law and equity courts existed. This plan, due mainly to historical causes, does not rest upon any logical basis and has been generally abandoned, so that both legal and equitable remedies may be administered by the same tribunal. This has always been true in the case of the Federal courts.

Injunctions and Contempt of Court.—An injunction is a restraining order issued by a court forbidding the commission of an act causing injury to another person by violating his personal or property rights. It may be a temporary order, in which case it is known as an interlocutory injunction, or it may be made permanent. Violation of an injunction constitutes contempt of court and subjects the guilty person to summary punishment by the court itself without trial by jury. It has been held that

The power to punish for contempts is inherent in all courts; its existence is essential to the preservation of order in judicial proceedings, and to the enforcement of the judgments, orders and writs of the courts, and consequently to the

[1] Art. III, sect. 2, cl. 1.

due administration of justice. The moment the courts of the United States were called into existence and invested with jurisdiction over any subject, they became possessed with this power.[1]

Contempt of court may be either direct or indirect. Direct contempt consists of acts of disrespect or disorder in the presence of the court, while indirect contempt consists in violating the orders of the court elsewhere. Contempt of court may also be either civil or criminal. Civil contempt is committed through an act of disrespect or disobedience to the court without, however, violating any criminal statute, while criminal contempt is committed through the violation of both a criminal statute and also an order of the court.

The injunction has frequently been used in cases affecting labor and in industrial disturbances due to strikes. Thus, during the Chicago railroad strike of 1894, the United States Government, finding that interstate commerce and the carriage of the mails were forcibly obstructed by the strikers, applied to the Federal circuit court for an injunction to restrain such obstruction. The injunction having been issued and one Eugene Debs, a leader of the strikers, having been arrested and sentenced to imprisonment for contempt because of violation of it, he petitioned the Supreme Court of the United States for a writ of habeas corpus to secure his release, alleging lack of constitutional authority in the circuit court to issue the injunction. The Supreme Court, however, declined to grant the petition, holding that the Federal courts had implied authority, aside from any statute especially granting it, to assist in preventing interference with the exercise by the Federal Government of its interstate commerce and postal powers. The fact that the acts enjoined might be prohibited by criminal statute did not dispossess the courts of their power summarily to punish such acts as contempt of court without trial by jury.[2]

The Debs case and similar decisions in later cases aroused the opposition of organized labor against this use of the injunction in industrial disputes, which was denounced as "government by injunction." The injunction for violation of which Debs was punished did not name Debs specifically but, like many other injunctions, was of the blanket variety, running against any person who might commit the forbidden acts. Since these acts were also forbidden by criminal statutes, the practice of the courts in punishing summarily for indirect criminal contempt enabled them to do away with indictment and trial by jury in cases to which they would otherwise apply.[3]

In deference to this opposition, Congress, in passing the Clayton Anti-Trust Act of 1914, inserted certain provisions intended to restrain

[1] *Ex parte* Robinson, 19 Wall. 505 (1873).
[2] *In re* Debs, 158 U. S. 564 (1895).
[3] *Cf.* McBain, H. L., *The Living Constitution*, pp. 264–271.

to some extent the use of the injunction in cases affecting labor and requiring trial by jury, upon demand of the accused, in cases of indirect criminal contempt.[1] The validity of this section of the Clayton Act was attacked in the Supreme Court of the United States. That tribunal held that the jury provision of the act is mandatory, but that, reasonably construed, the statute relates exclusively to criminal contempts and does not interfere with the power to deal summarily with contempts committed within the presence of the court. In conclusion, the Supreme Court held that giving a right to trial by jury in cases of proceedings for contempt in violation of injunctions by acts which are also criminal is not unconstitutional as interfering with the inherent power of courts to punish for contempt.[2]

The Clayton Act has not been so interpreted as to prevent the issuance of injunctions of very far-reaching character, as, for example, the injunction issued in 1922 by the Federal district court for the northern district of Illinois and known as the Daugherty injunction.[3]

The provision of the Clayton Act allowing trial by jury in certain contempt cases does not apply to violation of any order issued by the court in any "suit or action brought or prosecuted in the name of, or on behalf of, the United States." Its operation is confined to orders issued by the courts in suits instituted by private individuals or corporations.

It should also be noted that the provision of the Clayton Act limiting the power of the courts to punish summarily in cases of indirect criminal contempt applies only to violation of orders issued by the district courts of the United States or by any court of the District of Columbia. Since these inferior courts are created by Congress, they are peculiarly subject to its control. Whether Congress could similarly limit the power of the Supreme Court, deriving its existence and powers from the Constitution, is doubtful.[4]

In addition to the use of the injunction above described, it should also be noted that an injunction may sometimes be issued by a Federal court addressed to a state court. This may be done to prevent interference by the state court with the jurisdictional rights of the Federal court.[5] Under certain circumstances, Federal courts may also issue injunctions to restrain state officers from enforcing state acts alleged to be in conflict with the Constitution of the United States.[6]

Admiralty and Maritime Jurisdiction.—The judicial power of the United States is declared by the Constitution to extend to "all cases of

[1] 38 U. S. Stat. at L. 738–740, reprinted in Mathews and Berdahl, *Documents and Readings in American Government*, pp. 377–378.

[2] Michaelson v. United States, 266 U. S. 42 (1924).

[3] Text in MATHEWS and BERDAHL, *op. cit.*, pp. 379–384.

[4] *Cf. Ex parte* Robinson, cited *supra*.

[5] French v. Hay, 22 Wall. 250 (1875).

[6] Federal Judicial Code, sect. 266.

admiralty and maritime jurisdiction." This is a phase of jurisdiction not included under either common law or equity. The Constitution does not undertake to define the words "admiralty and maritime," and, under these circumstances, the usual rule is that such terms are to be taken in the sense in which they were generally used at the time of the adoption of the Constitution. Such jurisdiction had been exercised in England by the Courts of the Admiral of the British Navy. Between the issuance of the Declaration of Independence and the adoption of the Constitution of the United States, admiralty courts also existed in various states of the Union. The Confederate Congress also established a court of appeal in prize cases, which entertained appeals from the admiralty courts of the states. Upon the adoption of the Constitution, state admiralty courts went out of existence and thereafter the Federal courts exercised exclusive jurisdiction in admiralty and maritime cases. No special Federal admiralty courts were created, however, jurisdiction in such cases being exercised by the Federal district courts. Appeals in prize cases may be taken directly from the district courts to the Supreme Court. In other cases appeals may be taken to the Circuit Court of Appeals.

The principal subjects of admiralty jurisdiction have thus been stated by the Supreme Court:

(1) Contracts, claims, or service, purely maritime and touching rights and duties appertaining to commerce and navigation, are cognizable in admiralty. (2) Torts or injuries committed on navigable waters, of a civil nature, are also cognizable in the admiralty courts. Jurisdiction in the former case depends upon the nature of the contract, but in the latter depends entirely upon locality.[1]

The Constitution does not expressly confer upon Congress power to determine the substantive law which is administered by the courts in admiralty cases. It has been held, however, that "As the Constitution extends the judicial power of the United States to 'all cases of admiralty and maritime jurisdiction,' and as this jurisdiction is held to be exclusive, the power of legislation on the same subject must necessarily be in the national legislature."[2]   In other words, the power of Congress to legislate on this subject may be considered as derived by implication from the judiciary article, and not from the grant of power to regulate commerce. In the absence of acts of Congress upon the subject, the courts will enforce the general rules of admiralty which have been developed among civilized nations. The states of the Union also have a limited power to enact legislation upon the subject but, curiously enough, such state laws are enforcible not in the state courts but in the Federal courts. The limits within which such state laws may be enacted are not very well defined, but, as a rough general rule, it may be said that such laws are

[1] The Belfast, 7 Wall. 624 (1868).
[2] Quoted *in re* Garnett, 141 U. S. 1 (1891), from an earlier case.

valid if not conflicting with acts of Congress, if applying to matters which are local in character, and if not changing the general maritime law nor interfering with the "proper harmony or uniformity of that law in its international or interstate regulations."[1]

It thus appears that Congress has paramount authority to enact laws on this subject, within the limits of admiralty and maritime jurisdiction as granted in the Constitution. The Federal courts, however, have final authority to determine what these limits are.[2]

The views of the courts as to the spatial extent of admiralty and maritime jurisdiction has gone through an interesting development. Originally, in England, this jurisdiction extended only to cases arising on the high seas or on rivers as far as the ebb and flow of the tide extended. In the United States, the Federal courts at first adopted the same rule in testing the locality of admiralty jurisdiction.[3] In England, however, tide water and navigable water are substantially identical, but this is not true in the United States. By the middle of the nineteenth century, commerce on the Great Lakes, on which there is no ebb and flow of the tide, had become important. The same was true of the principal rivers. Consequently, the Supreme Court overruled the earlier cases and adopted actual navigability as the test of admiralty jurisdiction.[4]

Both by act of Congress and by decision of the courts, the admiralty jurisdiction has been held to extend over the navigable waters of the United States, *i.e.*, over the public waters, lakes, and rivers of the United States which are navigable in fact. The navigable waters of the United States, as distinguished from the navigable waters of the states, have been defined as those which "form in their ordinary condition by themselves, or by uniting with other waters, a continued highway over which commerce is or may be carried on with other states or foreign countries in the customary modes in which such commerce is conducted by water."[5] Such waters may be wholly within the boundaries of a particular state, provided they constitute connecting links or means of passage for interstate or international commerce. In the case just cited, for example, the Grand River, a stream wholly within the State of Michigan and

[1] Grant-Smith-Porter Ship Co. v. Rohde, 257 U. S. 469 (1922). It will be noticed that the line of division here drawn between Congressional and state powers is not unlike that drawn between these powers in regulating interstate commerce. A New York State workmen's compensation act was held unconstitutional as applied to employees whose work is maritime in nature (Southern Pacific Co. v. Jensen, 244 U. S. 205), but, in a later case, a state law giving a right of action on account of a maritime tort committed on navigable waters was upheld. Western Fuel Co. v. Garcia, 257 U. S. 233 (1921).

[2] The Lottawanna, 21 Wall. 558 (1874).

[3] The Thomas Jefferson, 10 Wheat. 428 (1825).

[4] The Genesee Chief, 12 How. 443 (1851).

[5] The Daniel Ball, 10 Wall. 557 (1861).

flowing into Lake Michigan was held to be navigable water of the United States. The same ruling was also made in the case of the Fox River of Wisconsin, although that stream contains falls around which portages had to be made.[1] The admiralty jurisdiction of the United States has also been held to extend to cases arising on canals used as highways for interstate or foreign commerce, in spite of the fact that the ships involved were canal boats drawn by mules or horses walking on land.[2]

Under the Constitution Congress is given power to exercise exclusive legislation in all cases whatsoever over such places as forts, arsenals, and dockyards purchased by the United States from a state.[3] No such general political jurisdiction over navigable waters, however, attaches to the Federal Government by virtue of the grant of admiralty and maritime jurisdiction. The states still continue to exercise general political jurisdiction over navigable streams within their boundaries, and ordinary crimes, not involving violation of Federal law, occurring on such streams or on territorial waters within three miles of their shores are punishable in state courts.[4]

Congress, however, retains full power to pass such legislation as may be necessary in order to render admiralty and maritime jurisdiction effective and in order to maintain or improve the navigability of streams and lakes. Bridges over, or tunnels under, navigable rivers which may interfere with their navigability cannot be constructed or maintained without the consent of Congress or of some officer, such as the secretary of war, to whom this power has been delegated. The same is true of the withdrawal of water from large lakes by states or local units of government to such an extent as to interfere with their navigability.[5] Congress also exercises conclusive judgment as to what power plants, works, or constructions in or over a stream may or may not conduce to the maintenance and improvement of its navigability.[6]

Admiralty and maritime jurisdiction extends not only over cases arising on the navigable waters of the United States within the boundaries of states but also over those arising on the high seas. The latter class

---

[1] The Montello, 20 Wall. 430 (1874).

[2] The Robert W. Parsons, 191 U. S. 17 (1903).

[3] Art. I, sect. 8, cl. 17.

[4] United States v. Bevans, 3 Wheat. 336 (1818).

[5] Thus, under an act of Congress, the secretary of war has been authorized to issue an order limiting the amount of water which may be withdrawn from Lake Michigan by the Sanitary District of Chicago and the attorney-general of the United States may enter suit in the Federal courts to enjoin the District from withdrawing water in excess of that amount. Sanitary District of Chicago v. United States, 266 U. S. 405 (1925).

[6] United States v. Chandler-Dunbar Water Power Co., 229 U. S. 53 (1913). *Cf.* West Chicago St. Ry. v. Illinois, 201 U. S. 506 (1906) (removal of obstructing tunnel); Union Bridge Co. v. United States, 204 U. S. 364 (1907) (removal of obstructing bridge).

of cases may involve either American citizens or American ships or both. They may be either civil or criminal. Congress is of course specifically granted the power "to define and punish piracies and felonies committed on the high seas."[1] It has been held that this grant enables the United States to take jurisdiction even of piracies committed by aliens on foreign ships on the high seas.[2]

Cases of Diverse Citizenship.—Among the cases which come before the Federal courts on account of the parties and without regard to the subject matter are those of diverse citizenship, *i.e.*, where the plaintiff and defendant are respectively citizens of different states or one of the parties is a citizen of one of the states of the Union and the other is a citizen or subject of a foreign state. The law involved in such cases is not Federal law but state law and these cases are brought before the Federal courts for adjudication not because there is a Federal question involved but because the framers of the Constitution thought (and rightly) that a Federal court would be likely to be a more impartial tribunal for the determination of such cases than would be the court of either of the states of which the parties are citizens.

Inasmuch as no vital national interest is involved in such cases, it is not necessary that the Federal courts should have exclusive jurisdiction of them. They may be brought in the first instance in the state court at the option of the plaintiff, but, before final decision by the state court, they may be removed, at the option of the defendant, into the Federal district court. In order, however, not to clog the Federal courts with a large number of minor cases, Congress has provided in the Federal Judicial Code that, in cases of diverse citizenship, the jurisdiction of the Federal courts is limited to those in which more than $3,000 is involved.

In order to be considered a case of diverse citizenship, the parties must be not merely residents but citizens of different states. If there are two or more plaintiffs and two or more defendants in a case, each of the plaintiffs must be a citizen of a different state from that of which each of the defendants is a citizen in order to sustain the Federal jurisdiction. Under this rule a firm of partners in one state might bring suit in the Federal court against a firm of partners domiciled in another state. The same rule was also at first applied to corporations, it being held in early cases that, in order to sustain Federal jurisdiction, all the stockholders of a plaintiff corporation must be citizens of a different state from that of which the defendants were citizens.[3] This decision, however, was later overruled, and it has now for a long time been held that, for purposes of Federal jurisdiction, all the stockholders of a corporation are conclu-

[1] Constitution, Art. I, sect. 8, cl. 10.

[2] *Cf.* WILLOUGHBY, W. W., *Constitutional Law of the United States*, 2d ed., vol. III, p. 1359.

[3] Bank of United States v. Deveaux, 5 Cranch 61 (1809).

sively presumed to be citizens of the state by which the corporation is chartered.[1]   Under this doctrine, which is a legal fiction, a corporation is practically considered to be a citizen of the state in which it has been incorporated.   This seems to be almost the only sense in which corporations come within the meaning of the word "citizen" as used in the Constitution.

Suits between States.—Under the Articles of Confederation, as we have seen, the judicial power of the Confederate Congress extended to controversies between states.   Such disputes might be settled by special tribunals set up under the supervision of the Congress.   The question of enforcing the decisions of these tribunals, however, presented difficulties.

Under the Constitution the states are prohibited from making war or making treaties with each other; nor do they have regular diplomatic relations with each other.   These have been the usual methods resorted to by sovereign foreign nations for the purpose of settling international controversies.   Since the states cannot resort to these methods, it was desirable, if not necessary, that some other method should be provided. This other method is found in that provision of the Constitution which declares that the judicial power of the United States shall extend to controversies between two or more states.   Furthermore, the Supreme Court of the United States is granted original jurisdiction in cases to which a state is a party.[2]

In hearing and deciding controversies between states, the Supreme Court may be said to perform a function analogous to that of international tribunals, except that the latter have not usually had compulsory jurisdiction over such cases.   In the absence of applicable municipal law, federal or state, the Supreme Court may apply to the decision of interstate controversies the rules which have developed in the relations between nations, commonly called international law.

Many controversies to which states were parties have been brought before the Supreme Court for settlement, especially within recent decades. A considerable number of boundary disputes have been settled in this way, sometimes by the mutual consent of the parties.[3]   Other controversies between states have arisen in connection with alleged torts and contract debts.   Since the states cannot collect damages for torts or money due under contracts of debt, such cases are regarded as justiciable by the Supreme Court.   This is true even when the plaintiff state has no direct interest as such but is acting on behalf of its citizens or a

---

[1] Ohio and Mississippi R. R. Co. v. Wheeler, 1 Black 286 (1862).   When a corporation is sued by one of its own stockholders, however, there is no such presumption.

[2] Constitution, Art. III, sect. 2.

[3] One of the earliest instances of an interstate boundary dispute in the Supreme Court was Rhode Island v. Massachusetts, 12 Pet. 657 (1838), in which the jurisdiction of the Court to decide such a dispute was upheld.

portion of them. Thus, the Supreme Court entertained a suit by Missouri against Illinois which sought an injunction forbidding the pollution of the Mississippi River, which was used by some of the inhabitants of Missouri as a source of water supply.[1] Again, the Supreme Court took jurisdiction of a suit brought by Kansas against Colorado to prevent the latter state from unduly depleting the waters of the Arkansas River for irrigation purposes and held that each state was entitled to an equitable apportionment of the water.[2]

An interstate controversy which aroused considerable interest culminated in a suit brought by Arizona against California and five other states and also against the secretary of the interior to enjoin the carrying out of the Boulder Dam project on the Colorado River, which had been authorized by act of Congress. The Supreme Court declined to grant the injunction, holding that the authority to construct the dam and reservoir is a valid exercise of Congressional power and that the Boulder Canyon Project Act does not abridge the right of Arizona to make additional appropriations of water flowing within the state or on its boundaries.[3] Under this ruling, work on the Boulder Dam project has proceeded in spite of Arizona's objections.

Virginia v. West Virginia.—A number of cases between states have arisen in the Supreme Court involving questions of debt based on contract or quasi-contract. Among the most interesting of these was that of Virginia v. West Virginia.[4] At the time West Virginia was admitted into the Union in 1863, she agreed to assume a just proportion of the public debt of Virginia, of which state she had previously been a part. In 1906, Virginia began proceedings in the Supreme Court of the United States to compel the carrying out of this undertaking. After numerous actions had been brought, the Court in 1915 entered a judgment fixing the amount of West Virginia's indebtedness at approximately twelve millions of dollars. Two further actions were then brought by Virginia to compel West Virginia to pay the amount thus fixed. In the first action Virginia petitioned the Court for a writ of execution upon the judgment. The court denied the petition upon the ground that the legislature of West Virginia should be given an opportunity to provide for payment, and it had not met since the judgment was entered. Another obstacle to granting such a remedy, which was pointed out by counsel for West Virginia, was that presumably the State of West Virginia had no prop-

---

[1] Missouri v. Illinois, 180 U. S. 208 (1901); 200 U. S. 496 (1906).

[2] Kansas v. Colorado, 185 U. S. 125 (1902); 206 U. S. 46 (1907). On interstate cases in the Supreme Court, see J. B. Scott (ed.), *Judicial Settlement of Controversies between States of the American Union*, 2 vols. (1918); Charles Warren, *The Supreme Court and Sovereign States* (1924); and H. A. Smith, *The American Supreme Court as an International Tribunal*.

[3] Arizona v. California, 283 U. S. 423 (1931).

[4] 246 U. S. 565 (1918).

erty not used by it for public governmental purposes and therefore had no property subject to seizure to satisfy the judgment.

In the second of the two actions, Virginia, instead of renewing her petition for a writ of execution, prayed that an order or mandamus should be entered by the Court directing the levy of a tax by the legislature of West Virginia to pay the judgment. The Court was thus brought almost face to face with the question as to what should or could be done when a state failed or refused voluntarily to comply with a judgment rendered against her by the highest judicial tribunal in the land. The Court held that a state could be compelled to pay a judgment rendered against her. As to the means of compulsion, the Court made two suggestions. The first was that appropriate action might be taken by Congress. Since Congress had given its consent to the agreement of West Virginia to pay her share of the joint debt, it was necessarily implied that Congress had both the power and the duty to see that the agreement was carried out. Congress also had the power to create new remedies for the enforcement of judicial authority.

The second suggestion was that appropriate judicial remedies might be found under existing legislation. A further hearing at a later date was ordered to determine what these judicial remedies were—whether to award the mandamus to the legislature of West Virginia, to direct the levy of a tax, or to deal in an equitable proceeding with the rights, funds, or taxable property of that state. Before this hearing was held, however, West Virginia finally in 1919 made provision for the payment of the judgment.

The Eleventh Amendment.—The Constitution as originally adopted provided that the judicial power of the United States should extend to controversies "between a state and citizens of another state."[1] In view of the well-established principle of law that a sovereign state is not suable without its consent, Hamilton argued in *The Federalist*[2] that the provision of the Constitution just quoted would not give the Federal courts jurisdiction of suits against a state by a citizen of another state. In the Virginia ratifying convention, Marshall and Madison took the same view. As it turned out, however, it would seem that these able statesmen were probably mistaken. This was soon evidenced by the decision of the Supreme Court in the case of Chisholm v. Georgia,[3] decided in 1793, which was a suit brought by one Chisholm, a citizen of South Carolina, against the State of Georgia. The Court took jurisdiction of the case, holding that the language of the constitutional provision was broad enough to cover not only suits brought by a state but also those brought against her. Upon the State of Georgia's failing to make any

---

[1] Art. III, sect. 2, cl. 1.
[2] No. 81.
[3] 2 Dall. 419. (Justice Iredell dissented.)

defense to the suit because she refused to recognize the jurisdiction of the Court, the case was decided against her by default.

Vehement protests against the decision of the Court in this case were made by several states and especially by Georgia, which refused to allow the Court's decree to be enforced. To hold a state amenable to suit was deemed by many persons derogatory to its dignity, and, in order to prevent any similar decisions in the future, an amendment to the Constitution was proposed and adopted and went into force in 1798. This became the Eleventh Amendment and provides that "the judicial power of the United States shall not be construed to extend to any suit in law or equity, commenced or prosecuted against one of the United States by citizens of another state, or by citizens or subjects of any foreign state." This does not prevent such suits from being brought in the courts of the state sued, but that can be done only with the state's consent. Moreover, it has been held that the spirit of the Eleventh Amendment prevents a state from being sued by one of its own citizens without its consent even when a Federal Constitutional question is involved.[1] The amendment does not deprive the Federal courts of jurisdiction over suits brought by a state against a citizen of another state, and this arrangement is advantageous because such a suit in the plaintiff state's own courts would hardly be feasible and in the courts of the defendant's state would hardly be proper.[2]

The Eleventh Amendment "recalled" the decision in Chisholm v. Georgia, and since its adoption the Federal courts can no longer entertain a suit against a state unless it is brought by another state or by the United States or by a foreign state.[3] This leaves a state legally free to repudiate debts which it owes to private citizens, whether residing in another state or in a foreign state or within its own boundaries. This has been done by some states, especially in the case of the debts incurred by certain Southern states during the "carpet-bag" *régime* shortly after the Civil War.

Various attempts have been made in the Supreme Court to enforce the payment of these repudiated state bonds. Thus, in New Hampshire

---

[1] Hans v. Louisiana, 134 U. S. 1 (1890). In this case the Court also declared *obiter* that the decision in Chisholm v. Georgia had been erroneous, thus upholding the dissenting opinion of Justice Iredell as the correct position, even though the Eleventh Amendment had not been adopted.

[2] If a state takes the initiative in instituting a suit and wins the case in the lower court, it waives its immunity against being made defendant in error in the higher court to which the case may be taken by the original defendant.

[3] Although the amendment in terms merely prohibits suits brought by "citizens," that term is in this instance broad enough to include also suits brought by corporations, foreign or domestic. On the other hand, a corporation may be sued by a citizen or by another corporation, even though the state which created the defendant corporation is one of its stockholders.

v. Louisiana,[1] it appeared that certain individual owners of these bonds had assigned them to the plaintiff state for collection. Under the law of the plaintiff state, the money recovered in the suit, if any, in excess of the expense of litigation, was to be paid over to the assignors of the bonds. In effect, therefore, the state, through the Supreme Court, was attempting to act as a collection agency for its citizens. Since the real parties in interest were the individual bondholders, the suit was obviously an attempt to evade the spirit of the Eleventh Amendment, and the Court therefore dismissed the suit.

In a later case, however, brought by one state against another for the collection of a debt, the situation was different. In South Dakota v. North Carolina,[2] it appeared that the repudiated state bonds had been donated by individual owners to the plaintiff state without reservation of interest in them. The entire ownership and interest in the bonds was vested in the plaintiff state, and the suit was brought on behalf of the state rather than on behalf of the former individual bondholders. The Supreme Court therefore took jurisdiction and rendered judgment against the defendant state, which was accordingly paid.

When Is a Suit One against the State?—No very clear or satisfactory test has yet been formulated by the courts for the purpose of determining when a suit is to be considered one against the state which the Eleventh Amendment forbids them to entertain. In an early case it was declared that a suit is not one against a state unless the state is a party on the record,[3] but this test was soon abandoned. A number of cases have arisen in which the Court has been called upon to decide whether a suit against a state officer is one against the state and therefore forbidden by the Eleventh Amendment. It was held that a suit against the governor of a state in his official capacity to compel him to act in respect to property legally in his possession was thereby forbidden.[4] The Court has also refused to issue a mandamus to compel a state officer to execute a duty devolving upon him under a contract made by the state, but which he refuses to perform under color of an unconstitutional law.[5] It thus appears that, even if a state impairs the obligation of a contract, it cannot be sued. The same would be true if it should take property without due process of law. But a law impairing the obligation of a contract or under which property may be taken without due process may be judicially resisted and held void in proper cases.

[1] 108 U. S. 76 (1883).

[2] 192 U. S. 286 (1904). This was a five-to-four decision, the four dissenting judges holding the view that to entertain such a suit was to violate the spirit of the Eleventh Amendment.

[3] Osborn v. Bank of the United States, 9 Wheat. 738 (1824).

[4] Governor of Georgia v. Madroza, 1 Pet. 110 (1828).

[5] Louisiana v. Jumel, 107 U. S. 711 (1882); *cf.* Hans v. Louisiana, 134 U. S. 1 (1890).

In another case it was held that "a suit against the officers of a state to compel them to do the acts which constitute a performance by it of its contracts is in effect a suit against the state," but that, on the other hand, a suit against state officers

. . . whether brought to recover money or property in the hands of such defendants, unlawfully taken by them in behalf of the state, or for compensation in damages, or in a proper case where the remedy at law is inadequate, for an injunction to prevent such wrong and injury, or for a mandamus in a like case, to enforce upon the defendant the performance of a plain legal duty, purely ministerial, is not within the meaning of the Eleventh Amendment an action against the state.[1]

In a recent case it was held that when the unconstitutionality of a state statute is not open to much doubt and where its operation would work irreparable injury to the plaintiff, an injunction will issue to restrain a state officer from enforcing it.[2] Although no clear distinction between suits which are, and those which are not, against the state has been drawn, it is obvious that the mere fact that a person is a state officer does not in all cases render him immune or exempt from suit. As the Court declared in the Arlington case, "No man in this country is so high that he is above the law. No officer of the law may set that law at defiance, with impunity. All the officers of the Government, from the highest to the lowest, are creatures of the law and are bound to obey it."[3]

Suits to Which the United States Is a Party.—As we have seen, a state cannot be sued by individuals without its consent, and this would probably be true even in the absence of the Eleventh Amendment. The same principle applies to the National Government. Unless it gives its consent, it is likewise immune from such a suit. The Constitution provides that the judicial power of the United States shall extend to "controversies to which the United States shall be a party." This provision, however, does not change the rule of the nonsuability of the National Government without its consent. It merely enables the United States Government to bring suit in the Federal courts and also enables Congress to provide for the bringing of suits against the United States in either the regular or general Federal courts or in a tribunal specially created for the purpose, such as the Court of Claims. Such a tribunal, as we have seen, merely passes upon the legality of the claim and an appropriation by Congress is necessary in order to pay the judgment.

Officers or agents of the United States who act in excess of their authority may be made legally liable in a suit for damages brought against them. In the Arlington case, cited above, the United States was in possession of the Robert E. Lee homestead through a tax sale.

[1] Pennoyer v. McConnaughy, 140 U. S. 1 (1891).
[2] Massachusetts State Grange v. Benton, 272 U. S. 525 (1926).
[3] United States v. Lee, 106 U. S. 196 (1882).

Lee's heir, claiming that the title thus acquired was invalid, brought a suit in ejectment against the Federal officers in charge. The majority of the Supreme Court held that this was not a suit against the United States but against the Federal officers and that, if the title of the United States was found to be invalid, these officers could be ejected.[1] It is the general rule that, if an officer acts beyond his legal powers, his act is to be considered as one not of his government but his private act for which he is responsible, even though the act was one performed while he was in the discharge of his official duties.

On the other hand, if the officers are acting within their legal authority, the suit against them is one against the United States Government and will not be entertained by the courts unless that Government has given its consent to be sued. Such consent has been given, as a rule, only in cases based on contract and not in those based on tort. In a mandamus suit against the secretary of the navy to compel him to deliver to the highest bidder a cruiser which had been offered for sale, the Court held that the suit was one against the United States and could not be entertained.[2]

Suits Affecting Ambassadors and Consuls.—The Constitution provides that the judicial power of the United States shall extend to "all cases affecting ambassadors, other public ministers, and consuls" and also provides that in all such cases the Supreme Court shall have original jurisdiction.[3] Ambassadors and ministers representing foreign governments in the United States are entitled, under the general rules of international law, to exemption from the jurisdiction of American courts. There is no judicial redress that the courts of this country can afford for wrongful acts which they may commit while holding their official positions. The only remedy is recall or dismissal.

The effect of the above-quoted constitutional provisions is to enable ambassadors, public ministers, and consuls to bring suit in the Federal courts against private individuals. They also enable the Federal courts to intervene in cases where a state court may have, without legal authority, assumed jurisdiction over foreign ambassadors or ministers. Consuls are not entitled under international law to all of the privileges and

---

[1] United States v. Lee, 106 U. S. 196 (1882). It has also been held that an action against a Federal collector of internal revenue to recover back the amount of a tax alleged to have been illegally collected is personal and not against the United States. Graham v. Goodcell, 282 U. S. 409 (1931).

[2] United States *ex rel.* Goldberg v. Daniels, 231 U. S. 218 (1913). Suit may not be maintained against the United States in any case not clearly within the terms of the statute by which it consents to be sued. United States v. Michel, 282 U. S. 656 (1931).

[3] Since the Federal courts do not have general jurisdiction in divorce actions, a suit for divorce against a foreign vice consul must be brought in the state courts. Ohio *ex rel.* Popovici v. Agler, 280 U. S. 379 (1930).

immunities accorded to ambassadors and ministers. In the absence of treaty stipulation, they are subject to suit or prosecution in the courts of the country in which they are stationed. In the United States, Congress is empowered to confer upon the Federal courts jurisdiction with reference to them, without violating international law.

CHAPTER XV

SPECIAL PHASES OF JUDICIAL POWER

The Law Administered by the Federal Courts.—The question has sometimes been raised as to whether there is a common law of the United States, just as there is a body of common law found in each of the states except Louisiana. In answering this question it is necessary to distinguish between the criminal and civil aspects of the common law. It has long been well established that there is no criminal common law of the United States.[1] Offenses against the United States must consist of violations of the Constitution, treaties, or of acts of Congress. Offenses against the United States may be tried in the state courts as well as in the Federal courts if the laws of Congress so provide, but the state courts probably could not be compelled by the Federal Government to exercise jurisdiction in such cases.

On the civil side, it is also the general rule that there is no common law of the United States, but to this rule there are some exceptions. There are, as we have seen, several classes of cases, such as those of diverse citizenship, over which the Federal courts have jurisdiction because of the character of the parties and not because Federal law is involved. In deciding such cases the Federal courts may virtually be considered state tribunals for this special purpose. They decide such cases in accordance with the rules of state law. Section 34 of the judiciary act of 1789, which is still in force, provides that "the laws of the several states, except where the Constitution, treaties, or statutes of the United States otherwise require or provide, shall be regarded as rules of decision in trials at common law, in the courts of the United States, in cases where they apply." The provision thus definitely excludes equity cases.

When, in cases of diverse citizenship, a Federal court administers state law, it is of course necessary for it to discover what is state law. This is found in the Constitution and statutes of the state as construed by the highest judicial tribunal of the state in its latest settled adjudications, *i.e.*, a series of decisions which settle the rule. Where a state court has changed its former interpretation of the state law relating to real property, the Federal Supreme Court has likewise changed, in order to conform with the latest construction by the state court.[2]

[1] United States v. Hudson, 7 Cranch 32 (1812).
[2] Green v. Neal's Lessee, 6 Pet. 291 (1832).

The Federal Supreme Court follows the latest settled adjudications of the state courts in cases involving state statutes and the law of real property, but in certain other branches of law the Federal court has adopted a more independent attitude. This is especially true in the branch of general commercial law, where both state and Federal courts are called upon to ascertain what is the true exposition of a contract or instrument upon general reasoning and legal analogies. Thus, in an early case coming up from New York involving the law of negotiable instruments, the Federal Supreme Court held itself not to be bound by the decision of the New York state court.[1] This independent position has been maintained by the Federal court in later cases with the result that there has been built up what may be called a body of Federal common law relating to commercial transactions. This has led to some confusion because it produces varying rules of common law administered in a given state by state and Federal courts.

In controversies between states which come before the Federal Supreme Court for decision, that tribunal may find that the laws of the litigant states upon the question at issue vary and it is consequently under the necessity of evolving a rule of law from general reasoning and analogy. As was pointed out by the Court in the course of its opinion in such a case, "through these successive disputes and decisions this court is practically building up what may not improperly be called interstate common law."[2]

In so far as it is applicable, Federal courts administer international law, composed of that body of rules, partly written and partly unwritten, which govern the conduct of nations in their relations with one another. This body of law is recognized by our courts not so much because of its own force but because it has been adopted in large part by the United States through its own law and usage. The Federal Constitution expressly recognizes the force of international law in that provision which authorizes Congress to define and punish offenses against the law of nations.[3] The Supreme Court of the United States has also declared that:

International law is part of our law, and must be ascertained and administered by the courts of justice of appropriate jurisdiction, as often as questions of right depending upon it are duly presented for their determination. For this purpose, where there is no treaty, and no controlling executive or legislative act or judicial decision, resort must be had to the customs and usages of civilized nations.[4]

Since international law has no independent or inherent force but only such force as it derives from its voluntary adoption by the United States,

[1] Swift v. Tyson, 16 Pet. 1 (1842).
[2] Kansas v. Colorado, 206 U. S. 46 (1907).
[3] Art. I, sect. 8, cl. 10.
[4] The Paquete Habana, 175 U. S. 677 (1900).

it is subject to such statutes as may be passed by Congress for its modification or repeal.

Judicial Review of Legislation.—The power exercised by the courts of declaring laws unconstitutional is one of fundamental importance. Although this is a weapon of large caliber, it may be exercised by any of the regular judicial tribunals from the highest to the lowest and whether state or Federal. Both state and Federal courts have in many cases exercised this extraordinary power of refusing to apply to a case before them a statute which they deem to be in excess of the power of the legislature to enact on account of constitutional limitations resting upon the exercise of legislative power. The Federal courts may declare state or Federal laws invalid if in conflict with the Federal Constitution, while the state courts may declare state laws invalid if in conflict with either the state or Federal Constitution and may declare Federal laws invalid if in conflict with the Federal Constitution.

When a case is brought before a court for determination, it is the duty of the court to decide the case in accordance with such law as it may find applicable. If, however, there are two laws both of which are applicable to the case, but they are in irreconcilable conflict with each other, the court must make a choice between them, applying one but giving no effect to the other. If these conflicting laws are of equal grade or if they are enacted by the same legislative body, the general rule is that the court applies the one of later date and ignores the earlier. The distinction between different grades of law, however, early became well established in this country. Thus, acts of colonial legislatures might be disallowed by the Judicial Committee of the Privy Council in England if in conflict with the provisions of the colonial charter. The charter limited the powers of the legislature just as the instructions from a principal limit the authority of his agent. The courts are bound to obey both the Constitution and the statutes but in every case of conflict between the two, the Constitution, being the highest written law, must prevail.

It is passing strange that a power of such fundamental importance should not have been expressly conferred upon the Federal courts by the Federal Constitution but should have been left to be derived by implication. On this account the exercise by them of this function has been deemed in some quarters to be a usurpation of power. This view, however, is not generally held and there is good ground for believing that it is incorrect.

The principle that the government should be one of laws and not of men was expressly embodied in the Massachusetts Constitution of 1780 and was familiar to the men who framed the Federal Constitution. Prior to the holding of the Federal Convention of 1787 there had been several instances in which state courts had held invalid provisions of state statutes in conflict with the state constitution, and with these cases the members of that Convention were doubtless familiar.[1] They inserted in the Federal Constitution a provision that the judicial power of the United States should extend to all cases in law and equity arising under this Constitution.[2] This provision was apparently deemed to be sufficient to authorize judicial review of legislation.

Contemporaneous Evidence.—The papers of the *Federalist* give contemporaneous evidence as to the meaning attached to the Constitution by some of the members of the Convention of 1787. The authors of those papers realized that a mere paper limitation upon the powers of the several departments of government would not necessarily keep them from exceeding those limitations. They believed that there was a need for some practical security against unconstitutional excesses of power. They did not consider it practicable constantly to recur to the people to correct such breaches of the Constitution. Although they probably did not foresee the extent to which the courts would come to exercise the power of declaring legislative acts unconstitutional, they argued very earnestly in favor of the need for the exercise of this power in a limited government. Thus Hamilton, in one of the papers of *The Federalist*, declared that:

By a limited constitution, I understand one which contains certain specified exceptions to the legislative authority . . . Limitations of this kind can be preserved in practice no other way than through the medium of courts of justice, whose duty it must be to declare all acts contrary to the manifest tenor of the constitution void . . .

There is no position which depends upon clearer principles, than that every act of a delegated authority, contrary to the tenor of the commission under which it is exercised, is void. No legislative act, therefore, contrary to the Constitution, can be valid . . .

The courts were designed to be an intermediate body between the people and the legislature, in order, among other things, to keep the latter within the limits assigned to their authority. The interpretation of the laws is the proper and peculiar province of the courts. A constitution is, in fact, and must be regarded by the judges, as a fundamental law. It, therefore, belongs to them to ascertain its meaning, as well as the meaning of any particular act proceeding from the legislative body. If there should happen to be an irreconcilable variance between the two, that which has the superior obligation and validity ought, of course, to be preferred; or, in other words, the Constitution ought to be preferred to the statute, the intention of the people to the intention of their agents.[3]

Another practically contemporaneous evidence of the belief that the courts should exercise the power of passing upon the constitutionality of

---

[1] See HAINES, C. G., *The American Doctrine of Judicial Supremacy.*

[2] Art. III, sect. 2, cl. 1.

[3] *The Federalist*, No. 78.

laws is found in the Judiciary Act passed in 1789 at the first session of Congress which contained a number of prominent men who had been members of the Constitutional Convention of 1787. One of the sections of this act provides that

. . . a final judgment . . . in the highest court of a state . . . where is drawn in question the validity of a treaty or statute of the United States, and the decision is against their validity . . . may be reexamined and reversed or affirmed in the Supreme Court of the United States upon a writ of error.[1]

This section clearly recognized the competence of the Supreme Court to hold an act of Congress unconstitutional.

Marbury v. Madison.—Although there had been earlier opportunities for the Supreme Court to hold acts of Congress unconstitutional, the first case in which it actually did so was that of Marbury v. Madison,[2] decided in 1803. The Federalists, having lost the election of 1800 and control of the political departments of the government, sought to retain control of the judiciary. A number of judicial appointments were made by President Adams just before the expiration of his term in March, 1801. Among these appointments was that of Marbury to be a justice of the peace of the District of Columbia. His commission had been signed by President Adams and countersigned and sealed by John Marshall, his secretary of state. It then became Marshall's duty to deliver the commission, but he failed to do so. Naturally the Anti-Federalist leaders, President Jefferson and his secretary of state Madison did not remedy this omission by delivering the commission, and Marbury thereupon brought an original proceeding in the Supreme Court applying for a writ of mandamus directed to Madison commanding him to deliver the commission.

The judiciary act of 1789 had undertaken to confer upon the Supreme Court power to issue writs of mandamus "to any courts appointed or persons holding office under the authority of the United States." The Supreme Court, speaking by Chief Justice Marshall, held that the petitioner had a right to the commission and that the issuance of the writ of mandamus was the proper remedy if the court to which the petitioner was applying had jurisdiction to issue the writ. The Court held, however, that the issuance of the writ was an original proceeding but was not within the original jurisdiction of the Supreme Court as defined in the Constitution.[3] Consequently, the provision of the Judiciary Act of 1789 which purported to confer upon the Court jurisdiction to issue the writ was in conflict with the Constitution and could not be applied by the Court.

[1] Sect. 25.
[2] 1 Cranch 137 (1803).
[3] Art. III, sect. 2, cl. 2.

The argument which Marshall used in this case to justify the Court in refusing to apply the act of Congress followed in part that of Hamilton contained in the passage from *The Federalist* quoted above. He declared that the theory that an act of the legislature, repugnant to the Constitution, is void "is essentially attached to a written constitution." That the courts have the power to declare such an act void he derived by implication from three provisions of the Constitution. The first was that which extends the judicial power of the United States to all cases arising under the Constitution.[1] The second was that which requires all judicial officers, both of the United States and of the several states, to be bound by oath or affirmation to support the Constitution.[2] The third was that which declares that the Constitution and such laws of the United States as are made in pursuance thereof shall be the supreme law of the land.[3]

The argument with which Marshall supports the power of the courts to declare legislative acts void is not very strong. It is absurd to say that such a power is essentially attached to a written constitution in view of the fact that in most modern governments the courts do not assume to exercise such a power. As far as the judge's oath to support the Constitution is concerned, it may be pointed out that the President and members of Congress also take such an oath and there is no more reason for supposing that the oath will be violated in one case than in the other. Again, it would seem that the provision declaring laws of the United States made in pursuance of the Constitution to be the supreme law of the land was intended to insure the supremacy of Federal law over state law rather than to give the courts the power to declare laws of Congress unconstitutional.

In 1825, Justice Gibson of the supreme court of Pennsylvania effectively answered some of Marshall's arguments. In the course of an opinion, he said:

It is the business of the judiciary to interpret the laws, not scan the authority of the lawgiver; and without the latter, it cannot take cognizance of a collision between a law and the Constitution. So that to affirm that the judiciary has a right to judge of the existence of such collision, is to take for granted the very thing to be proved . . . The oath to support the Constitution is not peculiar to the judges, but is taken indiscriminately by every officer of the government, and is designed rather as a test of the political principles of the man, than to bind the officer in the discharge of his duty . . . But granting it to relate to the political conduct of the judge, as well as every other officer, and not to his political principles, still it must be understood in reference to supporting the Constitution, only as far as that may be involved in his official duty; and, consequently, if his

[1] Art. III, sect. 2, cl. 1.
[2] Art. VI, cl. 3.
[3] Art. VI, cl. 2.

official duty does not comprehend an inquiry into the authority of the legislature, neither does his oath.[1]

By way of criticism of Marbury v. Madison it may also be pointed out, first, that, since Marshall himself had signed the commission which the Court was asked in this case to compel the delivery of, he was an interested party and a proper respect for judicial ethics would have required him not to participate in the decision of the case. As has been pointed out, "he appears in the rôle of advocate rather than of judge, passing judgment upon his own case."[2] In the second place, Marshall took a narrower view regarding the extent of the jurisdiction of the Supreme Court than has been taken by that tribunal in both earlier and later cases. As a result of Marbury v. Madison, however, Federal officials can be mandamused only through the lower courts, with the resulting delay and unnecessary costs of appeals.[3] In short, it would appear that in this case Marshall violated the rule that the courts will not hold a statute unconstitutional if either the statute or the Constitution can be construed so as to avoid conflict between them. One can hardly avoid the conclusion that, in reaching a decision in this case, he was influenced by the fact that, since the Federalists controlled the judiciary and the Jeffersonians were in the majority in Congress, it would strengthen the control of the Federalists over the government if the power of the courts to annul such acts of Congress as they deemed unconstitutional were clearly established. The case shows that even the best of judges, in passing on constitutional questions, are not always uninfluenced by political considerations.

Marshall doubtless considered himself justified in the stand which he took because he identified the strongly nationalistic aims of the Federalists with the best interests of the country as a whole. At any rate, even though the reasons which he gave for holding that the courts have the power to pass on the constitutionality of laws are unconvincing, it does not necessarily follow that the conclusion which he reached was either incorrect or inexpedient. Moreover, even if it could be shown that the assumption of this power by the courts was a usurpation (which it cannot), the validity of its exercise has been established by continual use and the acquiescence therein of public opinion. It is true that after the Marbury case no act of Congress was declared unconstitutional until fifty-four years later in the Dred Scott case.[4] Altogether, however,

---

[1] Eakin v. Raub, 12 S. & R. 330 (1825). *Cf.* the view of Blackstone that "to set the judicial power above that of the legislature . . . would be subversive of all government." *Commentaries*, Bk. I, p. 91.

[2] GRANT, J. A. C., "Marbury v. Madison Today," *Amer. Polit. Sci. Rev.*, vol. 23, p. 678 (August, 1929).

[3] *Ibid.*, p. 677.

[4] Dred Scott v. Sandford, 19 How. 393 (1857).

nearly sixty acts of Congress have been so declared, and there have been many more instances in which the Court has asserted the power without actually exercising it.

Declaring State Laws Unconstitutional.—Whatever ground there might originally have been for believing that the Federal courts were usurping power in declaring unconstitutional the acts of Congress, a coordinate branch of the government, there was none for holding that they were doing so when declaring state laws void because of conflict with the Federal Constitution. This was equally true whether the state law in question was constitutional or statutory. If the Federal courts had never assumed to exercise the power to declare acts of Congress unconstitutional, it is probable that no fundamentally serious results would have followed. But if the Federal courts could not have held state laws void when in conflict with the Federal Constitution, there would doubtless have resulted a very far-reaching difference in the nature of our Federal system. It is expressly declared in that instrument that the Constitution, laws, and treaties of the United States "shall be the supreme law of the land, and the judges in every state shall be bound thereby, anything in the constitution or laws of any state to the contrary notwithstanding."[1] It is indicated with sufficient clearness that Federal judges are also bound thereby. The framers of the Constitution showed by the provision quoted that they realized the special need for judicial review of state legislation alleged to be in violation of that instrument.

State laws may be declared unconstitutional either because they conflict with express limitations upon the states found in the Federal Constitution or because they encroach upon the sphere of the National Government as determined by that instrument. An example of the former class of laws was that declared invalid in the Yazoo land fraud case,[2] in which the Supreme Court held void an act of the legislature of Georgia which purported to rescind a grant of land made in a previous act. The later act was declared invalid on the ground that it impaired the obligation of a contract in violation of the express prohibition of the Federal Constitution. An example of the latter class of state laws was the statute of Maryland taxing the note issues of the branch Bank of the United States, which was held unconstitutional as encroaching upon the power of Congress to establish such a bank.[3] Hundreds of state laws have been declared unconstitutional, while relatively few—less than sixty—acts of Congress have been so declared. Apparently no instance has occurred in which a treaty of the United States has been declared unconstitutional, but there is no question that, in a proper case, this could be done.

[1] Art. VI, cl. 2.
[2] Fletcher v. Peck, 6 Cranch 37 (1810).
[3] McCulloch v. Maryland, 4 Wheat. 316 (1819).

Limitations upon the Power to Hold Laws Unconstitutional.—The courts will not, as a rule, hold a law unconstitutional unless it is necessary to do so in order to decide the case. They are not empowered to go out of their way in order to review and annul legislation. If, in the course of an opinion, the suggestion should be made that a particular statute is unconstitutional but such a determination is not necessary to the decision of the case, the suggestion is a mere *obiter dictum* and has no more legal effect than any other personal opinion of the judge. As a rule, the courts attempt, if possible, to avoid declaring a law unconstitutional and thus setting their judgment up against that of the legislative body.

It is to be assumed that the legislature will not intentionally violate the Constitution, and in cases of reasonable doubt the benefit of doubt, as a rule, is given in favor of the constitutionality of legislation. Although the doctrine of reasonable doubt is not always strictly followed by the courts in practice, it is more likely to be applied in cases where the law in question has been enacted by a coordinate legislative body. It must be remembered, however, that, in most instances, the Court acts by majority vote, so that, if a bare majority of the Court think that a law is without doubt unconstitutional, they may so declare it, regardless of the contrary views of the minority. Under such circumstances, it might reasonably be supposed that the Court, taken as a group, entertains some doubt as to the constitutionality of the statute, which, under the rule, should be resolved in its favor. In respect to this matter, however, the Court acts not as a group, but individually. If, in the minds of the majority judges, there is no doubt as to the invalidity of the statute, they are bound so to decide. They are not bound to take into consideration the dissenting views of the minority judges any more than they are those of other distinguished lawyers.[1]

The fact that eminent lawyers and jurists may honestly disagree over questions of the constitutionality of laws is due to the lack of preciseness in meaning of some constitutional provisions. It is true that there are some provisions of the Constitution which are fairly definite and precise and lay down hard and fast rules which cause little or no difference of opinion regarding their interpretation. Such a provision would be that which requires that direct taxes, if levied, shall be apportioned among the states in accordance with population.[2] On the other hand, many constitutional limitations are either ambiguous or broad and indefinite in character, so that there is room for wide differences of opinion as to their meaning and application in particular cases. An example of such a limitation is that which prohibits the states from

---

[1] CUSHMAN, R. E., "Constitutional Decisions by a Bare Majority of the Court," *Mich. Law Rev.*, vol. 19, p. 793 (June, 1921).

[2] Art. I, sect. 2, cl. 3.

depriving any person of life, liberty, or property without due process of law.   Since there are no exact juridical standards for determining whether or not a state law is in conflict with this provision, the element of personal judgment as to the expediency or desirability of the state law is likely to enter into the determination of its constitutionality.   Such judgment depends in turn upon the views of the judges regarding social, economic, and political questions.   These naturally differ widely among equally able lawyers and jurists.

Since judges are human, it is difficult to avoid the conclusion that they are sometimes influenced, in deciding questions of constitutionality, by their views as to the wisdom or expediency of the statute involved. Strictly speaking, however, they are to this extent encroaching upon the proper sphere of the legislature.   If a statute is within the constitutional competence of the legislature to enact, the court has no right to declare it null and void, regardless of how unreasonable it may appear to be. For example, if Congress should pass a law providing that each member of that body should receive for his services a compensation of one million dollars per annum, it would be outside the province of the courts to declare such a law unconstitutional.   The proper remedy in such cases is not the check of the judicial veto, but the disapproval of popular opinion, as indicated at the ballot box.   As the Supreme Court itself has declared:

If the statute is beyond the constitutional power of Congress, the court would err in the performance of a solemn duty if it did not so declare.   But if nothing more can be said than that Congress erred . . . the remedy for the error and the attendant mischief is the selection of new senators and representatives.[1]

The power of the Federal courts to declare laws unconstitutional may be indirectly limited through the power of Congress to regulate their jurisdiction.   Thus, under the Constitution, Congress is empowered to regulate the appellate jurisdiction of the Supreme Court.[2]   In 1868, when it appeared that the Court was about to declare unconstitutional one of the reconstruction acts, Congress hastily enacted a law withdrawing from the Court jurisdiction in such cases.   When, therefore, the case came on for decision, the Court dismissed it for want of jurisdiction.[3]

Finally, the Federal courts will not pass on the constitutionality of statutes, either existing or proposed, in mere hypothetical or moot cases. In other words, they will not hand down advisory opinions upon such questions but will wait until the matter comes before them for decision in a *bona fide* case or controversy to which there are parties having

[1] Northern Securities Co. v. United States, 193 U. S. 197 (1904).
[2] Art. III, sect. 2, cl. 2.
[3] *Ex parte* McCardle, 7 Wall. 506 (1869).

adverse interests which will be affected by the enforcement of a law actually on the statute book. The Supreme Court has also taken the position that it cannot hand down declaratory judgments or decrees.[1]

Effect of an Unconstitutional Statute.—Strictly speaking, the phrase "an unconstitutional law" is a contradiction in terms: if it is a law, it cannot be unconstitutional, while, on the other hand, if it is unconstitutional, it cannot be a law. In legal theory, the courts, when confronted by a conflict between the constitution and a statute, do not annul the statute or declare it unconstitutional. They simply ignore it or refuse to apply it to the case before them, on the ground that it never was a law *ab initio* or from the beginning. Being in excess of the power of the legislature to enact, it was merely a futile and unsuccessful attempt on the part of the legislature to pass a law. According to this theory, such an act by the legislature has no legal effect whatever, so that no legal rights or duties can be based upon it. This view was well expressed by Justice Field as follows: "An unconstitutional act is not a law, it confers no rights, it imposes no duties, it affords no protection, it creates no office; it is, in legal contemplation, as inoperative as though it had never been passed."[2] The effect of the act of the courts in declaring a law unconstitutional, therefore, is not exactly equivalent to the repeal of such law by the legislature, for, in the latter case, the law had presumably full force and effect up to the date of its repeal.

The *ab initio* doctrine, however, as so sententiously stated by Justice Field, while true as a general rule, is subject practically to certain modifications. Thus, a law declared unconstitutional may not be completely dead but merely in a state of suspended animation, so that, if the condition which rendered the law unconstitutional is changed, the law may revive and have full force without being reenacted by the legislature. This might happen, for example, when a state insolvency law is held invalid because in conflict with the bankruptcy law of Congress but is revived without reenactment when the law of Congress is repealed.[3] Again, it is sometimes held that a statute which was in conflict with the Constitution as it stood at the time of the enactment of the statute and was so declared by the courts may be subsequently revived by an amendment of the Constitution, either expressly or by implication.[4] It may also be noted that a statute authorizing the levying and collecting of taxes, even though later declared unconstitutional, has force to the extent that a taxpayer who has paid taxes under such statute without protest cannot recover. Individuals acting in good faith under a statute

---

[1] Arizona v. California, 283 U. S. 423 (1931).

[2] Norton v. Shelby County, 118 U. S. 425, 442 (1886).

[3] Tua v. Carriere, 117 U. S. 201 (1886).

[4] Upon this point, however, the courts are divided. This question, as we have seen, was involved in the Newberry case. See above (p. 94, note 2).

later declared unconstitutional may be indemnified by legislative appropriation.[1] As to whether a person acting in reliance on a law later declared unconstitutional may or should be held criminally liable, the courts are divided. The better view would seem to be that he should not. It has happened sometimes that courts have first declared a law unconstitutional and later have held the law constitutional, or *vice versa*. The judges who by the later decision have admitted that they were mistaken in the earlier decision are not themselves civilly liable for any injuries which such mistake may have caused. It would seem that individuals acting in reliance upon such mistaken decision should also not be held liable, but upon this point the courts are divided. At any rate, sufficient has been said to show that the *ab initio* doctrine is not invariably applied in practice.

Partial Unconstitutionality.—It sometimes happens that some provision of a statute conflicts with the Constitution, while others do not. If, under these circumstances, that part of the statute which is in conflict with the Constitution is separable from the remainder, the courts will declare unconstitutional the former part only while the remainder will be enforced. If, however, the constitutional and unconstitutional parts of a statute are so closely connected that the legislature could not be assumed to have intended one part to stand without the other, the courts will declare the whole statute unconstitutional.[2]

Criticism of Judicial Review.—It has been generally recognized, at least since the Civil War, that, in order to maintain the supremacy of the Federal Constitution and laws, the Supreme Court should have the power to declare unconstitutional those state enactments which conflict therewith.[3] Criticism of that tribunal has rather been based upon its practice in declaring unconstitutional the acts of Congress, a coordinate department of the government. The theory of the Constitution is that the departments of government are organs of limited powers. This is as true of the judicial department as it is of the others. The constitutional limits upon the legislative and executive departments are enforced by the Supreme Court, but how are such limits upon the power of that tribunal itself to be enforced? Who will oversee the overseers? In the absence of appeal to the ultimate source of authority—the people —in every case of dispute as to whether or not constitutional limitations have been exceeded—a totally impracticable procedure—it is necessary that final interpretation of constitutional limitations should be vested in one of the organs of the government. Since the primary function of

---

[1] United States v. Realty Co., 163 U. S. 427 (1896).

[2] Pollock v. Farmers' Loan and Trust Co., 158 U. S. 601 (1895).

[3] It should be noted, however, that the Supreme Court may, and not infrequently does, declare unconstitutional state laws which do not threaten Federal supremacy nor indeed relate to the line of division between Federal and state power.

the judiciary is to construe and apply the law, it is the department of the government which seems to be best fitted for this purpose.   In passing upon the validity of laws, the judiciary is likely in most cases to consider the question more disinterestedly than would the department in which the laws originated.   If this seems to make the judiciary paramount over the other departments of the government, it should be remembered that the judiciary is, on the whole, the weakest department of the government and its powers are narrower than those of the others.   It neither holds the purse nor wields the sword.   The President in nominating, and the Senate in confirming, appointments to the Supreme Court exercise general control over the character of the men who sit on that tribunal.   If Congress should fail to make any financial provision for the maintenance of the Court, there is no legal method whereby it could be compelled to do so.   Congress controls the appellate jurisdiction of the Supreme Court even to the extent, as we have seen, of depriving it of the right finally to decide a case pending before it.   It may reduce the number of judges on the Supreme Court bench and may abolish the lower Federal courts.

It must be admitted, however, that the exercise by the courts of the power of declaring laws unconstitutional has given rise to considerable popular dissatisfaction at times because it seemed to stand in the way of social reforms the need for which was widely and keenly felt.   The two decisions of the Supreme Court holding unconstitutional acts passed by Congress for the purpose of remedying the child labor evil are excellent examples of this.   Social legislation has sometimes been held void as being in conflict with broad constitutional guaranties, such as that relating to due process of law, the meaning of which is so vague and indefinite that their construction depends very largely upon the social, economic, and political philosophy of the particular judges rendering the decision, and upon their views as to the desirability or expediency of the legislation in question.   In such cases the judges are frequently accused of adopting a reactionary attitude and of maintaining unduly the sanctity of private rights where they conflict with the general welfare. Declaring laws unconstitutional is in reality frequently the exercise of a discretionary and political act.   The result is almost or practically equivalent to the exercise of the legislative power of repealing a statute, which is clearly a political act.

It is not within the proper province of the courts to lead reform movements or to espouse particular social theories.   It is their duty rather to apply the law as they find it.   If their decisions on constitutional questions sometimes seem ultraconservative, the fault may lie not with the judges but with the Constitution which may not be in all respects abreast of modern conditions or in harmony with preponderant public opinion.   Under these circumstances, it may be that it is the

Constitution, rather than the social philosophy of the judges, which needs to be amended.

Proposals for Reform of Judicial Review.—At various times in our history, opposition to the power of the courts of declaring laws unconstitutional has manifested itself in the formulation of proposals for the withdrawal or modification of this power. Jefferson and his political associates were especially incensed on account of the practice of the Federal courts of declaring state laws unconstitutional. They proposed that the judges be required to render their opinions *seriatim*, in accordance with the custom in English courts; and then if a particular judge persisted in this obnoxious practice, he might render himself liable to impeachment. During the reconstruction period after the Civil War, several bills were introduced in Congress declaring that no court had a right or power to declare any act of Congress unconstitutional. None of these bills passed Congress. In the exercise of its power to regulate the appellate jurisdiction of the Supreme Court, however, Congress did, as we have seen, pass an act withdrawing from that tribunal the power to pass on the constitutionality of one of the reconstruction acts of Congress in a case then pending before the Court.[1]

Most of the proposed reforms of the power of judicial review have not undertaken to abolish the power altogether but to introduce certain modifications in it. One of the most prominent of these proposals for modification is that which would allow Congress to reverse any judicial decision holding an act of that body unconstitutional by repassing the law, either by a bare majority or by a two-thirds vote. Probably the earliest forerunner of proposals of this sort was the resolution of Senator Johnson of Kentucky introduced in 1821 and providing that the Constitution should be amended so as to give the Senate appellate jurisdiction in cases wherein state laws are drawn in question. The proposal that Congress should be given the power of validating laws declared unconstitutional by repassing them by a two-thirds vote has been brought into prominence within recent years through its advocacy by Senator LaFollette of Wisconsin. This proposal has special reference to the situation where the Supreme Court declares an act of Congress unconstitutional.

The principal argument made in favor of the LaFollette proposal is that, in declaring an act of Congress unconstitutional, the Court is frequently exercising a power which is not strictly judicial but rather political in character and the decision of the Court will be determined in accordance with the views of the judges on social, economic, and political questions. Although the judges thus exercise a political power, the argument runs, they are not subject to political responsibility as are members of Congress by the necessity of popular election or reelection. Therefore, the decision rendered by the Court in the exercise of such

[1] *Ex parte* McCardle, 7 Wall. 506 (1868).

political power should be subject to the revisory authority of Congress, which is a political body *par excellence*. This would bring the decision more in harmony with the wishes of the people and with the current trend of public opinion.

In opposition to these arguments, however, it is pointed out that the LaFollette proposal would virtually make Congress the judge in its own case by giving it final authority to pass on the constitutionality of its own acts. It would destroy the desirable judicial check upon the partisan passion or prejudice of Congress and thus place the rights of the minority at the mercy of the majority. It would make the Constitution mean whatever Congress, through the whim or caprice of the moment, might choose to make it mean.[1]

In case the amendment granting this power to Congress should be adopted, it has been suggested as a possibility that

. . . the very first statute passed by Congress might be a statute taking away all power in the court to pass upon the constitutionality of Federal statutes; then, after the court holds such a statute unconstitutional, suppose Congress passes the statute a second time . . . Thereafter no act of Congress could be held either invalid or valid by the court. Consequently, Congress would be unlimited in power, uncheckable by any court, and bound by no provision of the Constitution, except so far as it chose to regard it.[2]

The second main proposal for the modification of the power of judicial review is aimed especially at the much denounced "one-man judgments" or five-to-four decisions. It embodies the requirement of an extraordinary majority of the Court in order to declare a law unconstitutional. The first to make this suggestion seems also to have been Senator Johnson of Kentucky who in 1823 introduced a bill requiring a unanimous vote of the Court in order to adjudge a law unconstitutional. Since then, this proposal has been frequently made, varying only in the size of the majority required in order to exercise the power. The most frequently suggested requirement seems to be that of a two-thirds vote. In 1867, during the excitement in Congress over the possibility that the Supreme Court might declare the reconstruction acts unconstitutional, a bill embodying the two-thirds requirement was actually passed in the House of Representatives but failed in the Senate. Senator Borah of Idaho and others would require a vote of all but two of the judges. Former Justice John H. Clarke of the Supreme Court has suggested that the two-thirds requirement be adopted not by act of Congress but by a rule voluntarily adopted by the Court itself. Others, fearing that an act of Congress would not be sufficient to impose such a requirement on the Court, have suggested that it be embodied in a constitutional amend-

[1] *Cf.* MONROE, A. H., "The Supreme Court and the Constitution," *Amer. Polit. Sci. Rev.*, vol. 18, p. 755 (November, 1924).

[2] WARREN, CHARLES, *Congress, the Constitution and the Supreme Court*, p. 142.

ment. Such a requirement, it may be noted, has already been embodied in the constitutions of one or two states of the Union.

The requirement of a two-thirds vote of the Court in order to declare unconstitutional acts of Congress is in harmony with the provision in certain other cases where one department of the government exercises a power affecting the function or personnel of another. This is true in case of the presidential veto, the impeachment of officers, and the approval of treaties by the Senate. The requirement has been objected to, however, on the ground that, while it prevents a bare majority of the Court from declaring a law unconstitutional, it virtually enables a minority of the Court to declare a law constitutional.[1] Moreover, it has been pointed out that if the members of the Court did not wish to acquiesce in such a requirement, they could render it ineffective by making an agreement among themselves that, "in the event of a five-to-four decision, a sufficient number of the minority will record themselves with the majority in order to meet the requirement of the law."[2]

There is evidently considerable dissatisfaction, especially in Congress, with reference to the exercise by the Court of the power to declare laws unconstitutional, but no unanimity of opinion as to what should be done about it. Although popular dissatisfaction with the Federal courts cannot be expressed through refusal to reelect Federal judges, public opinion is not a force regarding which such judges can be altogether indifferent. Moreover, it may happen that the attitude of the judiciary in particular cases, although giving rise to some popular dissatisfaction for the time being, will ultimately be approved by the sober second thought of the people. The power of the courts rests at bottom upon the support of public opinion, and their continued exercise of the power of declaring legislative acts unconstitutional must ultimately depend upon the fact that their policy and practice meet with general popular approval.

Judicial Control over the Executive.—Control of the judiciary over executive officers may in proper cases be exercised through the issuance of various extraordinary writs. Thus, by writ of *quo warranto*, the judiciary may inquire into the legal right or title of an officer to his office. By the writ of *habeas corpus*, persons who claim to be held in the custody of executive officers without just ground or legal authority may have the court pass upon the validity of their detention. As a general rule, executive and administrative officers act as agents for the enforcement of various laws. If, however, they assume to act without authority of law or under color of authority purported to be granted by an unconstitutional law, and individual rights are thereby injured, the courts may interfere through the issuance of the writ of injunction restraining the officers from continuing such acts. Officers may also

[1] MONROE, A. H., *loc. cit.* p. 758.
[2] MCBAIN, H. L., *The Living Constitution*, 263.

be held civilly liable in damages by decision of a law court for injuries to individual rights committed while acting in their official capacity but without legal authority or under an unconstitutional statute.

The writ of mandamus is another means which may be used by the courts to control executive action. Unlike the injunction, which is negative, the writ of mandamus is positive in character and undertakes to command an officer to perform his duty as required by law in cases where his failure to do so would result in injury to individual rights. The courts, however, will not issue this writ to compel the performance of discretionary or political acts. It may properly be issued to compel the performance of a mere ministerial or nondiscretionary act. The writ of mandamus will not be issued, as a rule, to the legislative branch of the government, since its powers are political and discretionary in character and, furthermore, it occupies a position in the government coordinate with that of the judiciary. The courts, moreover, will probably not issue the writ of mandamus to the chief executive, even to compel the performance of ministerial duties, since he also is head of a coordinate branch of the government. Much less would the courts be likely to issue the writ to compel him to perform a discretionary or political duty.

In Mississippi v. Johnson[1] it appeared that Congress had passed certain "reconstruction" acts providing for placing certain Southern states under military government and President Johnson had vetoed them on the ground that they were unconstitutional. They had, however, been repassed over his veto and if the President had then refused to enforce them he would have rendered himself liable to impeachment. He was therefore proceeding to enforce them when Mississippi brought suit in the Supreme Court to restrain him from doing so, on the ground of their alleged unconstitutionality. It was argued on behalf of the plaintiff that, since the President had vetoed the acts, his enforcement of them was not the exercise of discretion and the issuance of the writ by the Court would therefore not be an attempt to control his discretion. The Court, however, refused to restrain the President by injunction from carrying into effect the allegedly unconstitutional acts. To do so, the Court said, quoting Marshall, would be "an absurd and excessive extravagance." The impropriety of issuing the writ, the Court declared, was clearly shown by the fact that if the President should refuse obedience, the Court would be without power to enforce its process. This would follow from the fact that the President, as commander-in-chief of the army, is in control of the machinery which must ultimately be depended upon for the enforcement of law.

The attempt to secure an injunction restraining the President having failed, an action was then brought by Georgia seeking to have an injunc-

[1] 4 Wall. 475 (1866).

tion issued restraining Stanton, secretary of war, and other military officials from enforcing the reconstruction acts in that state. The Court, however, again refused to issue the writ.[1] In giving its reason for this refusal, the Court pointed out that the petition or bill in equity presented a non-justiciable question. It presented no case of threatened infringement of private rights or private property. It called rather for the judgment of the Court upon political questions and for the protection by the Court of the political and governmental rights of a state. The power of the judiciary did not extend to the protection of such rights or to the decision of such questions.

The Courts and Political Questions.—The exercise of political powers and the determination of political questions—involving matters of public policy—are primarily within the province of the political departments— the legislature and the executive—rather than of the judiciary. Among such questions are those relating to the existence and territorial extent of sovereignty. Whether the sovereignty of the United States extends over a given district or territory is a political question which the courts will not settle on their own initiative or authority; but if a judicial decision regarding private rights depends upon the determination of such a question, the courts will follow the determination which has been made by either or both of the political departments of the government.[2] This is true not only as to the territorial extent of American sovereignty but also as to which of two foreign countries shall be deemed to be the *de jure* sovereign over a particular foreign territory.[3]

Questions concerning the foreign relations of the United States are peculiarly within the province of the political departments of the government. Among such questions are those as to the beginning and termination of war; as to whether a treaty between the United States and a foreign government shall be deemed to be still in force or terminated by adverse breach or other circumstance; and as to whether a person claiming diplomatic immunity on the ground that he is a member of the staff of a foreign ambassador accredited to the United States is really such or not.[4] As to such questions the Supreme Court has declared that:

The conduct of the foreign relations of our government is committed by the Constitution to the executive and legislative—the political—departments of the government, and the propriety of what may be done in the exercise of this political power is not subject to judicial inquiry or decision.[5]

[1] Georgia v. Stanton, 6 Wall. 50 (1867).

[2] See, for example, Foster v. Neilson, 2 Pet. 253 (1829); Wilson v. Shaw, 204 U. S. 24 (1907).

[3] Williams v. Suffolk Insurance Co., 13 Pet. 415 (1839).

[4] *Cf. ex parte* Baiz, 135 U. S. 403 (1890); Doe v. Braden, 16 How. 635 (1853).

[5] Oetjen v. Central Leather Co., 246 U. S. 297 (1918), following the action of the political departments of the Government of the United States in recognizing the Carranza Government in Mexico first as the *de facto* and later as the *de jure* government of that country.

In all such matters the courts feel themselves bound by the action of the political departments of the government. If private justiciable rights are involved, however, they will not decline to take jurisdiction and pass on such rights merely because political questions are also involved. They will, however, in such cases base their decisions regarding private rights upon the determination of political questions made by the political departments of the government.

One of the leading cases which aptly illustrates the points stated above is that of Luther v. Borden.[1] The decision in this case depended upon the determination of the question as to which of two separate governments in Rhode Island was the legitimate one. These were the old charter government and a newly established one under a rebel named Dorr, each claiming to exercise constitutional authority. The Court declared that the question as to which of these governments was the rightful one was political and therefore refused to decide it or even to examine the evidence bearing upon it. The Court did, however, feel it incumbent upon itself to decide the question of private right between the two individual parties to the case, because this was a justiciable and non-political question. Luther was an adherent of the Dorr government and brought an action against Borden to recover damages for breaking and entering his house. Borden claimed justification for this action on the ground that an insurrection existed, that martial law had been declared, and that, as a member of the militia of the old charter government, he had been ordered to arrest Luther.

The question presented to the Court then depended on the further question as to which was the rightful government. If the Dorr government was legitimate, Borden had had no right to break into his house and arrest him, and Luther in that case would be entitled to recover damages. On the other hand, if the old charter government was legitimate, Borden was acting within his authority and Luther would not be entitled to recover. The Court found that the President, acting under authority granted to him by an act of Congress, had threatened to intervene by military force on behalf of the old charter government and had thus recognized it as the legitimate government. The Court merely followed this decision of the political question involved as made by the political department of the Federal Government and based thereon its decision of the question of private rights involved, holding that Luther was not entitled to recover.

In a more recent case,[2] it was alleged that the insertion in the state constitution of Oregon of a provision for direct legislation through the popular initiative and referendum deprived it of a republican form of government as guaranteed by the Federal Constitution and thereby

[1] 7 How. 1 (1849).

[2] Pacific States Telephone and Telegraph Co. v. Oregon, 223 U. S. 118 (1912).

rendered invalid a tax which the state had levied upon the plaintiff company. The Court declined to go into the question as to whether the state had a republican form of government, on the ground that this was political. There had been no determination by the political departments of the Federal Government that the state government was not republican in form, and the Court therefore refused to hold invalid the tax levied by the state.

Advisory Opinions.—As pointed out above, the courts will not, as a rule, pass on the constitutionality of statutes, either existing or proposed, in mere hypothetical or moot cases. They have exhibited a distinct aversion to handing down advisory opinions or rendering declaratory judgments.[1] A fabricated or merely collusive suit will not usually be considered on its merits.

The Federal Constitution extends the judicial power of the United States to "cases" and to "controversies."[2] These words are generally construed to refer to those *bona fide* cases and controversies to which there are parties having adverse interests which will be affected by the decision of the court. A proceeding instituted merely for the purpose of obtaining an opinion as to the constitutionality of legislation is not a case or controversy to which the judicial power of the United States extends.[3] Furthermore, such power does not extend to the decision of cases from which an appeal may be carried to executive or legislative authorities. Appeals from judicial decisions can be carried only to higher courts.

Some state constitutions require their supreme courts to give advisory opinions to the governor or legislature when requested by them to do so, and with such constitutional requirements the courts are naturally bound to comply. Advisory opinions handed down in compliance with such requests, however, are not usually rendered in the light of opposing arguments of counsel and are therefore not likely, on an average, to be so well considered as are opinions handed down in cases involving real controversies. They are therefore not considered as binding precedents and may be departed from without violating the rule of *stare decisis*, if subsequently a *bona fide* case involving similar circumstances should arise.

The Constitution of the United States contains no provision requiring the Federal courts to give advisory opinions.[4] Consequently, when, in

[1] A declaratory judgment is determinative of the rights of the parties to the case, while an advisory opinion is one rendered by the court at the request of the executive or legislative departments of the government. The Supreme Court has distinctly stated that "this tribunal cannot issue declaratory decrees." Arizona v. California, 283 U. S. 423 (1931).

[2] Art. III, sect. 2, cl. 1. The difference between a case and a controversy is that the word "case" covers all kinds of suits or actions, whether civil or criminal, while the word "controversy" refers especially to a civil suit.

[3] Muskrat v. United States, 219 U. S. 346 (1911).

[4] A proposal made in the Constitutional Convention of 1787 to require the Supreme Court to give advisory opinions was not adopted.

1793, President Washington, through his secretary of state, requested the Supreme Court to give an advisory opinion regarding a proposed treaty, that tribunal declined to do so, and this has become the well-established rule.[1] For this reason, it may sometimes happen that a law remains on the statute book for a long time before its constitutionality is passed upon by the courts in an actual controversy. For example, the Missouri Compromise Act passed by Congress in 1820 remained presumably in force for thirty-seven years before it was finally declared unconstitutional by the Supreme Court in the Dred Scott case.[2]

[1] Apparently the only exception to this rule was an instance occurring in President Monroe's administration, when the Supreme Court rendered an advisory opinion regarding the constitutionality of a proposed act of Congress appropriating money to be expended wholly within a single state.

[2] Dred Scott v. Sandford, 19 How. 393 (1857).

CHAPTER XVI

TAXATION AND FISCAL POWERS

Taxation in General.—No government can be energetic or self-sufficient unless it has adequate means of raising revenue. By far the most important source of governmental revenue is taxes. A tax is an enforced contribution made by an individual or by a corporation for the support of the government. The individual is required to pay it without regard to any special benefit which he may receive from the government. In this respect a tax differs from a fee, which is a payment made to the government in return for a special privilege granted by public authority. Thus, a license to form a corporation is a special privilege in return for which the individual or group of individuals especially benefited may be required to pay a fee to the government.

A tax should also be distinguished from the taking of property by eminent domain. When the government wishes to take land or other private property for a public use, such as the site of a public building, it may do so by what is known as the right of eminent domain. When this right is exercised by the Federal Government, the Constitution requires that just compensation shall be paid to the person whose property is taken.[1] When, however, property is taken by taxation, the owner of the property is entitled to no particular compensation aside from the general benefit which he derives from the existence and protection of the government. This general benefit does not necessarily bear any exact relation to the amount of the taxes he is required to pay; nor is it necessary to justify the tax by showing that he will receive any benefit at all from the expenditure of the proceeds therefrom. In the case of "special assessments," however, there is a relation between the amount of the assessment and the benefit to be derived from the expenditure of the proceeds.

The real burden of a tax may not always be borne by the person who actually pays it to the government. Goods imported from abroad may be taxed upon their entrance into the United States. The importer pays the tax to the government but ordinarily adds the tax to the price of the article when he sells it. The ultimate purchaser or consumer is therefore the one who really bears the burden of the tax, but he does not always realize it, because he pays it not in the form of a tax but in the form of a price. Such indirect methods of taxation are a favorite source

[1] Amendment V.

227

of governmental revenue, since they are not likely to arouse very much protest from the ultimate taxpayer.

Taxation under the Confederation.—Under the Articles of Confederation the states could levy imposts or custom duties provided they did not interefere with any stipulations in certain treaties. The central government, on the other hand, had no power of levying taxes directly on individuals. It was authorized to make requisitions upon the various states for funds in proportion to the amount of improved land in each state, but in practice such requests were to a large extent ignored by most of the states. One of the weaknesses of the central government was that it had no means of compelling the states to heed such requests. It was not surprising that a government financially so powerless soon fell into disrepute and could not long endure under these conditions.

Taxation under the Constitution.—In order to remedy this situation, the framers of the Constitution determined to endow the new National Government with ample power of levying taxes directly upon individuals, independently of the states. They granted to Congress the power "to lay and collect taxes, duties, imposts, and excises."[1] These words are sufficiently comprehensive to include all forms of taxation needful to meet the financial requirements of the Government. "Taxes" is a general term. The words "duties" and "imposts" are usually applied to custom dues levied upon goods imported from foreign countries, while the term "excises" denotes internal revenue taxes levied on the use, sale, manufacture, or transfer of property within the country. Subject to limitations found in the Constitution, this grant of power enables Congress to tax any individual and any property, tangible or intangible, whether owned by an individual or private corporation, within the country. Moreover, there is apparently no limit to the rate of taxation or to the amount of property which the Government may take in the form of taxation, for, as Chief Justice Marshall declared in a leading case: "The power to tax involves the power to destroy . . . The only security against the abuse of this power is found in the structure of the government itself."[2]

As in the case of other important grants of power in the Constitution, however, it was found necessary, in the matter of taxation, to make certain concessions, or compromises, in order to secure the main object in view. Consequently, we find that in the Constitution several limitations were placed upon the taxing power of Congress. These limitations are partly expressed and partly implied. Among the express limitations we find, in the first place, that taxes may be levied not for any purpose whatever but only in order "to pay the debts and provide for the common

[1] Art. I, sect. 8, cl. 1.
[2] McCulloch v. Maryland, 4 Wheat. 316 (1819).

defense and general welfare of the United States."[1] This means, in other words, that they can be levied, and the proceeds of taxes can be appropriated, only for a public, as distinguished from a private, purpose.

In the next place, we find certain express limitations upon the manner in which Congress may levy taxes. Thus, it is required that "all duties, imposts, and excises shall be uniform throughout the United States."[2] Congress, moreover, is prohibited from giving any preference "by any regulation of commerce or revenue to the ports of one state over those of another."[3] Direct taxes (with the exception of income taxes) are required to be apportioned among the several states in accordance with population.[4] Finally, an express limitation upon the objects which may be taxed is found in that provision which declares that "no tax or duty shall be laid on articles exported from any state."[5]

The provisions mentioned are the only express limitations upon the taxing power of Congress. There are, however, implied limitations found in other parts of the Constitution, especially in the due-process-of-law clause of the Fifth Amendment. There is also the limitation implied in the general nature of the Federal Government that Congress cannot tax the instrumentalities of the state governments.

The Purpose of Taxation.—The requirement that taxes can be levied for public purposes only is fundamental and is applicable to the taxing power not only of Congress but also of the states and local governments. This power is vested in the legislatures to be exercised in trust for the benefit of the people in general and can therefore be used for a public purpose only. In the leading case of Loan Association v. Topeka,[6] the city of Topeka had issued bonds to raise money as a gift to a bridge company to aid or induce it to locate its plant in that city. Upon the city's subsequently failing to pay interest upon the bonds, the plaintiff brought suit in the Federal Court on the ground of diversity of citizenship, but the Court upheld the city on the ground that the bonds were invalid because issued for a private purpose. "If," said the Court, "in the given case no tax can lawfully be levied to pay the debt, the contract itself is void for want of authority to make it." One judge dissented on the ground that no definite constitutional provision was violated by the legislative act under authority of which the city issued the bonds. It would seem, however, that the Court might have held that taxation for a private purpose would amount to a deprivation of property without due process of law in violation of the Fourteenth Amendment.

[1] Art. I, sect. 8, cl. 1.
[2] *Ibid.*
[3] Art. I, sect. 9, cl. 6.
[4] Art. I, sect. 2, cl. 3; Art. I, sect. 9, cl. 4; Amendment XVI.
[5] Art. I, sect. 9, cl. 5.
[6] 20 Wall. 655 (1875).

The Supreme Court did not lay down in Loan Association v. Topeka any general test to differentiate between public and private purposes. In a more recent case, the Court refused to invalidate the sale of bonds in North Dakota to finance a program of state-owned enterprises, such as a bank, grain elevators, and flour mills.[1]

In the case of Congress, the power to levy taxes and to appropriate money is not merely ancillary to other powers granted to that body by the Constitution but may be exercised independently, so long as it is for a public purpose or, as expressed by that instrument, "to pay the debts and provide for the common defense and general welfare of the United States." This clause indicates two fairly specific purposes of taxation, and one other of such a broad and general nature that it does not operate as a very stringent limitation on the taxing power of Congress. Moreover, it is seldom possible successfully to attack a taxing law on the ground that it is for a private purpose. Taxes are not usually levied for any definitely indicated purpose but merely to provide revenue for the Government.

After taxes have been collected and paid into the treasury of the United States, they cannot be paid out except on authority of an act of Congress. The purpose for which the proceeds of taxes are to be used is not usually indicated until Congress passes an appropriation act. In order successfully to attack an appropriation act as not being for a public purpose, the plaintiff must show that as a taxpayer he has sufficient financial interest in the matter to entitle him to relief and to give him a standing in court. It is usually difficult to show this to the satisfaction of the Court. Because this had not been shown, the Supreme Court refused to declare invalid the maternity act of 1921 carrying an appropriation by Congress to cooperate with the states in protecting the health and lives of mothers and infants.[2] The appropriating power of Congress is evidently very broad, including the authorization of money to be spent for such purposes as world's fairs, higher institutions of learning, vocational education, industrial rehabilitation, soldiers' bonuses, and battlefield grounds and monuments. Some question, however, might be raised as to whether Congress could constitutionally grant subsidies to private corporations.

Taxation for Ulterior Purposes.—The normal public purpose for which taxes are levied is to raise revenue for the support of the Government and to carry out its functions. It sometimes happens, however, that taxes are levied not for revenue, or not primarily for revenue, but for purposes of regulation or even of prohibition. For example, it has

[1] Green v. Frazier, 253 U. S. 233 (1920).

[2] Frothingham v. Mellon. 262 U. S. 447 (1923). *Cf.* Massachusetts v. Mellon, *ibid.*, where the Court declined to hold the Maternity Act invalid on the ground that it encroached on the reserved powers of the states.

been the practice of Congress from the beginning to levy tariff duties not only for revenue but also for the protection of American industries. Curiously enough, the constitutionality of this practice was not passed upon by the Supreme Court until recently. The tariff act of 1922 was attacked on the ground that the power of Congress extends only to laying duties for the purpose of revenue and not for protection. The Court, however, denied this contention and upheld the act.[1] The decision was based in part on the long-established practice of Congress in laying protective tariffs and partly on the ground that, as long as the motive of raising revenue existed, other motives were immaterial. The act might also have been sustained under the power to regulate foreign commerce.

An example of the use of the taxing power for purposes of regulation was the act of Congress of 1882 which levied on shipowners a tax of fifty cents on each passenger brought from abroad into the United States. This law was objected to on the ground that it was not intended to raise revenue for the common defense or general welfare. Upon this point the Supreme Court declared that

. . . the true answer to all these questions is, that the power exercised in this instance is not the taxing power. The burden imposed upon the ship-owner by this statute is the mere incident of the regulation of commerce, of that branch of foreign commerce which is involved in immigration . . . The money thus raised, though paid into the Treasury, is appropriated in advance to the uses of this statute, and does not go to the general support of the government . . . If this is an expedient regulation of commerce by Congress, and the end to be attained is one falling within that power, the act is not void because, within a loose and more extended sense than was used in the Constitution, it is called a tax.[2]

The power of Congress formally to levy taxes may be used not only for regulation but also for prohibition. If Congress has the power to tax, the rate of taxation is within its discretion and may be made so high as to be prohibitive. Thus, in 1866 Congress levied a 10 per cent tax on the note issues of state banks. This was only in form a tax law. It raised no revenue and was not intended to do so. It was intended to prohibit the issuance of paper money by state banks, so as to prevent competition with the note issues of the recently established national banks, and it had that effect. It was nevertheless upheld by the Supreme Court, not as an exercise of the taxing power but rather as an exercise indirectly of the expressly granted power to regulate the currency.[3] It thus appears that when Congress has the express power to regulate a

[1] Hampton v. United States, 276 U. S. 394 (1928).
[2] Head money cases, 112 U. S. 580 (1884).
[3] Veazie Bank v. Fenno, 8 Wall. 533 (1869).

matter, a prohibitory regulation may take the form of taxation, even though the law could probably not be sustained under the taxing power.

Congress may tax articles manufactured within a state, even though it has no power to prohibit such manufacture. This was illustrated by the McCray case, decided in 1904, which involved the constitutionality of an act of Congress levying a tax of ten cents a pound upon oleomargarine artificially colored in imitation of butter. This act had apparently been passed not to raise revenue but to protect the dairy interests from the competition of the manufacturers of oleomargarine. Since Congress had no constitutional power to carry out the latter purpose, the law could not be sustained on that ground. The Supreme Court nevertheless upheld the act on the ground that on its face it appeared to be a revenue measure and that it was not the duty of the Court to inquire into the ultimate effect of the law nor into the motives of Congress in passing it.[1]

The decision in the McCray case appeared to interpret very broadly the power of Congress to levy excise taxes and seemed to open the way for Congress, under the guise of the taxing power, to enact social legislation for purposes of regulation and even prohibition or destruction. Such laws, for example, have been enacted by Congress for the purpose of prohibiting the manufacture of white phosphorus matches and of narcotic drugs, and of the sale of cotton on future contracts.

The Child Labor Tax Case.—Encouraged by the failure of the courts to declare these laws unconstitutional, and relying upon the doctrine of the Supreme Court in the McCray case, Congress in 1919 attacked the child labor problem by passing a law levying a tax of 10 per cent upon the annual net profits of business concerns which, at any time during the year, employed children in violation of stipulated regulations as to age, hours, etc. A case was thereupon brought before the Supreme Court to test its constitutionality.[2]

Since Congress has no power directly to regulate the employment of children within the states, the only ground upon which it could be sustained was as an exercise of the taxing power. Since concerns employing child labor presumably made more profits through the use of such cheap labor, it would seem that they could be singled out for taxation on such profits. The Court held, however, that the law showed upon its face that it was not a revenue measure. "The so-called tax," declared that tribunal, "is imposed to stop the employment of children within the age limits prescribed." It was an attempt to regulate child labor through the use of the so-called tax as a penalty. That it was a penalty rather than a tax was shown by the provision that the so-called tax was not to be imposed unless the employer *knowingly* employed children under the

[1] McCray v. United States, 195 U. S. 27 (1904).
[2] Bailey v. Drexel Furniture Co., 259 U. S. 20 (1922).

age limit. "*Scienters*," said the Court, "are associated with penalties, not with taxes."

However desirable a national child labor law might be from the social point of view and however delinquent some of the states were in protecting children of tender years from the stunting effects of long hours of labor, the Court did not feel itself thereby justified in upholding an attempt on the part of Congress to regulate child labor, a power which by the Tenth Amendment is reserved to the states. The Court might have refused to inquire into the motives of Congress and have sustained the law upon the precedent of the McCray case, but it declined to do so. In taking this position, the Court was probably influenced by the consideration that Congress by various laws was showing a tendency to encroach upon the reserved powers of the states and, unless the Court called a halt somewhere, the tendency might develop so far as very seriously to limit such state powers. The McCray case was distinguished from the instant case on the ground that the former did not show upon its face an attempt to regulate a matter which is entirely under state control. This distinction, however, does not seem to be either necessary or fundamental.[1] The child labor case is one of the few recent cases of importance in which the Supreme Court has decided against the extension of national power at the expense of states' rights.

Direct Taxes.—As noted above, a limitation upon the Federal taxing power found in the Constitution is that direct taxes are required to be apportioned among the several states in accordance with population.[2] No definition of direct taxes is contained in the Constitution and it cannot be assumed that the distinction between direct and indirect taxes is the same in constitutional law as in economics. The Constitution clearly implies, however, that capitation or poll taxes are to be considered direct. What other taxes are to be classed as direct was a question left by the framers for future determination.

In an early case it was held that a tax on carriages was not direct and therefore did not need to be apportioned.[3] One reason given by the Court for this decision was that it was not practicable to apportion such a tax and the framers of the Constitution could not have intended that a tax should be considered direct unless it were apportionable. The Court also intimated that probably the only direct taxes under the Constitution are capitation taxes and taxes on land. Although this statement was *obiter*, it was substantially the position which the Court continued to hold until almost the end of the nineteenth century. Direct taxes in

[1] *Cf.* the Doremus case, 249 U. S. 86, in which the Court upheld the Harrison Narcotic Drug Act, which was obviously intended to regulate the sale of drugs, not to raise revenue.

[2] Art. I, sect. 2, cl. 3; Art. I, sect. 9, cl. 4.

[3] Hylton v. United States, 3 Dall. 171 (1796).

this limited sense have been levied only a few times in our history, the last instance being during the Civil War.

Federal Income Taxes.—The most important question which has been raised in connection with the interpretation of the constitutional provision for direct taxes is that as to whether or not income taxes are to be classed as direct.   It was not until the time of the Civil War that Congress resorted to income taxes as a source of revenue.   The provisions of the income tax law passed at that time showed that Congress was of the opinion that an income tax is not a direct tax, because it was not apportioned among the several states in accordance with population. The failure to include such a provision for apportionment was the ground for an attack upon the law and a case involving this point reached the Supreme Court for decision in 1880.   That tribunal nevertheless unanimously upheld the law on the ground that an income tax is not a direct tax and therefore does not need to be apportioned.   The Court made the definite statement that direct taxes, within the meaning of the Constitution, include only capitation taxes and taxes on real estate.[1]

This interpretation, however, of the meaning of direct taxes was destined to be overthrown.   In 1894, Congress passed a law levying a tax of 2 per cent upon incomes in excess of $4,000.   It contained no provision for apportionment among the states in accordance with population. Inasmuch as most incomes taxable under this law were to be found in the Northeastern part of the country, it was not surprising that the law was enacted as the result of a sectional contest in Congress in which the West and South were successful.   The Congressional contest, however, was only the preliminary skirmish, and the struggle was then transferred to the courts.   On the ground that the law was unconstitutional, one Pollock, a stockholder in the Farmers' Loan and Trust Company of New York, sought to have the company enjoined from paying the tax upon its income, which was derived mainly from real estate and from stocks, bonds, and other personal property.[2]

Two hearings were held by the Supreme Court in the Pollock case. In the first hearing the Court, starting from the admitted premise that taxes upon real estate are direct taxes, held that taxes upon the rents or income from real estate are also direct because the two taxes are indistinguishable.   In the rehearing, the chief question was whether taxes on personal property, such as stocks and bonds, and on the income (dividends and interest) derived therefrom were also direct.   This question the Court answered in the affirmative, but by the bare majority of five to

---

[1] Springer v. United States, 102 U. S. 586 (1880).   It had previously been held that an inheritance tax was an indirect tax upon the privilege of the beneficiary to inherit rather than a direct tax upon the property transmitted.   Scholey v. Rew, 23 Wall. 331 (1874).

[2] Pollock v. Farmers' Loan and Trust Co., 157 U. S. 429 and 158 U. S. 601 (1895).

four.[1] Thus the Hylton case and the Springer case were both overruled and the interpretation of direct taxes which had been deemed established for a hundred years was overthrown. In view of the changed construction of the term "direct," the act of 1894, not providing for apportionment among the states in accordance with population, was declared unconstitutional. This exercise of the judicial veto was a victory for the North and East. The West and South, however, were still destined to have the last word.

The Sixteenth Amendment.—The decision in the Pollock case had hardly been rendered when agitation began for the adoption of an amendment to the Constitution which would overcome the effect of that decision and enable Congress to levy income taxes without apportionment. The criticism of the decision both by the dissenting judges and also by lawyers and laymen apparently was not without some effect on the Court, for it did not extend the doctrine of the Pollock case but, on the contrary, in subsequent cases rather tended to limit it. Thus, when the constitutionality of an act of Congress of 1909 levying a 1 per cent tax upon the annual net income of corporations was attacked in the Supreme Court on the ground (among others) that it was an unapportioned direct tax, that tribunal held that the tax was an excise or indirect tax and consequently did not need to be apportioned.[2] This tendency of the Court toward a more liberal interpretation of the constitutional provision regarding direct taxes, however, was not sufficient to satisfy the more liberal, progressive, or radical leaders in the country, who continued to insist upon the adoption of a constitutional amendment. Congress in 1909 passed the necessary joint resolution which was submitted to the states and adopted in 1913. This Sixteenth Amendment provides that: "The Congress shall have power to lay and collect taxes on incomes, from whatever source derived, without apportionment among the several states, and without regard to any census or enumeration."

By this means the decision of the Supreme Court in the Pollock case was "recalled." Since the adoption of the amendment, it is no longer important whether income taxes are classed as direct or indirect. The Court has nevertheless intimated that the effect of the amendment is to convert income taxes into excise or indirect taxes.[3] They must therefore conform to a geographical uniformity but may be progressive.

One of the principal questions which arose at the time of the adoption of the Sixteenth Amendment was as to the meaning of the phrase "from whatever source derived." If this language is taken literally at its face value, it would seem to be broad enough to enlarge considerably the

---

[1] It is to be remembered that the Court was here construing the term "direct taxes" in the constitutional, and not in the economic, sense.

[2] Flint v. Stone Tracy Co., 220 U. S. 107 (1911).

[3] Brushaber v. Union Pacific R. R., 240 U. S. 1 (1916).

kinds of incomes which Congress can tax. In several of the state legislatures to which the proposed amendment was submitted, the objection was raised that this provision of the amendment would enable Congress to tax the salaries of state officers and the interest from state and municipal bonds—a power which it had not hitherto possessed. Even able lawyers, such as Governor Hughes of New York, himself later a member of the Supreme Court, were opposed to the amendment on this ground. These fears, however, were baseless, for the Supreme Court, in decisions rendered since the adoption of the amendment, has held that it does not enable Congress to tax any incomes which it did not have the power to tax before its adoption. Its effect was merely to avoid the rule laid down in the Pollock case.[1] The scope of the taxing power of Congress had not been enlarged, but merely the method of taxation had been changed.

As illustrating this position of the Court, may be cited the case of Evans v. Gore,[2] in which it was held that, in spite of the broad language of the amendment, the salaries of Federal judges were not subject to a Federal income tax. Their constitutional exemption against diminution of their compensation during continuance in office remained unimpaired. This doctrine was applied even to judges appointed after the passage by Congress of the income tax law.[3]

Shortly after the adoption of the Sixteenth Amendment, Congress passed an income tax law, which, with changes and amendments made since then, has come to be one of the principal sources of revenue of the Federal Government. An interesting case which arose under this law involved the question as to whether or not stock dividends are to be considered as income which may be taxed. On the theory that such a dividend merely splits the stock into a larger number of parts without increasing the assets, a bare majority of the Court held that it was not income.[4] This decision was followed by a great increase in the number of stock dividends issued by large corporations. The Court also held that "rights," issued by a corporation to stockholders enabling them to subscribe for additional stock at less than the market price, are not income.[5] If new stock or rights thus issued, however, are sold, the proceeds are of course income and subject to tax.

Indirect Taxes.—It is required by the Constitution that "all duties, imposts, and excises shall be uniform throughout the United States."[6] By these terms the framers of the Constitution included all taxes that

[1] *Ibid.*
[2] 253 U. S. 245 (1920).
[3] Miles v. Graham, 268 U. S. 501 (1925).
[4] Eisner v. Macomber, 252 U. S. 189 (1920).
[5] Miles v. Safe Deposit and Trust Co., 259 U. S. 247 (1922).
[6] Art. I, sect. 8, cl. 1.

are not direct. "Duties" and "imposts" properly refer to taxes on imports, while "excises" are internal revenue taxes levied on rights, franchises, and privileges or upon the manufacture, sale, and transfer of property rather than upon the property itself. The meaning of the phrase "uniform throughout the United States" was not definitely passed upon by the Supreme Court until a case came before it involving the constitutionality of the inheritance tax law enacted by Congress during the Spanish-American War.

This law levied a succession tax upon legacies. The grounds upon which the law was attacked were that, if the tax was direct, it was unconstitutional because not apportioned; while, if indirect, it was equally invalid because not uniform inasmuch as legacies worth less than $10,000 were exempted from the tax, while, in the case of legacies above that amount, the rate of the tax varied progressively according to the amount of the legacy and also according to the degree of relationship of the legatee or beneficiary. It was further contended that the law was invalid because, if it were a tax on the right of succession to property, it invaded a field reserved to the states.

All of these objections were considered in the opinion of the Court.[1] Upon the question as to whether an inheritance tax is a direct or an indirect tax, the Court took the position that such a tax is not on the property inherited but rather upon the right of the beneficiary to inherit. The tax does not take part of a person's property but intercepts a part of it on the way to him. This distinction seems rather tenuous but is nevertheless well established. From this line of reasoning the Court concluded that the tax was an excise and therefore indirect. Consequently, it did not need to be apportioned, but it had to meet the requirement of uniformity.

The second question involved in the case was as to whether or not the law was in conformity with the constitutional requirement of uniformity. Upon this point the Court declared that an intrinsic uniformity could not have been intended, for this interpretation would render the words "throughout the United States" mere surplusage. It was held, therefore, that geographical uniformity was all that was required. If property of the same amount or rights of the same value are taxed at the same rate wherever found in the United States, the requirement is complied with. As was pointed out by the Court in another case: "The tax is uniform when it operates with the same force and effect in every place where the subject of it is found."[2] The law was therefore upheld against attack on this ground.

The Court also denied the validity of the third objection to the law mentioned above, declaring that

[1] Knowlton v. Moore, 178 U. S. 41 (1900).
[2] Head money cases, 112 U. S. 580 (1884).

. . . the thing forming the universal subject of taxation upon which inheritance and legacy taxes rest is the transmission or receipt, and not the right existing to regulate . . . A tax placed upon an inheritance or legacy diminishes, to the extent of the tax, the value of the right to inherit or receive, but this is a burden cast upon the recipient and not upon the power of the state to regulate.

By an act of 1926 Congress provided that, if payers of the Federal inheritance tax also paid state inheritance taxes, they would be entitled to a refund of the amount paid the state, provided this was not more than 80 per cent of the Federal tax.   By constitutional provision, Florida prohibits the levying of inheritance taxes.   Consequently, residents of that state paying Federal inheritance taxes would not become entitled to the stated refund.   Florida therefore attacked the validity of this provision on the ground that it did not comply with the constitutional requirement of uniformity.   This contention, however, the Court denied, holding that

. . . Congress cannot accommodate its legislation to the conflicting or dissimilar laws of the several states nor control the diverse conditions to be found in the various states which necessarily work unlike results from the enforcement of the same tax.   All that the Constitution requires is that the law shall be uniform in the sense that by its provisions the rule of liability shall be alike, in all parts of the United States.[1]

On account of the difference in the methods of levying direct and indirect taxes as required by the Constitution, the Supreme Court has been called upon in a number of cases to decide whether a given tax falls in one or the other class.   In addition to the inheritance tax, other taxes which the Court has held to be indirect are duties on immigrants,[2] taxes on sugar refining, and on the manufacture and sale of tobacco.   Taxes upon sales or income resulting from the exercise of a license or privilege have been held to be indirect.   Thus, a tax upon sales or contracts of sale at exchanges or boards of trade was held to be indirect because it was an excise tax upon the privilege of engaging in such business at these places.[3]   Likewise, a tax upon the net income of corporations was an excise tax upon the privilege of engaging in business in the corporate capacity, the value of the privilege being measured by the amount of the income.[4]

[1] Florida v. Mellon, 273 U. S. 12 (1927).   Cf. Poe v. Seaborn, 282 U. S. 101 (1930), in which the Court, while allowing a husband and wife to file separate Federal income tax returns, each treating one-half of the community income as their separate incomes, if they reside in a state in which the wife has a vested property right in the community property equal with that of her husband, nevertheless ruled that "differences of state law, which may bring a person within or without the category designated by Congress as taxable, may not be read into the Federal income tax laws to spell out a lack of uniformity."

[2] Head money cases, 112 U. S. 580 (1884).

[3] Nicol v. Ames, 173 U. S. 509 (1899).

[4] Flint v. Stone Tracy Co., 220 U. S. 107 (1911).

Taxes on Exports.—In order to placate the Southern states, which were engaged mainly in agriculture and desired freedom from interference by taxation in the exportation of their surplus agricultural products, the framers of the Constitution placed upon Congress the express limitation that "no tax or duty shall be laid on articles exported from any state."[1] It may be noted in this connection that the states are also prohibited, without the consent of Congress, from laying imposts or duties on imports or exports, except what may be absolutely necessary for executing their inspection laws.[2] It is therefore virtually impossible for any government in the United States to levy taxes on exports. Although the Constitution is not clear upon the point, the term "export" has been construed by the Court to mean articles taken from the United States to a foreign country and therefore does not comprise articles transported from one state of the Union to another.[3]

It will be noticed that the limitation upon Congress does not prohibit that body from levying taxes on exports from the territories or dependencies of the United States but merely from the states of the Union. Moreover, in one of the insular cases decided shortly after our acquisition of outlying territories during the Spanish War, it was held that Congress could levy a tax on goods carried from New York to Porto Rico.[4] This seems to have been considered, however, as an import into Porto Rico rather than as an export from New York.

An export tax is one levied upon articles exported or upon the right to export them. In an early case a state statute levying a license fee on the right to sell imports was held invalid.[5] By analogy, it would seem that a license fee levied on exporters as such would also be invalid. A tax which is levied upon articles which are intended to be exported and singles them out because of this intention is also an export tax, even though the actual process of exportation has not yet begun. The constitutional prohibition against export taxes, however, does not prevent the application of a general property tax to goods intended ultimately for export, provided they are not discriminated against on this account and provided also that the actual movement towards exportation has not yet begun.[6]

A number of cases have been brought to the Supreme Court in which that tribunal has been called upon to decide whether a given tax is or

[1] Art. I, sect. 9, cl. 5.
[2] Art. I, sect. 10, cl. 2.
[3] Woodruff v. Parham, 8 Wall. 123 (1868).
[4] Dooley v. United States, 182 U. S. 222 (1901), 183 U. S. 151 (1901).
[5] Brown v. Maryland, 12 Wheat. 419 (1827).
[6] Turpin v. Burgess, 117 U. S. 504 (1886). *Cf.* Coe v. Errol, 116 U. S. 517 (1886) wherein it was held that the process of interstate transportation does not begin until the goods are started on their journey beyond the state or delivered to a common carrier for that purpose.

is not an export tax within the constitutional prohibition. Among taxes held to be export taxes and therefore invalid are stamp taxes on foreign bills of lading which evidence the exports and stamp taxes upon policies of marine insurance on articles being exported. On the other hand, it has been held that a tax levied upon the income or profits of a domestic corporation derived from its business of exporting goods to a foreign country is not an export tax.[1]

In conclusion, it may be noted that the constitutional prohibition regarding export taxes does not prevent Congress from regulating the export trade in ways other than by taxation. This power of regulation may, under some circumstances, even go as far as prohibition, as in the case of the embargo act of 1807.

Federal Taxation of State Agencies.—One of the implied limitations upon the taxing power of Congress is that it cannot tax the agencies or instrumentalities of the state governments. The converse of this proposition is also true, *viz.*, that the states cannot tax the instrumentalities of the National Government. The leading case in which the latter principle was laid down was McCulloch v. Maryland,[2] decided in 1819, in which it was held that a state did not have the right to tax the essential operations of a branch of the Bank of the United States. In the course of his opinion in this case, Chief Justice Marshall made use of the famous phrase: "The power to tax involves the power to destroy." This was the major premise from which he derived the corollary that a state cannot tax the instrumentalities of the National Government.

With reference to this proposition, it may be admitted that, from a strictly legal point of view, there is little doubt that a power to tax may involve the power to destroy. If the taxing authority has the power to levy a tax of 1 per cent, there is no definite limit implied upon the rate of taxation, which might conceivably reach 100 per cent. This, however, would amount to confiscation and, from a fiscal point of view, would be suicidal. It would be "killing the goose that lays the golden egg." Looking at the matter from a more practical or fiscal point of view, destruction of the thing taxed is only a very remote possibility, unless the tax should be a discriminatory one, singling out a particular object or group of objects and placing on it a special tax burden. Except in the case of a discriminatory tax, therefore, the principle that the power to tax is the power to destroy does not seem to be one to which much weight should be attached. In subsequent cases, however, the Court has followed the doctrine laid down by Marshall and has applied it to Federal taxes as well as state taxes.

Collector v. Day.—The leading case with reference to Federal taxes on state instrumentalities is Collector v. Day,[3] decided in 1870, in which

[1] National Paper and Type Co. v. Bowers, 266 U. S. 373 (1924).
[2] 4 Wheat. 316 (1819).
[3] 11 Wall. 113 (1870).

the Court was called upon to determine whether the salary of a Massachusetts probate judge was subject to taxation under a general income tax law passed by Congress. The tax was not a discriminatory one. Nevertheless, the Court held that a state judge is not subject to such a tax on his salary. The reasoning of the Court is shown by the following passage from the opinion:

If the means and instrumentalities employed by that [the National] Government to carry into operation the powers granted to it are, necessarily and for the sake of self-preservation, exempt from taxation by the states, why are not those of the states depending upon their reserved powers, for like reasons, equally exempt from Federal taxation? Their unimpaired existence in the one case is as essential as in the other. It is admitted that there is no express provision in the Constitution that prohibits the General Government from taxing the means and instrumentalities of the states, nor is there any prohibiting the states from taxing the means and instrumentalities of that government. In both cases the exemption rests upon necessary implication, and is upheld by the great law of self-preservation—as any government, whose means employed in conducting its operations, if subject to the control of another and distinct government, can only exist at the mercy of that government. Of what avail are these means if another power may tax them at discretion?

The references in this passage to "self-preservation" show that the Court had in mind the possible destructive effects of taxation. The Court tacitly assumed that a general income tax may be destructive—an assumption which is economically unsound. It is true, theoretically at least, that the National Government has no right by the indirect method of taxation to destroy the essential instrumentalities of the states, for this would be tantamount to destroying the states themselves. If Congress can tax the salaries of state officers at all, so the argument runs, there is no definite point at which the rate of taxation may be limited, and the rate may be so heavy that the officers' net salaries may be reduced to such a negligible amount that states will be unable to find persons to fill its offices, except those who are willing to serve without compensation. Here again, this deduction is not valid economically, except on the assumption that the tax is a discriminatory one. It is true that constitutional law and economics do not need to agree, but, if they do not, the result is likely to be unfortunate.

Another ground on which the decision in this case was based was the coordinate relation of the national and state governments in the Federal Union. Since, upon this assumption, these governments stand on an equal plane to each other, an implied limitation upon the taxing power of the states is equally valid as applied to the National Government. This is in striking contrast with other cases in which the supremacy of the National Government has been maintained in the exercise of its granted powers, even though they conflict with those of the states. In explanation of the attitude of the Court in the principal case, it may be noticed that it was rendered during the reconstruction period after the Civil War when the Court was engaged in endeavoring to stem the tendency in Congress toward extreme centralization at the expense of state rights, which, if it had been allowed to proceed unchecked, might have engulfed the states completely in the rising tide of nationalism.

However much the doctrine of Collector v. Day may be criticized, it has nevertheless been followed in subsequent cases and is now well established. It applies not only to the states but also to municipalities and other local governmental subdivisions of the states. It applies not only to officers but also to employees. This means that the vast army of state and local officers and employees are not subject to a Federal income tax on their official salaries or wages. They may, however, be required to pay such a tax on any income, above the exempted amount, which they receive from other sources. In this connection, a distinction must be made between officers and employees on the one hand and contractors on the other. A person who, for example, contracts with the state or municipality to construct a road or building is not a regular officer or employee and is subject to Federal income tax on the profit which he makes from such enterprise. The Supreme Court has held that fees received for professional services by consulting engineers from states and local subdivisions are subject to Federal taxation.[1] They are neither officers nor employees nor do they bear such a close relation to the state or local subdivision as to be classed as an instrumentality of such government, and a Federal tax upon their fees does not impair their ability to discharge their obligations under their contract with the state.

Under the doctrine of Collector v. Day it has also been held that the bonds, and the interest therefrom, issued by states and local governmental subdivisions are not subject to Federal taxation.[2] In the case cited, the Court declared that

. . . the same want of power to tax the property or revenues of the states or their instrumentalities exists in relation to a tax on the income from their securities and for the same reason . . . It is obvious that taxation on the interest therefrom would operate on the power to borrow before it is exercised, and would have a sensible influence on the contract, and that the tax in question is a tax on the power of the states and their instrumentalities to borrow money, and consequently repugnant to the Constitution.

One effect of this doctrine has been to make it possible for people to evade the Federal income tax by investing their funds in the bonds of

[1] Metcalf v. Mitchell, 269 U. S. 514 (1926).
[2] Pollock v. Farmers' Loan and Trust Co., 157 U. S. 429, 158 U. S. 601 (1895). Four justices dissented in this case, but not in regard to this point.

states and municipal corporations. The rate of interest on these bonds is lower than on those of private corporations, but, for persons with incomes in the higher brackets, it is advantageous to sacrifice the difference in interest return in order to evade the higher rates of the Federal income tax. It results from this situation that a medium of investment is created which affords persons of large wealth a means of evading the share of Federal taxation which they would otherwise have to bear. Another effect of the legal exemption of state and municipal bonds from Federal taxation is to create a demand for such securities which makes it easier to float them. Although this may be advantageous to a certain extent, it also sometimes tempts states and cities to indulge in unnecessary and extravagant borrowing.

In the Federal taxation of state agencies, it would seem that a distinction should be made between those agencies used in the discharge of the ordinary or essential functions of government and those used for carrying out what may be regarded as more suitable for private enterprise. This distinction is illustrated by the South Carolina dispensary case, in which the Court was called upon to decide whether state agents engaged in dispensing liquor were subject to a Federal internal revenue tax.[1] The majority of the Court held that they were subject to such tax because the selling of liquor is not an ordinary governmental function. They also held that, if the state could monopolize the business of selling liquor, it could do the same with reference to other commodities to such an extent that, if such businesses should be thereby withdrawn from the Federal taxing power, the latter would be seriously interfered with. Three dissenting judges took the stronger ground of holding that the state, in taking over the liquor business, was exercising its police power and, in order to be consistent with previous decisions, the state agents engaged therein should not be subject to Federal tax. If the state so desired, it could prohibit the liquor business altogether, and this was not true with reference to the business of selling ordinary commodities. The majority of the Court seem to have been influenced by the feeling that the state was engaged in a socialistic (and therefore improper) enterprise.

There are other apparent exceptions to the doctrine of Collector v. Day, or rather situations which do not fall within the rule of that case. Thus, a private corporation created by the state is not a state agency employed in the exercise of ordinary or essential governmental functions and is therefore subject to Federal taxation.[2] The tax is upon the business of the private corporation and not upon the right of the state to create corporations. Similarly, a Federal inheritance tax is valid in spite of the fact that the regulation of succession to property is under the

[1] South Carolina v. United States, 199 U. S. 437 (1905).
[2] Flint v. Stone Tracy Co., 220 U. S. 107 (1911).

control of the state. The Federal tax is not upon the power of the state to regulate, but upon the transmission or receipt of the property inherited.[1] In the case just cited the Court also held that an inheritance tax is not levied upon the property inherited. This being true, it was held in a later case that a Federal inheritance tax is valid, even though levied upon bequests to states or municipal corporations.[2]

With reference generally to the rule of the reciprocal exemption of governmental instrumentalities from taxation, the Supreme Court has taken the position that it will not be applied mechanically and without regard to the consequences upon the operations of government.[3] This rule must be given "such a practical application as will not unduly impair the taxing power of the one or the appropriate exercise of its functions by the other."[4]

The doctrine of Collector v. Day is not in conflict with the decision in an earlier case,[5] in which a prohibitive Federal tax on the note issues of state banks was held valid, because the former had to do with a tax on a right reserved to the states, while the latter had to do with a tax on a matter which the Constitution grants to Congress the power to regulate. The doctrine of Collector v. Day was not affected by the adoption of the Sixteenth Amendment, because the latter, as we have seen, did not enlarge the scope of the taxing power of Congress.

National Borrowing.—The ordinary revenues of the Government are not likely to be sufficient to meet emergencies and extraordinary expenditures, such as the construction of the Panama Canal or the waging of the World War. Consequently, on such occasions the Government must resort to borrowing. This necessity was foreseen by the framers of the Constitution, who provided that Congress should have power "to borrow money on the credit of the United States."[6] Unlike some states and most local governments, the National Government is legally unlimited as to the amount or other conditions of its borrowing. During the World War, the total of loans floated by the Government ran into billions of dollars, and much of this has not yet been paid off. Constitutionally, the Government is under no necessity to provide for the payment of its debt, but considerations of honor and of sound finance require that all national bonds be paid at or before maturity.

The Currency and Legal Tender.—In addition to the power to borrow money, Congress is also given the power to coin money and to regulate

---

[1] Knowlton v. Moore, 178 U. S. 41 (1900).

[2] Snyder v. Bettman, 190 U. S. 249 (1903). Three justices dissented.

[3] Educational Films Corporation v. Ward, 282 U. S. 397 (1931).

[4] Susquehanna Power Co. v. State Tax Commission of Maryland, 283 U. S. 291 (1931).

[5] Veazie Bank v. Fenno, 8 Wall. 533 (1869).

[6] Art. I, sect. 8, cl. 2.

the value thereof.[1] As implied in these powers, Congress was early held to have the implied power to establish a national bank with authority to conduct a banking business including the issuance of bank notes.[2]

Prior to the adoption of the Constitution, the currency of the country was in a badly demoralized condition. Paper money unsupported by specie was issued in large quantities by both Congress and the states, with the natural result that it depreciated in value very rapidly. Trade and commerce became thereby impeded and unsettled. With this situation in mind, the framers of the Constitution inserted a provision prohibiting the states from coining money, emitting bills of credit, or making anything but gold and silver coin a legal tender in payment of debts.[3] The National Government was not prohibited from emitting bills of credit. On the other hand, no express grant of such a power was made to it. At one stage in the development of the draft of the Constitution, such an express grant was inserted but was later stricken out. This action seems to have been due not to a desire to withdraw this power from Congress but rather to a feeling that an express grant of the power was unnecessary, since it was implied in the power to borrow money. After the adoption of the Constitution, the existence of this power was assumed without question.

At the time of the Civil War, however, a more serious question arose when Congress undertook not only to emit bills or notes on the credit of the United States but also to make them legal tender in the payment of debts between private individuals. This was known as the "greenback" issue. As far as the intention of the framers of the Constitution can be ascertained, it would seem that they did not intend that Congress should make anything but metallic money a legal tender. When, shortly after the Civil War, the first of the legal tender cases arose in the Supreme Court, that tribunal held that Congress had exceeded its constitutional powers in making these greenbacks a legal tender.[4] Such a power, the Court held, was not essential to the effective exercise of the borrowing power, and, if creditors could be compelled to accept the greenbacks in payment of debts, they would be deprived of property without due process of law.

In this first legal tender case, three justices dissented. Shortly afterwards, two vacancies occurred on the Supreme Court bench and their places were filled by appointees who agreed with the views of the minority, who thereby became the majority. Thereupon the question was again brought before the Court and the decision in the first legal tender case was overruled by a vote of five to four.[5] In the second legal

[1] *Ibid.*, cl. 5.
[2] McCulloch v. Maryland, 4 Wheat. 316 (1819).
[3] Art. I, sect. 10, cl. 1.
[4] Hepburn v. Griswold, 8 Wall. 603 (1869).
[5] Knox v. Lee, 12 Wall. 457 (1870).

tender case, the Court upheld the power of Congress to issue legal tender notes mainly as a legitimate exercise of the war power. This conclusion was also supported by the powers granted to Congress to borrow and to coin money. It was not necessary, said the Court, to deduce a power as implied from some one expressly granted power: it might be deduced from a group of powers. The Court further denied that making such notes a legal tender deprived a creditor of his property without due process of law. As an indirect result of such legislation, the individual creditor might suffer loss, but this was no more a legal deprivation of property than would be a loss due to a change in the purchasing power of money.

After the decision in the second legal tender case, the only question which still remained to be settled was as to whether Congress had the power to issue legal tender notes not only in time of war but also in time of peace. This question came up a few years later in the third legal tender case.[1] With only one justice dissenting, the Court in this case upheld the power of Congress to issue legal tender notes even in time of peace. It followed the preceding case in deriving this power from a group or aggregate of powers, including those to lay taxes, pay debts, borrow money, coin money, and regulate the value thereof and also other powers implied in these express powers. The Court also adverted to the fact that the power in question is one exercised by sovereign governments generally but did not rest its decision solely upon that dangerous ground.

Public Expenditures.—Under the Constitution no money may be drawn from the treasury of the United States except "in consequence of appropriations made by law."[2] The term "law" here means an act of Congress. This provision concentrates upon Congress the responsibility for appropriations, subject to the veto power of the President. Appropriations, however, may be made in lump sums and placed at the disposal of the President, the detailed expenditures from such appropriation to be made in accordance with his discretion. He may even be authorized to make such expenditures without specifically accounting therefor, as in the case of his secret service fund. The fact that such secret fund exists, however, cannot be kept secret, because the Constitution requires a periodical publication of the receipts and expenditures of all public money.[3]

---

[1] Juilliard v. Greenman, 110 U. S. 421 (1884).

[2] Art. I, sect. 9, cl. 7.

[3] *Ibid.*

CHAPTER XVII

THE REGULATION OF COMMERCE

The Commerce Clause.—Next to the power of levying taxes upon individuals, the most important power granted to Congress by the Constitution is the power to regulate commerce. While the power of Congress to levy taxes is mainly concurrent with that of the states, the power of regulating that portion of commerce placed under the control of Congress is, by its very nature, largely exclusive in character.

The need which the business interests of the country felt for more centralized control over the regulation of commerce was, as we have seen, one of the leading causes which led to the adoption of the Constitution. Under the Articles of Confederation each state could levy duties upon and regulate the passage of goods across its boundaries to such an extent that the situation became intolerable. The framers of the Constitution desired to give the country the great blessing of freedom of commerce across state lines. The value of this freedom will be appreciated by anyone who has traveled in Europe and been subjected to the inconveniences of customs inspections at international boundaries.

The commerce clause, as finally drawn up, contained the broad grant to Congress of the power to "regulate commerce with foreign nations, and among the several states, and with the Indian tribes."[1] Of the several limitations placed by the Constitution upon the exercise of this power, the only one of considerable importance was that which prohibits Congress from levying any tax or duty on articles exported from any state.[2] This prohibition, as we have seen, was inserted as a concession to the agricultural interests of the South but does not prevent Congress from regulating exports in any other way than by taxation.

It will be noticed that the regulatory power granted to Congress extends to three kinds of commerce. Of these, that with the Indian tribes has become of increasingly less importance. Such tribes were formerly regarded very much like foreign nations, and the power of Congress to regulate commerce with them extended even to those tribes located entirely within the boundaries of states. The tribes are now regarded more in the nature of domestic dependent nations. Moreover, an increasing number of Indians are living outside the tribal relation.

[1] Art. I, sect. 8, cl. 3.
[2] Art. I, sect. 9, cl. 5.

The power of Congress to regulate foreign commerce is broader than its power to regulate interstate commerce because, with respect to the former, other sources of constitutional power may be drawn upon, such as the treaty power and others concerning the management of foreign relations. Congress can lay general or special embargoes upon the importation of goods, can exclude all or certain classes of alien immigrants, and can prohibit foreign vessels of all or of certain nationalities from entering our ports. The power of exclusion includes the power of admission under certain conditions.

Besides the three kinds of commerce which Congress is given the power to regulate, there remains the commerce which is entirely within the boundaries of a particular state, or intrastate commerce. As a general rule, the power to regulate such commerce still remains within the control of the state. The distinction between interstate and intrastate commerce is somewhat arbitrary and is not based upon economic considerations. The language of the Constitution, however, makes it necessary for the student of the fundamental law to draw this distinction.

The commerce clause has become the most important provision of the Constitution concerning the relation between the Government and business. More decisions of the Supreme Court interpreting it have been rendered than in the case of any other provision of the Constitution except the due-process clause of the Fourteenth Amendment. The interpretation of the commerce clause, however, was slow in developing, only a few decisions regarding it having been rendered prior to the middle of the nineteenth century.

What Is Commerce?—At the time of the adoption of the Constitution, commerce was in the stagecoach period of development. Its volume was small and its instrumentalities were rudimentary. It is therefore remarkable that the language of the Constitution on this subject should still be found applicable to the enormous volume and elaborate facilities of commerce of the present day. This is due in part to the simplicity of the language used by the framers, in dealing with this matter, and in part to the broad and liberal construction which has been placed upon such language by the courts.

This broad view was taken by the Supreme Court in the first case involving this clause which came before it—a case which is still a leading one on this topic. This was the case of Gibbons v. Ogden,[1] which arose out of an act passed by the New York state legislature granting to Fulton and Livingston the exclusive privilege or monopoly of navigating by steam the waters of the state. Under the act no one could engage in such navigation without a license from such grantees. Such a license was secured by Ogden to navigate the Hudson River between New York City and points in New Jersey. The same waters were navigated by

[1] 9 Wheat. 1 (1824).

Gibbons who was engaged in the coasting trade under authority of an act of Congress. Ogden sought to enjoin Gibbons from violating his exclusive right and won the case in the New York state court, whereupon Gibbons appealed to the Supreme Court of the United States.

Chief Justice Marshall, in one of his greatest opinions, supported the contention of Gibbons and held that he had the right to engage in the navigation of these waters in spite of the attempt of New York state to create a monopoly for its grantees. On this account the case has been called the first of the great anti-trust decisions. In the course of his opinion, Marshall pointed out that the argument had been made that commerce is confined to traffic, to buying and selling, or the interchange of commodities. Marshall, however, repudiated this narrow doctrine and declared that "commerce, undoubtedly, is traffic, but it is something more—it is intercourse. It describes the commercial intercourse between nations, and parts of nations, in all its branches . . . All America understands, and has uniformly understood, the word 'commerce' to comprehend navigation."

It is not quite clear from this language whether Marshall intended to confine the meaning of commerce to commercial intercourse or to give it the broader meaning of intercourse in general. This question, however, has been settled by subsequent adjudications in favor of the broader view. Thus, it has been held that the thousands of people who daily pass and repass over a bridge spanning the Ohio River between Ohio and Kentucky "may be as truly said to be engaged in commerce as if they were shipping cargoes of merchandise from New York to Liverpool."[1] Undoubtedly, some of these thousands of people were not engaged in business or traffic in the ordinary sense but were crossing the bridge merely for pleasure. Yet, in the constitutional sense, they were engaged in interstate commerce. It follows that a pleasure yacht sailing back and forth across a river which is a boundary line between two states, or a man swimming from shore to shore of such a river, or a person taking a walk for his health across a state line, would be engaged in interstate commerce. So would also a man crossing a state line in his own automobile with goods intended not for sale but for his own use.[2]

Not only the passengers or shippers of goods across state lines are engaged in interstate commerce but also the common carriers, whether railroad, motor-truck, or other companies which agree to transport such

[1] Covington Bridge Co. v. Kentucky, 154 U. S. 204 (1894). In this case the element of commercial enterprise was not wholly lacking, because the bridge was operated by its owners for profit. In other cases, however, the Court has indicated that mere transportation or transmission across state lines with no element of profit involved constitutes interstate commerce. Cf. United States v. Simpson, 252 U. S. 465 (1920), wherein the transportation of liquor by its owner in his own automobile across state lines for his personal use was held to be interstate commerce.

[2] United States v. Simpson, 252 U. S. 465 (1920).

goods or passengers. The transportation of oil, gas, or water through pipe lines across state boundaries is also interstate commerce. It is not necessary, however, that the thing which crosses a state line should be material or tangible. The mere transmission of intelligence across state lines by means never dreamed of by the framers of the Constitution is a form of interstate commerce. Examples of this are the sending of communications across state lines by telephone, telegraph,[1] or by the wigwag system and the sending of wireless messages or radiograms. Moreover, the message need not be in words, either code or ordinary, but may be in the form of music. A band or orchestra playing so that the notes may be heard across state lines, either by the propulsion of sound waves or through a radio broadcasting station, is engaged in interstate commerce. These illustrations indicate the broad scope of such commerce and the broad power of regulation conferred upon Congress.

A drummer who acts as an agent for a company in one state and takes orders in another state for goods to be shipped into the latter state is engaged in interstate commerce.[2] On the other hand, a peddler who sells goods which he carries with him, even though they have been imported from another state, is not engaged in such commerce, because his business is essentially local in character.

It has been held that the business of a correspondence school which has pupils in other states is interstate commerce, because it involves the sending of books, papers, and information across state lines in exchange for the fees received.[3] On the other hand, it was held at an early date that an insurance company which makes contracts of insurance with customers in other states is not engaged in interstate commerce.[4] In this case the Court declared that contracts of insurance are not articles of commerce in any proper sense of the word and that they are not interstate, but local, transactions. The particular form of insurance involved in this case was fire insurance, but the same rule has been applied by the courts to life, marine, and other forms of insurance generally. This case arose shortly after the Civil War, when the Supreme Court was stemming the excessive tide towards nationalism. If the same question should arise today for the first time, the Court might possibly take a broader view of it. At any rate, the doctrine of the case is well established, with the result that the vastly important business of insurance is within the regulatory power of the respective states rather than of Congress.

Another form of activity which is not commerce is manufacturing and production generally, including farming, fishing, lumbering, and mining.

[1] Pensacola Telegraph Co. v. Western Union Telegraph Co., 96 U. S. 1 (1877).
[2] Robbins v. Taxing District of Shelby County, 120 U. S. 489 (1887).
[3] International Textbook Co. v. Pigg, 217 U. S. 91 (1910).
[4] Paul v. Virginia, 8 Wall. 168 (1869).

These activities, therefore, are subject to regulation by the states and no such power is conferred upon Congress by the commerce clause. Undoubtedly, however, most of the articles produced by such activities are intended for ultimate shipment into other states and over such interstate shipments Congress, of course, has regulatory power.

When Is Commerce Interstate?—The transportation of goods or passengers or the transmission of messages across state lines constitutes interstate commerce, to which the regulatory power of Congress extends. The exercise of this power is, of course, not confined to the instant of time at which the state boundary is crossed but extends to the whole of the interstate journey or even to the entire commercial transaction which involves the crossing of a state line. As Marshall pointed out in Gibbons v. Ogden, "the power of Congress does not stop at the jurisdictional lines of the several states," but "must be exercised within the territorial jurisdiction of the several states."

Where the journey involves two or more states, it is interstate.[1] This is true even though the beginning and termination of the journey are points within the same state, provided the route passes through another state. It is logical that, where the transaction involves two or more states, the power of regulation should be in Congress because no one state would be jurisdictionally competent to regulate adequately and the combined regulations of the several states affected might be conflicting and unduly burdensome upon such commerce. The power of Congress extends to the subject of its regulation wherever it is found, even though intermingled with the purely internal commerce of a state. Thus, a small steamer plying on a river between points wholly within the state of Michigan but carrying some goods to or from points outside that state was held to be engaged in interstate commerce.[2]

The Beginning and Termination of Interstate Commerce.—Since Congress has no power to regulate the purely internal commerce of a state, it is important to determine when persons or goods in transit within a state cease to be intrastate, and become interstate, commerce. *Vice versa*, it is equally important to determine when they cease to be interstate, and become intrastate, commerce. Manufacture and production, as we have seen, are not interstate commerce, even though the goods produced are intended for ultimate transportation into other states. But at some point or stage in the course of the business transaction, they

[1] It has been held, however, that the business of selling oil and gasoline by an oil company to fish packers in the same state is not interstate commerce even though the articles are sent by the packers to their agents in another state with a bill of lading indicating that the articles remain the property of the oil company until delivered to the packers' agents. This was an attempt to make the transaction have the appearance of interstate commerce in order to avoid local taxation. Superior Oil Co. v. Mississippi *ex rel.* Knox, 280 U. S. 390 (1930).

[2] The Daniel Ball, 10 Wall. 557 (1871).

become interstate commerce. This point is when the goods are started on a continuous journey between two states or are delivered to a railroad company or other common carrier for that purpose. The continuity of the journey, however, may be temporarily interrupted by incidents happening in the course of transportation. Thus, logs being floated down a river may be temporarily halted on account of low water. Again, goods being shipped by train may be temporarily sidetracked, or transferred from one car to another, or even wrecked and scattered about the ground but they do not thereby cease to be interstate commerce. The same is true of cattle which are temporarily halted during an interstate journey to be fed, watered, or pastured.[1]

The local movement of goods preparatory to being delivered to a common carrier is not part of the interstate journey. Thus, the moving of logs from the forest to the banks of a river to wait for seasonal high water in preparation for floating down the river and into another state is not a part of the interstate journey.[2] Similarly, if a shipper hires a drayman to haul goods to a railroad freight station preparatory to being delivered to the freight agent for an interstate journey, the trip to the station is not a part of that journey. If the drayman were an agent of the railroad company, however, the situation would be different. Again, if a person hires a taxicab to take him between his hotel and the railroad station either before or after an interstate journey by rail, the trip in the taxicab is not a part of that journey. But if the railroad company sells a passenger a ticket which includes transportation to or from his hotel by taxicab, the trip in the taxicab is a part of the interstate journey.

Since the states cannot tax interstate commerce, goods shipped from one state into another are not subject to taxation by the latter state until the interstate journey has ended. The same rule applies also to goods shipped into a state from a foreign country. The most usual object of importation is sale. If goods imported could not be sold, the privilege of importation would be of little value. A state cannot, therefore, by prohibition or taxation, interfere with the first sale of goods imported from another state or foreign country.

The Original-package Doctrine.—On the other hand, Congress cannot regulate the purely internal commerce of a state. It is necessary, therefore, to determine the point at which commerce ceases to be interstate or foreign and becomes intrastate. For this purpose the "original-package" doctrine was formulated by Chief Justice Marshall in an early case which involved the constitutionality of an act of Maryland forbidding the selling by wholesale of articles imported from foreign countries without securing and paying for a license therefor.[3] In this case, the Court

---

[1] The driving of sheep across a state line is interstate commerce. Kelley v. Rhoads, 188 U. S. 1 (1903).

[2] Coe v. Errol, 116 U. S. 517 (1886).

[3] Brown v. Maryland, 12 Wheat. 419 (1827).

held that not only is the act of importing goods exempt from state taxation but also the goods after being imported, so long as they remain unsold in the original package. In the course of his opinion the Chief Justice declared that

. . . when the importer has so acted upon the thing imported, that it has become incorporated and mixed up with the mass of property in the country, it has, perhaps, lost its distinctive character as an import, and has become subject to the taxing power of the state; but while remaining the property of the importer, in his warehouse, in the original form or package in which it was imported, a tax upon it is too plainly a duty on imports to escape the prohibition of the Constitution.

The statute of Maryland involved in this case was held unconstitutional because it conflicted not only with the grant to Congress to regulate foreign commerce but also with that provision of the Constitution which prohibits the states, without the consent of Congress, from taxing imports.[1] Goods carried from one state to another, however, are not imports within the meaning of this provision, so that the constitutional prohibition against state taxation does not apply to interstate shipments after they have reached their destination.[2] The state may levy a tax upon goods which have been brought in from other states, even while still remaining in the original packages, provided it is not a special or discriminatory tax upon such goods, because of having thus been brought in, but falls equally upon all goods of the same class or kind regardless of the place of origin. The distinction between foreign and interstate commerce with respect to state taxation rests not only upon the difference in the language of the Constitution but also upon the logical basis that, since foreign goods are imported at the ports of comparatively few states, the power of those states to tax imports would enable them virtually to levy tribute upon inland states having no ports of entry for foreign goods.

The police power of the state does not apply to goods shipped from other states while remaining in the original packages, unsold, unbroken, and unused.[3] For example, before the adoption of the Eighteenth Amendment, a case arose involving the constitutionality of an Iowa statute which prohibited the manufacture, transportation into and sale within the state of liquor brought in from other states. The state was within its rights in prohibiting manufacture because this is not interstate commerce, but it could not prohibit transportation of liquor into its territory. Since sale is an essential element of interstate commerce, it

[1] Art. I, sect. 10, cl. 2.

[2] Brown v. Houston, 114 U. S. 622 (1885); Woodruff v. Parham, 8 Wall. 123 (1868).

[3] It would seem, however, that the police power of a state may extend to articles imported from other states, such as explosives, firearms, and diseased meat, even while they remain in the original packages, provided they are being used in such a way as to menace the public health or safety.

was held that the state could not prohibit the first sale of liquor imported in the original packages.[1]   Congress, however, could, and subsequently did, prohibit the transportation of intoxicating liquor into "dry" or prohibition states.[2]

When the original package in which goods are imported into a state is broken and the goods are offered for sale, they lose their character as interstate commerce and become subject to state taxation or regulation. Thus, it was held that the city of New Orleans had the right to tax packages of towels offered unbroken for sale after they had been taken out of the large wooden boxes in which they had been originally imported from abroad.[3]

The application of the original-package doctrine is sometimes difficult. It must be remembered that it is a rough rule of thumb and cannot be applied literally in all cases.   The line must be drawn somewhere and it is convenient to make it at the point where there is a change in the form of the goods imported.   The Tennessee cigarette case involved an attempt to use the original-package doctrine in order to evade the law of that state prohibiting the sale of cigarettes.   These articles were imported into that state from North Carolina in small paper boxes, each containing ten cigarettes, and dumped from an open basket upon the counter of the importer and offered by him for sale.   The Court held that this was an evasion of the spirit of the doctrine and that "the whole theory of the exemption of the original package from the operation of state laws is based upon the idea that the property is imported in the ordinary form in which, from time immemorial, foreign goods have been brought into the country."[4]   The Court added that "if there be any original package at all in this case, we think it is the basket and not the paper box."   It would seem, however, that the original-package doctrine was not applicable to this case.[5]

Sometimes imported articles are contained in no package of any sort. For example, new automobiles may be driven from the factory in Detroit to the agent's showroom in Chicago.   In such cases, the goods should be considered interstate commerce until sold.   When, as in such case, the original-package doctrine is not applicable, some other test must be applied to determine when the goods imported cease to be interstate commerce.

Federal Regulation of Interstate Commerce.—An attempt has been made above to indicate the meaning of the word "commerce" as used

[1] Leisy v. Hardin, 135 U. S. 100 (1890).

[2] Webb-Kenyon Act of 1913, 37 Stat. at L. 699, which was upheld in Clark Distilling Co. v. Western Maryland Ry. Co., 242 U. S. 311 (1917).

[3] May & Co. v. New Orleans, 178 U. S. 496 (1900).

[4] Austin v. Tennessee, 179 U. S. 343 (1900).

[5] *Cf.* Cook v. Marshall, 196 U. S. 261 (1905), where there was not even a basket.

in the constitutional provision. Another important word in that provision, whose meaning it is next in order to consider, is "regulate." The power given Congress to regulate commerce enables it to lay down the rule which shall guide the course or conduct of commerce. This includes not only the power to protect and promote but also to restrict and even to prohibit certain kinds of commerce.

The power of Congress to regulate commerce directly was not exercised in any important way until the latter half of the nineteenth century. During the early part of that century, commerce was largely local and state regulation, therefore, was deemed sufficient for the purpose. This situation, however, gradually changed and, in 1886, the Supreme Court handed down its decision in the Wabash Railway case, which was the immediate occasion for the establishment of the Interstate Commerce Commission in the following year. In this case it was held that a state was without power to regulate the rates charged for that portion of an interstate journey entirely within its own boundaries.[1] If a state could not do this, it was necessary for Congress to act in order that such rates should not be entirely without regulation. Legally, Congress might have acted directly and prescribed the rates, but practically this function seems more suitable for exercise by an administrative, than by a legislative, body. Consequently, in 1887, Congress created the Interstate Commerce Commission and by acts passed at various times has given it extensive powers of regulation over interstate commerce. These extend to all such commerce as is carried on by railroads, oil pipe lines, and express, sleeping-car, telegraph, telephone, cable, and wireless companies. The commission has power to fix rates charged by these companies, to require them to make reports, and to maintain a uniform system of accounting.

In 1890, Congress passed the Sherman Anti-Trust Act, which prohibits and penalizes contracts or combinations in restraint of interstate or foreign commerce. This was an attempt by Congress to exercise control over trusts and monopolies which had begun to be formed about that time. At first the courts adopted such an unsympathetic attitude toward the purpose of this act that it remained almost a dead letter. This was illustrated by the decision of the Supreme Court in the sugar trust case,[2] decided in 1895, in which it was held that a combination of sugar manufacturing plants, which together controlled practically the entire output of sugar in the United States, was not within the prohibition of the Sherman Act. It is true, of course, that manufacturing, considered by itself, does not come within the interstate commerce power of Congress, but, since much of the sugar manufactured was to be shipped beyond state lines, interstate commerce was almost necessarily affected by the creation of such a monopoly.

[1] Wabash, St. L. and P. Ry. Co. v. Illinois, 118 U. S. 557 (1886).
[2] United States v. E. C. Knight Co., 156 U. S. 1 (1895).

A more liberal attitude was taken by the courts toward the Sherman Act in later cases, notably in the Northern Securities case,[1] decided in 1904, wherein a holding company formed for the purpose of acquiring and holding the majority of the stock of several interstate railway systems which had previously competed with each other was held to be a violation of the Sherman Act. Although the transaction involved was merely the purchase of railroad stock, the Court nevertheless held that the purpose and probable result of the transaction was to curtail, if not to eliminate, competition between the railroads and thus to affect interstate commerce.

An interesting point of statutory construction which may be mentioned in this connection was the decision of the Supreme Court handed down in 1911 in the Standard Oil and American Tobacco Company cases.[2] Overruling earlier opinions of the Court that every contract or combination in restraint of trade was prohibited by the Sherman Act, the Court held in these cases that only those combinations were prohibited that were in unreasonable restraint of trade. In other words, a distinction was made between good and bad trusts. This was the famous "rule of reason" and is a notable instance of judicial legislation.

Commerce and the National Police Power.—By the police power is meant fundamentally that power of government which is exercised for the protection and promotion of public health, order, safety, and morals, through restraint upon the individual. This is one of the most important of the powers reserved to the states. The Constitution makes no express grant of police power to the National Government, but such power may be exercised by it as implied in certain expressly granted powers, especially the postal power and the commerce power.

Among examples of police regulations under the commerce power are the series of safety appliance acts passed by Congress beginning in 1893. They are intended to protect the safety of passengers and employees by requiring air brakes and other safety devices on all cars of interstate trains, even though some of the cars are engaged in merely intrastate commerce.

The national police power may be exercised not only in the form of positive regulations but also in the form of the prohibition of the carriage in interstate commerce of articles or persons for purposes which are or may be detrimental to public health, safety, or morals.[3] Among the articles or persons excluded from interstate commerce by acts of Congress are lottery tickets, impure or misbranded foods and drugs, meat not

---

[1] Northern Securities Co. v. United States, 193 U. S. 197 (1904).

[2] 221 U. S. 1 (1911).

[3] It should be noted that the power of Congress to exclude from the mails and also its power to exclude from foreign commerce are broader than its power to exclude from interstate commerce.

properly inspected, obscene literature, women or girls for immoral purposes, prize-fight films, and stolen automobiles. Congress has also prohibited the transportation in interstate commerce of intoxicating liquor into "dry" or prohibition states.[1] Furthermore, Congress has prohibited railroads from transporting in interstate commerce any commodity which they own wholly or in part, except such articles as they use and except timber and its manufactures.[2]

The Lottery Case.—The power of Congress to prohibit the transportation of articles in interstate commerce was considered by the Supreme Court in the lottery case.[3] This case involved the constitutionality of an act of Congress passed in 1895 which prohibited the shipment of lottery tickets into any state from another state or from a foreign country. The act was upheld by the Court upon the following grounds. In the first place, lottery tickets were held to be articles of commerce in spite of the objection that they should be considered to be in the same class as contracts of insurance which, as we have seen, had been held not to be articles of commerce.

Having disposed of this objection, the Court was confronted with two other objections based upon peculiar features of the act. One objection was that the carrying of lottery tickets in interstate commerce was not detrimental to such commerce and did not interfere with its safety or efficiency in any way. The Court, however, held that the power of Congress was not confined merely to protecting the safety and efficiency of interstate commerce but extended also to the protection of the morals of persons to whom lottery tickets might be sent through the channels of such commerce. This argument assumed the correctness of the generally prevalent view in Congress and in the country that the traffic in lottery tickets was detrimental to public morals.

Finally, it was objected that the power of Congress to regulate commerce enabled it to prescribe the rule according to which such commerce should be carried on but did not enable that body absolutely to prohibit it from being carried on. The Court also overruled this objection, holding that Congress had the implied power under the commerce clause to prohibit activities of such obnoxious character as might be prohibited by the states under their police power. The power of the states over lotteries, however, did not extend to the prohibition of the shipment of tickets in interstate commerce. The Court was undoubtedly influenced in its decision by the consideration that, if Congress did not have the power in question, there would be no governmental power anywhere in the United States to deal adequately with the lottery evil.

[1] By the Webb-Kenyon Act of 1913. See Clark Distilling Co. v. Western Maryland Ry. Co., 242 U. S. 311 (1917).

[2] By the Hepburn Act of 1906.

[3] Champion v. Ames, 188 U. S. 321 (1903).

Largely upon the authority of the lottery case, the Supreme Court has also upheld the prohibitions contained in the White Slave Act,[1] the stolen automobile act,[2] and the Food and Drugs Act.[3] The last-named act was intended not to protect interstate commerce but to protect the public health. The provision against misleading labels was intended to protect the public against fraud.

Although in the lottery case and in later cases upholding prohibitory acts, the Court has broadly construed the commerce power of Congress, it should be noted that the Court did not go so far as to hold that Congress has the arbitrary power to exclude from interstate commerce any article which in its discretion it sees fit to exclude. That there is a limit to this power of Congress was shown in the first child labor case.

The First Child Labor Case.—In 1916, Congress passed an act excluding from shipment in interstate commerce the products of mines and manufacturing establishments in which, at any time during the preceding month, children under certain ages had been employed. This was an attempt on the part of Congress to reach the child labor evil which had grown to serious proportions in some states. That it would be held constitutional was confidently predicted by its supporters who relied upon the lottery case and other cases in which the power of Congress to exclude certain articles from interstate commerce had been upheld. These prophets, however, turned out to be mistaken, for, when it came before the Supreme Court in 1918 in the first child labor case,[4] it was held unconstitutional by a court dividing five to four upon the question.

The grounds upon which the majority of the Court held the act invalid were, first, that it was not properly a regulation of interstate commerce, because it did not promote the safety or efficiency of the carrying on of such commerce nor prevent harmful results from following it. The products of child labor, after the work upon them was finished, the Court pointed out, were harmless in themselves. In these respects the act differed from previous exclusion acts which had been upheld by the Court. In the second place, the majority held that the act was really a regulation of manufacture and production rather than of transportation and therefore encroached upon the reserved powers of the states. The majority then considered the argument that the act would

---

[1] Hoke v. United States, 227 U. S. 308 (1913).

[2] Brooks v. United States, 267 U. S. 432 (1925).

[3] Hipolite Egg Co. v. United States, 220 U. S. 45 (1911); McDermott v. Wisconsin, 228 U. S. 115 (1913). Congress had previously passed an act in 1884 prohibiting the transportation in interstate commerce of animals suffering from contagious diseases. 23 Stat. at L. 31.

[4] Hammer v. Dagenhart, 247 U. S. 251 (1918). This is called the first, in order to distinguish it from the second, child labor case, Bailey v. Drexel Furniture Co., 259 U. S. 20 (1922), which held unconstitutional the act of Congress attempting to reach the same evil through its taxing power. See above (Chap. XVI).

operate to protect against the unfair competition of child-made goods manufacturers in states where child labor is prohibited by state law. To this argument the majority answered that many causes, such as minimum wage laws, may operate to give one state an economic advantage over others, but the commerce clause was not intended to give Congress general authority to equalize such conditions.

A strong argument in favor of the validity of the act was made by the minority in a dissenting opinion written by Justice Holmes. After citing the lottery and other cases in support of his position, he declared:

I had thought that the propriety of the exercise of a power admitted to exist in some cases was for the consideration of Congress alone, and that this court always had disavowed the right to intrude its judgment upon questions of policy or morals. It is not for this court to pronounce when prohibition is necessary to regulation if it ever may be necessary—to say that it is permissible as against strong drink, but not as against the product of ruined lives.

The act does not meddle with anything belonging to the states. They may regulate their internal affairs and their domestic commerce as they like. But when they seek to send their products across the state line they are no longer within their rights. If there were no Constitution and no Congress their power to cross the line would depend upon their neighbors. Under the Constitution, such commerce belongs not to the states but to Congress to regulate. It may carry out its views of public policy whatever indirect effect they may have upon the activities of the states. Instead of being encountered by a prohibitive tariff at her boundaries, the state encounters the public policy of the United States which it is for Congress to express. The public policy of the United States is shaped with a view to the benefit of the nation as a whole.

It does not appear from this argument that Justice Holmes would admit that there is any limit upon the power of Congress to exclude from interstate commerce any articles whatever for the accomplishment of any indirect results which it deems desirable. But is there no limit? Would it be admitted, for example, that Congress could prohibit cigarette smokers or divorced persons from crossing state lines or from shipping goods across state lines for the purpose of indirectly remedying the cigarette smoking or divorce evils? Justice Holmes's argument would apparently go this far. According to this view, there would be no limit to the power of Congress to exclude from interstate commerce except its own judgment as to the propriety of the act. Possibly this might be a sufficient limit, but it must be admitted that such an extreme view would extend the power of Congress over labor conditions generally and over many matters which have heretofore been considered to be within the reserved powers of the states.

In order to adopt Justice Holmes's extreme view, it seems to be necessary to assume that the right to engage in interstate commerce is one of Federal creation, which cannot exist except by Federal permission. The majority, however, assume that this right exists irrespective of, and antecedent to, any act of Congress and that the power granted to Congress is merely one to regulate and to protect against state control.   Under the latter assumption, the power of Congress to exclude from interstate commerce is not arbitrary but extends only to those articles which are intrinsically harmful or whose conditions of consumption are harmful.[1] Probably the Court could have sustained the act in question on the ground of previous decisions without too serious a break with precedents, but it felt that the line must be drawn somewhere and that this case afforded a proper opportunity to draw this line against the encroachment of the power of Congress upon the reserved powers of the states.

It should be borne in mind that the power of Congress to regulate commerce is not absolute but is limited not only by the reserved powers of the states but also by the limitations and guarantees of the Constitution for the protection of individual rights, such as those providing that private property shall not be taken for public use without just compensation and that no person shall be deprived of life, liberty, or property without due process of law.[2]

Interstate Commerce and Labor.—Although the Supreme Court has refused to uphold child labor legislation of Congress, there are a number of other phases of Congressional labor legislation which it has upheld, only a few of which can be considered here.   For example, it upheld an act of Congress passed in 1907 which undertook to limit the number of hours per day which employees upon interstate railroads should be allowed or required to work.[3]   The reasoning of the Court was that, if employees work for long hours, their fatigue may cause accidents, and a reasonable limitation of hours is therefore conducive to the safety and efficiency with which interstate commerce is carried on.

In 1916, in the face of an extreme emergency threatening a nation-wide strike of railroad employees and the apparent inability of the companies and their employees to reach an agreement upon matters in dispute, Congress virtually undertook the compulsory arbitration of the controversy by passing the Adamson Act which not only specified eight hours as the standard length of a day's work for employees upon interstate railroads but also laid down the rate of wages to be paid them for a standard day's work and also for overtime.   The Court had no difficulty in upholding the provision of the act with reference to hours of labor, but that portion which undertook to regulate wages was upheld only by the narrow margin of one vote.[4]   The five majority judges upheld the

[1] *Cf.* WILLOUGHBY, W. W., *Constitutional Law of the United States*, 2d ed., vol. II, p. 991.

[2] United States v. Chicago, M., St. P. & P. R. R. Co., 282 U. S. 311 (1931).

[3] Baltimore & Ohio R. R. Co. v. Interstate Commerce Commission, 221 U. S. 612 (1911).

[4] Wilson v. New, 243 U. S. 332 (1917).

wage regulation as necessary to prevent the interruption of interstate commerce through the threatened nation-wide strike. Except in such an emergency, the act would probably not be upheld and the case does not support a general power of Congress to regulate the wages of interstate railroad employees.

Another matter connected with labor which Congress has undertaken to regulate is the liability of the carriers for injuries sustained by employees in the course of their employment. The first attempt of Congress to regulate this matter, made in 1906, was unsuccessful because it went too far in that it applied to all employees of interstate carriers, whether or not they were engaged in interstate commerce at the time of injury. In order to remedy this defect, Congress in 1908 passed the second employers' liability act which followed the provisions of the preceding act except that its application was expressly confined to injuries or deaths of employees while actually engaged in interstate commerce or transportation. It abrogated the usual common-law defences of assumption of risk and fellow-servant rule, which employers had enjoyed against suits of employees for damages in injury cases, and transformed the doctrine of contributory negligence into one of comparative negligence. The Supreme Court, in upholding the constitutionality of the act, laid down the premise that the power "to regulate, in the sense intended, is to foster, protect, control, and restrain, with appropriate regard for the welfare of those who are immediately concerned and of the public at large," and then declared that:

The natural tendency of the changes described [in the common law] is to impel the carriers to avoid or prevent the negligent acts and omissions which are made the bases of the rights of recovery which the statute creates and defines; and as whatever makes for that end tends to promote the safety of the employees and to advance the commerce in which they are engaged, we entertain no doubt that in making those changes Congress acted within the limits of the discretion confided to it by the Constitution.[1]

Although the act does not regulate interstate commerce directly, it does so indirectly by regulating the liability of the railroads in carrying it on. It tells them to be careful, under penalty for failing to do so, of being liable in damages for injuries to their employees, even though such injuries were due to the fault of employees and not of the railroad. Moreover, it is no objection that the fellow employee through whose fault the injury occurred was not himself engaged in interstate commerce.

A number of cases have arisen under the act in which the Court has been called upon to determine whether or not the employee injured was engaged in interstate commerce. This question has involved some rather fine points. Thus, it has been held that an employee who was

---

[1] Second employers' liability cases, 223 U. S. 1 (1912).

injured by being struck by an intrastate train, while carrying bolts to repair a bridge over which interstate trains ran, was engaged in interstate commerce and was therefore entitled to recover damages under the act.[1] Similarly, it was held that a man employed as cook for a group of men employed in repairing an interstate railroad was engaged in interstate commerce. This was on the theory that the services of the cook were essential to the efficiency of the repair gang. However, a barber employed to trim the beards of the repair gang probably would not be engaged in interstate commerce, since the efficiency of the gang would not be appreciably affected by the extent of their hirsute adornment.

Congressional Regulation of Intrastate Commerce.—The general rule, as stated above, is that the power of Congress is confined to the regulation of interstate commerce, while the regulation of intrastate commerce is reserved to the states. If we examine the situation more closely, however, we find that this general rule is subject to exceptions. These exceptions are, first, that Congress has impliedly the power to regulate intrastate commerce incidentally; while, in the second place, the states may, under certain circumstances, make regulations which to some extent affect interstate commerce.

The adoption of the first of these exceptions by the Supreme Court was foreshadowed in the Minnesota rate case,[2] decided in 1913, which involved certain state laws and orders of the railroad commission of Minnesota fixing maximum charges for the hauling of intrastate freight and passengers. It was alleged that the indirect economic effect of these laws and orders was to place an undue burden upon interstate commerce. Recognizing the importance of the case from the standpoint of state powers, arguments were presented in the case by several state governors and railroad commissions, acting in accordance with a resolution of the Conference of Governors. Although the Court declined to set aside the state laws and orders, it indicated the possibility of doing so in case they interfered with the policy of Congress regarding interstate commerce.

This position was finally taken squarely by the Court the following year in what is known as the Shreveport rate case.[3] This case can be better understood in the light of the geographical situation of Shreveport, which is a distributing center for points in eastern Texas, including Marshall, only forty-two miles away. The rates for carrying freight between Shreveport and Marshall were regulated by the Interstate Commerce Commission. The Texas Railway Commission fixed rates between points in Texas so much lower than those fixed by the Interstate Commerce Commission that it was possible to ship freight from Houston and Dallas to Marshall at a lower rate than from Shreveport to Marshall,

[1] Pederson v. D. L. & W. Ry., 229 U. S. 146 (1913).
[2] 230 U. S. 352.
[3] Houston, East & West Texas Ry. Co. v. United States, 234 U. S. 342 (1914).

less than one-third of the distance. This situation placed Shreveport at such a disadvantage that, in spite of her greater proximity to Marshall, merchants in the latter town could buy their supplies more cheaply in Dallas and Houston. The orders of the Texas commission, while applying directly to intrastate transportation only, indirectly worked to the disadvantage of interstate commerce. Complaint regarding this situation was made to the Interstate Commerce Commission, which might have equalized conditions by lowering the interstate rates it had fixed to meet the rates fixed by the Texas commission. However, an order to this effect would, in the opinion of the Interstate Commerce Commission, have made its rates unreasonably low. The other alternative was to order the rates for intrastate hauls to be raised to a point where they did not discriminate against interstate commerce, and this was accordingly done. The controversy was thereupon taken to the Supreme Court of the United States which sustained the order of the Interstate Commerce Commission. This decision established for the first time the doctrine that, under some circumstances, a Federal agency may directly order the carriers to make a change in the intrastate rates as fixed by a state agency. These circumstances are when such order is necessary for the purpose of protecting interstate commerce from discrimination, obstruction, or undue burden produced by the order of the state agency.

The fundamental reason for the decision in the Shreveport case is that interstate and intrastate commerce are actually so blended and intermingled that it is difficult if not impossible for Congress to exercise its plenary power of regulating interstate commerce without incidentally regulating intrastate commerce. "This," declared the Court in its opinion as written by Justice Hughes, "is not to say that Congress possesses the authority to regulate the internal commerce of a state, as such, but that it does possess the power to foster and protect interstate commerce, and to take all measures necessary or appropriate to that end, although intrastate transactions of interstate carriers may thereby be controlled."

The doctrine of the Shreveport case was applied even more broadly in a case which arose under the transportation act of 1920,[1] some provisions of which were doubtless an attempt to embody in the law the doctrine of the Shreveport case, and the powers of the Interstate Commerce Commission were accordingly enlarged so as to authorize it to prevent discrimination against interstate commerce. The act also required that the Interstate Commerce Commission should fix rates so that the railroads would be able to earn a fair return upon the value of their property. The case arose out of the situation existing in Wisconsin where a state statute had fixed a maximum rate of two cents a mile for

[1] Railroad Commission of Wisconsin v. Chicago, B. & Q. Ry. Co., 257 U. S. 563 (1922).

carrying passengers between points within the state. The Interstate Commerce Commission, however, in exercising its powers under the transporation act of Congress, had fixed 3.6 cents per mile as a fair rate for the carrying of interstate passengers in this region. On account of the wide difference between the interstate and intrastate rates, the practice grew up whereby passengers making what was really an interstate journey would buy new tickets when crossing state lines and be thus nominally classified as intrastate passengers in order to get the benefit of the lower rate. The situation thus worked a discrimination against interstate commerce. It caused the roads to suffer a loss of revenue from their interstate traffic which would prevent them from securing a fair return upon their property unless intrastate rates were increased or unless interstate and intrastate rates were equalized. In view of this situation, the Interstate Commerce Commission thereupon issued an order increasing intrastate rates, state law to the contrary notwithstanding, so as to remove the discrimination against interstate commerce. This order was upheld by the Supreme Court in an opinion written by Chief Justice Taft in which he aptly stated the reasoning of the Court as follows:

Commerce is a unit and does not regard state lines, and while, under the Constitution, interstate and intrastate commerce are ordinarily subject to regulation by different sovereignties, yet when they are so mingled together that the supreme authority, the nation, cannot exercise complete, effective control over interstate commerce without incidental regulation of intrastate commerce, such incidental regulation is not an invasion of state authority.

Another provision of the transportation act of 1920 was that in accordance with which the excess profits of those railroads which earned more than a fair return were "recaptured" by the Government to be used for the benefit of the weaker roads. A portion of the profits thus recaptured were derived from intrastate commerce. Nevertheless, this provision of the act was upheld by the Supreme Court as part of the general plan of Congress to foster and promote a comprehensive system of transportation for the country.[1]

State Legislation Affecting Interstate Commerce.—Another exception to the general rule laid down above is that state legislation may to some extent be valid, even though it affects interstate commerce. The power of Congress to regulate interstate commerce is not expressly made exclusive. In Gibbons v. Ogden[2] a state regulation of interstate commerce was held invalid because it conflicted with a valid act of Congress regulating the same subject matter. As to whether or not the state act would have been valid in the absence of any conflicting act of Congress was not

[1] Dayton-Goose Creek Ry. Co. v. United States, 263 U. S. 456 (1924).
[2] 9 Wheat. 1 (1824).

settled by that case.   In the middle of the century, however, a case arose which very largely cleared up this question.   In Cooley v. Board of Port Wardens,[1] the Supreme Court upheld the validity of a state statute of Pennsylvania requiring all vessels entering or leaving the port of Philadelphia to employ a licensed pilot, even though they were engaged in interstate or foreign commerce.   This was a local regulation and did not conflict with any act of Congress.   With reference to such local matters, which by their nature require a diversity of regulation, the Court held that the states are competent to deal with them in the absence of any conflicting Congressional regulation.   Over such local matters relating to interstate commerce, the states and Congress have concurrent authority in the sense that either (but not both) may act.

"The power to regulate commerce," declared the Court in the Cooley case,

> . . . embraces a vast field, containing not only many, but exceedingly various subjects, quite unlike in their nature; some imperatively demanding a single uniform rule, operating equally on the commerce of the United States in every port; and some, like the subject now in question, as imperatively demanding that diversity, which alone can meet the local needs of navigation.

The Court added that "whatever subjects of this power are in their nature national, or admit only of one uniform system, or plan of regulation, may justly be said to be of such a nature as to require exclusive legislation by Congress."   In other words, state laws dealing with phases of interstate commerce requiring uniform regulation would be invalid even though there were no conflicting Congressional legislation.   The Court, however, failed to lay down any clear criteria to determine whether a matter is one requiring uniform national, or local and varying, regulation.   In practice the courts decide such questions as they arise, although they would seem to be more suitable for legislative, than for judicial, determination.

State laws affecting interstate commerce which are valid in the absence of conflicting Congressional legislation are, in the main, enacted by the state in the exercise of its police power.   Not every exercise of the state police power affecting interstate commerce would be valid, however, even though not conflicting with an act of Congress.   Thus, as we have seen in the Wabash case, the attempt of the state to regulate rates for that portion of an interstate journey which lies within its boundaries was held invalid.[2]   There was no conflicting act of Congress. The Court in effect held that the regulation of interstate rates is not a local matter and therefore can be regulated only by Congress.

---

[1] 12 How. 299 (1851).

[2] Wabash Ry. Co. v. Illinois, 118 U. S. 557 (1886).   The Court had previously taken a contrary position.   Peik v. Chicago & N. W. Ry. Co., 94 U. S. 164 (1876).

The valid exercise of the state police power, however, as affecting interstate commerce has been broadly construed as extending not only to the fundamental objects of the protection of public health and safety but also to the promotion of the public comfort and convenience. Examples of regulations of a local character falling under this head which have been upheld in the absence of conflicting Congressional legislation are those requiring passenger trains to stop at county seats and at places having more than a certain population. Such regulations are upheld if considered by the Court to be reasonably conducive to the convenience of the traveling public without placing an undue burden on interstate commerce. A regulation, however, requiring all trains to stop at all stations or at all grade crossings would quite clearly be going too far and would be held invalid. Such a regulation would not only place an undue burden on interstate commerce but could not be upheld as necessary for the public convenience.

Most of the state police regulations affecting interstate commerce which are valid in the absence of conflicting Congressional legislation are those enacted in the protection of the public health and safety. Thus, a state may absolutely exclude the introduction from other states of diseased cattle or articles which might be a menace to the public health. Again, the state may prohibit the use of common drinking cups or towels even on interstate trains. For the protection of public safety, the state may require the examination and licensing of locomotive engineers on passenger trains, may require the proper guarding of grade crossings, and may prohibit the heating of wooden passenger coaches with coal stoves.

State Taxation and Interstate Commerce.—Taxation is not only a means of obtaining revenue but is also a form of regulation. It follows that, since the states cannot regulate interstate commerce, they cannot tax it. More specifically, the states cannot levy taxes on goods or persons in transit between points in different states. Nor can the states tax the agencies of interstate commerce, nor the right of persons or corporations to engage in it, nor (which is equivalent to the same thing) the gross receipts derived by them from engaging in it. Subject to necessary quarantine provisions, persons have the right freely to move from one state to another. The attempt of Nevada to levy a tax of one dollar on every passenger leaving the state was therefore held invalid.[1] Logs cut in Maine and floated down a river passing through New Hampshire were temporarily detained in the latter state by low water. It was held that while so detained they were still legally in transit between states and could not be taxed by New Hampshire.[2] On the other hand,

---

[1] Crandall v. Nevada, 6 Wall. 35 (1868).
[2] Coe v. Errol, 116 U. S. 517 (1886).

logs cut in New Hampshire and merely drawn overland to the bank of a tributary preparatory to being consigned to the river at high water had not yet begun their interstate journey and were therefore subject to taxation by New Hampshire.[1]

The states may not levy taxes on articles imported from foreign countries while remaining unsold and in their original packages.[2] The same rule, however, does not apply to articles brought from one state to another.[3] The Constitution prohibits the states from taxing imports or exports without the consent of Congress, except to the extent necessary for executing their inspection laws,[4] but goods transported from one state to another are not imports within the meaning of this provision.[5] Consequently the state may tax articles which have been transported from other states and which have reached their destination even though still unsold and in the original package, provided the tax makes no discrimination on account of the extrastate origin of the goods.[6]

In connection with the taxing power of the state, a distinction must be made between a drummer and a peddler. As pointed out above. a drummer who merely carries a sample with him and takes orders for goods to be shipped in from another state is engaged in interstate commerce and the state in which he takes orders cannot levy a license tax upon him for the privilege of engaging in such business.[7] On the other hand, a peddler, who carries with him the articles which he sells, is deemed to be engaged in local business and may be required to pay a license fee for this privilege, even though the goods which he sells were brought in from another state, provided there is no discrimination against peddlers who sell goods brought from other states.[8]

Although the state may not directly tax interstate commerce, or its agencies, or the right to engage therein, it may nevertheless impose taxes which indirectly or incidentally affect interstate commerce. The various forms of property utilized in carrying on interstate commerce, such as right of way, road bed, rolling stock, and freight and passenger stations, are located within the boundaries of a state and receive its protection. Such property is subject to taxation by the state, provided there is no discrimination on account of its use in interstate commerce.

---

[1] *Ibid.*

[2] Brown v. Maryland, 12 Wheat. 419 (1827).

[3] Brown v. Houston, 114 U. S. 622 (1885).

[4] Art. I, sect. 10, cl. 2.

[5] Woodruff v. Parham, 8 Wall. 123 (1868).

[6] The state police power, however, does not extend to articles brought in from other states so long as they remain unsold and in the original package unless Congress specifically divests such articles of their interstate character.

[7] Robbins v. Shelby County Taxing District, 120 U. S. 489 (1887).

[8] In Welton v. Missouri, 91 U. S. 275 (1875), a state tax on peddlers was held to be invalid because it was discriminatory.

Such taxation is not deemed to place a direct burden upon interstate commerce or to interfere with carrying it on. The distinction is between *operation* and *property*. Although the state cannot by taxation place a direct burden upon the operation or carrying on of interstate commerce, it may place a nondiscriminatory tax upon the property of interstate commerce carriers.

Is a state tax on the receipts derived from carrying on interstate commerce one on operation or on property? In answering this question, a distinction must be made between gross and net receipts. A tax cannot be levied by the state upon the gross receipts as such, for this would be a direct and immediate burden upon operation. A tax on net receipts, on the other hand, would be only an indirect and incidental burden and could be levied in the form of a general income tax or other nondiscriminatory exaction. Net receipts, moreover, constitute the fund out of which all taxes are normally paid.[1]

Although gross receipts as such cannot be taxed, they may be used as a basis of measuring the value of the carrier's property within the state, and a tax levied upon this basis will be upheld, provided it is a substitute for, and no heavier in amount than, a reasonable property tax. The enforcement of the tax must be by ordinary methods, and the right to engage in interstate commerce cannot be made dependent upon the payment of the tax. This is true of any tax upon the property of interstate carriers.

In attempting to tax that portion of the road bed or rolling stock of an interstate carrier which lies within a particular state, difficulties have been encountered in determining the valuation of such portion of the property for purposes of assessment. An arbitrary section of the property within the boundaries of a state may have little value in itself, for the property can only be intelligently valued as a unit. To meet this difficulty, the "unit rule" has been adopted, whereby the assessed valuation within the state is taken to be an amount which bears the same proportion to the total valuation that the mileage within the state bears to the total mileage. This is merely a rough rule, however, and cannot always be applied with justice, because the expense of construction per mile may vary considerably from one state to another. Moreover, the rule does not take into account expensive terminals found in some states and not in others.

A state may tax not only the tangible, but also the intangible, property of interstate carriers. Thus, a tax may be levied upon the franchise of a corporation engaged in interstate commerce. The franchise may be considered as the right granted to the corporation to engage in business and, where the business extends through several states, the unit rule is

---

[1] United States Glue Co. v. Oak Creek, 247 U. S. 321 (1918).

used in ascertaining the value of the franchise for taxation in any one state.

A state may also tax the capital stock of a corporation engaged in interstate commerce, but a distinction must be made between domestic and foreign corporations. A state may tax the entire capital stock of a domestic corporation created by it when the tax can be considered as one on the corporation as an entity and not on the property of the corporation which may be located in part in other states. The capital stock of foreign corporations, however, may be taxed only to the extent that it represents property located within the state.

Kansas attempted to levy a percentage tax upon the entire capital stock of foreign corporations engaged in both interstate and intrastate commerce as a condition of their continuing to do local business within the state. The Western Union Telegraph Company refused to pay this tax and was upheld in its refusal by the Supreme Court both on the ground that it was virtually a tax on property outside the state and also because it operated as a burden upon the interstate business of the company.[1] This decision followed from the fact that the intrastate and interstate parts of the company's business were so closely connected that a tax upon the right to engage in the former placed a burden upon the latter. Under such circumstances, the power of the state to regulate intrastate commerce in this manner cannot be exercised.[2]

The Postal Power.—In connection with the discussion of interstate commerce, brief mention may be made of the postal power, with which it has points both of similarity and of difference. The Constitution authorizes Congress to "establish post offices and post roads"[3] and this grant of power has been broadly construed as giving Congress the general power of establishing and maintaining a comprehensive postal system. This grant enables Congress not only to designate the roads over which the mails shall be carried but also to establish those roads. It may also adopt such means as may be necessary to protect the mails from interference and for this purpose may utilize the judicial arm of the Federal Government and the armed forces of the United States.[4] The same means may be used to protect interstate commerce. The postal service differs from interstate commerce in that the Federal Government creates and not merely regulates the former. The extent of the control of the Government over the postal service is therefore greater. It extends to mail matter carried between points within a given state as well as to that carried across state lines. Moreover, the power of Congress over the postal system is exclusive and monopolistic. No state or private

[1] Western Union Telegraph Co. v. Kansas, 216 U. S. 1 (1910).
[2] *Cf.* the doctrine of the Shreveport case, cited above.
[3] Art. I, sect. 8, cl. 7.
[4] *In re* Debs, 158 U. S. 564 (1895).

organization is permitted to establish a rival postal system and operate it for hire.

The power of Congress over the mails includes the power to prohibit the carriage through the mails of articles deemed to be injurious to the morals, health, or safety of the public or of postal employees. Thus, Congress may exclude and has excluded from the mails lottery tickets and obscene pictures, magazines, or books. The postmaster-general has also been authorized by act of Congress to issue fraud orders excluding from the mails letters or circulars of a fraudulent character. During the World War, Congress also prohibited the transmission through the mails of newspapers or other printed material containing seditious or treasonable matter or statements calculated to hinder and embarrass the Government in the prosecution of the war. In exercising its power of exclusion from the mails, Congress is ordinarily limited by the constitutional safeguards relating to freedom of speech and the press, due process of law, and unreasonable searches and seizures.

CHAPTER XVIII

FOREIGN RELATIONS AND THE TREATY POWER[1]

The determination of the control of foreign relations in the United States is especially complicated for two main reasons: first, because of our Federal form of government and, second, because of the prevalent application of the principle of separation of powers, with which the principle of checks and balances is closely connected. In countries whose government is based on the federal plan, it is necessary to consider the amount, if any, of control over foreign relations which is assigned to the divisional governments.

The American States and Foreign Relations.—Experience under the Articles of Confederation showed that, if foreign relations were to be efficiently conducted, they should be concentrated in the hands of the central government. Consequently, the Constitution provides positively that they shall be concentrated in that government and undertakes to accomplish the same purpose negatively by placing prohibitions in this respect upon the states. Thus, the Constitution expressly assigns the diplomatic, treaty-making, and war powers to the central government. If, for example, a French citizen residing in Pennsylvania claims to have suffered injuries or indignities at the hands of the authorities of that state, the French Government cannot take the matter up directly with the Pennsylvania authorities but must deal only with the National Government at Washington. The Constitution not only assigns diplomatic, treaty, and war powers to the central government but also prohibits the states from engaging in these activities. By way of exception, however, the states are allowed, with the consent of Congress, to enter into compacts with foreign governments and even to engage in war if invaded or threatened with invasion.

Although the states cannot directly control foreign relations, they may indirectly affect such relations by taking action or failing to take action regarding the rights of aliens residing within their boundaries. Thus, in 1891, the chief of police of New Orleans having been assassinated, certain Italians accused of this crime were lynched by a mob in Louisiana. The lynchers were not promptly prosecuted and brought to justice by the Louisiana authorities. The Italian Government protested against

[1] This chapter is based upon the author's work, *American Foreign Relations: Conduct and Policies*, Chaps. X, XII, XVI, XVII, XIX–XXV (New York, 1928), to which the reader is referred for more detailed discussion.

this treatment of her citizens, but the protest, of course, was not sent directly to Louisiana but to the authorities of the National Government. The latter Government, however, was not in a position to interfere with the administration of criminal justice within a state. All that it could do was to recommend that Congress pass an appropriation to compensate the families of the deceased Italians, and this was accordingly done.

If, on the other hand, a state enacts a law which adversely affects the rights of aliens residing therein as guaranteed to them by treaties between the United States and the countries of which such aliens are citizens, their treaty rights may be vindicated by appeal to the courts. Since treaties made under the authority of the United States are declared by the Constitution to be a part of the supreme law of the land, regardless of conflicting provisions of state constitutions or laws, the Federal and state courts are both bound to uphold the treaty in preference to the state law in case of conflict. If the state courts fail to afford redress for violation of an alien's treaty rights, the Federal courts may be appealed to. A case involving a treaty between the United States and Switzerland regulating the right of aliens to inherit land having been taken to the Supreme Court, that tribunal upheld the treaty, even though it conflicted with the law of Virginia, in which the land was situated.[1]

Even though a state law is attacked on the ground that it conflicts with a treaty, it will not be declared invalid on this account if the Court finds that there is no conflict between the law and the treaty. For example, California and Washington passed laws prohibiting aliens ineligible to citizenship from leasing land for agricultural purposes. This was alleged to be in conflict with a treaty with Japan securing to Japanese citizens residing in the United States the right to engage in trade therein. The Court, however, found no conflict and upheld the state law.[2] In any case of conflict, however, between a valid treaty and a state law, the latter must yield, at least to the extent of the conflict.

Foreign Relations and the Separation of Powers.—In addition to the division of governmental powers between the National Government and the states, the powers of the former government are also divided among the three departments, legislative, executive, and judicial, in accordance with the principles of separation of powers and checks and balances. The framers of the Constitution of the United States thought that the application of these principles was necessary in order to prevent tyranny, autocracy, despotism, and a government of men rather than of laws. They applied these principles to the conduct and control of foreign relations as well as the other phases of governmental organization and

---

[1] Hauenstein v. Lynham, 100 U. S. 483 (1880).
[2] Terrace v. Thompson, 263 U. S. 197 (1923).

activity. At the time our Constitution was drawn up, the control of foreign relations in other modern governments belonged almost exclusively to the executive. The framers of the Constitution introduced an innovation by dividing this control between the President, the Senate, and Congress. Such divided control may prevent autocratic or one-man power but, on the other hand, may lead to deadlocks and lack of concentrated responsibility for the conduct of foreign relations.

Presidential Direction of Foreign Relations.—The Constitution gives a voice to the Senate in making treaties and to Congress in declaring war. In most matters connected with foreign relations, however, such as appointing and receiving diplomatic representatives, negotiating treaties, communicating with foreign governments, and formulating American foreign policies, the President has a pretty free hand. In such matters he usually takes the initiative and it is not often that his control is subject to any serious check by the other branches of the government.

Diplomatic Intercourse.—Although appointments made by the President to regular diplomatic and consular posts abroad must be confirmed by the Senate, the power of receiving diplomatic representatives from foreign governments is vested in him alone. Foreign consuls in the United States must also be recognized by the President before entering upon their duties. In maintaining American diplomatic and consular representatives abroad, the President is, of course, dependent upon Congress for appropriations to pay their salaries and expenses.

The President has developed the power of appointing special diplomatic agents without the consent of the Senate. This is to some extent an anomalous practice and scarcely authorized by the theory of the Constitution, but it is nevertheless well established.

By virtue of his general diplomatic powers, as well as his treaty or war powers, the President may provide for the participation of the United States in an international conference. Instructions to the delegates to such a conference generally proceed from the President.

The President may at any time sever diplomatic relations with any country by recalling our representative and dismissing the representative of that country in the United States. Such severance of diplomatic relations may be the forerunner to the outbreak of war between the two countries but may nevertheless be brought about by the President without consultation with either Congress or the Senate.

The Power of Recognition.—No express grant of the power of recognizing foreign governments is contained in the Constitution, but that this power is vested in the President is inferred from his powers of sending and receiving diplomatic representatives and of negotiating treaties. Although, with reference to some of these matters, the Senate may participate, the President has ample power of extending recognition, if he so desires, without consulting the Senate. Inasmuch as the President is in control of more authentic sources of information upon which to base intelligent action, it is natural that to him, rather than to the Senate, should gravitate control in this, as in other phases, of American foreign relations. When the President has acted in extending recognition, the courts consider such action binding upon "the judges as well as upon all the other officers and citizens of the government."[1]

The Treaty-making Power.—A treaty may be defined as a contract between two or more independent states, entered into for the purpose of creating or defining rights and/or duties. Under the Constitution, treaties are made by the President "by and with the advice and consent of the Senate, provided two-thirds of the Senators present concur."

In considering the relative influence and control wielded by the President and the Senate in treaty making, it is desirable to bear in mind the various steps or stages commonly followed in the process of making treaties. As a rule, there are four distinct steps: (1) negotiation, including the advice and consent of the Senate to ratification; (2) ratification; (3) exchange of ratifications; and (4) proclamation. Treaties are proclaimed by the President and are published in the Statutes at Large as a means of officially acquainting the people with their texts, which forthwith become parts of the supreme law of the land. Such proclamation, however, has no direct bearing on foreign relations and is not necessary to the validity of a treaty in international law.[2] The function of the Senate in treaty making is popularly spoken of as ratification. But this is an error. The advice and consent of the Senate is a necessary prerequisite to the ratification of a treaty; the act of ratification itself is performed by the President (or his agents), as is also the exchange of ratifications with the representative of the foreign government.[3] In reality, therefore, the President alone fully controls the last three steps,[4] and he and the Senate are associated together in the first step only, *i.e.*, negotiation. This limitation of the Senate's authority to the first stage is not expressly set up by the Constitution but is brought about in part through international usage and diplomatic practice in treaty making and in part through the implications of certain provisions of the Constitution, other than the treaty-making clause, which combine to make

[1] Ricaud v. American Metal Co., 246 U. S. 304 (1918).

[2] The issuance of the proclamation is a mere ministerial act which follows as a matter of course after the first three stages have been completed, although it is not compellable by mandamus.

[3] The fact that the President ratifies treaties is often lost sight of even by writers on international law. Thus, A. S. Hershey says: "Of course there has never been any question of the right to refuse ratification in the case of States in which, like the United States, the power of negotiation and ratification are in different hands." *Essentials of International Public Law*, p. 315, note 16.

[4] Except, of course, that the consent of the foreign government must be had to the exchange of ratifications.

the President the spokesman of the nation in foreign relations. These causes, in turn, rest upon fundamental differences in organization between the executive and the legislature, or the upper branch thereof.

Although the Senate's authority is confined to the first stage, that body need not be consulted by the President during the preliminary negotiations leading up to the drafting of the treaty. This is the usual practice. On the other hand, he may, if he sees fit, consult the Senate during this period and may appoint senators on the commission to negotiate the treaty. Occasionally, he submits the nomination of treaty negotiators to the Senate for confirmation, but this is not customary.

The Senate is legally free to exercise an independent judgment in regard to the terms of a proposed treaty, and, as already indicated, it may consent to ratification without change, may reject absolutely, or may consent to ratification with amendments. Speaking strictly, the Senate cannot amend a treaty. But it can propose amendments and such amendments become parts of the instrument when accepted by the President and by the foreign government concerned. When, therefore, the Senate proposes amendments, the President, unless he elects to drop the treaty entirely (as he has sometimes done), must renew negotiations looking to the acceptance of such amendments by the foreign government. Practically, the Senate may thus participate in negotiations, although only, of course, through the voluntary agency of the President.

The President is at all times in control of the treaty-making process to the extent that he can prevent any treaty that he dislikes from being adopted. He cannot, however, positively secure the adoption of a treaty if a favorable two-thirds vote in the Senate is unobtainable. Under present conditions, therefore, a minority of the Senate may block a treaty. It would seem that the country would be amply safeguarded against objectionable treaties if their making were placed in the hands of the President and a bare majority of the Senate. To this combination it might be worth while to add the consent of a bare majority of the House of Representatives.

Executive Agreements.[1]—The Constitution contains no express recognition of the President's power to make international agreements without the consent of the Senate, but a practice has developed whereby he effects certain agreements without such consent. There are three kinds of executive agreements, classified according to the immediate source of the President's power to make them. In the first place, his power may be implied from the provisions of the Constitution conferring on him diplomatic powers, making him commander-in-chief of the army and navy, and requiring that he see that the laws are faithfully executed.

---

[1] The section on Executive Agreements is reprinted by permission from a part of the author's article on the same subject in the *Encyclopaedia of the Social Sciences*, vol. V, pp. 685–686.

Agreements of this kind may be entered into without either prior authorization or subsequent approval by the Senate. For example, the Rush-Bagot agreement of 1817, whereby the United States and Great Britain undertook mutually to limit their naval armaments on the Great Lakes, was negotiated under the power of the President as commander-in-chief of the navy. The frequent settlement by executive agreement of American citizens' claims against foreign governments is incidental to his power of conducting foreign relations.

In the second place, Congress, by virtue of its commerce, postal, or other powers, may authorize the President or a cabinet member acting on his behalf to make international agreements relating to the subject matter of such powers. Reciprocal tariff agreements and postal conventions have been entered into in this way. Finally, the President may be authorized by general treaties to make special executive agreements for the purpose of carrying out the treaty provisions. Such are the agreements on extradition of particular individuals arrived at on the basis of an extradition treaty.

Although the embodiment of a large part of important international understandings in executive agreements may virtually evade the constitutional requirement that treaties be submitted to the Senate, nevertheless executive agreements are useful and often practically necessary in the conduct of foreign relations.

The Scope of the Treaty Power.—The Constitution provides that all treaties made under the authority of the United States shall be a part of the supreme law of the land. It might be argued that any treaty made by the President and two-thirds of the Senate is made "under the authority of the United States" and is therefore valid; but this argument is clearly erroneous. Although the courts have never declared a treaty unconstitutional, there seems to be no question as to the possibility of a conflict between the subject matter of a treaty and the Constitution, in which case, of course, the treaty would be invalid. It would hardly be contended that the treaty power could provide for the imposition of an export tax, or enact a bill of attainder, or transfer the power to declare war from Congress to the President. If this were possible, then the Constitution could be formally amended by treaties, but there seems to be no question that the method of formally amending the Constitution, as provided in that instrument, is exclusive.

Even though a treaty does not conflict with any express provision of the Constitution, it would probably not be valid if it relates to a matter of purely domestic concern, which is not an appropriate subject of international agreement. The distinction, however, between matters of domestic, and of international, concern is shadowy, and in case of doubt the courts would probably hold that this is a political question, to be decided by the treaty-making authorities rather than by the courts.

A treaty may deal with a matter which, under the general principles of the Constitution, is within the reserved powers of the states but may nevertheless be valid if it relates to an appropriate subject of international agreement. For example, any treaty with foreign nations dealing with the rights and status of their citizens residing in the United States is such an appropriate subject, because it is a matter of common concern between the two countries. It would therefore be valid, even though it conflicts with state laws on the same subject. The United States could, therefore, nullify by treaty all anti-alien state laws. But the treaty power could not infringe upon the reserved powers of a state where the interests of a foreign nation are not concerned. Thus, the United States could not by treaty regulate generally the labor of children within the states but could do so with reference to such children as are aliens.

The regulation of the shooting and hunting of birds generally is within the reserved powers of the states. If, however, the birds are migratory and cross the international boundary, the treaty power may adopt regulations for their protection. A treaty was made between the United States and Great Britain containing regulations for the protection of such birds and promises on the part of each party to enact further legislation on the subject. Although Congress probably could not have legislated on this subject in the absence of a treaty, both the treaty and the act of Congress passed for its enforcement were upheld as constitutional.[1] From this case it appears that the treaty power may regulate matters within the reserved powers of the states which cannot be reached by Congress in the absence of a treaty on the subject. Moreover, through the making of such a treaty, the legislative power of Congress may be extended.

Treaties and Acts of Congress.—With respect to the method of enforcement, treaties may be divided into self-executing and non-self-executing. The first class usually relate to the rights of aliens which they undertake presently to establish. They may be enforced by the courts as law of the land without auxiliary Congressional legislation. The second class usually involve political questions or promises of future action by the political departments of the Government. They are not enforceable by the courts without auxiliary legislation. An example of a non-self-executing treaty was the treaty of alliance made with France in 1778 promising that, under certain circumstances, the United States would take warlike action on behalf of that country. Such a promise might be broken through failure of Congress to take the stipulated action, but the courts could do nothing to coerce Congress, because this is a political question.

---

[1] Missouri v. Holland, 252 U. S. 416 (1920).

Again, a treaty might require an appropriation of money to put it into effect. Money cannot be appropriated by treaty but only by act of Congress. If Congress fails to pass the appropriation, there is, in constitutional law, no legal remedy for this situation.[1]

Under the Constitution bills to raise revenue must originate in the House of Representatives. It is doubtful whether the treaty power could enact a tariff law and put rates of duty into force different from the rates provided in existing acts of Congress. In practice this is, not usually done, but the treaty merely contains a promise that certain rates will be enacted by Congress. The enforcement of the treaty then depends upon the voluntary action of Congress.

The treaty power may undertake to bind the legislative power in a negative way. Thus, the United States may enter into arbitration or conciliation treaties whereby we agree not to go to war under certain circumstances or within a given time. From the constitutional point of view, however, the power of Congress to declare war cannot be taken away or restricted by treaty.

If Congress can virtually nullify a treaty as law of the land by failing to pass legislation to carry it out, it follows *a fortiori* that it may do so by passing legislation conflicting with a treaty. In general, it would seem that treaties and acts of Congress are regarded as being on a parity with each other. Consequently, when there is a conflict between the two, the usual rule prevails that the one of later date supersedes the earlier, at least to the extent of the conflict. An exception to this rule, however, is that a non-self-executing treaty does not supersede an earlier act of Congress with which it conflicts. But all acts of Congress supersede earlier conflicting treaties. Thus, Congress passed an act providing a head tax on immigrants coming to the United States in spite of earlier treaties providing for their free admission. The Supreme Court upheld the act of Congress, declaring that "so far as a treaty made by the United States with any foreign nation can become the subject of judicial cognizance in the courts of this country, it is subject to such acts as Congress may pass for its enforcement, modification, or repeal."[2]

The passage by Congress of an act conflicting with a treaty does not affect the validity of the international obligation thereby imposed upon the United States. The other party to the treaty may justly protest through diplomatic channels and accuse the United States of bad faith. But as law of the land or from the Constitutional point of view, the treaty is nullified and will not be enforced by the courts. The complaint of the other party, as the Supreme Court has declared,

[1] *Cf.* MATHEWS, J. M., "The League of Nations and the Constitution," *Mich. Law Rev.*, vol. 18, pp. 385–386 (1920).

[2] Head money cases, 112 U. S. 580 (1884).

"must be made to the political department of our Government, which is alone competent to act upon the subject . . . The question whether our Government is justified in disregarding its engagements with another nation is not one for the determination of the courts."[1]

The Termination of Treaties.—Any treaty may be terminated through the making of a new treaty either expressly or by implication superseding the earlier one.   This is ordinarily the only way to terminate a treaty which contains no provision for its own termination.   Even such a treaty, however, if violated by one party, may be considered void, and thus terminated, at the option of the other party.   When fully executed, a treaty thereby terminates.   As already indicated, treaties may be terminated as law of the land or in the domestic sense when Congress passes conflicting legislation, or even when Congress fails to pass legislation for the enforcement of non-self-executing treaties. Treaties frequently contain provisions whereby they terminate on a given date or whereby either party may terminate them upon giving notice to the other.   In the case of the United States, such notice is, of course, given by the President.   He probably has authority to give such notice upon his own initiative but usually waits until authorized to do so by Congress or the Senate.   The outbreak of war between two countries terminates such treaties as are inconsistent with that condition or at least suspends them for the period of the conflict.

[1] Chae Chan Ping v. United States, 130 U. S. 581 (1889).

CHAPTER XIX

MILITARY AND WAR POWERS[1]

Centralization of the War Power.—Even under the Articles of Confederation, the Congress had power to declare war, although it could be done only by a vote of nine states, and, except in unusual circumstances, the states were prohibited from engaging in war without the consent of Congress. The power to build and equip a navy was conferred upon Congress, but, in order to raise land forces, Congress was dependent upon making requisitions upon the states to furnish their quotas, in proportion to the number of white inhabitants in each state. The furnishing of such forces depended, in reality, upon the voluntary action of the states. Congress, moreover, had no control over the state militia.

In order to strengthen the military and war powers of the central government under the Constitution, that instrument provided that Congress should have the power to raise and support armies; to maintain a navy; to govern the land and naval forces; to provide for calling out the militia and for organizing, arming, and disciplining them. Congress was also empowered to "declare war, grant letters of marque and reprisal, and make rules concerning captures on land and water." These provisions give evidence of the intention of the framers of the Constitution to give the central government power adequate to defend itself against both foreign and domestic enemies. At the same time, the states were prohibited, without the consent of Congress, from keeping regular troops or ships of war in time of peace or "engaging in war, unless actually invaded or in such imminent danger as will not admit of delay." These provisions do not deprive the states of police power to maintain the militia and to preserve domestic order but prevent them from usurping the authority of the central government to decide on the question of war or peace.

The President as Commander-in-chief.—By the Constitution, the President is made the commander-in-chief both of the regular army and navy of the United States and also of the "militia of the several states when called into the actual service of the United States." He may also be required to use force in connection with the performance of his duty to see that the laws of the United States are faithfully executed. He

[1] This chapter is based in part upon the author's *American Foreign Relations: Conduct and Policies*, Chaps. XXVII–XXIX (New York, 1928) to which the reader is referred for more detailed discussion.

is, of course, dependent upon Congress to supply the necessary forces. Congress determines the organization, size, and equipment of the army and navy and makes appropriations for their maintenance, including pay of officers and men and other expenses. Subject to the limitation that it cannot appropriate money for the support of the army for a longer term than two years, Congress exercises all necessary legislative power in connection with the maintenance and government of the land, naval, and aerial forces, during both war and peace.

The President, however, may supplement the laws of Congress with detailed regulations, which have the force of law as long as they are issued in pursuance of the President's constitutional or statutory authority. Moreover, when appropriations have been made and forces have thus been placed at the disposal of the President, he may appoint the military and naval officers and has full control over the direction of the movements of the forces, not only in this country but also on the high seas and abroad. He may even take personal command of the forces in the field if he so desires. It is doubtful whether Congress could even indirectly control the President's power as commander-in-chief to direct the movement of the forces through provisions in appropriation bills making funds available for the support of the army only on condition that it is employed in a certain way or upon certain territory. In governing invaded or conquered territory, the President exercises full control through the military officers until Congress passes an act for the establishment of civil government in such territory. Although, even in time of peace, the President's power as commander-in-chief in directing military and naval operations is considerable, his power in this capacity naturally expands greatly in time of war.

Forcible Measures Short of War.—It may become necessary for the President to exercise his power as commander-in-chief in directing the movement of the forces in the performance of warlike acts, even though there has been no formal declaration of war. For example, the President has authority to use the forces in order to repel sudden attacks or to repel the invasion of our territory and it would also be his duty to defend the country under these circumstances, even though Congress is not in session or there is not sufficient time to issue a formal declaration. As the Supreme Court declared in the Prize Cases, "if a war be made by invasion of a foreign nation, the President is not only authorized but bound to resist force by force. He does not initiate the war, but is bound to accept the challenge without waiting for any special legislative authority."[1]

Any invasion of our territory, moreover, would almost necessarily interfere with the enforcement of the laws of the United States, which

---

[1] 2 Black 635 (1862).

the President is bound to see executed.   Moreover, even though there has been no formal declaration, it has been held that the President may recognize the existence of a state of war.   This he did at the opening of the Civil War by issuing his proclamation of blockade and the Supreme Court held in the Prize Cases that the issuance of this proclamation, which was binding on the Court, was conclusive evidence of the existence of a state of war.   It was not until nearly three months later that Congress passed a law validating retroactively the acts of the President.   With respect to this situation, however, it is probably true that the President's power of recognizing a state of war is greater in case of civil, than of foreign, war.   A foreign war can be legally started only by declaration of Congress.

In the absence of a formal declaration of war, the President's power of using the armed forces may be exerted not only to repel invasion and to put down rebellion but also to protect the rights and interests of the American Government and citizens in foreign countries and upon the high seas.   In many instances, by order of the President, our forces have been landed in Latin-American and Asiatic countries in order to protect the lives and property of American citizens.   In some cases this action was authorized by treaty between the United States and such countries.   But in other important instances the President on his own authority has sent forces into foreign countries when there was no treaty authorizing it.   Examples are the sending of forces into China in 1900 and into Mexico in 1914.   In these cases there was no declaration of war.   Again, during the World War President Wilson sent troops into Russia, although we were not at war with that power.

Under Congressional authorization, but without a formal declaration of war, the United States has sometimes adopted the policy of armed neutrality, which differs but little from limited or partial war.   As already indicated, the Constitution empowers Congress to "grant letters of marque and reprisal" or, in other words, to authorize privateering.   In 1798, Congress authorized the President to issue such letters to owners of private armed vessels of the United States during our partial or limited war with France.

In 1917, after the severance of diplomatic relations with Germany, President Wilson requested Congress to authorize him to arm our merchant ships for defense but, at the same time, claimed that he had the authority to do so "without special warrant of law, by the plain implication of my constitutional duties and powers."   When Congress failed to give him the requested authority, he proceeded to exercise the power on his own initiative.   There seems little doubt as to the constitutionality of his act.   As commander-in-chief of the navy, he could have directed our warships to convoy and protect our merchant ships on the high seas.

The Beginning of War.—Unlike the arrangement existing in most modern governments at the time of the adoption of our Constitution, the framers vested the power of formally declaring war in Congress, rather than in the executive. This followed the precedent of the Articles of Confederation in which, as we have seen, Congress had that power. A more important reason, however, was that, since war profoundly affects the lives and fortunes of the mass of the people, the control over its initiation should be vested in the most broadly representative branch of the government. Moreover, this arrangement would be in accordance with the principle of checks and balances, for, while Congress could declare war, the waging of war would be in the hands of the President.

Formal declarations of war are drawn up in the form of acts or joint resolutions and are submitted to the President for his approval or disapproval. They almost invariably take the form of recognizing a state of war thrust upon us by the hostile acts of foreign powers, rather than declaring that war shall be begun.

In spite of the theory of the Constitution that Congress initiates war, this matter in practice is virtually under the control of the President. This comes about by virtue of the power of the President to manipulate the situation through the exercise of his military or diplomatic powers so as to secure or prevent a declaration of war by Congress. For example, the President was instrumental in bringing on the Mexican War through sending our forces into disputed territory and in bringing on the Spanish War through sending the battleship *Maine* into Havana harbor. Moreover, in the latter case the President did not accept Spain's offer to submit all differences arising from the destruction of the *Maine*, to arbitration and thus, through the exercise of his diplomatic powers, made war more difficult to avoid.

On account of the President's control of essential information on which to base an intelligent decision regarding war or peace, it has become an established "convention" of the Constitution that Congress accepts almost without question the President's leadership in this matter. Legally, Congress could pass an act or resolution declaring war regardless of the President's wishes and could even repass it over his veto. This, however, has never happened and is never likely to happen so long as Congress follows the hitherto established practice of not adopting a declaration of war unless the President recommends it and of always adopting it when he does recommend it.[1]

Raising Military Forces.—Congress has power to "raise and support armies" and to "make rules for the government and regulation of the land and naval forces." It has never been the policy of the United States, however, to maintain a large standing army. Until the time of

[1] With reference to the proposal for a national popular referendum on war, see J. M. Mathews, *American Foreign Relations: Conduct and Policies*, pp. 247–249.

the Civil War, voluntary enlistment was the sole method resorted to for raising troops. The President may ask for volunteers but cannot legally adopt more drastic measures for raising troops without the authorization of Congress. It is true that, at the opening of the Civil War, President Lincoln by proclamation and on his own initiative increased the size of the standing army, but his act was subsequently ratified and validated by Congress.

During the Civil War, conscription was first resorted to and Congress passed several draft acts for compelling military service. The constitutionality of this legislation was upheld in a case before a state court, but the question was not brought before the Federal courts.

Shortly after the entrance of the United States into the World War in 1917, Congress passed the selective draft law providing for compulsory military service by all able-bodied men between certain ages, except those expressly exempted. The constitutionality of this law was attacked on various grounds, among which were, first, that no such power had been granted to Congress in the Constitution; second, that it was involuntary servitude in violation of the Thirteenth Amendment; and, third, that it encroached upon the constitutional power of the states over the state militia. All of these contentions were denied, however, by the Supreme Court, which upheld the law in a unanimous opinion.[1]

It was held in these cases that the power of Congress to compel military service was implied in its powers to declare war and to raise and support armies. Such service did not constitute involuntary servitude within the meaning of the Thirteenth Amendment but was the performance of a duty owed by the citizen to the government. Furthermore, the Court held that such control as the states exert over the militia is subject to the superior authority of Congress to raise armies, which power is not affected by constitutional limitations upon the use of the militia for Federal purposes. Finally, the position of the Court in upholding this law was strengthened by the consideration that conscription is a power exercised by other sovereign nations and that the United States, as such a nation, must be deemed to have a similar power. This conclusion is further strengthened by the fact that the exercise of this power may be necessary for the nation's self-preservation.

Courts-martial.—The members of the armed forces, whether raised by voluntary enlistment or conscription, are governed by such disciplinary measures as may be adopted by Congress and the President. For the purpose of administering such measures, military tribunals are set up. Such tribunals, known as courts-martial, are established, not under the power to create Federal courts but under the power to govern the military forces. Since they are not a part of the Federal judicial system, the provision of the Sixth Amendment regarding trial by jury in

[1] Selective draft law cases, 245 U. S. 366 (1918).

criminal cases does not apply to them. Moreover, by the express terms of the Fifth Amendment, "cases arising in the land or naval forces, or in the militia, when in actual service in time of war or public danger" are excepted from the requirement that criminal prosecutions must be instituted by presentment or indictment by a grand jury.

During time of war, military tribunals have jurisdiction to try criminal offenses not only of members of the military forces but also of civilians who commit acts directly or indirectly assisting the enemy. Even during time of war, however, military courts cannot try civilians for such offenses in places which are not the scene of actual military operations and in which the regular civil courts are open.[1]

National Authority over the Militia.—The framers of the Constitution placed special stress on the militia, because they regarded it as a substitute for the dreaded standing army. By the Second Amendment, it was declared that a "well-regulated militia" is "necessary to the security of a free state."

The state militia is composed of all able-bodied male citizens between the ages of eighteen and forty-five, with certain exceptions, and including alien declarants of their intention to become citizens. It is divided into two parts: first, the organized militia or National Guard, a relatively small body of citizens who volunteer for part-time military training and service, and, second, the remaining members of the militia who are unorganized and untrained.

The militia is frequently used by the states in time of peace for the purpose of maintaining order and putting down local disturbances.[2] The Constitution authorizes Congress to "provide for organizing, arming, and disciplining the militia." When not called into the service of the United States, however, the militia is under the control and management of the states in respect to the appointment of their officers and their training, except that the latter is carried out according to the discipline prescribed by Congress. Beginning in 1886, Congress undertook to enforce national standards with respect to the militia through the system of grants-in-aid, *i.e.*, through conditions attached to Congressional appropriations for arming and equipping the militia. The National Defense Act passed by Congress in 1916 changes the name of the organized militia to the National Guard and provides for such an extension of national supervision and control over this force as to make it "a nationally organized body of state troops auxiliary to the regular army, and similarly equipped and disciplined."[3]

---

[1] *Ex parte* Milligan, 4 Wall. 2 (1866).

[2] For the use of Federal troops in quelling domestic disorder in the states, see pp. 61–62.

[3] MACDONALD, A. F., quoted in Mathews and Berdahl, *Documents and Readings in American Government*, p. 538.

The Constitution authorizes Congress "to provide for calling forth the militia to execute the laws of the Union, suppress insurrections, and repeal invasions." In pursuance of this power, Congress in 1795 passed an act (which still remains in force) delegating to the President the function of calling out the militia for the above purposes. In exercising this power, the President is the sole and exclusive judge as to whether the exigency is such as to warrant the calling out of the militia.[1] When called into the service of the United States, the militia comes under the command of the President.

The three purposes enumerated in the Constitution for which the militia may be called into the national service seem to contemplate service within the United States rather than abroad. In addition, however, to the express authority for calling out the militia for the three purposes mentioned, there is also the implied power of calling it out in time of war. In the exercise of this power, Congress drafted the members of the militia into the national service at the opening of the World War. They were thereby discharged from the militia and were required to take an oath of allegiance to the United States. There was then, of course, no difficulty about sending them abroad at the discretion of the President.

War Powers and Constitutional Limitations.—During war the powers of both Congress and the President expand enormously. When war is declared, the implied power may then be exercised of taking such measures as are calculated to carry it on efficiently and to bring it to a successful conclusion. Consequently, many powers the exercise of which would be unconstitutional in time of peace become quite legitimate in time of war. Such powers may be exercised not only during actual hostilities but as long as the technical state of war continues. This situation is to some extent expressly recognized by the Constitution, which impliedly permits the suspension of the writ of habeas corpus in time of war but prohibits its suspension at times when the public safety is not threatened.

The maxim that the safety of the state is the highest law, if not expressly recognized in the Constitution, is largely followed in practice when conditions seem to warrant. The carrying on of war is the exercise of the police power in its most extreme form. While, in the exercise of the police power by the states, individual rights which stand in the way must be sacrificed, the exercise of this extreme form of the police power by the National Government involves the sacrifice not only of individual rights but also of state rights. The ordinary line of demarcation between the reserved powers of the states and the delegated powers of the National Government may become less distinct, if not entirely effaced, during time of war.

---

[1] Martin v. Mott, 12 Wheat. 19 (1827).

The extent of the war power is shown by actual experience during the two most important wars in which the United States has been engaged—the Civil War and the World War. During the Civil War President Lincoln, on his own initiative, carried out measures which would have been shockingly unconstitutional in time of peace. Among other things, he liberated the slaves and confiscated other property of enemy persons, in violation both of the Constitution and of international law. Even with reference to persons in the loyal states, he suspended the writ of habeas corpus,[1] suppressed newspapers, carried out searches and arrests without warrant, and declared martial law in places remote from the scene of hostilities and wherein the regular courts were open. Most of his acts, however, were retroactively validated by Congress.

President Wilson exercised powers in the World War equally extreme as those of President Lincoln, but with the difference that he usually secured the prior authorization of Congress. Among the extraordinary powers exercised by the National Government during the World War were the regulation of the price of fuel, the commandeering of ships and the output of factories, the virtual suppression of the freedom of speech and of the press,[2] the taking over of what would ordinarily be a police power of the states through the enforcement of national prohibition prior to the adoption of the Eighteenth Amendment, the taking over and operation of the railroads and telegraph lines, and the regulation of intrastate commerce and rates.

When the question of the constitutionality of war acts was raised, the courts hesitated to render decisions which might interfere with the efficient prosecution and successful termination of the war. In doubtful cases they were inclined to resolve the doubt in favor of the constitutionality of governmental acts and to uphold them if they had even an indirect or remote relation to the successful prosecution of war. If such a relation could be shown, then acts could be upheld which would otherwise have been invalid as lacking in due process or running counter to some other constitutional limitation.

Nevertheless, in spite of the great extent of the war power, the courts do not admit that it is unlimited. The issuance of a declaration of war does not have the effect of suspending the Constitution. As was declared in the war-time prohibition case, "the war power of the United States, like its other powers and like the police power of the states, is subject to applicable constitutional limitations."[3] Just what limitations are applicable, however, is not perfectly clear. But in at least one case the Court held that Congress had overstepped the bounds. The Lever Food Control Act, which made it a criminal offense to make an unreasonable

---

[1] On the location of the power to suspend the writ of habeas corpus, see Chap. XXIII.

[2] On freedom of speech and press in war time, see Chap. XXIV.

[3] Hamilton v. Kentucky Distilleries and Warehouse Co., 251 U. S. 146 (1919).

charge in dealing in the necessities of life, was held to be lacking in due process because it set up no definite standard of guilt.[1] The Court took occasion to declare that " . . . the mere existence of a state of war could not suspend or change the operation upon the powers of Congress of the guaranties and limitations of the Fifth and Sixth Amendments . . . " It would also seem clear that any constitutional limitation upon Congress which is both express and fairly definite, such as those against passing *ex post facto* laws and levying export taxes, would be upheld by the courts even in time of war.

The Termination of War.—Hostilities may be brought to an end through an armistice or capitulation, but in a legal sense war may, and usually does, continue after the cessation of actual fighting. As commander-in-chief of the army and navy, the President has full authority to terminate hostilities through agreeing to an armistice, such as that of November 11, 1918. It is clear that the armistice did not legally terminate the war, for Congress passed the war-time prohibition act after the armistice had been declared and provided therein that the prohibition should be continued "until the conclusion of the present war." Since the Eighteenth Amendment had not then been adopted, Congress would have had no power to pass such a law except during time of war. When, however, the validity of the act was attacked partly on the ground that the war had terminated, the Supreme Court denied the contention and upheld the validity of the act.[2]

Although the President may terminate hostilities, the question as to whether he could, on his own authority, bring war to an end in the legal sense, is another matter. It is true that, in the case of the Civil War, both the Supreme Court and Congress adopted the date of presidential proclamation as that on which the war legally came to an end.[3] If, however, Congress had adopted a different date as the end of the war, it would seem that the Court would probably have followed Congress rather than the President.[4]

The only method of terminating war apparently contemplated by the framers of the Constitution is that by treaty. This, in fact, is the only way whereby wars to which the United States was a party have actually been terminated, with the exception of the Civil War. Even in the case of foreign wars, however, it is quite conceivable that some other method of ending the conflict legally might have to be found. Thus, on account of difference of opinion between the Senate and President Wilson regarding the Treaty of Versailles, a deadlock ensued which was not broken during his administration. Finally, in 1921, nearly three years

[1] United States v. Cohen Grocery Co., 255 U. S. 81 (1921).
[2] Hamilton v. Kentucky Distilleries and Warehouse Co., 251 U. S. 146 (1919).
[3] *The Protector*, 12 Wall. 700 (1871).
[4] United States v. Anderson, 9 Wall. 56, 70 (1870).

after the armistice, the war with Germany was terminated by a separate treaty.

It might also conceivably happen that, in a foreign war, the enemy's government would be completely overthrown, so that there would be no authorities competent to sign a treaty. Under these circumstances, some other method would have to be found. Although the question is undecided, it would seem reasonable that, since Congress is empowered to recognize a state of war, it would by implication have the power under these circumstances to recognize also a state of peace. In the absence of such a Congressional declaration of peace, the war might possibly be terminated by Presidential proclamation.

CHAPTER XX

TERRITORIES AND DEPENDENCIES

Territorial Expansion.—The territorial expansion of the United States may be divided into three periods, *viz.*, 1783–1853, 1853–1898, and 1898–1917. The treaty of peace of 1783 with Great Britain recognized that the territory of the United States extended west to the Mississippi River. During the first period, we extended our territory across the continent to the Pacific Ocean. This was brought about mainly through the purchase of the vast Louisiana Territory from France in 1803. Likewise, in 1819, we acquired Florida from Spain. In 1845, Texas was annexed. In the following year, the Oregon Territory was acquired and by agreement with Great Britain our Northwest boundary, which had been in doubt, was drawn along the forty-ninth degree of latitude, where it now stands. Territory in the Southwest was acquired in 1848, at the conclusion of the war with Mexico. The first period of territorial expansion was brought to an end in 1853 through the Gadsden Purchase from Mexico, which rounded out our continental area.

The second period was one of comparative inactivity, as we were busy developing the territory we already possessed. In 1856, Congress passed an act authorizing the acquisition of the Guano Islands. The most important territory acquired during this period was Alaska, which was purchased from Russia in 1867. In the same year, the Midway Islands were brought under our control, while Horseshoe Reef in Lake Erie had been ceded to us by Great Britain in 1850. The territory acquired during this period was, for the first time, not contiguous to our continental area.

The third period was ushered in by the Spanish-American War; but we had already been negotiating for the acquisition of the Hawaiian Islands and this plan was finally carried out in the same year. As a result of the war with Spain we acquired in 1898 the insular possessions of Porto Rico, the Philippine Islands, and Guam, and a protectorate over Cuba. By the Anglo-German-American partition treaty of 1899 the United States acquired a portion of the Samoan Islands, including Tutuila, and in the same year took possession of Wake Island in the Pacific. In 1904, we came into possession of the Panama Canal Zone. Finally, in 1917, we purchased from Denmark the Virgin Islands in the Caribbean Sea. Prior to this purchase the United States had acquired protectorates over certain backward countries of the Caribbean region, including Haiti, San Domingo, and Nicaragua. In this connection, it should also be noted that, by treaty arrangement, American consuls have exercised extraterritorial jurisdiction in China and other countries.

The United States acquired no territory as a result of the World War. In 1920, President Wilson submitted to Congress a request for authority to assume a mandate over Armenia, but Congress declined to grant it. A mandate over the Island of Yap, an important cable station lying midway between Guam and the Philippines, was conferred upon Japan, but at the Washington Conference of 1922 an agreement was effected whereby Japan conceded to the United States cable and certain other rights in the island.

Differentiation of Territorial Status.—Originally the United States consisted merely of states and of territory destined to be admitted into the Union as states. During our national history, however, a process of differentiation has developed, so that the "American empire," as Chief Justice Marshall called it,[1] may now be said to consist of seven kinds of territory or territorial jurisdiction, which, though subject to some overlapping, have distinguishing characteristics. These are as follows:

1. States.
2. Incorporated territories, such as Alaska.
3. Unincorporated territories, such as the Philippines.
4. The District of Columbia.
5. Territory under military or naval government, such as Guam
6. Extraterritorial jurisdiction.
7. Protectorates or quasi-protectorates.

The Power to Acquire Territory.—In view of the enormous territorial expansion of the United States, it is curious that the Constitution contains no express grant of the power to acquire territory. Consequently, those who were inclined to construe the Constitution strictly were at first somewhat doubtful whether such a power existed. Thus, President Jefferson, when confronted with the question of the acquisition of the Louisiana Territory, if not doubtful as to the bare power to acquire territory, was at least doubtful as to whether it was constitutionally permissible to incorporate newly acquired territory into the United States. He none the less took the initiative in making the treaty of 1803 with France for the annexation of Louisiana Territory but suggested that a constitutional amendment should be adopted validating such action. No such amendment was ever proposed by Congress and, as it turned out, it was unnecessary, for ample authority to acquire territory may be found in the Constitution.

The main provisions of the Constitution from which the power to acquire territory may be derived are:

1. The power to admit new states into the Union.
2. The power to declare and wage war.
3. The power to make treaties.

[1] Loughborough v. Blake, 5 Wheat. 317 (1820).

In addition to these sources, the United States, as a sovereign state, is also held to have such power to acquire territory as any other sovereign state is recognized by the rules of international law to have, as by discovery, conquest, and occupation.

With reference to the power to admit new states into the Union, it is true that this is a somewhat restricted source of the power to acquire territory, since this provision of the Constitution was apparently intended to authorize the transformation of already acquired territory into the status of a state, rather than the acquisition of new territory.   None the less two states—Texas and California—were annexed and admitted into the Union, without going through the territorial status.

More ample sources of the power to acquire territory are found by implication in the war and treaty powers.   Through one or both of these powers most of our territory has been acquired, including Louisiana, Florida, Alaska, Porto Rico, and the Philippines.   In 1828, Chief Justice Marshall declared, as if it were a self-evident proposition, that "the Constitution confers absolutely upon the government of the Union the power of making war and of making treaties; consequently that government possesses the power of acquiring territory, either by conquest or by treaty."[1]   The acquisition of territory may thus be an incidental result of the exercise of the war or treaty powers.

Had none of the foregoing constitutional sources of power existed, however, it would still have been possible for the United States to acquire territory under the doctrine that, in its external relations, the United States has such powers as sovereign nations are recognized by international law to have.   Discovery and occupation as methods of acquiring territory are recognized by international law and have to some extent been utilized by the United States for this purpose, in cases where none of the three constitutional sources of power would be applicable.

An example of acquisition on this basis is found in the guano island act passed by Congress in 1856, which provided that whenever any citizen of the United States should discover a guano island, not within the lawful jurisdiction of any other government, and should take peaceable possession of it, such island might, "at the discretion of the President, be considered as appertaining to the United States."[2]   The statute further provided that crimes committed on such an island should be punishable in the Federal courts in accordance with the law of the United States. In a criminal case arising under this provision, the Supreme Court was called upon to pass upon the validity of American title to the island and, in the course of its opinion, declared that:

By the law of nations, recognized by all civilized states, dominion of new territory may be acquired by discovery and occupation, as well as by cession

[1] American Insurance Co. v. Canter, 1 Pet. 511 (1828).
[2] 11 Stat at L. 119.

or conquest; and when citizens or subjects of one nation, in its name and by its authority or with its assent, take and hold actual, continuous, and useful possession . . . of territory unoccupied by any other government or its citizens, the nation to which they belong may exercise such jurisdiction and for such period as it sees fit over territory so acquired. This principle affords ample warrant for the legislation of Congress concerning guano islands.[1]

The Court thus recognized a source of power for the acquisition of territory based on international law but not enumerated in the Constitution. The upholding of the validity of the guano island act was, however, a foregone conclusion in view of the well-established doctrine which the Court in the Jones case stated as follows: "Who is the sovereign, *de jure* or *de facto*, of a territory is not a judicial, but a political question, the determination of which by the legislative and executive departments of any government conclusively binds the judges, as well as all other officers, citizens, and subjects of that government."[2]

The Modes of Acquiring Territory.—The foregoing discussion of the sources of the power of acquiring territory has indicated also to some extent the manner of acquiring territory, as by treaty. Certain other modes of acquiring territory, however, have been followed from time to time. Although the usual method of acquiring territory has been by treaty, this plan has been followed only when there was a ceding power with which a treaty could be made and which continued to exist as an independent government after the annexation of the transferred territory to the United States. In other words, this method has been followed when a portion of the territory of a foreign state has been ceded to us, but not when its entire territory has been ceded. Examples of the latter case are Texas and Hawaii which, upon annexation, became wholly merged with the United States. It is true that, in the case of both Texas and Hawaii, an attempt was first made to annex them by the treaty method, which failed on account of inability to secure a two-thirds vote necessary in the Senate for approval of the treaty. Thereupon, the political expedient was adopted of annexation by joint resolution of Congress, which requires only a majority vote. It is questionable, however, whether the treaty method would have been appropriate in view of the fact that, in both of these cases, there was no government with

---

[1] Jones v. United States, 137 U. S. 202 (1890). *Cf.* Fleming v. Page, 9 How. 603 (1850), in which Chief Justice Taney, while holding that a war declared by Congress can never be presumed to be waged for the purpose of conquest or the acquisition of territory, none the less admitted that, by the laws and usages of nations, conquest is a valid title. The Supreme Court has recognized in other cases that the United States has all powers in international relations that other sovereign and independent nations have. *Cf., e. g.,* Fong Yue Ting v. United States, 149 U. S. 698 (1893).

[2] *Ibid. Cf.* Williams v. Suffolk Insurance Co., 13 Pet. 415 (1839); Pearcy v. Stranahan, 205 U. S. 257 (1907).

which to make a treaty except the government of the territory annexed, which ceased to have an independent existence at the moment of annexation. It is true, however, that, even if the treaty method had been followed, the annexation would not have been invalidated by the courts, even supposing that the question could have been brought directly before them.

Texas may be considered as having been annexed in pursuance of the express grant to Congress of the power to admit new states into the Union—a power which may be exercised in the form either of an act or of a joint resolution. Hawaii, however, was not admitted as a state, so that the admission of Texas cannot be regarded as a precedent for the annexation of Hawaii. The latter act represents a greater extension of Congressional power. It may be justified, however, on the same grounds of international usage on which the guano island act was upheld. Since the Hawaiian Islands were acquired in order to form a strategic base for naval operations and in order to assist in promoting American commerce in the Pacific region, the power to annex them might also possibly be implied from the war and commerce powers.

The method of acquisition of territory represented by the guano island act was that of annexation by the President under authority conferred upon him by act of Congress. In a few cases, however, the President has proceeded to acquire territory on his own initiative without waiting for express authority from Congress. Examples of this are Horseshoe Reef, Midway and Wake Islands, and American Samoa. Thus, through cession from Great Britain, Horseshoe Reef in Lake Erie was acquired by the President by means of a simple executive agreement, without submission of the question to the Senate. Generally speaking, however, these acts of the President were subsequently ratified by Congress either expressly or by implication. Horseshoe Reef was ceded on the condition that the United States should erect and maintain a lighthouse thereon, and this naturally required an appropriation act by Congress, which impliedly sanctioned the acquisition.

The Purpose of Acquiring Territory.—At the time of the adoption of the Constitution, the prevalent view as to the purpose for which territory should be acquired or held by the United States was in order that it might ultimately be admitted into the Union as states. Such territory consisted of potential or embryo states. This is shown by the language of the ordinance of 1787 providing that the Northwest Territory should be divided into from three to five parts and each part should ultimately be admitted into the Union as a state. The views of American statesmen generally before the Civil War were that it was incompatible with the genius of our institutions to acquire or hold territory not intended ultimately for statehood. This view was also supported by judicial opinion as, for example, by that of Chief Justice Taney in the Dred Scott case, in which he declared that territory "is acquired to become a state, and not to be held as a colony and governed by Congress with absolute authority."[1] As to when it is in a suitable condition to become a state is a matter within the discretion of Congress. As late as 1894, it was declared by the Supreme Court that:

The territories acquired by Congress whether by deed or cession from the original states, or by treaty with a foreign country, are held with the object, as soon as their population and condition justify, of being admitted into the Union as states upon an equal footing with the original states in all respects.[2]

In respect to this matter, however, a definite change of opinion took place in 1898 at the beginning of the third period of our territorial expansion. That the territory acquired during this period should not be considered as destined ultimately for statehood is not surprising in view of the fundamental change in the character of that territory.

The Power to Govern Territory.—As we have seen, the Articles of Confederation were delayed in going into effect on account of the difficulty caused by the conflicting claims of various states to Western territory. This difficulty was finally settled through the cession by these states of their territorial claims to the central government. In 1787, the Confederate Congress passed the famous Northwest Ordinance for the government of the territory which had been thus ceded by the states.[3] Congress, however, had no constitutional power either to accept this cession or to provide a form of government for the territory ceded. Madison admitted this fact but justified the action of Congress on the ground of public interest and the necessity of the case.[4]

The defectiveness of the Articles of Confederation in not empowering Congress to govern territory was remedied by the insertion in the Constitution of a provision that "Congress shall have power to dispose of and make all needful rules and regulations respecting the territory or other property belonging to the United States."[5] Shortly after the Constitution went into effect, the Northwest Ordinance was reenacted by Congress in order to remove any doubts as to its validity. This ordinance became the model for many subsequent laws enacted by Congress for the government of the territory of the United States.

The clause of the Constitution quoted above, empowering Congress to "make all needful rules and regulations," has usually been held by

---

[1] Dred Scott v. Sandford, 19 How. 393 (1857).

[2] Shively v. Bowlby, 152 U. S. 1 (1894).

[3] Text of the ordinance will be found in Mathews and Berdahl, *Documents and Readings in American Government*, pp. 480–486.

[4] *The Federalist*, No. 38. If this were a usurpation of power, however, no objection was raised by the states and their acquiescence, combined with the cession of territory, might possibly be construed as a grant of power to take and govern it.

[5] Art. IV., sect. 3, par. 2.

the courts to be amply sufficient to authorize Congress to govern not only the territory originally held at the time of the adoption of the Constitution but also territory subsequently acquired.[1]

It had been held by the majority of the judges in the Dred Scott case, however, that the provision applied only to the original territory and, moreover, was not a general grant of governing power but merely a grant of the somewhat restricted power of making such regulations as were needful. Consequently, the tendency of the courts since the decision in that case has been to rely upon other sources of power. In the first place, the power to govern territory is implied from the power to acquire it. This position was foreshadowed by Chief Justice Marshall as early as 1810 in a case wherein he remarked that "the power of governing and of legislating for a territory is the inevitable consequence of the right to acquire and hold territory."[2] It is thus a power which is implied in a power which is itself implied. This position has been confirmed by later judicial statements, such as that in which it was declared that "it would be absurd to hold that the United States has the power to acquire territory and no power to govern it when acquired."[3]

In the second place, the power to govern territory has been derived from the fact that, since the states are incompetent to govern territory not within their boundaries, the National Government must necessarily be construed to have the power. As Chief Justice Marshall declared in an early case:

Perhaps the power of governing a territory belonging to the United States, which has not, by becoming a state, acquired the means of self-government, may result necessarily from the facts that it is not within the jurisdiction of any particular state, and is within the power and jurisdiction of the United States.[4]

This position was confirmed many years later in one of the insular cases, in which the Court declared that the power to govern territory "arises not necessarily from the territorial clause of the Constitution, but from the necessities of the case, and from the inability of the states to act upon the subject."[5]

Modes of Governing Territory.—The mode of governing territory acquired by the United States, or at least temporarily under its control, may in general be either presidential or Congressional. This distinction corresponds somewhat, though not exactly, to that between military and civil government. Although presidential government is administered by military or naval officers acting under the President, such government does not necessarily connote conquest. It may be applied to

---

[1] Mormon Church v. United States, 136 U. S. 1 (1890).

[2] Sere v. Pitot, 6 Cranch 332 (1810).

[3] Mormon Church v. United States, 136 U. S. 1 (1890).

[4] American Insurance Co. v. Canter, 1 Pet. 511 (1828).

[5] De Lima v. Bidwell, 182 U. S. 1 (1901).

territory which has been obtained by peaceful means. American Samoa, for example, has been governed by the President through a naval officer appointed for the purpose. In this instance the President acts by virtue of his power and duty to see that the applicable laws of the United States are observed and peace maintained in territory subject to American control.

More usually, however, presidential government is applied to territory either temporarily or permanently under our control through conquest by our military and/or naval forces. In this instance the President exercises authority by virtue of his position as commander-in-chief. For example, Porto Rico and the Philippines were taken by our forces in 1898 and remained under the immediate control of our military commanders acting under the President even after Spain had formally ceded them to us by treaty. On account of unsettled conditions in those dependencies, presidential or military government was continued until 1900 in Porto Rico and until 1901 in the Philippines. On those dates, acts of Congress went into effect which established forms of civil government for those dependencies respectively and thereby changed their governments from presidential to Congressional. Congress might constitutionally have taken this action from the moment those territories were brought under the control of our forces, but, for reasons of expediency, presidential or military government was allowed to continue temporarily, since it is a more effective form for purposes of pacification and the restoration of order. It might also be allowed to continue after the ratification of the treaty of peace ceding the territory to the United States. During the period of such military government, the President, as commander-in-chief of the army and navy, exercised almost absolute control over the conquered territory, limited only by the laws and usages of war. Such absolute control is justified only on the ground of military necessity, so that, when order has been restored and the territory has been formally annexed to the United States, the President's power probably ceases to be quite so unlimited, even prior to the establishment of civil government by act of Congress.

When Congress undertakes to establish civil government in place of military control in territory acquired by the United States, it may either legislate for the territory directly or may delegate its legislative authority to such local governmental agencies as may be set up for the purpose. Just as the states may delegate legislative power to municipalities, so the doctrine that legislative power cannot be delegated does not apply to the relation of Congress to the territories. In legislating for the territories, Congress combines the powers of both Federal and state authorities and has full discretion to establish such form of government as it sees fit. The government set up need not be republican in form; it need not embody the principle of separation of powers; and the inhabitants need not be given rights of self-government. The usual policy, however, has been to grant as large a measure of self-government as seems feasible.[1] In general, the model of the Northwest Ordinance has been followed, with such variations as may have seemed necessary to meet special conditions.

By virtue of the complete authority of Congress over the form of government to be established in the territories, whether incorporated or unincorporated, it is not subject to certain constitutional provisions which limit it in creating agencies within the continental area of the United States. Thus, the judges of lower Federal courts which are created by Congress from time to time, hold their offices during good behavior, while the term of judges of the territorial courts may, in the discretion of Congress, be fixed at a short period of years.[2] In the latter case, Congress is acting under its territorial power rather than under its power to establish lower Federal courts.

Incorporation of Territory into the United States.—During the Mexican War, American forces were in temporary military control of the port of Tampico. The United States tariff law then in force imposed duties upon goods imported into the United States from foreign countries. The question arose as to whether Tampico was foreign within the meaning of this law during the time it was under American military control. The Supreme Court held that it was and that the duties were properly levied.[3] Chief Justice Taney, who rendered the opinion, declared that, although other nations generally were bound to regard Tampico as part of the territory of the United States, from the standpoint of our constitutional or domestic law, Tampico was not a part of the Union. The mere conquest of Tampico by military forces under the President did not "enlarge the boundaries of this Union nor extend the operations of our institutions and laws beyond the limits before assigned to them by the legislative power."[4] In other words, such conquest, regardless of whether the territory is held temporarily or permanently, does not, in and by itself, effect its formal annexation to the United States. Much less does it incorporate such territory into the United States.

It will be noticed that Tampico was merely under our temporary military control and it was not ceded to the United States by treaty.

[1] This statement is made from the legal point of view. Practically, self-government is a capacity for managing affairs which is acquired by practice rather than granted by higher authority.

[2] American Insurance Co. v. Canter, 1 Pet. 511 (1828).

[3] Fleming v. Page, 9 How. 603 (1850).

[4] *Ibid. Cf.* United States v. Rice, 4 Wheat. 246 (1819), in which it was held that when Castine, Maine, was under temporary military control of British forces during the War of 1812, goods imported into Castine were not imported into the United States and the Congressional tariff act was not applicable to them. From the international point of view, these two cases seem to conflict, but from the Constitutional point of view, they are reconcilable.

During that period of military control it was a part of the United States in an international sense but not in a domestic sense. With respect to the operation of our tariff laws, it was foreign to the United States in a domestic sense, but in the international sense it was not foreign, so that the American military commander at Tampico could probably have collected duties on goods imported there from countries other than the United States. The question as to whether he could do so was not before the Court in the Fleming v. Page case, but a similar question was presented to the Court in a later case involving the authority of the American military commander in California. In this case,[1] the action of the commander in collecting duties on goods imported at San Francisco from countries other than the United States prior to the ratification of the treaty of 1848, whereby Mexico ceded California to the United States, was upheld as an exercise of the war power.

In the case just cited, the question was also presented to the Court as to the status of California after the ratification of the treaty of 1848. It was held that California became domestic territory immediately upon the ratification of the treaty, or, in the language of the Court, it "became a part of the United States" and, consequently, the tariff laws of the United States then in force became *ipso facto* applicable to it, even though no act of Congress had been passed expressly extending them to it. Any other view, the Court intimated, would be contrary to the provision of the Constitution which enjoins that "all duties, imposts and excises shall be uniform throughout the United States."[2]

The position of the Court in this case would seem to be that annexation of territory by the treaty power is sufficient, in and by itself, to incorporate such territory into the United States. If so, this position, as we shall see, was not sustained by the Court in the insular cases, decided a half century later.

Does the Constitution Follow the Flag?—As a result of the acquisition of new territory of a different character at the time of the Spanish-American War in 1898, the question naturally arose as to how far the Constitution is applicable to such territory or, in other words, to what extent Congress is limited by the Constitution in dealing with such territory.

The Constitution was designed to be the fundamental law for a nation composed of states and of territory obviously destined for statehood and inhabited by a largely homogeneous population having the same predominantly Anglo-Saxon legal and political traditions and institutions. It is not surprising, therefore, that, prior to the Spanish War, it was generally supposed that Congress, in dealing with the territories, was limited by the Constitution to the same extent that it was thereby limited in dealing with the same matters within the states. It was recognized,

[1] Cross v. Harrison, 16 How. 164 (1853).
[2] Art. I, sect. 8, cl. 1.

of course, as we have seen, that Congress had complete authority over the form of government to be established in the territories. Furthermore, with respect to the political rights of the inhabitants of the territories, Congress had such wide control that it might deny or abolish the right to vote altogether. But with respect to the civil rights of the inhabitants, Congress was generally supposed to be subject to the same constitutional limitations under which it operates in dealing with the residents of the states.

Thus, the majority of the judges in the Dred Scott case[1] took the position that Congress, in dealing with the territories, was limited by the provision of the Fifth Amendment which prohibits the deprivation of property without due process of law. Although, as far as the slaves were concerned, this position was rendered untenable by the adoption of the Thirteenth Amendment, the proposition that Congress, in dealing with the inhabitants of the territories, is limited by the constitutional bill of rights was not repudiated by that amendment. In fact, as late as 1897, the year before the Spanish War broke out, the Supreme Court upheld the principle that Congress, in dealing with the territories, is limited by the provision of the constitutional bill of rights regarding trial by jury.[2]

In spite of the general trend of judicial opinion, however, certain indications may be found, even prior to the Spanish War, which logically point in the direction of such differentiation of territory that the power of Congress may be different in dealing with different areas.

In the first place, as we have seen, the constitutional requirement of a life tenure for judges was held not to bind Congress in establishing courts in the territories.

In the second place, the guano island act of 1856, upheld by the Supreme Court, recognized that there might be territory which was not a part of the United States proper but merely appertained to the United States.

In the third place, as we have seen, the Supreme Court held in the Tampico case that territory might be under our military control and a part of the United States in an international sense but not a part of the United States in the domestic sense.

Fourth, it should be mentioned in this connection that the Thirteenth Amendment, adopted in 1865, in abolishing slavery "within the United States, or any place subject to their jurisdiction," clearly indicated that, in the minds of the framers, there might be territory subject to American control but not within the United States.[3]

[1] Dred Scott v. Sandford, 19 How. 393 (1857).

[2] Springville v. Thomas, 166 U. S. 707 (1897), confirmed (as to Alaska) in Rasmussen v. United States, 197 U. S. 516 (1905).

[3] The Fourteenth Amendment, adopted in 1868, also uses the phrase "the United States and subject to the jurisdiction thereof," while the Eighteenth Amendment uses an almost identical phrase.

Finally, it may be noted in this connection that it was held by the Supreme Court in 1891 that the Anglo-Saxon principle of trial by jury, as provided for in the Constitution, is not applicable to cases tried in American consular courts in the Orient. An American seaman named Ross had committed murder on board an American vessel in the harbor of Yokohama, Japan, in which country the United States at that time exercised extraterritorial jurisdiction. The offender was convicted in a trial before the American consular court without either a grand or petit jury. Ten years later, while serving a life sentence in the United States, he applied for a writ of habeas corpus on the ground that his conviction without trial by jury was unconstitutional. The Supreme Court held, however, that the Constitution of the United States can have no operation in another country and that Congress, therefore, in regulating the procedure in consular courts, is not limited by the bill of rights of the Constitution. As a further reason for its opinion, the Court pointed out that it would ordinarily be impracticable to operate the jury system in such courts, on account of the difficulty of obtaining a competent grand or petit jury.[1]

If we analyze the limitations upon Congress in the Constitution as to the territorial extent of their applicability, we find that they may be classified into four groups, as follows:

1. Prohibitions upon Congress with reference to the states, as, for example, that "no tax or duty shall be laid on articles exported from any state."[2]

2. Prohibitions upon Congress applicable in every place to which the acts of Congress may extend, as, for example, the prohibition against slavery.

3. Prohibitions on Congress which apply only within the United States, as, for example, the requirement that "all duties, imposts, and excises shall be uniform throughout the United States."[3]

4. Prohibitions on Congress in connection with which no statement is made indicating the territorial extent of the prohibition, as, for example, those contained in the first eight amendments or constitutional bill of rights.

It was especially in connection with the last two classes of prohibitions that the courts were called upon in the insular cases to express an opinion as to their applicability to the new territory acquired from Spain as a result of the war of 1898.

The Insular Cases.—In a group of cases decided by the Supreme Court shortly after the Spanish War, that tribunal was confronted with a number of puzzling questions regarding the status of the newly acquired

---

[1] *In re* Ross, 140 U. S. 453 (1891).

[2] Art. I, sect. 9, cl. 5.

[3] Art. I, sect. 8, cl. 1.

territory and of its inhabitants.   It was, as we have seen, opposed to the genius of our institutions and to the theory of the Constitution that the United States should hold territory and its inhabitants in a permanent condition of inferiority to the states and to their residents.   Those judges, therefore, who held that this could not be done had logic and precedent on their side.   The United States, however, was confronted in 1898 with an unprecedented situation.   The broad question was as to whether the Constitution could be construed in such a flexible manner as to adapt it to the new conditions.   The Supreme Court had to deal not with a theory but with a condition and the solution of the problem had to be based fundamentally on practical rather than on legal considerations.

As will be remembered, the situation of the territories acquired in 1898 was radically different from that of the territory acquired before that date.   The earlier territory had practically all been on the continent of North America and, with the exception of Alaska, had been contiguous to the territory that we already possessed.   Moreover, it had been only sparsely populated and, excepting the greater part of Alaska, was in a temperate climate, so that, in both these respects, it was suitable for settlement by American citizens.   On the other hand, the territory acquired in 1898 was separated from our continental area by the high seas. Moreover, it was in a tropical climate and already densely inhabited by an essentially alien race of people who were unfamiliar with the rules of the common law and with the working of our political institutions.   For these reasons, regardless of what the Constitution might be thought to say on the subject, it did not seem to most informed observers that it would be wise or expedient to extend at once and automatically to these territories such peculiarly Anglo-Saxon institutions as indictment by grand jury and trial by petit jury.

These were doubtless the fundamental considerations which led the majority of the Supreme Court in the insular cases to construe the Constitution in such a flexible manner as to adapt it to the new conditions.   The Court, however, was badly divided over the question, with the result that several of the more important of these cases were decided by a bare majority of the Court, and, in the most important case of all, although the Court reached a decision, there was no opinion of the Court, since not more than four out of the nine judges were able to agree on any one opinion[1].

It is not necessary to go into a consideration of all the ramifications of the arguments contained in the opinions of the respective judges, whether concurring or dissenting, in the insular cases.   For the most part, the concurring opinion written by Justice White in the case of Downes v. Bidwell has come to be regarded as the established doctrine of the Court. In this case it was held that Porto Rico, even after it was annexed by

[1] Downes v. Bidwell, 182 U. S. 244 (1901).

treaty with Spain, was not a part of the United States within the meaning of the constitutional provision that "all duties, imposts, and excises shall be uniform throughout the United States," and, consequently, the Congressional act of 1900 levying duties on goods imported into the United States from Porto Rico was constitutional. Porto Rico was held to be merely a territory appurtenant and belonging to the United States. In the international sense or from the standpoint of other nations, however, Porto Rico was a part of the United States as soon as the treaty of annexation became effective, but it continued to be foreign to the United States in a domestic sense.

In the Downes and other insular cases, the majority of the Court laid down three important propositions: first, that the territories of the United States may be classified into incorporated and unincorporated; second, that the treaty-making power, although able to annex territory to the United States in the international sense, is not competent to incorporate territory fully into the United States in a constitutional or domestic sense; and, third, that Congress, in dealing with the civil rights of the inhabitants of the unincorporated territories, is not subject to all of the constitutional limitations which govern it in dealing with those of the residents of states and incorporated territories.

Distinction between Incorporated and Unincorporated Territories.— The distinction between these two kinds of territory as laid down by the Supreme Court is not very clear. The distinction is not the same as that between organized and unorganized territory, since an organized territory, such as Porto Rico or the Philippines, may be unincorporated. In order that a territory be incorporated, there must be an act or joint resolution of Congress expressing or implying an intention on its part to that effect. Where no indication of such intention can be found, the territory must be regarded as unincorporated or merely appurtenant to the United States.

All of the territories formerly existing in the continental area of the United States were incorporated, but this incorporation was not brought about by the mere fact of the annexation of such territory through treaty. The treaties annexing those territories might and did contain provisions promising future incorporation, but in order to bring this about, the consent of Congress was required. It is doubtful whether our government would ever have consented to the annexation of territory by treaty if the necessary result were immediately to incorporate it fully into the United States and to confer American citizenship upon native inhabitants who were largely alien to our traditions, customs, and political institutions.

The position of the Court that the incorporation of territory in the domestic sense can be effected by act of Congress but not by treaty has been criticised on the ground that it is contrary to the provision of the Constitution which "places treaties upon a plane of equality with the statutes of Congress."[1]   This criticism, however, emphasizes the language of the Constitution while disregarding its operation.   From the latter point of view, treaties and acts of Congress are not equal in a domestic sense because treaties are not always self-executing but may require ancillary legislation to put them into effect, while a statute goes into effect without further Congressional action.[2]

Our only incorporated territories are Hawaii and Alaska.   From the time of its annexation in 1898, however, until the enactment by Congress in 1900 of the organic law for Hawaii, that territory remained unincorporated.   Even though the joint resolution of 1898 had provided for the annexation of Hawaii "as part of the the territory of the United States, and subject to the sovereign dominion thereof," it was held that Hawaii was not thereby incorporated into the United States to such an extent that certain provisions of the constitutional bill of rights automatically and by their own force applied to that territory.[3]   The reasoning of this opinion seems somewhat doubtful, but by the organic law of 1900, at any rate, it was clearly the intention of Congress fully to incorporate Hawaii and to bring it under all the applicable provisions of the Constitution.

With respect to Alaska, it was held that the treaty of cession and the action of Congress thereunder clearly indicated an intention to incorporate it into the United States.[4]   The treaty had provided that the inhabitants of the ceded territory, except the uncivilized native tribes, should be admitted to the enjoyment of all the rights, advantages, and immunities of citizens of the United States.   This was the usual formula found in earlier treaties for the cession of territory, such as Louisiana and Florida.   It was substantially the formula used to express the purpose to incorporate the territory into the United States.   This purpose was confirmed by the fact that, in 1868, the year following the treaty ceding Alaska, Congress extended the customs and internal revenue laws to it and established a collection district therein.

Status of the Inhabitants of the Territories.—The question may be raised as to how far the inhabitants of the territories are protected by the provisions of the Constitution designed to safeguard individual rights. In other words, to what extent is Congress limited by such provisions in regulating the rights of territorial inhabitants?   With respect to the inhabitants of the incorporated territories, it would seem that Congress is restricted by all the constitutional limitations which rest upon it when dealing with the same matters within the states.   This was the view held

---

[1] WILLOUGHBY, W. W., *Constitutional Law of the United States*, 2d ed., vol. I, p. 493.

[2] For this reason a statute supersedes, in the domestic sense, an earlier conflicting treaty, while a treaty does not always or necessarily supersede an earlier conflicting statute, but only when the treaty is self-executing.   On this matter, see J. M. Mathews, *American Foreign Relations: Conduct and Policies*, Chap. XXIII.

[3] Hawaii v. Mankichi, 190 U. S. 197 (1903).

[4] Rasmussen v. United States, 197 U. S. 516 (1905).

by the courts prior to the insular cases, but they were considering merely the status of inhabitants of incorporated territories. The insular cases made no change in this respect. In these cases, however, the Court was confronted with the question as to the status of the inhabitants of unincorporated territories. Face to face with this problem, the Court took the position that some provisions of the Constitution are fundamental and others are not and that Congress, in dealing with the rights of inhabitants of the unincorporated territories, is limited only by the fundamental provisions, *i.e.*, by those prohibitions which go to the very root of the power of Congress to act at all, irrespective of time and place. The Constitution is everywhere and at all times potential, in so far as its provisions are applicable, but only the fundamental provisions are applicable to the unincorporated territories. It would seem that these provisions extend to such territories of their own force and do not need to be extended by act of Congress. The inhabitants of such territories, therefore, are not under the absolute control of Congress in all respects nor completely subject to its unlimited will.

The Court has not undertaken to make a complete enumeration of those provisions of the Constitution which are to be deemed fundamental. It has intimated, however, that among the fundamental provisions are those declaring that "no bill of attainder or *ex post facto* law shall be passed" and that "no title of nobility shall be granted." These were among the prohibitions described by Justice White in Downes v. Bidwell as "not mere regulations as to the form and manner in which a conceded power may be exercised, but an absolute denial of all authority under any circumstances or conditions to do particular acts."

On the other hand, it has been held that the provisions of the constitutional bill of rights with reference to indictment by grand jury and trial by petit jury are not fundamental. These were among the rights described by Justice Brown in Downes v. Bidwell as "artificial or remedial rights which are peculiar to our own system of jurisprudence," as distinguished from "certain natural rights enforced in the Constitution by prohibitions against interference with them."

With reference to the status of the inhabitants of Hawaii after the Congressional joint resolution of 1898 for its annexation but before its incorporation in 1900, it was held that the conviction of a person who had been prosecuted merely on information and convicted by a non-unanimous jury was legal, although not in accordance with the Fifth and Sixth Amendments to the Constitution.[1] These provisions were not formally extended to Hawaii until the act of 1900.

The same rule, of course, applied to any other unincorporated territory, such as the Philippine Islands. The treaty with Spain whereby these islands were annexed clearly evidences an intention that they should

[1] Hawaii v. Mankichi, 190 U. S. 197 (1903).

not be incorporated into the United States. Congress was left a free hand in dealing with them, for it was expressly provided in the treaty that "the civil rights and political status of the native inhabitants of the territories hereby ceded to the United States shall be determined by the Congress." In 1902, Congress passed an act providing, among other rights of the inhabitants of those islands, that no person should be held for a criminal offense without due process of law. No mention, however, was made of trial by jury and, on the authority of the Mankichi case, the Supreme Court upheld the trial of crimes in the islands without a jury.[1]

On the other hand, in the case of Alaska which, as we have seen, is an incorporated territory, it was held that the provision of the Sixth Amendment, providing for the trial of crimes by jury, was operative in Alaska by its own force and, consequently, an act of Congress, depriving inhabitants of Alaska of the right to trial by a common-law jury, was repugnant to the Constitution and void.[2]

Although the nonfundamental provisions of the Constitution do not, of their own force, extend to the unincorporated territories, they may be extended to them by act of Congress. Thus, by act of 1902, Congress extended to the inhabitants of the Philippines immunity against double jeopardy for crime provided for in the Fifth Amendment to the Constitution.[3] The question may be raised as to whether or not, when Congress has made such an extension, its act is irrevocable and irrepealable. In his concurring opinion in the Rasmussen case, Justice Brown declared that, once the provisions of the Constitution are extended to such territories, that action, in his opinion, is irrevocable. It is true that some acts of Congress are irrevocable. It would hardly be contended, for example, that, when Congress has passed an act admitting a state into the Union, it could subsequently oust that state by repealing the act of admission. In general, however, Congress can pass no irrepealable act, and it is not clear that Congress could not withdraw from inhabitants of unincorporated territories the benefit of rights contained in non-fundamental provisions of the Constitution which it had previously extended to them.

Citizenship in the Territories.—As already noted, in treaties entered into prior to the Spanish-American War for the annexation of territory, it was generally provided that the inhabitants of such territories should be admitted as soon as possible to the enjoyment of all the rights, advantages, and immunities of the citizens of the United States. Although this provision left some discretion to Congress, it nevertheless embodied substantially the general rule of international law that, when territory is

[1] Dorr v. United States, 195 U. S. 138 (1904).
[2] Rasmussen v. United States, 197 U. S. 516 (1905).
[3] Kepner v. United States, 195 U. S. 100 (1904).

transferred from one nation to another, the allegiance of the inhabitants is similarly transferred.

From the standpoint of constitutional law, such inhabitants, while ceasing to be aliens, do not necessarily acquire full citizenship by virtue of the transfer of territory. In the case of the territories acquired from Spain in 1898, the treaty of cession, as we have seen, left full discretion to Congress, providing that "the civil rights and political status of the native inhabitants . . . shall be determined by the Congress." The native inhabitants of Porto Rico and of the Philippines were by acts of Congress of 1900 and 1902 declared to be citizens of those respective dependencies. They were neither aliens nor full-fledged citizens but occupied an intermediate status. Since they are under the jurisdiction of the United States, they may, from the standpoint of international law, be spoken of as "nationals."

The Fourteenth Amendment provides that all persons born in the United States, provided they are also subject to our jurisdiction, are American citizens. It would seem, however, that the term "United States," as used in this provision, does not include the unincorporated territories, so that their inhabitants do not thereby become American citizens in the full constitutional sense. By virtue of its power of naturalization, however, Congress may extend citizenship to such inhabitants. Thus, in 1917, Congress extended full American citizenship to the Porto Ricans and, in 1927, to the inhabitants of the Virgin Islands. The inhabitants of the incorporated territories—Alaska and Hawaii—are also citizens of the United States.

The District of Columbia.—This District might be classified in certain respects as an incorporated territory of the United States, but it seems better to consider it as in a class by itself. It comes under a special provision of the Constitution which empowers Congress "to exercise exclusive legislation in all cases whatsoever over such district (not exceeding ten miles square) as may by cession of particular states, and the acceptance of Congress, become the seat of the government of the United States."[1] The purpose of this provision was to provide a seat of National Government which should not be under the jurisdiction of any particular state. Since this territory was once part of a state, it has been held that those provisions of the Constitution applying generally to the United States, apply also to the District and no change was made in this respect by the cession of the District to the United States.[2] Out of superabundant caution, however, Congress in 1871 expressly extended the provisions

---

[1] Art. I, sect. 8, cl. 17.

[2] By Justice Brown in Downes v. Bidwell, 182 U. S. 244 (1901). In an early case it was held that the District is a part of the United States within the meaning of the Constitutional provision that "all duties, imposts, and excises shall be uniform throughout the United States." Loughborough v. Blake, 5 Wheat. 317 (1820).

of the Constitution to the District. Certain provisions of the bill of rights, such as the right to trial by jury in civil and criminal cases, which were held in the insular cases to be nonfundamental parts of the Constitution, have been held to be applicable to the District.[1] The common law of Maryland still prevails in the District, except in so far as it is inconsistent with local conditions or has been modified by Congressional or local legislation.

Congress may exercise within the District all legislative powers that the legislature of a state may exercise within a state. In the case of the territories, as we have seen, Congress may delegate to them the exercise of legislative power. In view of the constitutional provision, however, empowering Congress to exercise "exclusive legislation" over the District, it would seem that Congress cannot delegate legislative power to the District, but it may authorize it to exercise municipal powers. Legislative power of a national character or corresponding to that exercised by a state legislature must be exercised by Congress. At least that is the assumption and the well-established rule in practice. Congress has created a commission to exercise executive powers in the District, but Congress itself is the law-making body. In 1878, Congress abolished the right of suffrage in the District completely.

In some respects the District of Columbia is regarded as if it were a state and in other respects as if it were not. Unlike a state, it has no representation in Congress nor in the presidential electoral college. Unlike a state, or even a territory, it is suable without its consent. In this respect, it is more like a municipality. It has also been held that it is not a state within the meaning of the constitutional provision which confers on the Federal courts jurisdiction over suits between citizens of different states.

On the other hand, the District was classified as a state within the meaning of the constitutional provision regarding direct taxes, so that, if Congress levies a direct tax within the District, it must be apportioned in accordance with population.[2] It has also been held that in the international sense, or with respect to foreign nations, the District may be regarded as a state. Thus, in 1890, the question arose whether a French citizen is entitled to own, by inheritance from an American citizen, property situated in the District. The treaty of 1853 with France granted this right with reference only to property situated in "all the states of the Union." The Supreme Court construed this provision broadly enough to include the District.[3]

Places Purchased.—In addition to the power of exclusive legislation over the District of Columbia, Congress is also empowered "to exercise

---

[1] Callan v. Wilson, 127 U. S. 540 (1888); Capital Traction Co. v. Hof, 174 U. S. 1 (1899).

[2] Loughborough v. Blake, 5 Wheat. 317 (1820).

[3] De Geofroy v. Riggs, 133 U. S. 258 (1890).

like authority over all places purchased by the consent of the legislature of the state in which the same shall be for the erection of forts, magazines, arsenals, dockyards, and other needful buildings."[1]   Over land acquired for such purposes and with such consent, Congress exercises political jurisdiction or governmental authority and that of the state is ousted. If Congress should purchase land within a state, whether or not through its power of eminent domain, without the consent of the legislature of such state, the political jurisdiction of the state would not be ousted, and the National Government would occupy substantially the position of an ordinary proprietor, except that such national property would not be subject to state taxation.[2]

The Alienation of Territory.—In some instances of boundary disputes, the United States has surrendered territory which it had previously claimed, but the surrender of the territory may be construed as an admission that the claim was not well founded.   Aside from the settlement of such disputes, there has been no instance of the alienation of American territory.   The matter has been considered, however, in *obiter* statements by the Supreme Court.   If the territory in question is that of one of the states of the Union, there is general agreement that it could be alienated with the combined consent of the National Government and of the state in question.   In one case, however, the Supreme Court stated that "it would not be contended that it (the treaty-making power) extends so far as to authorize what the Constitution forbids, or a change in the character of the government, or in that of the states, or a cession of any portion of the territory of the latter, without its consent."[3]

It would seem, however, that, just as territory may be acquired by the treaty-making power, so, if it should be desired to cede any of the territory of a state to a foreign nation, the making of a treaty would be the proper method.   And although it would be good policy to obtain the consent of the state in question to such cession, its consent, if not formally given, might, in cases of necessity, be presumed.   The supremacy of the National Government in international relations is sufficient to enable it to make such a cession, because this is a power which, by international usage, may be exercised by sovereign nations generally.   Such cession might be indispensable to purchase peace or, as Justice White pointed out in one of the insular cases, "from the exigency of a calamitous war or the necessity of a settlement of boundaries, it may be that citizens of the United States may be expatriated by the action of the treaty-making power, impliedly or expressly ratified by Congress."[4]   If the territory

---

[1] Art. I, sect. 8, cl. 17.

[2] Ft. Leavenworth R. R. Co. v. Lowe, 114 U. S. 525 (1884); Van Brocklin v. Tennessee, 117 U. S. 151 (1885).

[3] De Geofroy v. Riggs, 133 U. S. 258 (1890).

[4] Downes v. Bidwell, 182 U. S. 244 (1901).

of a state could be alienated without its consent, it follows without question that that of an incorporated or unincorporated territory could be.

If any portion of American territory should rebel against the authority of the United States Government and should establish a *de facto* government acting independently of that of the United States, such independence could be recognized by treaty with the *de facto* government. If, however, there is no purpose of ceding territory to a foreign nation but merely of granting independence to one of our territories, such as the Philippines, in the absence of the prior establishment of such independence in fact, the proper method of procedure would not be by treaty but by act or joint resolution of Congress. That body would be enabled to exercise this power, both by virtue of the constitutional grant to "dispose of . . . the territory . . . belonging to the United States"[1] and also by virtue of the fact that, in such matters, the National Government, acting through Congress, is to be deemed to have such powers as sovereign nations generally possess. At any rate, if Congress should assume to exercise the power, there is little chance that the courts would interfere, for the question as to the extent of American territorial jurisdiction is a political, rather than a judicial, one.

[1] Art. IV, sect. 3, cl. 2.

PART III
GOVERNMENT AND THE INDIVIDUAL

CHAPTER XXI

CITIZENSHIP AND NATURALIZATION

Citizenship in General.—A citizen of a given nation may be defined as a natural person who owes it allegiance and is entitled to its protection. In other words, he is a member of the nation. From the standpoint of international law or foreign relations, the members of a nation are called "nationals" and are deemed to be a homogeneous body of persons, without distinction as to status or rights. From the point of view of constitutional law, however, the citizens of a nation may be classified into various groups with differing rights. They may be classified, for example, into native-born and naturalized citizens. Again, they may differ in respect to the extent of their political rights. Minors are citizens in the sense that they owe allegiance and are entitled to protection equally with adults. But they are generally excluded from the right to vote and the right to hold office. In other words, they do not enjoy all the privileges which have been conferred upon adult citizens. While it is thus true that not all citizens are voters, it is also true that some voters are not citizens. Thus, some states have conferred the right to vote upon aliens who have merely declared their intention to become citizens of the United States.[1] It will thus be seen that there is no necessary connection between citizenship and suffrage.[2]

Two principal rules for determining citizenship have been adopted by modern civilized nations. One is by parentage and the other is by place of birth. The former is called the *jus sanguinis* and the latter is known as the *jus soli*. Generally speaking, the former has been followed by the nations of Continental Europe, while the latter has usually been adhered to by England and the United States. A given nation, however, may to some extent follow both rules at the same time, and this is true of the United States.

National and State Citizenship.—The subject of citizenship in the United States is especially complicated on account of the Federal system of government. On account of this dual system of government, there exists also a dual citizenship. Prior to the adoption of the Constitution there was state citizenship but probably no citizenship of the United States. That instrument, however, clearly recognizes a dual citizenship, and since its adoption both state and national citizenship have existed. Prior to the adoption of the Fourteenth Amendment, there was no uni-

---

[1] No state, however, now does this.
[2] Minor v. Happersett, 21 Wall. 162 (1875).

313

form rule as to state citizenship, but, under the original Constitution, Congress was given the exclusive power of establishing a uniform rule of naturalization, *i.e.*, of prescribing the method by which aliens may become citizens.

Although the Constitution mentions both state and national citizens several times, it contained, as originally drawn up, no definition of citizenship and no indication as to the relationship existing between the two kinds of citizenship. This omission of the Constitution left in doubt which of the two citizenships was anterior to, or more fundamental than, the other. Consequently, a controversy over this question arose between the nationalists and the states' rights advocates. The latter declared that state citizenship was primary and more fundamental than national citizenship. They held that, if a person were a citizen of the United States, he became such, except in the case of naturalized citizens and those residing in a territory, by virtue of the fact that he was in the first place a citizen of one of the states. According to this view, therefore, national citizenship, with these exceptions, was derivative from, and subordinate to, state citizenship.

The issue thus presented finally came before the Supreme Court in the celebrated Dred Scott case, decided in 1857.[1] Although the judges were badly divided on some of the issues involved in this case, the majority adopted the states' rights point of view regarding the priority of state over national citizenship. They also held that, although, in general, a person acquires citizenship by being born within the country, this is not true of a native-born negro, even though free, who could not become a citizen of the United States, by either state or Federal action.[2]

The Fourteenth Amendment.—The decision of the Supreme Court in the Dred Scott case was, in a certain sense, "recalled" by the Fourteenth Amendment, which reversed the two holdings of the Court mentioned above. That amendment for the first time places in the Constitution a definition of citizenship, which is that "all persons born or naturalized in the United States and subject to the jurisdiction thereof, are citizens of the United States and of the state wherein they reside." This definition continues the original idea of two citizenships but clearly makes national citizenship primary and more fundamental than state citizenship. Mere birth within the United States makes a person a citizen of the United States without any requirement of residence, provided he is subject to its jurisdiction. This is broad enough to include the former slaves, who, by the Thirteenth Amendment, had been generally freed.

---

[1] Scott v. Sandford, 19 How. 393.

[2] The holding of the Court in this case regarding the citizenship of free negroes was, strictly speaking, *dicta*, but this would undoubtedly have been the holding, had the question actually been before the Court for decision.

While state citizenship is retained under the Fourteenth Amendment, it is now of less importance, for it practically means nothing more than residence within the state. It is now subordinate to, and derivative from, national citizenship. The paramountcy of national citizenship is further indicated by the provision of the amendment that "no state shall make or enforce any law which shall abridge the privileges or immunities of citizens of the United States." A state has no right to treat as an alien any person who by national law is a citizen of the United States nor to refuse to accept as one of its citizens any citizen of the United States who establishes a residence within the state. It would seem, however, that a state may extend its citizenship to persons who are not citizens of the United States, although this question has not been definitely decided by the Supreme Court of the United States. At any rate, it is clear that a state may extend to aliens the privileges ordinarily attaching to citizenship and may even vest the right to vote in aliens who have declared their intention to become citizens of the United States.

On the other hand, there may be persons who are citizens of the United States without being citizens of any state. For example, persons born abroad of parents who are American citizens are not residents of any state but may, under an act of Congress, remain citizens of the United States by taking an oath of allegiance to this country, provided the father has at any time resided in the United States. To this extent, the United States follows the rule of *jus sanguinis*. Another example of a citizen of the United States who is not a state citizen is that of an American citizen residing in the District of Columbia or in one of the incorporated territories of the United States. As declared by the Supreme Court in the Slaughter House cases:

Not only may a man be a citizen of the United States without being a citizen of a state, but an important element is necessary to convert the former into the latter. He must reside within the state to make him a citizen of it, but it is only necessary that he should be born or naturalized in the United States to be a citizen of the Union.[1]

Citizenship by Birth.—The provision of the Fourteenth Amendment conferring citizenship upon persons born in the United States was intended primarily to extend this status to the newly freed negroes, but the language is broad enough to cover persons of any race or color, regardless of the citizenship of the parents. It even applies to persons born in this country whose parents are not only aliens but, under our naturalization laws, are ineligible to become citizens of the United States. This was the doctrine laid down by the Supreme Court in the leading case of Wong Kim Ark, a Chinaman, who, although admittedly born within the United States, was denied admission by the immigration

[1] 16 Wall. 36 (1872).

officers upon his return from a temporary visit to China. They did so on the ground that, since Wong was born of alien Chinese parents, he was not a citizen of the United States and, therefore, under the exclusion act of Congress, should not be admitted to the country. The Court, however, held that Wong was a citizen of the United States and ordered that he be admitted. It declared that the Fourteenth Amendment "affirms the ancient and fundamental rule of citizenship by birth within the territory, in the allegiance and under the protection of the country, including all children here born of resident aliens."[1]

To the general rule as thus laid down, however, the Court recognized the existence of certain exceptions introduced by the requirement of the Fourteenth Amendment that, in order to be a citizen by birth, a person must not only be born in the United States but must also be "subject to the jurisdiction thereof." Certain classes of persons, although born on our soil, are not citizens of the United States because they do not meet this requirement. As listed by the Court in the Wong Kim Ark case, these exceptional classes of persons are "children of (1) foreign sovereigns or their ministers, or (2) born on foreign public ships, or (3) of enemies within and during a hostile occupation of part of our territory, and with the single additional exception (4) of children of members of the Indian tribes owing direct allegiance to their several tribes."

Under international law and usage, diplomatic representatives of foreign governments accredited to the United States are not considered to be under the jurisdiction of our government. Consequently, their children, although born on our soil, are not citizens of the United States. This is not true, however, of the children of foreign consuls resident in the United States, who are in the same situation as the children of aliens occupying no official position.

Formerly, the members of Indian tribes stood in a peculiar relation to the Government of the United States. The tribes were regarded as domestic dependent nations, with which our government dealt through treaties. After 1871, however, this method was abandoned and Congress assumed the authority to legislate with reference to them. Nevertheless, it was held by the Supreme Court in 1884 that children of Indians living in tribes, even though born and residing on American soil, were not citizens of the United States under the Fourteenth Amendment.[2] Such Indians were under tribal jurisdiction rather than under the jurisdiction of the United States. Certain Indians not living in tribes, however, were naturalized by act of Congress. Finally, by act of 1924, Congress authorized the issuance of certificates of citizenship to Indians living in tribes, so that all Indians born within the jurisdiction of the United States are now citizens.

[1] United States v. Wong Kim Ark, 169 U. S. 649 (1898).
[2] Elk v. Wilkins, 112 U. S. 94 (1884).

Citizenship by Naturalization.—Prior to the adoption of the Constitution, each state controlled the determination of citizenship by naturalization, and, as Madison pointed out in *The Federalist*,[1] the dissimilarity of the rules of the different states laid the "foundation for intricate and delicate questions." In order to remedy this situation, Congress was authorized by the Constitution to establish a uniform rule of naturalization throughout the United States.[2]

In some early cases it was held that the power of naturalization is concurrent between Congress and the states, but in 1817 Chief Justice Marshall declared that the power is vested exclusively in Congress.[3] This has ever since been recognized as the established doctrine. State courts of record, however, are used by Congress as agencies for carrying out the process of naturalization. This is merely an authorization of the exercise of a power, and one which the state courts could not be compelled to exercise.

By naturalization, not only are the disabilities of the alien status removed but the aliens are transformed into full-fledged citizens of the United States, and of the state in which they reside, with all the rights and privileges which native-born citizens enjoy, except that naturalized citizens are not eligible to hold the office of President or Vice-President of the United States. Naturalized citizens who return to the country of their former allegiance, and are impressed into military service therein, will not be protected against such service by our Government.

Naturalization may be either individual or collective. The conditions under which individuals may be naturalized are specified in detail by act of Congress. The act, however, of granting naturalization papers to particular individuals in accordance with these conditions is a function which is performed by the Federal courts and, as already noted, by state courts of record. Such a proceeding is judicial in character because, since the United States is always potentially an adverse party, it is a case or controversy within the meaning of those words as used in the Constitution. The action of a court in granting a certificate of naturalization is not necessarily final and conclusive. If it can be shown that the grant was made as the result of fraudulent representations or perjured testimony, it may be canceled or revoked.

When an alien becomes a naturalized citizen of the United States, the effect is to make naturalized citizens also of his minor children residing in the United States. Formerly an alien wife eligible to American citizenship also became a citizen through the naturalization of her husband, but, by the Cable Act passed by Congress in 1922, a more independent status is granted to married women. Under this act, they not only do

---

[1] No. 42.

[2] Art. I, sect. 8, cl. 4.

[3] Chirac v. Chirac, 2 Wheat. 269 (1817).

not become citizens of the United States through the naturalization of their husbands, but they do not lose their American citizenship through marrying an alien, unless they choose to renounce it. Prior to 1931, however, if an American woman married an alien ineligible to American citizenship, she lost her American citizenship, but this was changed by an act passed in that year, so that marriage now has substantially no effect upon a woman's citizenship.

Who May Be Naturalized?—Not only does Congress specify the process of naturalization but also determines what classes of persons shall or shall not be eligible to citizenship by this process.[1] Such determination is a matter of statutory, rather than of constitutional, law. Nevertheless, it may be noted that anarchists and polygamists cannot be naturalized and, during time of war, alien enemies may also be excluded. More important, however, is the provision of the law that only such persons as are white or of African nativity or of African descent are eligible for naturalization. This has the effect of excluding most Asiatics, such as Chinese, Japanese, and Hindus. The question as to whether Filipinos may be naturalized has not been authoritatively decided by the Supreme Court, but the better opinion seems to be that the exclusion of the yellow and brown races from naturalization applies only to aliens. If this view is correct, the Filipinos, not being aliens but rather nationals of the United States and owing it allegiance, may, if they have established a residence in any state of the Union, become naturalized. American Indians are not eligible for individual naturalization under the general law, but, as already noted, a special act was passed in 1924 extending citizenship to them.

Collective Naturalization.—In addition to individuals, a group of persons may be naturalized *en masse*, without special consideration of the fitness of particular individuals in the group. This is known as collective naturalization and may be effected by act of Congress. It has usually been exercised with reference to the inhabitants of territories and dependencies acquired by the United States. From the standpoint of international law, the inhabitants of territories acquired by the United States cease to be aliens and become nationals of the United States. From the standpoint of domestic or constitutional law, however, they do not necessarily become full-fledged citizens. Their status in this respect is to be determined at the discretion of the annexing power. The inhabitants of unincorporated territories, even when born after the annexation of the territory to the United States, are probably not "born or naturalized in the United States" within the meaning of those words as used in the Fourteenth Amendment.[2] Provision as to their status, therefore, is

---

[1] Aliens who will not agree to bear arms to defend the country in time of war are excluded from becoming citizens by naturalization. United States v. Schwimmer, 279 U. S. 644 (1929); United States v. MacIntosh, 283 U. S. 605 (1931).

[2] Downes v. Bidwell, 182 U. S. 244 (1901).

usually made by treaty or act of Congress. The treaty of annexation may promise that the inhabitants shall be admitted as soon as possible to the enjoyment of all the rights and immunities of citizens of the United States. This was done in the cases of the Louisiana Territory, Florida, and Alaska, with the exception of the uncivilized native tribes in Alaska. Beginning in 1898, a change of policy occurred. By the treaty of peace with Spain, made in that year, it was provided that the cession of Spanish colonies to the United States was not to operate as a naturalization of their native inhabitants, but that the "civil rights and political status of the native inhabitants of the territories hereby ceded to the United States shall be determined by Congress." In accordance with this provision Congress at first declared the Porto Ricans and Filipinos to be citizens of their respective islands.[1] This is the status still retained by the Filipinos, but, by act of 1917, Congress made the Porto Ricans citizens of the United States. Other examples of collective naturalization are found in the cases of Texas, whose inhabitants were made citizens of the United States by resolution of Congress at the time of its annexation in 1845; of the Hawaiian Islands, upon whose inhabitants was conferred American citizenship by an act of Congress passed in 1900; and of the Virgin Islands, whose inhabitants received American citizenship by a law enacted by Congress in 1927.

Expatriation.—A person is expatriated from a country when he renounces his allegiance to it and assumes the citizenship of another country. Nothing is said in the Constitution with reference to expatriation but, since Congress has the power to nationalize, it has impliedly the power to expatriate, subject to the limitations of due process.

Until comparatively recent times, foreign nations have not generally recognized the right of one of their subjects to renounce his allegiance. It was not until 1870 that Great Britain abandoned the doctrine: "Once a British subject, always a British subject." Prior to 1868, there was some variation in the policy of the different departments of the United States Government with reference to the right of expatriation. In that year, however, Congress passed an act declaring in explicit terms that the "right of expatriation is a natural and inherent right of all people, indispensable to the enjoyment of the rights of life, liberty, and the pursuit of happiness," and declaring further that the naturalized citizens of the United States are not to be considered as owing allegiance to any foreign government.

It may be questioned, however, in spite of this act, whether expatriation is a natural or inherent right. The better view is that it is one which rests upon the consent of the Government, although this consent may be given tacitly. Except in time of war, when the right of expatriation is

[1] In Gonzales v. Williams, 192 U. S. 1 (1904), the Supreme Court held that the Porto Ricans were not aliens.

not recognized, there is no question, at least since 1868, that an American citizen may voluntarily expatriate himself. In 1907, Congress for the first time provided formally how this might be done, *viz.*, through becoming naturalized in any foreign state or through taking an oath of allegiance to any foreign state. The act of 1907 also provided that a naturalized citizen who shall have resided for two years in the foreign state from which he came, or for five years in any other foreign state, shall be presumed to have ceased to be an American citizen. This presumption, however, may be overcome by the presentation of counter-vailing evidence.

The Supreme Court has taken the view that citizenship is of tangible worth and therefore a person cannot be arbitrarily deprived of it, for this would be a denial of due process. As a punishment for crime or for desertion from the military or naval forces, a person may be deprived of the rights of citizenship, but this is not expatriation, for the obligations of citizenship remain.

Privileges and Immunities of Citizens of the United States.—After defining citizenship, the Fourteenth Amendment proceeds to forbid any state from making or enforcing "any law which shall abridge the privileges or immunities of citizens of the United States." It will be noticed that this clause does not mention the privileges of state citizens nor undertake to protect them against state action. In view of the fact that in the preceding sentence, the distinction between national and state citizenship had been clearly recognized, the failure to mention the privileges of state citizenship in the clause under discussion is significant. It shows that it is only those privileges which attach to United States citizenship as distinguished from state citizenship which are protected against state action by the amendment.

What are the privileges and immunities of United States citizenship as distinguished from those of state citizenship, however, was left in doubt by the amendment and remained to be cleared up by decision of the Supreme Court. This question came before that tribunal in the famous Slaughter House cases,[1] decided in 1873, in which its decision is of fundamental importance, since a different decision would have radically changed the nature of our government. The facts of these cases were that the State of Louisiana, in the exercise of its police power, had passed a law conferring upon a certain corporation the exclusive right of slaughtering animals for food within the city of New Orleans. The constitutionality of the law was attacked by the butchers of the city on various grounds, among which was that engaging in the slaughtering business was one of the privileges or immunities of citizens of the United States which the Fourteenth Amendment prohibits the states from abridging through the making or enforcement of any law. In other words, the

[1] 16 Wall. 36.

contention was that that Amendment protected against state action the ordinary and everyday civil rights which were recognized by either the common law or state constitutional or statutory provisions as attaching to state citizens. Since Congress was given the power to enforce the amendment by appropriate legislation, this contention, if sustained, would have meant that the whole body of civil rights of citizens would have been placed under the legislative control and protection of Congress, while the police powers of the states would have been made subject to Federal judicial scrutiny. The states would thus have been reduced to a much more subordinate position in the American governmental system.

Confronted with a question of such fundamental importance, a bare majority of the Supreme Court, laboring under a due sense of the gravity of the issue, declared that it could not be presumed that Congress in proposing, and the state legislatures in ratifying, the amendment had intended by the language used to transform the nature of the government and they could therefore not sustain the contention of counsel for the New Orleans butchers in the absence of language in the amendment having necessarily that effect. They also referred to the well-known historical circumstance that the pervading purpose of the amendment had been primarily to extend citizenship to the former slaves and to protect them in the exercise of their privileges as citizens of the United States from possible encroachment by the states. It had not been the purpose of the amendment to transfer the control and protection of the whole domain of ordinary civil rights from the states to the National Government.

What Are Privileges and Immunities of United States Citizenship?— As to what are the peculiar privileges and immunities attaching to national citizenship as distinguished from state citizenship, the majority of the Court held that this question was not directly before them but nevertheless proceeded to answer it, at least in part. Among the privileges of a citizen of the United States, they indicated, are to go to the seat of government to assert any claim he may have upon it or to petition for redress of grievances; to move freely from state to state; to have free access to the seaports of the country; to demand the care and protection of the National Government over his life, liberty, and property when on the high seas or within the jurisdiction of a foreign government; to engage in interstate commerce and to use the navigable waters of the United States, however they may penetrate the territory of the several states; to assert all rights secured to our citizens by treaties with foreign nations; and to become a citizen of any state of the Union by a *bona fide* residence therein.

It will be noticed that the privileges enumerated are those which have a special and peculiar relation to the National Government and are not the great mass of ordinary and fundamental rights of citizens which they enjoy by virtue of the common law or of state statutory or constitutional provisions. The amendment thus refers only to such privileges and immunities as were before its adoption especially designated in the Constitution or necessarily implied as belonging to citizens of the United States. This being the case, as Justice Field pointed out in his dissenting opinion, this prohibition of the amendment

. . . was a vain and idle enactment, which accomplished nothing, and most unnecessarily excited Congress and the people on its passage. With privileges and immunities thus designated no state could ever have interfered by its laws, and no new constitutional provision was required to inhibit such interference. The supremacy of the Constitution and the laws of the United States always controlled any state legislation of that character.

This statement is correct, so that this provision of the amendment, in effect, is merely declaratory of the situation which would have existed without it. It is true that the war amendments generally represented a reaction from the states' rights doctrine and a movement toward increasing the power of the National Government at the expense of the states, but as far as any effect in this direction was intended to be brought about by the provision of the Fourteenth Amendment under consideration, such effect was nullified by the decision of the Court in the slaughter house cases.

What Are Not Privileges and Immunities of United States Citizenship?—As indicated in the preceding paragraph, the great mass of the ordinary rights of citizens conferred upon them by the common law or by state law are not privileges or immunities of national citizenship. Moreover, the mere fact that a right is mentioned in the Federal Constitution, such as the privilege of the writ of habeas corpus, does not necessarily make it a privilege peculiarly belonging to citizens of the United States. Many of these privileges or immunities, such as the immunity against deprivation of life, liberty, or property without due process of law, attach to persons or to the people generally, rather than to citizens as such.

The same is true with reference to the long list of privileges and immunities enumerated in the first eight amendments to the Constitution, such as freedom of speech, of religion, and of the press. It was early held that the prohibitions in these amendments against infringement of the rights enumerated constitute limitations on the National Government and not on the states.[1] In a later case it was argued that the fundamental rights recognized by the first eight amendments are privileges and immunities of citizens of the United States which, by the Fourteenth Amendment, no state could abridge. The Supreme Court, however, denied this contention, holding that the mere fact that certain rights are protected against encroachment by the National Government does not

[1] Barron v. Baltimore, 7 Pet. 243 (1833).

make them peculiarly privileges and immunities of national citizenship.[1] The rights mentioned in the first eight amendments, declared the Court, are not privileges and immunities "belonging to the individual as a citizen of the United States, but they are secured to all persons as against the Federal Government, entirely irrespective of such citizenship."

From the above discussion, it will be seen that the Fourteenth Amendment did not create or recognize any new privileges or immunities attaching to national citizenship.

Privileges and Immunities Protected against State Action Only.—The prohibition in the Fourteenth Amendment against the abridgment of the privileges or immunities of citizens of the United States is expressly directed against state action. This is to be taken as excluding action by individuals, which is not prohibited by the amendment, unless those individuals are state officers.

In 1875, Congress passed the so-called "civil rights act" which prohibited the owners of hotels, theaters, and other places of public resort from discriminating against any person on account of his race or color. This act indicated that Congress conceived that it not only had the power to define and create privileges and immunities of national citizenship but also to protect them against encroachment by private individuals. The Supreme Court, however, held the act unconstitutional.[2] "Individual invasion of individual rights," declared the Court, "is not the subject matter of the Amendment. It has a deeper and broader scope. It nullifies and makes void all state legislation and state action of every kind, which impairs the privileges and immunities of citizens of the United States . . . "

As to whether the failure of the state to protect individuals against mob violence is to be construed as a denial or abridgment of individual rights by action of the state in violation of the amendment is a question not yet decided. Such a question may be presented to the courts if the anti-lynching bill introduced in Congress, and providing for levying a Federal fine on counties in which a lynching occurs, should be passed. It would seem that such an act of Congress probably would not be upheld by the courts, not only because the failure of the state to act is not the state action prohibited by the amendment but also because the right of which the victim is deprived by a lynching mob is not a privilege or immunity of United States citizenship.[3]

---

[1] Maxwell v. Dow, 176 U. S. 581 (1900).

[2] Civil rights cases, 109 U. S. 3 (1883).

[3] Unless the victim is lynched in order to prevent him from exercising a Federal right, such as the right to vote for a representative in Congress.

CHAPTER XXII

THE SUFFRAGE

The suffrage or elective franchise may be regarded, from different points of view, either as a right or as a privilege or as an office. It is not, however, a natural right in the sense that anyone has a right to have it conferred upon him. It is rather a privilege or an office which is conferred, theoretically at least, only upon such persons or classes of persons as seem best fitted to exercise it and whose exercise of it seems likely to be most conducive to the general welfare. It is a political privilege, as distinguished from a civil right, because it is a means whereby the individual may participate in public affairs. Since only a comparatively small percentage of the people ever have the opportunity to hold office or to serve on juries, the elective franchise is by far the most important way in which the average person exerts a direct influence upon the conduct of the government.

The determination of who shall have the privilege of exercising the suffrage is considered to be a matter of such fundamental importance that it is usually fixed in the constitution rather than left to statutory regulation. The first state constitutions, which were adopted during the period of the Revolutionary War, contained provisions on this subject. These provisions were usually highly restrictive, confining the suffrage to those who could meet certain property qualifications. Racial, moral, and religious qualifications were also sometimes laid down, with the result that, as a rule, only a comparatively small proportion of the adult male population was privileged to vote.

Suffrage in the Original Constitution.—The desirability of a restricted suffrage, as shown by the practice of the states, represented the spirit of the times, which was naturally reflected in the convention that drew up the Federal Constitution. The majority of the members of that convention had no great faith in the political capacity of the people. They made no provision for the popular suffrage in the choosing of presidential electors or United States senators, nor in the adoption of constitutional amendments. It is true that, in the case of presidential electors, popular choice was not excluded. The method of choice being left to the discretion of the state legislatures, those bodies might provide, and with the growth of democratic feeling have provided, for choosing the presidential electors by popular vote. It should be remembered, however, that this is not required but merely permitted by the Constitution.

The only instance in which the Constitution, as originally drawn up, makes definite provision for direct popular vote is in the election of representatives in the lower house of Congress. Even in this instance, no particular qualifications for voters are laid down in the Constitution. Had this been done, such qualifications would naturally have been uniform throughout the country. The Convention was unable to agree upon any such set of uniform qualifications. As noted in another chapter, the specification of uniform qualifications would have had the effect of creating a national electorate distinct from that of the state electorate in some, and possibly all, of the states. This would have been due to the fact that the qualifications for voting for state officers were not only not uniform but varied considerably from state to state. The difficulty thus presented to the Convention was overcome through the device of adopting, as the qualifications of voters for representatives in the lower house of Congress, those laid down in each state for voters for the lower, or more numerous, branch of the state legislature.[1] The specific qualifications, therefore, for voters for representatives in Congress can be found only by consulting the state constitutions or statutes. It may happen that a person who is qualified to vote for such representatives in one state would not be in another. However, with the growth of democracy and adult suffrage, qualifications for voting in the several states have become more nearly uniform and, consequently, the difference between the members of the national and state electorates respectively has become less.

Some question has been raised as to whether the constitutional provision just mentioned may be regarded as conferring upon the states the power of determining the qualifications of voters for representatives in the lower house of Congress. Indirectly it does confer this power upon them. Nevertheless, the right to vote for members of Congress is not derived merely from state constitutions or laws but has its foundation in the Federal Constitution.[2] If a state confers upon any class of persons the right to vote for members of its lower legislative body, then such persons automatically acquire the right to vote for representatives in Congress, and the state cannot bar them from doing so, because their right is derived fundamentally from the Federal Constitution and is guaranteed to them, provided they meet the qualifications as laid down by state law. The state does not confer the right to vote for members of Congress but merely lays down the actual qualifications for doing so. This distinction was brought out by the Supreme Court in one of the Ku Klux cases.[3]

[1] Art. I, sect. 2, cl. 1.
[2] Wiley v. Sinkler, 179 U. S. 62 (1900).
[3] *Ex parte* Yarborough, 110 U. S. 651 (1884). See quotation from this case on p. 91.

The Regulation of Elections.—The Constitution makes it mandatory upon the state legislatures to regulate the "times, places, and manner of holding elections for senators and representatives" in Congress.[1]   There would seem, however, to be no way of enforcing this mandate.   But the need to do so is not likely to arise, because Congress is permitted by the Constitution not only to change any state regulations on the subject but also to make new ones.[2]   The regulations of Congress supersede those of the states in so far as they conflict with each other, but no farther; so that Congressional and state regulations may operate on different phases of the subject simultaneously.   The states' regulations on the subject were not disturbed until 1842, when Congress for the first time exercised the power conferred upon it by providing that representatives in the lower house of Congress should be elected by districts rather than on a general ticket.   Thirty years later, Congress specified a day uniform throughout the country on which such elections should take place.

In the Ku Klux case, cited above, the Supreme Court intimated that the right to vote for members of Congress is a right derived from the Federal Constitution and that Congress is empowered to protect it against violence or intimidation on the part of mobs or private individuals.   It was not only the power but also the duty of Congress to afford such protection, not only because of the interest of the voter,

. . . but from the necessity of the government itself that its service shall be free from the adverse influence of force and fraud practiced on its agents, and that the votes by which its members of Congress and its President are elected shall be the *free* votes of the electors, and the officers thus chosen the free and uncorrupted choice of those who have the right to take part in that choice.[3]

Since Congress has the power to regulate the proper conduct of Congressional elections and to protect the voters who participate therein from violence and intimidation, it follows that Congress might, if it chose, provide for the appointment of Federal officers to conduct such elections. If members of Congress alone were chosen at such elections, this would undoubtedly be done.   It is not necessary that any other elections should occur on the same day as Congressional elections, but, as a matter of convenience, the states have scheduled elections for various state and local officers on that date.   These combined state and Congressional elections were supervised by Federal officers in the South during the reconstruction period, but nowadays they are in charge of state or local officers.   Congress can control combined state and Congressional elec-

[1] Art. I, sect. 4, cl. 1.

[2] *Ibid.* This provision purports to except the places of choosing senators from the power of Congress to make or alter regulations, but, since the adoption of the Seventeenth Amendment for popular election of senators, this exception no longer has any significance.

[3] *Ex parte* Yarborough, 110 U. S. 651 (1884).

tions to the extent necessary to protect the interests of the National Government but has no right to assume full control of them. To the extent that state officers have charge of Congressional elections, they may be regarded as virtually officers or agents of the National Government acting in this capacity. Congress may adopt the state laws relating to Congressional elections and may provide for punishing a state officer of election for violating his duty under a state statute pertaining to the election of a representative in Congress.[1]

Under its power of regulating the manner of holding elections for senators and representatives, Congress undertook in 1910 to pass a law limiting the amount of money which a candidate for representative in Congress might spend in securing not only his election but also his nomination. In spite of the obviously close connection between nomination and election as parts of the same general process, the Supreme Court in the Newberry case held this law unconstitutional in so far as it applied to the nomination of candidates, on the ground that this part of the process was not included in the word "elections" as used in the Constitution.[2]

Suffrage Provision of the Fourteenth Amendment.—Although the determination of the qualifications for voting is left mainly to the states, this power has been subjected to certain limitations. The Civil War marked a reaction away from the extension of state power and this is noticeable in connection with the suffrage as well as in other matters. After that war a feeling developed that the newly freed negroes would not be able to maintain the civil rights incident to freedom unless they were also endowed with political rights, the most important of which is the right to vote. Consequently, in the second section of the Fourteenth Amendment, adopted in 1868, the attempt was made to secure the right of suffrage for the negroes through the operation of minatory inducements upon the states. That section provides that whenever any of the adult male citizens of the United States are excluded from the right to vote in any national or state election in any state, the basis of representation of such state in the lower house of Congress shall be reduced in the proportion which the number of citizens thus excluded shall bear to the whole number of adult male citizens in such state.

This section of the amendment clearly recognizes the right of a state to adopt suffrage qualifications which exclude certain of its adult male citizens from voting. It is a mistake, therefore, to say that such exclusion is a violation of this section. It is correct to say, however, that such exclusion brings on a situation in which the representation of the state in Congress may be reduced. Such reduction of representation, however,

[1] *Ex parte* Siebold, 100 U. S. 371 (1880).
[2] Newberry v. United States, 256 U. S. 232 (1921). For further discussion of this case, see p. 94.

is not automatic, in spite of the mandatory language of the Constitution. Whether or not the representation of any state shall actually be reduced is left to the discretion of Congress. The provision for reduction seems impracticable and, at all events, has never been put into operation, in spite of the fact that a number of states have laid themselves open to the infliction of the penalty. The failure of Congress to exercise the power of reducing the representation of states in which negroes are prevented from voting seems to be due mainly to the following causes: (1) the general tone of public opinion on the matter throughout the country seems to be rather apathetic; (2) it would be difficult to determine the exact number of persons disqualified from voting by state law, for many persons, otherwise qualified, do not take the trouble to register or, if registered, fail to vote; (3) any plan of reduction would probably affect not only Southern states in which negroes are prevented from voting, but also some Northern states in which literacy qualifications are found; and (4) the real contest in Southern states takes place in the Democratic party primary from which negroes are largely excluded, and this section of the Fourteenth Amendment does not apply to exclusion of voters from primaries held to nominate candidates for office.[1] It has been held, however, that a state law specifically excluding negroes as such from participating in the Democratic party primary is invalid as violative of the equal-protection-of-the-law provision found in the first section of the Fourteenth Amendment.[2]

The Fifteenth Amendment.—When it appeared that the threat of reduction of representation contained in the Fourteenth Amendment would have no effect in inducing the Southern states to extend the suffrage to the negroes, the Fifteenth Amendment was adopted which prohibited both the United States and the states from making any discrimination among citizens of the United States in the matter of voting, on account of race, color, or former slavery. Congress was empowered to enforce the provisions of the amendment, and, as long as national power was exerted to this end, negroes were able to vote in large numbers. When the force exerted by the National Government to maintain negro suffrage was withdrawn, however, the exercise by negroes of the elective franchise was very largely suppressed. This was accomplished at first by intimidation and other irregular methods, but later legal methods of excluding negroes were adopted, as far as this was possible within the limitations of the Fifteenth Amendment.

That amendment, it will be noticed, unlike the Fourteenth, is a limitation not only upon the states but also upon the National Government. Against the latter, however, it has never been necessary to invoke the provisions of the amendment. Its application has actually been

[1] MATHEWS, J. M., *American State Government*, pp. 82–83 (New York, 1924).
[2] Nixon v. Herndon, 273 U. S. 536 (1927).

confined to action by the states alleged to be in violation of it. It does not apply to the action of private individuals and cannot be invoked by Congress to punish private persons who by violence or intimidation attempt to prevent negroes from voting on account of their color or race.[1] As we have seen, however, Congress may, under the provisions of the original Constitution, pass laws to protect, as against individual action, the freedom of elections at which members of Congress are to be chosen.

If a state constitution contains the word "white" in listing the qualifications of those upon whom the elective franchise is conferred, such a provision is automatically rendered null and void by the operation of the Fifteenth Amendment. No legislation of Congress is necessary in order to bring about this effect. It is a mistake, however, to say that the amendment confers upon, or guarantees to, the negro the right to vote.[2] All it confers upon him is immunity from being discriminated against, in the matter of voting, on account of his race, color, or former slavery. The right to vote, at least for state officers, is still derived from the state. The power to prescribe the qualifications for voting, whether in state or in national elections, is still vested in the state, subject to the limitation that it cannot disqualify anyone on account of his race, color, or former slavery.

The Fifteenth Amendment is not violated by a state unless it discriminates against citizens on the prohibited grounds. The inference is sometimes drawn that, when persons are prevented from voting and those persons are negroes, therefore the exclusion is on account of race, etc.; but this may be an unwarranted presumption. It is hardly probable that any qualification for voting that a state might set up would operate to exclude an equal proportion of both races. It is conceivable that, in a given state, a property qualification might operate to exclude nearly all negroes but almost no white persons. In spite of this effect, however, such a qualification would not come within the prohibition of the amendment. The only kind of discrimination which the amendment prohibits is that based on race, color, or former slavery. On this ground, the Supreme Court held unconstitutional an act of Congress which purported to punish state officers for excluding persons from voting, without confining the operation of the statute specifically to cases where the exclusion was on account of race, color, or former slavery.[3]

While it is clear that the amendment prohibits only such discrimination as is based on the grounds of race, color, or former slavery, it is by no means always clear whether or not a given state statute or constitutional provision operates to exclude persons on the prohibited grounds. This question has given rise to several adjudications. By constitutional

[1] James v. Bowman, 190 U. S. 127 (1903).
[2] *Cf.* a dictum to this effect in the slaughter house cases, 16 Wall. 36 (1873).
[3] United States v. Reese, 92 U. S. 214 (1875).

provision Mississippi required that each voter must be able to read any section of the Constitution, or to understand the same when read to him, or to give a reasonable interpretation thereof. There was nothing on the face of this provision which discriminated against negroes as such. Objection might be made to the wide discretion conferred upon election officers in administering the understanding clause. The Supreme Court, however, refused to declare the provision invalid, holding that it did not on its face discriminate between the races and that, while evil was possible under it, no proof had been adduced to show that its actual administration was evil.[1] The provision might operate in fact to disfranchise more negroes than white persons, but this in itself would not be sufficient evidence that the discrimination was based on race.

A different fate befell a provision found in a number of Southern state constitutions, known as the "grandfather clause." Such a clause was contained in the Oklahoma constitution, which, as amended in 1910, provided a literacy test for voting but exempted from its operation all persons who were entitled to vote in 1866 or earlier, together with the lineal descendants of such persons. It will be noticed that the clause did not expressly discriminate against negroes on the grounds prohibited by the Fifteenth Amendment. But a court must be blind if it looks merely at the language of a provision and ignores its obvious purpose, effect, and operation. The date 1866 in the clause under consideration was obviously selected because it preceded the adoption of the Fifteenth Amendment and the purpose of establishing the 1866 standard was evidently to restore the conditions which the amendment had been intended to abolish. The suffrage provision of the Oklahoma constitution, containing the grandfather clause, was therefore in conflict with that amendment and was declared unconstitutional by the Supreme Court when, in 1915, it came before that tribunal for adjudication.[2] By implication from this decision, substantially similar clauses in other state constitutions also became invalid. In general, however, it would seem that the purpose of the disfranchising provisions of the Southern state constitutions had already for the most part been accomplished. The letter of the Fifteenth Amendment is observed, but its spirit is violated.

The Nineteenth Amendment.—By this amendment, adopted in 1920, both the states and the National Government were deprived of the right to discriminate among citizens of the United States in the matter of voting on account of sex, and since its adoption women have had the privilege of voting on an equality with men throughout the nation.[3] This

---

[1] Williams v. Mississippi, 170 U. S. 213 (1898).

[2] Guinn v. United States, 238 U. S. 347 (1915).

[3] This amendment has been held by the Supreme Court to have been validly adopted. Leser v. Garnett, 258 U. S. 130 (1922); Fairchild v. Hughes, 258 U. S. 126 (1922).

was the greatest single step taken during our history in the extension of suffrage. It is true that women voted to some extent before the adoption of this amendment. In a considerable number of states they had been given the right to vote in certain local and school elections. In Illinois, an act of the legislature had extended to them the right to vote for all state and local officers of statutory creation. In several states, they had even been given, by constitutional amendment, the full right to vote on an equality with men. The adoption of the Nineteenth Amendment was thus the culmination of long agitation and of a long series of state acts.[1]

Regarded from the historical point of view, the Nineteenth Amendment is properly called the woman-suffrage amendment, because its purpose was to give equal suffrage rights to women throughout the country and especially in those states which had not already done so. Its language, however, is so broad that it might conceivably be invoked to protect a man against the abridgment of his right to vote on account of his sex. Its language follows that of the Fifteenth Amendment word for word, except that the word "sex" is substituted for the phrase "race, color, or previous condition of servitude." As in the case of the Fifteenth Amendment, the act of denial or abridgment prohibited is that performed by the state or National Government and not that of private individuals. The act of the latter, however, may be in violation of state law. Similarly, the discrimination prohibited by the Nineteenth Amendment is solely that based on sex. It does not prevent a state from excluding women from voting on any other ground, nor from establishing a test for voting which disqualifies more women than men. The adoption of the amendment has conferred upon women a new Federal immunity—that of exemption from discrimination in the matter of voting on account of sex.

It should be added that this amendment is confined strictly to the exercise of the right to vote and does not apply to the holding of public office or service on juries. It does not prevent the states from making or keeping women ineligible to hold the latter positions.

[1] MATHEWS, J. M., *American State Government*, pp. 83–84 (New York, 1924). As early as 1874 a Mrs. Minor brought suit to compel election officers to accept her vote on the ground that she had a right to vote by virtue of being a citizen of the United States. The Supreme Court, however, held that the right to vote was not a necessary privilege of citizenship. Minor v. Happersett, 21 Wall. 162 (1874).

CHAPTER XXIII

PROTECTION OF PERSONS ACCUSED OF CRIME

Introduction.—Very elaborate safeguards are found in the Constitution of the United States for the protection of persons accused of crime. In view of the current laxness in the administration of justice and of the difficulties now encountered in bringing criminals to justice, these safeguards appear to be much more elaborate and extensive than is necessary for the adequate protection of such persons. Their existence can hardly be explained in the light of current need but only in that of their historical development. The English criminal law at the time of the adoption of our Federal Constitution was very severe. Capital punishment could be inflicted for a large number of offenses, many of which have come to be regarded as rather trivial, such as the theft of property valued at more than five shillings. The criminal law was also sometimes used by the Government as a means of punishing political offenders. Moreover, criminal procedure was at first very hard on the accused, but later a tendency developed to remedy this situation in order to offset to some extent the severity of the substantive law.

Since our independence was declared as a result of what we deemed to be the oppressive conduct of the British Government towards us, it was natural that we should wish to safeguard the liberty of the individual against any similar conduct which might possibly develop in our own government. The tendency to soften the harshness of criminal procedure, already developed to some extent in England, was accentuated in the United States, as was evidenced by the provisions of bills of rights in state constitutions. The substantive law of crimes in the states was found partly in the statutes and partly in the common law, the latter being the body of law developed through the centuries by the decisions of the English courts and transplanted to the English colonies in America, together with acts of Parliament which were in force in the colonies at the time of their separation from the mother country. The body of common law thus transplanted has been modified to suit the different conditions found in the New World and has also been molded and developed so as the better to meet new conditions as they arise in the various states. This modification and development of the common law have been brought about in part by formal legislative enactment and in part by judicial decision and the gradual accretion of precedent.

Crime and Criminal Procedure in the Federal Constitution.—After a period of doubt on the subject, it was decided in 1812 that there is no common law of crimes of the United States.[1] The basis of this decision was that the power of the National Government to punish for crime is only such as is derived from the Federal Constitution, which has not adopted the common law of crimes. Consequently, the crimes punishable by the National Government are those only which are defined by the Federal Constitution or by act of Congress.[2] Only a small number of crimes are specifically mentioned in the Constitution. These are treason, piracies and felonies committed on the high seas, offenses against the law of nations, and counterfeiting the securities and current coin of the United States. Congress is expressly empowered to provide for the punishment of certain of these specifically mentioned crimes. By far the larger number of Federal crimes, however, are those which Congress has made punishable under its implied powers. Congress is empowered to provide for the punishment of crimes to the extent that may be necessary and proper as a means of carrying into effect its constitutionally granted powers. This means that Congress is empowered to provide for the punishment as crimes of acts which violate the laws enacted under its constitutional powers.

In spite of the theory that Congress has no powers except those granted to it in the Constitution, that document, as originally drawn up, contains some limitations upon the power of Congress with reference to criminal procedure, such as those relating to *ex post facto* laws, bills of attainder, and the writ of habeas corpus. Most of the limitations on Congress relating to criminal procedure, however, are found in the bill of rights or first eight amendments. We shall consider, first, the crimes specifically mentioned in the Constitution; second, the limitations on criminal procedure found in the original Constitution; and, third, those found in the amendments.

Treason.—Congress cannot define the crime of treason, since it is defined in the Constitution as consisting only in levying war against the United States, or in adhering to its enemies, giving them aid and comfort.[3] The power to punish for treason had been abused in England to such an extent that a large number of offenses were declared by the laws of that country to be treasonable, including such a venial political offense as criticism of the acts of the crown. It was to prevent the repetition of such abuses in this country that the definition of treason was inserted in the Constitution. As Madison declared in the Federalist:

[1] United States v. Hudson, 7 Cranch 32 (1812).
[2] An apparent exception is that the violation of regulations issued by the President or executive departments may be made a crime, by authority of an act of Congress. The statute, not the regulations, fixes the penalty. United States v. Grimaud, 220 U. S. 506 (1910).
[3] Art. III, sect. 3, cl. 1.

But as new-fangled and artificial treasons have been the great engines by which violent factions, the natural offspring of free government, have usually wreaked their alternate malignity on each other, the Convention have, with great judgment, opposed a barrier to this peculiar danger by inserting a constitutional definition of the crime, fixing the proof necessary for conviction of it, and restraining the Congress, even in punishing it, from extending the consequences of guilt beyond the person of its author.[1]

Treason against the United States may be committed by anyone who owes it allegiance. This includes not only citizens but also aliens temporarily residing in the United States, who, during such residence, owe it temporary or qualified allegiance.

In order to constitute a levying of war against the United States, within the meaning of the constitutional definition of treason, it has been held that there must be an actual assembling of a body of men for the purpose. A mere conspiracy to levy war or overthrow the government is not sufficient.[2] Resistance by armed force to the enforcement of law is not treason unless such resistance is aimed at laws in general or at the overthrow of the government. Not even the assassination of the President would be treason under the constitutional definition. On the other hand, not only the furnishing of materials to the enemy but assisting him by supplying him with information of military value would constitute giving him aid and comfort, within the meaning of the definition.

The Constitution not only defines treason but also specifies the character of the evidence on which a conviction for this offense may be secured. It requires the testimony of two witnesses to the same overt act, or confession in open court. This provision was intended to replace the English practice according to which conviction might be secured on the testimony of one witness and confessions were sometimes wrung from victims by torture.

The English practice, whereby a person convicted of treason was attainted, and his property, as well as that of his descendants, forfeited to the crown is modified by our Constitution, which protects innocent persons by limiting the punishment for treason to the person found guilty of it. Conviction of treason does not work "corruption of blood."

Treason may be committed not only against the United States but also against one of the states of the Union. Within the due process of law and other limitations of the Federal and state constitutions, each state government may define the offense of treason and the punishment therefor.

Counterfeiting.—The power to punish the counterfeiting of the securities and current coin of the United States is a concurrent power which may be exercised not only by Congress but also by the states, so

---

[1] *The Federalist*, No. 42.
[2] *Ex parte* Bollman, 4 Cranch 75 (1807).

that a given act of counterfeiting may be an offense against both the National Government and a state. This power is expressly granted to Congress in the Constitution,[1] but this provision is surplusage, since in its absence the power would have been implied in the power to coin money and regulate the value thereof. In the power to punish counterfeiting there is also implied the power to punish the passing of counterfeited money into circulation. Congress also has the implied power to punish the bringing of counterfeit money into the country from abroad. Nothing is said in the Constitution as to the power of Congress to punish the counterfeiting on our soil of the coin and securities of foreign governments, but it has nevertheless been held to have this power, which is derived from its expressly granted power to define and punish offenses against the law of nations.[2]

Offenses against the Law of Nations.—The Constitution expressly empowers Congress to "define and punish piracies and felonies committed on the high seas, and offenses against the law of nations."[3] We thus have in our fundamental law a formal recognition of the relation of international law to our own system of jurisprudence. In the Arjona case, just cited, the Court indicated that our Government not only has the power but is also under the implied obligation to punish offenses against international law. "The law of nations," said the Court, "requires every national government to use 'due diligence' to prevent a wrong being done within its own dominion to another nation with which it is at peace, or to the people thereof." Consequently, when the President has proclaimed the neutrality of the United States in a war being waged between two or more foreign nations, it is both the power and the duty of Congress to pass laws prohibiting unneutral acts from being committed by our citizens. Among such unneutral acts forbidden by act of Congress is the fitting out on our soil of expeditions to take part in such foreign wars.

Piracy, or the commission of depredations at sea without governmental authority, is also an offense against international law which Congress may punish. Congress may either provide for the punishment of this offense as defined by international law or may itself define it. Thus, Congress has declared the slave trade to be piracy.

Congress is also authorized to punish felonies committed on the high seas: that is to say, on the salt waters beyond the three-mile limit from the low-water mark. This provision gives express support to a power which would probably have been implied in the admiralty and maritime jurisdiction of the United States. Although the waters within the three-mile limit are within the territorial jurisdiction of the adjacent country, the

[1] Art. I, sect. 8, cl. 6.
[2] United States v. Arjona, 120 U. S. 479 (1887).
[3] Art. I, sect. 8, cl. 10.

high seas cannot, under international law, be brought within the exclusive control of any one nation or group of nations. A vessel on the high seas, however, flying the flag of a given nation is deemed to be under the jurisdiction of that nation. Moreover, by treaty with Great Britain, the United States has extended to twelve miles from its shore line the right to search and seize British rum runners found to be engaged in violating our national prohibition laws.

The Writ of Habeas Corpus.—One of the few provisions inserted in the original Constitution for the protection of the individual against the possible arbitrary or tyrannical action of the National Government is that which prohibits the suspension of the writ of *habeas corpus* except in cases of rebellion or invasion, when the public safety may require it.[1] This is a writ issued by a judge and directed to a jailer or other officer who may have a prisoner in custody, directing him to have the body of the prisoner in court at a certain time specified in the writ, at which time the sufficiency of the reason for his detention may be inquired into, and, if the court finds the reason insufficient, it may order his discharge from custody. It appears, therefore, that the purpose of the writ is to prevent a person from being kept in prison without sufficient cause. The privilege of this writ was preserved to English citizens by the Habeas Corpus Act, passed by Parliament in 1679, but on subsequent occasions Parliament had passed special acts suspending the privilege of the writ for what seemed to lovers of liberty insufficient reasons. It was in order to prevent Congress from doing likewise that the provision cited above was inserted in the Constitution.

It is not clearly indicated in the Constitution who may suspend the privilege of the writ in time of invasion or rebellion. During the Civil War, President Lincoln thought that this was a power attaching to the chief executive office and proceeded to exercise it. The courts were nevertheless free to issue the writ, but the suspension of the privilege by the President was deemed by jailers to whom the writ was directed sufficient legal ground to refuse to obey it. Nevertheless, Chief Justice Taney disagreed with President Lincoln, holding that the power to suspend the privilege rests in Congress and not in the President.[2] As basis for this decision, he pointed out that the provision regarding the writ is found in the article of the Constitution dealing with the powers of Congress.

It is now generally agreed that Taney was correct in his contention and that the power of suspension is vested only in Congress, but Congress may authorize the President to exercise it. In the case of President Lincoln's suspension of the writ, Congress validated his act by retroactive legislation. In a theater of war, where martial law is declared, the privi-

---

[1] Art. I, sect. 9, cl. 2.

[2] *Ex parte* Merryman, Taney's Reports, 246 (1861).

lege of the writ is suspended, because at such time and place the civil power as represented by the courts is superseded by the military. Congress, however, is not empowered to suspend the privilege of the writ except by reason of actual necessity and therefore cannot suspend it in regions remote from the scene of hostilities, in which the civil courts are open.[1]

The provision of the Federal Constitution regarding the writ of habeas corpus is a limitation on the National Government and not on the states. If a state, however, without violating its own constitution, should suspend the privilege of the writ without cause, a prisoner held in custody of state authorities during such suspension might apply to a Federal court for the writ and secure his release on the ground that he was being deprived of his liberty without due process of law in violation of the Fourteenth Amendment.

Bills of Attainder.—Both the National Government and the states are prohibited by the Constitution of the United States from passing bills of attainder.[2] These have been defined by the Supreme Court as legislative acts which inflict punishment without a judicial trial. Such arbitrary and unjust acts were sometimes passed by the English Parliament, especially during the Stuart *régime*, as in the celebrated case of the Earl of Strafford, upon whom the death penalty was inflicted in accordance with such a bill. If a penalty less than death was inflicted, it was called a bill of pains and penalties. The latter is included within our constitutional prohibition against bills of attainder.

In order to constitute a bill of attainder, it is not necessary that the person punished should be mentioned by name in the legislative act, nor is it necessary that the punishment inflicted should be either death, imprisonment, or a fine. Thus, a statute excluding from this country Chinese who are citizens of the United States has been held to be a bill of attainder.[3] During the Civil War, the State of Missouri adopted a constitution which imposed a test oath of loyalty as a qualification for holding office or engaging in the professions of law, teaching, or ministry. These disabilities were held to be penalties and the constitutional provision a bill of attainder.[4] Likewise, the Supreme Court held invalid as a bill of attainder an act of Congress passed in 1865 requiring a similar oath of all persons practicing as attorneys in the Federal courts.[5]

Ex Post Facto Laws.—Another limitation found in the original Constitution and applicable to both Congress and the state legislatures is that which prohibits the passage of *ex post facto* laws. Such laws are construed

---

[1] *Ex parte* Milligan, 4 Wall. 2 (1866).
[2] Art. I, sect. 9, cl. 3; Art. I, sect. 10, cl. 1.
[3] *In re* Yung Sing Hee, 36 Fed. 437 (1888).
[4] Cummings v. Missouri, 4 Wall. 277 (1866).
[5] *Ex parte* Garland, 4 Wall. 333 (1866).

to be those which are retroactive in their operation. As used in our Constitution, however, the provision does not prohibit all retroactive laws. In the first place, it does not apply to retroactive laws that are civil in character. In the second place, it does not apply to all retroactive criminal laws, but only to those which operate to the disadvantage of persons accused of crime.

The courts have held three different kinds of laws to be *ex post facto:* first, those that make an action done before the passing of the law, and which was innocent when done, criminal; second, those that increase the degree of a crime or attach to it a greater penalty than the law annexed at the time of its commission; and, third, those that change the rules of criminal procedure in such a way as to make it more difficult for a defendant to avoid conviction.[1] All such laws are unconstitutional. But legislative acts which decrease the penalty attached to a crime or change the rules of procedure, so as to make it easier for a defendant to be acquitted, are valid, even though retroactive.

The rule against *ex post facto* laws does not apply to judicial decisions, so that a virtual change in the law by judicial legislation to the disadvantage of a person accused of crime is not prohibited by the rule.   It applies, however, not only to statutes enacted by Congress or the state legislatures but also to state constitutional provisions and municipal ordinances. The Missouri constitutional provision, mentioned above, which required a test oath of loyalty of those engaged in certain professions, although not penal in form, was nevertheless held to be invalid not only as a bill of attainder but also as *ex post facto*. It was held that participation in rebellion did not affect the fitness of a person to engage in such professions, and that exclusion therefrom operated as a penalty which was not attached to such participation at the time it occurred.

In a New York state court, it was held that a law changing the punishment for an offense from death to life imprisonment was *ex post facto*, as applied to such an offense committed before the law was passed.[2] Most courts, however, in other jurisdictions hold that such a law would not be *ex post facto*, as thus applied, because it lessens the severity of the punishment.

A number of states have enacted habitual-offender laws, inflicting heavier penalties for a second than for a first offense.   The contention has been made that such law is *ex post facto* when enacted after the commission of the first offense. This contention has been denied by the Supreme Court, however, which held that the heavier penalties are not for the first offense but for the later offense committed after the passage of the law.[3]

[1] *Cf.* Calder v. Bull, 3 Dall. 386 (1798); Thompson v. Missouri, 171 U. S. 380 (1898).
[2] Shepherd v. People, 25 N. Y. 406 (1862).
[3] McDonald v. Massachusetts, 180 U. S. 311 (1901).

Another example of an *ex post facto* law which may be mentioned was that found in the constitution of Utah which changed the size of the trial jury in criminal cases from twelve to eight.[1] This law changed the procedure to the disadvantage of the accused, because it is easier to avoid conviction by the unanimous verdict of twelve men than it is by that of eight men.

It should be remembered that the *ex post facto* laws mentioned above are invalid only as applied to offenses committed before the passage of the law. As to future offenses they are not unconstitutional through conflict with the prohibition against *ex post facto* laws, although they may be unconstitutional through conflict with some other provision of the Constitution.

The First Eight Amendments.—The bill of rights contained in the group of amendments adopted immediately after the Constitution went into effect was inserted in that instrument, as we have seen, in order to allay the fears of those persons who desired safeguards for private rights against the possible oppression and tyranny of the new National Government. It is therefore in accordance with their historical origin that they should be, and are, construed as limiting that Government and not the states.[2] They limit the legislative power of Congress but not of the state legislatures, and they apply to cases in the Federal courts but not to those in state tribunals. The states, however, are limited by identical or similar provisions found in the state constitutions and in the Fourteenth Amendment to the Federal Constitution. The first eight amendments are mainly, although not exclusively, concerned with the protection of persons accused of crime.

Indictment by Grand Jury.—A person may be indicted by a grand jury before he is arrested, but, if first arrested, he is usually brought before the United States commissioner, who decides whether the accused shall be dismissed or held for the action of the grand jury. The Fifth Amendment requires that "no person shall be held to answer for a capital, or otherwise infamous crime, unless on presentment or indictment of a grand jury." This operates as a protection to the person accused of crime, because otherwise the prosecution would be entirely in the hands of the United States district attorney or other prosecuting officer. The grand jury was evolved originally for the purpose of injecting an element of popular control into the administration of justice and of protecting accused persons against arbitrary action or persecution by the government. In some states, however, the grand jury has been abolished and for it has been substituted the filing of an information by the prosecuting attorney. The provision of the Fifth Amendment just quoted does not limit the states. It applies only to the National Government and to the

[1] Thompson v. Utah, 170 U. S. 343 (1898).
[2] Barron v. Baltimore, 7 Pet. 243 (1823).

prosecution of crimes against the United States. The United States district attorney presents the evidence to the grand jury, which may or may not return an indictment, depending on whether or not it believes there is a *prima facie* case against the accused.[1] The sessions of the grand jury are secret and the proceedings are *ex parte; i.e.*, it hears only evidence against the accused person, who is not usually allowed to present, either in person or by attorney, evidence in his favor.

The Fifth Amendment protects not merely citizens but persons generally, and this is broad enough to include aliens. It is not necessary, however, to resort to the procedure of indictment by grand jury in deporting an alien who has unlawfully entered the country.

It will be noticed that the procedure of indictment by grand jury is not required in the case of every person accused of crime, but only in the case of those accused of capital or otherwise infamous crimes. It is not entirely clear what is meant by an infamous crime, but in general it depends upon the character or extent of the punishment which may be inflicted. A crime punishable with death is, of course, infamous. Furthermore, a crime has been held to be infamous when the penalty attached is imprisonment in a penitentiary for at least a year. Still other crimes might come within the definition of infamous if the public opinion of the time so regards them.

In the case of petty offenses, such as misdemeanors, indictment by grand jury is not required. Moreover, it is not required in cases arising in the unincorporated territories, nor in the consular courts of the United States,[2] nor "in cases arising in the land or naval forces, or in the militia, when in actual service in time of war or public danger." Cases of the latter class are tried in courts martial, in accordance with military law.

Trial by Jury.—Trial by jury is a long-established institution of Anglo-Saxon judicial procedure, dating back to the Middle Ages. It was transplanted from England to the American colonies and was highly regarded by the colonists as a bulwark against governmental oppression. One of their charges against the British monarch contained in the Declaration of Independence was that he had "combined with others" in "acts of pretended legislation for depriving us in many cases of the benefits of trial by jury."

It is not surprising, therefore, that the framers of the Constitution made ample provision in that instrument for safeguarding this venerable institution. It is doubly protected by provisions in both the original Constitution and in the bill of rights. The former declares that "the

[1] A presentment differs from an indictment in that it is returned upon the initiative of the grand jury on the basis of evidence in its possession, while an indictment is returned on the basis of evidence laid before it by the prosecuting attorney.

[2] *In re* Ross, 140 U. S. 453 (1891).

trial of all crimes, except in cases of impeachment, shall be by jury,"[1] while the Sixth Amendment further declares that "in all criminal prosecutions the accused shall enjoy the right to a speedy and public trial by an impartial jury of the state and district wherein the crime shall have been committed." These two provisions both relate solely to criminal cases, but by the Seventh Amendment the right of trial by jury is also preserved in civil suits, where the value in controversy exceeds twenty dollars. The three provisions thus found in the Federal Constitution relating to jury trial apply to cases tried in the Federal courts and not to cases tried in state courts. This is true not only in the case of the regular Federal courts but also of those in the District of Columbia and in those territories which have been incorporated into the United States.

As in the case of many other terms used in the Constitution, the word "crimes" as used in the provision relating to jury trial is to be interpreted in the light of the meaning attached to it by the common law at the time of the adoption of the Constitution. In this technical sense, it does not include all those for which criminal punishment may be inflicted but only those of a more serious character, conviction for which may involve deprivation of liberty, as contrasted with petty offenses. The distinction here made, however, is not that between felonies and misdemeanors, since those tried for certain classes of misdemeanors, for which the punishment may be imprisonment, are also entitled to trial by jury.[2]

It has been held that the framers of the Constitution probably intended to limit the right of trial by jury as provided by the Sixth Amendment to those who, under the Fifth Amendment, were subject to indictment or presentment by grand jury.[3] Persons accused of such petty offenses as gambling or violation of certain provisions of the Pure Food and Drugs Law, or of the Oleomargarine Act, for which the punishment is not imprisonment but merely a fine, are not entitled to trial by jury and may be summarily proceeded against in any court having jurisdiction of the case. Moreover, a person accused of contempt of court, such as, for example, the violation of an injunction issued by the court, may also be summarily punished without trial by jury.[4] Furthermore, an alien against whom proceedings are brought for his deportation

---

[1] Art. III, sect. II, cl. 3.

[2] Callan v. Wilson, 127 U. S. 540 (1888). It has been held that a person charged with driving an automobile, not merely at an excessive rate of speed, or recklessly, but so as to endanger property and individuals, has a constitutional right to a jury trial. In other words, this is not a petty offense. District of Columbia v. Colts, 282 U. S. 63 (1930).

[3] *Ex parte* Milligan, 4 Wall. 123 (1866).

[4] By the Clayton Anti-Trust Act of 1914, however, Congress extended the right to trial by jury to accused persons in cases of indirect criminal contempt, and this provision was held to be not unconstitutional. Michaelson v. U. S., 266 U. S. 42 (1924).

is not entitled to trial by jury. Such proceedings are brought merely for the purpose of determining whether or not the conditions exist which, by act of Congress, permit his continuance in the country. The order of deportation is not a punishment for crime. The question as to the admission of an alien into the country is one which may be left to the determination of an administrative officer and his decision may be made conclusive.[1] It is also true, of course, that juries are not employed in military tribunals.

Although United States commissioners are not allowed to accept pleas of guilty in prohibition cases, this may be done by the Federal courts and, in such cases, no jury is employed, because there is then no fact for the jury to determine. This represents a great saving of time to the Federal prosecuting attorney, so that, in return for a plea of guilty, he is frequently willing to agree to the imposition of a fine without the addition of imprisonment. Under the national prohibition laws, it is possible to proceed against places where liquor is sold through the issuance of injunctions padlocking them for a year as public nuisances. In such equity cases, no juries are employed and the judge passes summarily on both the law and the facts. Such padlocking of the premises is equivalent to a fine, but violation of the injunction constitutes contempt of court, which, as indicated above, is punishable as a criminal offense without trial by jury. By this method the constitutional provision regarding trial by jury may be substantially evaded.

The right to trial by jury includes all the substantial incidents which attached thereto according to the common law as it existed at the time of the adoption of the Constitution and of the first ten amendments. In the light of this requirement, the jury to trial by which the accused is entitled is composed of twelve "true and lawful men." They are chosen from the district in which the crime is alleged to have been committed. Furthermore, in order to reach a verdict, the jury must be unanimous. Although the states of the Union, if allowed by their constitutions, may provide for conviction by less than a unanimous verdict of a jury or by a jury of less than twelve (and in some instances have done so), such a provision by act of Congress would be unconstitutional. The three essential common-law elements embodied in trial by jury, as pointed out by the Supreme Court, are " (1) that the jury should consist of twelve men, neither more nor less; (2) that the trial should be in the presence of and under the superintendence of a judge having power to instruct them as to the law and advise them in respect of the facts; and (3) that the verdict should be unanimous."[2]

Waiver of Jury Trial.—It does not follow that, because a person accused of crime has a right to trial by jury, he may not waive that right. Although the provision for jury trial in the third article of the original

---

[1] United States v. Ju Toy, 198 U. S. 253 (1905).
[2] Patton v. United States, 281 U. S. 276 (1930).

Constitution is couched in mandatory language, it must be read in the light of the more or less permissive language of the Sixth Amendment. In case of conflict between the two provisions, the amendment, as the later expression of the will of the framers, should be deemed to prevail. Consequently, it would seem that a person accused of crime who, under either or both of these provisions is entitled to trial by jury, may waive that right. It has long been recognized that he could do so in certain minor cases, especially if authorized to do so by statute. Thus, Congress passed an act providing that, in police court prosecutions in the District of Columbia, the accused might waive jury trial and elect to be tried by the judge. This authorization of waiver was upheld by the District of Columbia court, which pointed out that the statute "is not only an expression of the increasing necessity of dealing summarily with the minor crimes that harass our society; it is likewise an expression fully justified by experience of the ability of the courts of law to deal justly with the accused, without the intervention of juries."[1]

Although the courts have taken contrary views on the question, it has been generally supposed that the accused could waive a jury trial in minor cases, such as misdemeanors, but that he could probably not do so in felony cases. This was the common-law rule. The variation in the decisions on this question has been due to difference of opinion among the courts as to whether the right to trial by jury has been extended to the accused merely for his benefit or also in the interests of the state and society in general. This question, however, has now been settled by the Supreme Court in a case in which the accused was indicted for conspiracy to bribe a Federal prohibition officer, a crime punishable by imprisonment. The accused having been put on trial and one juror becoming incapacitated, it was agreed by both sides to waive objection and to proceed with the remaining eleven jurors. Upon conviction, the defendant appealed and the question was certified to the Supreme Court, which held that the agreement to be tried by eleven jurors was equivalent to waiving jury trial altogether but nevertheless upheld the conviction in spite of the waiver. The Court based its decision on grounds of public policy, holding that the purpose and effect of the constitutional provisions were not to establish jury trial as an essential part of the structure of government but merely to guarantee the privilege of jury trial for the benefit of the accused.[2] Consequently the right to trial by jury may be waived, even though the offense is a felony.

Incidents of Jury Trial.—Since the Sixth Amendment entitles the defendant to trial by an impartial jury, it follows that he has the right to challenge any prospective juror for cause. He is also entitled "to be informed of the nature and cause of the accusation." This means that he

[1] Belt v. United States, 4 App. Cas. (D. C.) 32 (1894).
[2] Patton v. United States, 281 U. S. 276 (1930).

must be furnished with a copy of the indictment against him a sufficient length of time before the trial to enable him to prepare his defence. The Sixth Amendment further provides that the accused is entitled "to be confronted with the witnesses against him, and to have compulsory process for obtaining witnesses in his favor." With the exception of death-bed depositions, it was required by the common law that witnesses against an accused person must appear personally in court and give their testimony orally, and this rule is embodied in the amendment. The purpose of the rule is to enable the defendant or his counsel to cross-examine the witnesses and thus test their credibility. It is a right, however, which may be waived by the defendant.

Since the Government which prosecutes criminal offenses has means at its disposal to compel the appearance of witnesses against the defendant, it is deemed but fair that the latter should be entitled to a similar privilege. This privilege of a defendant extends even to summoning as witnesses members of Congress (except during sessions), judges, and other officers, provided it does not interfere with the performance of their official duties. Diplomatic representatives of foreign governments in the United States are, under international law, exempt from being compelled to appear in court as witnesses. This is a privilege, however, which they may waive with the consent of their respective governments. By treaty, the same privilege of exemption may also be extended to foreign consuls.

Finally, the defendant is guaranteed the assistance of counsel for his defence. This provision was intended to change the ancient rule of the common law which did not give the right to counsel. It also operates for the benefit of impecunious defendants who are unable to employ an attorney to defend them. Under these circumstances, it becomes the duty of the court to appoint an attorney to do so.

Place of Trial.—The original Constitution provides that the "trial of all crimes . . . shall be held in the state where the said crimes shall have been committed; but when not committed within any state, the trial shall be at such place or places as the Congress may by law have directed."[1] The Sixth Amendment goes farther and requires that the trial shall be by an impartial jury "of the state and district wherein the crime shall have been committed, which district shall have been previously ascertained by law." These provisions show the importance which the framers of the Constitution and the early amendments attached to the principle that the trial should not take place far from the scene of the crime. They still remembered the condition against which the colonists complained in the Declaration of Independence when they accused the British King of "transporting us beyond seas to be tried for pretended offenses." It was also an ancient rule of the common law that the jury should be drawn from the "vicinage," because it was supposed

[1] Art. III, sect. 2, cl. 3.

that residents near the scene of the crime would be better acquainted with the circumstances of the case and therefore more competent to bring in a correct verdict. On the other hand, public opinion in the locality of a crime may be so aroused and inflamed against a person accused of it that he would hardly be able to secure a fair trial. If it is a state case, a change of venue may under these circumstances be granted from one county to another.[1] In Federal cases, however, there can be no change of venue from one state to another. By act of Congress the country has been divided into judicial districts, and crimes are tried in that district in which committed. It may happen, however, that a crime is committed in two or more districts. For example, if a person mails a bomb in New York addressed to a person in Chicago and the latter is injured by its explosion upon delivery, a crime has been committed in both places. It has been provided by act of Congress that, under these circumstances, the perpetrator of the crime may be tried either in the district in which the crime was begun or in that in which it was completed. A shipper who secures transportation of goods in interstate commerce at less than the carrier's published rates may be prosecuted in any district through which the goods are carried.[2]

The provision of the original Constitution that, when a crime is "not committed within any state, the trial shall be at such place or places as Congress may by law have directed" refers to offenses committed in the territories or upon the high seas on vessels flying the American flag. In the first Crimes Act, passed by Congress in 1790, it was provided that "trial of crimes committed on the high seas, or in any place out of the jurisdiction of any particular state, shall be in the district where the offender is apprehended, or into which he may first be brought."[3] It is clear that the act of Congress designating the place of the trial must antedate the trial and it would seem that it should also antedate the commission of the offense.

Speedy and Public Trial.—The old adage "justice delayed is justice denied" embodies the reason underlying the requirement in the Sixth Amendment that the defendant in a criminal case is entitled to a speedy trial. The word "speedy" here refers both to the shortness of time elapsing between the defendant's arrest and the time of the beginning of his trial and also to the celerity with which the trial is pushed forward to a conclusion after it has begun. This requirement of the amendment, however, is to be regarded as largely directory rather than mandatory. The Supreme Court has declared that "the right of a speedy trial is

[1] The state or prosecution, however, is not usually allowed the right to change of venue, even though public sentiment in favor of the accused is so great that it is impossible to secure a conviction in the face of incontrovertible evidence of guilt.

[2] Armour Packing Co. v. United States, 209 U. S. 56 (1908).

[3] 1 Stat. at L. 114.

necessarily relative. It is consistent with delays and depends upon circumstances. It secures rights to a defendant. It does not preclude the rights of public justice."[1]

Where a court hears both civil and criminal cases, preference in the matter of speediness is usually given to the criminal cases. It unfortunately sometimes happens that a court is so far behind its docket even in the disposal of criminal cases that excessive delays occur. Even in criminal cases, however, where time is required to secure witnesses and gather evidence, a certain amount of delay may be reasonable and justifiable. An innocent defendant, who naturally desires speedy vindication, will not as a rule seek any unnecessary delay in his trial. On the other hand, consciousness of guilt on the part of the defendant may cause him to seek delay, and criminal procedure provides so many opportunities for obstructive tactics that in the end he may escape merited punishment. A defendant cannot, however, resort to such tactics and later move to have his case dismissed on the ground that the constitutional requirement of a speedy trial has not been complied with.

The provision of the Sixth Amendment for a "public trial" was intended to prevent the introduction into the Federal courts of such star-chamber proceedings in passing on the guilt of the accused as had sometimes been resorted to in England. The provision requires that the case must be heard in open court. It does not necessarily follow, however, that any and all persons must be admitted to the trial up to the capacity of the court room. It seems clear that the constitutional requirement does not deprive the judge of the right to exclude from the court room immature persons or those attracted merely by morbid curiosity, when the testimony is not fit for them to hear or the details of the crime are of such character as may tend to corrupt public morals. If, in a case where no such considerations are involved, the judge excludes from the court room all persons except members of the bar, relatives of the defendant, and newspaper reporters, there would seem to be a difference of opinion as to whether or not the constitutional requirement of a public trial has been complied with.[2]

Self-incrimination.—The Fifth Amendment provides that no person shall be compelled in any criminal case to be a witness against himself. The privilege thus extended applies not only to the defendant in a criminal case but also to other persons who are not on trial but are summoned to testify as witnesses. It applies to proceedings not only in court but also before a grand jury. In a criminal case before a court, the defendant may waive this privilege and voluntarily take the witness stand, but he cannot be compelled to do so. Moreover, it is improper for the judge or the opposing counsel to call the attention of the jury to, or to comment

---

[1] Beavers v. Haubert, 198 U. S. 86 (1905).

[2] *Cf.* Davis v. United States, 247 Fed. 394 (1917).

adversely upon, his failure to take the stand in his own defense. The privilege thus extended by the amendment is a corollary from the principle of the common law that an accused person is presumed to be innocent until he is proved guilty. In this respect our law differs from the civil law as found in France and other Continental European countries, where apparently an accused person is presumed to be guilty until he has been proved innocent, and, consequently, he may be compelled to testify in his own case. The rule of evidence as embodied in the amendment operates to excuse a witness in a criminal case from answering any question which might disclose facts rendering him liable to criminal prosecution. It does not, however, excuse him from testifying to facts which may impair his reputation for probity or tend to disgrace him.[1] Moreover, it does not excuse him from answering questions which might disclose criminal conduct on his part, if such conduct is no longer subject to prosecution because the statute of limitations has run, or because he has been granted a pardon,[2] or because he has been guaranteed by statute immunity from prosecution. Such statutes guaranteeing immunity are frequently passed in order to secure the testimony of persons implicated in certain classes of crimes where their testimony is needed in order to convict others who are regarded as the principal parties to the crime. In order to deprive such witnesses of their constitutional privilege to refuse to testify or, in other words, to avoid the application of the constitutional provision against self-incrimination, it is necessary that absolute immunity be granted against prosecution on account of any matter concerning which they may testify. Such immunity, however, applies only to prosecution in the same jurisdiction in which it is granted, so that a grant of immunity by Federal statute does not prevent prosecution in the state courts, and conversely.

A witness in a criminal case does not have the conclusive power to determine that his answer to a question would tend to incriminate him. It is for the judge to decide whether his answers will reasonably have such a tendency or furnish a link in the chain of evidence necessary to convict him. If, however, it appears that the witness is in danger, "great latitude should then be allowed to him in judging for himself of the effect of any particular question."[3]

The constitutional privilege against self-incrimination includes not only the right to refuse to answer incriminating questions but also the right to refuse to produce private books, documents, or papers which would have an incriminating effect. This, however, as the Supreme Court has pointed out, "is purely a personal privilege of the witness. It was never intended to permit him to plead the fact that some third

---

[1] Hale v. Henkel, 201 U. S. 43 (1906).
[2] Provided the pardon has been accepted. Burdick v. U. S. 236 U. S. 79 (1915).
[3] Foot v. Buchanan, 113 Fed. 160 (1902).

person might be incriminated by his testimony, even though he were the agent of such person."[1] In the case just cited, Hale, secretary and treasurer of a certain corporation, was served with a *subpoena duces tecum* requiring him to appear before the grand jury and to bring with him various documents and papers relating to the business of the corporation. He refused to obey on the ground that to produce such papers would violate the constitutional provision against self-incrimination. This contention, however, was overruled on the ground that a corporation is a creature of the state, incorporated for the benefit of the public, and that an officer or agent of a corporation cannot refuse to testify because his testimony may incriminate the corporation. Substantially, it would seem that a corporation is not a person within the meaning of the con-stitutional provision against self-incrimination. Moreover, it has been held that an officer of a corporation who holds its books and papers in his possession does not do so in his private capacity, and, even although they may tend to incriminate him, he is not entitled to refuse to produce them in answer to a *subpoena duces tecum*, as he might if they were absolutely his own.[2]

The provision of the Fifth Amendment against self-incrimination places no prohibition upon the states, nor does the due-process clause of the Fourteenth Amendment prevent a state from enacting a statute compelling defendants or witnesses in criminal cases to give self-incrimi-nating testimony.[3] Most state constitutions, however, limit the state legislatures in this respect.

Unreasonable Searches and Seizures.—The Fourth Amendment is based on the ancient rule that a man's house is his castle. It protects not only persons accused of crime but also others who are merely sus-pected of crime as well as the innocent.[4] It contains, in the first place, a general prohibition against "unreasonable searches and seizures" of "persons, houses, papers, and effects," and, in the second place, it prohibits the issuance of search warrants except "upon probable cause, supported by oath or affirmation, and particularly describing the place to be searched, and the persons or things to be seized." It will be noticed that the framers of this amendment endeavored to maintain a balance between the two more or less conflicting considerations of individual liberty and governmental necessity. Although exempting the individual to some extent from searches and seizures, it does not prohibit them if they are reasonable. Moreover, it permits the issuance of definitely descriptive search warrants based upon probable cause but "prevents the

---

[1] Hale v. Henkel, 201 U. S. 43 (1906).

[2] Wilson v. United States, 221 U. S. 361 (1911); Essgee Co. v. United States, 262 U. S. 151 (1923).

[3] Twining v. New Jersey, 211 U. S. 78 (1908).

[4] Go-Bart Importing Co. v. United States, 282 U. S. 344 (1931).

issue of warrants on loose, vague, or doubtful bases of fact. It emphasizes the purpose to protect against all general searches."[1] Historically, the amendment was aimed at the prevention of the issuance of such general warrants as the "writs of assistance," under which British officers searched the houses of the colonists for smuggled goods—a procedure which, although entirely legal at that time, was eloquently denounced by James Otis in 1761 as being tyrannical and unreasonable.

Since the Fourth Amendment does not prohibit all searches but only those that are unreasonable, large discretion is left to the courts in passing upon the reasonableness of the search. There is no formula for the determination of reasonableness, and each case is to be decided on its own facts and circumstances.[2] The courts have construed the Fourth Amendment as being closely connected with the Fifth. In other words, if a person's papers and effects are seized in violation of the Fourth Amendment, or if he is required by *subpoena duces tecum* to produce them, and they are used as evidence against him in a criminal case, he is subjected to compulsory self-incrimination, in violation of the Fifth. This would, in effect, be making his papers speak against him or, in other words, making him a witness against himself. The Supreme Court has held that, where incriminating papers had been taken from a defendant in a criminal case by the United States marshal or Federal prohibition officer without a warrant or legal authority, they will, upon his demand, be returned to him in spite of the desire of the Government to use them as evidence against him.[3] The evidence thus illegally obtained was inadmissible.

The common-law rule, however, is that the admissibility of evidence is not affected by the illegality of the means by which it was obtained. The cases just cited, therefore, recognize an exception to this rule when the evidence is obtained by government officials in violation of the Fourth Amendment. The common-law rule, however, is adhered to when there has been no illegal search or seizure by governmental officials. An example of the latter class of cases was that in which certain incriminating papers were stolen from the owner and turned over by the thief to a prosecuting officer of the Federal Government. It was held that the officer could not be prevented from using the papers as evidence, simply because some other person had stolen them.[4] In other words, the Fourth Amendment affords protection only against illegal action on the part of governmental officials. A strong dissent was filed in this case in which it was declared that "respect for law will not be advanced by

---

[1] *Ibid.*

[2] Go-Bart Importing Co. v. United States, cited *supra* (1931).

[3] Weeks v. United States, 232 U. S. 383 (1914); Go-Bart Importing Co. v. United States, cited *supra* (1931).

[4] Burdeau v. McDowell, 255 U. S. 313 (1921).

resort, in its enforcement, to means which shock the common man's sense of decency and fair play."

Another case in which evidence was admitted because it had been obtained by government officers without illegal search or seizure was the "wire-tapping" case, decided in 1928.[1] In this case Federal prohibition officers had secured evidence against a gang of rum runners and bootleggers by tapping the telephone wires running from their headquarters and making a record of their telephone conversations. This record conclusively proved the guilt of the defendants, but they objected to the admission of this evidence on the ground that it was obtained by an unreasonable search and seizure and that its admission as evidence would amount to compulsory self-incrimination. Those contentions, however, were denied by the Supreme Court in a five-to-four decision, in which Chief Justice Taft, speaking for the majority, declared: "There was no searching. There was no seizure. The evidence was secured by the sense of hearing, and that only. There was no entry of the houses or offices of the defendants." It was admitted that the opening by government officers of mailed sealed letters would constitute an unreasonable search, in violation of the Fourth Amendment, but it was denied that this was a precedent for the instant case. The United States takes no such care of telegraph or telephone messages as of mailed sealed letters, although Congress might, by direct legislation, protect the secrecy of telephone messages by making them inadmissible as evidence and thus alter the common law of evidence. But the courts may not do this, he averred.

It was also admitted that the method of obtaining the evidence was unethical and even a violation of the state law. On this account, Justice Holmes, in his dissenting opinion, denounced it as "dirty business." He pointed out that

. . . we must consider the two objects of desire both of which we cannot have and make up our minds which to choose. It is desirable that criminals should be detected, and to that end that all available evidence should be used. It is also desirable that the government should not itself foster and pay for other crimes, when they are the means by which the evidence is to be obtained . . . For my part I think it a less evil that some criminals should escape than that the government should play an ignoble part.

The majority, however, took the opposite view, feeling that where there is a conflict between the interests of society at large and those of individual criminals, the courts, in the absence of controlling legislation by Congress, should uphold the former. As Chief Justice Taft declared, "A standard which would forbid the reception of evidence if obtained by other than

[1] Olmstead v. United States, 277 U. S. 438 (1928).

nice ethical conduct by government officials would make society suffer and give criminals greater immunity than has been known heretofore."

In addition to the wire-tapping case, a number of other cases relating to search and seizure have been decided by the Supreme Court since the adoption of national prohibition. As pointed out above, it has been held that, while government officials cannot obtain evidence by unreasonable searches and seizures and use it in a criminal case, nevertheless if the evidence is stolen and turned over to them by private individuals, it may be used. The same is also true where the evidence is obtained by state police officers, provided Federal officers do not participate in the raid and provided the state has a prohibition law. If the state does not have a prohibition law, the state officers who seize the evidence must be deemed to be acting on behalf of the United States, so that the evidence thus obtained is the result of an unreasonable seizure and cannot be used in securing a conviction.[1]

It has been held that, under some circumstances, searches and seizures may be deemed reasonable and the evidence obtained therefore admissible, even though made without a warrant. These are, first, when a violation of law is committed in the presence of officers, as when liquor is sold to disguised prohibition agents; and, second, when officers have probable cause to suppose that a boat, automobile, or other vehicle is being used as a means of transporting liquor. Under these circumstances, the officers must act at once in order to secure the evidence before it disappears, and it would be unreasonable to require them to obtain a warrant.[2] They have no right, however, to enter private dwelling houses without a warrant on mere suspicion that liquor is being manufactured or even sold there.

From the above discussion it clearly appears that the Eighteenth Amendment has not had the effect of repealing or nullifying the Fourth.

Double Jeopardy.—A venerable rule of the common law is embodied in that provision of the Fifth Amendment which declares that no person shall "be subject for the same offense to be twice put in jeopardy of life

---

[1] Gambino v. United States, 275 U. S. 310 (1927). The evidence held inadmissible in this case was liquor seized from defendant's car by New York state troopers, who were not agents of the Federal Government but thought that they were assisting in the enforcement of the national prohibition law. At the time this case arose, New York's state prohibition law had been repealed.

[2] Carroll v. United States, 267 U. S. 132 (1925). In Husty v. United States, 282 U. S. 694 (1931), it was held that, to show probable cause justifying search of an automobile for intoxicating liquor without search warrant, it is sufficient if the apparent facts would induce a reasonably discreet and prudent man to believe that liquor was illegally possessed in the automobile to be searched. Search based on such information without search warrant is upon probable cause even though sufficient time had elapsed between the time of receiving the information and the time when the suspected persons started away with the automobile to have enabled the officer to procure a search warrant.

or limb." The phrase "life or limb" is a relic of the times when barbarous punishments were occasionally inflicted, but the word "limb" is now to be interpreted as meaning liberty. This rule against double jeopardy has been broadly construed so as to prohibit a person not only from being twice punished for the same offense but also from even being put on trial twice for the same offense.

When may a person be said to be put in jeopardy? On this point, there has been some difference of opinion among different courts. In general, however, it seems to be the doctrine of the Federal courts that a person is put in jeopardy whenever he is put on trial before a court of competent jurisdiction and the jury has been impaneled and sworn.[1] If it should turn out that the court did not have jurisdiction to try the case, then the prisoner was not in jeopardy, even though the trial had reached the point where he confronted the jury. Moreover, it should be remembered that the preliminary examination of a person arrested on suspicion of a crime is not a trial; and his discharge by the magistrate upon such an examination is not an acquittal.[2] Even the finding of an indictment, followed by arraignment, pleading thereto, repeated continuances, and eventually dismissal at the instance of the prosecuting officer, on the ground that there was not sufficient evidence to hold the accused, does not constitute jeopardy.[3]

To the general rule that the prisoner is in jeopardy when put on trial before a competent tribunal and the jury has been inpaneled and sworn, it should be noted as an exception that the prisoner is not in jeopardy if the jury finds itself unable to agree on a verdict of either guilty or not guilty and is, on this account, discharged by the judge. "Such a discharge constitutes no bar to further proceedings and gives no right of exemption to the prisoner from being again put upon trial."[4] Furthermore, it has been held that the prisoner is not in jeopardy when it is discovered after the beginning of a trial that a juror is biased or has been a member of the grand jury which found the indictment.

The general rule as to jeopardy stated above holds good regardless of what verdict the jury reaches, and the accused is equally put in jeopardy at the first trial, whether acquitted or convicted. The immunity against double jeopardy, however, is a constitutional privilege which the accused may waive. This he does when he asks for a new trial or appeals to a higher court from the decision holding him guilty in his first trial. In his second trial, however, he runs the risk of being convicted of a more serious offense than that for which he was convicted at his first trial.

[1] Kepner v. United States, 195 U. S. 100 (1904).
[2] Collins v. Loisel, 262 U. S. 426 (1923).
[3] Bassing v. Cady, 208 U. S. 386 (1908).
[4] United States v. Perez, 9 Wheat. 579 (1824). The second trial under these circumstances is regarded as a continuation of the first one.

For example, if convicted of manslaughter on his first trial, he might, at the second trial, be convicted of murder. His conviction of manslaughter constitutes an acquittal of murder, but, if he appeals, he waives his immunity against being tried again and being convicted of murder.[1]

On the other hand, if the prisoner is acquitted on the first trial, the judgment in his favor is final and conclusive. The government or the prosecution does not have the right to obtain a new trial or to take an appeal to a higher court. The second trial for the same offense, although involving no danger of second punishment, would involve double jeopardy in violation of the amendment.[2] In 1909, Congress passed an act allowing the Government to take a criminal case by writ of error from the lower Federal courts to the Supreme Court in order to review questions of law, but with the proviso that "no writ of error should be taken by or allowed the United States in any case where there has been a verdict in favor of the defendant."[3]

The rule against double jeopardy as found in the Fifth Amendment does not limit the states, but the Federal Government only. Moreover, it applies only to cases arising in the Federal jurisdiction and not to offenses against state law. If, therefore, it should happen that a given act is an offense against both Federal and state law, the offender may be tried in both jurisdictions without violating the constitutional rule against double jeopardy, because, although there is only one act, there are, strictly speaking, two separate offenses. For example, fraud or corrupt practices at an election, at which both state officers and members of Congress are chosen, or passing counterfeit coin of the United States are offenses against both the state and the Federal Government. The offender in such a case, if tried in one jurisdiction, whether acquitted or convicted, has no right to plead double jeopardy as a defense when also tried in the other.

It is also true that a single act may sometimes constitute two offenses even in the same jurisdiction. For example, a motorist in the District of Columbia drove his car at an excessive rate of speed along the wrong side of the street. He thereby violated two distinct traffic regulations, *viz.*, that limiting the speed of vehicles and that requiring all vehicles to pass to the right. He could be tried for each of these violations as separate offenses, in spite of the fact that they were committed by one act, and could not plead double jeopardy at the second trial. The test is whether different evidence is required to prove the violations charged. If so, there are two offenses regardless of the fact that the charges grow out of one transaction.

[1] Trono v. United States, 199 U. S. 521 (1905).
[2] Kepner v. United States, 195 U. S. 100 (1904).
[3] 34 Stat. at L. 1246.

Although the principle stated above—that a person who violates both state and national law by the same act is not protected by the double-jeopardy clause against being tried twice—has been long established, its importance has greatly increased since the advent of national prohibition. Congress and most of the states have passed laws for the enforcement of the Eighteenth Amendment. These laws generally make the sale of intoxicating liquor a criminal offense, so that by a single act of sale a person may commit an offense against both the National Government and the state in which the sale took place. He may be tried for this offense by the state and, whether acquitted or convicted and punished, may later be tried in the Federal courts for a similar offense growing out of the same act. For example, a case came before the United States Supreme Court in 1922 in which one Lanza, who had been convicted and fined in the Washington state courts for transporting liquor in violation of state law, was put on trial and convicted in a lower Federal court for violating the Volstead act or national prohibition law by the same act of transportation. His claim that the second trial placed him in double jeopardy in violation of the Fifth Amendment was denied by the lower Federal court and this decision was affirmed by the Supreme Court.[1] The latter tribunal declared that

. . . we have here two sovereignties, deriving power from different sources, capable of dealing with the same subject matter within the same territory . . . It follows that an act denounced as a crime by both national and state sovereignties is an offense against the peace and dignity of both, and may be punished by each.

Although the principle of law as thus enunciated by the Court is well established, it hardly seems fair to the average man that a person should be subject to double punishment for the same act. Although this legal liability exists, the number of prohibition cases is so large that little attempt is made to prosecute offenders twice and in fact this is seldom done. If it is thought desirable to prevent this altogether, it could be accomplished by an act of Congress prohibiting prosecution in the Federal courts for an act when punishment for such act in violation of state prohibition law has been imposed. It is doubtful, however, whether it would be wise for Congress to do this in view of the fact that, if the penalty under state prohibition law should be unduly light, an offender might avoid the heavier penalty imposed for violating Federal law by surrendering to the state authorities and pleading guilty in the state courts. If, in any state, it is generally felt that double punishment for the same act is unjust, it may be prevented by the repeal of the state prohibition law, and this has been done in some states.

Most state constitutions contain a provision against double jeopardy, but this does not prevent a person from being tried by the state for a

[1] United States v. Lanza, 260 U. S. 377 (1922).

violation of its law even though he has already been tried for the same act in the Federal courts. A question which arises in this connection, however, is whether a person can be prosecuted by both a state and by a municipality within the state for an act which is a violation both of state law and of municipal ordinance. Although there is a difference of opinion upon this question, the weight of authority is that prosecution by both the state and the municipality does not constitute double jeopardy.[1] The opposite view, however, held by some courts, seems to embody the wiser policy and some states have by law or constitutional provision prohibited double prosecution for the same act or omission. This is also in accordance with the opinion regarding an analogous situation held by the United States Supreme Court, which has declared that, after a defendant has been prosecuted in the territorial court of the Philippines, he cannot be again prosecuted for the same act under a Federal statute. Here the same act does not constitute two offenses, because both Federal and territorial courts exert their powers under the authority of the same government.[2]

Bail and Fines.—The Eighth Amendment provides that "excessive bail shall not be required, nor excessive fines imposed, nor cruel and unusual punishments inflicted." This amendment is copied from similar provisions of the English Bill of Rights of 1689, which were intended to do away with certain barbaric practices which had previously prevailed in the administration of the criminal law. Although the English bill was intended primarily as a limitation upon the king's courts rather than upon Parliament, the Eighth Amendment has been construed as a limitation upon both Congress and the Federal judiciary. It does not limit the states.

Bail is the pledge of money or property by an accused person or his sureties in order to assure his appearance for trial. It is a means whereby a person arrested for a criminal offense may obtain his liberty while awaiting trial. It may also sometimes be granted, even after conviction in the trial court, pending appeal to a higher court. Although excessive bail cannot be required, the question as to what is "excessive" leaves a large amount of discretion to the courts, subject to any statutory regulations of the matter that may have been enacted. In determining this question, there are two things which the court should consider; first, the seriousness of the offense and, second, the financial resources of the accused person. If he is charged with a very grave offense, such as one

---

[1] KNEIER, C. M., "Prosecution under State Law and Municipal Ordinance as Double Jeopardy," *Cornell Law Quart.*, vol. 16, No. 2, p. 201.

[2] Grafton v. United States, 206 U. S. 333 (1907), quoted by C. M. Kneier, *op. cit.*, p. 207. It was also held in this case that trial and acquittal of an accused person by a court martial is a bar to a second trial in a Federal civil court, since they are both tribunals of the same jurisdiction.

for which the penalty is death, the temptation to "skip bail" would be too great to be overcome, no matter what its amount, and, under these circumstances, bail may properly be refused altogether. In the cases involving lesser offenses, however, the amendment by implication directs that bail shall not be refused. To demand, in such cases, an amount of bail more than the accused person could possibly furnish would constitute a requirement of excessive bail in violation of the amendment.

When a person is convicted of a criminal offense, a fine or money exaction may frequently be imposed as one form of punishment. In order to avoid conflict with the amendment, the amount of the fine should be proportionate to the seriousness of the offense. If Congress should levy a fine of twenty-five dollars for each flower picked in the parks of the District of Columbia, this would probably be held to be excessive. On the other hand, the mailing of each of a number of letters with intent to defraud may properly be regarded as a separate offense with a separate fine attached. Similarly, a separate fine of $100 may be imposed upon a railroad company for each failure to obey the order of the railroad commission, which the legislature has empowered it to issue.

Cruel and Unusual Punishment.—If, in spite of the elaborate safeguards provided in the bill of rights for the protection of a person accused of crime, he is nevertheless finally convicted, he still has the benefit of the constitutional provision that cruel and unusual punishment cannot be inflicted upon him. There are two ways in which this constitutional prohibition may be violated: first, by the imposition of punishment which is, in itself, cruel and unusual, and, second, by the imposition of punishment which, although not in itself cruel and unusual, is out of all proportion to the offense.

The unnecessary cruelty involved in such punishments as torture and lingering death has been prohibited by the amendment. Summary execution, however, whether by hanging, shooting, electrocution, or lethal gas, is not in itself a cruel and unusual punishment. It may be noted, however, that capital punishment has been abolished in some states and that, with the changing conceptions of propriety in methods of social control, punishments now generally regarded as legitimate may in time come to be considered by the public generally as cruel and unusual, and therefore unconstitutional.[1]

The amendment requires that the extent or nature of the punishment should bear some relation to the degree of the offense. A habitual-offender law, however, which inflicts a heavier penalty for the second and

---

[1] Technical terms used in the Constitution which had a meaning at common law at the time of its adoption are to be interpreted in the light of that meaning. "Cruel and unusual punishment," however, is not such a term and may, therefore, be interpreted in the light of the meaning attached to it by public opinion at the time the case arises.

later offenses does not run counter to the constitutional prohibition.[1] An example of cruel and unusual punishment which was held by the Supreme Court to violate the amendment was the provision of the Philippine Penal Code which provided that, for falsification of public records, a public official should be subject to fine and imprisonment at hard and painful labor for from twelve to twenty years, during which he should wear a chain at wrist and ankle and should be deprived of civil and political rights.[2]

Although there are now many more criminal offenses than formerly, punishments are on the whole much less severe for the lesser offenses than they were a century or more ago. Looking at the matter from the practical point of view, therefore, the elaborate safeguards for the protection of the accused, found in the bill of rights, seem now to be rather antiquated and unnecessary.

[1] McDonald v. Massachusetts, 180 U. S. 311 (1901).
[2] Weems v. United States, 217 U. S. 349 (1910).

CHAPTER XXIV

THE PROTECTION OF CIVIL RIGHTS

Certain individual rights and privileges under the Constitution are considered in other chapters. These are the rights of life, liberty, and property, the privileges of Federal and state citizenship, the right to vote, and the rights or immunities of persons accused of crime. In this chapter, a few other important civil rights, protected by the Constitution, will be considered, *viz.*, the right to freedom, religious liberty, freedom of speech and press, the right to assemble and petition for redress of grievances, and the right to bear arms.

The Right to Freedom.—At the time of the adoption of the Constitution, slavery existed to some extent in most of the states. The original Constitution did not expressly mention slavery but impliedly recognized it in several provisions, such as that regarding the return of fugitive slaves,[1] the temporary prohibition of Congressional legislation forbidding the importation of slaves,[2] and the phrase "other persons," who, in addition to all "free persons," were to be fractionally counted in determining the basis of direct taxes and representation in the lower house of Congress.[3]

Thus, as far as anything in the original Constitution was concerned, the question of slavery in the states, including its continuation, extension, modification, or abolition, was legally left with the states. In the Northwest Ordinance of 1787, however, the Confederate Congress had provided that "there shall be neither slavery nor involuntary servitude in the said territory, otherwise than in the punishment of crimes, whereof the party shall have been duly convicted." This language was almost identical with that later used in the Missouri Compromise Act of 1820 and finally in the Thirteenth Amendment itself. The Missouri Compromise Act, however, which undertook to abolish slavery and involuntary servitude in all that portion of the Louisiana Territory north of a certain degree of latitude was declared unconstitutional by the Supreme Court shortly before the Civil War, on the ground that it took property without due process of law in violation of the Fifth Amendment.[4]

[1] Art. IV, sect. 2, cl. 3.
[2] Art. I, sect. 9, cl. 1.
[3] Art. I, sect. 2, cl. 3.
[4] Dred Scott v. Sandford, 19 How. 393 (1857). This holding was, strictly speaking, *obiter* because, since the Court held that Dred Scott was not a citizen but rather a piece of property, it did not have jurisdiction to pass on the merits of the case.

After the battle of Antietam, President Lincoln determined upon the issuance of his emancipation proclamation which went into effect on the first day of 1863. This undertook to free the negroes within such territory as was occupied by the Federal armies. This was a war measure carried out under the authority of the President as commander-in-chief and was admittedly impotent to abolish slavery as a legal institution after military control had ceased. The abolition of this institution generally over the whole country and in time of peace could be accomplished only by a change in the Constitution, and the Thirteenth Amendment was accordingly adopted in 1865. This follows substantially the language of the Northwest Ordinance, quoted above, except that the spatial extent of the prohibition contained in the amendment is broadened so as to apply not only to the United States but to "any place subject to their jurisdiction." Consequently, slavery is prohibited not only in the continental area of the United States but also in our outlying territories and dependencies, whether incorporated or unincorporated.

The amendment is a limitation upon both the state and national governments, so as to prevent them from legalizing slavery or involuntary servitude. While thus withdrawing power, it at the same time grants to Congress a power not before possessed, *viz.*, that of passing legislation to enforce its provisions. The amendment is a limitation not only on governments but also on individuals, so as to prevent them from subjecting anyone to slavery or involuntary servitude, and Congress in its enforcement legislation has made criminal the action of anyone who does so. It is also to be noted that, although the amendment was intended to apply primarily to negroes, its language is broad enough to protect persons of any race, color, or nationality. Thus, it may be construed to prohibit slavery incidental to Mexican peonage or the Chinese coolie labor system.

Peonage may be defined as compulsory service based on debt and is a form of involuntary servitude prohibited by the amendment. The term is ordinarily confined to compulsory work for a private master, but the amendment has been construed by the Supreme Court broadly enough to prohibit criminal punishment for breach of a contract whereby a debtor agrees to render personal services.[1] In the case just cited the Court declared that "although the statute in terms is to punish fraud, still its natural and inevitable effect is to expose to conviction for crime those who simply fail or refuse to perform contracts for personal service in liquidation of debt." It would seem that if a state can make mere breach of contract a crime, the exception in the amendment would virtually destroy the prohibition.

In certain exceptional cases, however, breach of contract for personal services may be criminally punished or the person undertaking such service under a contract may be compelled to render them. For example,

[1] Bailey v. Alabama, 219 U. S. 219 (1911).

an act of Congress providing that a seaman who deserts his vessel in violation of his contract may be arrested and either punished by imprisonment or returned to his vessel for service has been upheld by the Supreme Court.[1] The decision was based in the main upon the fact that seamen have from time immemorial been treated as in an exceptional class and their services should therefore not be regarded as within the purview of the amendment.   Their work is also of a semipublic character.   Others who have contracted to furnish services and whose work is of a public service character are policemen, firemen, and members of a traincrew. They have no right to desert their positions during an emergency or in such a way as to endanger life or property under their charge or protection.

A servitude knowingly and willingly entered into cannot be regarded as involuntary.   Without violating the amendment, however, the state or government may require the performance of certain services not based on contract.   Thus military service may be compelled,[2] as may also jury service, and certain persons may be required to furnish a stipulated amount of labor annually upon the public highways.   Such requirements are, of course, for the public benefit and not for that of any private employer and are therefore to be regarded as legitimate exercises of the police power.   They illustrate the fact, however, that the right to freedom, like other individual rights protected by the Constitution, is relative and not absolute.

Extreme claims have sometimes been put forth as to the extent of the protection afforded by the Thirteenth Amendment. Thus, it was claimed in an early case that a state statute, which granted to a certain company a monopoly of the slaughtering business and thereby compelled others to resort to that company for the slaughtering of their cattle, reduced them to involuntary servitude.[3] This contention, however, the Court summarily brushed aside.   In the Civil Rights Acts of 1875 Congress provided that negroes should not be discriminated against in hotels, theaters, and public conveyances.   The act was supported in part upon the theory that such discrimination constitutes a badge of slavery in violation of the amendment, but the Court refused to construe the amendment so broadly and held the act unconstitutional.[4]

Religious Liberty.—Although, even in the absence of the First Amendment of the Constitution, Congress would have had no power to make a law respecting an establishment of religion, or prohibiting the free exercise

[1] Robertson v. Baldwin, 165 U. S. 275 (1897).

[2] Selective draft law cases, 245 U. S. 366 (1918).

[3] Slaughter house cases, 16 Wall. 36 (1872).

[4] Civil rights cases, 109 U. S. 3 (1883).   In a later case the Court denied that a state statute requiring separate accommodations for white and colored people on railroads violates the Thirteenth Amendment. Plessy v. Ferguson, 163 U. S. 537 (1896).

thereof, nevertheless it was deemed desirable to insert in that amendment an express limitation upon the power of Congress in this respect. Furthermore, the original Constitution had provided that "no religious test shall ever be required as a qualification to any office or public trust under the United States."[1]

Congress has never attempted to make any law for the establishment of religion, and the principle of separation of church and state has been adhered to in this country, except in the case of a few states at an early period. Congress may and has, however, enacted laws making criminal certain practices or actions opposed to public policy, even though they may be regarded by the members of some church or sect as being enjoined by their religion. The leading case on this point was one involving a statute of Congress making polygamy criminal in the territories. A member of the Mormon Church, who contracted a polygamous marriage, was tried for violating the statute but set up the defense that, since polygamy was enjoined by the doctrines of the Mormon Church, the statute was void on account of conflict with the First Amendment. The Supreme Court, however, upheld the statute, holding that the principle of religious freedom forbids interference with matters of conscience, dogma, or opinion, but that the government may interfere when such opinion breaks out into overt acts against peace or good order.[2]

In another statute Congress excluded from the right to vote in the territories all members of orders or sects that teach or encourage polygamy, and this statute was also upheld as not in violation of the First Amendment. In the course of its opinion in this case, the Court declared that the religious-freedom provision of that amendment

. . . was intended to allow every one under the jurisdiction of the United States to entertain such notions respecting his relations to his Maker and the duties they impose as may be approved by his judgment and conscience, and to exhibit his sentiments in such form of worship as he may think proper, not injurious to the equal rights of others, and to prohibit legislation for the support of any religious tenets, or the modes of worship of any sect. The oppressive measures adopted, and the cruelties and punishments inflicted by the governments of Europe for many ages, to compel parties to conform in their religious beliefs and modes of worship to the views of the most numerous sect, and the folly of attempting in that way to control the mental operations of persons, and enforce an outward conformity to a prescribed standard, led to the adoption of the amendment in question. It was never intended or supposed that the amendment could be invoked as a protection against legislation for the punishment of acts inimical to the peace, good order, and morals of society. With man's relations to his Maker and the obligations he may think they impose, and the manner in which an expression shall be made by him of his beliefs on those subjects, no interference can be permitted, provided always the laws of

[1] Art. VI, cl. 3.
[2] Reynolds v. United States, 98 U. S. 145 (1878).

society, designed to secure its peace and prosperity, and the morals of its people, are not interfered with. However free the exercise of religion may be, it must be subordinate to the criminal laws of the country, passed with reference to actions regarded by general consent as properly the subjects of punitive legislation.[1]

Thus it appears that religious liberty is a relative and not an absolute right. No one is at liberty to indulge in antisocial practices and shield himself from the consequences by hiding behind religion. Otherwise, every man would be a law unto himself.

In the Selective Draft Act, passed by Congress in 1917, certain classes of persons, including ministers of religion and members of religious sects whose doctrines forbid participation in war, were exempted from regular military service. The act was attacked on the ground, among others, that this exemption was a violation of the religious-liberty provision of the First Amendment, but this contention the Court summarily brushed aside.[2]

The provisions of the First Amendment, like those of the first eight amendments generally, are limitations on the National Government and not on the states. There is nothing in the First Amendment which prevents a state from enacting a law respecting an establishment of religion, nor does that amendment protect the citizens of a state against a state statute infringing on their religious liberties. A state statute, however, providing for the establishment of religion or favoring one religious sect over another would doubtless violate the equal-protection-of-the-laws clause of the Fourteenth Amendment. Moreover, the states generally have in their own constitutions provisions similar to the religious liberty clause of the First Amendment.

Within the limits of the state constitutional provisions, the states may exempt property used for religious purposes from taxation, provided, of course, no discrimination is made for or against the property of any particular religious sect or denomination. Charitable institutions, such as orphanages, operated by or under the supervision of a religious denomination are also sometimes exempted from taxation, provided, at least, persons in need of such charity are received as inmates regardless of their religious affiliations. In some states appropriations for public financial aid to charitable institutions maintained under denominational auspices is forbidden, while in other states it is permitted on the basis of a proportional payment per inmate, provided no one is excluded merely on the ground of his religious beliefs.[3]

A state statute which requires a parent to provide medical treatment for a child suffering from disease is not unconstitutional, even if not in

[1] Davis v. Beason, 133 U. S. 333 (1890).
[2] Selective draft law cases, 245 U. S. 366 (1918).
[3] *Cf.* Trost v. Manual Training School, 118 N. E. 743 (1918).

accordance with the religious tenets of the parent. State statutes setting aside Sunday as a day of rest and prohibiting labor on that day, except work of necessity, have generally been upheld. Such decisions have been based not on the religious requirement of the observance of the Sabbath, but rather on the secular idea that one day of rest in seven conduces to the well-being of society and the day to be selected by the law for this purpose may be the one favored by the preponderant majority of the people.

On the question of the reading of the Bible in the public schools, the courts are badly divided. Since such schools are maintained at public expense, the courts of some states hold that the reading of the Bible therein is unconstitutional because it virtually places the taxpayer under the obligation to support religious worship.[1] In other states the courts take the view that the Bible may be regarded as a textbook with a legitimate place in the school curriculum.[2]

Freedom of Speech and Press.[3]—The First Amendment provides that "Congress shall make no law . . . abridging the freedom of speech or of the press." The adoption of this amendment was brought about through the leadership of such men as Madison and Jefferson, who felt that the original Constitution was deficient in not protecting these fundamental rights against possible encroachment by the new National Government.

Twenty-five years before the adoption of this amendment, Blackstone laid down the rule that

. . . the liberty of the press . . . consists in laying no previous restraints upon publications and not in freedom of censure from criminal matter when published. Every freeman has an undoubted right to lay what sentiments he pleases before the public; to forbid this is to destroy the freedom of the press; but if he publishes what is improper, mischievous or illegal, he must take the consequence of his own temerity.[4]

This was the established rule of the common law both in England and also in the American colonies. Undoubtedly, the First Amendment was intended at least to prevent Congress from enacting a law providing for a censorship or previous restraint upon publication. It seems clear, however, that the framers of this amendment intended to establish in America a more liberal rule respecting this particular right than that embodied in the common law, for, as has been pointed out, "the liberty of the press might be rendered a mockery and a delusion, and the phrase itself a by-word, if, while every man was at liberty to publish what he pleased, the

---

[1] *Cf.* People v. Board of Education, 245 Ill. 334 (1910).

[2] Church v. Bullock, 104 Tex. 1 (1904), and *cf.* Evans v. Selma Union High School District, 222 Pac. 801 (1924).

[3] For the special freedom of speech accorded to legislators, see pp. 98–99.

[4] *Commentaries*, vol. 4, pp. 151, 152.

public authorities might nevertheless punish him for harmless publications."[1]   Madison went so far as to declare that "to the press alone, chequered as it is with abuses, the world is indebted for all the triumphs which have been gained by reason and humanity over error and oppression."[2]   It has come to be generally recognized that popular government cannot be maintained except upon the basis of free discussion of public questions, which may involve criticism of governmental policies.

On the other hand, it must not be supposed that the First Amendment establishes a right of exemption from responsibility for what one publishes, either orally or by written or printed word.   Here, as in the case of other individual rights, the right of free speech is not absolute but rather is relative to circumstances and conditions.   The extent of one person's right of free speech, for example, is limited by the correlative right of other persons to reputation.   The law of slander and libel has not been abolished.   The purveyor of baseless and malicious charges which injure another's reputation lays himself open to a civil suit for damages.   Such charges may also constitute the public offense of seditious libel, when directed against the government or its officers, and may render the libeler subject to criminal punishment.   If, however, the stated charges are not baseless or malicious but are published for the promotion of the general welfare, this would usually be considered an adequate defense, at least against a suit for damages.   Moreover, well-founded charges of official misconduct may create a public scandal, but to penalize the person who publicly but without malice calls attention to such misconduct would ordinarily be a more serious evil.

Again, the relative or conditional nature of the right of free speech is shown by the fact that it may not be exercised in such a way as to endanger the public safety or morals.   This supposed right would not protect a man who falsely raises a cry of fire in a crowded theater so as to cause a panic, especially if there is nothing to lead a reasonable man to suppose that a fire exists.   Moreover, it would not protect a man who corrupts public morals by publishing obscene matter, especially if circulated among immature persons.   "A state, in the exercise of its police power, may punish those who abuse this freedom by utterances inimical to the public welfare, tending to corrupt public morals, incite to crime, or disturb the public peace."[3]   Congress may also prohibit the sending of obscene or defamatory matter or lottery advertisements through the mails.

Again, the ancient rule that the safety of the state is the highest law still operates.   The constitutional safeguard of free speech "does not deprive a state of the primary and essential right of self-preservation,

---

[1] COOLEY, *Constitutional Limitations*, 8th ed., vol. 2, p. 885.
[2] Madison's *Works*, vol. 4, p. 544.
[3] Gitlow v. New York, 268 U. S. 652 (1925).

which, so long as human governments endure, they cannot be denied."[1] Consequently, the constitutional right of free speech and press does not protect a person who publishes seditious or treasonable statements intended to bring about revolution or the overthrow of the government, or who is not content with merely criticising a law and advising its repeal or modification but advocates or encourages its violation.[2] This is especially true in time of war, for, as has been pointed out, words may sometimes have all the effect of force.

Free Speech in War Time.—The discussion, both judicial and popular, with reference to the scope and effect of the constitutional safeguards of free speech and press, has occurred principally during time of war or of public danger and excitement. In 1798, there was considerable public excitement over the foreign policy of the Adams administration, which led to such bitter attacks upon it that, in the opinion of the Federalists, the safety of the government was endangered. Consequently, in that year Congress passed the Sedition Act, one section of which provided criminal punishment for anyone who published false and malicious statements with intent to defame the Government, Congress, or the President, or to bring them into contempt or disrepute or to excite hatred against them. Several convictions under this act were obtained in the lower Federal courts, but its constitutionality was not passed upon by the Supreme Court and it expired by self-limitation in 1801. The act aroused widespread popular indignation, especially among the Anti-Federalists. The section mentioned was generally regarded as unconstitutional, and Congress subsequently remitted the fines of persons convicted under it. The Virginia and Kentucky resolutions were drafted in protest against the assumption of power by Congress embodied in the act.

In spite of the political reaction which resulted from the Sedition Act of 1798, the lesson of that incident seems not to have been learned, and the same extreme measures were adopted by the government during the World War. The Espionage Act of 1917, however, was comparatively mild. It prohibited the making of false statements intended to interfere with the successful prosecution of the war and also prohibited acts obstructing recruiting or causing insubordination in the military and naval forces of the United States. This act was upheld as constitutional by the Supreme Court, in a unanimous decision.[3] Justice Holmes, speaking for the Court, laid down the rule that "the question in every case is whether the words used are used in such circumstances and are of such a nature as to create a clear and present danger that they will bring

[1] *Ibid.*
[2] United States v. Burleson, 255 U. S. 407 (1921).
[3] Schenck v. United States, 249 U. S. 47 (1919).

about the substantive evils that Congress has a right to prevent.   It is a question of proximity and degree."

The Espionage Act, however, was not deemed by the Government to go far enough, and consequently in 1918 the more drastic Sedition Act was passed.[1]   In addition to the prohibitions of the Espionage Act, this Sedition Act provided severe penalties for those who,

> . . . when the United States is at war, shall willfully utter, print, write, or publish any disloyal, profane, scurrilous, or abusive language about the form of government of the United States, or the Constitution of the United States, or the military or naval forces of the United States, or the flag of the United States, or the uniform of the army or navy of the United States, or any language intended to bring the form of government of the United States, or the Constitution of the United States, or the military or naval forces of the United States, or the flag of the United States, or the uniform of the army or navy of the United States into contempt, scorn, contumely or disrepute.

In addition, the postmaster-general was given authority to prevent the use of the mails by anyone in violation of the provisions of the act.

The Sedition Act of 1918 seems broad enough to overthrow the doctrine of fair comment on public affairs and of legitimate criticism of public policies which had been supposed to be set up by the First Amendment and, indeed, to underlie democratic government.   When the act came before the Supreme Court for adjudication, that tribunal abandoned the "clear and present danger" test which had been adopted in the Schenck case and set up in its stead the "remote and indirect tendency" test, by which almost any criticism of the government could be brought within the prohibition of the Sedition Act, especially when such tendency was itself held to show the defendant's intent to bring about the evils specified in the act.[2]

It is true that many things which could be freely said in time of peace without harm may be validly forbidden in time of war.   As already pointed out, the right of free speech and press is relative to time and circumstance, and this relativity of the right is especially illustrated in time of war when men's passions run high.   Then, Congress has implied power to do everything which may be conducive to the winning of the war, even to the extent of limiting those expressions of opinion which may interfere with its successful conduct.   The power of Congress to limit free expression is greater in time of war because of the greater danger confronting the country.   As Justice Holmes has declared, "When a nation is at war many things that might be said in time of peace are such a hindrance to its effort that their utterance will not be endured so long as

[1] 40 Stat. at L. 553.
[2] Debs v. United States, 249 U. S. 211 (1919); Abrams v. United States, 250 U. S. 616 (1919).

men fight and that no court could regard them as protected by any constitutional right."[1] Nevertheless, even during time of war, as the Supreme Court declared shortly after the Civil War, the provisions of the Federal bill of rights are not suspended.[2] It was certainly true, however, that during the World War, limitation of freedom of expression went much farther than had been supposed constitutionally possible—farther than necessary, it would seem in the soberer light of postwar years. As Justice Holmes pointed out in his dissenting opinion in the Abrams case, "only the emergency that makes it immediately dangerous to leave the correction of evil counsels to time warrants making any exception to the sweeping command" of the First Amendment. Again, as he aptly remarked, "with effervescing opinions, as with not yet forgotten champagnes, the quickest way to let them get flat is to let them get exposed to the air."

Free Speech in Peace Time.—The Sedition Act of 1918 was in terms limited to time of war. It seems probable that, in time of peace, such extreme limitation on freedom of expression as that act contained would not generally be upheld by the courts. Nevertheless, in the first peace-time case involving free speech to come before the Supreme Court, that tribunal upheld a conviction under the New York Criminal Anarchy Act of 1902.[3] It is true that, as already pointed out, the First Amendment does not apply to nor limit the states. None the less, the term "liberty" as used in the due-process clause of the Fourteenth Amendment had been broadly enough construed so that it might include the concept of free speech and press as embodied in the First Amendment. This, in fact, was the position which the Court took in the Gitlow case, holding that "freedom of speech and of the press—which are protected by the First Amendment from abridgment by Congress—are among the fundamental personal rights and 'liberties' protected by the due-process clause of the Fourteenth Amendment from impairment by the states."

Gitlow, the defendant in this case, was indicted under the state act for circulating various writings advocating the adoption of violent measures against the Government in order to secure the rights of the working class. There was no evidence, however, that these writings had any concrete result or effect. The Court nevertheless upheld the constitutionality of the state law as a reasonable exercise of the police power of the state for the protection of its peace and safety against threatened danger. The Court adopted the state legislature's determination that the natural tendency and probable effect of the prohibited writings were to bring about the substantive evil which the legislative body might prevent. The Court thus followed the "remote and indirect

[1] Schenck v. United States, 249 U. S. 47 (1919).
[2] *Ex parte* Milligan, 4 Wall. 2 (1866).
[3] Gitlow v. New York, 268 U. S. 652 (1925).

tendency" test laid down in the Abrams case. Justices Holmes and Brandeis dissented, the former declaring that

. . . there was no present danger of an attempt to overthrow the government by force on the part of the admittedly small minority who shared the defendant's views . . . If, in the long run, the beliefs expressed in proletarian dictatorship are destined to be accepted by the dominant forces of the community, the only meaning of free speech is that they should be given their chance and have their way.

After the passions aroused by the World War had died down, the Supreme Court began to show a more liberal attitude in its interpretation of the constitutional safeguards of free speech and press. Thus, in 1931, two significant cases were decided. The first was that in which the Court reversed the conviction of one Yetta Stromberg for violating the California "red flag" law.[1] This law prohibited the display of a red flag as a symbol or emblem of opposition to organized government. The Court, speaking by Mr. Chief Justice Hughes, recognized emphatically that the state may punish "those who indulge in utterances which incite to violence and crime and threaten the overthrow of organized government by unlawful means." It held, however, that the conviction could not be sustained because the provision of the law cited was too ambiguous and indefinite and might be construed to prohibit peaceful and orderly opposition to government by legal means. The Court then went on to declare that:

The maintenance of the opportunity for free political discussion to the end that government may be responsive to the will of the people and that changes may be obtained by lawful means, an opportunity essential to the security of the Republic, is a fundamental principle of our constitutional system. A statute which upon its face, and as authoritatively construed, is so vague and indefinite as to permit the punishment of the fair use of this opportunity is repugnant to the guaranty of liberty contained in the Fourteenth Amendment.[2]

The decision in the California red flag case foreshadowed the decision rendered shortly afterwards in an even more important case—that involving the Minnesota "press gag" law.[3] This law, enacted in 1925, provided for the abatement, as a public nuisance, of a "malicious, scandalous, and defamatory" newspaper or other periodical, and anyone guilty of maintaining such a nuisance might be enjoined. The statute thus provided a separate and distinct remedy from a suit for libel. Under this statute, action was brought to enjoin the publication of *The Saturday Press* of Minneapolis, which was alleged to contain malicious, scandalous, and defamatory articles charging the mayor, chief of police, and other

[1] Stromberg v. California, 283 U. S. 359 (1931).
[2] Justices McReynolds and Butler dissented.
[3] Near v. Minnesota *ex rel.* Olson, 283 U. S. 697 (1931).

public officials with participation in graft and neglect of duty. No proof was offered to show that the charges were untrue, and, under the statute, it was not necessary to prove this in order to obtain an injunction. Nor was it necessary to prove malice in fact, but malice was inferred from the mere publication of the defamatory matter. The injunction was issued by the lower state court, affirmed by the state supreme court, and, from this judgment, the defendant appealed to the Supreme Court of the United States.

In a five-to-four decision, Mr. Chief Justice Hughes again delivering the opinion, the Federal Supreme Court, without going into the question of the truth of the charges made in the defendant's newspaper, reversed the judgment of the state court and held that the statute was an unconstitutional restraint upon publication and an infringement of the liberty of the press guaranteed by the Fourteenth Amendment. One of the chief ingredients of that guarantee, the Court pointed out, is the prevention of censorship or previous restraints upon publication. The statute in question not only operated to suppress offending newspapers but put the publisher under an effective censorship, because, unless the publisher could satisfy the judge that the charges are true and made with good motives and for justifiable ends, his newspaper is suppressed and further publication made punishable as contempt of court. This the Court held to be the essence of censorship.

The Court admitted that punishment for the abuse of the liberty accorded to the press is essential to the protection of the public but held that the proper remedy for abuse of the liberty is a damage suit for libel when merely the reputation of private individuals is injured, or a prosecution for criminal or seditious libel when illegal and unreasonable attacks are made on the government or its officers, or even punishment for contempt of court when publications directly tend to prevent the proper discharge of judicial functions. The statute in question, however, did not deal with punishment but with suppression and restraint upon publication. In conclusion, the Court pointed out that "the fact that the liberty of the press may be abused by miscreant purveyors of scandal does not make any the less necessary the immunity of the press from previous restraint in dealing with official misconduct."

In this liberal and enlightened decision, the Supreme Court reinvigorated the principle of a free press as applied, at least, to time of peace.

Freedom of Assembly and Petition.—The First Amendment also provides that Congress shall make no law abridging "the right of the people peaceably to assemble, and to petition the government for a redress of grievances." It is hardly necessary to say that this, like the other provisions of the bill of rights, is a limitation on the National Government and not on the states. The amendment does not create these rights but merely undertakes to protect them against interference by

Congress. If the people assemble to petition Congress for a redress of grievances, or for anything connected with the powers and duties of the National Government, they are exercising a privilege of national citizenship, which is under the protection of, and guaranteed by, the United States.[1]

The rights of peaceable assembly and petition are properly regarded as implied in the very idea of democratic government. Nevertheless, like other individual rights, they are not absolute but relative. Riotous or disorderly assemblies are not protected by the amendment. The right of assembly is limited by the reasonable exercise of the police power for the protection of public health, safety, morals, or convenience. Moreover, in time of war it would seem that petitions of a sort that would be harmless in time of peace may be forbidden, although this is a doctrine which may be carried to dangerous extremes. Finally, it may be noted that the right of petition seems to carry with it no legal requirement that the petition shall be considered. This was illustrated by the fate of the numerous anti-slavery petitions presented to Congress before the Civil War. The remedy in such cases is not legal but political.

The Right to Bear Arms.—The Second Amendment provides that "a well regulated militia, being necessary to the security of a free state, the right of the people to keep and bear arms, shall not be infringed." The right to bear arms is not granted by this amendment, but it merely prohibits Congress from abridging the right. The word "arms" as used here refers to the ordinary arms of a soldier and is used in the military sense. It does not refer to such weapons as daggers or pistols which are used in private affrays. The amendment is not violated by laws prohibiting the carrying of concealed weapons[2] or of weapons capable of being concealed.

The purpose underlying this amendment is indicated by its language, *viz.*, to obtain security through a well-regulated militia, which the framers considered to be the best substitute for the dreaded standing army. The amendment prevents Congress from disarming the state militia. Although it does not limit the states, nevertheless it may be noted that the paramount control over the militia is vested in Congress by virtue of its military powers granted in the Constitution.[3]

Finally, it is of interest to note that the Second Amendment, as originally drafted, contained a proviso that "no person religiously scrupulous of bearing arms shall be compelled to render military service in person," but this proviso was eliminated before the Amendment was submitted for ratification.

[1] United States v. Cruikshank, 92 U. S. 542 (1875).

[2] Robertson v. Baldwin, 165 U. S. 275 (1897). *Cf.* Presser v. Illinois, 116 U. S. 252 (1886); Miller v. Texas, 153 U. S. 535 (1894).

[3] Art. I, sect. 8, cl. 16. *Cf.* Houston v. Moore, 5 Wheat. 1. (1820).

CHAPTER XXV

THE PROTECTION OF CONTRACTS

A contract is a mutual and legally enforceable agreement between at least two parties whereby each or both undertake to do or to refrain from doing certain things. In order to be valid in the eyes of the law, there must be a consideration on both sides. Contracts may be of various kinds: express and implied, written and unwritten, executory and executed. The parties may be the United States, the states or governmental sub-divisions thereof, corporations, and individuals. The conduct of modern business and society in general is largely based on contract. Most contracts are complied with without question through the good faith of the parties. But this is not always sufficient, and, unless there were some legal means of enforcing contracts, great uncertainty and insecurity in everyday relations would exist. The state and national governments, therefore, through their courts and other law-enforcing agencies, under-take to secure the enforcement of valid contracts. If a party to a valid contract fails to perform the obligation which he has assumed thereunder, the other party, provided he is not also delinquent in the performance of his obligation, has one or both of two kinds of remedies. He may sue in a law court for damages, or he may sue in a court of equity for a writ of specific performance. The latter remedy would be granted in certain cases where the award of damages would not be an adequate remedy, or where the proper amount of damages could not be estimated.

In several of the states, prior to the adoption of the Federal Constitution, state bankruptcy laws were passed in order to relieve the condition of debtors and the obligation of contracts was impaired through laws making depreciated paper money a legal tender in payment of debts. Such money, it seems, was not issued in Massachusetts, but in 1786 a rebellion broke out in that state under the leadership of one Daniel Shays for the purpose of compelling the issue of credit money by that state. The framers of the Constitution thought that something should be done to protect creditors from the effects of such laws and it was doubtless this situation which led them to incorporate into the Constitution a provision which declares that "no state shall pass any law impairing the obligation of contracts."[1] It will be noticed that this prohibition rests merely on the states and the framers placed no such prohibition in the Constitution upon the National Government, probably because they supposed that

[1] Art. I, sect. 10, cl. 1.

371

ordinary business relationships would be regulated by the states rather than by the National Government. The term liberty, however, as used in the Fifth Amendment, as well as in the Fourteenth, includes the right to enter into contracts. Thus, both the national and state governments are forbidden to deprive any person of this right without due process of law. Assuming, however, that there is no denial of due process, the National Government may impair contract obligations, as in the instance of the legal tender acts.

A contract when entered into is a form of property, the right to which the due-process clauses of the Fifth and Fourteenth Amendments also protect against illegal infringement or confiscation by the national and state governments. Such property as well as other kinds may be taken by the National Government under its power of eminent domain, but in such case the Fifth Amendment requires that just compensation shall be paid.

The contract clause of the Constitution has been the subject of interpretation in the Supreme Court more frequently than any other limitation upon the states except that relating to due process. On the whole it has been liberally construed by the Court and has not been confined in its application to the special evils which the framers intended to prevent.

State Legislation Only Prohibited.—Courts and judges may be considered for practical purposes to be to some extent law-making agencies, and this is even true also in the case of executive and administrative bodies and officers. Their action may, however, impair the obligation of a contract without violating the contract clause of the Constitution. After rendering a decision on the strength of which contracts have been made, the court may come to the conclusion that it was mistaken and may reverse itself in a subsequent case. The obligation of such contracts is impaired, but the contract clause has not been violated. The act of a corporation or private individual in rendering a contract unenforceable and thus impairing its obligation is also, of course, not prohibited by this clause. The words "pass a law" as used in this clause refer to the action of a state legislature in enacting a law, or similar action taken by the legislative body of a political subdivision of the state, such as a municipal council. The action of the people of a state in adopting a constitution or amendments thereto would also come within the meaning of the contract clause.

When Is the Obligation of a Contract Impaired?—The obligation of a contract may be defined as the legally enforceable duty which one of the parties assumes at the time of entering into the agreement and the right of the other party to a remedy at law or in equity in case of a failure to perform such duty. More briefly, it may be defined as the law which binds the parties to perform their agreement. If the obligation which was assumed by either party to a contract was enforceable by the law as it stood at the time the contract was made, but the legislature subsequently changes the law so that the contract is no longer legally enforceable, the obligation of the contract has been impaired. The contract clause means that no state shall pass a law which conflicts with the law binding the parties to perform the contract. Furthermore, even if the subsequent law does not make the contract absolutely unenforceable but does make it decidedly more difficult to enforce, the obligation has been impaired. By parity of reasoning, it is also true that the obligation has been impaired if adequate remedy for the enforcement of the contract has been taken away. Not every change in the remedy, however, impairs the obligation. Thus, at one time it was possible in some states for a creditor to have a debtor put in jail for failure to pay the debt. An act of the legislature abolishing imprisonment for debt even as applied to preexisting debts was held to be constitutional, because the creditor still retained the generally adequate remedy of suing the debtor in a court of law.[1]

The contract clause was probably intended to apply primarily to contracts between individuals. Under the Constitution the states have the power, concurrently with Congress, of enacting bankruptcy or insolvency laws. These are laws which compel a creditor to accept, in full discharge of the bankrupt debtor's liability, less than the total amount of the debt due him. They are intended not so much to relieve the debtor of further liability, as to assure the creditor of receiving his *pro rata* share of the bankrupt debtor's assets. Although, in 1898, Congress passed a law covering this subject which had the effect of setting aside or suspending state bankruptcy laws, the matter had previously been to some extent regulated by the states. The contract clause of the Constitution, however, prevented state bankruptcy laws from having retroactive operation, so as to invalidate contracts already made, but did not prevent the application of such laws to future contracts. A contract made after the enactment of the state bankruptcy law was not impaired thereby, because the law was impliedly a part of the contract. These propositions were laid down by the Supreme Court in early cases in which the defendant had executed certain promissory notes prior to the enactment of the state bankruptcy law which was in terms applicable to the discharge of both past as well as future insolvent debtors. The Court held, however, that while the law was valid as to future debts, it ran counter to the contract clause of the Constitution and was therefore invalid in so far as it applied to debts contracted before the enactment of the law.[2] Although state bankruptcy laws are now suspended, since

---

[1] Beers v. Houghton, 9 Pet. 329 (1835).

[2] Sturges v. Crowninshield, 4 Wheat. 117 (1819); Ogden v. Saunders, 12 Wheat. 213 (1827).

Congress has taken over this field of legislation, under its general grant of power to pass bankruptcy laws, nevertheless, as pointed out above, contracts are a form of property the right to which is protected against illegal impairment or confiscation on the part of the Federal Government by the due-process clause of the Fifth Amendment. A discharge under Federal bankruptcy law, however, will relieve the insolvent debtor of liability under contract debts made both before and after the enactment of such Federal law.

Contracts to Which a State Is a Party.—The first case in which the interpretation of the contract clause came before the Supreme Court was that of Fletcher v. Peck,[1] decided in 1810. The facts of this case were that in 1795 the legislature of the state of Georgia passed a bill granting to one James Gunn and others a large tract of land. Subsequently it came to light that the passage of the bill had been secured through bribery and corruption. Thereupon the legislature, in order if possible to wipe out this blot upon the good name of the state, passed another act annulling and rescinding the law under which the conveyance to the original grantees had been made. Meanwhile, however, the land had passed into the hands of innocent purchasers, who contested the validity of the rescinding act on the ground that the original grant was a contract the obligation of which the rescinding act unconstitutionally impaired. Chief Justice Marshall, in rendering the opinion of the Court, pointed out that there were two principal questions to be decided. The first question was as to whether a grant made by a state to an individual in the form of a legislative act is a contract within the meaning of the contract clause of the Constitution. The second question was as to whether that clause applies to executed as well as to executory contracts. Chief Justice Marshall answered both of these questions in the affirmative.

As pointed out above, the contract clause was probably intended to apply primarily to contracts between individuals. If so, judicial interpretation has expanded it so as to include contracts to which a state is a party. It was doubtless natural that Marshall, considering his strong tendency in the direction of increasing national power while limiting that of the states, should have seized this opportunity of construing the contract clause so as to cover not only contracts between individuals but also those to which a state is a party.

Since the adoption of the Fourteenth Amendment in 1868, the construction of the contract clause by the court in Fletcher v. Peck as covering executed contracts is probably not of much significance since such contracts are a form of property the right to which is protected by that amendment against illegal impairment or confiscation by a state.

[1] 6 Cranch 87.

State Bonds.—Although the contract clause of the Constitution applies to contracts to which a state is a party, it is nevertheless true that an individual who has a contract with the state may not always be able to compel the state by legal means to observe the terms of the contract. Thus, an individual or corporation may have a contract with the state to build an addition to the state capitol. In case of difference of opinion between the state and the contractor as to the amount of compensation which the latter should receive, he has no right to sue the state without its consent. Again, if the state fails to pay the interest on one of its bonds or the principal of the bond when it falls due, the holder, if an individual, whether a citizen of that state or of another state, cannot compel payment by suit against the state without its consent. If, however, the bond is held by another state, suit may be brought. Many states have passed laws providing for suits to be brought against them by individual claimants, and such laws may be in force at the time the contract is made or the bond is issued. Nevertheless, there also exists at the same time the general principle of law that the state is not suable by individuals without its consent. Consequently if, during the life of the bond, the state repeals the law allowing itself to be sued by individuals, such repealing law does not unconstitutionally impair the obligation of the contract. In such case, the individual bondholder has no direct legal remedy against the state. In collateral proceedings, however, he may have some remedy. If, at the time the bond was issued, a law was on the statute books providing for levying a tax, the proceeds from which were to be devoted to paying the interest on the bond and to providing a sinking fund to liquidate the principal of the bond when due, a repeal of this law prior to the maturity of the bond could doubtless be successfully attacked in court as an unconstitutional impairment of the obligation of the contract.

Municipal Bonds.—A municipal corporation is in a different position from a state, inasmuch as it is suable by individuals without its consent. Consequently, an ordinance passed by a city council which purported to make invalid bonds of the city which were valid at the time they were issued would render the city liable to suit in which such ordinance would be held to be in violation of the contract clause. Violation of the clause, however, is likely to be brought about by more indirect methods. This is illustrated by a case which arose shortly after the Civil War. The city of Quincy, Illinois, issued bonds in aid of railroads under the authority of an act of the state legislature which provided for the levying of a special tax upon the property in the city, the proceeds of which should be devoted to paying the interest on the bonds. A subsequent act of the legislature reduced the city's taxing powers to such an extent that the proceeds were insufficient to pay the interest on the bonds in addition to the general running expenses of the city. One Von Hoffman, a holder of one of the bonds, sued for a writ of mandamus to compel the city and its officers to levy the taxes as provided in the original act, notwithstanding the later repealing act. The Supreme Court of the United States granted his petition, holding that the repealing act was unconstitutional, because in conflict with the contract clause of the Constitution of the United States.[1]

It follows from this case that laws providing for levying taxes, the proceeds of which are applicable to the payment of municipal debts, are a part of the obligation of the contract and a repeal of such laws is unconstitutional. The usual remedy is a writ of mandamus directed to the taxing officers of the city to proceed under the original taxing laws. If a city is annexed to another or two cities are consolidated, the holders of the bonds of the two cities have a right to look to the consolidated city to discharge the obligations under the bonds, and any state law which undertakes to prevent them from doing so would unconstitutionally impair the obligation of the contract debt. If, however, a municipal corporation should be abolished and no new municipality erected in its place, or if the taxing officers of a city should resign and no new officers be elected in their places, holders of the bonds of such city would be unable to compel their payment by judicial process during the continuance of such conditions.

The Dartmouth College Case.—This case, known as Trustees of Dartmouth College v. Woodward[2] and decided by the Supreme Court in 1819, is the leading case on the interpretation of the contract clause and has also other features of special interest. The charter of Dartmouth College, granted by the English Crown in 1769, created a board of trustees of twelve members, with authority to choose its president and to fill vacancies in its membership by cooptation. In 1816, the legislature of New Hampshire passed an act amending the charter in such a way as to bring the board of trustees and the college under state control. The board was enlarged, the additional members to be appointed by the governor of New Hampshire and a state board of overseers was created with power to inspect and control the most important acts of the trustees. The old trustees refused to recognize the validity of the statute of 1816 and, having lost their suit in the New Hampshire state court, carried the case by writ of error to the Supreme Court of the United States. In the latter court, Daniel Webster appeared as attorney for the old trustees, making an able and justly celebrated argument, and Chief Justice Marshall rendered the opinion of the Court.

There were two questions involved in the case: first, whether the charter of the college was a contract the obligation of which could not be impaired without violating the Constitution of the United States and,

[1] Von Hoffman v. Quincy, 4 Wall. 535 (1866).
[2] 4 Wheat. 518 (1819).

second, if so, whether its obligation had been impaired by the New Hampshire statute of 1816. Marshall answered both of these questions in the affirmative, holding that the college was a private eleemosynary corporation and not a state institution.

The general doctrine of the Dartmouth College case still stands. Like the case of Fletcher v. Peck, it holds that the contract clause extends to contracts to which a state is a party, but it is broader than the latter case in that it extends the meaning of the contract clause so as to cover charters or franchises granted by the state to private corporations. The chief justice admits that it is quite probable that such an extension was not within the intention of the framers of the Constitution. He answers this objection, however, by saying that

. . . it is not enough to say that this particular case was not in the mind of the convention when the article was framed, nor of the American people when it was adopted. It is necessary to go further, and to say that, had this particular case been suggested, the language would have been so varied as to exclude it, or it would have been made a special exception.

This principle of interpretation is frequently invoked by the courts.

Although the particular corporation involved in the Dartmouth College case was an eleemosynary corporation, the rule has since been extended to private commercial corporations organized for profit.

Grants Which Are Not Contracts.—Had the college been a public institution, such as a state university, admittedly the decision would have been different. The chief justice also admitted that the contract clause of the Constitution was not intended to restrain the states in the regulation of their civil institutions, adopted for internal government. In other words, the charter of a municipal corporation is not a contract within the meaning of this clause. He also allowed as an exception the general right of the state legislature to legislate on the subject of divorces. It may even grant a divorce unless restrained by the state constitution from doing so.[1] Marriage, although a contract, is also a status and does not come within the meaning of the contract clause. Another exception is a license granted by a state or city, which is not a contract within the meaning of the clause but is the grant of a special privilege which may be legally withdrawn at the pleasure of the grantor, because the subject matter covered by the license falls within the scope of the police power, which may not be contracted away. An example of such a license was the charter granted by the legislature of Mississippi in 1867 to conduct a lottery. The Court, in holding that the legislature might withdraw the grant, said:

All that one can get by such a charter is suspension of certain governmental rights in his favor, subject to withdrawal at will. He has in legal effect nothing

[1] Maynard v. Hill, 125 U. S. 190 (1888).

more than a license to enjoy the privilege on the terms named for the specified time, unless it is sooner abrogated by the sovereign power of the state. It is a permit, good as against existing laws, but subject to future legislative and constitutional control or withdrawal.[1]

Still another exception is that an office holder does not have a vested right to the office by virtue of a contract with the state, and the state may therefore remove him from office prior to the expiration of his term without violating the contract clause of the Constitution. The clause does, however, protect his claim to the salary which he earned while holding the office.

The Rule of Strict Construction.—The doctrine of the Dartmouth College case was subjected to much criticism on the ground that it enables the legislatures to make irrevocable grants of special privileges which are against public policy. On account of the value of such grants, it may also tend to promote bribery and corruption of the legislature. Even in the absence of bribery, the legislature may sometimes make reckless and improvident grants. Although the courts have not overturned the doctrine of the case, they have adopted the rule of strict construction of all legislative grants, of denying that substantial privileges may be granted by implication, and of resolving doubts as to the meaning of grants in favor of the state and against the private corporations, especially those organized for private profit.

It was natural and fitting that the leading case in which this view was adopted was one in which the opinion was handed down by Chief Justice Taney, who was a much stronger believer in the desirability of maintaining the powers of the states than was Chief Justice Marshall. The case in question was the Charles River bridge case, decided in 1837.[2] In 1785, the legislature of Massachusetts had passed a law granting to the proprietors of the Charles River bridge a franchise to construct a bridge and to collect tolls therefrom for a period of seventy years. In 1828, the legislature granted another franchise to the proprietors of the Warren bridge empowering them to construct another bridge within a few rods of the first bridge and providing that in not more than six years it should become a free bridge. The latter grant had the effect of destroying the value of the franchise of the Charles River bridge, whose proprietors sought to enjoin the erection and use of the Warren bridge, claiming that by implication the grant made to them was an exclusive one, and that the grant to the proprietors of the Warren bridge therefore impaired the obligation of their contract with the state. The Supreme Court denied that the state was bound by any such supposed implication and refused to issue the injunction. In applying the rule of strict construction, the

---

[1] Stone v. Mississippi, 101 U. S. 814 (1879).
[2] Charles River Bridge v. Warren Bridge, 11 Pet. 420.

Court held that grants of special privileges must be clearly and expressly made. When it is doubtful whether certain rights have been granted, the interests of the general public as represented by the state require that the rights should be considered as not having been granted, and the obligation of the contract is not impaired by the passage of laws based on the assumption that the rights in question have not been granted. The rule thus laid down has been consistently followed by the courts.

State Reservation of Right of Revocation.—Although the doctrine of strict construction is of some assistance to the state in maintaining its regulatory powers, it is of no help in cases where there is no doubt that special privileges have been granted. In order to overcome the hindering effect of the contract clause in preventing a state from altering corporate charters or revoking rights granted therein, it has become the usual practice of the states to insert in their constitutions or general laws provisions to the effect that the grant of all special privileges in corporate charters is made subject to the right of the state to alter or revoke such privileges at its pleasure. If the state then elects to exercise such a right, the obligation of the contract is not impaired, because the law reserving to the state this right is impliedly as much a part of the contract as if it had been expressly stipulated therein. Such a reservation by the state thus effectively evades the limitation of the contract clause, but it does not follow that the state is free to revoke any or all privileges it has granted, for to do so may adversely affect property rights in violation of the due-process clause of the Fourteenth Amendment.

May the State Deprive Itself by Contract of Essential Governmental Powers?—In cases, however, where the state has not undertaken to reserve a right of revocation or alteration, the question may arise as to whether one state legislature may so contract away the governmental powers of the state as to bind a subsequent legislature not to interfere with the exercise of the rights or immunities granted. Upon this question the courts have not adopted a perfectly consistent attitude. In a few cases they have held that certain governmental powers may be bargained away in particular instances. Among these is the power of taxation. When railroads first began to be built, they were regarded as speculative enterprises which needed financial encouragement from the state, which was sometimes given in the form of immunity from state taxation. Subsequently, when the enterprise proved to be lucrative and prosperous, and the legislature undertook to reverse its former policy and to levy taxes on the railroads, it encountered hostile court decisions holding that the immunity from taxation which had been granted was a contract, the obligation of which the state might not impair. The grant of immunity from taxation has also been held to bind the state in the case of other enterprises, such as banks. Thus, an Ohio statute of 1845 authorizing the incorporation of banks granted them exemption from the state general property tax. Six years later, however, the legislature attempted to subject them to such a tax. The Court, however, held that the state was bound by its earlier agreement and the tax, therefore, was invalid.[1]

Criticism of This Doctrine.—Cases holding that the state may bargain away certain essential governmental powers in particular instances have been subjected to much criticism, some of which is found in dissenting opinions filed in such cases. Thus, one dissenting judge declared that "to hold that any of the annual legislatures can, by contract, deprive the state forever of the power of taxation, is to hold that they can destroy the government which they are appointed to serve,"[2] which is a *reductio ad absurdum*. In the Mississippi lottery case mentioned above, the Court itself declared that "no government dependent on taxation for support can bargain away its whole power of taxation, for that would be substantially abdication,"[3] or, in other words, state suicide. The better view is that the legislature is not competent to make a wholesale grant of essential governmental powers, because, since such powers are held by it in trust for the people, to grant them away irrevocably would constitute a betrayal of the trust. In more recent cases, the courts, while not overturning the earlier doctrine with reference to the powers of taxation and rate making, have been inclined to limit it as much as possible. They have held, for example, that a municipality has no inherent power to contract away the power of rate regulation unless such power has been delegated to it by the state, and the delegation of such power must be made in explicit terms.[4] More important still, the courts have held that there are certain important governmental powers, *viz.*, eminent domain and the police power, which cannot be contracted away.

Eminent Domain and the Contract Clause.—The power of eminent domain is an essential power that may be exercised either by the Federal Government or by the several states or by the political subdivisions thereof or by public service corporations to which it has been delegated. It is a power whereby private property may be taken for a public use, but the constitutions require that just compensation shall be paid for all property so taken. Now, contracts, grants, or franchises are forms of private property which may be taken for a public use under the power of eminent domain. This is true whether the state is a party or the contract is between individuals. The action of the State of Vermont in condemning a toll bridge with an exclusive franchise and converting it into a free bridge was upheld.[5] Again, the city of Brooklyn took over by eminent domain the property and franchises of the Long Island Water Supply

---

[1] Piqua Branch of State Bank of Ohio v. Knoop, 16 How. 369 (1853).
[2] Justice Miller dissenting in Washington University v. Rouse, 8 Wall. 439 (1869).
[3] Stone v. Mississippi, 101 U. S. 814 (1879).
[4] Freeport Water Co. v. Freeport, 180 U. S. 587 (1901).
[5] West River Bridge Co. v. Dix, 6 How. 507 (1848).

Company.   The Court, in denying the contention of the company that such condemnation was an impairment of the obligation of the contract, declared that "all private property is subject to the demands of a public use."[1]   Therefore, if a city desires to engage in municipal ownership of its public utilities, it does not have to wait until the expiration of the franchises before taking them over by eminent domain.   This, however, would be subject to the conditions that the state has delegated it authority to do so and that it has the financial resources to make just compensation.   To permit the state or city to take over contracts by eminent domain does not impair their obligation, because all contracts are made subject to the implied condition that they are liable to condemnation, either directly or indirectly, by the state.   It is not necessary that any express stipulation to this effect be made in the contract or franchise, bcause the power of eminent domain is an essential governmental power which cannot be bargained away.

The Police Power and the Contract Clause.—Another essential governmental power of the state is that known as the police power.   In considering its relation to the contract clause, it is necessary to distinguish between the exercise of the police power for the promotion of the fundamental objects of social welfare, such as health, safety, and morals, and its exercise for the promotion of less fundamental objects, such as economic interests, comfort, and convenience.   In the latter category falls such a power as that of rate making.   As already indicated, the courts have held that the state may make a binding contract with a public service corporation granting to it the right to make its own rates.   Again, the grant of the exclusive franchise to supply gas to a city has been held to be a binding contract which cannot be impaired through the exercise of the police power for the promotion of mere comfort and convenience.[2]

In more recent cases, however, the courts have evinced a more liberal attitude toward the police power of the state when alleged to be in conflict with the contract clause, so that this clause now operates as a comparatively slight, if any, limitation on the police power.[3]   This is especially true in the case of the exercise of the police power for the promotion of the fundamental objects of social welfare, such as health, safety, and morals. The old maxim that "the safety of the people is the highest law" is applicable here.   The state government has no right to bargain away this essential governmental power as exercised for the promotion of these fundamental objects.

---

[1] Long Island Water Supply Co. v. Brooklyn, 166 U. S. 685 (1897).

[2] New Orleans Gas Co. v. Louisiana Light Co., 115 U. S. 650 (1885).

[3] *Cf.* Atlantic Coast Line Ry. Co. v. Goldsboro, 232 U. S. 548 (1913); Union Dry Goods Co. v. Georgia Public Service Corp., 248 U. S. 372 (1919); Producers' Transportation Co. v. Railroad Commission, 251 U. S. 228 (1920).

This principle may be illustrated by the following cases. In the Mississippi lottery case, cited above, it appeared that the state had granted to a certain company a charter authorizing it to conduct a lottery for a period of twenty-five years. Shortly afterwards the state by constitutional and statutory provision made the conduct of lotteries in the state illegal. The lottery company contended that this impaired the obligation of its contract. The action of the state, however, was upheld as a legitimate exercise of its police power for the protection of public morals.[1] Again, for the same reason, it has been held that the state has the power to enforce a prohibition law against a corporation to which it had granted a charter authorizing it to manufacture alcoholic beverages.[2] Since the police power is paramount to charter provisions, it may be said that there virtually exists in such charters an implied power of subsequent legislative regulation. Thus, a railroad may be required to adopt safety appliances or, even in spite of a previous express agreement to the contrary, to eliminate grade crossings in the interests of public safety.[3]

Another illustration of the principle under discussion arose in Illinois in 1878. In accordance with a charter granted a few years before by the state, the Northwestern Fertilizing Company had established its works for the manufacture of fertilizer within the limits of the village of Hyde Park. The works were located in territory that was swampy and practically uninhabited. Subsequently, however, the village grew rapidly and the operations of the fertilizer works became so obnoxious to the residents of the neighborhood as to constitute a public nuisance. Thereupon the village, acting by authority from the state, passed an ordinance forbidding the conduct of these offensive operations within its limits. The Supreme Court of the United States held that the company had no vested right to continue these obnoxious operations in the locality originally selected after the character of the neighborhood changed, and that the village ordinance was a valid exercise of the police power for the protection of the public health.[4]

In some more recent cases, the courts have evinced a tendency to extend the doctrine of the above cases so as to uphold the exercise of the police power of the state for the promotion of public comfort, convenience, or general welfare. Thus, a Missouri law required railroads which constructed embankments along their right of way to make suitable openings for water drainage and made the requirement applicable to embankments already constructed before the passage of the law. In upholding the law as a legitimate exercise of the police power, the Court declared that this

[1] Stone v. Mississippi, 101 U. S. 814 (1879).
[2] Beer Co. v. Massachusetts, 97 U. S. 25 (1878).
[3] Chicago, B. & Q. Ry. Co. v. United States, 170 U. S. 57 (1898).
[4] Fertilizing Co. v. Hyde Park, 97 U. S. 659 (1878).

power "embraces regulations designed to promote the public convenience or the general welfare and prosperity, as well as those in the interest of public health, morals, or safety" and "is inalienable even by express grant."[1] This doctrine, however, is doubtless applicable only to public service corporations or other businesses affected with a public interest, which are peculiarly subject to public regulation.

The contracts which in the above cases were held not to limit the state in the exercise of its police power were contracts to which the state was a party. The same doctrine, however, applies also to contracts between individuals. Thus, a contract between two individuals for the sale of intoxicating liquor becomes invalid upon the going into force of a state prohibition law. Again, a contract between a tenant and a landlord, whereby the former agrees to pay a certain amount of rent, may be set aside in times of emergency, involving a building shortage, by a state law providing that tenants need pay only a reasonable rent, and forbidding the landlord to dispossess the tenant for breach of contract.[2] In the case of Manigault v. Springs,[3] the latter had contracted to remove a dam across a stream so as to allow the former a clear passage, and this was done. Subsequently, however, the state legislature passed an act authorizing Springs to erect another dam across the stream in order to drain low and swampy land. The law was upheld by the Court as a legitimate exercise of the police power, even though it set aside the contract between the two individuals.

[1] Chicago and Alton R. R. Co. v. Tranbarger, 238 U. S. 67 (1915).

[2] Marcus Brown Holding Co. v. Feldman, 256 U. S. 170; Block v. Hirsh, 256 U. S. 135 (1921); Levy Leasing Co. v. Siegel, 258 U. S. 242 (1922).

[3] 199 U. S. 473 (1905).

CHAPTER XXVI

DUE PROCESS OF LAW[1]

One of the most important concepts of constitutional law is that involved in the phrase "due process of law." Under an absolutism or autocratic form of government, the most valuable of individual rights—life, liberty, and property—are completely at the mercy of the government. The advance of democracy and of constitutional government has had for its primary aim the safeguarding of these valuable rights from arbitrary or tyrannical governmental action.

Development of Due Process.—In Anglo-American jurisprudence the concept of due process of law may be traced back to Magna Carta of 1215, in Chapter 39 of which it was provided that: "No freeman shall be arrested, or imprisoned, or disseized, or outlawed, or exiled, or in any way molested; nor will we proceed against him, unless by the lawful judgment of his peers or by the law of the land."

In later statutes of English law and commentaries thereon, the phrase "law of the land" and the phrase "due process of law" came to be used interchangeably. The Petition of Right of 1628 prayed that "freemen be imprisoned or detained only by the law of the land, or by due process of law, and not by the King's special command without any charge." It is clear that due process of law at that time was intended and understood as a limitation on the King and not upon Parliament. If the King could be constrained to act only in accordance with the laws of Parliament, individual rights, it was thought, would be sufficiently safeguarded.

The concept of due process of law was introduced into the Constitution of the United States in the Fifth Amendment, adopted in 1791. This, as in the case of the other amendments adopted at the same time, was intended as a limitation upon the National Government only. A similar limitation upon the states was introduced by the adoption of the Fourteenth Amendment in 1868. The Declaration of Independence spoke of the rights of "life, liberty, and the pursuit of happiness." The vague idea of "pursuit of happiness" was changed by the framers of the constitutional amendments to the more definite concept of "property." They provided that no person should be deprived of "life, liberty, or property, without due process of law."

[1] On the subject matter of this and of the next four chapters, see R. L. Mott, *Due Process of Law, passim* (1926).

Although more cases have arisen in the courts involving the due-process clause than any other provision of the Constitution, the first case in which the Supreme Court considered this clause of the Fifth Amendment was not decided until 1855.   In this case,[1] the Court departed from the meaning of due process as it had been understood in England and held that it operated as a limitation not only on the executive but also on the other departments of the Government.   "The article," declared the Court, "is restraint on the legislative as well as on the executive and judicial powers of the Government, and cannot be so construed as to leave Congress free to make any process 'due process of law' by its mere will."   Therefore, while the contract clause of the Constitution limits merely the legislative department, the due-process clause limits all branches of the government.[2]

In the case just quoted, however, the Court apparently regarded due process as a limitation on procedure merely rather than on the substance of governmental action, thus following the interpretation which had been given to this principle in England.   So long as the manner of determining individual rights was fair and sound, the requirement of due process was not violated.   This is still an important phase of the application of the due-process clause.   Gradually, however, and at first somewhat hesitantly, the courts have broadened the meaning of due process until by the end of the nineteenth century it became well established that the due-process clauses of both the Fifth and Fourteenth Amendments limit not only the manner but also the substance of governmental action.   Even though procedural rights are not infringed, laws either of Congress or of the state legislatures which are arbitrary or oppressive in content or purpose are lacking in due process and therefore void.

The Nature of Due Process.—The due-process clause embodies a general principle of justice the meaning of which is rather vague.   It cannot be thoroughly understood without a somewhat detailed consideration of its various applications in concrete cases.   The courts do not undertake to give an exact definition of due process.   As the Supreme Court itself has declared:

Few phrases in the law are so elusive of exact apprehension as this.   This court has always declined to give a comprehensive definition of it, and has preferred that its full meaning should be gradually ascertained by the process of inclusion and exclusion in the course of the decisions of cases as they arise.[3]

A broad indication of the nature of due process, however, has been given by the Supreme Court in the course of certain opinions.   Thus, in a vague way it has been spoken of as requiring "a course of legal proceed-

---

[1] Murray's Lessee v. Hoboken Land and Improvement Co., 18 How. 272 (1855).

[2] For a case holding that due process of law may be denied by judicial decision, see Brinkerhoff-Faris Trust and Savings Co. v. Hill, 281 U. S. 673 (1930).

[3] Twining v. New Jersey, 211 U. S. 78 (1908).

ings according to those rules and principles which have been established in our system of jurisprudence for the protection and enforcement of private rights."[1]   In another opinion the Court spoke of the two clauses as imposing upon national and state power "the limits of those fundamental principles of liberty and justice which lie at the base of all our civil and political institutions."[2]   In the case just cited, the Court also quoted with approval Daniel Webster's familiar definition of due process contained in his argument in the Dartmouth College case, in which he described it as "the general law, a law which hears before it condemns; which proceeds upon inquiry, and renders judgment only after trial," so "that every citizen shall hold his life, liberty, property and immunities under the protection of the general rules which govern society."   From this definition it results, the Court points out, that the following are void because lacking in due process: "Acts of attainder, bills of pains and penalties, acts of confiscation, acts reversing judgments, and acts directly transferring one man's estate to another, legislative judgments and decrees, and other similar special, partial, and arbitrary exertions of power under the forms of legislation."   It appears, then, that the provisions found in the original Constitution prohibiting Congress and the states from passing bills of attainder[3] are unnecessary, since the exercise of such a power is prohibited by the due-process clauses.

The purpose of the due-process clause is to protect against arbitrary governmental action the most precious rights of the individual, viz., life, liberty, and property.   Even these rights, however, may be taken away, provided the taking is in accordance with due process.   We thus have a conflict between governmental power and individual rights with the courts holding the balance between the two.   The discretion thus placed in the hands of the courts is very great, because there are no exact juridical standards for determining what is due process.   Whether a given law or administrative proceeding complies with the requirements of due process or not depends very largely upon the opinion of the court as to its reasonableness, expediency or wisdom, and upon the judges' sense of justice and fair play.

The Protection of Liberty.—The terms "life," "liberty," and "property" are not defined in the Constitution, and their meaning therefore is also left largely for judicial determination.   The meaning of "life" is fairly clear.   The term "liberty" has been broadly construed by the Supreme Court as meaning

. . . not only the right of the citizen to be free from mere physical restraint of his person, as by incarceration, but the term is deemed to embrace the right

[1] Pennoyer v. Neff, 95 U. S. 714 (1877).
[2] Hurtado v. California, 110 U. S. 516 (1884).
[3] Art. I, sects. 9 and 10.

of the citizen to be free in the enjoyment of all his faculties; to be free to use them in all lawful ways; to live and work where he will; to earn his livelihood by any lawful calling; to pursue any livelihood or avocation; and for that purpose to enter into any contracts which may be proper, necessary, and essential to his carrying out to a successful conclusion the purposes above mentioned.[1]

It is thus clear that the term as used in the due-process clause means not only liberty of person but also liberty of action. Liberty, however, must be distinguished from license; it does not mean absence of all restraint. Liberty of contract has been defined as "freedom from arbitrary restraint—not immunity from reasonable regulation to safeguard the public interest."[2] From one point of view liberty may be defined as the right of a person to do what he pleases, provided he does not infringe upon the rights of others. Real liberty for all can be assured only under a system in which the rights of each individual are not absolute but merely relative to the rights of others. The liberty of an individual may be restrained, provided the restraint is not arbitrary but reasonable and for the public interest. Thus, a man may be compelled against his will to submit to vaccination in order to protect the community against disease.[3]

Recently, the Supreme Court has radically enlarged its interpretation of the term "liberty" as contained in the due-process clause of the Fourteenth Amendment. This enlargement was foreshadowed in 1923 when, in an *obiter dictum*, the opinion was expressed that liberty

. . . denotes not merely freedom from bodily restraint, but also the right of the individual to contract, to engage in any of the common occupations of life, to acquire useful knowledge, to marry, establish a home and bring up children, to worship God according to the dictates of his own conscience, and, generally to enjoy those privileges long recognized at common law as essential to the orderly pursuit of happiness by free men.[4]

In the case just cited a state statute prohibiting the teaching of German in private schools was held invalid as a deprivation of liberty without due process of law in violation of the Fourteenth Amendment. It was held to interfere arbitrarily "with the calling of modern language teachers, with the opportunities of pupils to acquire knowledge, and with the power of parents to control the education of their own children." This decision had reference to the application of the statute to private rather than public schools. In the latter the state may prescribe the curriculum.

[1] Allgeyer v. Louisiana, 165 U. S. 578 (1897).
[2] By Mr. Justice McReynolds in Liberty Warehouse Co. v. Burley Tobacco Growers' Cooperative Assoc., 276 U. S. 71 (1928), upholding the validity of a Kentucky statute authorizing cooperative marketing associations.
[3] Jacobson v. Massachusetts, 197 U. S. 11 (1905).
[4] Meyer v. Nebraska, 262 U. S. 390 (1923).

Later, the Court held unconstitutional an Oregon statute requiring all children of school age to attend the public schools, on the ground that it was a deprivation of the liberty guaranteed by the due-process clause.[1]

In view of this enlargement of the definition of liberty in the due-process clause, the question arose as to whether the term included those guarantees of individual rights contained in the first eight amendments to the Constitution, such as freedom of speech and press. It is well established that these amendments are limitations on the National Government only. But if the term liberty, as used in the due-process clause of the Fourteenth Amendment, is enlarged so as to include the rights mentioned in those amendments, the practical result would be the same as if they were also limitations on the states. This is substantially what the Supreme Court held in the Gitlow case, decided in 1925, in which the Court, speaking by Mr. Justice Sanford, declared that "for the present purposes we may and do assume that freedom of speech and of the press—which are protected by the First Amendment from abridgment by Congress—are among the fundamental rights and 'liberties' protected by the due process clause of the Fourteenth Amendment from impairment by the states."[2] The doctrine thus enunciated is of fundamental importance, because it transfers the ultimate protection of civil liberty in the United States from the states to the National Government.

The doctrine that freedom of the press is protected by the due-process clause of the Fourteenth Amendment was reiterated by the Supreme Court in a recent case involving the constitutionality of a Minnesota law for the suppression of newspapers containing defamatory matter. The Court declared that "it is no longer open to doubt that the liberty of the press, and of speech, is within the liberty safeguarded by the due process clause of the Fourteenth Amendment from invasion by state action." The Court thereupon held the law to be an infringement of the liberty of the press guaranteed by the Fourteenth Amendment.[3]

The Protection of Property.—The term "property" as used in the due-process clauses has also been broadly construed by the courts. It comprises not only the use, enjoyment, and disposal of one's belongings for lawful purposes but also the right to acquire property in any lawful manner. The right to enter into contracts, whether with regard to persons or to property, has been held to be an incident of the right not only of liberty but also of property. On account of the broad way in which the terms liberty and property have been construed, the courts have many opportunities of declaring unconstitutional both state and Federal laws as lacking in due process. Although there is no express constitutional prohibition against the passage by Congress of laws impair-

[1] Pierce v. Society of Sisters, 268 U. S. 510 (1925).
[2] Gitlow v. New York, 268 U. S. 652 (1925).
[3] Near v. State of Minnesota ex rel. Olson, 283 U. S. 697 (1931).

ing the obligation of contracts, nevertheless, since contracts are a form of property protected by the due-process clause, such a law might be held void as a violation of due process.

The Persons Protected.—The rights guaranteed by the due-process clauses are extended in terms to "any person." This phrase is broad enough to include not only citizens but also aliens and, in fact, "all persons within the territorial jurisdiction, without regard to any differences of race, or color, or of nationality."[1] Moreover, the term person as here used includes not only natural but also artificial persons or corporations. This is especially true in regard to the right of property. The right to life doubtless attaches to natural persons only and this is probably also true of the right to liberty, at least in the narrow sense. But this works little hardship on corporations in view of the broad sense in which the term property has been construed.

[1] Yick Wo v. Hopkins, 118 U. S. 357 (1886).

CHAPTER XXVII

DUE PROCESS AND PROCEDURE

As pointed out in the preceding chapter, the concept of due process of law as a limitation upon the substance of governmental power is a comparatively recent development. Historically, the main purpose of the concept has been to protect individual rights by limiting the manner or procedure of governmental action, and this is still an important phase of the subject.

Flexibility of Due Procedure.—The Supreme Court has fortunately adopted a progressive attitude regarding the question as to what kind of procedure is consonant with due process. That tribunal recognizes that, although the principle of justice embodied in due process is relatively permanent, the means of securing justice may change. It is true that, in an early case, the Court declared that the settled usages and modes of proceeding existing in the common and statute law of England, before the emigration of our ancestors, and transplanted in this country are due process.[1] This statement, however, is not to be construed as implying that a new method of governmental action is necessarily lacking in due process. If so, the procedure of the seventeenth century would be fastened upon American jurisprudence like a straight jacket, which could only be unloosed by constitutional amendment.[2]

In 1879, the constitution of California provided that criminal offenses previously prosecuted through indictment by grand jury might be prosecuted either by indictment or by information filed by the prosecuting attorney. A person prosecuted for murder upon an information contended that the procedure was not due process because it did not follow the settled usage of indictment by grand jury. The objection was not because California had changed her procedure but was based on the ground that indictment by grand jury was an essential right under the due-process clause of the Fourteenth Amendment. The Court, however, denied this contention, holding that prosecution by information is consistent with the fundamental principles of justice. So long as the requirement of justice is met, the procedure is not invalid merely because it is new. Any other interpretation of the due-process clause "would be to deny every quality of the law but its age, and to render it incapable of

[1] Murray v. Hoboken Land and Improvement Co., 18 How. 272 (1855).
[2] Twining v. New Jersey, 211 U. S. 78 (1908).

progress and improvement."[1] From this decision it follows, as the Court pointed out, that "any legal proceeding enforced by public authority, whether sanctioned by age and custom or newly devised in the discretion of the legislative power, in furtherance of the general public good, which regards and preserves these principles of liberty and justice, must be held to be due process of law." This decision was important because, by allowing flexibility and capacity for growth in the modes of procedure, it opened the way for improvements and adaptation to new conditions.

Legislative Procedure.—In matters of procedure, due process limits all three departments of government but not in the same way. In judicial procedure, notice and hearing are required, but no such requirements limit the legislature in enacting laws. The legislatures are limited, however, by the provisions of the Federal and state constitutions as to the formalities to be complied with in the procedure of enacting laws. If a law should be published which had not been enacted in accordance with the constitutional requirements as to procedure, it would be a fraud upon the people and lacking in due process.

Jurisdiction.—Due process in matters of procedure, however, is much more important as applied to the judiciary than to the legislature. A prime requisite of due process in judicial procedure is that the court shall have jurisdiction over the person, thing, or relation affected by the judgment rendered. If a suit involves the question as to the personal liability of the defendant, he must be brought within the jurisdiction of the court by service of process within the state or by his voluntary appearance.[2] If the defendant is domiciled within the state and is served with the process of the court, he is thereby brought within the control of the court and the requirement as to jurisdiction is complied with. Service on nonresidents by publication is lacking in due process. If, however, either one of the parties to a proceeding in which a divorce is granted is a resident of the state, service of the other party by publication is deemed to be sufficient. This is not a proceeding *in personam* but rather *in rem* to determine status. If the judgment sought in a state court is one concerning property, the court has jurisdiction if the property is within the state, regardless of the residence of the owner.

Notice and Hearing.—The fundamental idea of justice embodied in due process forbids that a person's legal rights should be affected when he may be unaware that such proceedings are going forward and may therefore have no opportunity of presenting his side of the case. This is one reason why, as noticed above, it is required that process should be served upon the defendant in a civil suit. The notice to which a person whose legal rights are to be determined or affected is entitled is due notice; *i.e.*, it must be given a reasonable length of time before the proceedings take

[1] Hurtado v. California, 110 U. S. 516 (1884).
[2] Pennoyer v. Neff, 95 U. S. 733 (1877).

place in order that a defense may be prepared. The hearing to which he is entitled must enable him to present such arguments, testimony, or evidence as may be pertinent or relevant to the case. Moreover, the trial must be carried on in an orderly manner before an impartial tribunal of competent jurisdiction, but not necessarily before a judicial court.

Impartial Tribunal.—In a trial before a court, the impartiality of the judge may be questioned if it can be shown that he has such a personal interest in the result of the case as may reasonably affect the fairness of his decision. For example, a law of Ohio under which the judge received a part of the costs for convictions for violation of the prohibitory liquor law was held to be lacking in due process.[1] In its opinion in this case, the Supreme Court declared that "it certainly violates the Fourteenth Amendment and deprives a defendant in a criminal case of due process of law to subject his liberty or property to the judgment of a court, the judge of which has a direct, personal, substantial pecuniary interest in reaching a conclusion against him in his case." The provision thus held invalid was a device especially introduced in order to secure the effective enforcement of the prohibitory liquor law. Long-established procedure, however, has generally been held to be due process. Moreover, if the pecuniary advantage which the judge derives from a conviction is so small as to be negligible, due process is probably not denied, in accordance with the principle *de minimis non curat lex*.

In order to maintain the impartiality of the tribunal, that body must be not only willing but able to accord a fair hearing to the defendant. If the court should be overawed and dominated by threats of violence or intimidation by a mob clamoring for conviction, it would not be able to give the defendant a fair hearing and due process would be denied.[2]

Due Procedure in Criminal Trials.—The various provisions of the Federal bill of rights relating to procedure in criminal trials do not limit the states. In such trials, the only limitation upon the states found in the Federal Constitution is the due-process clause of the Fourteenth Amendment. This clause, as already shown, requires that the court shall have jurisdiction and that the defendant shall have due notice and a fair hearing. Provided these conditions are fulfilled, the methods of procedure in criminal trials are within the control of the state. The due-process clause prevents arbitrary procedure but does not require any particular procedure. It does not, as we have seen, require indictment by grand jury, nor does it require trial by jury, either as a general proposition or when trial by jury is established by the state constitution or laws.[3]

[1] Tumey v. Ohio, 273 U. S. 510 (1927).

[2] Moore v. Dempsey, 261 U. S. 86 (1923), with which *cf*. Frank v. Magnum, 237 U. S. 309 (1915).

[3] Jordan v. Massachusetts, 225 U. S. 167 (1912).

It does not prevent a state from providing that the trial jury shall consist of eight instead of twelve men,[1] nor from allowing a verdict of guilty by less than a unanimous jury.   Due process does not require the right of appeal, nor does it require that the defendant in a criminal trial be exempt from compulsory self-incrimination.[2]

Due Procedure and Administrative Action.—Due process is not necessarily judicial process.   On account of the increasing need for prompt governmental action in dealing with the complicated economic and social conditions of modern times, a larger measure of discretion must necessarily be accorded to the administrative authorities.   It would not be consistent with due process to give an administrative officer authority to enforce obedience to his orders in criminal cases by a judgment of fine or imprisonment.[3]   In civil cases, however, and even in quasi-criminal cases, an administrative officer may be given conclusive authority to determine questions of fact upon which an individual's legal rights depend. Thus, it was held in an early case that an administrative officer might be given final authority to decide with regard to facts justifying the issuance of a distress warrant against a revenue collector to compel payment of a balance due the United States.[4]   In this case there had been no notice nor hearing granted and the procedure was rather high handed but was probably justifiable as governmental self-help, and also because this particular procedure had long been the settled usage.   Ordinarily, however, even in administrative proceedings, notice and hearing are required when a person's liberty or property is affected by the decision.   In some cases of emergency, however, such as the slaughter of diseased cattle or the destruction of houses in the path of a conflagration, it may be impracticable to accord notice and hearing prior to the destruction, but the owner has a right to a hearing later and to recover damages if the destruction was without legal justification.

Another requirement of due process is that the administrative officer must be acting within his jurisdiction and he cannot be given final authority to decide the extent of his own jurisdiction.   This is a question of law upon which an appeal to the courts must be allowed.   Other questions of law may sometimes be decided by administrative tribunals, but this is exceptional.

Administrative tribunals are frequently granted not only administrative, but also quasi-legislative and quasi-judicial power.   The delegation

[1] Maxwell v. Dow, 176 U. S. 581 (1900).

[2] Twining v. New Jersey, 211 U. S. 78 (1908).

[3] An act of Congress was upheld, however, which levied a fine of $100 upon transportation companies for bringing into the country aliens who, as determined by an administrative officer, were suffering from detectable disease and prohibited clearance of company's vessels from port until the fine was paid.   Oceanic Steam Navigation Co. v. Stranahan, 214 U. S. 320 (1909).

[4] Murray's Lessee v. Hoboken Land and Improvement Co., 18 How. 272 (1855).

of such powers to the tribunal does not violate due process. Thus, the legislature may create a public utilities commission and set up the general standard that rates charged by the utilities shall be reasonable, leaving it to the commission to fix the detailed rates within this general requirement. When the commission or administrative tribunal exercises the quasi-legislative power of promulgating rules and regulations, due process no more requires notice and hearing than it does when the legislature enacts a law. When the tribunal exercises the quasi-judicial power of holding a hearing to determine the rights of persons coming within its jurisdiction, it may adopt summary methods of procedure and need not observe the technical rules of judicial procedure relating to such matters as pleading and the admissibility of evidence.

The extent to which conclusiveness attaches to the determinations of administrative tribunals or officers varies with the nature of the case. The greatest conclusiveness in determining questions of fact attaches when such officers exercise essential governmental powers which affect individual privileges rather than rights. An example of this is the power of the postmaster-general to issue "fraud orders" excluding certain persons from the use of the mail because of fraud.[1] The exclusion of aliens from the country is also an essential governmental power and the entry of an alien is a privilege rather than a right. A citizen, however, ordinarily has a right to reenter the country, but, even where the question of fact presented is whether a person requesting permission to enter is an alien or a citizen, the determination of the immigration authorities upon this question has been held to be final and conclusive.[2] In such cases, due process is preserved by the right of appeal to the courts regarding any questions of law involved, and regarding any abuse of authority or lack of jurisdiction on the part of the administrative officer.

[1] Public Clearing House v. Coyne, 194 U. S. 497 (1904).
[2] United States v. Ju Toy, 198 U. S. 253 (1905).

CHAPTER XXVIII

DUE PROCESS IN TAXATION

Taxation in General.—In general, a government can exist and carry on its functions only through contributions made by the citizens. For this purpose, voluntary contributions would not be sufficient and therefore the force of government may be used to compel their payment. The two principal governmental powers by which such contributions may be compelled are taxation and eminent domain. Of these, taxation is more important because it is much more frequently used and touches everybody, whereas only comparatively few people are affected by the power of eminent domain. In the exercise of the latter power, the constitutions require that just compensation be given to the owner of the property taken. In the case of taxation, however, no special compensation need be, or is, given. Such compensation as the taxpayer receives is the general return which he derives from living under a government which affords protection to his property and person, educates his children, and performs many other functions for the benefit of the citizens. The fact, however, that a particular taxpayer derives no direct benefit from the performance of certain of these functions does not relieve him from the payment of taxes for their support.

It would, of course, be fatal to the efficiency of government for the Constitution to place serious limitations upon the legitimate exercise of the taxing power. The due-process clauses of the Fifth and Fourteenth Amendments are not to be so construed. They do, however, prevent an illegitimate exercise of the taxing power, whereby a person's property is taken away from him for wrong purposes or in an arbitrary, tyrannical, or discriminatory manner. Taxation is not lacking in due process if (1) it is levied for a public purpose; (2) the state has jurisdiction of the subject matter of the tax; and (3) due procedure has been followed in levying and collecting the tax. In addition, there must be no arbitrary discrimination or classification.

What Is a Public Purpose in Taxation?—The general opinion as to what constitutes a public purpose in taxation changes from time to time and depends on conditions found in particular localities. In a general way the legitimate purposes of government are admirably stated in the preamble to the Federal Constitution: to "establish justice, insure domestic tranquillity, provide for the common defense, promote the general welfare, and secure the blessings of liberty to ourselves and our posterity." Differences of opinion may arise, however, as to what specific functions the government should undertake to perform for the accomplishment of such a purpose as the promotion of the general welfare. Formerly the view prevailed that the government should attend only to those functions which could not be satisfactorily performed by individuals.

This individualistic view of the functions of government is no longer widely held. Modern industrial, social, and economic conditions have become so complex that the need for the intervention of the government has become much greater in recent decades. The functions of government have expanded in accordance with this need. The government nowadays performs many more functions than the minimum allowed under the individualistic theory. Among other things, it operates a system of public schools, maintains charitable institutions, protects the public health, promotes agriculture, builds good roads, and regulates traffic, commerce, and public utilities. There is no question that these are now generally considered to be legitimate public purposes for which the government may spend the proceeds of taxes.

Some people would have the government go further and acquire and operate mines, railroads, and other public utilities. Public opinion does not yet generally demand that the government go this far, but, if it should, the Constitution would probably not stand in the way. This was indicated by the decision of the Supreme Court handed down in 1920 upholding legislation of North Dakota promoted by the Nonpartisan League, which represented probably the greatest departure ever undertaken by any state of the Union from the principle of private enterprise. This legislation provided, among other things, for the ownership and operation by the state of a bank, grain elevators, and flour mills, and the establishment of a Home Building Association to buy, sell, and lease homes to citizens of the state. This program naturally involved the expenditure of funds raised by taxation. The Court nevertheless held that such taxation was not for a private purpose and was therefore constitutional.[1]

In rendering this decision, the Supreme Court was doubtless influenced by the social and economic conditions prevailing in North Dakota, which is mainly an agricultural state. When a business enterprise is of such a character that private capital cannot be induced to undertake it but the conduct of such business is deemed to be promotive of the general welfare, it becomes a legitimate public purpose for the state to raise and spend money to carry it on. Thus, during the internal improvement period before the Civil War, the credit of the state and local governmental subdivisions was pledged to the financial support of railroads and similar enterprises which were at that time regarded as too hazardous to attract private capital. However unwise this policy may have been, such

[1] Green v. Frazier, 253 U. S. 233 (1920).

support was not unconstitutional as involving taxation for a private purpose. Now, however, the situation in this respect has changed, since such enterprises now attract adequate private capital.

On the other hand, enterprises which were formerly and usually considered of such a private character that a state or city could not undertake them may, on account of change of circumstances, come to be considered legitimate public enterprises. Thus, the establishment of a public fuel yard by a city during a time of fuel shortage has been upheld.[1] There was no element of financial profit involved, as the fuel was sold at cost and the purpose was to supply the citizens with a necessity of life and health which in this time of emergency could otherwise be obtained only with great difficulty.

The answer, therefore, to the question as to whether or not a particular activity involves taxation for a public or for a private purpose depends on time and circumstance. Sometimes different courts may answer the same question differently. Thus, the question was presented to the supreme courts of North Dakota and Kansas as to whether or not it was a public purpose to furnish seed grain for farmers in time of widespread financial distress and was answered differently by the two courts.[2] In a state engaged principally in agriculture, it would seem that this should be considered a public purpose. In time of disaster or widespread suffering, the state may legitimately appropriate money to relieve the destitute. The payment of pensions in the form of deferred compensation to soldiers, policemen, firemen, teachers, or other employees, is a legitimate public purpose. A number of states have also enacted old-age pension laws.

Exemption from taxation is practically equivalent to public financial aid to the owner of the property exempted and would probably be unconstitutional unless some public purpose is to be subserved by such exemption. Property used for religious purposes is frequently exempted from taxes, and this exemption is constitutional, provided there is no discrimination for or against the property of any particular religious denomination.

Jurisdiction for Taxing Purposes.—If property is taxed which is not within the jurisdiction of the taxing authority, such taxation is a taking of private property without legal warrant and therefore without due process of law. Although the general principle, as thus stated, is very simple, complications arise in applying it to certain forms of property. There is no difficulty, however, in applying the principle to real property, which has a fixed *situs* and is taxable at that place, regardless of the domicile of the owner. A mortgage on real estate, however, may be

[1] Jones v. City of Portland, 245 U. S. 217 (1917).
[2] State v. Osawkee Township, 14 Kan. 418 (1875); State v. Nelson, 1 N. D. 88 (1890).

taxed either at the place where the real estate is located or at the place where the mortgagee is domiciled, or in both places.

In applying the general principle to personal property, it is necessary, in the first place, to classify this form of property into tangible and intangible. Household furniture, automobiles, rolling stock, and cattle are examples of tangible personal property. The rule for determining jurisdiction for taxing purposes over such property is the same as that for real property; *viz.*, it is taxable at the place where it is actually located, regardless of the domicile of the owner. Tangible property, whether real or personal, which has a permanent *situs* in a given state, is taxable only by that state.

In the case of such property as the rolling stock of a railroad, which is constantly moving back and forth across state lines, there is no particular group of cars which remain within the jurisdiction of any one state for taxing purposes. Nevertheless, the state can tax a percentage of the total number of cars operated by the railroad corresponding to the average number of cars within the state as compared with the total number of cars operated by the railroad in all states through which it runs.

In the case of a corporation operating in several states, such as a railroad, telegraph company, or express company, it is obvious that the value of that portion of the company's property located within one state cannot be adequately assessed if considered as separate from the remainder of the system found in other states. In order to determine true value for taxing purposes, the entire system must be considered as a unit. In practice, the states apply this "unit rule" to corporations engaged in interstate business by determining the total value of the system, including property both inside and outside the state, or by determining total earnings from business transacted both inside and outside the state, and levying a tax upon the corporation measured by the proportion of its mileage within the state to its entire length. This would be track mileage or wire mileage in the case of a railroad or telegraph company. Apportionment may also be made upon the basis of receipts from business transacted within the state as compared with total receipts. Even though a part of the corporation's earnings is derived from interstate commerce, such a tax apportioned on the basis of earnings merely as a measure of the relative value of the company's property within and without the state, and levied in lieu of other taxes, has been upheld by the Supreme Court.[1]

Although the apportionment on the basis of track mileage is generally reasonable and therefore upheld by the courts, there may be special cases in which taxation on this basis would be unreasonable and therefore invalid. An example of this would be where a railroad has a large

[1] See, for example, Adams Express Co. v. Ohio, 165 U. S. 194 (1897); rehearing in 166 U. S. 185 (1897).

percentage of its trackage in one state but very valuable terminal property in another state.

Jurisdiction in Taxing Intangible Property.—Such property must, of course, be within the jurisdiction of the taxing state. The general rule with respect to the location of intangible property for purposes of taxation is embodied in the phrase *mobilia sequuntur personam*. That is to say, the *situs* of intangible property, such as stocks, bonds, and certificates of indebtedness, for taxing purposes is in the state in which the owner or creditor has his domicile. If the certificate of stock or paper evidencing a debt, such as a promissory note, is actually located in a state different from that in which either the obligor or the obligee resides, such state cannot tax the property represented by such paper.[1]

The Supreme Court, speaking by Mr. Justice McReynolds, has declared that there have been four different views or theories concerning the *situs* for taxation of negotiable public obligations, such as state or municipal bonds. "One fixes this at the domicile of the owner; another at the debtor's domicile; another at the place where the instruments are found—physically present; and the fourth within the jurisdiction where the owner has caused them to become integral parts of a localized business."[2] He goes on to point out, however, that if each state can adopt any one of these and tax accordingly, the same bonds may be taxable in four states at the same time—an absurd conclusion which suggests a wrong premise. Although the Court does not go so far as to hold that the mere fact of taxation of an object by one state necessarily excludes the right of another state to tax the same object, it evinces a decided tendency to limit within narrow bounds the possibility of double or multiple taxation. In the case just cited it is declared that "existing conditions . . . imperatively demand protection of choses in action against multiplied taxation, whether following misapplication of some legal fiction or conflicting theories concerning the sovereign's right to exact contributions."

The general principle of taxing intangible property on the basis that *mobilia sequuntur personam* is subject to several exceptions. The Court declines to follow this principle slavishly or mechanically in cases where it seems to result in injustice, whether through double taxation or otherwise. This principle is a legal fiction and yields to the fact of actual control elsewhere.[3] The *situs* of intangible property may, for purposes of taxation, be separated from the domicile of the owner. Thus, as pointed out above, mortgages are taxable by the state in which the mortgaged property is located, regardless of the domicile of the mortgagee. Again, a special franchise tax on a corporation may be levied only by the

[1] Buck v. Beach, 206 U. S. 392 (1907).
[2] Farmers Loan and Trust Co. v. Minnesota, 280 U. S. 204 (1930).
[3] Safe Deposit and Trust Co. v. Virginia, 280 U. S. 83 (1929).

state granting it, but, in applying the unit rule, another state may levy a property tax on the assets of a foreign corporation, including the franchise.

Inheritance Taxes.—The right or privilege of succession to property is entirely subject to the control of the state in which the deceased person was domiciled. Inheritance taxes are levied by a state, not upon the property inherited but upon the privilege of succession to the property. It follows that the state of the deceased person's domicile may levy inheritance taxes, the amount of which is determined by the value of the property transmitted. This does not prevent other states, having control over some of the property transmitted, from also levying taxes measured by the value of such portion of the property.

An inheritance tax of Connecticut was applied to a bequest made by a resident of that state in the form of a partnership interest in a business located in New York and government bonds kept in the latter state. These were both forms of intangible personal property and the Court, following the rule of *mobilia sequuntur personam,* upheld the tax as applied to such property.[1] In a later case, the facts were that a resident of New York died leaving a large amount of bonds issued by the state of Minnesota. These bonds were kept in New York and had no connection with any business carried on in Minnesota. New York levied an inheritance tax on the transfer of the bonds, the legality of which was not disputed. The State of Minnesota also attempted to levy an inheritance tax on the same transfer. The latter tax was held void by the Supreme Court,[2] on the ground that such a tax was a taking of property without due process of law because the bonds were not within the jurisdiction of the state. The majority of the Court in this case took a rather firm stand against double taxation of intangible property and expressly overruled an earlier case[3] in which it had been held that debts or choses in action are taxable both at the domicile of the debtor and also at that of the creditor.

Income Taxes.—In the case of income taxes, states derive jurisdiction to levy such taxes from two sources: first, because the person receiving the income is a resident of the state and, second, because the property or business from which the income is derived is located in the state. In the former case, the tax is nevertheless valid even though the income is derived from outside the state. In the latter case, the state can levy an income tax even though the recipient of the income is a nonresident, but it cannot, of course, levy a higher tax on nonresidents than on residents.

Procedure in Taxation.—The requirements of due process in relation to procedure in taxation are not so elaborate as in the case of criminal

[1] Blodgett v. Silberman, 277 U. S. 1 (1928). *Cf.* Baldwin v. Missouri, 281 U. S. 586 (1930).

[2] Farmers Loan and Trust Co. v. Minnesota, 280 U. S. 204 (1930).

[3] Blackstone v. Miller, 188 U. S. 189 (1903).

procedure. In matters of taxation the rights of the individual are not so strictly guarded because of the recognition of the need of the government for an efficient taxing system. In indicating the requirements of procedure in taxation, it is necessary to make a distinction between specific and *ad valorem* taxes. A specific tax is a tax of a given amount levied upon each article owned, such as head of cattle or acre of land. In the case of such a tax, due process does not require notice or hearing. In the absence of any dispute as to the number of taxable articles owned by a particular individual, the obligation to pay the tax is complete upon the enactment of the law. As a general rule, all persons in the state are bound by the laws enacted by the legislature, regardless of whether they have notice of the law, either before or after its enactment.

In the case of an *ad valorem* tax, the amount of which depends on the value of the property taxed, it is necessary that an administrative official make an assessment involving the exercise of judgment, about the correctness of which there may be a difference of opinion. In order to prevent arbitrary administrative action in assessing property for *ad valorem* taxes, due process requires some sort of notice and the opportunity, at least, of a hearing. The notice need not be personal but may be constructive, as by publication of the assessment list or by a law fixing the time and place of hearing. The hearing, at which the taxpayer may present arguments regarding the assessment of his property, need not be held prior to the making of the assessment. It is usually held before a board of review and the requirements of due process are met if it takes place before the amount of the tax is finally determined.

CHAPTER XXIX

DUE PROCESS IN EMINENT DOMAIN

Constitutional Basis.—The term "eminent domain" signifies literally paramount ownership, but, in practice, it is used as referring to the power of the government to take private property when needed for a public purpose. This is a power which is inherent in the state or government and does not, therefore, need to be expressly conferred. When the power of taxation is exercised, no direct compensating benefit is conferred upon the taxpayer, but merely the general benefit of living under the government. In the case of the exercise of the power of eminent domain, however, the Federal and state constitutions require that just compensation be paid to the owner of the property. This provision as found in the Fifth Amendment of the Federal Constitution limits only the National Government and is in addition to the limitation of that amendment that property shall not be taken without due process of law. It might be inferred from this circumstance that the limitation regarding just compensation is not included in the due-process provision and that, when the due-process clause was placed in the Fourteenth Amendment as a limitation on the states without mentioning the requirement of just compensation for the taking of private property, the latter requirement is also not included in the due-process provision. This inference, however, has been clearly repudiated by the courts.[1] As construed by them, the due-process clause limits the power of eminent domain in three respects: in the first place, private property cannot be taken at all for a private purpose; second, when private property is taken for a public purpose, just compensation must be given; and, third, the owner of the property to be taken is entitled to notice and hearing.

Practical Application.—The power of eminent domain is an essential governmental power, the need for the exercise of which frequently arises in order to carry on necessary governmental functions. The property subject to condemnation may be not only land but such intangible property as franchises and contracts.[2] Thus, during the World War, the United States Shipping Board Emergency Fleet Corporation requisitioned certain contracts for the construction of vessels, and this was held

[1] Chicago, B. & Q. Ry. Co. v. Chicago, 166 U. S. 226 (1897).
[2] This does not constitute the impairment of the obligation of the contract but rather its acquisition.

to be a taking for public use entitling the owner to compensation.[1] During that war, the President, by virtue of the authority vested in him by the National Defense Act, requisitioned all the electrical power produced by a certain power company. This was held to be a taking of private property for public use, although the Government did not use the power, but, in consideration of the power company's waiver of compensation, permitted it to sell such power to private manufacturers.[2]

Delegation of Eminent Domain.—As already pointed out, the power of eminent domain is inherent in the government and may not be contracted away.[3] It may, however, be delegated by the state to a governmental subdivision of the state, such as a municipal corporation. It may also be delegated to corporations organized primarily for private profit, provided they are engaged in a business affected with a public interest. The best example is a railroad, which, in many instances, could not be constructed if it did not have the power to condemn land for its right of way. In this case, the taking of property, although primarily for the benefit of the railroad, is also incidentally for the public good. The power of eminent domain might even be delegated to a private individual, if his use of it is for the public good, but this is seldom done. The exercise of the power by private corporations or individuals is allowable only when the taking or use of certain land is essential to the conduct of the enterprise. An individual or corporation desiring to construct a hotel in a city would not have the right to condemn land for the purpose, because, although the enterprise may incidentally be of public benefit, the taking of no particular plot of land is essential to its conduct.

National Eminent Domain.—The power of eminent domain may be exercised not only by the states and local subdivisions thereof but also by the National Government. As exercised by the latter Government, however, it must be incidental to the accomplishment of the purposes for which it is established or to the carrying out of the powers granted to it in the Federal Constitution. It may be classed as a resulting power. For example, the National Government may condemn land in the District of Columbia for the erection of public buildings. It may also exercise a similar power in the states for the erection of post offices, custom houses, etc.

Conflicts of Authority in Eminent Domain.—A state cannot condemn land within its borders which is being used by the National Government for governmental purposes. On the other hand, it would seem that, if the National Government should need the site of a state capitol for the erection of a fort and no other site was suitable for the purpose, it probably

---

[1] Russian Volunteer Fleet v. United States, 282 U. S. 481 (1931).

[2] International Paper Co. v. United States, 282 U. S. 399 (1931). By the law of New York the right to take such power was a corporeal hereditament and real estate.

[3] See Chap. XXV.

could condemn it. This case has not actually arisen. It has been held, however, that the National Government may condemn land for a public park at the site of the battlefield of Gettysburg in Pennsylvania, even though a part of this land comprised the route of a state electric road.[1]

A somewhat different situation may arise when two railroad companies desire to condemn the same land for railroad purposes. Where their rights of way cross each other, it may be consistent with the efficient operation of each road for the two companies to use the intersection jointly. When this is not feasible, the legislature may by special act authorize one railroad to take land occupied by another railroad for less essential railroad purposes.[2] In the case just cited, the railroad which was authorized to take the land needed it for a passenger station, whereas it was being used by the other railroad merely for a freight yard. Under these circumstances, the first railroad could probably have condemned the land under the general power of eminent domain in the absence of a special legislative act. But if the second railroad had also been using the land for a passenger station, the first railroad could probably not have been authorized even by special legislative act to condemn it, because no public use could be shown.

In connection with the exercise of the power of eminent domain, three important questions may arise which, in general, are finally to be settled by the courts. They are, first, what is a public use in eminent domain; second, what constitutes a taking of property in eminent domain; and, third, what is the measure of compensation in eminent domain?

What Is a Public Use?—It is within the discretion of the legislature to determine in the first instance whether the public convenience and necessity require that property shall be condemned, as well as the amount of land and the extent of the estate in it which shall be taken. The final determination of what is a public use in eminent domain, however, is within the control of the courts rather than of the legislature. Some uses are so clearly public that no question is likely to arise with regard to them. For example, the condemnation of land by a state for a capitol or a highway, by a city for a city hall or public school, and by a railroad for its right of way, are clearly public uses. Likewise, public utilities may condemn land for use in transporting gas, water, and electric current. As already pointed out, however, land could not be condemned for the erection of a hotel, or for the establishment of an ordinary business, such as a grocery store. It would also be unconstitutional for a private grain elevator to condemn land.[3] but this could be done by a public grain elevator.

[1] United States v. Gettysburg Electric Ry. Co., 160 U. S. 668 (1896).
[2] Eastern R. R. Co. v. Boston & Maine R. R., 111 Mass. 125 (1872).
[3] Missouri Pacific Ry. Co. v. Nebraska, 164 U. S. 403 (1896).

Land may be condemned for the establishment of public works which promote the public health, safety, or welfare, such, for example, as a public park. As to whether property may be condemned for purely aesthetic purposes, there has been some difference of opinion among the courts, but the better view would seem to be that this may be done. Thus, it has been held that the height of buildings around a city square may be limited for the sake of architectural symmetry, provided just compensation were made to the owners.[1]

An interesting group of cases relating to what is a public use in eminent domain are those construing the mill acts passed in various states. These acts authorize riparian owners to dam rivers and erect mills, resulting in the flooding of land previously used for agricultural purposes, provided, of course, just compensation be made to the owners of such land. The attitude of the courts as to the constitutionality of such acts differs, depending upon the particular circumstances of the time and place. Such acts would be upheld in states where, and at a time when, the development of water power for milling is considered more essential to the public welfare than agriculture. In other states where agriculture is more important and in later times in which the advent of steam and electricity has decreased the importance of water power, such acts are not upheld.

Another group of cases illustrating the changing conception of public use in eminent domain is that relating to irrigation in the arid region of the West. Under such circumstances, acts authorizing a private individual to condemn a right of way across his neighbor's land for an irrigation ditch to convey water to his own land have been upheld.[2] In this case there was really no public use, but the fact of public benefit to be derived from the operation of such acts was deemed to be sufficient. Such an act, however, probably would not be upheld in other states where similar conditions do not prevail.

By analogy, it has been held that an individual mine owner may be authorized to condemn a right of way across adjacent property for an aerial bucket line to convey his products to a railroad.[3]

What Is a Taking of Property?—In considering the question as to what constitutes a taking of property in eminent domain, it is necessary at the outset to bear in mind that property does not consist of things but rather of the right to the use and enjoyment of things. Consequently, as we have seen in connection with the mill acts, the flooding of land

[1] Attorney-General v. Williams, 174 Mass. 476 (1899). As to whether a city may condemn more land than is actually needed for a public improvement, *i.e.*, exercise the power of excess condemnation, has not yet been finally determined by the courts. As throwing some light upon this question, however, see City of Cincinnati v. Vester, 281 U. S. 439 (1930).

[2] Clark v. Nash, 198 U. S. 361 (1905).

[3] Strickley v. Highland Boy Gold Mining Co., 200 U. S. 527 (1906).

constitutes a taking of property for which compensation must be made, although the title to the flooded land is not necessarily disturbed. Of course, if the title is changed, the property is taken. On the other hand, interference with the full enjoyment of property by noise or smoke has not been held to be a taking for which compensation may be obtained.

Again, if A holds land subject to an easement whereby B has a right of way over it, the exercise by B of this right is obviously not a taking of A's property. Similarly, the ownership by a private individual of the bed of a navigable stream may be subject to a public right of navigation, in which case the exercise by the public of this right does not entitle the owner of the bed of the stream to compensation. By analogy, the ownership of land is subject, without compensation, to the public right of aerial navigation over it. By the same line of reasoning, it has been held that lands abutting on rivers are subject to a servitude in favor of the public, whereby such portions thereof as are necessary for the purpose of making and repairing public levees may be taken, in pursuance of law, without compensation.[1] In other words, there was in this case no taking of private property in eminent domain.

Somewhat analogous to the situation of riparian owners along a navigable stream is that of abutting landowners along a street or highway. In the latter case, the city may own the street in fee, in which case the abutting property owners have easements in the street of air, light, access, and lateral support. Or the city may merely have an easement in the street to use it for legitimate highway purposes, the fee being held by the abutting property owners. In either case the main question which arises is: what are reasonable and legitimate purposes for which the street may be used? If the purposes are reasonable, the abutting landowners are not entitled to compensation, even though the carrying out of such purposes may interfere with their rights to air, light, access, or lateral support.

As to some purposes for which a street may be used, there is no difference of opinion that they are reasonable and legitimate. Among these are street railways, water mains, gas and sewer pipes, and electric lighting posts when used to light the streets. In order to increase the usefulness of a street for highway purposes, it is also legitimate to grade it by cutting through ridges and filling in ravines. Houses adjacent to a cut may have their access and lateral support interfered with, while those adjacent to a fill may have their air, light, and access restricted, but the owners are not entitled to compensation. As to whether elevated railroads and subways constitute reasonable street uses, the courts are divided. It would seem clear, however, that the use of streets for steam railroads is not legitimate.

[1] Eldridge v. Trezevant, 160 U. S. 452 (1896).

Compensation in Eminent Domain.—The just compensation to which a person whose property is taken in eminent domain is entitled is the market value of the property. In case of dispute as to what is market value, the question is one for determination by a court or administrative tribunal. But it is customary for the court to submit the question to a master in chancery who is an expert in property values and to base its decision upon the report of the master.

If an entire tract or piece of property is taken, compensation must be made in money at the market value. But if only part of a tract of land is taken, as, for example, through the construction of a highway, it would seem that the owner of the tract may be required to take a part of his compensation in the form of benefits or increased market value, which accrue to the remainder of his land, provided, at least, such benefits attach specially to his land and not generally to all land in the locality.

On the other hand, the taking of a portion of a man's land may result not in benefit but in injury to the remainder. In this case the owner is entitled to compensation equal to the fair value of the portion taken plus the amount of damage to the remainder.

When property is merely damaged and not taken, *i.e.*, when there is no transfer of title, the Federal Constitution does not require compensation, but many states by statute or constitutional provision require compensation in such case, provided the damage would be actionable if caused by an individual. As already noted, the courts have not yet come to the view that damage caused by smoke or noise requires compensation, although logically it would seem that it should.

Notice and Hearing.—Finally, it should be pointed out that due process requires that the owner of property which it is proposed to take under the power of eminent domain shall have notice and hearing. These constitute what are known as condemnation proceedings. In some cases constructive notice, as by publication, is sufficient when personal service is impracticable.

As noted above, the hearing need not be before a court but may be before an administrative tribunal and, if before the latter, the right of appeal to a court on questions of fact is not required, nor is it necessary that a jury should be employed, provided the procedure followed is reasonably calculated to secure a fair determination of the question.

CHAPTER XXX

DUE PROCESS AND THE POLICE POWER

General Principles Underlying the Police Power.—The police power is among the most important and comprehensive of all governmental powers. It may be broadly defined as the regulation of conduct for the promotion of the general welfare. The principle on which the exercise of the police power is based is that all individual rights of liberty and property are held subject to such reasonable limitations and regulations as may be necessary and expedient for the protection of the common good and the general welfare.[1] This principle is succinctly expressed in the maxim "so use your own property as not to injure that of others." It represents a departure from the individualistic philosophy of *laissez faire* and an approach toward collectivism. This development has been rendered practically necessary on account of the increasing complexity of social, economic, and industrial conditions in modern times.

It will be seen that, in every exercise of the police power, there are two essential ingredients: first, a limitation upon the individual in respect to his liberty or property and, second, the promotion of the common good or general welfare. The first ingredient is not a good in itself but is merely a means for the accomplishment of the second ingredient, which is the end in view. If any particular limitation upon individual liberty or property rights is not reasonably conducive to the promotion of the general welfare, it is not a legitimate exercise of the police power and would be prohibited by the due-process clauses of the Fifth or Fourteenth Amendment.

The police power is one of the inherent or reserved powers of the states, but it is not a transcendent or all-inclusive power and, although somewhat vague in extent, is subject to constitutional limitations. It should be distinguished from other powers of government, such as those of taxation and eminent domain. By the latter power, as we have seen, private property may be taken for public use, provided just compensation be given. Property may also be taken under the police power, but only when the use of such property is deemed to be detrimental to the public interests, and, in this case, no compensation need be given.[2] Ordinarily,

---

[1] Commonwealth v. Alger, 7 Cush. 53 (1851).

[2] It would seem that the police power may be exerted, without compensation, to dynamite buildings in the path of a conflagration. American Print Works v. Lawrence, 23 N. J. L. 590 (1851). In such case, the destruction of some property is reasonably necessary in order to save the property of the other residents.

however, property is merely regulated by the police power and not actually taken.[1]

The National Government, as well as the states, may exercise a police power. There is no express grant of this power to the National Government in the Federal Constitution, but, incidentally to the exercise of powers expressly granted to that Government, a national police power may be exercised. Thus, as we have seen, Congress has excluded lottery matter and obscene literature from the mails and has passed pure food and drugs acts and meat inspection laws, as incidental to the exercise of its postal and commerce powers. The states, however, are able to exercise a broader and more general police power than that of the National Government. The states, as we have seen, may even exercise a police power which indirectly affects interstate commerce, provided the regulation is local in character and does not conflict with any legislation of Congress. Thus, a state may regulate the speed of interstate trains at crossings and the method of heating and sanitary conditions on such trains in the absence of conflicting Congressional regulations.[2] The states may exercise the police power directly, or they may delegate it to municipal corporations within their borders.

Although, as already pointed out, the purpose of the exercise of the police power is the promotion of the general welfare, this statement gives only a vague idea of its scope. To put the matter more definitely, it may be said that the scope of the police power includes two main divisions: first, that relating to fundamental objects of social welfare, such as the promotion of the public safety, health, morals, and peace or order, and, second, that relating primarily to economic welfare. The first division is not only more fundamental but is the traditional content of public welfare regulations. The promotion of economic welfare is a later development which has been brought about by the abandonment of the *laissez faire* doctrine and the adoption of a more paternalistic attitude of government toward business and economic interests.

The exercise of the police power under either of these divisions must be in harmony with the constitutional guarantee of due process. One of the most important functions of the courts is that of keeping a proper balance between these opposing considerations, *viz.*, the necessity of governmental regulation for the promotion of the general welfare and the enforcement of the constitutional guarantees for the protection of

[1] MATHEWS, J. M., "State Power and Individual Rights," *Ill. Law Quart.*, vol. 4, pp. 253–262 (June, 1922). The police power is sometimes exerted in the guise of a tax law. Thus, a provision for a dog tax may be designed primarily to promote public safety rather than to produce revenue. Requirements of the payment of license taxes before engaging in certain occupations, deemed to be potentially dangerous to health or morals, may be in reality police regulations.

[2] Southern Ry. Co. v. King, 217 U. S. 524 (1910); New York, etc., Ry. Co. v. New York, 165 U. S. 628 (1897).

individual rights. Every exercise of the police power interferes to some extent with individual rights, but such exercise will nevertheless, as a rule, be upheld by the courts if they are of the opinion that it is reasonably conducive to the promotion of the general welfare and does not arbitrarily interfere with the rights of individuals. A certain regulation, however, which only slightly conduces to the promotion of the general welfare might not be upheld by the courts if it involves a severe or extreme interference with individual rights. Of these two opposing considerations, the promotion of the general welfare is the more weighty, but the constitutional provisions regarding due process are nevertheless very considerable limitations upon the governmental exercise of the police power. As has been pointed out, "the boundary between the liberty of the individual and the police power of the state is an indeterminate zone rather than a definite line. It is not for the courts to draw that line, but only to call a halt when the legislature has passed over that zone."[1]

It is impracticable to enumerate all the concrete examples of the exercise of the police power, because they are exceedingly numerous. But a few examples will indicate the general characteristics of each group. Many of them may be classified under more than one head, but we may consider them in accordance with that division in which they seem primarily to fall.

The Promotion of Public Health.—Under the head of measures designed to protect the public health may be mentioned those providing for the establishment of quarantines and the abatement of nuisances, and pure food and drug acts, prohibiting the selling or keeping for sale of unwholesome or adulterated foods, requiring the inspection of milk, meat, and other provisions, and prohibiting the selling of poisonous drugs, unless properly labeled. By these measures both liberty and property may be interfered with, but such interference does not invalidate the regulations in question if they are reasonably necessary to the protection of the public health. On the other hand, the establishment of a strict quarantine might be regarded by the courts as unreasonable and therefore invalid if the disease were very mild and only slightly contagious. Again, a statute of Pennsylvania which required all stockholders of a corporation owning drug stores to be licensed pharmacists was held invalid as arbitrary and lacking in due process because there is no real and substantial relation between the public health and ownership of stock in a drug company.[2]

A good example of the exercise of the police power for the protection of the public health is the requirement of vaccination against smallpox. In many states vaccination is required of children as a condition of

[1] KEASBY, E. Q., "The Courts and the New Social Questions," *Green Bag*, vol. 24, p. 120 (1912).

[2] Liggett Co. v. Baldridge, 278 U. S. 105 (1928).

attending the public schools. A statute of Massachusetts went further and required the vaccination of adults whenever, in the opinion of local boards of health, it was necessary for the protection of the public health. One Jacobson refused to comply with such an order of the Cambridge board of health, contending that vaccination is a useless and dangerous procedure, but this contention was denied by the courts and the order of the board was upheld.[1] In this case, smallpox was actually prevalent in the community wherein the board of health ordered compulsory vaccination. If, however, there have been no cases of smallpox in the community and no danger of contagion, the board's order of compulsory vaccination might have been held to be an unreasonable deprivation of personal liberty. On the other hand, the order might have been upheld, even under these circumstances, if it were regarded by public opinion generally as reasonable.

A decision based in part upon the exercise of the police power for the promotion of public health but having broad social implications was that involving a Virginia statute of 1924 providing for the sterilization of mental defectives confined in public institutions. In holding the law constitutional as not lacking in due process, Justice Holmes, speaking for the Court, declared that, "It is better for all the world, if instead of waiting to execute degenerate offspring for crime, or to let them starve for their imbecility, society can prevent those who are manifestly unfit from continuing their kind."[2]

The Regulation of Occupations.—Among the recognized rights of the individual, falling within the scope of the term "liberty" as used in the due-process clauses, is that of entering into lawful callings and occupations for the purpose of earning a livelihood. Many occupations, however, are of such nature as to affect not only the individuals who enter them but also the public generally who may avail themselves of the services of those engaged in such occupations or professions. On account of this larger public interest involved, the police power may be exerted for the purpose of limiting the privilege of engaging in certain occupations to those having the requisite qualifications, so that no one may have a right to practice these professions unless licensed by proper authority. Such occupations are those in which certain degrees of professional skill and probity are necessary in order to protect the health and safety of the public, or to prevent fraud and deception. Among the occupations subject to regulation for the protection of public health are those of physician, druggist, dentist, and nurse. Other occupations frequently regulated are those of lawyer, banker, barber, plumber, and undertaker. If the regulation of such occupations seems to be primarily for the purpose of reducing

[1] Jacobson v. Massachusetts, 197 U. S. 11 (1905).
[2] Buck v. Bell, 274 U. S. 200 (1927).

competition and has very slight relation to the public health or safety, it will probably not be upheld by the courts.

An example of the regulation of occupations for the protection of public health was the statute of Minnesota requiring the possession of a diploma from a dental college in good standing as a prerequisite to being examined for a license to practice dentistry. The statute was upheld as not being a denial of due process or equal protection of the law.[1]

The Promotion of Public Morals.—The police power is exerted for the protection of public morals through the enactment of laws to curb gambling, intoxication, sexual irregularities, and obscenity. Among forms of gambling which are or may be prohibited or regulated under the police power are lotteries, selling stocks on margin, betting at race tracks, and games of chance. In order to curb obscenity, theaters, moving picture houses, and other places of amusement may be regulated and their exhibitions censored. Indecent or obscene publications, prize fights, and the transportation of prize-fight films may be prohibited.

The Promotion of Public Safety and Order.—For the purpose of promoting the public safety or order, laws may be enacted prohibiting the carrying of concealed weapons without a license, prohibiting the holding of meetings in the streets and parks without a license, requiring that electric wires shall be placed under the surface, that dogs shall be muzzled, that gunpowder shall not be transported or stored in populous areas, and that tanks within city limits for the storage of petroleum or other inflammable liquids shall be buried underground.[2] Numerous building regulations have been made for the promotion of public safety, designed especially to eliminate fire risks, such as requirements that buildings within certain zones shall be constructed of fire-resisting materials, that buildings of more than a certain height shall be equipped with fire escapes, and that theaters shall be equipped with asbestos curtains and doors opening outward.

Many traffic regulations also come under the head of exertions of the police power for the promotion of public safety. Among these may be mentioned measures requiring vehicles to turn to the right, to be equipped with lights after dark, and to travel at not more than a reasonable rate of speed. Railroad trains may be required to slow down in cities, to blow the whistle at crossings, and to be heated in some other way than by stoves, and locomotives may be required to carry a particular type of headlight.[3]

Another illustration of a safety regulation was the law of Illinois which was designed to protect property owners against damage caused by mobs or riots. The law imposed on the municipality in which the property

---

[1] Graves v. Minnesota, 272 U. S. 425 (1926).
[2] Standard Oil Co. v. Maryville, 279 U. S. 582 (1929).
[3] Atlantic Coast Line Ry. Co. v. Georgia, 234 U. S. 280 (1914).

was situated liability for such damage. A peculiar feature of the law was that such liability was absolute and irrespective of any fault on the part of the municipality. The law was nevertheless upheld as a legitimate exercise of the police power.[1]

Public Convenience.—The courts have sometimes frankly held that the police power may be exercised to promote aims other than the primary objects of health, safety, and morals. Thus, the Supreme Court of the United States, speaking by Justice Harlan, has declared:

We hold that the police power of a state embraces regulations designed to promote the public convenience or the general prosperity as well as regulations designed to promote the public health, the public morals, or the public safety . . . And the validity of a police regulation must depend upon the circumstances of each case and the character of the regulation, whether arbitrary or reasonable and whether really designed to accomplish a legitimate public purpose.[2]

In 1899, the same Court, speaking by the same justice, upheld the constitutionality of a state statute requiring railroads to stop certain trains at towns having a population of 3,000, although there was no question of health, morals, or safety involved, but simply a matter of public convenience.[3] It is true, of course, that the promotion of the public comfort or convenience is not so urgent a matter as the promotion of the primary and more fundamental objects of the police power—health, safety, and morals. For this reason the exercise of the police power for the former purpose is restricted within narrower limits and is usually, though not invariably, upheld only when applied to restrain public service corporations. Even with reference to such corporations, it will not be upheld if exercised for the convenience of a particular individual rather than of the general public.[4]

Aesthetic Purposes.—The courts have not heretofore been inclined to uphold attempted exercises of the police power for merely aesthetic purposes. "Aesthetic considerations," it has been declared, "are a matter of luxury and indulgence rather than of necessity, and it is necessity alone which justifies the exercise of the police power to take private property without compensation."[5] This question has arisen frequently in connection with the attempts of cities to regulate billboards and to require the establishment of building lines. Such regulations

[1] Chicago v. Sturgis, 222 U. S. 313 (1911).

[2] Chicago, B. & Q. Ry. Co. v. Illinois, 200 U. S. 561 (1906). The same position was taken in Chicago & Alton R. R. Co. v. Tranbarger, 238 U. S. 76 (1915).

[3] Lake Shore & M. S. Ry. Co. v. Ohio, 173 U. S. 285 (1899).

[4] Chicago, St. P., M. & O. Ry. Co. v. Holmberg, 282 U. S. 162 (1930), holding invalid the order of a state railroad commission requiring a railroad company, at its own expense, to construct an underpass connecting farm lands on both sides of the tracks, solely for the convenience of the landowner.

[5] City of Passaic v. Paterson Bill Posting Co., 72 N. J. L. 285 (1915).

have usually been held invalid if capable of being supported on no other than aesthetic grounds.[1]   But they will be sustained if capable of being supported on the ground of safety or morals.[2]   Thus, it would of course be valid, in the interest of morals, to prohibit the exhibition of indecent posters on billboards; and, in the interest of safety, their location and strength of construction might be regulated.

Zoning ordinances, which have been passed in many cities, limiting the uses to which land in different sections of the city may be put, are intended partly, although not mainly, for aesthetic purposes. If they are not clearly arbitrary or unreasonable and have some relation to the public health, safety, morals, or general welfare, such ordinances are upheld.[3]

Race Legislation.—That the police power of the states with reference to the regulation of the civil rights of their citizens was not taken away by the Fourteenth Amendment was decided by the Supreme Court of the United States in the Slaughter House and Civil Rights Cases.[4] Consistently with that amendment, the states may, under their police powers, enact laws introducing or maintaining racial distinctions, provided they are not unduly or unreasonably discriminatory. The question has arisen principally in connection with the enactment of laws embodying racial distinctions in the public schools and in public conveyances. Separate public schools for the white and colored races have been established in a number of states, and there is no doubt as to the power of the state to make such separate arrangements, provided substantially equal facilities are accorded to each race. Where the number of colored children are few, a state may, under some circumstances, suspend temporarily a colored high school, while continuing to maintain a white high school.[5] In the Berea College case it was held that a state may prohibit the instruction of white and colored persons at the same time and place even in private educational institutions.[6]

With reference to racial distinctions in public conveyances, a state cannot require that persons of both races shall have the same privileges in public conveyances plying between two or more states, since this would conflict with the power of Congress over interstate commerce.[7] But a state may require a railroad to provide equal, but separate, accom-

---

[1] Eubank v. Richmond, 226 U. S. 137 (1912).   But *cf.* St. Louis Advertising Co. v. City of St. Louis, 249 U. S. 269 (1918).

[2] Cusack v. Chicago, 242 U. S. 526 (1917).

[3] Euclid v. Ambler Realty Co., 272 U. S. 365 (1926).   For further consideration of zoning ordinances, see Chap. XXXI.

[4] 16 Wall. 36, 21 Law. ed. 394 (1873); 109 U. S. 3, 27 Law. ed. 835 (1883).

[5] Cumming v. Board of Education, 175 U. S. 528, 44 Law. ed. 202 (1899).

[6] Berea College v. Commonwealth, 123 Ky. 209, 211 U. S. 45, 53 Law. ed. 81 (1908).

[7] Hall v. De Cuir, 95 U. S. 485, 24 Law. ed. 547 (1878).

modations for white and colored passengers on intrastate journeys, as this would not be a denial of the equal protection of the laws.[1]

Classification by race, however, may go too far. Thus, the residential block segregation ordinance of Louisville, Kentucky, was held invalid because it deprived members of both races of the right to live where they wished and of the right to sell property to a member of the opposite race, while it could not be sustained as preventing race riots or the depreciation of property.[2]

Liquor Legislation.—The business of manufacturing and selling intoxicating liquor for consumption as a beverage has been deemed to have such an important effect upon the public health, safety, and morals as to require special regulation and even prohibition. The exercise of the police power with reference to the liquor traffic has been a continual progression. Starting with mild regulation, it developed into highly drastic and stringent regulation, and, when this did not prove satisfactory, the final step of complete prohibition was taken. This last step, however, was really a series of steps, the first being taken in the localities under local option laws. State-wide prohibition followed, and, finally, by the Eighteenth Amendment, nation-wide prohibition was introduced. A step intermediate between regulation and complete prohibition is the state dispensary system, which was introduced in South Carolina, whereby all private traffic in liquor is abolished and the state assumes a monopoly of the subject.

The provisions of the Eighteenth Amendment are supposed to be enforced by the concurrent legislation of the states and of Congress. This amendment does not invalidate state prohibition laws previously enacted, but, on the contrary, it makes them constitutional if they were not so already, provided they do not conflict with the amendment nor with the laws of Congress enacted for its enforcement. State laws cannot legalize a laxer enforcement of the amendment than the laws of Congress provide, but they might set up a stricter rule of prohibition than that embodied either in the amendment or in the enforcement laws of Congress.

The due-process clause does not protect the liquor business against state regulation or prohibition, even though property invested in the business at a time when it was legal is virtually rendered worthless through the operation of the state prohibitory law.[3] All property is held under the implied obligation that the owner's use of it shall not be injuri-

[1] Plessy v. Ferguson, 163 U. S. 537, 41 Law. ed. 256 (1896). In the absence of statutory authority, a railroad may segregate the races even in interstate transportation. Chiles v. C. & O. Ry. Co., 218 U. S. 71, 54 Law. ed. 936 (1910).

[2] Buchanan v. Warley, 245 U. S. 60, 62 Law. ed. 149 (1917). On race legislation see G. T. Stephenson, *Race Distinctions in American Law* and C. W. Collins, *The Fourteenth Amendment and the States*, Chaps. V and VI (1912).

[3] Mugler v. Kansas, 123 U. S. 623 (1887).

ous to the community.[1]   A liquor license, therefore, is not a vested right. In the Mugler case, the Court even recognized the power of the legislature to prohibit individuals from manufacturing intoxicating liquors for their own use as a beverage, on the ground that, if this were allowed, the prohibitory plan might fail.   On the same ground, even the mere possession of intoxicating liquor may be prohibited.[2]

The Promotion of Economic Welfare.—In addition to the objects mentioned, the police power also undertakes to promote the general welfare by restricting those economic activities of individuals and corporations which may endanger it.   Some examples will indicate in a general way the scope of this branch of the police power.   Thus, laws passed for the conservation of natural resources, such as laws establishing closed seasons for fish and game and forbidding the waste of gas or oil and the pumping out of natural mineral springs, have been upheld under the police power.[3]

On account of the ever-changing conception of the general welfare, new subjects are continually coming within the scope of the police power. Numerous laws have been passed for the protection of the public against various forms of fraud, such as the sale of merchandise in bulk without notice to creditors.[4]   In order to prevent the economic oppression of the debtor class, laws have been enacted forbidding the charging of usurious rates of interest.   Laws prohibiting the misbranding of foods and drugs are intended not only for the protection of health but also for the prevention of fraud.

Blue-sky Laws.—A large amount of worthless stock is annually sold to people throughout the country by concerns having little more tangible assets than so many feet of blue sky.   In order to protect the public against this form of fraud, many states have enacted what are known as "blue-sky" laws, prohibiting the sale of securities without a license from a designated state officer.   From the standpoint of constitutionality, blue-sky laws had rough sailing at first, several of them being declared unconstitutional in the lower courts.   The grounds on which they were attacked were that they constituted an undue interference with interstate commerce, delegated judicial power to an administrative officer, deprived persons of liberty or property without due process of law, and abridged the privileges and immunities of citizens of the United States.   In 1917, however, these contentions were negatived by the Supreme Court of the United States in a case involving the Ohio blue-sky law, holding it to be a valid exercise of the state police power.[5]

[1] Beer Co. v. Massachusetts, 97 U. S. 25 (1878).

[2] Crane v. Campbell, 245 U. S. 304 (1917).

[3] Ohio Oil Co. v. Indiana, 177 U. S. 190 (1900); Lindsley v. Natural Carbonic Gas Co., 220 U. S. 61 (1911).

[4] Lemieux v. Young, 211 U. S. 489 (1909).

[5] Hall v. Geiger-Jones Co., 242 U. S. 539 (1917).   For cases upholding similar laws in other states, see Caldwell v. Sioux Falls Stock Yards Co., 242 U. S. 559 (1917);

Regulation of Banking and Insurance.—For the protection of the public against fraud or loss, many laws have been enacted regulating the banking business. Thus, in Wisconsin a statute was enacted which forbade the conduct of the banking business in other than the corporate form. This was objected to on the ground that it infringed the common-law right of every citizen to engage in the banking business. The supreme court of that state, however, held that banking is a quasi-public business and that, although the legislature could not prohibit its conduct altogether, it could, under the police power, make such a reasonable regulation as the requirement of incorporation.[1]

Although state banks are subject to supervision and inspection by state officers, nevertheless defalcations may occur and for this or other reasons a bank may fail with loss to depositors. In order to guard against the latter contingency, Oklahoma, in 1907, enacted a statute providing for the creation of a depositors' guarantee fund by assessments upon every state bank's average daily deposits. If any such bank failed, depositors were protected against loss through payments from this fund. The banks objected to the exaction, arguing that the assessment was a taking of private property for private use without compensation. The Supreme Court of the United States, however, speaking by Justice Holmes, upheld the statute as a valid exercise of the state's police power. He pointed out that "an ulterior public advantage may justify a comparatively insignificant taking of private property for what, in its immediate purpose, is a private use," and further declared that "the police power extends to all the great public needs. It may be put forth in aid of what is sanctioned by usage, or held by the prevailing morality or strong and preponderant opinion to be greatly and immediately necessary to the public welfare."[2]

Attempts were later made to secure an injunction against the collection of special assessments upon banks under a similar bank depositors' guarantee law of Nebraska. The Supreme Court admitted that such a police regulation, although valid when made, might become, by reason of later events, arbitrary and confiscatory but in this case refused to enjoin such collection on the ground that the assessment was not so confiscatory or unreasonable as to be violative of the due-process clause.[3]

It has also been held that the insurance business is so far affected with a public interest that the state under its police power may regulate rates and also the amount of the commissions allowed to the local agents.[4]

Merrick v. Halsey & Co., 242 U. S. 568 (1917); and Stewart v. Brady, 300 Ill. 445 (1921).

[1] Weed v. Bergh, 141 Wis. 569 (1910). *Cf.* Shallenberger v. First State Bank of Holstein, 219 U. S. 114 (1911).

[2] Noble State Bank v. Haskell, 219 U. S. 104 (1911).

[3] Abie State Bank v. Bryan, 282 U. S. 765 (1931).

[4] O'Gorman & Young v. Hartford Fire Insurance Co., 282 U. S. 251 (1931).

Business Affected with a Public Interest.—Another important way in which it is attempted by public authority to promote the economic welfare of the people is through regulation of the rates and service of public service corporations and other concerns which, in the language of the Supreme Court, are "clothed with a public interest."[1] In the case just cited, the Court was presented with the question as to the constitutionality of an act of the Illinois legislature fixing the maximum charges for the storage of grain in warehouses or elevators. The law was attacked as a deprivation of property without due process of law. The Court nevertheless held that the operation of grain elevators is a business sufficiently clothed with a public interest to justify the legislature in regulating the rates charged. It pointed out that property becomes

. . . clothed with a public interest when used in a manner to make it of public consequence, and affect the community at large. When, therefore, one devotes his property to a use in which the public has an interest, he, in effect, grants to the public an interest in that use, and must submit to be controlled by the public for the common good, to the extent of the interest he has thus created.

In an *obiter dictum* in the Munn case, the Court declared that for protection against abuses by legislatures in fixing rates of businesses affected with a public interest, the "people must resort to the polls, not to the courts." This doctrine, however, was later repudiated. It was later declared that there can be no doubt of the power and duty of the courts to inquire whether a body of rates prescribed by a legislature or a commission is unjust and unreasonable so as to work a deprivation of property without due process of law.[2]

This position was reaffirmed a few years later in a case involving the validity of a railroad rate laid down by legislative enactment. In invalidating the rate, the Court held that due process not only requires judicial review of the reasonableness of rates fixed by the legislature but also requires that the rate fixed shall allow the railroad a fair return upon a fair valuation of its property. In determining what is a reasonable rate in accordance with these principles, a number of factors have to be taken into consideration, which were described by the Court as follows:

The basis of all calculation as to the reasonableness of rates to be charged by a corporation maintaining a highway under legislative sanction must be the fair

[1] Munn v. Illinois, 94 U. S. 113 (1876).

[2] Reagan v. Farmers' Loan and Trust Co., 154 U. S. 362 (1894). The courts will also inquire into the reasonableness of an order made by a state directly or through a commission relating to the service to be furnished by a public service corporation. Thus, the Supreme Court upheld the order of the California Railroad Commission requiring certain railroad companies to construct a union passenger station in the city of Los Angeles as not depriving the companies of property without due process of law. Atchison, T. & S. F. Ry. Co. v. Railroad Commission, 283 U. S. 380 (1931).

value of the property used by it for the convenience of the public. And, in order to ascertain that value, the original cost of construction, the amount expended in permanent improvements, the amount and market value of its bonds and stock, the present as compared with the original cost of construction, the probable earning capacity of the property under particular rates prescribed by statute, and the sum required to meet operating expenses, are all matters for consideration and are to be given such weight as may be just and right in each case . . . What the company is entitled to ask is a fair return upon the value of that which it employs for the public convenience. On the other hand, what the public is entitled to demand is that no more be exacted from it for the use of a public highway than the services rendered by it are reasonably worth.[1]

It would appear that the various businesses affected with a public interest and thus subject to public regulation may be classified into three groups: first, those discharging functions, such as transportation, which might appropriately be discharged by the government itself; second, those requiring public franchises, such as the use of the public streets and the exercise of the power of eminent domain; and, third, those of vital importance to the public welfare, especially if monopolistic in character. Since monopolies cannot be regulated by competition, the exercise of the police power for this purpose is more necessary. It is principally in connection with the third class mentioned that difference of opinion arises as to whether a given business should be included. Thus, there are judicial decisions on both sides of the question as to whether a news-gathering and disseminating concern, such as the Associated Press, is a business so affected with the public interest as to justify public regulation.

It has been held that theaters are not businesses affected with a public interest and that, consequently, public regulation of their prices is a deprivation of due process. This was the position taken by the majority of the Supreme Court in 1927 in a five-to-four decision holding unconstitutional a New York statute which declared the charge for admission to

[1] Smyth v. Ames, 169 U. S. 466 (1898). The phrase quoted: "a fair return upon the value of that which it employs for the public convenience" has been later construed to mean that "there must be a fair return upon the reasonable value of the property at the time it is being used for the public," or, in other words, "cost of replacement less depreciation." Willcox v. Consolidated Gas Co., 212 U. S. 19 (1908); Minnesota rate cases, 230 U. S. 352 (1913).

In the Baltimore Street Railway case, the Court included the franchise in the admitted valuation of the company's property, computed depreciation upon the basis of present, rather than original, cost and held that, in determining what is a fair return, the circumstances, locality, and risk of the particular company must be taken into consideration. United Railways and Electric Co. v. West, 280 U. S. 234 (1930). *Cf.* St. Louis & O'Fallon Ry. Co. v. United States, 279 U. S. 461 (1929) and Smith v. Illinois Bell Telephone Co., 282 U. S. 133 (1930). In the last-named case, the Court pointed out that an order of a state commission fixing rates of a public utility, which is confiscatory when made may cease to be confiscatory, or one which is valid when made may become confiscatory at a later period.

theaters a matter affected with a public interest and forbade the resale of tickets of admission at a price in excess of fifty cents more than the price printed on the face of the ticket.[1] Similarly, the business of selling gasoline has been held not to be affected with a public interest, and consequently a state statute fixing the price of gasoline is invalid as a deprivation of property without due process of law.[2]

The business of an employment agency has been held to be affected with a public interest to an extent necessary to justify police regulation, but not to an extent necessary to justify regulation of the charges made for its services.[3] In this case, Justice Stone in a dissenting opinion declared that the term "affected with a public interest" is vague, indefinite, and not founded on the Constitution. He describes it as applying to any business "whenever any combination of circumstances seriously curtails the regulative force of competition, so that buyers or sellers are placed at such a disadvantage in the bargaining struggle that a legislature might reasonably anticipate serious consequences to the community as a whole."

Emergency Measures.—A business which in ordinary times is not subject to regulation under the police power may be regulated in time of emergency. Thus, it was held that, during and after the World War while an acute housing shortage existed, the police power could be exerted to prohibit landlords from charging more than a reasonable rent, and to restrain them from evicting their tenants for failure to pay more than a reasonable rent, even though the tenant had contracted to pay more.[4] In another case, however, it was held that such businesses as those of producing food, clothing, and fuel were not clothed with a public interest to the extent of justifying the state in requiring the compulsory settlement of labor arising in such industries.[5] But in time of acute shortage of such necessities of life, such a regulation might be upheld.

[1] Tyson v. Banton, 273 U. S. 418 (1927). In a strong dissenting opinion, Justice Holmes suggested the abandonment of the police power doctrine, declaring that "the notion that a business is clothed with a public interest and has been devoted to the public use is little more than a fiction intended to beautify what is disagreeable to the sufferers. The truth seems to me to be that, subject to compensation when compensation is due, the legislature may forbid or restrict any business when it has a sufficient force of public opinion behind it . . . But if we are to yield to fashionable conventions, it seems to me that theatres are as much devoted to public use as anything well can be . . . I am far from saying that I think this particular law a wise and rational provision. That is not my affair. But if the people of the state of New York, speaking by their authorized voice, say that they want it, I see nothing in the Constitution of the United States to prevent their having their will."

[2] Williams v. Standard Oil Co., 278 U. S. 235 (1928).

[3] Ribnik v. McBride, 277 U. S. 350 (1928). *Cf.* Adams v. Tanner, 244 U. S. 590 (1917).

[4] Marcus Brown Holding Co. v. Feldman, 256 U. S. 170 (1921); Block v. Hirsh, 256 U. S. 135 (1921); Levy Leasing Co. v. Siegel, 258 U. S. 242 (1922).

[5] Wolff Packing Co. v. Court of Industrial Relations, 262 U. S. 525 (1923).

Labor Legislation.—An important phase of the police power of the state, in both its social and economic aspects, is that which embraces the regulations adopted by the state for the betterment of the conditions of labor. In spite of the more liberal attitude of the courts toward social legislation, questions of constitutionality are still of great importance, and a number of labor laws have been held void, even within recent years, as infringing the limitations of the Constitution. The most important of these limitations is that found in both Federal and state constitutions to the effect that no person shall be deprived of "life, liberty, or property without due process of law."

With the introduction of the factory system and the development of modern industry, bringing about great concentration of laborers in industrial establishments, the matter of health and safety of the workers became of pressing importance. In recognition of the fact that the workers, on account of the inferior economic position which they have hitherto occupied, would not, as a rule, be able to secure proper conditions of work without governmental aid, the states have enacted many measures to regulate such conditions. These have had reference mainly to hazardous or unhealthful occupations and to the employment of women and children. There is no question as to the constitutionality of laws limiting the hours of labor for children.

The courts have, in general, upheld laws limiting the hours of labor of women. An Oregon statute of 1903 limited to ten hours a day the labor of women in factories, laundries, and mechanical establishments. This was attacked as depriving women of freedom of contract and of the equal protection of the law. In 1908, the Supreme Court of the United States finally held the law constitutional as a valid exercise of the police power for the protection of the health of women. The physical difference between the sexes, the Court said, was sufficient to justify a different rule as to hours of labor, and such protective legislation seemed necessary to enable women to secure a real equality of right. The Court took judicial notice of social facts indicating the injurious effects of long hours of labor upon the health of women.[1] In 1915, the same Court also upheld the more drastic California statute limiting the labor of women in certain industries to eight hours a day and forty-eight hours a week, as a reasonable exercise of protective authority within the domain of legislative discretion.[2] Within recent years the courts of most of the states have also become more liberal in their attitude toward hour legislation for women.[3]

---

[1] Muller v. Oregon, 208 U. S. 412, 52 Law ed. 551 (1908).

[2] Miller v. Wilson, 236 U. S. 373, 59 Law ed. 628 (1915).

[3] As illustrations of this, compare People v. Schweinler, 214 N. Y. 395, 108 N. E. 639 (1915), overruling People v. Williams, 189 N. Y. 131, 81 N. E. 778 (1907), holding invalid a statute prohibiting night work for women; and Ritchie v. Waymen, 244 Ill.

Hour legislation for men, or for workers generally without regard to sex or age, has been a comparatively slow growth. It developed first in hazardous employments, such as mining, and in public work. As early as 1898, the Supreme Court of the United States decided in favor of the validity of a Utah statute which prohibited the employment of workmen in mines for more than eight hours a day.[1] The act was admittedly a limitation upon the legal freedom of contract, but the Court held that such freedom was not absolute but subject to the lawful exercise of the police power of the state for the protection of the health of a class of workers engaged in an industry which the legislature had reasonable ground to believe was detrimental to health if too long pursued.

The further question remains as to whether the legislature may limit the hours of labor of adult men in private employments of a nonhazardous nature. Upon this question the Supreme Court of the United States at first adopted an adverse attitude. In 1905, it held unconstitutional a New York statute which prohibited the employment of any person in bakeries for more than ten hours a day, on the ground that it was "not, within any fair meaning of the term, a health law, but an illegal interference with the rights of individuals, both employers and employees, to make contracts regarding labor upon such terms as they may think best."[2] As to whether it was properly a health measure, however, the Court substituted its own judgment for that of the legislature upon a question which should have been recognized as within the domain of legislative discretion. In his dissenting opinion, which has had great influence upon subsequent decisions, Justice Holmes said:

This case is decided upon an economic theory which a large part of the country does not entertain . . . The Fourteenth Amendment does not enact Mr. Herbert Spencer's Social Statics . . .

A constitution is not intended to embody a particular economic theory, whether of paternalism and the organic relation of the citizen to the state or of *laissez faire* . . . I think that the word "liberty," in the Fourteenth Amendment, is perverted when it is held to prevent the natural outcome of a dominant opinion, unless it can be said that a rational and fair man necessarily would admit that the statute proposed would infringe fundamental principles as they have been understood by the traditions of our people and our law.

The influence of the views of Justice Holmes and the distance which the Court had traveled since the Lochner case were shown twelve years

---

509, 91 N. E. 695 (1910), upholding a ten-hour law for women, although the same court held an eight-hour law invalid in Ritchie v. People, 155 Ill. 98, 40 N. E. 454 (1895).

[1] Holden v. Hardy, 169 U. S. 366, 42 Law ed. 780 (1898).
[2] Lochner v. New York, 198 U. S. 45, 49 Law ed. 937 (1905).

later by the Bunting case in which the Oregon ten-hour law for men employed in factories was upheld as constitutional by the Supreme Court.[1] This decision represents a more realistic view of labor legislation on the part of the Court. It might be difficult, however, under present conditions to sustain a general eight-hour law as a mere health measure. Where an employment is neither unhealthful nor dangerous, the state is still generally held to have no more right to limit hours of labor than the other economic terms of the labor contract. "Even an eight-hour day established by law would probably constitute an unwarranted invasion of the constitutional liberty of private action."[2] Laws providing for one day of rest in seven, however, might be sustained on the analogy of Sunday legislation.

The conflict between the legal theory of freedom of contract and social need has also appeared in connection with the payment of wages. It is true that there have long been on the statute books of many states laws giving mechanics and laborers liens on the real or personal property benefited by their labor. But a difference of opinion has arisen as to the validity of laws which undertake to regulate the time or manner of paying wages, as well as the amount of wages to be paid. Such laws undoubtedly limit to some extent the legal freedom of contract, but such freedom, as we have seen, is subject to the exercise of the police power in proper cases, and such laws, moreover, may be necessary to secure a real equality between employer and employee. This view, however, has not been adopted by some of the state courts. Difference of opinion has arisen as to the validity of laws prohibiting the practice adopted by employers in some businesses, such as mining, of paying their employees in scrip or store orders instead of cash or legal tender. In Pennsylvania such a law was declared void on the ground that it interfered with the freedom of contract.[3] The Supreme Court of the United States, however, held valid a statute of Tennessee which required the redemption in cash of store orders issued by employers in payment of wages.[4] The Court found that the act did not conflict with any provision of the Constitution of the United States protecting freedom of contract. The same Court adopted a similarly liberal attitude towards a statute of Arkansas which prohibited coal mine operators from using screens to reduce the amount of wages due to miners working at quantity rates. "The right of freedom of contract," declared the Court, "has been held not to be unlimited in its nature, and when the right to contract or carry on business conflicts with laws declaring the public policy of the state, enacted for the protection of the public health, safety, or welfare, the

[1] Bunting v. Oregon, 243 U. S. 246, 61 Law ed. 830 (1917).
[2] FREUND, E., *Amer. Lab. Legis. Rev.*, vol. 4, p. 129.
[3] Godcharles v. Wigeman, 113 Pa. St. 431, 6 Atl. 354 (1886).
[4] Knoxville Iron Co. v. Harbison, 183 U. S. 13, 46 Law ed. 55 (1901).

same may be valid notwithstanding they have the effect to curtail or limit the freedom of contract."[1]

The Minimum Wage.—Probably the most important single item in the labor contract is that specifying the amount of wages to be paid. State interference in this matter goes to the very essence of the theoretical right of freedom of contract.   Here again, however, the police power may be invoked in so far as it is necessary to protect the health, morals, and welfare of employees from the consequences of a wage too low to enable them to purchase the minimum of subsistence.   Outside of labor on public work, however, where the state may regulate wages as a proprietory function, the proscription of minimum wages by the states has been confined to women and minors.   These classes of employees have been most in need of protection because their wages have been lowest; there is a greater proportion of unskilled workers among them and their unions have been weaker than those of adult men.

The constitutionality of minimum wage laws rests upon the same general principles as those on which hour legislation for women and children has been upheld.   In 1914, the question first came before the supreme court of Oregon which declared valid the minimum wage law of that state.[2]   This case was appealed to the Supreme Court of the United States, which, by an equal division, affirmed the decision of the state court.[3]   The highest courts of a number of other states, including Arkansas, Minnesota, Washington, and Massachusetts, have also upheld the validity of minimum wage legislation.[4]   These decisions are based on the ground that such legislation is proper for the protection of the health of the employees, and that the state may constitutionally interfere with the freedom of contract between employer and employee in the legitimate exercise of its police power.

In 1923, however, the Supreme Court of the United States declared unconstitutional the minimum wage law of the District of Columbia in so far as it applied to adult women.[5]   The court held that women of mature age are *sui juris* and therefore not entitled to special consideration.   The statute in question was held to violate the principle of freedom of contract as established by the Fifth Amendment, and the standard of a living wage set up by the statute was declared to be too vague.

[1] McLean v. Arkansas, 211 U. S. 539, 63 Law ed. 315 (1909).   *Cf.* Rail and River Coal Co. v. Yaple, 236 U. S. 338, 59 Law ed. 607 (1915), sustaining a similar law of Ohio.

[2] Stettler v. O'Hara, 69 Ore. 519, 139 Pac. 743.

[3] 243 U. S. 629 (1917), 61 L. ed. 937, Mr. Justice Brandeis did not sit on the case since he had been of counsel in favor of the validity of the law.   According to the rules of the Supreme Court in such cases, no opinion was rendered.

[4] State v. Crone, 179 S. W. 4; Williams v. Evans, 165 N. W. 495; Larson v. Rice, 171 Pac. 1037; Holcombe v. Creamer, 120 N. E. 354.

[5] Adkins v. Children's Hospital, 261 U. S. 525 (1923).

Employer's Liability and Workmen's Compensation.—With the introduction of the factory system and the multiplication of machinery, accidental injuries to employees naturally increased. If the employer did not voluntarily look after the employee in such cases, the latter had, under the common law, no other recourse than to bring suit against the employer. If he could prove that the employer had not exercised due care in providing safe conditions of work, he might recover damages. But in such litigation the courts gradually recognized certain important defenses to which the employer was entitled. The first of these was the doctrine of contributory negligence, according to which the employee could not recover if he was himself guilty of negligence, which, however slightly, contributed to the injury.[1] The second defense was based upon the fellow-servant rule which provided that if the injury was due to the negligence of a fellow employee, the injured employee could not recover.[2] The third defense was that of assumption of risk, which implied that, when the employee entered the employment, he assumed any unusual risk which might be involved. These three common-law defenses may not have been particularly unjust at the time they originated, but, as conditions changed, they caused the odds to be so strongly against the employee that he failed to bring suit against the employers in many cases of injury, and, when he did so, he seldom recovered damages. Employers frequently adopted the plan of protecting themselves against damage suits by taking out liability insurance in private companies, and the latter employed expert legal talent in defending any suits that might be brought, while the plaintiffs in such cases were not as a rule financially able to secure similar representation. The result was that the great burden of accidental injuries fell almost entirely upon the workers and their dependents. The feeling grew that this condition should be remedied by positive legislation, so as to throw the burden of industrial injuries upon the industry and thereby indirectly upon the community as a whole. Accordingly, in all but a very few states, the three common-law defenses mentioned above have been abolished by statute, and provision made for workmen's compensation without the necessity of a lawsuit.

Nearly all the states have now passed compensation laws, although they differ considerably in their detailed provisions. Most of the early laws were elective. Most of the elective laws, however, contained provisions, known as "club legislation," whereby employers who failed to come under the law were deprived of the common-law defense of contributory negligence, negligence of a fellow servant, and assumption of risk. This feature was attacked on the ground that it made the law practically compulsory and therefore unconstitutional. This contention, however,

---

[1] Butterfield v. Forester, 11 East 60 (1809).
[2] Farwell v. Boston & W. R. Co., 4 Metc. 49 (1842).

was denied by the courts,[1] and compensation laws which are not only practically coercive but legally compulsory have now been upheld by the Supreme Court of the United States.   In 1917, the New York compulsory law was held valid by that Court on the ground that, although no doubt limiting to some extent the freedom of contract between employer and employee, it was nevertheless a legitimate exercise of the police power of the state for the protection of the health, safety, and welfare of an important class of individuals.[2]   The same Court has also held that a state may make a workmen's compensation statute compulsory for coal mines, although elective for other enterprises except railroads, which are excluded entirely.   The peculiar conditions of labor in coal mines are held to justify special treatment, while the exclusion of railroads is upheld on the ground that many of the injuries to railroad employees come within the Federal employers' liability act.[3]

[1] Borgnis v. Falk Co., 147 Wis. 327, 133 N. W. 209 (1911); State ex rel. Yaple v. Creamer, 85 Ohio St. 349, 97 N. E. 602 (1912).

[2] New York Central Ry. Co. v. White, 243 U. S. 188, 61 Law ed. 667 (1917). This law had previously been upheld by the New York court in Jensen v. Southern Pacific Co., 109 N. E. 500 (1915).

[3] Lower Vein Coal Co. v. Industrial Board of Indiana, 255 U. S. 144 (1921), 65 Law ed. 383.   In Arizona, the injured employee was given the option, after injury, to accept compensation or to sue for damages.   This was objected to as imposing liability without fault and without restriction as to the amount, but was upheld by the Supreme Court of the United States in the Arizona employer's liability cases, 250 U. S. 400, 63 Law ed. 1058.

CHAPTER XXXI

EQUAL PROTECTION OF THE LAWS

The provision of the Fourteenth Amendment which prohibits the states from denying to any person within their jurisdiction the equal protection of the laws embodies a special application of the principle contained in the due-process clause. Since there is no specific equal-protection clause in the Fifth Amendment, the National Government is not expressly limited in this respect, but this difference is more apparent than real, because it would be difficult to cite any violation of the equal-protection clause which would not also be a violation of the due-process clause. To this extent, the two clauses overlap. On the other hand, it may happen that the due-process clause is violated without the equal-protection clause's being involved.

The Persons Protected by the Equal-protection Clause.—In the light of the situation existing at the time of the adoption of the Fourteenth Amendment, it is clear that the equal-protection clause was intended primarily to protect the newly freed negroes against discriminatory state legislation. In the slaughter house cases,[1] decided shortly after the adoption of the amendment, the Supreme Court, speaking by Justice Miller, went so far as to say that "we doubt very much whether any action of a state not directed by way of discrimination against the negroes as a class, or on account of their race, will ever be held to come within the purview of this provision." This prediction, however, turned out to be wide of the mark. By far the large majority of the cases interpreting and applying the equal-protection clause have not involved negroes.

It will be noticed that the protection afforded by the clause is not confined to citizens but extends to "persons." This term is broad enough to include aliens. Nor is it confined to natural persons but includes also corporations. Many cases involving corporations have arisen under this clause. It is not to be understood that laws may not be passed which single out aliens or corporations for special treatment, but such treatment must be based on a reasonable distinction.

The persons protected by this clause must be within the jurisdiction of the state. A natural person is within the jurisdiction of a state when he is physically present therein or maintains therein his legal abode. A corporation is within the jurisdiction of a state by which it has been incorporated or by which it has been admitted to do business.

[1] 16 Wall 36 (1873).

Protection Afforded against State Action Only.—The equal-protection clause is a prohibition upon the states only and does not forbid individuals or corporations from discriminating between different classes of persons. The Civil Rights Act, passed by Congress in 1875 for the enforcement of the Fourteenth Amendment, seems to have been predicated upon the mistaken theory that individual action is thereby prohibited. It undertook to forbid proprietors of hotels, theaters, and other places of public resort from making discrimination against persons or from refusing to accommodate them on account of race, color, or previous condition of servitude. In holding the act unconstitutional, the Supreme Court declared that "it is state action of a particular character that is prohibited. Individual invasion of individual rights is not the subject matter of the amendment."[1] It follows that there is nothing in this clause to prevent a railroad, on its own initiative, from segregating its passengers on the basis of race, even in interstate commerce.[2] As already pointed out, although a state cannot require that persons of both races shall have the same privileges on interstate trains,[3] it may require a railroad to provide equal, but separate, accommodations for white and colored passengers on interstate journeys.[4]

Although the equal-protection clause does not operate against individuals as such, it does apply to those individuals who occupy state office, since it is only through them that the state can act. This is equally true whether the officer is acting on the supposed authority of an unconstitutional law or is acting beyond the authority granted to him by state law. A Virginia county judge was charged with excluding negroes from the jury lists on account of their race, color, and previous condition of servitude, in violation of an act of Congress. The state law under which he was acting made no such discrimination. The judge was nevertheless guilty of violating the equal-protection clause, because he was the official agent or instrument through which the state was acting.[5] In another case decided at about the same time, a negro was tried and convicted of murder in West Virginia before a jury composed exclusively of white male

[1] Civil rights cases, 109 U. S. 3 (1883). This civil rights act, however, if passed by a state, would probably be valid under its police power.

[2] Chiles v. C. & O. Ry. Co., 218 U. S. 71 (1910).

[3] Hall v. De Cuir, 95 U. S. 485 (1878).

[4] Plessy v. Ferguson, 163 U. S. 537 (1896).

[5] *Ex parte* Virginia, 100 U. S. 339 (1880). In this case, it would seem that not only the particular negro who was on trial was denied the equal protection of the laws but also the negroes of the county generally. The question may be raised as to how sitting on a jury affords protection. Children are everywhere excluded from jury service and, in many states, women are also still excluded. And yet, in their case, such exclusion does not involve deprivation of the equal protection of the laws. The reason for this distinction would seem to be that the exclusion of women is not arbitrary, while, in the case of negroes, it is. Or, if this is not the reason for the distinction, there is a historical basis for it.

citizens as required by state law. This law was held by the Supreme Court of the United States to deny the negro the equal protection of the laws, and his conviction was therefore reversed.[1]

The Rights That Are Protected.—In general it may be said that the rights protected by the equal-protection clause are primarily civil rather than political. Civil rights are more fundamental, while political rights may, from one point of view, be considered as ancillary to civil rights in the sense that, in order to protect the latter, political rights are granted. It was formerly supposed that the equal-protection clause does not prevent a state from making discriminations in the matter of voting on account of race, color, or previous condition of servitude. This was the position taken by Justice Field in an early case in which he argued that the equal-protection clause did not prevent discrimination in the matter of voting on such accounts because, in order to accomplish that purpose, a new amendment (the Fifteenth) was required.[2] However, in the Texas white primary case, decided in 1927, Justice Holmes, speaking for the Court, held invalid a statute of that state barring negroes from voting in the Democratic primary election on the ground that it deprived them of the equal protection of the law.[3]

Reasonable Classifications Not Forbidden.—The equal-protection clause means that persons shall be entitled to the protection of equal laws. It forbids discrimination between persons who are in substantially similar circumstances or conditions. Without violating this clause, persons may be classified into groups and such groups may be differently treated if there is a reasonable basis for such difference or distinction. In other words, the classification must be not merely arbitrary but based upon a difference which bears a just and proper relation to the attempted classification. It should be emphasized that the equal-protection clause does not require that all persons, all property, or all occupations must be treated alike. In fact, the public welfare requires that persons, property, and occupations be classified and be subjected to differing and appropriate legislation under the police power or the power of taxation.

For example, regulations not applying to adults may be made which prohibit children from entering into certain occupations; or regulations as to hours of labor may be made which apply exclusively to children or

---

[1] Strauder v. West Virginia, 100 U. S. 303 (1880). If the question should be raised as to why illiterates or women, if excluded by law from jury service, could not be held to be deprived of the equal protection of the laws, the answer would seem to be that the law assumes that there may be prejudice or discrimination against the negro race but none against women or illiterates. It has been held by the Supreme Court that, on trial of a negro charged with killing a white man before a white jury, the refusal of the trial court to permit prospective jurors to be interrogated as to racial prejudice is reversible error. Aldridge v. United States, 283 U. S. 308 (1931).

[2] *Ex parte* Virginia, 100 U. S. 339 (1880).

[3] Nixon v. Herndon, 273 U. S. 536 (1927).

minors.   Moreover, persons may be prohibited from engaging in certain professions, such as medicine or dentistry, unless they hold a diploma from a reputable medical or dental school, because there is a reasonable relation between completion of a course in such school and proficiency in the practice of such profession.   Another example of a valid classification was that made in the New York statute of 1923 aimed at the Ku Klux Klan.   It provided that any society, corporation, or association having more than twenty members and requiring an oath as a condition of membership, except labor unions and benevolent orders, must file with the secretary of state a copy of its constitution and by-laws and a list of its officers and members.   The Court, recognizing that classification may be somewhat flexible, upheld the statute on the ground that the societies covered by it bear a different relation to the public welfare from labor unions and benevolent orders.[1]

Discrimination between localities is constitutional if reasonable. Thus, a law of Missouri was upheld which allowed appeal from lower courts to the state supreme court in all parts of the state except in St. Louis and certain other counties, in which an appeal was allowed only to the St. Louis court of appeals.[2] A state might establish two state universities for two halves of the state and limit the students in each to the residents of each half.

The constitution of Ohio provides that "no law shall be held unconstitutional and void by the [state] supreme court without the concurrence of at least all but one of the judges, except in the affirmance of a judgment of the court of appeals declaring a law unconstitutional and void." Since there are several courts of appeals in the state, this provision may so operate that a given statute may be upheld in one case and declared void in another.   It was therefore attacked in the Supreme Court of the United States on the ground, among others, that it denied the equal protection of the laws.   That tribunal, however, refused to invalidate the provision on the ground that neither the equal-protection clause nor any other provision of the Federal Constitution requires that "the state shall adopt a unifying method of appeals which will insure to all litigants within the state the same decisions on particular questions which may arise," and it was therefore not the business of the Court "to intervene to protect the citizens of the state from the consequences of its policy."[3]

Discrimination may be based on size if size is an index to an admitted evil which the law is attempting to correct.   For example, workmen's compensation laws or laws regulating wage contracts in mines may exempt from their operation small establishments employing fewer than

[1] Bryant v. Zimmerman, 278 U. S. 63 (1928).

[2] Missouri v. Lewis, 101 U. S. 22 (1880).

[3] State of Ohio ex rel. Bryant v. Akron Metropolitan Park District, 281 U. S. 74 (1930).

a certain number of persons.[1] Again, a law was upheld that required hotels to provide night watchmen but applied only to hotels having more than fifty rooms.[2]

Discrimination against Aliens.—In passing upon the question as to whether a particular discrimination made by the law is or is not based upon a reasonable distinction, the courts may exercise a considerable range of discretion. In some cases, however, the courts exhibit a tendency to refuse to substitute their own judgment for that of the legislature as to the existence of reasonable grounds for the distinction. For example, a municipal ordinance prohibiting the granting of pool- or billiard-room licenses to aliens but allowing such grants to citizens was upheld, the Court declaring that

> . . . the ordinance, in the light of facts admitted or generally assumed, does not preclude the possibility of a rational basis for the legislative judgment and we have no such knowledge of local conditions as would enable us to say that it is clearly wrong. Some latitude must be allowed for the legislative appraisement of local conditions and for the legislative choice of methods for controlling an apprehended evil.[3]

The same Court also upheld a state law which prohibited aliens from hunting wild game or owning a gun for such a purpose.[4] Discrimination against aliens may go too far, however, as in the case of the Arizona law requiring that when any employer had as many as five employees, at least 80 per cent of them must be citizens of the United States. This was held to deny aliens the equal protection of the laws by preventing them from engaging in the ordinary means of earning a livelihood.[5]

When, in the opinion of the courts, the legislature has gone beyond a rational basis for the distinction, they do not hesitate to declare the legislative determination to be lacking in equal protection. For example, an act of Oklahoma requiring a showing of public necessity for the issuance of licenses to individuals to operate a gin, but not requiring such showing when a license is issued to a cooperative association, was held void as an arbitrary classification.[6]

Discrimination against Railroads.—For some purposes railroads may be placed in a group and dealt with by special legislation, and for other purposes they may not be. As illustrating the fine line sometimes drawn by the courts between what is, and what is not, equal protection, may be mentioned two cases relating to railroads decided by the Supreme Court

---

[1] McLean v. Arkansas, 211 U. S. 539 (1909).

[2] Miller v. Strahl, 239 U. S. 426 (1915).

[3] Ohio *ex rel.* Clarke v. Deckelbach, 274 U. S. 392 (1927).

[4] Patsone v. Pennsylvania, 232 U. S. 139 (1914).

[5] Truax v. Raich, 239 U. S. 33 (1915).

[6] Frost v. Corporation Commission, 278 U. S. 515 (1928). Three justices dissented.

of the United States. In the first case, the Court held invalid a law of
Texas which imposed a special penalty upon railroads for failure to pay
any small debt. This was in the form of an attorney's fee collectible by
the claimant. It was held that there was no good reason why railroads
should be singled out from other corporations and penalized for the
nonpayment of debts not peculiar to the railroad business.[1] This law
not only discriminated against railroads but also treated persons who
have claims against railroads better than those who have claims against
other corporations. In this case the Court did not give the benefit of
doubt in favor of the legislative determination, for, as it declared,

> . . . while good faith and a knowledge of existing conditions on the part of a
> legislature is [sic] to be presumed, yet to carry that presumption to the extent
> of always holding that there must be some undisclosed and unknown reason for
> subjecting certain individuals or corporations to hostile and discriminating legisla-
> tion is to make the protecting clauses of the Fourteenth Amendment a mere rope
> of sand, in no manner restraining state action.[2]

In the other of the two cases mentioned, the Court upheld a state law
which imposed a similar penalty upon railroads, *i.e.* allowed the plaintiff
to collect a reasonable attorney's fee in actions for damages due to the
negligent escape of fire from trains.[3] This was an action for a matter
more nearly peculiar to railroads, and the additional penalty was imposed
under the police power in order to induce greater care on the part of the
railroads in the operation of their trains.

A recent statute of Florida required private carriers by motor vehicles
operating on highways over regular routes to obtain a certificate of necessity and convenience and to take out insurance to protect the public
against injuries. From these requirements, however, transportation
companies engaged in transporting agricultural, dairy, or other farm
products were exempted. The statute was held void as an unconstitutional discrimination.[4]

Thus, in the case of the equal-protection clause, as in that of other
provisions of the Constitution, the full meaning is "gradually ascertained
by the process of inclusion and exclusion in the course of decisions as they
arise."[5]

Equal Protection and the Police Power.—The nature of the police
power has been described and some illustrations of its relation to the

---

[1] Gulf, C. & S. F. Ry. Co. v. Ellis, 165 U. S. 150 (1897).

[2] *Cf.* Western & A. R. Co. v. Henderson, 279 U. S. 639 (1929), in which a statute
providing that any collision between a railroad train and a person or vehicle was to be
presumed to be due to the negligence of the railroad was held invalid.

[3] Atchison, T. & S. F. Ry. Co. v. Matthews, 174 U. S. 96 (1899).

[4] Smith v. Cahoon, 283 U. S. 553 (1931).

[5] Twining v. New Jersey, 211 U. S. 78 (1908).

requirement of equal protection have already been given,[1] to which the following may be added.

In the exercise of its police power for the promotion of the fundamental purposes of public health, safety, and morals, the state may find it necessary or desirable to classify the objects of regulation, whether persons, property, or occupations. If such classification is not merely arbitrary class legislation but is based on a reasonable distinction, the equal-protection clause is not violated. If there is a substantial or essential difference in the situation of some persons or some property from that of others, the former may be regulated under the police power while the latter are left unregulated, or else differing regulations may be applied to the two classes. On the other hand, arbitrary class legislation is invalid, even though admittedly enacted for the promotion of legitimate purposes of the police power.

In the field of criminal law, it has been held that habitual criminals may be put in a class separate from first offenders and heavier penalties may be inflicted upon the former.[2] It has also been held that a heavier penalty for assault with a deadly weapon may be imposed upon life convicts than upon others.[3]

Persons engaged in occupations having particular relation to the public health, such as physicians, dentists, nurses, and milk dealers, may be subjected to special regulation. An ordinance of San Francisco prohibited night work in laundries within a certain section of the city. This was alleged to violate the equal-protection clause, because it discriminated against those engaged in the laundry business and also against those located in the prescribed section of the city. The ordinance was nevertheless upheld against both these attacks as a reasonable protection against fire.[4]

Zoning.—Ordinances whereby a city is divided into residential, commercial, and manufacturing districts, and whereby buildings not appropriate to a particular district are prohibited therein and different heights prescribed for buildings in different districts, have been upheld.[5] It is generally held necessary to their validity, however, that such ordinances should not be arbitrary or unreasonable and should have some relation to the public health, safety, morals, or general welfare.[6] Build-

---

[1] See Chap. XXX.

[2] McDonald v. Massachusetts, 180 U. S. 311 (1901).

[3] Finley v. California, 222 U. S. 28 (1911).

[4] Barbier v. Connolly, 113 U. S. 27 (1885).

[5] Welch v. Swasy, 214 U. S. 91 (1909); Hadacheck v. Sebastian, 239 U. S. 394 (1915).

[6] Euclid v. Ambler Realty Co., 272 U. S. 365 (1926). But *cf.* Nectow v. Cambridge, 277 U. S. 183 (1928), in which the arbitrary inclusion of a person's land within the residence zone was held to deprive him of property without due process of law. *Cf.* also Seattle Trust Co. v. Roberge, 278 U. S. 116 (1928), in which it was held invalid

ings erected after the passage of the ordinance may be kept back a certain distance from the street in the interest of health and safety.[1] By a zoning ordinance of Los Angeles, certain territory was declared to be residence territory in which certain establishments, such as public laundries, were prohibited. This ordinance, even though applying retroactively to laundries already established at the time it was passed, was held valid as a reasonable exercise of the police power to promote the comfort of the residents in that territory.[2] Another ordinance of the same city, however, which suddenly and arbitrarily changed the limits within which gas works might be operated, was held invalid as a discriminatory and unreasonable exercise of the police power.[3] It has also been held that the police power does not extend to the prohibition in certain sections of the city of establishments, such as store buildings, that do not injure or infringe the lawful rights of others.[4]

Labor Legislation.—Within the limits of the equal-protection clause, labor legislation may be enacted which applies to children and not to adults. Regulation of hours of labor may be made which applies to women and not to men,[5] or which applies to especially unhealthful occupations and not to others.[6] In respect to minimum wage legislation, however, it has been held that women are *sui juris* and cannot be placed in a separate class from men.[7]

It has been held that a state statute which denies to employers the right to have the benefit of a court injunction in labor disputes, but not denying to employees the same right, is a deprivation of the equal protection of the laws.[8]

The equal-protection clause in relation to the police power may also be involved in legislation classifying persons according to race and subjecting them to different regulations.[9]

Classification for Taxing Purposes.—Prominent among recent movements for tax reform in the states is that for a departure from the uniform rule of the general property tax and the adoption of classification of the

---

as a denial of due process of law to refuse to allow the erection of an old people's home in a certain residential district, where such exclusion was not necessary to the carrying out of the general zoning plan, merely because two-thirds of the neighboring property owners declined to consent.

[1] Gorieb v. Fox, 274 U. S. 603 (1927).

[2] *Ex parte* Quang Wo, 161 Calif. 220 (1911). *Cf.* the decision of the Supreme Court of the United States upholding a zoning ordinance in Reinman v. Little Rock, 237 U. S. 171 (1915).

[3] Dobbins v. Los Angeles, 195 U. S. 223 (1904).

[4] State *ex rel.* Lachtman v. Houghton, 158 N. W. 1017 (1916).

[5] Muller v. Oregon, 208 U. S., 412 (1908).

[6] Holden v. Hardy, 169 U. S. 366 (1898).

[7] Adkins v. Children's Hospital of the District of Columbia, 261 U. S. 525 (1923).

[8] Truax v. Corrigan, 257 U. S. 312 (1921).

[9] This topic has been discussed above (see pp. 414–415).

objects of taxation.   As already pointed out, the equal-protection clause
of the Fourteenth Amendment does not forbid the making of reasonable
distinctions.   The courts, in fact, are somewhat more liberal in allowing
distinctions for taxing purposes than in the exercise of the police power,
because taxation is the more essential of the two governmental powers.
Different rates of taxation may be levied upon different classes of property,
or some classes may be exempted from taxation altogether.[1]   The classification must not, of course, be an arbitrary one but must be based upon
a genuine distinction and a uniform method and rate must be applied to
all objects properly falling within the same class.   The distinctive
economic characteristics of different kinds of property naturally place
them in separate classes for taxing purposes.   For example, railroads,
mines, forests, household goods, express companies, money, credits, bonds
and shares of stock may be classified separately for purposes of taxation.[2]

An example of classification for taxing purposes which was upheld
by the courts was involved in the statute of Louisiana imposing a license
tax upon all persons or corporations engaged in the business of refining
sugar and molasses, based upon the gross annual receipts from such
business, but exempting from the tax planters and farmers refining their
own products.   It was held that the discrimination was a reasonable
one for the encouragement of agriculture and did not deny to persons or
corporations engaged in the general refining business the equal protection
of the laws.[3]   The Court has even gone so far as to uphold a statute of
Montana which taxed hand laundries operated by men or in which over
two women were employed,[4] but this was clearly a close case.

A recent case of considerable importance from the economic point of
view was that in which the Supreme Court, in a five-to-four decision,
upheld the Indiana chain-store tax law.   This law imposed an occupation
tax upon the operation of mercantile establishments, graduated according
to the number of stores owned.   The majority of the Court held that such
a tax was justified by differences in organization, management, and type
of business transacted, between the business of chain stores and other
types of store.[5]   The Court laid down the general principle that the equal-
protection clause "does not compel the adoption of an iron rule of equal
taxation, nor prevent variety or differences in taxation, or discretion in

---

[1] Different classes of property may also be assessed for taxes at different per-
centages of their full value.   Thus, stock may be assessed at its full sale price, while
land is assessed at only 75 per cent of its sale price.   Klein v. Board of Tax Super-
visors, 282 U. S. 19 (1930).

[2] A state may tax both a corporation and also the holders of the corporation's
stock but is not required by the Constitution to do so.   Klein v. Board of Tax Super-
visors, 282 U. S. 19 (1930).

[3] American Sugar Refining Co. v. Louisiana, 179 U. S. 89 (1900).

[4] Quong Wing v. Kirkendall, 223 U. S. 59 (1912).

[5] State Board of Tax Commissioners of Indiana v. Jackson, 283 U. S. 527 (1931).

the selection of subjects, or the classification for taxation of properties, businesses, callings, or occupations." It further held that "the fact that a statute discriminates in favor of a certain class does not make it arbitrary if the discrimination is founded upon a reasonable distinction, or if any state of facts reasonably can be conceived to sustain it."

Inheritance Taxes.—A special form of tax resorted to by the National Government as well as by the states is that upon inheritances, or rather upon persons receiving property by inheritance. This tax is held by the courts to be an excise tax upon the right of the decedent to transmit the property or upon the right of the beneficiary to receive it rather than upon the property itself. In most of the states which have adopted the inheritance tax, small estates are exempted from taxation altogether, while in the case of estates above the exempted amount the tax is a graduated or progressive tax, the rate increasing with the amount of the estate transmitted. Furthermore, the rate sometimes varies according to whether the estate goes to lineal descendants, to collateral heirs, or to strangers in blood. All of these features of the inheritance tax laws have been attacked in the courts on the ground that they violate the equal-protection clause, but they have nevertheless been generally upheld.

An Illinois inheritance tax law of 1895 provided varying rates depending on the circumstances just mentioned and was attacked on these grounds but was nevertheless upheld by the Supreme Court of the United States, which pointed out that the equal-protection clause of the Fourteenth Amendment "does not require exact equality of taxation. It only requires that the law imposing it shall operate on all alike, under the same circumstances."[1] It should be noted, however, that while the distinctions mentioned in the law are reasonable in themselves, the law might also be sustained on the ground that the succession to property is a privilege resting entirely upon the permission of the state, and the state may therefore attach such conditions as it sees fit to the enjoyment of the privilege, provided these conditions do not arbitrarily discriminate between different successors to property. A statute of Wisconsin which provided that gifts made within six years of death should be conclusively presumed to have been made in contemplation of death and imposing a graduated inheritance tax upon such gifts was held invalid as a violation of the equal-protection clause.[2]

Income Taxes.—Another form of tax adopted by the National Government and also by some states is the income tax. The laws providing for this form of tax usually exempt small incomes, and, on incomes above the exempted amount, the tax rate becomes higher as the amount of the income increases. These distinctions are reasonable and do not violate the equal-protection clause. That clause would be violated,

[1] Magoun v. Illinois Trust and Savings Bank, 170 U. S. 283 (1898).
[2] Schlesinger v. Wisconsin, 270 U. S. 230 (1926).

however, if a certain class of persons, such as doctors or lawyers, were singled out to bear a special income tax that did not apply to other classes of persons having the same amounts of income, or if they were granted special exemptions that did not apply to others. In the matter of exemptions, a state is also debarred from discriminating between its own citizens and those of other states.

Some state constitutions require that all property taxes shall be levied at a uniform rate. This requirement of uniformity would probably also apply to taxes on income from property but would probably not apply to taxes on income from other sources, such as salaries and wages.

Special Assessments.—Another special form of taxation is the special assessment, such as is levied, for example, upon abutting property owners whose property is benefited by a public improvement, such as the paving of a street. The property owners of the city generally are not taxed although they may derive some benefit from the use of the street. Nevertheless, the classification of property owners into abutting and non-abutting is reasonable and does not violate the equal-protection clause. It frequently happens that property on near-by or intersecting streets not actually abutting on the improvement is also assessed for a portion of the cost, but the abutting property owners have no right to object if this is not done. If some abutting property owners were assessed and others equally benefited were not, there would of course be an unconstitutional discrimination and lack of equal protection of the laws. The amount of the assessment need only approximately equal the benefit conferred. The assessment would not be invalid because it somewhat exceeded the value of the benefit, provided it is not out of all proportion to such value.[1]

Conclusion.—The cases cited in the last few chapters show that due process and equal protection are such general terms that a wide discretion is left to the judiciary in construing them. Quite frequently the court substitutes its judgment for that of the legislature and holds the statute invalid if it strikes the majority of the judges as being unwise or unreasonable. Some of the Supreme Court judges take the view that the judiciary ought not to substitute its judgment for that of the legislature but ought to uphold a statute which seems to them unreasonable if its reasonableness is a debatable question and if a reasonable man might deem the statute to be reasonable. The latter judges, however, have usually been in the minority.[2]

[1] French v. Barber Asphalt Paving Co., 181 U. S. 324 (1901); Martin v. District of Columbia, 205 U. S. 135 (1907).

[2] For a statement of this latter view, see the dissenting opinion of Justice Holmes in Schlesinger v. Wisconsin, 270 U. S. 230 (1926).

APPENDIX

CONSTITUTION OF THE UNITED STATES OF AMERICA

We, the people of the United States, in order to form a more perfect union, establish justice, insure domestic tranquillity, provide for the common defense, promote the general welfare, and secure the blessings of liberty to ourselves and our posterity, do ordain and establish this Constitution for the United States of America.

ARTICLE I

SECTION I

All legislative powers herein granted shall be vested in a Congress of the United States, which shall consist of a Senate and House of Representatives.

SECTION II

The House of Representatives shall be composed of members chosen every second year by the people of the several States, and the electors in each State shall have the qualifications requisite for electors of the most numerous branch of the State legislature.

No person shall be a Representative who shall not have attained the age of twenty-five years, and been seven years a citizen of the United States, and who shall not, when elected, be an inhabitant of that State in which he shall be chosen.

Representatives and direct taxes shall be apportioned among the several States which may be included within this Union, according to their respective numbers, which shall be determined by adding to the whole number of free persons, including those bound to service for a term of years, and excluding Indians not taxed, three-fifths of all other persons. The actual enumeration shall be made within three years after the first meeting of the Congress of the United States, and within every subsequent term of ten years, in such manner as they shall by law direct. The number of Representatives shall not exceed one for every thirty thousand, but each State shall have at least one Representative; and until such enumeration shall be made, the state of New Hampshire shall be entitled to choose three, Massachusetts eight, Rhode Island and Providence Plantations one, Connecticut five, New York six, New Jersey four, Pennsylvania eight, Delaware one, Maryland six, Virginia ten, North Carolina five, South Carolina five, and Georgia three.

When vacancies happen in the representation from any State, the executive authority thereof shall issue writs of election to fill such vacancies.

The House of Representatives shall choose their Speaker and other officers, and shall have the sole power of impeachment.

SECTION III

The Senate of the United States shall be composed of two Senators from each State, chosen by the legislature thereof, for six years; and each Senator shall have one vote.

Immediately after they shall be assembled in consequence of the first election, they shall be divided as equally as may be into three classes. The seats of the Senators of the first class shall be vacated at the expiration of the second year; of the second class, at the expiration of the fourth year, and of the third class, at the expiration of the sixth year, so that one-third may be chosen every second year; and if vacancies happen by resignation or otherwise during the recess of the legislature of any State, the executive thereof may make temporary appointments until the next meeting of the legislature, which shall then fill such vacancies.

No person shall be a Senator who shall not have attained to the age of thirty years, and been nine years a citizen of the United States, and who shall not, when elected, be an inhabitant of that State for which he shall be chosen.

The Vice-President of the United States shall be President of the Senate, but shall have no vote, unless they be equally divided.

The Senate shall choose their other officers, and also a President *pro tempore* in the absence of the Vice-President, or when he shall exercise the office of the President of the United States.

The Senate shall have the sole power to try all impeachments. When sitting for that purpose, they shall be on oath or affirmation. When the President of the United States is tried, the Chief Justice shall preside: and no person shall be convicted without the concurrence of two thirds of the members present.

Judgment in cases of impeachment shall not extend further than to removal from office, and disqualification to hold and enjoy any office of honor, trust, or profit under the United States; but the party convicted shall, nevertheless, be liable and subject to indictment, trial, judgment, and punishment, according to law.

SECTION IV

The times, places, and manner of holding elections for Senators and Representatives shall be prescribed in each State by the legislature thereof; but the Congress may at any time by law make or alter such regulations, except as to the places of choosing Senators.

The Congress shall assemble at least once in every year, and such meeting shall be on the first Monday in December, unless they shall by law appoint a different day.

SECTION V

Each house shall be the judge of the elections, returns, and qualifications of its own members, and a majority of each shall constitute a quorum to do business; but a smaller number may adjourn from day to day, and may be authorized to compel the attendance of absent members, in such manner, and under such penalties, as each house may provide.

Each house may determine the rules of its proceedings, punish its members for disorderly behavior, and with the concurrence of two thirds, expel a member.

Each house shall keep a journal of its proceedings, and from time to time publish the same, excepting such parts as may in their judgment require secrecy, and the yeas and nays of the members of either house on any question shall, at the desire of one fifth of those present, be entered on the journal.

Neither house, during the session of Congress, shall, without the consent of the other, adjourn for more than three days, nor to any other place than that in which the two houses shall be sitting.

SECTION VI

The Senators and Representatives shall receive a compensation for their services, to be ascertained by law and paid out of the Treasury of the United States. They shall, in all cases except treason, felony, and breach of the peace, be privileged from arrest during their attendance at the session of their respective houses, and in going to and returning from the same; and for any speech or debate in either house they shall not be questioned in any other place.

No Senator or Representative shall, during the time for which he was elected, be appointed to any civil office under the authority of the United States, which shall have been created, or the emoluments whereof shall have been increased, during such time; and no person holding any office under the United States shall be a member of either house during his continuance in office.

SECTION VII

All bills for raising revenue shall originate in the House of Representatives; but the Senate may propose or concur with amendments as on other bills.

Every bill which shall have passed the House of Representatives and the Senate shall, before it become a law, be presented to the President of the United States; if he approves he shall sign it, but if not he shall return it, with his objections, to that house in which it shall have originated, who shall enter the objections at large on their journal and proceed to reconsider it. If after such reconsideration two thirds of that house shall agree to pass the bill, it shall be sent, together with the objections, to the other house, by which it shall likewise be reconsidered, and if approved by two thirds of that house it shall become a law. But in all such cases the votes of both houses shall be determined by yeas and nays, and the names of the persons voting for and against the bill shall be entered on the journal of each house respectively. If any bill shall not be returned by the President within ten days (Sundays excepted) after it shall have been presented to him, the same shall be a law, in like manner as if he had signed it, unless the Congress by their adjournment prevent its return, in which case it shall not be a law.

Every order, resolution, or vote to which the concurrence of the Senate and House of Representatives may be necessary (except on a question of adjournment) shall be presented to the President of the United States; and before the same shall take effect, shall be approved by him, or being disapproved by him, shall be repassed by two thirds of the Senate and House of Representatives, according to the rules and limitations prescribed in the case of a bill.

SECTION VIII

The Congress shall have power to lay and collect taxes, duties, imposts, and excises, to pay the debts and provide for the common defense and general welfare of the United States; but all duties, imposts, and excises shall be uniform throughout the United States;

To borrow money on the credit of the United States;

To regulate commerce with foreign nations and among the several States, and with the Indian tribes;

To establish an uniform rule of naturalization, and uniform laws on the subject of bankruptcies throughout the United States;

To coin money, regulate the value thereof, and of foreign coin, and fix the standard of weights and measures;

To provide for the punishment of counterfeiting the securities and current coin of the United States;

To establish post-offices and post-roads;

To promote the progress of science and useful arts by securing for limited times to authors and inventors the exclusive right to their respective writings and discoveries;

To constitute tribunals inferior to the Supreme Court;

To define and punish piracies and felonies committed on the high seas and offenses against the law of nations;

To declare war, grant letters of marque and reprisal, and make rules concerning captures on land and water;

To raise and support armies, but no appropriation of money to that use shall be for a longer term than two years;

To provide and maintain a navy;

To make rules for the government and regulation of the land and naval forces;

To provide for calling forth the militia to execute the laws of the Union, suppress insurrections, and repel invasions;

To provide for organizing, arming, and disciplining the militia, and for governing such part of them as may be employed in the service of the United States, reserving to the States respectively the appointment of the officers, and the authority of training the militia according to the discipline prescribed by Congress;

To exercise exclusive legislation in all cases whatsoever over such district (not exceeding ten miles square) as may, by cession of particular States and the acceptance of Congress, become the seat of the Government of the United States, and to exercise like authority over all places purchased by the consent of the legislature of the State in which the same shall be, for the erection of forts, magazines, arsenals, dockyards, and other needful buildings; and

To make all laws which shall be necessary and proper for carrying into execution the foregoing powers, and all other powers vested by this Constitution in the Government of the United States, or in any department or officer thereof.

SECTION IX

The migration or importation of such persons as any of the States now existing shall think proper to admit shall not be prohibited by the Congress prior to the year one thousand eight hundred and eight, but a tax or duty may be imposed on such importation, not exceeding ten dollars for each person.

The privilege of the writ of habeas corpus shall not be suspended, unless when in cases of rebellion or invasion the public safety may require it.

No bill of attainder or ex post facto law shall be passed.

No capitation or other direct tax shall be laid, unless in proportion to the census or enumeration hereinbefore directed to be taken.

No tax or duty shall be laid on articles exported from any State.

No preference shall be given by any regulation of commerce or revenue to the ports of one State over those of another; nor shall vessels bound to or from one State be obliged to enter, clear, or pay duties in another.

No money shall be drawn from the Treasury but in consequence of appropriations made by law; and a regular statement and account of the receipts and expenditures of all public money shall be published from time to time.

No title of nobility shall be granted by the United States; and no person holding any office of profit or trust under them shall, without the consent of the Congress, accept of any present, emolument, office, or title, of any kind whatever, from any king, prince, or foreign State.

SECTION X

No State shall enter into any treaty, alliance, or confederation; grant letters of marque and reprisal; coin money; emit bills of credit; make anything but gold and silver coin a tender in payment of debts; pass any bill of attainder, ex post facto law, or law impairing the obligation of contracts, or grant any title of nobility.

No State shall, without the consent of Congress, lay any imposts or duties on imports or exports, except what may be absolutely necessary for executing its inspection laws; and the net produce of all duties and imposts, laid by any State on imports or exports, shall be for the use of the Treasury of the United States; and all such laws shall be subject to the revision and control of the Congress.

No State shall, without the consent of Congress, lay any duty of tonnage, keep troops or ships of war in time of peace, enter into any agreement or compact with another State or with a foreign power, or engage in war, unless actually invaded or in such imminent danger as will not admit of delay.

ARTICLE II

SECTION I

The executive power shall be vested in a President of the United States of America. He shall hold his office during the term of four years, and together with the Vice-President, chosen for the same term, be elected as follows:

Each State shall appoint, in such manner as the legislature thereof may direct, a number of electors, equal to the whole number of Senators and Representatives to which the State may be entitled in the Congress; but no Senator or Representative, or person holding an office of trust or profit under the United States, shall be appointed an elector.

The electors shall meet in their respective States and vote by ballot for two persons, of whom one at least shall not be an inhabitant of the same State with themselves. And they shall make a list of all the persons voted for, and of the number of votes for each; which list they shall sign and certify, and transmit sealed to the seat of government of the United States, directed to the President of the Senate. The President of the Senate shall, in the presence of the Senate and House of Representatives, open all the certificates, and the votes shall then be counted. The person having the greatest number of votes shall be the President, if such number be a majority of the whole number of electors appointed; and if there be more than one who have such majority, and have an equal number of votes, then the House of Representatives shall immediately choose by ballot one of them for President; and if no person have a majority, then from the five highest on the list the said House shall in like manner choose the President. But in choosing the President the votes shall be taken by States, the representation from each State having one vote; a quorum for this purpose shall consist of a member or members from two thirds of the States, and a majority of all the States shall be necessary to a choice. In every case, after the choice of the President, the person having the greatest number of votes of the electors shall be the Vice-President. But if there should remain two or more who have equal votes, the Senate shall choose from them by ballot the Vice-President.

The Congress may determine the time of choosing the electors and the day on which they shall give their votes, which day shall be the same throughout the United States.

No person except a natural-born citizen, or a citizen of the United States at the time of the adoption of this Constitution, shall be eligible to the office of President; neither shall any person be eligible to that office who shall not have attained to the age of thirty-five years, and been fourteen years a resident within the United States.

In case of the removal of the President from office, or of his death, resignation, or inability to discharge the powers and duties of the said office, the same shall devolve on the Vice-President, and the Congress may by law provide for the case of removal, death, resignation, or inability, both of the President and Vice-President, declaring what officer shall then act as President, and such officer shall act accordingly until the disability be removed or a President shall be elected.

The President shall, at stated times, receive for his services a compensation, which shall neither be increased nor diminished during the period for which he shall have been elected, and he shall not receive within that period any other emolument from the United States or any of them.

Before he enter on the execution of his office he shall take the following oath or affirmation:

"I do solemnly swear (or affirm) that I will faithfully execute the office of President of the United States, and will to the best of my ability preserve, protect, and defend the Constitution of the United States."

SECTION II

The President shall be commander-in-chief of the army and navy of the United States, and of the militia of the several States when called into the actual service of the United States; he may require the opinion, in writing, of the principal officer in each of the executive departments, upon any subject relating to the duties of their respective offices, and he shall have power to grant reprieves and pardons for offenses against the United States, except in cases of impeachment.

He shall have power, by and with the advice and consent of the Senate, to make treaties, provided two thirds of the Senators present concur; and he shall nominate, and, by and with the advice and consent of the Senate, shall appoint ambassadors, other public ministers and consuls, judges of the Supreme Court, and all other officers of the United States, whose appointments are not herein otherwise provided for, and which shall be established by law; but the Congress may by law vest the appointment of such inferior officers, as they think proper, in the President alone, in the courts of law, or in the heads of departments.

The President shall have power to fill up all vacancies that may happen during the recess of the Senate, by granting commissions which shall expire at the end of their next session.

SECTION III

He shall from time to time give to the Congress information of the state of the Union, and recommend to their consideration such measures as he shall judge necessary and expedient; he may, on extraordinary occasions, convene both houses, or either of them, and in case of disagreement between them with respect to the time of adjournment, he may adjourn them to such time as he shall think proper; he shall receive ambassadors and other public ministers; he shall take care that the laws be faithfully executed, and shall commission all the officers of the United States.

SECTION IV

The President, Vice-President, and all civil officers of the United States shall be removed from office on impeachment for and conviction of treason, bribery, or other high crimes and misdemeanors.

Article III

SECTION I

The judicial power of the United States shall be vested in one Supreme Court, and in such inferior courts as the Congress may from time to time ordain and establish. The judges, both of the supreme and inferior courts, shall hold their offices during good behavior, and shall, at stated times, receive for their services a compensation which shall not be diminished during their continuance in office.

SECTION II

The judicial power shall extend to all cases, in law and equity, arising under this Constitution, the laws of the United States, and the treaties made, or which shall be made, under their authority; to all cases affecting ambassadors, other public ministers, and consuls; to all cases of admiralty and maritime jurisdiction; to controversies to which the United States shall be a party; to controversies between two or more States; between a State and citizens of another State; between citizens of different States; between citizens of the same State claiming lands under grants of different States, and between a State, or the citizens thereof, and foreign States, citizens, or subjects.

In all cases affecting ambassadors, other public ministers, and consuls, and those in which a State shall be a party, the Supreme Court shall have original jurisdiction. In all the other cases before mentioned the Supreme Court shall have appellate jurisdiction, both as to law and fact, with such exceptions and under such regulations as the Congress shall make.

The trial of all crimes, except in cases of impeachment, shall be by jury; and such trial shall be held in the State where the said crimes shall have been committed; but when not committed within any State, the trial shall be at such place or places as the Congress may by law have directed.

SECTION III

Treason against the United States shall consist only in levying war against them, or in adhering to their enemies, giving them aid and comfort. No person shall be convicted of treason unless on the testimony of two witnesses to the same overt act, or on confession in open court.

The Congress shall have power to declare the punishment of treason, but no attainder of treason shall work corruption of blood or forfeiture except during the life of the person attainted.

ARTICLE IV

SECTION I

Full faith and credit shall be given in each State to the public acts, records, and judicial proceedings of every other State. And the Congress may by general laws prescribe the manner in which such acts, records, and proceedings shall be proved, and the effect thereof.

SECTION II

The citizens of each State shall be entitled to all privileges and immunities of citizens in the several States.

A person charged in any State with treason, felony, or other crime, who shall flee from justice, and be found in another State, shall, on demand of the executive authority of the State from which he fled, be delivered up, to be removed to the State having jurisdiction of the crime.

No person held to service or labor in one State, under the laws thereof, escaping into another, shall, in consequence of any law or regulation therein, be discharged from such service or labor, but shall be delivered up on claim of the party to whom such service or labor may be due.

SECTION III

New States may be admitted by the Congress into this Union; but no new State shall be formed or erected within the jurisdiction of any other State; nor any State be formed by the junction of two or more States or parts of States, without the consent of the legislatures of the States concerned as well as of the Congress.

The Congress shall have power to dispose of and make all needful rules and regulations respecting the territory or other property belonging to the United States; and nothing in this Constitution shall be so construed as to prejudice any claims of the United States or any particular State.

SECTION IV

The United States shall guarantee to every State in this Union a republican form of government, and shall protect each of them against invasion, and on application of the legislature, or of the executive (when the legislature cannot be convened), against domestic violence.

ARTICLE V

The Congress, whenever two thirds of both houses shall deem it necessary, shall propose amendments to this Constitution, or, on the application of the legislatures of two thirds of the several States, shall call a convention for proposing amendments, which in either case shall be valid to all intents and purposes as part of this Constitution, when ratified by the legislatures of three fourths of the several States, or by conventions in three fourths thereof, as the one or the other mode of ratification may be proposed by the Congress; provided that no amendments which may be made prior to the year one thousand eight hundred and eight shall in any manner affect the first and fourth clauses in the ninth section of the first article; and that no State, without its consent, shall be deprived of its equal suffrage in the Senate.

ARTICLE VI

All debts contracted and engagements entered into, before the adoption of this Constitution, shall be as valid against the United States under this Constitution as under the Confederation.

This Constitution, and the laws of the United States which shall be made in pursuance thereof, and all treaties made, or which shall be made, under the authority of the United States, shall be the supreme law of the land; and the judges in every State shall be bound thereby, anything in the Constitution or laws of any State to the contrary notwithstanding.

The Senators and Representatives before mentioned, and the members of the several State legislatures, and all executive and judicial officers both of the United States and of the several States, shall be bound by oath or affirmation to support this Constitution; but no religious test shall ever be required as a qualification to any office or public trust under the United States.

ARTICLE VII

The ratification of the conventions of nine States shall be sufficient for the establishment of this Constitution between the States so ratifying the same.

Done in convention by the unanimous consent of the States present, the seventeenth day of September, in the year of our Lord one thousand seven hundred and eighty-seven, and of the independence of the United States of America the twelfth. In witness whereof, we have hereunto subscribed our names.[1]

AMENDMENTS

ARTICLE I

Congress shall make no law respecting an establishment of religion, or prohibiting the free exercise thereof; or abridging the freedom of speech or of the press; or the right of the people peaceably to assemble, and to petition the government for a redress of grievances.

[1] The signatures are here omitted.

ARTICLE II

A well-regulated militia being necessary to the security of a free State, the right of the people to keep and bear arms shall not be infringed.

ARTICLE III

No soldier shall, in time of peace, be quartered in any house without the consent of the owner, nor in time of war, but in a manner to be prescribed by law.

ARTICLE IV

The right of the people to be secure in their persons, houses, papers, and effects, against unreasonable searches and seizures, shall not be violated, and no warrants shall issue but upon probable cause, supported by oath or affirmation, and particularly describing the place to be searched, and the person or things to be seized.

ARTICLE V

No person shall be held to answer for a capital or otherwise infamous crime, unless on a presentment or indictment of a grand jury, except in cases arising in the land or naval forces, or in the militia, when in actual service in time of war or public danger; nor shall any person be subject for the same offense to be twice put in jeopardy of life or limb; nor shall be compelled in any criminal case to be a witness against himself, nor be deprived of life, liberty, or property, without due process of law; nor shall private property be taken for public use without just compensation.

ARTICLE VI

In all criminal prosecutions the accused shall enjoy the right to a speedy and public trial, by an impartial jury of the State and district wherein the crime shall have been committed, which district shall have been previously ascertained by law, and to be informed of the nature and cause of the accusation; to be confronted with the witnesses against him; to have compulsory process for obtaining witnesses in his favor, and to have the assistance of counsel for his defense.

ARTICLE VII

In suits at common law, where the value in controversy shall exceed twenty dollars, the right of trial by jury shall be preserved, and no fact tried by a jury shall be otherwise re-examined in any court of the United States, than according to the rules of the common law.

ARTICLE VIII

Excessive bail shall not be required, nor excessive fines imposed, nor cruel and unusual punishments inflicted.

ARTICLE IX

The enumeration in the Constitution of certain rights shall not be construed to deny or disparage others retained by the people.

ARTICLE X[1]

The powers not delegated to the United States by the Constitution, nor prohibited by it to the States, are reserved to the States respectively, or to the people.

[1] The first ten amendments seem to have been in force from Nov. 3, 1791.

Article XI[1]

The judicial power of the United States shall not be construed to extend to any suit in law or equity, commenced or prosecuted against one of the United States by citizens of another State, or by citizens or subjects of any foreign State.

Article XII[2]

The electors shall meet in their respective States and vote by ballot for President and Vice-President, one of whom, at least, shall not be an inhabitant of the same State with themselves; they shall name in their ballots the person voted for as President, and in distinct ballots the person voted for as Vice-President, and they shall make distinct lists of all persons voted for as President and of all persons voted for as Vice-President, and of the number of votes for each; which lists they shall sign and certify, and transmit sealed to the seat of the government of the United States, directed to the President of the Senate. The President of the Senate shall, in the presence of the Senate and House of Representatives, open all the certificates and the votes shall then be counted. The person having the greatest number of votes for President shall be the President, if such number be a majority of the whole number of electors appointed; and if no person have such majority, then from the persons having the highest numbers not exceeding three on the list of those voted for as President, the House of Representatives shall choose immediately, by ballot, the President. But in choosing the President the votes shall be taken by States, the representation from each State having one vote; a quorum for this purpose shall consist of a member or members from two thirds of the States, and a majority of all the States shall be necessary to a choice. And if the House of Representatives shall not choose a President whenever the right of choice shall devolve upon them, before the fourth day of March next following, then the Vice-President shall act as President, as in the case of the death or other constitutional disability of the President.

The person having the greatest number of votes as Vice-President shall be the Vice-President, if such number be a majority of the whole number of electors appointed; and if no person have a majority, then from the two highest numbers on the list the Senate shall choose the Vice-President; a quorum for the purpose shall consist of two thirds of the whole number of Senators, and a majority of the whole number shall be necessary to a choice. But no person constitutionally ineligible to the office of President shall be eligible to that of Vice-President of the United States.

Article XIII[3]

Section 1. Neither slavery nor involuntary servitude, except as a punishment for crime whereof the party shall have been duly convicted, shall exist within the United States or any place subject to their jurisdiction.

Section 2. Congress shall have power to enforce this article by appropriate legislation.

Article XIV[4]

Section 1. All persons born or naturalized in the United States and subject to the jurisdiction thereof, are citizens of the United States and of the State wherein they reside. No State shall make or enforce any law which shall abridge the privileges or immunities of citizens of the United States; nor shall any State deprive any person of

[1] Proclaimed in force Jan. 8, 1798.
[2] Proclaimed Sept. 25, 1804.
[3] Proclaimed Dec. 18, 1865.
[4] Proclaimed July 28, 1868.

life, liberty, or property, without due process of law; nor deny to any person within its jurisdiction the equal protection of the laws.

SECTION 2. Representatives shall be apportioned among the several States according to their respective numbers, counting the whole number of persons in each State, excluding Indians not taxed. But when the right to vote at any election for the choice of electors for President and Vice-President of the United States, Representatives in Congress, the executive and judicial officers of a State, or the members of the legislature thereof, is denied to any of the male inhabitants of such State, being twenty-one years of age, and citizens of the United States, or in any way abridged, except for participation in rebellion, or other crime, the basis of representation therein shall be reduced in the proportion which the number of such male citizens shall bear to the whole number of male citizens twenty-one years of age in such State.

SECTION 3. No person shall be a Senator or Representative in Congress, or elector of President and Vice-President, or hold any office, civil or military, under the United States or under any State, who, having previously taken an oath as a member of Congress, or as an officer of the United States, or as a member of any State legislature, or as an executive or judicial officer of any State, to support the Constitution of the United States, shall have engaged in insurrection or rebellion against the same, or given aid or comfort to the enemies thereof. But Congress may, by a vote of two thirds of each house, remove such disability.

SECTION 4. The validity of the public debt of the United States, authorized by law, including debts incurred for payment of pensions and bounties for services in suppressing insurrection or rebellion, shall not be questioned. But neither the United States nor any State shall assume or pay any debt or obligation incurred in aid of insurrection or rebellion against the United States, or any claim for the loss or emancipation of any slave; but all such debts, obligations, and claims shall be held illegal and void.

SECTION 5. The Congress shall have power to enforce, by appropriate legislation, the provisions of this article.

ARTICLE XV[1]

SECTION 1. The right of citizens of the United States to vote shall not be denied or abridged by the United States or by any State on account of race, color, or previous condition of servitude.

SECTION 2. The Congress shall have power to enforce this article by appropriate legislation.

ARTICLE XVI[2]

The Congress shall have power to lay and collect taxes on incomes, from whatever source derived, without apportionment among the several States, and without regard to any census or enumeration.

ARTICLE XVII[3]

The Senate of the United States shall be composed of two Senators from each State, elected by the people thereof, for six years; and each Senator shall have one vote. The electors in each State shall have the qualifications requisite for electors of the most numerous branch of the State legislature.

When vacancies happen in the representation of any State in the Senate, the executive authority of such State shall issue writs of election to fill such vacancies:

[1] Proclaimed Mar. 30, 1870.

[2] Proclaimed Feb. 25, 1913.

[3] Proclaimed May 31, 1913.

Provided, That the legislature of any State may empower the executive thereof to make temporary appointment until the people fill the vacancies by election as the legislature may direct.

This amendment shall not be so construed as to affect the election or term of any Senator chosen before it becomes valid as part of the Constitution.

ARTICLE XVIII[1]

SECTION 1.   After one year from the ratification of this article, the manufacture, sale, or transportation of intoxicating liquors within, the importation thereof into, or the exportation thereof from the United States and all territory subject to the jurisdiction thereof, for beverage purposes, is hereby prohibited.

SECTION 2.   The Congress and the several States shall have concurrent power to enforce this article by appropriate legislation.

SECTION 3.   This article shall be inoperative unless it shall have been ratified as an amendment to the Constitution by the legislatures of the several States, as provided in the Constitution, within seven years from the date of the submission hereof to the States by the Congress.

ARTICLE XIX[2]

The right of citizens of the United States to vote shall not be denied or abridged by the United States or by any State on account of sex.

Congress shall have power to enforce this article by appropriate legislation.

PROPOSED ARTICLE XX[3]

SECTION 1.   The terms of the President and Vice President shall end at noon on the 20th day of January, and the terms of Senators and Representatives at noon on the 3d day of January, of the years in which such terms would have ended if this article had not been ratified; and the terms of their successors shall then begin.

SECTION 2.   The Congress shall assemble at least once in every year, and such meeting shall begin at noon on the 3d day of January, unless they shall by law appoint a different day.

SECTION 3.   If, at the time fixed for the beginning of the term of the President, the President-elect shall have died, the Vice President-elect shall become President.   If a President shall not have been chosen before the time fixed for the beginning of his term, or if the President-elect shall have failed to qualify, then the Vice President-elect shall act as President until a President shall have qualified; and the Congress may by law provide for the case wherein neither a President-elect nor a Vice President-elect shall have qualified, declaring who shall then act as President, or the manner in which one who is to act shall be selected, and such person shall act accordingly until a President or Vice President shall have qualified.

SECTION 4.   The Congress may by law provide for the case of the death of any of the persons from whom the House of Representatives may choose a President whenever the right of choice shall have devolved upon them, and for the case of the death of any of the persons from whom the Senate may choose a Vice President whenever the right of choice shall have devolved upon them.

SECTION 5.   Sections 1 and 2 shall take effect on the 15th day of October following the ratification of this article.

SECTION 6.   This article shall be inoperative unless it shall have been ratified as an amendment to the Constitution by the Legislatures of three-fourths of the several States within seven years from the date of its submission.

[1] Proclaimed Jan. 29, 1919.

[2] Proclaimed Aug. 26, 1920.

[3] Passed by Congress and submitted to the states on March 2, 1932.

TABLE OF CASES

INDEX

A

Ab initio doctrine, 216–217

Acceptance of pardon, 169–170

Adamson Act, the, 260

Adjournment of Congress, 99

Administrative action and due process, 393–394

Administrative determination, conclusiveness of, 394

Administrative ordinances, 116–117, 166–167

Admiralty and maritime jurisdiction, 193–197

Admission of states, 50–56

Advisory opinions, 215, 225–226

Aesthetic purposes, condemnation of property for, 405
exercise of police power for, 413–414

Agencies, Federal taxation of state, 240*ff.*

Agreements, executive, 275–276

Alaska, incorporation of, 304, 306

Alien and sedition laws, 29

Aliens, deportation of, 340–342
discrimination against, 431
treaty rights of, 271–272

Ambassadors, suits affecting, 204–205

Amendment, of the Constitution, 32*ff.*
Sixteenth, 235, 236

Amnesty, 168–169

Annapolis convention, 17

Annexation of territory, 293–294

Appeals, methods of taking, 185–186

Appointment of officers, 150–158

Apportionment of representatives, 82–84

Armed neutrality, 282

Arms, right to bear, 370

Articles of Confederation, and acquisition of territory, 295
commerce under, 247

Assembly and petition, freedom of, 369–370

Assessments, special, 437

Assistance, writs of, 349

Attainder, bills of, 337

B

Bail, excessive, 355–356

Ballot, short, 150

Bank depositors' guarantee fund, 417

Banking, regulation of, 417

Bankruptcy laws, 373–374

Banks, state, taxation of, 231

Bicameral System, the, 81–82

Bill of rights, 339

Billboard regulation, 413–414

Bills, approval and veto of, 138–144
of attainder, 337
of credit, 245
revenue, 118–119
submission of, 137

Blue-sky laws, 416

Bonds, municipal, 375–376
state, 375

Bootleggers, 350

Borrowing, national, 244

Boulder Dam case, 77, 199

Budget, executive, 144

Budget and Accounting Act, 161, 165

C

Cabinet, President's, 85–86, 124, 148–149

"Cases and controversies," 225

Caucus, Congressional, 127

Censorship of publication, 363, 369

Certiorari, writ of, 186, 187

Chain-store tax law, 435–436

Charter, colonial, 208

Chicago railroad strike, 192

Child labor case, first, 258–260

Child labor tax case, the, 232

Citizens, privileges of, 65–67, 320–323

Citizenship, 313*ff.*
by birth, 315–316
cases of diverse, 197–198, 206
and Fourteenth Amendment, 314–315
of Indians, 316
of married women, 317–318
national and state, 313–314

461